RECIPE ANNUAL
1996 Edition

Every *Sunset Magazine* recipe and
food article from 1995

KEVIN CANDLAND

*A fine winter trio: hazelnuts, Satsuma mandarins,
and Comice pears (page 285).*

By the Editors of *Sunset Magazine*
and Sunset Books

Sunset Publishing Corporation ■ **Menlo Park, California**

SUNSET BOOKS

President & Publisher
Susan J. Maruyama

Director, Finance & Business Affairs
Gary Loebner

Director, Sales & Marketing
Richard A. Smeby

Marketing & Creative Services Manager
Guy C. Joy

Production Director
Lory Day

Director, New Business
Kenneth Winchester

Editorial Director
Bob Doyle

Coordinating Editor
Cornelia Fogle

Assistant Editor
Kevin Freeland

SUNSET PUBLISHING CORPORATION

Chairman
Jim Nelson

President/Chief Executive Officer
Robin Wolaner

Chief Financial Officer
James E. Mitchell

Publisher
Stephen J. Seabolt

Circulation Director
Robert I. Gursha

Vice President, Manufacturing
Lorinda Reichert

Editor, Sunset Magazine
William R. Marken

Managing Editor
Carol Hoffman

Executive Editor
Melissa Houtte

Senior Editor, Food & Entertaining
Jerry Anne Di Vecchio

Cover: Asian Noodle Salad with Grilled Chicken (page 82). Cover design by Susan Bryant. Photography by Kevin Sanchez. Food styling by Merilee Hague. Prop styling by Carol Starling.

Back cover photographers: (Left) Peter Christiansen; (center) Deborah Jones; (right) Peter Christiansen.

Illustrations: David Broad (*Chefs of the West*) Alice Harth (*Kitchen Cabinet*)

First printing November 1995

Copyright © 1995 Sunset Publishing Corporation, Menlo Park, CA 94025. First edition. All rights reserved, including the right of reproduction in whole or in part in any form.

ISBN 0-376-02699-5 (hardcover)
ISBN 0-376-02698-7 (softcover)
ISSN 0896-2170
Printed in the United States

♻ printed on recycled paper

Material in this book originally appeared in the 1995 issues of *Sunset Magazine.* All of the recipes were developed and tested in the Sunset test kitchens. If you have comments or suggestions, please let us hear from you. Write us at:

Sunset Books
Cookbook Editorial
80 Willow Road
Menlo Park, CA 94025

If you would like to order additional copies of any of our books, call us at 1-800-634-3095 or check with your local bookstore. For special sales, bulk orders, and premium sales information, call Sunset Custom Publishing Services at (415) 324-5577.

KEVIN CANDLAND

Taco Bowl Salad with Grilled Chicken (page 188)

Share Our Experiences

Join us for a celebration of good food as we share another year's experiences in this annual collection.

As always, you'll find plenty to stimulate your interest and appetite. Throughout the year, our food writers traveled the West, learning more about contemporary cooking and the latest food trends. We reported on the booming aquaculture industry and visited growing fields and produce markets. We sampled constantly— at renowned restaurants, country inns, ethnic eateries, family barbecues, and on some great picnics—and shared the best dishes with you after retesting them in our *Sunset* kitchens.

Because so many of you are trying to limit the fat in your diet, we continued to slim down favorite recipes; the no-fry, low-fat version of taco salad shown above is just one example. We've also instituted a new monthly feature, *Everyday Low-fat Cooking,* which began in July (page 163). And now you can find low-fat recipes in their own separate index (page 296).

Contents

A Letter from Sunset

DEAR READER,

It's curious how quickly we come to rely on the things that make life easier. We may get along fine without them for years—but once we have them, we can't imagine giving them up. For me, the fax is a prime example. One day I didn't know what it was; by the next, it was as indispensable to me as the telephone.

The new recipe format we introduced in July of this year may not affect you quite so dramatically, but it will certainly make the recipes easier to use. As you probably know, our *Recipe Annual* comes straight from the pages of *Sunset Magazine*—so to appreciate the updated design, just compare a recipe from, say, the June issue to a dish from July or later. Below each recipe title, you'll now find an at-a-glance review of some important information: cooking and preparation times; notes about practical details such as make-ahead steps and sources for ingredients; and the number of servings. Other useful changes include bigger and bolder type in ingredient lists, and numbered steps to help you keep your place as you cook.

Balanced nutrition is the backbone of this book. Because so many of you are keeping close tabs on the fat in your diet, we're supplying a bit more nutritional information. As before, we list the percentage of calories from fat for each recipe—but now we do the math for you and provide the actual number of fat calories as well.

If you are trying to cook and eat lean, you're sure to cheer our many low-fat recipes. Each one proves what experienced fat-trimmers already know: less fat does not mean less food and less flavor! In fact, the opposite is often true—for the total calories, lower-fat dishes may well offer heartier portions and livelier taste.

Slim recipes show up all year, from "Eat smart" in January to lightened-up cheese blintzes in March and Thai noodles in December. June brings a 13-page entertaining special, "Great dishes for a low-fat summer." And in July, we introduce *Everyday Low-fat Cooking*, a new monthly column by Elaine Johnson. Keep an eye on my Food Guide, too; you'll find some great low-fat recipes there, such as September's La Puerta Lasagne.

The Low-fat Recipes index on page 296 provides a complete list of dishes in which fat makes up no more than 30% of the total calories. For still more light choices, look past the percentages in other recipes to check the grams of fat. In many cases, the number of total calories per serving is so low that the amount of fat seems higher than it really is. For example, Parsley and Herb Salad (page 155) gets 72% of its calories from fat—but it provides just 4.3 grams of fat and a

AT FARMER'S MARKETS, *in supermarkets, and in the Sunset test kitchen, our team stays on top of the food scene. From left to right: ChristineWeber Hale, Jerry Anne Di Vecchio, Andrew D. Baker, Linda Lau Anusasananan, Betsy Reynolds Bateson, Barbara E. Goldman, Elaine Johnson, and Bernadette Hart.*

NORMAN A. PLATE

modest 54 calories per serving. The same situation holds true for Raw Fennel and Beet Salad (page 44), Party Garden Slaw (page 116), and many other selections in this book.

All your favorite features are still going strong. Tops among these, of course, is *Kitchen Cabinet*—and it's celebrated in September with an excerpt from our new, charmingly nostalgic cookbook, *Sunset's Kitchen Cabinet*, a compilation of the column's best recipes from 1929 to the present.

Chefs of the West is still a fixture, as is *Why?*, in which Linda Anusasananan answers your cooking questions. Among the topics she tackles this year: thickeners and how they work; advice on making custards; and tips for prize-winning cheesecakes. And, as always, Bob Thompson offers sage and sometimes surprising advice on wines in each month's Food Guide.

This year, we've given a number of familiar recipes a delicious new twist. In February, French onion soup goes Mexican and brownies get luxurious "grown-up" flavors. In April, tamales shed their wrappers and appear as spoonfuls of creamy masa topped with a chicken-chili sauce. In August, taco salad is served in flour tortilla "bowls" that are baked, not fried.

No *Recipe Annual* would be complete without holiday specialties. In October, enjoy our selection of gruesome—and awfully delicious!—Halloween treats. In November, we offer a short cut to a full-scale homemade Thanksgiving dinner—and for those who don't want to cook at all, we give advice on where and how to buy the whole works. In December, a cookie primer provides some fabulous recipes—and *Why?* addresses common cookie-making problems.

Our in-depth reporting keeps you up to date with the latest in Western food and dining. The subjects we cover include the new dim sum (January), wining and dining in the Napa Valley (April), aquaculture and the fish it puts on your plate (August), and the West's best Mexican cheeses (October).

Like every Recipe Annual, this book gives you great recipes that work, fresh ideas for family meals and entertaining, and wonderful ways to use all the ingredients your markets provide. So enjoy! Eat well, eat wholesomely, and don't forget to share your ideas and comments with us—by mail, by phone, by fax. . .and yes, even by internet.

Jerry DiVecchio

Senior Editor, Food and Entertaining
Sunset Magazine

THE LOOK OF SUNSET'S *food pages changed in July (right), when we adopted a new format designed to make recipes simpler to use and information easier to find.*

TO USE OUR NUTRITIONAL INFORMATION

Sunset recipes contain nutrition information based on the most current data available from the USDA for calorie count; grams of protein, total fat, saturated fat, and carbohydrates; and milligrams of sodium and cholesterol. Beginning in July, the percent and actual number of calories from fat are also included.

This analysis is usually given for a single serving, based on the largest number of servings listed for the recipe. Or it's for a specific amount, such as per tablespoon (for sauces) or by a unit, as per cookie.

The nutrition analysis does not include optional ingredients or those for which no specific amount is stated (salt added to taste, for example). If an ingredient is listed with an alternative, the figures are calculated using the first choice or a comparable food. Likewise, if a range is given for the amount of an ingredient (such as ½ to 1 cup butter), values are figured on the first, lower amount.

Recipes using regular-strength chicken broth are based on the sodium content of salt-free homemade or canned broth. If you use canned salted chicken broth, the sodium content will be higher.

Bass baked whole, dampening the fire of smoky chipotles, a seed mix for seasoning

By Jerry Anne Di Vecchio

Simpler foods taste better, lighter dishes make you feel better, uncomplicated meals are a relief in the aftermath of the holidays. One way I like to bring these qualities to the table is to serve striped bass baked the way Patrizio Sacchetto cooks it. The San Francisco chef-manager of Umberto's hails from Italy, where striped bass is a great favorite, and baking whole fish in a salt crust is a tradition. It's certainly easy and entertaining.

Striped bass has a lovely, delicate, sweet flavor and big, easy-to-find bones. In the West, it is a protected sport fish, but it is also farm-raised in ever-increasing amounts for restaurants and markets and sold whole. The fish is harvested at 1 to 3 pounds and is often sold in the round—with scales and innards (if you want it cleaned, ask when ordering). You may have to order ahead, or stop by a good Asian fish market. A 2-pounder costs $8 to $12 and adequately serves two or three.

The crust doesn't really affect the flavor, but it does keep the fish warm and juicy. When I lifted off the crust—now rock-hard—at a recent dinner, good smells poured forth. The only thing missing was some of Patrizio's infused red bell pepper oil (you need a juice extractor to make it), but sautéed red bell peppers plus little thin-skinned potatoes roasted in the oven with the fish worked nicely.

After you've baked the crust, you can recycle it if you like. Pull the crust from parchment or foil and put crust pieces in a heavy plastic bag. Put the bag inside another one. Smash with a mallet until crust is coarse crumbs. Pour several cupfuls at a time into a

food processor with motor running, and whirl until finely ground. Sealed airtight, the mixture keeps indefinitely. The next time you need a salt crust, beat up 4 more egg whites and add 6 more tablespoons cornstarch to crust mixture.

BACK TO BASICS

Taming chipotles

Dried chipotle chilies, according to author, artist, capsicum duenna, and official Pepper Lady Jean Andrews, are usually ripe jalapeños, but may be any number of other fleshy, hot chilies that are slowly dried over gentle smoke. Regardless of pedigree, the chilies develop a remarkable flavor. However, chipotles are their own worst enemy. As much as you like them, you can't indulge freely without risking gastric burnout—unless…

Yes, there is a way to have your chilies and good digestion, too.

If you soak the dried chilies—cover them generously with water, bring to a boil, and let stand until cool—they get soft. Then pull off the stems and open the chilies to remove the seeds and any veins. This gets rid of a tremendous amount of the hot taste. The soaked chilies don't irritate my skin, but I'm still careful to scrub my hands with soap and rinse well before touching my eyes.

Chipotles also come canned, usually in sauce. To cool these down, scrape off the sauce and rinse the chilies to remove seeds.

One way I indulge my fondness for these tempered chipotles is to tuck them into a grilled cheese sandwich. I also like to drop

KEVIN CANDLAND

8 to 10 sprigs rosemary

1 garlic clove, minced

Salt crust (directions follow)

Rinse fish and pat dry. Select a shallow casserole in which the fish can lie flat but are close together (if needed for fit, cut off fish heads just behind gills or let tails tip up). Coat casserole bottom with a little of the olive oil. Lay fish in casserole; on the top side of each, make 3 equally spaced slashes in the fleshiest part, cutting down to the bone. Cut several lemon slices in half and tuck them into the slashes along with a few thyme or rosemary sprigs. Sprinkle fish with garlic and scatter remaining lemon slices and herbs in casserole. Drizzle fish with a little more of the olive oil.

Cut a piece of cooking parchment or foil at least 2 inches longer and 2 inches wider than the casserole. Lay parchment on fish and pat salt crust onto parchment evenly, pressing paper to fit down along the sides of fish.

Bake fish in a 450° oven for 30 minutes. To serve, slip a knife tip or spatula under parchment to pry up slightly, then grasp crust with pot holders and lift it off fish. Test fish for doneness: meat should be moist but pull easily from the bone in thickest part (prod to test). If fish needs more cooking, set crust back in place and return to oven until fish tests done. Uncover fish, push off skin, and lift meat from the bones. Makes 4 to 6 servings.

Per serving: 174 cal. (37 percent from fat); 25 g protein; 7.2 g fat (1.3 g sat.); 2.4 g carbo.; 92 mg sodium; 88 mg chol.

Salt crust. In a deep bowl, beat 4 **large egg whites** on high speed until they hold soft peaks. In another bowl, mix 6 cups (about 2 lb.) **salt** with 6 tablespoons **cornstarch.** Add egg whites and stir to mix evenly. Use, or cover airtight and let stand up to 6 hours.

A MIX OF THESE SEEDS *will find its way into many recipes.*

soaked or rinsed chipotles into bean or lentil soups, braising meats, and meat sauces.

Regina Cordova, who lives in the Los Feliz district of Los Angeles, is a great authority on the Latin kitchen, partly because she has roots in Mexico and New Mexico, and mostly because she has made these foods a professional focus. She, too, dotes on chipotles. When I asked her to share some of her favorite quick dishes using these chilies, I quickly ran out of notepaper. Here you go:

For salsa that tastes the way it does in a cantina, buy mild salsa and add chopped soaked or rinsed chipotle chilies to taste. Or chop 1 soaked or rinsed chipotle chili and mix with 1 can (about 1 lb.) stewed tomatoes. Stir in enough red wine vinegar to make the tomatoes tart, some chopped onion for crunch, and salt to taste.

Slip soaked or rinsed chipotles *under chicken skin* before cooking. Grill or roast the chicken; the chipotle flavor soaks into chicken juices as the skin crisps.

For a fabulous sandwich, add flavor to ordinary mayonnaise with mashed soaked or rinsed chipotle chilies. Spread mayo onto a split and toasted French roll and add grilled chicken pieces, several avocado slices, a tomato slice, and salt to taste.

Sowing seed for flavor

At the heart of my personal kitchen is an aromatic seed mix that I make up by the batch—often to send home with guests. The seasonings are quite chameleon-like, exhibiting a different personality each time their background changes. Whole, the seeds can keep their flavor for years, but once in liquid, they become soft and easy to chew, while retaining

their individual integrity.

My daughter puts in an order for the mix now and then because she loves to dump the seeds generously into boiling water for artichokes; the flavor the artichokes soak up makes fattening butter or mayonnaise a distraction.

I often use the mix to make a fast carrot soup for one or two that relaxes the bones and is virtuously lean.

Yet another use for the aromatic seed mix is with meats such as oven-braised lamb shanks.

Aromatic seed mix. The proportions don't need to be precise. Roughly what you are aiming for has overtones of a mild, aromatic curry—without the color. Mix together ½ cup **mustard seed** (yellow, also called white), 1½ ta-blespoons **cumin seed,** 1½ tablespoons **coriander seed,** 1 tablespoon **dried thyme leaves,** and ¾ teaspoon **cardamom seed** (pods discarded). Sometimes I add 2 teaspoons **fennel seed,** 2 teaspoons **black peppercorns,** or 1 or 2 teaspoons **crushed dried hot chilies.** This makes about ⅔ cup.

Succulent lamb shanks. Fit 3 or 4 **lamb shanks** (3 to 4 lb. total) into a deep casserole and sprinkle with about 2 tablespoons **aromatic seed mix.** Add 1 tablespoon minced **fresh ginger,** 1 chopped large (about ½ lb.) **onion,** and about 2 inches **regular-strength chicken broth.** Seal the casserole with a tight lid or foil. Bake shanks in a 400° oven until the meat pulls easily from the bone, at least 2 to 2½ hours. About every hour, add more broth to maintain ½ inch liquid in casserole. Transfer shanks to a shallow casserole and return to oven to brown while you make the sauce. Skim and discard fat from juices. Boil juices in a frying pan over high heat until reduced to about 1 cup. Thicken, if you like, with **cornstarch** diluted with a little **water.** Serve sauce over shanks, adding **salt** to taste.

Per shank: 679 cal. (48 percent from fat); 75 g protein; 36 g fat (14 g sat.); 8.6 g carbo.; 230 mg sodium; 241 mg chol. ∎

Getting along with garlic

The first job of Sauvignon Blanc is to keep merry company with garlic. Any Sauvignon that can do that also will be companionable with sweet peppers, cilantro (coriander), and other flavor-rich ingredients of Mexican cookery, which means that this is not only a pan-Mediterranean wine, but also the right stuff to accompany Southwestern food.

There is no mystery to the flavor affinities. All over the world, Sauvignon (or Sauvignon Blanc or Fumé Blanc—the same grape goes by all three names) has an indelible taste of some leaf or stalk. Sometimes the exact flavor approaches that of asparagus, or a sweeter grass. Sometimes it falls somewhere between the sweetest of herbs and the muskiest of melons. Occasionally, when a year is so cool the grapes don't ripen fully, the flavor will make you think of eucalyptus, or the family cat.

The mystery is that garlic, herbs, and some of the most intensely flavored vegetables temper pungent Sauvignons without causing them to disappear into the wallpaper. Contrarily, mere power of flavor is not what allows Sauvignon to stand up to strong herb or vegetable flavors. Full body and firm texture count for as much.

The proper measuring stick for Sauvignon Blanc is a traditional dish from France's *cuisine mère* called Chicken 40 Cloves of Garlic. Measured by this dish, Sauvignon either has enough character or wimps out. The following examples will hold their own against at least 30 garlic cloves, probably all 40. Prices go from $8 to $20.

From northern Italy: Marco Felluga Collio Sauvignon, Alois Lageder Terlaner Sauvignon.

From California: St. Clement Napa Valley Sauvignon Blanc, Domaine Napa Napa Valley Sauvignon Blanc, Dry Creek Vineyard Dry Creek Valley Reserve Fumé Blanc, Handley Dry Creek Valley Sauvignon Blanc, Byron Santa Barbara Sauvignon Blanc.

From France's Graves: Château de Fieuzal, Château La Louvière.

PESTO-TOPPED *broiled swordfish crowns green beans, carrots, fennel, and small white beans in a vegetable-infused broth.*

Swordfish in an Italian setting

A California chef delivers a Tuscan-style plate of vegetables, pesto, and beans

IT'S NATURAL FOR A California chef who values fresh, seasonal foods to adopt the simple style of Tuscan cooking. Tuscany, a north-central region of Italy, is known for its homey, straightforward use of seasonal vegetables, olive oil, wine, and the white Tuscan bean.

Robert Montuori, chef at Kuleto's Trattoria in Burlingame, California, says his cooking has "a Tuscan theme, using a little of this and a little of that," and follows the particular season's wealth.

One of his Tuscan-style creations is a warm fish salad much like a stew that is seasoned richly with an aromatic broth, fresh vegetables, white beans, and basil pesto. Here we present the essence of his cold-weather fish dish with a few alterations for making it in your home kitchen.

Tuscan-style Swordfish with Vegetables

½ pound green beans, rinsed, ends snapped, broken into about 2-inch pieces

2 medium-size (about ¾ lb.) leeks

About 1 tablespoon olive oil

1 large (about ½ lb.) onion, chopped

2 cloves garlic, minced or pressed

About 2¼ cups regular-strength chicken broth

1 cup thinly sliced fennel

½ pound slender small or baby carrots

4 swordfish or halibut (or other firm-textured, white-flesh fish) fillets, each about 5 ounces and ¾ to 1 inch thick

Salt and pepper

1 can (15 oz.) small white beans, rinsed and drained

½ cup dry red wine, such as Chianti

About ¼ cup purchased refrigerated basil pesto

Fresh fennel sprigs (optional)

In a 10- to 12-inch frying pan over high heat, bring about 1 quart water to a boil. Add green beans and cook just until tender to bite, about 5 minutes. Drain, and immerse beans in ice water. When beans are cold, drain and set aside.

Trim and discard green ends from leeks; rinse leeks thoroughly to remove any dirt or grit. Thinly slice remaining white section. To frying pan over medium-high heat, add 2 teaspoons of the oil, leeks, onion, and garlic. Cook, stirring occasionally, until onion begins to brown and stick to pan, about 4 minutes. Add ⅓ cup of the broth and scrape pan to release browned bits; cook until liquid evaporates and onion begins to stick as in preceding step, about 3 minutes. Add another ⅓ cup broth and repeat process, cooking until onion is golden brown.

Add remaining broth, fennel, and carrots; cover, reduce heat, and simmer until vegetables are tender to bite, about 10 minutes.

Meanwhile, place fish fillets on a lightly oiled broiler pan, salt and pepper as desired, and drizzle with remaining oil. Broil fillets about 6 inches from heating element; turn fillets after 5 minutes. Cook fish until flesh is opaque when cut in the thickest section, about 5 minutes more.

To hot vegetable mixture, add white beans, dry red wine, and 2 tablespoons of the pesto. Cook until mixture is hot; stir in green beans at the last moment before serving. Evenly divide the vegetables among 4 dinner plates, place a fillet in the center of each plate, and top each fillet with about 1 teaspoon pesto. Garnish each plate with a fresh fennel sprig. Serve immediately. Makes 4 servings.

Per serving: 465 cal. (35 percent from fat); 38 g protein; 18 g fat (3.7 g sat.); 33 g carbo.; 480 mg sodium; 57 mg chol. ■

By Betsy Reynolds Bateson

WHAT IS THE NEW
DIM SUM ?

KEVIN CANDLAND

Dim sum is a collage

of filled dumplings, buns, soups, tarts, and many other little dishes more difficult to categorize. These examples are the work of chef Man Wei Lee at Fook Yuen Seafood Restaurant in Millbrae, California.

1 Chicken satay
(satay gai tran)

2 Fried shrimp in shell with salt and pepper (jew yim ha)

3 Steamed spinach and shrimp dumpling (bo choi gau)

4 Steamed pork dumplings
(siu mai)

5 Fried taro dumplings
(woo gok)

6 Fried sesame ball
(jin duey)

7 Steamed barbecued pork bun
(cha siu bau)

8 Baked custard buns
(nai won bau)

9 Baked custard tart
(don ta)

10 Baked barbecued pork pastry
(cha siu so)

11 Pan-fried pork and vegetable bun (sung jin bau)

12 Lotus leaf–wrapped rice tamale
(no mai gai)

13 Shark fin dumpling in soup
(quan tong gau)

14 Fried shrimp ball on sugarcane
(tzay ha)

15 Shrimp-stuffed bell pepper squares (jin nyung tzeng jew)

16 Steamed scallop and shrimp dumpling (dai tze gau)

17 Pan-browned chive and shrimp dumpling (gau choi gau)

18 Steamed shrimp dumplings
(ha gau)

ABLE FOR SIX FOR DIM SUM? THE HOSTESS HANDS ME A scrap of paper with 68 scribbled on it. Rumor has it that Hong Kong talent has landed here at Fook Yuen, a nondescript restaurant on the San Francisco Peninsula. It's still early this Sunday morning, and there's already a crowd—mostly Chinese—so we suspect the rumor is well-founded.

We wait for a table, tummies rumbling. Carts with stacks of steamer baskets careen among big round tables. Trays of crisp golden nuggets and sunny yellow tarts whiz by. Teas-ing aromas of pungent black beans, coconut custard, and cilantro shrimp mingle in the air as waitresses bark out names of dishes in Chinese. At last, 68 is called.

We are seated just outside the kitchen. Dining companion Jo Ann complains, but I rejoice. During peak dim sum hours, this is the best location: we can snag tempting morsels as they roll hot and fresh through the swinging doors. Even before tea arrives, two waitresses descend to offer plates of white cottony buns streaked with red filling and open-faced

BY LINDA LAU ANUSASANANAN

In San Francisco's financial district, a parade of dim sum at Yank Sing Restaurant rolls up to the table—just point at the dishes

dumplings dotted with orange. Famished, we point to both. The tea is poured as another cart glides up. *"Bo choi gau?"* asks the waitress. Puzzled, we ask for a peek. She lifts the lid. Pearly white dumplings glisten with steam but reveal no clue to their contents. We decide to give them a try. "Chicken *satay?*" asks another server. We nod yes. Our table is filling quickly with plates and small steamer sections. We opt to devour these foods while they're hot and wave away the next three carts.

Golden packets of mango crêpes arrive for our inspection. The fruit is in season, so we take some, mixing sweet dishes and savory ones with Chinese casualness. And when the tea is gone, we turn over the teapot top to signal for a hot water refill.

All around us in this noisy, crowded room are familiar favorites and little mysteries that demand explanation—or an educated palate. Thick porridges, jellyfish salads, cold and hot noodle dishes, curling chicken feet, leaf-wrapped sticky rice, and an uncalculated number of other dishes are being consumed with gusto and washed down with cup after cup of fragrant hot tea.

Just as the din reaches a crescendo, we ask for our bill. It's $60 for six, and we've had enough dim sum to make us feel as if we're waddling out the door.

A Cantonese revival in the West

Dim sum, a feast of tiny delectable morsels, is a social experience that Chinese often call *yum cha* (drink tea). This ancient custom dates from the 10th century, when chefs invented bite-size delicacies to tease the jaded palates of fickle royals and, hopefully, touch their hearts. Dim sum translates as *touch the heart.*

In the 13th century, Mongol invaders forced the royal court—and dim sum—south to the province of Guangdong and into the capital city of Guangzhou (formerly Canton). The Cantonese made dim sum their own, and added their own inventive dishes. Nibbling these tidbits—from morning to midafternoon—while sipping tea became part of the scenario for friends and associates who gathered to visit, gossip, or do business.

Where Cantonese migrated, dim sum went along. When communists came to power in China, many of the best dim sum chefs fled to Hong Kong, turning it into an epicurean capital where competition drove dim sum to greater refinement.

In recent years, political edginess about the 1997 mainland China takeover has had Hong Kong dim sum masters on the move again. Their favorite destinations are in the West—the San Francisco Bay Area; Los Angeles basin; Vancouver, British Columbia; and Honolulu (see our guide on page 14). They've brought world-class dim sum with them, incorporating tastes and customs of the West. Clifford Chow, manager of Harbor Village Restaurant in San Francisco, sums up the movement: "It's more refined, portions are smaller, quality is much higher, and the selection is greater than ever." And he ventures, "I think dim sum is better here than in Hong Kong."

Classically, dim sum enhances fresh, natural flavors with a few select seasonings. The new Western offerings take advantage of fresh produce and nontraditional ingredients from other

that catch your eye; more will follow.

STEPHANIE RAUSSER

ethnic cuisines, both of which abound in the West, and put them to use with classic techniques and a sensitivity to healthful eating.

Gearing up for dim sum

Eating dim sum is an off-the-wall adventure. Foods come in no particular sequence; you might be able to order, but often there is no menu and you have to point at what you want from a passing cart or tray. You may not know what you're eating until the first bite; even then you may be puzzled and possibly happier in ignorance. The server may not speak English. You are expected to share. The more people in your party, the more foods you can try. Exotic ingredients like tripe, chicken feet, and shark fin are common.

Yet in most places, dim sum dining is more user-friendly now than it was just a decade ago. Some restaurants, especially upscale ones, even take reservations and credit cards and communicate in English. Although brunch isn't a Chinese concept, the hours of dim sum service fit the time frame: 10 to 3.

Timing your visit could be critical to your enjoyment. Dim sum is enor-

mously popular with Chinese American families. On weekends in big cities, the crush occurs from about noon to 1:30. This is when you get the best and worst. If you can't make reservations, you have the longest wait. However, you can often call just as you leave for the restaurant and get your name put on a list (and receive an assigned number) that secures you a place in the waiting line. During the busiest time, you also get the best dim sum selection, as the maximum variety streams out of the kitchen to meet the oncoming crowd. Early customers have fewer choices as the specials of the day usually aren't ready. Latecomers often find the choicest morsels gone. To beat this catch-22, arrive a little before the mob—11 to 11:30 on weekends, 11:45 on weekdays. After several visits, you'll find the best time for your preferred restaurant.

Dim sum service usually follows a routine. Typically, you first choose a tea. If you like floral teas, ask for flowery jasmine (*mo lai fah* or *heung pin*) or fragrant chrysanthemum (*gou fa*). Dragon well (*long jing*), a green tea, and *sau mei,* a white unfermented tea, are especially delicate and light. For more depth, choose medium-bodied, semifermented *oolong* and black *bo lai*—which the Chinese feel has a cleansing quality. Some restaurants will blend teas on request. Two possibilities: add chrysanthemum to light sau mei or heavy bo lai to lend a gentle perfume.

A grab bag of surprises

Portions are small, so experimenting is a bargain. Often the server carries scissors to snip large portions into smaller pieces upon request. An array of 30 to 60 kinds of dim sum is not uncommon, with ample variations to please conservative and adventurous palates alike.

Pace yourself—it's tempting to order everything in sight. Hot foods are best hot, so gather them only as you can eat them. The exception is the crush hour; if you see something you want, grab it. It may never come again. Regular customers quickly figure out what's cooked in limited quantities.

Many morsels hide their identity under a wrapper. Here are clues.

White puffy buns: Steamed yeast bread may have savory or sweet fillings. Common ones are red barbecued pork, chicken, sweet bean paste, and custard.

Shiny golden buns: Baked, slightly sweet yeast bread may enclose barbecued pork or warm sweet custard.

Pearly white to translucent dumplings: Steamed, thin-skinned dumplings may be shaped as half-moons, crescents, bonnets, balls, even goldfish, and filled with seafood, ground pork, vegetables, or a combination of these ingredients. Pot stickers are dumplings that are pan-browned on the bottom.

Milky white, soft gelatinous rolls: Thin, steamed rice flour sheets are most commonly rolled around shrimp, barbecued pork, or beef and drizzled with dark, slightly sweet soy sauce.

Golden lumps, crisp or chewy: Deep-fried standards include mashed taro and pork with a lacy crust, fringed wonton wrappers containing shrimp, chewy thin-skinned dumplings filled with pork and vegetables, gummy sesame-coated rice balls filled with sweet bean paste.

Succulent meats: Choices include steamed chunks of pork spareribs with fermented black beans; shiny red spareribs; fried and braised chicken or duck feet; cilantro-scented ground beef balls; simmered strips of fine, white tripe with chili and fermented black beans; and mahogany-hued roast duck.

Leaf-wrapped tamales: Big olive drab lotus leaves encase sticky rice, sweet Chinese sausage, dried shrimp, and salted duck egg.

Golden flaky pastries: Shiny glazed oval turnovers may be filled with beef curry, rectangles with barbecued pork, tart shells with sweet custard.

Puddings and gelatins: White, almost-crisp almond gelatin is in cool cubes with fruit; bowls of eggy pearl tapioca come warm; and the pudding is probably mango or coconut.

Specials (vary): Shrimp fried in the shell with chili, little skewers of grilled chicken with spicy satay sauce, and even chicken salad.

Tallying up

Typically, each time you order a dish, the server marks an X on your ticket under the category small, medium, large, or special. This is how the dishes are priced. The range for a small to a large plate is $1.75 to $3.50. Specials, noodles, and large platters of vegetables and roasted meats may cost as little as $4 to $6. At the end of the meal, the Xs in each category are totaled. You'll also be charged for tea, probably 60 cents to $1 per person; special tea, such as chrysanthemum, will be a little more. The bill for a very satisfying dim sum meal is often $8 to $12 a person.

FINDING DIM SUM

The best dim sum are found where the greatest concentration of discriminating Chinese customers live. A select group of longtime dim sum aficionados, some Chinese, some not, suggested the following restaurants for dim sum because, as of press time, they match or exceed the best found in Hong Kong.

San Francisco Bay Area

City View Restaurant, 662 Commercial Street, San Francisco, (415) 398-2838; dim sum 11 to 2:30 weekdays, 10:30 to 2:30 Saturdays, closed Sundays. Reservations accepted. This financial district restaurant, next to Chinatown, is busiest on weekdays. Look for *siu mai* made with lean chicken as well as traditional pork.

Fook Yuen Seafood Restaurant, 195 El Camino Real, Millbrae, 692-8600; dim sum 11 to 2:30 weekdays, 10 to 3 weekends and holidays. To cut down your wait, call to reserve a place in line. Large variety of dim sum, some very seasonal.

Harbor Village Restaurant, 4 Embarcadero Center, Lobby Level, San Francisco, 781-8833; dim sum 11 to 2:30 weekdays, 10:30 to 2:30 Saturdays, 10 to 2:30 Sundays and some holidays. Reservations accepted weekdays. Enjoy views of San Francisco Bay.

Ritz Seafood Restaurant, 1528 S. El Camino Real, San Mateo, 571-6213; dim sum 11 to 2:30 weekdays, 10 to 2:30 weekends. Chive and shrimp dumplings are a specialty.

Ton Kiang, 5821 Geary Boulevard, San Francisco, 387-8273; dim sum 10:30 to 10 weekdays, 10 to 10:30 weekends. Reservations accepted. You can make selections from trays or a menu; dim sum are also on dinner menu. Notables include pea sprout dumplings.

Yank Sing Restaurant, 427 Battery Street, San Francisco, 781-1111; dim sum 11 to 3 weekdays, 10 to 4 weekends. Reservations accepted. An old-timer (opened in 1981) offering 60 kinds of dim sum every day, including Peking duck by the slice; full selection available throughout dim sum service hours.

Los Angeles Basin

Empress Pavilion, 988 N. Hill Street, Los Angeles, (213) 617-9898; dim sum 8 to 3 daily. Reservations accepted weekdays. Large restaurant, good variety, known for dumplings

ROWS OF GLISTENING *roast ducks await the chopping block; pieces go onto platters for dim sum.*

(steamed, fried, and in soup).

Harbor Village Restaurant, 111 N. Atlantic Boulevard, Third Floor, Monterey Park, (818) 300-8833; dim sum 10 to 2:30 weekdays, 9 to 2:30 weekends. Exceptional and artistic dim sum.

NBC Seafood Restaurant, 404 S. Atlantic Boulevard, Monterey Park, 282-2323; dim sum 8 to 3 daily. Modest prices, good variety.

Ocean Star Seafood Restaurant, 145 N. Atlantic Boulevard, Monterey Park, 308-2128; 10 to 3 weekdays, 9 to 3 weekends. Large and reliable.

Sam Woo Seafood Restaurant, Suite D, Fourth Floor, 140 W. Valley, San Gabriel, 571-8686; dim sum 10 to 3 daily. Excels in seafood dim sum.

Seafood City Restaurant, 7540 E. Garvey Avenue, Rosemead, 571-5454; dim sum 9 to 3 daily. Many kinds of seafood dumplings.

British Columbia, Canada

East Ocean Seafood Restaurant, Suite 108, 777 W. Broadway, Vancouver, (604) 876-8388; dim sum 11 to 3 daily. Reservations accepted. Consistent and reliable.

Fortune House Restaurant, Suite 608, 650 W. 41st Avenue, Oakridge Center, Vancouver, 266-7728; dim sum 11 to 3 Mondays through Saturdays, 10 to 3 Sundays and holidays. Reservations accepted. Innovative dim sum, such as tempura *nori* tofu roll and succulent scallop dumplings.

Grand King Seafood Restaurant, Holiday Inn, 705 W. Broadway, Vancouver; 876-7855; dim sum 11 to 2:30 weekdays, 10 to 2:30 weekends. Reservations accepted. Regularly offers interesting new items, seasonal choices; shark fin soup dumpling is especially popular.

Imperial Chinese Seafood Restaurant, the Marine Building, 355 Burrard Street, Van-couver, 688-8191; dim sum 11 to 2:30 weekdays, 10:30 to 2:30 weekends. Reservations accepted. You'll enjoy less rushed, more attentive service than is typical. View of the Burrard Inlet.

Kirin Seafood Chinese Restaurant, Suite 201, 555 W. 12th Avenue, City Square, Vancouver, 879-8038; dim sum daily 11 to 2:30. Reservations accepted. Dim sum made to order.

Maple Garden Restaurant, Suite 145, 4751 Garden City Road, Richmond, 278-2323; dim sum 8 to 3 daily. A second location at Suite 112, 3000 Lougheed Highway, Coquitlam, 464-2323; dim sum 11 to 3 weekdays, 9 to 3 weekends. Reservations accepted at both places. Good variety.

Sun Sui Wah Seafood Restaurant, Suite 102, 4940 No. 3 Road, Alderbridge Place, Richmond, 273-8208; dim sum 10:30 to 3 weekdays, 10 to 3 weekends. Reservations accepted on weekdays; weekends and holidays, call ahead to add your name to the waiting list. Arrive early for best selection.

Honolulu, Hawaii

Legend Seafood Restaurant, 108 Chinese Cultural Plaza, 100 N. Beretania Street, (808) 532-1868; dim sum 10:30 to 2 weekdays, 8 to 2 weekends. Reservations accepted. Good variety, quite traditional.

Panda Cuisine, 641 Keeaumoku Street, 947-1688; dim sum 10:30 to 2:30 weekdays, 8:30 to 2:30 weekends. Reservations accepted. As many as 60 kinds of dim sum daily.

Royal Garden Chinese Restaurant, Ala Moana Hotel, 410 Atkinson Drive, 942-7788; dim sum 11 to 2 daily. Reservations accepted. Consistent quality. ■

WARM, COMFORTING *chicken soup provides flavors that suit your energy needs.*

Chicken soup for whatever ails you

Remedies for the bedridden and the working wounded

STUFFY NOSE, DRY cough, feverish forehead? Have a bowl of homemade chicken soup. Steaming broth clears the head, and bites of succulent chicken restore strength to the body and soul. But not all soups have the same effect.

Want to just crawl into bed and suffer? The basic comfort version, chicken and noodles, will suit your mood. Need a gentle boost to get you out and about? Go for the invigorating variation spiced with turmeric. Big day at work you can't afford to miss? Better take a dose of the high-energy chicken spiked with chili; it'll wake you up.

A whole chicken, plopped into a pot with water and lots of seasonings, is the key element. Simmer away until the chicken pulls off the bones; dump the bones and return the chicken to the broth along with selected ingredients.

Soothing Chicken Soup

1   chicken (3½ to 4 lb.), rinsed

1   large (about ½ lb.) onion, thinly sliced

3   stalks (about ¼ lb. total) celery, sliced

3   medium-size (about ½ lb. total) carrots, sliced

3   cloves garlic, pressed or minced

4   sprigs (about 5 in.) parsley

2   dried bay leaves

2   teaspoons dried thyme leaves

1   teaspoon coriander seed

½   teaspoon black peppercorns

½   teaspoon whole allspice

¼   pound dried wide egg noodles

1   package (10 oz.) frozen petite peas

Salt

Remove and discard chicken skin, if desired. Place chicken in a 6- to 8-quart pan. Add onion, celery, carrots, garlic, parsley, bay, thyme, coriander, pepper, allspice, and 2 quarts water. Cover, and bring to boiling over high heat; reduce heat and simmer gently until chicken is no longer pink at bone in thigh (cut to test), about 1 hour total. Remove pan from heat; lift out chicken and set on a plate. Discard parsley. If making ahead, let broth cool uncovered, then cover and chill until cold or up to 1 day. Skim or lift chilled fat from broth and discard.

When chicken is cool, pull meat from bones. Discard bones and any skin. Tear meat into bite-size pieces. If making ahead, cover and chill meat up to 1 day.

Cover soup, and bring to a boil on high heat. Add noodles; cook until tender to bite, 6 to 8 minutes. Stir in peas and chicken and heat through, 3 or 4 minutes. Ladle into bowls. Add salt to taste. Makes 14 cups. Serves 6 to 7.

Per serving: 252 cal. (16 percent from fat); 28 g protein; 4.4 g fat (1 g sat.); 24 g carbo.; 169 mg sodium; 92 mg chol.

Invigorating Chicken Soup

Follow recipe for **soothing chicken soup** (preceding), adding along with the seasonings 1 can (28 oz.) **pear-shaped tomatoes** (cut up) and their juice, 1 teaspoon **ground turmeric,** and 1 teaspoon minced **fresh ginger.** Omit noodles and add 2 large (about 1 lb. total) **russet potatoes,** peeled and cut into ¾-inch chunks. Simmer, covered, until potatoes are tender when pierced, 20 to 25 minutes.

Omit peas when you return chicken meat to pan. Accompany soup with 6 cups hot cooked **basmati** or other long-grain white **rice** spooned equally into bowls. Garnish with **fresh cilantro (coriander) leaves.** Makes 18 cups, 9 to 10 servings.

Per serving: 327 cal. (8.5 percent from fat); 22 g protein; 3.1 g fat (0.7 g sat.); 52 g carbo.; 213 mg sodium; 53 mg chol.

High-energy Chicken Soup

Follow recipe for **soothing chicken soup** (preceding), adding along with the seasonings 1 teaspoon **cumin seed** and 2 or 3 **dried small hot red** or chipotle **chilies.** Omit noodles and peas and add 2 sprigs (about 4 in. each) **fresh mint;** 1 can (15 oz.) drained **garbanzos;** 1 pound **zucchini,** ends trimmed, cut into ½-inch cubes; and 3 large (about ½ lb. total) **Roma-type tomatoes,** cored and diced. Simmer, covered, until zucchini is tender when pierced, about 10 minutes. Discard mint sprigs; stir chicken into soup and heat through, 2 or 3 minutes. Makes 16 cups, 7 or 8 servings.

Per serving: 196 cal. (19 percent from fat); 24 g protein; 4.2 g fat (0.8 g sat.); 15 g carbo.; 161 mg sodium; 67 mg chol. ∎

By Linda Lau Anusasananan

PETER CHRISTIANS

Mushroom Fettuccine with Italian Sausage

• *Fill up on carbohydrate-rich pasta, about 1½ cups per person.*
• *Use meat as a condiment (2 ounces per person), and make your own extra-lean Italian sausage in the food processor.*
• *For a flavorful, nearly fat-free sauce, cook pasta in broth, then reduce liquid to concentrate.*

Beet, Grapefruit, and Romaine Salad

• *Skip the oil. Pectin powder (the kind sold for making jam) thickens fruit juice dressing so it clings to greens.*

Eat smart

Beyond New Year's resolutions: one nutritionist's ideas for healthy, delicious everyday eating

THAT SINKING feeling: the holiday parties are over and, unless the scales are lying, the near future holds nothing but broiled chicken and broccoli. But if Jane Rubey, a registered dietitian, had her way, dieting would be forbidden.

In Rubey's Bay Area cooking school, Nutritiously Gourmet, the goal isn't weight loss, though her ideas can work that way in the long run.

The goal is balance: learning to combine delicious foods so that calories come primarily from plant foods like grains, pasta, and produce (carbohydrates), with a much smaller proportion from fat-rich foods such as oils, cheeses, and many meats.

Everyone needs some fat, but an excess in the diet is implicated in obesity, heart disease, and cancer. How much is too much? Currently, about 34 percent of the calories Americans consume are from fat; the American Heart Association, National Cancer Institute, and U.S. Department of Health and Human Services recommend we cut back to 30 percent or less. Rubey sides with mavericks who shoot for only 20 percent.

Whether we're scrutinizing numbers or just trying to shed a few pounds, the first step is incorporating good recipes and useful principles like Rubey's into our everyday cooking.

FAT-SMART STRATEGIES

Take a look at fat's role in a dish: as a cooking medium (for sautéing vegetables or deep-frying chicken), spread or coating (on bread, in salad dressing, and sauces), or tenderizer (as in pastry and cakes). In the first and second roles, trimming or omitting fat is fairly easy, as explained below. Where fat is a structural component, as in baked goods, cutting back is trickier.

Go for lean cooking methods like poaching or roasting. Rubey "sautés" onions in only a teaspoon of oil in a nonstick frying pan; the braise-deglaze technique outlined in many *Sunset* recipes requires none.

Make fat work hard: small quantities of flavorful extra-virgin olive oil, sesame or nut oil, or browned butter go a long way. In recipes with nuts, toast them to augment their flavor. Strong cheeses satisfy in small amounts.

Intensify flavors. Fat carries flavors, so when Rubey cuts it back, she uses a bold hand with other seasonings: fresh herbs, citrus juices and zest, chilies, ginger, pepper, and salt (she thinks healthy people needn't worry much about sodium intake). Rich homemade broths like the recipe on page 94 go into her soups, stews, pasta dishes, even salad dressings.

Fat also smooths sharp flavors such as vinegar; when you take out the fat, experiment to achieve balance. For example, without the oil, a classic vinaigrette is too puckery. Rubey's salad dressing has a milder vinegar (balsamic), fruit juice, and honey.

Emulate fat without using it. Thicken sauces with cornstarch and liquid or puréed cooked vegetables instead of flour and butter.

Extend fats with nonfats: potato salad dressed with one part mayonnaise and two parts unflavored yogurt, lasagne layered with ricotta plus nonfat cottage cheese.

Use meat wisely. Select lean cuts, remove any external fat, and skim surface fats from cooking liquids.

Mushroom Fettuccine with Italian Sausage

2 to 2½ ounces (about 2 cups) mixed whole and sliced dried chanterelle, porcini, morel, or shiitake mushrooms

1 tablespoon extra-virgin olive oil

1 tablespoon minced fresh marjoram leaves or 1 teaspoon dried marjoram

Low-fat Italian sausage (recipe follows)

2 tablespoons balsamic vinegar

3 cups winter vegetable broth (recipe on page 18) or canned vegetable broth

8 ounces dried fettuccine

Fresh marjoram sprigs (optional)

Salt and freshly ground pepper

Place mushrooms in warm water to cover (about 2 cups) until soft, 20 to 40 minutes; stir occasionally. Rub while still in water to remove grit, then lift out. Reserve liquid. Discard any tough stems.

In a 10- to 12-inch nonstick frying pan over medium-

Low-fat Chocolate Chip Cookies

• *There are no forbidden foods—but this version of a classic trims fat from 50 percent of calories to only 29 percent.*

high heat, stir mushrooms, oil, and minced marjoram often until mushrooms are well browned, 7 to 10 minutes. Add sausage and vinegar; stir occasionally, keeping meat in chunks, until sausage is opaque, about 2 minutes. Remove from heat; cover to keep warm.

Meanwhile, pour mushroom liquid (except for residue in bottom of bowl) through a fine strainer into a 3- to 4-quart pan.

Add broth; bring to a boil over high heat. Add fettuccine; boil, uncovered, stirring occasionally, until barely tender to bite, about 6 minutes.

Strain fettuccine over a bowl. Measure liquid; you should have 2 cups. If needed, return broth to high heat and boil, uncovered, to reduce to 2 cups.

Combine liquid, pasta, and mushroom mixture. Garnish with marjoram sprigs; add salt and pepper to taste. Serves 4.

Per serving: 401 cal. (20 percent from fat); 22 g protein; 8.8 g fat (1.7 g sat.); 57 g carbo.; 73 mg sodium; 91 mg chol.

Low-fat Italian sausage. In a food processor, whirl 1 large clove **garlic,** 1 tablespoon packed **parsley leaves,** 2 teaspoons **all-purpose flour,** ½ teaspoon **fennel seed,** ¼ teaspoon **crushed dried hot red chilies,** and ⅛ teaspoon **dried oregano leaves** until minced. Trim ½ pound **pork tenderloin** of all fat and sinew; cut in 1-inch chunks. Add to processor with ¼ cup **dry white wine;** pulse until meat is coarsely chopped.

To make sausage without a food processor, mince seasonings and put in a bowl. Coarsely grind meat with a food chopper, then mix with seasonings and wine.

Winter Vegetable Broth

- ⅓ cup chopped shallots
- 2 tablespoons chopped garlic
- 1 cup chopped onion
- 2 teaspoons canola oil
- 5 quarts water
- 1 cup vermouth
- 4 cups chopped mushrooms
- 3 cups chopped celery
- 2 cups chopped fennel bulb with some leaves
- 1¾ cups chopped carrots
- ¾ cup parsley sprigs
- 1 teaspoon dried thyme
- 1 teaspoon peppercorns, cracked
- 2 dried bay leaves

In an 8- to 10-quart pan over medium heat, stir shallots, garlic, onion, and oil often until onion is golden, 8 to 10 minutes.

Add water, vermouth, mushrooms, celery, fennel, carrots, parsley, thyme, peppercorns, and bay leaves. Bring to a boil over high heat, then simmer, covered, for 1 hour.

Boil broth, uncovered, over high heat until reduced to 4½ quarts, 30 to 40 minutes. Pour through a fine strainer set over a heatproof container, pressing to extract liquid; discard seasonings. Use, chill airtight up to 5 days, or freeze. Makes 3 quarts.

Per cup: 37 cal. (22 percent from fat); 1 g protein; 0.9 g fat (0 g sat.); 6.8 g carbo.; 33 mg sodium; 0 mg chol.

Nutrition math demystified

Here's how to calculate percentages of calories from fats, protein, and carbohydrates. First, you need to know it takes 9 calories to burn 1 gram of fat and 4 calories to burn 1 gram of protein or carbohydrate.

To practice, use the nutrition information in the cookie recipe at right. One cookie has 4.6 grams of fat: 4.6 x 9 calories per gram = 41.4 calories. Divide 41.4 by 145 total calories, and you get 29 percent of calories from fat. Calories from carbohydrates = 25 grams x 4 calories / 145 calories, or 69 percent. Calories from protein = 2.3 grams x 4 calories / 145 calories, or 6 percent. (Because of rounded numbers, percentages don't equal exactly 100.)

Of course, most of us don't live on cookies alone. For a more accurate idea of how your diet shapes up, look at total intake over a day, or at least over one meal. Advanced math whizzes: this menu works out to 19 percent of calories from fat, 66 percent from carbohydrates, and 16 percent from protein.

Beet, Grapefruit, and Romaine Salad

- 2 large (2 lb. total) pink grapefruit
- Tarragon dressing (recipe follows)
- 2½ to 3 quarts (½ lb.) small whole romaine lettuce leaves (or larger leaves torn in pieces)
- 1 can (about 1 lb.) cooked small beets, drained and halved crosswise

Cut skin and white membranes from grapefruit; discard. Working over a large salad bowl to catch juices, cut between inner membranes to free grapefruit segments; set aside. Squeeze juice from inner membranes; discard them. Drain juice from bowl, reserving ¼ cup for dressing; save the rest for other uses.

In a bowl, gently mix romaine with half of dressing; arrange on a platter. Mix remaining dressing with grapefruit and beets; spoon over lettuce. Serves 4.

Per serving: 90 cal. (0 percent from fat); 2.3 g protein; 0.3 g fat (0 g sat.); 22 g carbo.; 183 mg sodium; 0 mg chol.

Tarragon dressing. Combine **reserved grapefruit juice;** 2 tablespoons **cider vinegar;** 1 tablespoon *each* **pectin powder,** minced **green onion, balsamic vinegar,** and **honey;** 2 teaspoons minced **fresh tarragon** (or ½ teaspoon dried tarragon); and **salt** and **freshly ground pepper** to taste. Stir until pectin dissolves. Let stand until slightly thickened, 15 to 20 minutes. Use, or chill airtight up to 2 days.

Low-fat Chocolate Chip Cookies

- 2 tablespoons butter, softened
- 2 tablespoons canola oil
- 1 cup firmly packed dark brown sugar
- 1 large egg
- ½ cup applesauce
- 1 teaspoon vanilla
- 1 teaspoon baking powder
- ½ teaspoon baking soda
- ½ teaspoon salt
- 1½ cups all-purpose flour
- 2 cups regular rolled oats
- 1 package (6 oz.) semisweet chocolate baking chips
- About 2 tablespoons granulated sugar

In the large bowl of an electric mixer, beat butter, oil, and brown sugar until smooth. Add egg, applesauce, and vanilla; beat until blended. Beat in baking powder, soda, and salt, then flour, until smooth. Scrape side of bowl, then stir in oats and chocolate.

Bake dough right away; if allowed to sit, cookies will be dry. Drop dough by 2-tablespoon portions onto 2 lightly oiled 12- by 15-inch baking sheets, spacing evenly. Dip fingertips in granulated sugar, then pat cookies into ⅓-inch-thick rounds.

Bake in a 350° oven until pale golden, about 10 minutes; switch pan positions after 5 minutes. Lift to racks; eat warm or cool. Makes 25.

Per cookie: 145 cal. (29 percent from fat); 2.3 g protein; 4.6 g fat (1.9 g sat.); 25 g carbo.; 104 mg sodium; 11 mg chol. ■

By Elaine Johnson

For fishing or trail food, muffins do the job

While chilies warm up schnitzel

POLENTA MUFFINS ARE GERALD Stone's quick getaway food. His recipe is easy to remember even in the cold light of dawn (it includes just one of practically everything), the ingredients take only a few minutes to mix, and the muffins bake while he showers and dresses. He eats a few before starting for trout country and carries along the rest as camp or trail nourishment.

Stone is not at all dogmatic about this recipe. He allows cornmeal instead of polenta (although the latter adds a satisfying crunch) and feels that fresh raspberries, dates, raisins, and even chopped red bell pepper can fill in for blueberries or cranberries.

Polenta Berry Muffins

1 cup all-purpose flour
1 cup polenta
2 tablespoons sugar
1 teaspoon baking powder
¼ teaspoon salt
1 large egg
1 cup low-fat milk
1 tablespoon melted butter or margarine
1 cup blueberries, rinsed and drained, or dried cranberries

In a large bowl, stir together flour, polenta, sugar, baking powder, and salt. In another bowl, beat egg to blend with milk and butter. Add egg mixture to dry ingredients, and stir just until moistened. Mix in berries. Spoon batter equally into 12 oiled 2½-inch muffin cups.

Bake in a 425° oven until muffins are brown, 20 to 25 minutes. Let cool 5 to 10 minutes, then invert from pan and serve warm or at room temperature. Makes 12 muffins.

Per muffin: 130 cal. (22 percent from fat); 3.3 g protein; 3.2 g fat (1.1 g sat.); 22 g carbo.; 112 mg sodium; 22 mg chol.

Berkeley

THE SANTA FE IN SANTA FE Schnitzel refers to the land of its birth. To be perfectly honest, Don Pichler sends this recipe from Albuquerque, but the alliteration in Santa Fe Schnitzel is irresistible in its euphony.

What is a schnitzel? The German word means small cut or slice: the exact equivalent of our cutlet. The classic Wiener (Vienna) Schnitzel is a breaded and fried veal cutlet. Variations often include lemon, anchovy, and capers. A Holstein Schnitzel tops the cutlet with a fried egg. Pichler's topping is sherried mushrooms and cheese—flavored with chilies, if you choose.

Santa Fe Schnitzel

1 pound boneless veal cutlets
  All-purpose flour
2 tablespoons butter or margarine
½ pound small mushrooms, rinsed and drained
½ cup dry sherry
½ teaspoon dried oregano leaves
¼ teaspoon garlic salt (optional)
½ teaspoon Worcestershire
1 package (1 lb.) frozen peas and pearl onions
½ cup shredded jack cheese
1 cup (¼ lb.) shredded mild or hot Mexican process cheese spread
2 teaspoons prepared drained capers
4 to 6 cherry tomatoes, halved
  Parsley or fresh cilantro (coriander) sprigs

Place cutlets between sheets of plastic wrap; pound gently and firmly with a flat mallet until slices are ⅛ to ¼ inch thick. Coat slices with flour and shake off excess.

In a 10- to 12-inch frying pan over medium-high heat, melt butter. When butter begins to brown faintly, fill pan with 1 layer of meat and cook just until edges turn white, about 1½ minutes. Turn and cook to lightly brown bottom of slices, about 1½ minutes more; as cooked, transfer pieces to an ovenproof platter and keep warm in a 200° oven. Continue to cook remaining meat.

Add mushrooms to pan and stir frequently until lightly browned, about 5 minutes. Stir in sherry, oregano, garlic salt, and Worcestershire. Boil on high heat, stirring often, until liquid is reduced to about 3 tablespoons.

Meanwhile, heat peas and onions according to package directions. Remove platter from oven; arrange meat across center, with slices overlapping. Cover meat evenly with cheeses.

Broil about 6 inches from heat until cheeses melt, 2 or 3 minutes. Sprinkle capers over meat; pour mushrooms onto platter on 1 side of meat, peas and onions on the other side. Garnish with tomatoes and parsley. Makes 4 to 6 servings.

Per serving: 292 cal. (37 percent from fat); 26 g protein; 12 g fat (6.5 g sat.); 20 g carbo.; 465 mg sodium; 93 mg chol.

Albuquerque

By Joan Griffiths, Richard Dunmire

BITE-SIZE POLENTA *triangles hold a topping of Chinese sausage, shiitake mushrooms, and cilantro.*

Cross-cultural appetizers

Chinese meets Italian and Mexican in these tasty tidbits

THE MOST POPULAR ingredients and flavor combinations used by the many ethnic groups that populate the West invariably break new ground in the hands of inventive neighbors. The results can be very tasty indeed, and these two harmonious appetizers prove the point.

Polenta Triangles with Chinese Sausage

Cook polenta at least 2 hours or up to 2 days ahead; it needs to cool and firm. Then make topping.

1 cup polenta

3½ cups regular-strength chicken broth

1 ounce (about 1¼ cups) dried shiitake mushrooms

½ pound Chinese sausages (*lop chong*) or bacon, coarsely chopped

2 cloves garlic, minced or pressed

2 tablespoons rice vinegar

1 tablespoon soy sauce

1 tablespoon cornstarch

2 tablespoons minced fresh cilantro (coriander)

Slivered green onions

Combine polenta and 3 cups broth in a 3- to 4-quart pan. Stir often over high heat until boiling. Reduce heat, and stir often (mixture spatters) until polenta is thick enough to hold its shape when mounded, about 10

minutes. Pour into a 9-inch square pan, and spread evenly. Cover and chill until firm, at least 2 hours or up to 2 days.

In a bowl, cover shiitakes with hot water and let stand at least 20 minutes. Gently rub mushrooms to release grit, then lift from water. Ladle out and save 3 tablespoons water; discard remainder. Discard stems, and finely chop the caps.

In a 10- to 12-inch frying pan over medium-high heat, stir sausages frequently until lightly browned, about 5 minutes. Pour off and discard fat. To sausages, add 2 tablespoons broth, shiitakes, 3 tablespoons of the soaking water, and garlic. Stir often until liquid evaporates and mushrooms are lightly browned, about 10 minutes.

Run a knife between polenta and pan rim. Invert pan to release polenta; cut polenta into 9 squares. Cut squares diagonally to make triangles. Transfer triangles to a lightly oiled 12- by 15-inch baking sheet. Bake in a 400° oven until triangles are warm and edges crisp, 15 to 20 minutes.

Meanwhile, mix remaining 6 tablespoons broth, vinegar, soy, and cornstarch until smooth. Add to sausage mixture; stir over high heat until boiling. Add cilantro; keep warm until polenta is ready.

Arrange warm polenta triangles on a platter. Mound sausage mixture equally on triangles; sprinkle with onions. Makes 18.

Per piece: 63 cal. (30 percent from fat); 2.4 g protein; 2.1 g fat (0.7 g sat.); 8.4 g carbo.; 157 mg sodium; 3 mg chol.

Mexican Potstickers

1 large (about ½ lb.) onion, finely chopped

2 tablespoons salad oil

½ pound ground turkey

½ teaspoon crushed dried hot red chilies

½ teaspoon ground cumin

½ teaspoon dried oregano leaves

¼ cup diced canned green chilies

¼ cup minced fresh cilantro (coriander)

¼ cup regular-strength chicken broth, smoothly mixed with 1 tablespoon all-purpose flour

3 dozen potsticker (gyoza) wrappers

Nonfat or regular sour cream

Combine onion and 2 teaspoons salad oil in a 10- to 12-inch frying pan. Stir often over medium-high heat until onion is browned, about 10 minutes. Add turkey, crushed chilies, cumin, and oregano; stir just until turkey is no longer pink and liquid evaporates, 5 to 8 minutes. Add green chilies, cilantro, and broth mixture; stir until boiling. Let cool.

Lay wrappers, 6 at a time, on a flat surface and mound 1 rounded teaspoon turkey filling in the center of each. Moisten wrapper edges with water. Fold edge of a wrapper over filling and press against opposite edge; pinch rim to seal. Repeat to seal remaining potstickers; cover wrappers not in use with plastic.

As potstickers are shaped, set pinched rim up and push down gently to flatten bottoms; place slightly apart on large flat pans. Cover with plastic wrap. (If making ahead, chill up to 4 hours; to store longer, freeze on pans, then transfer potstickers to freezer containers, seal, and freeze up to 3 months.)

Heat ½ the remaining oil in a nonstick 10- to 12-inch frying pan over medium-high heat. Fill pan with 1 layer (about ½ the batch) freshly made or frozen potstickers, flat bottom down. Cook, uncovered, until bottoms are golden, 1½ to 3 minutes. Add ⅓ cup water to pan. Reduce heat, cover tightly, and simmer until skins look translucent, about 4 minutes. Uncover and boil over high heat until liquid evaporates. Transfer to a platter as cooked; keep warm. Repeat, using remaining oil to cook the rest of the potstickers. Serve with sour cream. Makes 3 dozen.

Per piece: 35 cal. (33 percent from fat); 1.7 g protein; 1.3 g fat (0.2 g sat.); 3.9 g carbo.; 43 mg sodium; 5.1 mg chol. ■

By Christine Weber Hale

SUNSET'S KITCHEN CABINET

Creative ways with everyday foods—submitted by *Sunset* readers,
tested in *Sunset* kitchens, approved by *Sunset* taste panels

Apple-Cheese Cobbler

Molly Wynne, Manhattan Beach, California

8 large (about 4 lb. total) tart apples, such as Granny Smith or Newtown Pippin
½ cup dried cranberries or raisins
1 cup sugar
1½ teaspoons ground cinnamon
¼ cup (⅛ lb.) butter or margarine
1 cup (4 oz.) grated cheddar cheese
1 cup all-purpose flour

Core, peel, and slice apples into a deep, buttered 2- to 2½-quart baking dish. Stir in dried cranberries, ½ cup sugar, and cinnamon; set aside.

In a 2- to 3-quart pan over medium heat, melt butter and remaining sugar, about 2 minutes. Stir in cheese until melted. Remove from heat; immediately add flour. Drop spoonfuls of cheese mixture over apples; gently pat to spread topping (there may be gaps). Bake in a 350° oven until golden and apples are tender when pierced with a fork, about 1 hour; tent with foil if topping is becoming too brown. Makes 8 servings.

Per serving: 394 cal. (25 percent from fat); 5.5 g protein; 11 g fat (6.7 g sat.); 72 g carbo.; 147 mg sodium; 30 mg chol.

BAKED SLICED APPLES *and dried cranberries boast a golden cheese topping.*

Asian Cabbage Salad with Orange

Louise Ross, Elk Grove, California

6 medium-size (3 lb. total) oranges
10 cups (about 2 lb.) thinly shredded Napa cabbage
1 can (8 oz.) sliced water chestnuts, drained
⅓ cup seasoned rice vinegar
2 tablespoons *each* minced fresh ginger and soy sauce
1 tablespoon salad oil
2 teaspoons fermented black beans, minced (optional)
3 whole green onions, ends trimmed

Cut rind and white membrane from oranges; slice into ¼-inch rounds. Mix slices with cabbage and water chestnuts. If making ahead, cover airtight and chill up to 4 hours.

Whisk vinegar with ginger, soy sauce, oil, and fermented black beans. Pour dressing over cabbage mixture; gently mix to coat. Thinly slice 2 green onions and sprinkle over salad; garnish with remaining onion. Serves 8.

Per serving: 118 cal. (17 percent from fat); 2.8 g protein; 2.2 g fat (0.3 g sat.); 25 g carbo.; 467 mg sodium; 0 mg chol.

SHREDDED NAPA *cabbage, orange rounds, and water chestnuts combine with an Asian-inspired dressing.*

Beverly's Clam Chowder

Beverly Zegarski, Montara, California

1 tablespoon butter
2 large (1 lb. total) onions, chopped
2 large carrots, chopped
2 stalks celery, thinly sliced
½ pound mushrooms, thinly sliced
1 cup regular-strength chicken broth
4 cans (6.5 oz. each) chopped clams, juice drained and reserved
5 large (about 3 lb. total) russet potatoes, peeled and cubed
2 cans (12 oz. each) skim evaporated milk
1 package (10 oz.) thawed frozen corn kernels
Salt and pepper

In a 6- to 8-quart pan over high heat, melt butter; add onions, carrots, celery, mushrooms, and ⅓ cup broth. Cook, stirring often, until vegetables begin to brown and stick to pan bottom. Repeat browning process twice, adding ⅓ cup broth each time; then deglaze pan with reserved clam juice.

Add potatoes and milk. Reduce heat, cover; simmer until potatoes are just tender when pierced, about 20 minutes. Stir in clams and corn. Cook until hot; add salt and pepper to taste. Makes 14 cups, about 8 servings.

Per cup: 378 cal. (9 percent from fat); 27 g protein; 3.6 g fat (1.2 g sat.); 60 g carbo.; 246 mg sodium; 41 mg chol.

Compiled by Betsy Reynolds Bateson

CLAM CHOWDER *gains rich flavors from gently browned vegetables and corn.*

February
FOOD GUIDE

Fast apples and pork, how to work with masa flour, chocolate news you will love, and crisp, fizzy Muscats

By Jerry Anne Di Vecchio

A pples browned in a little butter don't take much effort, skill, or planning—which is why I suspect my mother succumbed so readily when we requested them, even at breakfast. They were grand with sizzling little pork sausages—and even better with cured pork loin roasts direct from my great-aunt Nora's smokehouse.

In fact, almost any part of a pig—roasts, chops, sausages, hams—is complemented by apples in one form or another. Over the years, I've learned a few tricks to keep butter-browned apples a family favorite, well ahead of applesauce, baked apples, and other such competitors.

Some apples get mushy when sautéed and need a politically incorrect amount of butter to keep them from sticking to the pan. Some need a calorically significant amount of sugar to round out their flavor. But Golden Delicious apples, one of my favorite varieties, skirt these pitfalls. Wedges of this apple usually hold their shape as they brown, while becoming creamy inside. And they need only a touch of sugar to emphasize their natural sweetness. Akane, Cortland, Empire, Idared, and Jonagold hold up almost as well.

Usually I sauté a few dried currants to go with the apples, because I like their chewy contrast and decorative speckling. When this dish is served with smoked pork loin roast, mashed potatoes, and a green vegetable such as spinach or broccoli rabe, you have an earthy

meal of exceptionally complementary flavors and textures. Best of all, it's a menu that works into a tight schedule.

Smoked pork loin roasts from the market come fully cooked and just need heating to serve. If guests are delayed, you can reduce oven temperature to 150° and keep the meat hot for at least an hour, no harm done. Carved, the chops are rosy pink and juicy.

And if mashed potatoes are too much work, scrub little ones and boil them whole.

Smoked pork loin roast. For 4 to 6 servings, buy a 4- to 6-bone (2½ to 3 lb.) **fully cooked smoked pork loin roast.** At the market, have the bones sawed through so you can cut between them easily. Set roast, bones down, in a slightly larger pan. Bake in a 350° oven until hot (about 120°) in center, 50 to 60 minutes. Slice into chops to serve. Makes 4 to 6 servings.

GREAT INGREDIENT

Masa moves mainstream

H omemade corn tortillas—which really are worth the effort at least once—represent my first serious commitment to Mexican cookery. I made them with dehydrated masa flour (corn tortilla flour) because fresh masa (ground lime–softened soaked dried corn) wasn't so easy to find. Dehydrated masa flour was, and still is, available at the supermarket. You may know the brand Masa Harina.

After I had made a batch of tortillas, I still had a lot of the dehydrated masa flour. Soon I

was dipping into the bag for everyday uses, because the distinctive masa flavor fits well with so many foods. Consider these uses:

Cornbread. Decrease each 1 cup **cornmeal** in the recipe by ¼ cup and replace it with ¼ cup **dehydrated masa flour.**

Biscuits or scones. Decrease each 1 cup **all-purpose flour** by ¼ cup and replace it with ¼ cup **dehydrated masa flour.**

Oven-fried chicken. Dip **chicken pieces** (skin on) in **broth,** milk, or water, then coat with **dehydrated masa flour;** shake off excess. Place chicken skin side up and slightly apart in a rimmed pan. Bake in a 375° oven until

KEVIN CANDLAND

well browned, 45 to 55 minutes; baste several times with pan drippings. Season to taste with **salt** and **pepper**.

Plain shortbread cookies. Decrease each 1 cup **all-purpose flour** by ¼ cup and replace with ¼ cup **dehydrated masa flour.**

Pan-fried fish. Rinse **fish steaks** or fillets, drain briefly, then coat with *dehydrated masa flour* and shake off excess. Pan fry as usual.

Soupy chili or beans. Instead of boiling to reduce liquid, blend **dehydrated masa flour** with enough **water** to make a smooth paste and stir into the boiling mixture until it thickens to preferred consistency.

GREAT TOOL

Get a lift with tongs

Chinese cookware and hardware stores carry a handy, inexpensive tool that makes it easy to retrieve containers with a lip—canning jars, pans, bowls, even plates—from hot water or a steamer.

It's a three-fingered tension tong that looks a lot like the gadget used to pull olives out of narrow-neck bottles. It works like tongs used for canning, but, for me, these hold objects more securely.

As you lift, the tong fingers are pulled tightly against the container. The tool's gripping capacity depends on the span

A TASTE OF THE WEST

Sautéed Apples and Currants

1 to 2 tablespoons dried currants

2 to 3 tablespoons butter or margarine

2 pounds (4 large) Golden Delicious apples, peeled

2 to 3 teaspoons sugar

Put currants in an 11- to 12-inch frying pan with about 1 teaspoon butter. Stir over high heat until currants puff, about 2 minutes. Pour currants from pan into a small bowl.

Cut apples in half, core, then cut each piece into 4 equal wedges.

Add remaining butter to frying pan and melt over medium-high heat. Lay apple wedges in pan and cook until wedges are lightly browned and feel soft when pressed, 15 to 20 minutes; turn slices occasionally with a wide spatula.

Sprinkle fruit with sugar and add currants to pan; shake pan to mix and brown apples just a touch more, 1 or 2 minutes. Makes 4 to 6 servings.

Per serving: 117 cal. (32 percent from fat); 0.3 g protein; 4.2 g fat (2.4 g sat.); 22 g carbo.; 39 mg sodium; 10 mg chol.

of the fingers. Mine can handle a 10-inch plate.

Frankly, tension tongs look cheap (mine have a fluorescent pink plastic grip) and are flimsy, but they only cost about $2. A caution: if not carefully handled or stored, the tongs are easily bent or broken. Once it's out of whack, it's more practical to replace it.

Even more for less... and chocolate, too

Walking up the steps of Alice Medrich's brownshingled house in Berkeley, California, I was inspired with the mad notion that the shingles might be made of chocolate. Only Alice would have such a home—so singular is her devotion to chocolate. It all began with her pursuit of the perfect chocolate truffle, after she had tasted her ideal in Paris, and it led to her award-winning, authoritative book *Cocolat: Extraordinary Chocolate Desserts* (Warner Books, 1990).

But, as Alice observes, times have changed. How could chocolate desserts retain the quality and taste appeal she set as standard while also meeting tougher dietary attitudes about fat?

I tasted her chocolate pound cake, and it is clear that Alice found the answer. Her new book, *Chocolate and the*

TENSION GRIPS *are cheap and handy.*

Art of Low-Fat Desserts (Warner Books, 1994; $35) brings together the results. Chocolate desserts dominate, but others, such as lemon bars and raspberry genoise, hold their own. None looks or tastes as if indulgence has been abandoned. Alice's goal has been not to make desserts taste light, but to make them taste rich and be light. Each recipe includes nutrition facts on calories, fat, protein, carbohydrates, and cholesterol.

Even if the book had no recipes, it would be worth owning for the chapter on the theory and practice of creating rich desserts with less fat. The tips and the philosophy Alice puts forth can be translated to all cooking, making foods lighter and better-tasting.

Nostalgic dining and a white salad

If you're in the mood for a little nostalgia, the Fly Trap Restaurant, south of

Market at 606 Folsom Street in San Francisco, offers it up with style. The Fly Trap's history predates the turn of the century, when it was known as Louie's. Rebuilt after the 1906 quake, it officially adopted its popular, rightfully earned moniker. The Fly Trap survived for many decades, faded from popularity, and then was revived by the Zolezzi family. The menu has plenty of contemporary offerings along with a delicious roster from its bawdier days: oysters Rockefeller, chicken Jerusalem, coq au vin, and great liver and onions.

I was particularly intrigued by the menu's understated description of a white salad. Executive chef and owner Walter Zolezzi uses all mayonnaise in his dressing and goat cheese on top; I also like the lighter touch and tang of yogurt in the dressing and shaved parmesan to finish.

White Salad

2 heads (about 5 oz. each) Belgian endive
¼ pound white mushrooms, rinsed and drained
1 cup sliced canned hearts of palm (about ½ of a 14 oz. can)
1 cup sliced water chestnuts, peeled fresh or rinsed and drained canned (8-oz. size)
3 to 4 tablespoons lemon juice

¼ cup reduced-fat or regular mayonnaise
¼ cup unflavored nonfat yogurt
1 tablespoon minced shallots
   Ground white pepper
   Salt
2 to 3 ounces unripened goat cheese, cut into ¼-inch slices, or about 1 ounce parmesan cheese, cut into thin shavings with a vegetable peeler
   A few slivers of red bell pepper
   Minced parsley

Rinse endive heads, wrap in a towel, and seal in a plastic bag; chill at least 15 minutes or up to several days.

Thinly slice mushrooms and combine in a bowl with hearts of palm, water chestnuts, and 2 tablespoons lemon juice. Remove and reserve 6 to 8 large outer endive leaves. Thinly slice remaining endive and mix with sliced vegetables. Stir to blend smoothly mayonnaise, yogurt, shallots, and remaining lemon juice (to taste). Add dressing to salad; mix well. Season to taste with white pepper and salt. Serve on salad plates, garnished with reserved endive leaves, cheese, bell pepper, and parsley. Makes 4 to 6 servings.

Per serving: 109 cal. (47 percent from fat); 4.8 g protein; 5.7 g fat (2.6 g sat.); 11 g carbo.; 288 mg sodium; 11 mg chol. ■

PETER CHRISTIANSEN

Muscat cuts the chill

Sometimes in the darkest hours of February you long for a breath of spring. When that moment arrives, set out a generous supply of cashews, scatter some bright yellow napkins, gather some friends, and open a bottle of Moscato d'Asti or one of California's light-hearted, low-alcohol, fizzy Muscats. A Moscato will not drive away rain or melt snow, but

it will make you feel that the sun will shine again.

If you happen to be someplace like Southern California, where February is not so dark, never mind. The airiest of Muscats are delicious outdoors on a springlike day, too, because they capture one thing to perfection: the luscious flavor of big, juicy, green-skinned Muscats hanging ripe on the vine.

Old-time Californians may recall going to Louis M. Martini, buying some Moscato Amabile, and heading home,

ears full of the admonition to put it in a refrigerator before it could warm. Nobody had the means to keep such wines from starting to ferment again as soon as they warmed up. With the advent of filters that can keep yeasts out of the bottle, the rest of us have been let in on the pleasures of crisp, fizzy, half-fermented young wine—wine that has about 6 percent alcohol and 8 percent residual sugar.

Look for Moscato d'Astis ($12 to $15) only at the shop of an import specialist with a

bent toward Italy. The Californians ($8 to $10) may be found at more wine shops.

Moscato d'Asti: La Spinetta (Giuseppe Rivetti), La Cascinetta (Vietti), La Caudrina (Rendento Dogliotti), Santo Stefano (Ceretto).

Californian light Muscats closely similar to Moscato d'Asti: Ca' del Solo Moscato del Solo (Bonny Doon Vineyard), Quady Electra, Louis M. Martini Moscato Amabile (sporadically available only from the winery).

NOEL BARNHURST

This napoleon's not for dessert

But chef Nancy Oakes's regal potatoes can fill several roles

POTATOES AREN'T usually the first food that comes to mind when one thinks of fine dining. But in the hands of Nancy Oakes, executive chef and owner of Boulevard in San Francisco, they transcend their humble reputation. Mashed potatoes are the foundation of one of her signature dishes, potato napoleon. The surprise element is more potatoes. Thin sheets of crisp baked potato are layered with the mashed potatoes for a positively addictive combination.

This dish has great versatility. Offer it as a hearty first course, as Oakes does, surrounded by sautéed mushrooms. Or present it with roasted vegetables and herbed butter sauce for a glorious vegetarian entrée, or dish it up in smaller portions to go with roasted meat or birds like squab or quail.

Unquestionably, lots of butter and milk have helped earn Oakes's potatoes widespread appreciation. But we think our lower-fat version is delicious, too—the choice is yours, and you can taste as you go.

Potato Napoleon

You can bake the potato galettes while boiling the potatoes to mash, or make them up to 4 hours ahead.

5 cups regular-strength chicken broth

2½ pounds (about 5 medium-size) russet potatoes, peeled and quartered

4 cloves garlic, peeled

¾ cup low-fat milk

3 tablespoons butter or margarine

Potato galettes (recipe follows)

Salt and pepper

Combine broth, potatoes, and garlic in a 5- to 6-quart pan; bring to a boil over high heat. Cover and simmer until potatoes and garlic are very tender when pierced, about 30 minutes.

About 5 minutes before potatoes are tender, combine milk and butter in a 1- to 1½-quart pan. Warm over medium heat until butter melts; keep warm.

Drain potatoes, reserving broth. In pan, mash potatoes with a masher or a mixer, adding warm milk and butter and ¼ cup of the reserved broth. If you want creamier potatoes, add more broth in small quantities until potatoes are desired consistency.

On 8 dinner plates, equally layer mashed potatoes and galette pieces, with galettes extending dramatically beyond the mashed potatoes. Finish the top layer of each stack with a galette piece standing upright (reserve your smallest galettes to use on top). Serve at once because galettes soften quickly; season to taste with salt and pepper. Makes 8 servings.

Per serving: 261 cal. (31 percent from fat); 6.2 g protein; 8.9 g fat (3.6 g sat.); 39 g carbo.; 105 mg sodium; 13 mg chol.

Potato galettes. Peel 3 medium-size (about 1½ lb. total) **russet potatoes.** Using a mandoline or vegetable slicer, cut potatoes in even slices about ⅟₁₆ inch thick. Coat 2 baking pans, each 10 by 15 inches, with about 1 tablespoon total **olive** or salad **oil.** Divide potatoes into 2 equal portions and lay slices evenly in pans to cover bottoms; overlap slices about ½ inch. Gently brush potatoes with another 2 teaspoons olive or salad oil. Bake in a 350° oven until potatoes are brown and crisp, 35 to 45 minutes. If some sections brown before others, cover dark parts lightly with foil. Cool galettes slightly, then loosen from pans with a spatula and break each sheet into 12 random shapes of approximately equal size. If making ahead, let cool on pans, cover airtight, and let stand up to 4 hours. To reheat, uncover and return to a 350° oven until crisp and hot to touch, about 5 minutes. Use warm. ∎

By Christine Weber Hale

The New Bistro Stews

California chefs put a spin on the French classics, and you can enjoy the best of them at home

ot au feu with rabbit? *Coq au vin* with yams? *Daube* with lamb? Classic French stews are being pushed beyond the bounds of tradition to stardom in California's new favorite restaurant—the bistro.

What makes these stews special? It's the meticulous care and creativity that go into their conception and preparation. It's classic French technique used in surprising ways with local ingredients, and the long, slow cooking needed to bring flavors to perfection.

As in France, such cooking can be found in neighborhood restaurants where friends and families gather for the convivial ambience as much as for the food. Bistro dishes are simple and homestyle, the ingredients basic, the portions generous. And quite often, the tab is as easy to swallow as the hearty meal.

It is the good value of this total package that has struck such a passionate chord. The bistro wave, which follows the Italian food invasion—which, ironically, displaced France's haute cuisine as

By
Christine Weber Hale
&
Elaine Johnson

CASSOULET at Pasadena's Twin Palms Bistro has all the good flavors of slow-cooked beans, duck, and sausage, but the nuances are distinctly Pacific Coast.
A TRIO OF OVEN-ROASTED root vegetables accompanies robustly flavored coq au vin at Pinot Bistro in Studio City; paper-thin root chips make crisp companions.

Recipes start on page 30.

LEAN, DELICATE RABBIT and tender young vegetables lighten the style of pot au feu at Savoy Brasserie in San Francisco.

the dining standard—represents much more than a passing trend. It is redefining Western dining.

Stew: the quintessential bistro food

Dozens of California bistro chefs and restaurateurs were polled for their interpretations of stew. Some stick with classic techniques and play around with ingredients; some tinker with technique but stick to classic ingredients. All, however, seem quite comfortable striking out on their own.

Octavio Becerra, executive chef at Pinot Bistro in Studio City, points out that lavish foods like lobster and caviar stand easily on their own. But it takes great care, skill, creativity, and time to bring out the best in tough cuts of meat like shanks and oxtails, typical founda-

tions for stews. "You have to reach down into your soul, your gut, to produce food with spirit," he says.

In agreement, chef Donia Bijan of L'Amie Donia bistro in Palo Alto stays true to the bistro concept—with some variations. "The timeless dishes," she says, "have so much depth, they can go on forever being reinterpreted."

Some chefs use ethnic flavors to create "fusion stews." Becerra and chef de cuisine Michael Otsuka offer Oxtails

SUCCULENT SHORT RIBS at San Francisco's Fringale are drenched with pan juices that get their richness from puréed vegetables.

from Little Saigon. Anise, coriander, cloves, dried chilies, ginger, and fish sauce season the fork-tender meat chunks served with rice noodles. Diners top individual portions with bean sprouts, basil, cilantro, lime juice, and fresh chilies.

"Deconstruction" is another approach. Loosely, it means ingredients that traditionally simmer together are cooked separately. This preserves textures and enhances the visual appeal of more fragile ingredients. All are arranged together when the dish is served.

Gerald Hirigoyen of Fringale in San Francisco makes Braised Short Ribs with Parsnips. Instead of simmering the parsnips with the short ribs, he cooks the parsnips separately and glazes them to a pale gold in a little butter.

Similarly, in Becerra's Coq au Vin with Caramelized Root Vegetables, the chicken doesn't cook with the vegetables. Some of the vegetables are roasted to bring out their sweetness, and some are sliced thin and deep-fried to become a crisp and crackling garnish for the stew.

Inevitable changes, but for the better?

Considering California chefs' appreciation for the essence of bistro stews, you might wonder why they depart from the original dishes with so little hesitancy. The reason is that they must adapt to California ingredients and Californians' tastes.

The meat cuts used for stews in France aren't quite the same as those used here. Some French cuts, such as the beef and veal cheeks the French prize for their tenderness and succulence, have never attained popularity over here. California chefs, however, may be changing attitudes. Some are incorporating these unfamiliar cuts. Others are adjusting dishes to use meats with more general appeal that yield comparable flavor and texture.

Some cuts once marbled with streaks of fat aren't what they used to be now that cattle and pork are bred for leanness. Loretta Keller, chef at Bizou in San Francisco, points out that today's lean beef chuck would not suit her standards for daube; instead she uses fatty oxtails or beef shanks with generous amounts of connective tissue that melt to add a rich taste.

But, surprisingly, these hearty stews have been quite easy for chefs to make leaner and more nutritionally attractive to the health-conscious diners of the West. Although some chefs still finish dishes with a goodly ration of butter or cream, many find these rich supplements just aren't needed. They're drawing the flavors from the ingredients themselves, and using innovative alternative low-fat cooking techniques to produce dishes that they—and their clients—like even better than more opulent versions.

Sauces are often thickened by vegetable purées or cornstarch instead of butter-flour roux. Stews feature leaner meats, such as poultry and rabbit. Also, abundant amounts of carbohydrate-rich root vegetables, legumes, and grains add wholesome bulk that nutritionally balances the fat.

Bistro stew and style— more than a trend

Bistros have established a stronghold that is likely to last quite a while. Simple, straightforward foods and good value fit the mood of the times. Loretta Keller sums up bistro food as "a sort of style that transcends the regions." Its rise in popularity does not surprise her. "It ends up being very satisfying and accessible to a lot of people. It's like 'everyone's food.'" ∎

BERLITZ FOR BISTROS

Though many California bistros keep menu French to a minimum, others have a freer hand. Here's a pocket guide to the most-used terms—with some California modifications.

Blanquette (blahn-*kett*). A light-colored stew of meat (lamb, veal, or poultry) that is not browned, but simmered in a sauce of broth or wine, often with mushrooms and onions. It's finished with cream and/or eggs.

Bouquet garni. A cluster of herbs tied together to season the dish in which it simmers. Typically, the combination might include bay leaf, thyme, and parsley, but this varies greatly.

Daube (dōb). Beef braised with red wine and usually seasoned with orange peel. California bistros may use lamb, veal, or even octopus, and add vegetables like artichokes.

Mirepoix (meer-*pwa*). Chopped onions, carrots, and celery cooked in a little oil or butter to develop flavor and color are an important seasoning foundation for stews and sauces.

Nage (nazh). Shellfish cooked in herb-flavored bouillon and served hot or cold with the broth. California bistro chefs may use fish instead of shellfish, and add seasonings such as star anise.

Navarin. Mutton and vegetable stew, often with root vegetables. In the West, lamb is just one of several choices, and the vegetables grow above or below the ground.

Pot au feu. Boiled meat (beef, chicken, and other choices) and vegetables flavor the broth they cook in. The meat is served with the vegetables, and the broth is served separately. California chefs don't hesitate to use rabbit and baby vegetables, and serve them in the broth; some of them even use fish.

Four really great stews

California bistros share their secrets

ESSENCES OF WELL-BROWNED *duck, pork, lamb, and sausage seep into tender white beans to give this streamlined cassoulet all the classic flavors.*

THESE STEWS highlight the innovative ways French classics have been reinvented in California restaurants—as described starting on page 26. Although the steps to make each of these dishes are simple, you need to allow up to several hours for them to cook. Once ingredients are assembled and prepped, they take little attention while simmering or baking. The reward of superb flavors is well worth the wait.

Twin Palms Streamlined Cassoulet
—Michael Roberts, Pasadena

1 pound dried white navy beans

1 duck (4 to 5 lb.), cut into 8 pieces

½ pound fat-trimmed, boned pork butt or shoulder, cut into 1½-inch cubes

½ pound fat-trimmed, boned lamb shoulder or neck

2 large (about 1 lb. total) onions, chopped

¼ pound bacon, chopped

2 tablespoons minced garlic

4 cups regular-strength chicken broth, heated to boiling

Bouquet garni (directions follow)

2 garlic sausages (about ½ lb. total), sliced

Italian parsley sprigs

Salt

Sort beans and discard debris. Rinse beans and put in a 4- to 5-quart pan; add 6 cups water. Cover and bring to boiling over high heat. Remove from heat and let stand at least 1 hour or up to 6 hours.

Meanwhile, rinse duck and pat dry. In an 11- to 12-inch frying pan over medium-high heat, brown duck pieces well, about 20 minutes. Do not crowd—cook pieces in sequence. As meat is browned, arrange pieces in a 6- to 8-quart casserole.

Discard fat in pan and add pork and lamb. Brown well over medium-high heat, about 10 minutes. As pieces

brown, add to duck.

Discard fat from pan and add onions, bacon, and garlic. Stir often until bacon is browned, about 10 minutes. Scatter mixture over meats in casserole. Drain beans and pour into casserole along with broth and bouquet garni; cover casserole tightly. Bake in a 325° oven until beans are tender to bite and liquid is mostly absorbed, about 3 hours. Gently mix in sausages, cover, and let stand until sausages are hot, about 10 minutes. Uncover, discard bouquet garni, and garnish cassoulet with parsley. Add salt to taste. Serves 8.

Per serving: 774 cal. (53 percent from fat); 47 g protein; 46 g fat (16 g sat.); 42 g carbo.; 598 mg sodium; 139 mg chol.

Bouquet garni. On a 9- to 10-inch cheesecloth square, place 12 **black peppercorns,** 4 **fresh** or dried **bay leaves,** 2 sprigs (3 or 4 in.) **fresh thyme,** and 1 sprig (about 3 in.) **rosemary.** Bring edges of cloth together and tie with cotton string to enclose seasonings.

Savoy Brasserie's Rabbit Pot au Feu
—Dean Max, San Francisco

1 rabbit (about 3 lb.), cut into 4 pieces

2 tablespoons olive oil

1½ cups diced onions

1¼ cups diced celery

½ cup diced carrot

6 cups low-sodium regular-strength chicken broth

Bouquet garni (directions follow)

1 head garlic, cut in half crosswise

½ pound smoked ham hock

12 tiny (about 1 in. wide, ½ lb. total) turnips, rinsed and ends trimmed

8 red or white tiny (about 1 in. wide, ½ lb. total) onions, peeled

2 leeks (about 1 in. wide), root ends and tough leaves trimmed, rinsed well, and cut crosswise into 16 equal pieces

16 tiny (about 4 in. long) carrots, scrubbed and tops discarded

8 medium-size (about 1-in.-wide caps, ½ lb. total) mushrooms, rinsed and stem ends trimmed

1 cup finely shredded red cabbage

Fresh chervil, parsley, or thyme sprigs

Salt

Freshly ground pepper

In a 5- to 6-quart ovenproof pan over medium-high heat, brown rabbit in oil without crowding, about 10 minutes. As pieces are browned, set aside in a rimmed pan; add remaining meat to oil to brown. To oil, add diced onions, celery, and diced carrot; stir often until vegetables are limp, about 10 minutes.

Stir broth into pan, then add bouquet garni, garlic, ham hock, rabbit, and any juices. Bring to a boil over high heat; cover pan tightly. Bake in a 300° oven until ham hock is tender when pierced, about 2 hours. With a slotted spoon, transfer rabbit pieces to rimmed pan; cover, and keep warm in a 150° oven. Lift out ham hock and let stand just until cool enough to handle. Pull or trim off ham hock skin, fat, and bone, and discard. Mince meat.

Meanwhile, pour broth mixture through a fine strainer into a bowl; press residue to extract liquid. Discard residue. Skim fat from broth.

Wipe cooking pan clean and return broth to it; bring to a boil over high heat. Add turnips, tiny onions, leeks, and whole carrots; cover and simmer for 3 minutes. Add mushrooms and cabbage; cover and simmer until all vegetables are barely tender to bite, 2 to 4 minutes more.

Divide rabbit and ham among 4 wide bowls. Ladle broth and vegetables into bowls. Garnish with fresh chervil; season to taste with salt and pepper. Makes 4 servings.

Per serving: 684 cal. (36 percent from fat); 66 g protein; 27 g fat (6.6 g sat.); 46 g carbo.; 598 mg sodium; 160 mg chol.

Bouquet garni. With cotton string, tie in a tight bundle 1 **fresh** or dried **bay leaf,**

4 or 5 **parsley sprigs,** and about 20 (about 4 in.) **fresh thyme sprigs.**

Pinot Bistro's Coq au Vin with Caramelized Roots and Chips

—Octavio Becerra, Studio City

2   chickens (each about 4½ lb.), cut up

2   tablespoons coarsely cracked black pepper

5   cups dry red wine

½   cup all-purpose flour

2   tablespoons salad oil

2   cups minced onions

2   cups thinly sliced mushrooms

1   cup minced celery

¼   cup minced garlic

¼   pound bacon, diced

     Bouquet garni (directions follow)

2   tablespoons cornstarch smoothly blended with ¼ cup water

     Caramelized root vegetables and chips (recipe follows)

     Italian parsley sprigs

     Salt

Rinse chicken and place in a bowl. Add pepper and wine, then cover and chill at least 2 hours or up to 1 day.

Lift chicken from bowl, reserving liquid. Pat chicken dry, coat with flour, and shake off excess. Pour oil into a 6- to 8-quart pan over medium-high heat. When oil is hot, add chicken, without crowding, and brown, about 5 minutes. As pieces brown, transfer to a rimmed pan.

Discard fat in pan and wipe pan clean. Add onions, mushrooms, celery, garlic, and bacon. Stir often over medium-high heat until bacon and vegetables are lightly browned, about 15 minutes. Return to pan the chicken, any juices, and the marinating liquid, and add the bouquet garni.

Bring mixture to a boil over high heat, then cover tightly and simmer until chicken is very tender when pierced, about 40 minutes. With a slotted spoon, transfer chicken to a rimmed pan and keep warm. Pour mixture in pan through a strainer into a bowl. Discard vegetable residue and skim fat from juices. Return juices to pan and boil over high heat, uncovered, until reduced to 3 cups, about 10 minutes. Stirring, add cornstarch mixture, and stir until boil resumes. Return chicken pieces to the wine sauce in pan and keep warm.

Mound caramelized vegetables on a large rimmed platter. Arrange chicken pieces beside vegetables and moisten with a little wine sauce. Garnish platter with chips and Italian parsley sprigs. Accompany with remaining sauce and add salt to taste. Makes 8 servings.

Per serving: 760 cal. (43 percent from fat); 65 g protein; 36 g fat (13 g sat.); 17 g carbo.; 268 mg sodium; 201 mg chol.

Bouquet garni. On a 9- or 10-inch cheesecloth square, combine 4 **fresh** or dried **bay leaves,** 3 whole **cloves,** 4 sprigs (3 or 4 in.) **fresh thyme,** 4 sprigs **parsley,** and 4 sprigs (4 or 5 in.) **fresh savory.** Bring edges of cloth together and tie with cotton string to enclose seasonings.

Caramelized Root Vegetables and Chips

8   large (about 2 lb. total) carrots, peeled

6   large (about 2¼ lb. total) parsnips, peeled

4   large (about 2 lb. total) yams, peeled

2   tablespoons butter or margarine, melted

     About 4 cups salad oil

¼   cup minced Italian parsley

     Salt

Cut all but 1 carrot and 1 parsnip diagonally into ½-inch-thick pieces. Cut 3 yams lengthwise into ½-inch-wide wedges. Mix cut vegetables with butter and 2 tablespoons oil in an 11- by 17-inch roasting pan. Bake in a 400° oven, turning occasionally with a wide spatula, until vegetables are tender when pierced and begin to brown at edges, about 1 hour. Use or keep warm up to 1 hour. If making ahead, let vegetables cool, transfer to a bowl, cover airtight, and chill up to 1 day. To reheat, return to roasting pan, cover with foil, and bake in a 350° oven until hot, about 30 minutes.

In a deep 4- to 5-quart pan, heat remaining oil to 300°. With a vegetable slicer, cut remaining carrot, parsnip, and yam into long, thin ribbons; keep each kind separate.

Drop a handful of vegetable strips, 1 kind at a time, into hot oil; regulate heat to maintain temperature. Fry vegetables until crisp and lightly browned; carrot takes about 1 minute and 10 seconds, parsnip 1 minute and 20 seconds, and yam about 2½ minutes. As cooked, quickly lift vegetable from pan with a slotted spoon and drain on paper towels. If making ahead, package airtight as soon as chips are cool and hold at room temperature up to 6 hours. Serve chips sprinkled with minced parsley and add salt to taste.

Per serving: 386 cal. (40 percent from fat); 3.9 g protein; 17 g fat (3.6 g sat.); 57 g carbo.; 85 mg sodium; 7.5 mg chol.

Fringale's Braised Short Ribs with Parsnips

—Gerald Hirigoyen, San Francisco

4   pounds beef short ribs, fat trimmed, separated and cut into 2½- to 3-inch pieces

1   tablespoon olive oil

1   cup diced carrots

1   cup diced onion

⅔   cup diced celery

6   cloves garlic, minced or pressed

1   cup dry white wine

4   cups regular-strength beef broth

     Bouquet garni (directions follow)

     About ¾ teaspoon freshly ground pepper

4   large (1½ lb. total) parsnips, peeled and cut into sticks ⅓ by 4 inches

2   tablespoons butter or margarine

     Chopped parsley and parsley sprigs

     Salt

In a 5- to 6-quart pan over high heat, brown short ribs well in oil, without crowding, 4 or 5 minutes. As pieces are browned, transfer to a rimmed pan; add remaining meat to hot oil.

When meat is removed, add carrots, onion, celery, and garlic to oil in pan. Stir often over medium-high heat until vegetables are limp and lightly browned, about 10 minutes.

Stir in wine and broth, then add meat and any juices, bouquet garni, and ½ teaspoon pepper. Bring to a boil over high heat, then reduce heat and simmer, covered, until meat is very tender when pierced, about 2¼ hours. Discard bouquet garni. With a slotted spoon, place ribs on a platter and sprinkle with about ¼ cup of the vegetables and juices; keep warm.

Skim fat from pan juices. Measure pan juices; if more than 1½ cups, boil over high heat, uncovered, stirring occasionally until reduced to this amount. Or if less, add water to make 1½ cups and heat to boiling. Smoothly purée pan juices in a blender or food processor; pour this sauce into a pitcher and keep warm.

Meanwhile, in an 11- to 12-inch frying pan over high heat, bring 1½ cups water to boiling and add parsnips. Cover and reduce heat; simmer until parsnips are tender when pierced, about 5 minutes. Drain, add butter to parsnips, and cook, uncovered, over medium-high heat until parsnips are lightly browned, 3 or 4 minutes; stir frequently or shake pan. Arrange parsnips next to meat. Scatter chopped parsley over meat and vegetables and garnish platter with parsley sprigs. Serve with the sauce; add salt and pepper to taste. Serves 4.

Per serving: 604 cal. (48 percent from fat); 42 g protein; 32 g fat (14 g sat.); 37 g carbo.; 183 mg sodium; 130 mg chol.

Bouquet garni. With cotton string, tie in a tight bundle 1 **fresh** or dried **bay leaf,** 4 or 5 **parsley sprigs,** and about 20 (about 4 in.) **fresh thyme sprigs.** ■

By Christine Weber Hale, Elaine Johnson

Mein, udon, soba…
a guide to Asian noodles

Choose them for their taste…and chew

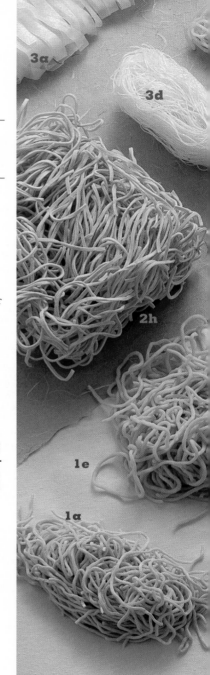

NOODLES ARE ASIA'S fast food. A dizzying selection of dishes based on them is sold throughout the Far East and Southeast Asia in noodle shops and by street vendors.

The noodles are thick or thin, served tender or crisp, hot or cold, and usually in delicious combinations that go together fast.

In the West, most supermarkets stock a good variety of the dried noodles next to the spaghetti and fettuccine, and fresh noodles are frequently found in refrigerated sections. For an even broader selection of noodles, visit Asian markets.

How do you decide which noodle to use? The photograph at right shows the basic noodles you can expect to find. Each behaves differently in some ways, but they all are very similar after being soaked or cooked in water.

In general, you choose a noodle for its texture and flavor, as in each of the following dishes. In the first, chewy fresh noodles, pan-browned, are the hot foundation for a main dish with eggs and sesame seed. In the second, wiry cellophane noodles made of rice or beans swell up instantly when fried to make an airy-crisp base for braised pork. Cold thin noodles support savory Chinese sausages in the third recipe. In the last dish, hot thin noodles go with a stir-fry of shrimp.

Look for the Asian seasonings for these recipes in a well-stocked supermarket. Chinese sausages are in the meat, refrigerator, or freezer section.

Chinese Noodle Cake with Eggs

If you can't find Shanghai-style noodles, serve the salad mixture on 6 cups hot, cooked thin wheat noodles.

- ¼ cup sesame seed
- 1 pound fresh Shanghai-style (thick wheat-flour) noodles
- 2 cups regular-strength chicken broth
  Soy dressing (recipe follows)
- 4 to 5 green onions (ends trimmed), cut diagonally into thin slices
- 4 hard-cooked large eggs, quartered

Stir sesame seed in an 8- to 10-inch frying pan on medium heat until golden, about 5 minutes; pour from pan and set aside.

Pull noodles apart to loosen and separate slightly. Lay gently in an even layer in the frying pan. Pour in broth. Bring to a boil over high heat, cover, and simmer gently until noodles are tender-firm to bite, 15 to 20 minutes. Do not stir noodles.

Uncover and boil on high heat until liquid has cooked away; watch to avoid scorching. Remove from heat and let stand 3 to 5 minutes. Slip a spatula under noodles to make sure they aren't stuck to the pan, but avoid breaking them apart. Invert onto the pan a 12- to 14-inch-diameter platter with a slight rim. Hold pan and platter to-

gether and flip over to unmold noodles.

Pour the soy dressing over noodles. Sprinkle with sesame seed and green onions. Arrange the egg pieces around the noodles. Cut noodles into wedges. Makes 4 servings.

Per serving: 584 cal. (22 percent from fat); 30 g protein; 14 g fat (2.8 g sat.); 85 g carbo.; 1,129 mg sodium; 274 mg chol.

Soy dressing. In a small bowl, stir or whisk together ¼ cup *each* **soy sauce** and **regular-strength chicken broth**, 3 tablespoons **rice vinegar**, 1 teaspoon **Oriental sesame oil**, and **chili-flavor oil** or cayenne to taste.

Hot Noodle and Pork Salad

- About 1 quart salad oil
- 3 ounces dried bean threads or rice sticks
- 2 quarts shredded napa cabbage or iceberg lettuce
  Braised pork (recipe follows)
- 2 to 3 green onions (ends trimmed), thinly sliced
- 1 cup lightly packed fresh cilantro (coriander) sprigs

Heat 1 to 1½ inches oil to 400° in a wok or 10- to 12-inch frying pan on high heat. Pull noodles apart into 4 or 5 portions. Drop 1 portion into hot oil. After 3 to 5 seconds, turn noodles. Cook until evenly puffed, 2 to 5 seconds longer. Quickly lift out noodles with a slotted spoon; drain on towels. Repeat to cook remaining noodles.

Pile noodles around edge

Which noodle to

Asian noodles are widely available fresh or dried. This sampler introduces you to some of the kinds that are

of a platter. Mound cabbage in the center, and spoon hot pork onto cabbage. Sprinkle with green onions and cilantro and serve at once (noodles soften quickly). Serves 6.

Per serving: 631 cal. (66 percent

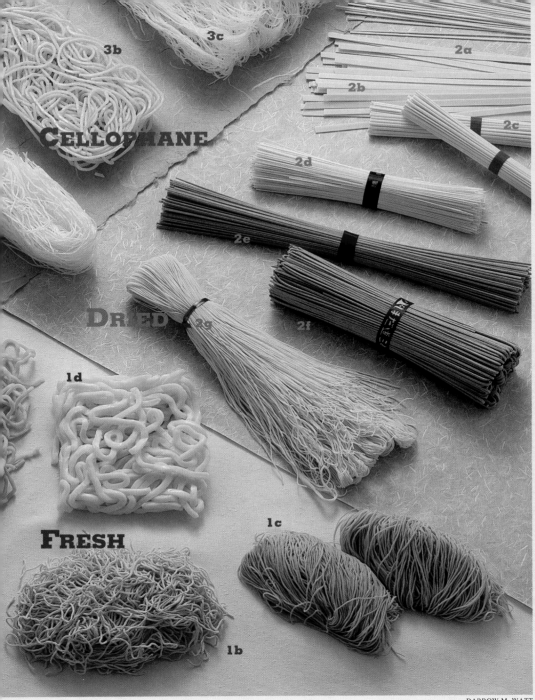

CELLOPHANE

DRIED

FRESH

3b
3c
2a
2b
2c
2d
2e
2f
2g
1d
1c
1b

DARROW M. WATT

have a distinctive, hearty taste. Cellophane noodles have a neutral, bland flavor.

Noodle shapes range from very fine strands to wide, thick, round or flat ribbons, and from straight bundles to tangled coils.

Chinese wheat-flour noodles are called *mein. Somen* are fine Japanese ones; *udon* are wider and thicker. Filipinos call noodles *pancit.* Wheat noodles can include egg or many other flavorings, such as shrimp. Japanese buckwheat noodles are called *soba.*

Use noodles of the same base and shape interchangeably.

Fresh noodles. Mein: thick (1a), medium (1b), and thin (1c). Udon: round and thick (1d). Pancit: round (1e).

Dried noodles. Mein: very fine (2a). Udon: flat (2b) or round (2c). Straight round noodles (2d) labeled somen, udon, or mein. Buckwheat soba: long (2e) or short (2f). Somen: folded (2g). Flour sticks (2h) are wheat-flour noodles, dried, fried, and ready to eat.

Cellophane noodles. Read labels carefully: noodles made of rice or bean flour will puff when fried. Yam (sometimes called potato) noodles won't.

These wiry, plastic-looking dried noodles have many names. Those made with rice flour (3a, 3b, 3c) might be called rice sticks, long rice, or rice noodles; in Chinese, they are *py mee fun, mai fun,* or *mi fun.*

Mung bean–flour noodles (3d) are called bean threads; *saifun* in Chinese; *harusame* in Japanese.

To prepare cellophane noodles, soak them in hot water for a few minutes until tender to bite; drain. (Or buy them soaked, canned or refrigerated.)

use? Fresh or dried; wheat, buckwheat, or cellophane?

easiest to find .

The noodles are made of wheat or buckwheat flour, or—if they are called cellophane (or transparent) noodles or rice sticks—the base can be rice, yam, or mung bean flour.

Dried wheat-flour noodles taste much like similarly shaped Italian-style pastas. Brown buckwheat noodles

from fat); 28 g protein; 46 g fat (14 g sat.); 26 g carbo.; 231 mg sodium; 110 mg chol.

Braised pork. In a 5- to 6-quart pan over medium heat, mix 2 pounds **boned pork butt** or shoulder, cut into 1-inch cubes; 1 large (about ½ lb.) **onion,** thinly sliced; 5 cloves **garlic,** minced; 3 tablespoons minced **fresh ginger;** and ½ cup **regular-strength chicken broth.**

Cover and cook until meat juices accumulate, about 30 minutes. Uncover; stir occasionally over medium-high heat until liquid evaporates, the meat begins to brown in its fat, and drippings are a rich brown color, about 20 minutes.

Add 1¼ cups additional regular-strength chicken broth and ½ cup **rice vinegar;** stir to free browned bits. Add ⅓ cup **canned Chinese bean sauce** (or soy sauce, to taste), and ½ to 1 teaspoon **cayenne,** to taste.

Cover and simmer until meat is very tender when

FAT FRESH NOODLES, left, make a crisp-chewy cake; serve hot, topped with hard-cooked eggs, green onions, and lots of toasted sesame seed. Thin cold noodles, right, are a tender base for Chinese sausages. Season with rice vinegar and fresh ginger; serve cool as a main dish.

mirin (sweet rice wine) or dry sherry; 2 teaspoons **Oriental sesame oil;** 1½ teaspoons **soy sauce;** and 1 teaspoon **sugar.**

Thin Noodles with Shiitake Mushrooms, Shrimp, and Oyster Sauce

- 2 cups (about 2 oz.) dried shiitake mushrooms
- 8 ounces dried thin noodles, or about 1 pound fresh thin noodles (see previous page)
- 2 teaspoons Oriental sesame oil
- 6 tablespoons oyster sauce
- 2 tablespoons salad oil
- 1 pound medium-size shrimp (31 to 35 per lb.), shelled and deveined
- ¼ pound cooked ham slices, cut into ⅛-inch-wide strips
- 1 tablespoon chopped fresh ginger
- 3 green onions (ends trimmed), cut into 1½-inch pieces

In a bowl, cover mushrooms with warm water; let stand until mushrooms soften, 10 to 15 minutes. Squeeze mushrooms dry. Cut off and discard stems. Slice caps into ¼-inch-wide strips.

In a 3- to 4-quart pan, bring 2 quarts water to a boil on high heat. Add noodles and cook, uncovered, stirring occasionally, until tender-firm to bite, 8 to 12 minutes for dried noodles, 3 to 5 minutes for fresh ones. Drain noodles; return to pan and mix with sesame oil and 3 tablespoons oyster sauce.

While noodles cook, place a wok or 10- to 12-inch frying pan over high heat. Add salad oil; when hot, add mushrooms, shrimp, ham, and ginger. Stir-fry until shrimp are opaque in center (cut to test), about 5 minutes. Stir in remaining oyster sauce and green onions.

Pour noodles into a wide bowl. Pour shrimp mixture onto noodles. Serves 4 or 5.

Per serving: 417 cal. (24 percent from fat); 31 g protein; 11 g fat (1.9 g sat.); 48 g carbo.; 1,320 mg sodium; 136 mg chol. ■

By Betsy Reynolds Bateson, Pam Eimers

pierced, about 45 minutes. Uncover and boil until most liquid evaporates, about 10 minutes; stir often. Drain 1 can (7 oz.) **sliced water chestnuts;** add to pork. Serve hot. If making ahead, cover and chill up to 1 day; reheat.

Cold Noodle Salad with Chinese Sausage

- 2 green onions, ends trimmed

  About ¼ pound Chinese link sausages or pepperoni, thinly sliced

- 6 ounces dried thin noodles, or 10 to 12 ounces fresh thin noodles (see previous page)

  Seasoning sauce (recipe follows)

  Fresh cilantro (coriander) sprigs

Cut onions into 3-inch sections; cut lengthwise into very thin strips. Put in a small bowl and cover with cold water. Cover and chill until strands curl, at least 15 minutes or up to 1 day.

In an 8- to 10-inch frying pan over medium-high heat, stir sausages often just until meat begins to crisp. Drain on towels.

Bring 2 quarts water to a boil in a 3- to 4-quart pan on high heat. Add noodles and cook, uncovered, stirring occasionally, until tender-firm to bite, 8 to 12 minutes for dried noodles, 3 to 5 minutes for fresh ones. Drain noodles; immerse in cold water until cool. Drain and mix noodles with seasoning sauce; pour onto a large platter. Drain onions and scatter over noodles, then add sausages and cilantro sprigs. Serves 3 or 4.

Per serving: 339 cal. (40 percent from fat); 12 g protein; 15 g fat (4.9 g sat.); 37 g carbo.; 710 mg sodium; 22 mg chol.

Seasoning sauce. In a bowl, stir together 2 tablespoons *each* **seasoned rice vinegar** (or 2 tablespoons rice vinegar and 2 teaspoons sugar), minced **fresh ginger,** and minced **cilantro;** 1 tablespoon *each* **lemon juice** and

PETER CHRISTIANSEN

GALANGAL, GINGER, *and ground turmeric from the same ginger species combine with chilies, lemon grass, seasonings, and fish sauce to form a classic Asian yellow curry paste.*

A curry classic

Keep this yellow paste on hand for seasoning a variety of dishes

A RECIPE SEARCH FOR A yellow curry paste led us to Asian cooking expert and restaurateur Bruce Cost. As a result of his thorough research into yellow curry pastes, he developed this classic version, which he uses at Ginger Club in Palo Alto, California, and Ginger Island in Berkeley.

Make the paste to use in Cost's recipe for noodles with curry, scallops, and chives— it's a perfect vehicle for showcasing the curry. Stir the remaining paste into fried rice, soups, scrambled eggs— even tuna salad. One batch will keep up to a month in the refrigerator.

Yellow Curry Paste

10 to 15 (about ¼ oz.) small dried hot red chilies

2 tablespoons coriander seed

1 tablespoon cumin seed

1 teaspoon black peppercorns

¾ cup chopped fresh cilantro (coriander), including stems

¼ cup *each* fresh lime juice and chopped garlic, about 12 cloves

2 tablespoons *each* fish sauce, chopped fresh ginger, and minced lemon grass core (about 1 large stalk, tough outer layers discarded and bottom bulb portion used)

1 tablespoon chopped fresh galangal or fresh ginger

2 teaspoons ground dried turmeric or 1½ tablespoons chopped fresh turmeric

2 teaspoons peanut oil

1 tablespoon ground fish sauce (anchovy cream or shrimp paste) or 1 tablespoon fish sauce

To an 8- to 10-inch frying pan, add chilies, coriander seed, cumin seed, and peppercorns. Cook over medium-high heat, stirring often, until fragrant and lightly toasted, about 2 minutes. With a mortar and pestle or a spice grinder, grind toasted ingredients to a coarse powder; set aside.

To a food processor or blender, add chopped fresh cilantro, lime juice, garlic, fish sauce, ginger, lemon grass, galangal, turmeric, and peanut oil; pulse or whirl to grind to a coarse paste. Add ground spice mixture and ground fish sauce; pulse or whirl until mixture is smooth. Use, or store airtight in the refrigerator up to 1 month. Makes about 1 cup.

Per tablespoon: 24 cal. (44 percent from fat); 0.8 g protein; 1.2 g fat (0.2 g sat.); 3 g carbo.; 2 mg sodium; 0 mg chol.

Noodles with Curry, Scallops, and Chives

¾ pound large scallops

2 teaspoons *each* cornstarch and Asian sesame oil

¾ pound fresh Chinese egg noodles

About 2 tablespoons peanut oil

½ cup regular-strength chicken broth

¼ cup yellow curry paste (from preceding recipe)

1 teaspoon sugar

2 cups 1½-inch pieces Chinese chives or green onions, ends trimmed

⅓ cup coarsely chopped roasted and salted peanuts

Fresh lime slices (optional)

Cilantro (coriander) sprigs (optional)

Slice each scallop crosswise into about 3 rounds, each about ⅓-inch thick. Mix with cornstarch and sesame oil; chill at least 15 minutes, or up to 4 hours.

Meanwhile, in a 5- to 6-quart pan, bring about 2 quarts water to a boil over high heat. Add noodles; cook just until tender to bite, about 4 minutes. Drain; rinse with cold water. Gently toss the noodles with 1 teaspoon peanut oil; set aside.

To a wok or 12-inch frying pan over high heat, add 2 tablespoons peanut oil; heat until hot. Add half the scallops, lower heat to medium, and quickly stir to separate rounds. Cook, turning often, until scallops are opaque but still moist-looking in center (cut to test), about 4 minutes. Remove scallops with a slotted spoon; drain on paper towels. Repeat process with remaining scallops.

To pan drippings, add broth, curry paste, and sugar. Stir briefly and add chives; cook 5 seconds. Add noodles and cook, stirring, 30 seconds more, then add scallops and cook just until hot. Divide among 4 dinner plates. Sprinkle with peanuts, and garnish with lime slices and cilantro sprigs; serve immediately. Makes 4 servings.

Per serving: 601 cal. (31 percent from fat); 31 g protein; 21 g fat (3.3 g sat.); 74 g carbo.; 223 mg sodium; 109 mg chol. ∎

By Betsy Reynolds Bateson

YELLOW CURRY *enlivens Chinese egg noodles with scallops.*

PAUL HAMMOND

DUMP STARCH *into hot liquid, and lumps are guaranteed.*

STIR DILUTED STARCH *into hot liquid, and it will blend in smoothly and thicken evenly.*

Why?

Why are gravies lumpy, sauces murky, and pies runny? It depends on the thickener and how it is used

What turns a thin liquid into a smooth, clinging sauce or gravy? Why are these mixtures sometimes shiny and clear, other times opaque and murky? What makes a pie filling firm enough to cut? These changes happen when liquids are thickened, and if you've used a starch to thicken them, the results depend on the kind of starch you've used and how you've used it.

The most common starch thickeners include flours or powders of wheat, corn, potato, arrowroot, and rice, and grainy-texture quick-cooking tapioca, which is made from manioc.

In each of these starches, bonded carbohydrate molecules—the gluey, thickening starch—are crammed into small granules. It is essential to physically separate these granules before heating them in liquid in order to tap their full thickening potential.

When the liquid is hot enough, the starch in the granules absorbs the liquid, swells dramatically, and bursts the granule shells, forming many tiny gels and thickening the liquid. The process is called gelatinization.

Why do I get lumps in gravies and sauces?

If you dump the dry starch thickener into simmering liquid, you get a lumpy mess. (The only exceptions are instant flour, which has been chemically altered, and quick-cooking tapioca.) Starch in the granules on the surface of each dry blob swells instantly when the granules hit hot liquid, forming a tight shell that keeps moisture from reaching the granules inside the clump—and their internal starch. As a result, you get a lot of lumps and a sauce that won't thicken. To rescue the mixture, you can rub it through a fine strainer or whirl it in a blender and re-heat. But these steps also reduce the thickening properties of the starch, and you will need to add more diluted starch and cook the mixture again to achieve the desired thickness.

To prevent lumps, you need to combine the starch with a medium such as a cool liquid, sugar, or a hot or cold fat, and then stir to keep the separate starch granules from sticking together as they cook. If you use a cold liquid, you'll get the smoothest results if you stir it, a little at a time, into the flour. If you mix starch with a liquid fat, the fat can be hot or cold.

How do I get the amount of thickening I want?

The ratio of starch to liquid for specific thickening is standardized: see the chart at the bottom of this page for how much of each to use.

You need to cook each starch just enough to reach its thickening potential (see chart); if cooked too long or mixed too vigorously, the mixture thins as the starch's bonding capacity breaks down. In traditional dishes thickened with a cooked roux, such as gumbos, jambalayas, and étouffées, wheat flour and fat are cooked and stirred just until blended or long enough to brown or almost blacken the flour. As the flour darkens, it loses its thickening power; as a result, a dark roux made with a cup of flour may have no more thickening ability than a couple of tablespoons of diluted flour—but of course, the flavor and color of the dish are quite different.

If a cooked mixture is thinner than you want, dilute more of the starch with water (or another liquid in the recipe) and stir, a little at a time, into the hot sauce until it has the consistency you want. If a sauce is too thick, add more liquid to thin it or cook the sauce longer (which also causes thinning) and add liquid to make up for the amount lost to evaporation as the mixture cooks.

If the mixture is to be served cold, keep in mind that some starch mixtures thicken and stiffen as they cool.

Why do some sauces look shiny and clear, others dull and opaque?

When starch absorbs liquid and swells with heat, it becomes gelatinized and transmits more light because the particles are no longer so tightly packed. Cornstarch, arrowroot, and potato starch produce the most transparent, shiny sauces. Wheat flour sauces are opaque and less glossy because the starch binds with protein in the flour, blocking the transmission of light.

"How can I get the filling of my lemon meringue pie to set up with cornstarch?"
—Nancy Mennel, Berkeley

Cooking the cornstarch filling with lemon juice can cause the filling to thin as it cools. The acid in the lemon juice breaks apart the starch bonds. This also happens when you cook other high-acid liquids, such as vinegar and other fruit juices, with wheat flour, potato starch, arrowroot, or rice flour.

Another ingredient that can reduce the thickening potential of these starches is sugar. Sugar, in concentrations above a specific level in the cooking liquid, literally hogs the water, and the starch can't get enough to swell and thicken as it cooks.

The solutions are simple: Make sure the starch is diluted by smoothly blending it with the cooking liquid before you add the sugar. Cook the starch-sugar-liquid mixture (including lemon peel for lemon pie), then take it off the heat and stir in the lemon juice (or other acid for different sauces). Pour the filling into the pastry, cover filling (hot or cool) with meringue, and bake to brown the topping. But don't serve the pie until the filling is cool. Commercially, lemon pies are made with vegetable gums and chemically altered cornstarch, both of which are resistant to acid.

Why does quick-cooking tapioca do such a good job of thickening fruit pies?

Acid does not alter tapioca's ability to thicken. In fruit pies, where acidity varies depending on the fruit used and its ripeness, tapioca gives consistent results. Also, tapioca mixed with sugar and then added to the fruit needs no liquid to dilute it. The sugar makes the fruit juicy, and the tapioca soaks up the juice. The particles of tapioca swell as they cook, become transparent, and continue to thicken the filling as it cools. When cut, the fruit mixture is not rigid but holds together.

More questions?

We would like to know what kitchen mysteries you're curious about. Send your questions to Why?, *Sunset Magazine*, 80 Willow Rd., Menlo Park, Calif. 94025. With the help of Dr. George K. York, extension food technologist at UC Davis, *Sunset* food editors will try to find solutions. We'll answer your questions in the magazine. ∎

By Linda Lau Anusasananan

STARCH THICKENERS: How much to use and how to cook with them

Thickener	Amount for 1 cup liquid	How to dilute	How to cook
All-purpose wheat flour	*Thin sauce:* 1 tablespoon *Medium sauce:* 2 to 2½ tablespoons *Thick sauce:* 3 to 4 tablespoons	Mix with cold liquid, in fat, or with sugar. Heat with liquid, or stir into hot liquid.	Stir until boiling. Cook 2 or 3 minutes to remove raw taste. Opaque. Thicker and rigid when cool.
Cornstarch	1 tablespoon = 2 tablespoons wheat flour	Same as for wheat flour.	Stir just until boiling. Transparent. Thicker and rigid when cool.
Potato starch and arrowroot starch	1 tablespoon = 2 tablespoons wheat flour	Same as for wheat flour.	Stir to cook; excessive stirring thins. Maximum thickness occurs at 176°, below the boiling point. Thins quickly if overcooked. Use in starch-egg mixtures or sauces when high heat is not desired. Very transparent. Semisoft when cool.
Sweet or white (waxy) rice flour	2 teaspoons = 1 tablespoon wheat flour	Same as for wheat flour.	Same as for wheat flour. Not inclined to lump. Same consistency hot or cool. Doesn't thin when frozen and thawed.
Quick-cooking tapioca	1 tablespoon = 2 tablespoons wheat flour	Mix in cold or hot liquid. Or mix with sugar, then fruit for pie fillings, and let stand until juicy, about 15 minutes.	Stir just until boiling. Gets gummy if stirred while cooling. Bake in pies until bubbling. Thicker when cool. Transparent, but tapioca particles visible. Soft gel.

Taking liberties with sticky buns

PHILADELPHIA IS ONE OF the cradles of our independence, but it has never been able to compete with Boston, New Orleans, or San Francisco in the Famous Regional Dishes sweepstakes. The Philly cheese-steak is a cardiologist's nightmare, scrapple is definitely an acquired taste, and pepper pot soup is of purely antiquarian interest. The Philadelphia sticky bun, on the other hand, is so suitable as a coffee companion that one is hard put to imagine a more perfect breakfast sweet bread.

Nevertheless, John Stearns has succeeded in gilding these gustatory lilies, giving them fruit and nut fillings and a caramel icing. If you can't decide between orange-pecan or apple-pecan filling, make both.

Caramel Breakfast Rolls

2 packages active dry yeast

¼ cup warm (110°) water

½ cup (¼ lb.) butter or margarine

½ cup milk

½ cup sugar

¼ teaspoon salt

About 4 cups all-purpose flour

3 large eggs

Orange-pecan filling or apple-pecan filling (recipes follow)

Caramel topping (recipe follows)

In a small bowl, sprinkle yeast over warm water; let stand until softened, about 5 minutes. In a 1- to 1½-quart pan over medium heat, occasionally stir butter, breaking into chunks, just until melted. Remove from heat and stir in milk, sugar, and salt. Pour into a large bowl and let cool until lukewarm. Add 2 cups flour, eggs, and yeast mixture. With a mixer, beat on low speed until evenly moistened, then mix at high speed until dough is stretchy, about 3 minutes. With a heavy spoon, stir 1½ cups flour into dough until well moistened, then stir in about ½ cup more flour to make soft dough. Scrape dough onto a lightly floured board and knead until smooth and elastic, 8 to 10 minutes; add more flour as required to prevent sticking. Place dough in a greased bowl; turn over to grease top. Cover with plastic wrap and let dough rise in a warm place until almost double, 1 to 1½ hours.

Knead dough on a lightly floured board to expel air, then divide equally. Roll 1 portion at a time into a 10- by 12-inch rectangle. Spread each rectangle with ½ the filling. Starting at a 12-inch side, roll each rectangle tightly to enclose filling; pinch seams to seal. Cut each roll into 10 to 12 equal slices and place, coil side down, in 2 lightly oiled 9-inch-diameter cake pans. Cover with plastic wrap and let rise until puffy, about 1 hour.

Bake, uncovered, in a 350° oven until rolls are well browned and feel firm when touched, about 30 minutes. Lay a rack on top of rolls in each pan; invert to release rolls. Invert a plate onto each batch of rolls and, holding rack and plate, turn the rolls over onto plates. Let rolls cool until warm or room temperature, then spread evenly with caramel topping. Serve, or if making ahead, cover and let stand up to 1 day; freeze to store longer. Makes 20 to 24.

Per roll with orange-pecan filling: 247 cal. (47 percent from fat); 5.3 g protein; 13 g fat (5.2 g sat.); 27 g carbo.; 133 mg sodium; 48 mg chol.

Per roll with apple-pecan filling: 272 cal. (43 percent from fat); 5.4 g protein; 13 g fat (5.2 g sat.); 34 g carbo.; 133 mg sodium; 48 mg chol.

Orange-pecan filling. Beat together 1½ cups (12 oz.) **neufchâtel** (light cream) **cheese** or part-skim ricotta cheese, ½ cup **orange marmalade,** 1 tablespoon finely grated **orange peel,** 1½ tablespoons **sugar,** and 1½ cups coarsely chopped **pecans.**

Apple-pecan filling. Beat together 1½ cups (12 oz.) **neufchâtel** (light cream) **cheese** or part-skim ricotta cheese, ¾ cup firmly packed **brown sugar,** 1½ teaspoons **ground cinnamon,** ⅛ teaspoon **ground nutmeg,** ¾ cup **golden raisins,** 2 cups peeled and chopped **tart apples,** and 1½ cups coarsely chopped **pecans.**

Caramel topping. In a 2- to 3-quart pan, combine ½ cup **sugar** and 1 tablespoon **water.** Bring to a boil over medium-high heat, stirring until sugar dissolves. Cook mixture, uncovered and without stirring, until a dark caramel color, 2 or 3 minutes; watch closely to prevent scorching as syrup darkens. At once add ½ cup **whipping cream;** simmer gently, stirring often, until caramel dissolves, 2 or 3 minutes. Remove from heat and stir in 2 tablespoons **butter** or margarine and ½ teaspoon **vanilla;** stir until mixture is smoothly blended. Let cool; if making ahead, cover and let stand up to 4 hours.

John W. Stearns

La Crescenta, California

By Joan Griffiths, Richard Dunmire

First-course drama

 PAIRING OF ORDINARY ROOT vegetables—leeks and beets—results in a quick, sophisticated starter.

Leeks in Beet Dressing

6   large (about 1½-in. diameter, 2½ lb. total) leeks

Beet dressing (recipe follows)

Thin lemon slices

Salt and pepper

Trim and discard root ends and tough dark green tops from leeks. Cut each leek in half lengthwise; rinse well. Tie halves back together around middle with cotton string. In a 5- to 6-quart pan, bring about 2 quarts water to a boil over high heat. Add leeks; cook, uncovered, over medium heat until tender when pierced, 6 to 8 minutes. Drain; immerse in ice water. When cool, drain. (If making ahead, cover and chill up to 1 day.)

Pour ⅙ of the beet dressing on each of 6 plates. Untie leeks; lay 2 halves on each plate. Garnish with lemon. Add salt and pepper to taste. Serves 6.

Per serving: 78 cal. (4.6 percent from fat); 1.6 g protein; 0.4 g fat (0 g sat.); 18 g carbo.; 168 mg sodium; 0 mg chol.

Beet dressing. In a blender or food processor, purée until smooth 1 can (8 oz.) **sliced pickled beets** including liquid. Add ¼ cup **water,** 2 tablespoons **lemon juice,** and 2 teaspoons **Dijon mustard;** whirl until blended. (If making ahead, cover and chill up to 1 day.) ■

By Linda Lau Anusasananan

POACHED LEEKS *in a pool of crimson dressing make a splashy first course.*

CRISP TORTILLA *strips bring onion soup to a different conclusion.*

A chili (and onion) soup for a chilly night

Mexican flavors turn a French classic on its ear

O NION SOUP, ONE OF FRANCE'S celebrated dishes, switches its national allegiance with the addition of warm Mexican spices. Chili, cumin, coriander, and oregano merge like natives with the sweetly braised onions. A sprinkling of jalapeño cheese and crisp tortilla strips topple the traditional cap of French bread and gruyère to create a memorable main-course soup for a chilly evening.

Mexican Onion Soup

6   large (about 3½ lb. total) onions, thinly sliced

About 7½ cups regular-strength chicken or vegetable broth

1   teaspoon ground cumin

½   teaspoon ground coriander

½   teaspoon dried oregano leaves

⅓   cup all-purpose flour

2   tablespoons ground dried New Mexico or California chilies

1¼ cups (about 5 oz.) shredded jack cheese with jalapeño chilies

Fried tortilla strips (recipe follows)

⅓   cup chopped fresh cilantro (coriander)

In a 5- to 6-quart pan, combine onions, 1 cup broth, cumin, coriander, and oregano. Cover and cook over medium-high heat, stirring occasionally, until most of the liquid evaporates, 25 to 30 minutes. Uncover pan and turn heat to high; stir often, scraping free brown film that forms on pan bottom, until onions are a rich caramel color, 15 to 20 minutes.

Meanwhile, smoothly mix 6½ cups broth with the flour. Add ground chilies to onions and mix well. Pour broth and flour mixture into pan. Stir over high heat until boiling; reduce heat to a gentle simmer and cook 15 to 20 minutes to blend flavors, stirring often. (If making ahead, cool, cover, and chill up to 1 day. Stir often over medium heat until steaming.)

Ladle soup into wide bowls and sprinkle with cheese, tortilla strips, and cilantro. Serves 5 or 6.

Per serving: 361 cal. (40 percent from fat); 14 g protein; 16 g fat (5.4 g sat.); 44 g carbo.; 299 mg sodium; 25 mg chol.

Fried tortilla strips. Cut 6 **corn tortillas** (6 in. wide) into ¼-inch-wide strips. Pour about ¼ inch **salad oil** into an 8- to 10-inch frying pan; place over medium heat. When oil reaches 350° on a thermometer, drop about ¼ of the strips into the oil. Stir until strips are golden and crisp, about 1 minute. Lift out with a slotted spoon and drain on paper towels.

Repeat to cook remaining tortillas. (If making ahead, cool and store airtight up to 1 day.) ■

By Linda Lau Anusasananan

A DUSTING OF CINNAMON *subtly reinforces the union of Mexican chocolate, piloncillo sugar, and toasted pine nuts.*

The adult brownie

Truffles and Mexican chocolate set these sweets apart

MORE SOPHISTICATED foods may become routine as we mature. But if you have a weakness for rich, gooey brownies, grown-up flavor is just what it takes to blast you out of blasé. Ingredients for adult consideration: Mexican chocolate and cinnamon or chocolate truffles. The resulting brownies make elegant dinner party finales or superb valentine offerings.

Espresso or a little brandy goes well with these brownies. But we must warn you—a glass of ice-cold milk is so tempting it can blow your mature cover.

Mexican Chocolate Brownies with Cinnamon

½ cup (3 oz.) pine nuts

4 ounces piloncillo or panocha sugar or ¾ cup firmly packed brown sugar

½ cup (¼ lb.) butter or margarine, cut into chunks

2 tablets (6½ oz.) Mexican chocolate, coarsely chopped

1 ounce unsweetened chocolate, coarsely chopped

2 large eggs

1 teaspoon vanilla

½ teaspoon ground cinnamon

½ cup all-purpose flour

Sweetened whipped cream and cinnamon sticks (optional)

Spread nuts out in an 8- or 9-inch-wide baking pan. Bake in a 350° oven until the pine nuts are golden brown, 8 to 10 minutes; shake often. Pour nuts from pan and set aside.

With a flat mallet or in a food processor, crush or whirl piloncillo until finely ground. In a 2- to 3-quart pan, combine sugar, butter, Mexican chocolate, and unsweetened chocolate. Stir often over low heat until chocolates are melted and smooth. Remove from heat, and beat in eggs, vanilla, and cinnamon until well blended. Mix in flour and pine nuts.

Pour batter into a lightly oiled 9-inch square pan. Bake in a 350° oven until brownie springs back in center when gently pressed, 20 to 25 minutes. Let cool on a rack. Cut into squares or triangles; top brownies with whipped cream to taste, and garnish with cinnamon sticks. Serves 8 or 9.

Per serving: 371 cal. (61 percent from fat); 5.6 g protein; 25 g fat (12 g sat.); 39 g carbo.; 129 mg sodium; 75 mg chol.

Truffle Brownies

½ cup (¼ lb.) butter or margarine, cut into chunks

3 ounces unsweetened or bittersweet chocolate, cut into chunks

1⅓ cups sugar

2 large eggs

1 teaspoon vanilla

½ cup all-purpose flour

About ¾ pound chocolate truffles, any flavor with solid centers, cut into 1-inch chunks

Sweetened whipped cream or vanilla ice cream (optional)

In a 2- to 3-quart pan, combine butter and unsweetened chocolate. Stir often over low heat until chocolate is melted and smooth. Remove from heat and beat in sugar, eggs, and vanilla to blend well. Stir in flour and truffle pieces. Pour batter into a lightly oiled 9-inch square pan.

Bake in a 350° oven until brownie springs back in center when gently pressed, about 25 minutes. Let cool in pan on a rack. Serve warm or cool, cut into squares or triangles. Top portions to taste with whipped cream. Serves 8 or 9.

Per serving: 487 cal. (55 percent from fat); 5.3 g protein; 30 g fat (18 g sat.); 55 g carbo.; 147 mg sodium; 95 mg chol. ∎

By Christine Weber Hale

SUNSET'S KITCHEN CABINET

Creative ways with everyday foods—submitted by *Sunset* readers, tested in *Sunset* kitchens

Reuben Casserole

Valerie Wiesner, Castro Valley, California

6½ cups (10 oz.) sliced rye bread in ¾-inch squares

3½ cups chopped green apples

1¼ cups slivered red onion

1 can or jar (16 oz.) sauerkraut, rinsed and drained

¼ cup *each* Dijon mustard and light mayonnaise

2 cups (½ lb.) grated Swiss cheese

½ pound thinly sliced corned beef, coarsely chopped, layers separated

Bake bread in a baking pan in a 400° oven until slightly crisp, about 10 minutes. Spoon half into a shallow 2½- to 3-quart baking dish. In a bowl, combine apples, onion, sauerkraut, mustard, mayonnaise, and half of cheese; spoon half over bread in dish, cover evenly with beef, then remaining mixture. Cover tightly with foil; bake until apples are very soft, 50 to 60 minutes. Sprinkle evenly with remaining bread, then cheese. Bake, uncovered, until cheese is melted and browned, about 20 minutes. Serves 6 to 8.

Per serving: 324 cal. (44 percent from fat); 16 g protein; 16 g fat (7.5 g sat.); 27 g carbo.; 978 mg sodium (less when sauerkraut is rinsed); 56 mg chol.

RUEBEN SANDWICH *components, plus tart apples, go into a casserole.*

Raised Sesame Seed Biscuits

Helen Knowlton, Eugene, Oregon

1 package active dry yeast

2 tablespoons warm (110°) water

¾ cup buttermilk

2 cups all-purpose flour

2 tablespoons sugar

½ teaspoon salt

⅓ cup butter or margarine

1 large egg white

⅓ cup sesame seed

In a bowl, dissolve yeast in water, about 5 minutes. Stir in buttermilk. In a large bowl, combine flour, sugar, and salt. With a pastry blender, cut in butter until fine crumbs form. Stir in buttermilk mixture; gather into a ball.

On a lightly floured board, knead dough until smooth, about 15 turns. Reflour board and pat dough into a 6-inch square. Cut into 9 equal pieces.

In a small bowl, beat white to blend. Dip top and bottom of each biscuit in white, then in sesame, to coat. Place slightly apart in a buttered 9-inch-square baking pan. Cover; let rise in a warm place until double, about 45 minutes. Bake in a 425° oven until deep golden, 18 to 20 minutes. Cool on a rack at least 15 minutes. Makes 9.

Per biscuit: 214 cal. (41 percent from fat); 5.2 g protein; 9.8 g fat (4.7g sat.); 26 g carbo.; 219 mg sodium; 19 mg chol.

GOLDEN, *yeast-leavened biscuits have a crunchy sesame seed coating.*

Grapefruit Tart

Tatiana Ovanessoff, San Diego

1¼ cups all-purpose flour

½ cup plus 2 tablespoons sugar

½ cup (¼ lb.) cold butter, cut in chunks

3 large eggs plus 1 large egg yolk

2 large (about 1 lb. each) pink grapefruit

¼ cup (⅛ lb.) melted butter

In a food processor or bowl, combine flour and 2 tablespoons sugar. Add butter; whirl or rub with fingers until fine crumbs form. Add yolk; whirl or mix with fork until dough holds together. Press into 9-inch tart pan with removable rim. Bake in 350° oven until deep golden, 20 to 23 minutes.

Grate 3 tablespoons colored part of peel from grapefruit. Cut all of outer membrane from 1 grapefruit. Catching juice in a bowl, cut between inner membranes to free segments; wrap segments airtight and chill up to 1 day. Squeeze juice from membranes into bowl; discard membranes. Ream enough juice from other grapefruit into bowl to make ⅔ cup total.

In processor or bowl, whirl or whisk juice, peel, ½ cup sugar, whole eggs, and melted butter until very well blended. Place empty tart shell in oven, add filling; bake until filling no longer jiggles when gently shaken, 15 to 20 minutes. Cool on rack; wrap airtight and chill at least 1½ hours or up to 1 day. Arrange reserved grapefruit segments on top. Serves 8 to 10.

Per serving: 272 cal. (53 percent from fat); 4.1 g protein; 16 g fat (9.3 g sat.); 28 g carbo.; 163 mg sodium; 123 mg chol. ∎

Compiled by Elaine Johnson

ARRANGE GRAPEFRUIT *segments on top of a refreshing citrus custard tart.*

A new venison, asparagus Milanese, the return of coffee bar syrups, and steely Chablis

By Jerry Anne Di Vecchio

Sue Jenkins lives in Blenheim, New Zealand, where she keeps bees, raises boys, and is the energy behind food activities at the Marlborough Wine & Food Festival. So when visitors like me show up, she hauls us around behind the scenes. And that's how I heard about cervena, a product of red deer, before it was official.

On our outings, we often passed these deer in high-fenced paddocks. They were brought to New Zealand by settlers, and like many introduced wild animals that have no predators, the population exploded. Sue's father was among the first ranchers to deal aggressively with their environmental destructiveness. He rounded them up and farm-fed them to create a new venison source. As production grew, strict quality controls were established for breeding, feeding, dressing, and packing. The result is called cervena. Leading supermarkets in the West now carry cervena, sometimes fresh, usually frozen—though you can always order it fresh. Only the tender, luxury cuts—from the loin section and the leg—are available, and they cost from 25 to 50 percent more than comparable beef cuts.

Cervena is darker red and more richly flavored than beef. It behaves a lot like beef when cooked, but because it is so much leaner, tender cuts are moistest if cooked very rare to rare (125° to 135°). Cervena is best seasoned by simple, classic red-meat sauces like the one here with brandy and green peppercorns.

If you can't locate cervena, call Cervena Co. at (800) 877-1187 for a nearby source.

A TASTE OF THE WEST

Cervena with Brandy Sauce

- 2 cervena tenderloins (about 1 lb. total)

  All-purpose flour

- 1½ teaspoons *each* butter or margarine and olive oil

- 2 tablespoons brandy
- ¼ cup minced shallots
- ½ teaspoon fresh or dried thyme leaves
- ¼ cup regular-strength chicken broth
- ¼ cup whipping cream
- 2 teaspoons drained canned green peppercorns

NOEL BARNHURST

About 2 teaspoons lemon juice (optional)

Fresh thyme sprigs

Salt and pepper

Trim and discard any fat or silver membrane on tenderloins. Rinse meat and pat dry. Cut across the grain into 4 equal pieces. Coat slices with flour, shake off excess.

In an 8- to 10-inch frying pan over high heat, melt butter in olive oil. When fat is hot, add meat and brown on each side, 4 to 6 minutes total (meat will be very rare; cook longer if you prefer rare or medium-rare). Add brandy and set aflame (not beneath a vent or near flammables). Shake pan until flame dies.

Transfer meat to a small, warm platter; keep warm.

To pan, add shallots and thyme leaves. Reduce heat to medium-high; stir often until shallots just begin to brown, about 2 minutes. Add broth, cream, and peppercorns. Boil on high heat, stirring often, until reduced by half, about 2 minutes. Drain any

juices from meat into pan; taste sauce and add lemon juice to give a mild tang. Spoon sauce around meat, garnish platter with thyme sprigs, and serve with salt and pepper to taste. Serves 4.

Per serving: 242 cal. (41 percent from fat); 27 g protein; 11 g fat (5.1 g sat.); 4 g carbo.; 87 mg sodium; 117 mg chol.

ASPARAGUS MILANESE *is just great with crusty bread, a green salad, and a glass of Merlot.*

NOEL BARNHURST

GREAT TOOL

Japanese cutting box

My food processor hasn't been replaced for nitty-gritty chopping and slicing. But a special treasure is the Japanese cutting box I first spotted among other slicer-grater-shredders in a grocery store in Los Angeles's Japan-town.

I use it to cut marvelously long, thin strands of citrus peel and hard cheeses like parmesan, hairlike strings of firm vegetables such as carrot and daikon (the white radish that's shredded to go with sushi), or uniformly paper-thin slices of all sorts of things.

The box has a lid. On this lid is a slot into which four different cutting blades can fit. The box gives good support as you push foods across the blades, while the slices collect neatly inside.

I recently bought another cutting box in San Francisco as a gift; prices start around $16 each.

To test a cutter's proficiency, try this salad; you'll appreciate how the box keeps staining beets contained.

Raw fennel and beet salad. Trim bruised or discolored areas from 2 **fennel** heads

SEASONAL NOTE

Spring and asparagus

Once those two words were synonymous. Now asparagus flows in from various points of the globe most of the year. But its quality and quantity bloom when the price drops in spring, and then it's time for Asparagus Milanese. This is one of the world's great supper dishes—even though it's just oven-fried eggs, parmesan cheese, and the asparagus. For a quick meal, it's heaven-sent; you cook it and serve from the pan. At Jack's Restaurant in San Francisco, one of the few establishments with this dish still on the menu, the eggs come sizzling on rather battered oval metal platters. Oval metal gratin pans or small frying pans work, too.

In our house, asparagus gets peeled. Some call this fussy. I call it practical. You can eat the whole peeled spear—and enjoy every tender bite. If you peel asparagus, use big fat spears to get more servings for your work. You can cook asparagus ahead; it takes only a few minutes to reheat and keeps its color better than if freshly boiled. Offer crusty bread for dunking into the yolks, and serve a green salad. For wine, Merlot is a smooth companion.

Asparagus Milanese. In a frying pan suitable for the table (6 to 8 in. wide, or 7 to 9 in. oval), melt 2 to 3 teaspoons **butter** or margarine over medium-high heat. Add **cooked asparagus** (following) and shake pan to roll spears in butter. Push them to the sides of the pan and break 1 or 2 **large eggs** into the cleared space. Cook just until egg begins to turn opaque on the bottom, about 1 minute. Sprinkle with 2 to 3 tablespoons finely shredded **parmesan cheese.** Bake in a 500° oven until yolk is as firm as you like, 2 to 3 minutes for soft. Sprinkle with **salt** and **pepper** and serve immediately. Makes 1 serving.

Per serving: 211 cal. (68 percent from fat); 13 g protein; 16 g fat (8.7 g sat.); 3.2 g carbo.; 370 mg sodium; 243 mg chol.

Cooked asparagus. For each serving, allow ¼ to ½ pound **asparagus.** Snap off tough spear ends and peel asparagus, if desired.

Drop asparagus into boiling **water** to cover; boil, uncovered, just until spears are tender when pierced, 2 to 4 minutes. Drain and use hot. If making ahead, immerse spears in ice water until cold, then drain; wrap airtight and chill up to 2 days.

SLICING AND SHREDDING *are easy with this box.*

(about 3 in. wide). Holding fennel stems, thinly slice heads; you should have about 2 cups. Save the feathery green leaves; discard stems. Put slices in a bowl and mix with 2 to 3 tablespoons **lemon juice,** 1 to 2 tablespoons **extra-virgin olive oil,** and **salt** and **pepper** to taste.

Peel 1 small (about 2 in. wide) **beet;** cut in thin strands. Mix, to taste, with about 1 tablespoon lemon juice and 1 tablespoon extra-virgin olive oil, salt, and pepper.

Arrange fennel mixture in a ring on a rimmed platter; spoon beet mixture into the center. Chop fennel leaves and sprinkle over the salad. Makes 4 or 5 servings.

Per serving: 61 cal. (84 percent from fat); 0.7 g protein; 5.7 g fat (0.8 g sat.); 2.7 g carbo.; 51 mg sodium; 0 mg chol.

GREAT INGREDIENT
Coffee bar syrups

Once upon a time in San Francisco's North Beach, when it was still full of old-timer Italians, there was a dark, cavernous place on Broadway called the Bocce Ball. In the bocce ball courts out back, aged gentlemen were at play while smoking incredibly smelly cigars imported from Lucca.

Inside, the entertainment was operatic and lively. I don't remember any food—I was all of 18 at the time. But there was a bar, and one shelf was lined with exotic syrups that intrigued me—tamarindo, orgeat, cassis, hazelnut, mint, tangerine.

One evening, an empathetic bartender let me taste each one, diluted in chilled club soda (very pre-Perrier) with a citrus twist. Tamarindo with lime became my favorite.

Eventually, the Bocce Ball ceased to be, and I forgot about the syrups.

But now, with the rebirth of coffeehouses, the syrups are everywhere. You'll find them in the liqueur section of fine grocery and department

stores, at Italian and other delicatessens, at liquor stores, and in coffee shops. Some, like the nut or caramel flavors, sweeten dark, thick espressos, foaming cappuccinos, and iced coffee drinks. Others are being poured over ice cream and desserts, and all are regaining attention as a way to enliven a refreshing glass of sparkling water.

Go one step further for these light variations on an ice cream float. First fill a glass with ice and sparkling water, then add to taste:

Tamarindo syrup and a scoop of **orange sorbet.**

Orgeat (almond) **syrup** and a scoop of **raspberry sorbet.**

Hazelnut syrup and a scoop of **toffee-candy vanilla ice cream.**

Raspberry syrup and a scoop of **passion fruit sorbet** or vanilla ice cream.

Tangerine syrup and a scoop of **strawberry sorbet.**

San Francisco's R. Torre & Co., manufacturers since 1925 of Torani Italian Syrups, will send you a free recipe book, *The Art of Flavor,* if you call (800) 775-1925. ∎

A SCOOP OF ORANGE SORBET *floats in tamarindo syrup–flavored sparkling water.*

BOB THOMPSON ON WINE
What is Chablis?

Olympia oysters and French Chablis do what they do, I think, because each is intensely evocative of one tiny place. Olympias come only from a couple of small bays in Puget Sound. Chablis comes only from the chalky hills around a small town in France.

People who try to be poetic about wine drive themselves daft in their search for the right words to describe Chardonnay as it grows in Chablis. Start with apples. More precisely, start with the freshly peeled skin of one of the powerfully redolent varieties. Add the faintest hint of burnt match.

This is not exact, but how many people are familiar

with the smell of gunflint, or whetstones, these days? After these, you have to chip in with your own details. However, once you have the basic outline, the grape will never confuse you again.

There is a hierarchy of Chablis wines. Most are called simply Chablis. From a dozen or so vineyards (some of them identified within quotation marks in the following list) comes Chablis Premier Cru, which costs more. Finally, just seven vineyards (some again named within quotes in the list) have the right to call themselves Grand Cru, and they charge carriage-trade prices.

Chablis of all three types smell and taste much like one another. Compared with regular Chablis, the costlier

Premiers Crus feel firmer, the Grands Crus outright steely. Steeliness is what makes Chablis more brilliant with oysters than Chardonnays from elsewhere. When the oysters happen to be Olympias, the more steel the better.

Chablis to try ($9 to $12): Laroche St.-Martin, J. Moreau, Long-Depaquit, La Chablisienne.

Chablis Premiers Crus ($15 to $20): Long-Depaquit Premier Cru, Long-Depaquit "Vaillons," Louis Michel "Montée de Tonnerre," Domaine Laroche "Vaudevey," Domaine Laroche "Fourchaume."

Chablis Grands Crus ($24 to $30): Long-Depaquit "Moutonne," Domaine Laroche "Blanchots," J. Moreau "Vaudésir."

the *Art* of ROASTING A CHICKEN

The best techniques and new recipes for simple, perfect feasting

W HO DOESN'T LOVE A GOOD ROAST chicken, with juicy meat and richly browned skin? Infinitely versatile, roast chicken is the cook's friend: just pop the bird in the oven, and before you know it, dinner is ready. Sounds ideal—yet, truth be told, we've all scratched our heads on occasion over those that fell short of perfection. To take the guesswork out of roasting a chicken, we revisited techniques, trying ovens hot to cooler, different equipment, and basting versus not. Here's what we learned.

By

Elaine

Johnson

MAGNIFICENTLY GOLDEN, rosemary-flecked bird roasts with

NOEL BARNHURST

garlic and has a simple gravy that's perfect with mashed potatoes, spring vegetables, and your favorite wine. See recipe on page 48.

MARCH

47

Oven temperature. Turn it up to 450° for the best browning, crispiest skin, and most succulent meat. At this temperature it isn't necessary to start the bird with breast down to enhance moistness.

The high heat will create some spattering, and you may need to switch on the fan; we say forget the clean oven and go for it. (If you add a little water to the roasting pan it will reduce spattering considerably, though the skin won't be quite as crisp.)

For the optional glazes (recipes below) and Mahogany Chicken (recipe on facing page), reduce the heat to 400° to prevent scorching; meat will still be moist.

Equipment. We tried roasting chickens directly in the pan and with different racks: the old-fashioned V-shaped rack, vertical roasters, even a spitlike suspension device. We found the V-shaped rack creates the most even browning.

Basting. Using pan juices for basting enhances browning nicely, and we find a brush more effective than a bulb baster with a chicken's modest amount of drippings.

LUCY I. SARGEANT

When's it done? Don't overcook the bird if you want moist meat. For greatest accuracy, use a meat thermometer. With the chicken breast side up on a V-shaped rack, pull back a drumstick and insert the thermometer into the thickest part of the thigh, angling it parallel to, but not touching, the thigh bone; cook until thermometer reaches 180°. The drumstick should wiggle easily, and thigh meat should no longer be pink.

Finally, if the golden bird before you cries out for carving skills you don't have, take the easy route. With poultry shears or strong kitchen scissors, cut the legs off at the joints. Then snip chicken to one side of the breastbone and right through the backbone into serving pieces.

Sunset's Basic Roast Chicken

Enjoy the simple perfection of a plain roast chicken, or try one of the options that follow: roasted with rosemary and garlic, or brushed with chili-lemon or apricot-Dijon glaze. If your chicken is smaller or larger than this size, adjust cooking time accordingly.

1 chicken, 3½ to 4 pounds
2 teaspoons olive oil
Salt and pepper

Remove giblets from chicken and save for other uses. Rinse chicken inside and out, pull off and discard lumps of fat, and pat chicken dry. Free wings if they are tucked behind chicken. Rub bird all over with oil, then sprinkle generously with salt and pepper.

Place chicken breast side up on a V-shaped rack in a 12- by 17-inch roasting pan. Insert a meat thermometer into thickest part of thigh. If desired, pour ⅛ inch water into pan to avoid oven spatters. For crispiest skin, omit water.

Bake chicken in a 450° oven until thermometer reaches 180°, drumstick wiggles easily, and thigh meat is no longer pink in center (cut to check), 45 to 50 minutes; after 30 minutes, baste bird occasionally with drippings.

When chicken is done, tip it so juices run into pan, then skim fat from juices and pour juices into a small bowl to spoon over chicken. (Juices may be modest or more generous, depending on the chicken.) Makes 4 to 6 servings.

Per serving: 312 cal. (55 percent from fat); 33 g protein; 19 g fat (5.2 g sat.); 0 g carbo.; 100 mg sodium; 104 mg chol.

TUSCAN-STYLE BREAD DRESSING with olives and fresh basil (recipe on facing page) bakes outside the bird.

Rosemary chicken with roasted garlic gravy

Prepare *Sunset's* basic roast chicken as directed above, first rubbing raw chicken all over with 1½ tablespoons chopped **fresh rosemary leaves**. Place 1 whole head **garlic** in pan next to chicken.

Roast chicken as directed. Roast garlic until very soft when squeezed, 40 to 45 minutes; cut the bulb in half horizontally and let it stand until it is cool enough to handle. Squeeze the garlic cloves into a blender or food processor. Add 1 cup **regular-strength chicken broth** and 1 tablespoon **cornstarch**; whirl until a smooth purée.

When chicken is done, remove to a platter. Skim and discard fat from roasting pan, then add garlic mixture. Place pan over 2 burners and whisk over high heat until bubbling, about 2 minutes. Scrape gravy into a bowl. Makes 4 to 6 servings.

Per serving: 340 cal. (53 percent from fat); 34 g protein; 20 g fat (5.4 g sat.); 5.6 g carbo.; 121 mg sodium; 104 mg chol.

Chili-lemon glaze

Follow directions for *Sunset's* basic roast chicken above. While chicken roasts, combine ¼ cup **fresh lemon juice**, 2 tablespoons **honey**, 1 tablespoon **chili powder**, ½ teaspoon salt (optional), and ¼ teaspoon *each* **ground cinnamon** and **cayenne**.

When thermometer in chicken reaches 170°, reduce oven to 400° and baste chicken with half of chili mixture. Roast 5 minutes and baste with remaining chili mixture. Continue to roast until thermometer reaches 180°, about 5 minutes more.

Serve pan juices as directed. Makes 4 to 6 servings.

Per serving: 340 cal. (50 percent from fat); 33 g protein; 19 g fat (5.2 g sat.); 7.5 g carbo.; 113 mg sodium; 104 mg chol.

Apricot-Dijon glaze

Follow directions for **chili-lemon glaze** above, but instead of chili mixture, stir together this combination: ¼ cup **apricot jam**, 2 tablespoons chopped **dried apricots**, 2 tablespoons **Dijon** mustard, 1 tablespoon chopped **shallot**, and 1 teaspoon **lemon juice**. Serves 4 to 6.

Per serving: 357 cal. (48 percent from fat); 33 g protein; 19 g fat (5.2 g sat.); 11 g carbo.; 226 mg sodium; 104 mg chol.

Mahogany Chicken and Shiitake Mushrooms

    1 chicken (3½ to 4 lb.)

       Sherry marinade (recipe follows)

       Soaked shiitake mushrooms
       (directions follow)

    ¼ cup soaking liquid from mushrooms,
       boiling

    1 pound hot, steamed edible-pod peas
       (with strings and stems removed)

Remove giblets from chicken and save for other uses. Rinse chicken inside and out, discard lumps of fat, and pat chicken dry. Place in a large bowl with sherry marinade and soaked shiitake mushrooms. Turn to coat, then cover and chill at least 2 hours or up to 24; turn chicken and mushrooms often.

Reserving marinade, lift out chicken and mushrooms. Place chicken breast side up on a V-shaped rack in a 12- by 17-inch roasting pan and insert a meat thermometer into thickest part of thigh (not touching bone).

Bake in a 400° oven 15 minutes, then arrange mushrooms in an even layer in pan and brush chicken and mushrooms with ⅓ of marinade. Bake until ther-

mometer reaches 180° and thigh meat is no longer pink in center (cut to check), 35 to 45 minutes more; every 15 minutes, turn mushrooms over and brush chicken and mushrooms with ⅓ of marinade and any pan juices.

Tip juices from chicken into pan. Lift out rack and slide chicken onto a platter. Place pan on heatproof surface and add boiling mushroom liquid. Stir to loosen browned bits. Tip juices into a corner of pan and skim fat, then stir in peas. Spoon pea mixture onto platter. Serves 6.

Per serving: 394 cal. (43 percent from fat); 37 g protein; 19 g fat (5.2 g sat.); 19 g carbo.; 507 mg sodium; 104 mg chol.

Sherry marinade. Combine ¾ cup **dry sherry**, ¼ cup **reduced-sodium soy sauce**, 2 tablespoons minced **fresh ginger**, 2 cloves **garlic** (minced), and 2 teaspoons **sugar**.

Soaked shiitakes. Place 2 ounces (about 2 cups) **dried shiitake mushrooms** in a bowl with warm water to cover. Let stand until softened, 30 to 40 minutes; stir occasionally. Swish in soaking liquid to remove grit. Lift out, then cut off and discard stems. Reserve ¼ cup soaking liquid.

Tuscan-style Bread Dressing

This takeoff on Italian bread salad is a great partner for the basic roast chicken.

    6 cups 1-inch chunks dense sourdough
       bread, ½ to ¾ pound

    1 tablespoon extra-virgin olive oil

    ¾ cup canned chopped Italian-style
       tomatoes in juice

    2 teaspoons red wine vinegar

    ¾ cup large green olives (unpitted or
       pimiento-stuffed)

    ¼ cup thinly sliced red onion slivers

    ¼ teaspoon *each* salt and pepper

    ⅔ cup coarsely chopped fresh basil
       leaves or 3 tablespoons dried basil
       leaves

       About 3 tablespoons chicken pan
       juices (fat skimmed) or regular-
       strength chicken broth

       Fresh basil sprigs (optional)

In a 10- by 15-inch rimmed baking pan, mix bread with oil to coat. Bake in a 450° oven until golden and slightly crisp to touch, 8 to 10 minutes; stir halfway through baking.

In a large bowl, combine tomatoes, vinegar, olives, onion, salt and pepper, and dried basil if used (do not add fresh basil). Gently mix in bread until evenly coated.

Evenly spread mixture in pan and bake until deep golden and slightly crisp to touch, 10 to 12 minutes. Add chopped fresh basil and chicken juices; stir to combine. Garnish with basil sprigs. Serves 6.

Per serving: 163 cal. (34 percent from fat); 4.7 g protein; 6.1 g fat (0.9 g sat.); 23 g carbo.; 779 mg sodium; 0.3 mg chol. ■

MAHOGANY CHICKEN and shiitakes get their rich color from the Asian marinade.

The delicious truth about polenta

What it really is, how to cook it just the way you like it, and other secrets

POLENTA MADE OF cornmeal ground the Italian way is inviting unadorned, yet in the hands of a creative cook, it is like an artist's canvas—immensely appealing used as the background for other foods.

Polenta can be soft, creamy, and fluid, or dense, firm, and shaped. It can be prepared quickly or simmer away slowly. It can quell the heartiest appetites, yet be delicate and sophisticated in an elegant presentation. It is lean enough to be classified low-fat, yet tastes deceptively rich.

As an added virtue, polenta is very forgiving. When you understand how it cooks, you can control it and get the results you want.

To start, consider the ingredient itself. *Polenta* means *mush* in Italian and can be made from several foods, including chestnut meal and buckwheat. We know it best made from ground dried corn. You can buy polenta as a fine, medium, or coarse meal; regular cornmeal is ground even finer. If the polenta grind isn't specified, it's most likely medium.

Purists cook polenta in water; others use all or part broth for flavor and often add wine and other seasonings.

When polenta cooks, the bits of ground corn soften as they absorb the hot liquid and swell. Once the raw starchy flavor is gone, within a quarter of an hour, polenta is ready to eat, but additional cooking makes the corn granules softer and the mixture thicker. Fine-ground polenta cooks most quickly and has the smoothest texture; coarse-ground retains the most texture, even with long cooking.

The amount of liquid used determines how soft or stiff the polenta will be—use more liquid for creamy (3 to 4 cups for each 1 cup polenta), less for firm (about 2 cups for each 1 cup polenta). Should you misjudge and the polenta is too soupy, just cook it longer to thicken it—some liquid will evaporate. If the polenta is stiffer than you want, simply mix in more liquid and continue to cook. Really thick polenta will hold the stirring spoon upright. No matter what you do, polenta thickens as it cools.

The traditional Italian method for cooking polenta is to whisk or stir it into boiling

VELVETY HOT POLENTA *is made even creamier with layers of teleme and parmesan cheeses. Serve this lavish combination with a crisp green salad.*

liquid, followed by about an hour of stirring and simmering. Because polenta spatters, and burns when it sticks, it's not only easier but also safer to mix it with cold liquid, stir it often as it heats to boiling, then simmer until the starchiness is replaced by a mellow taste. A long-handled spoon is fine, but a whisk works best to prevent lumps.

Besides the various grinds of yellow cornmeal, polenta also comes in other forms and flavors. For details, see "Polenta spin-offs,"on the facing page.

You don't need to move far from the basics to have winning polenta dishes. Here are three recipes that make use of polenta in various forms: soft and layered with cheese (the way Alice Guslani of Los Altos Hills, California, makes it), firm, and precooked. We also include tips for cooking polenta for a crowd.

Soft Polenta with Two Cheeses

To control spattering, use a large pan like the one specified in the directions.

2 cups polenta

3 cups water

3 cups regular-strength chicken broth

¾ pound teleme cheese, thinly sliced

About 1 cup (¼ lb.) shredded parmesan cheese

Fresh coarsely ground pepper

Extra-virgin olive oil or olive oil flavored with basil, chili, or another choice (optional)

Salt

In a 5- to 6-quart pan, stir polenta, water, and broth to mix well. Bring to a boil over high heat, stirring often with a whisk or a spoon to prevent lumps and sticking. Reduce heat; simmer uncovered, stirring often, until polenta feels creamy and smooth when tasted, at least 15 minutes. Ladle ½ the polenta into a large, shallow bowl (or 6 to 8 individual bowls) and cover with ½ the teleme and 1 cup parmesan. Cover with remaining polenta, and top with the rest of the teleme. Sprinkle with pepper. Accompany with more parmesan, olive oil, and salt to add to taste. Serves 6 to 8.

Per serving: 316 cal. (43 percent from fat); 18 g protein; 15 g fat (3.1 g sat.); 30 g carbo.; 533 mg sodium; 19 mg chol.

Shaped Polenta

It takes only a few minutes for hot polenta to get firm in a mold; then it's ready to tip out and serve. Or you can leave polenta in the mold until cool, invert from container, and reheat when ready to serve. Or slice cold polenta, brush with olive oil, and broil, grill, or pan-fry to lightly brown.

2 cups polenta

4 cups water or regular-strength chicken broth

Salt

In a 4- to 5-quart pan, stir polenta and water to mix well. Bring to a boil over high heat, uncovered; stir often with whisk or spoon to prevent lumps and sticking. Reduce heat and simmer, stirring often, until polenta is very thick and no longer tastes gritty, at least 15 minutes. Add salt to taste. Quickly scrape polenta into an oiled 4- to 5-cup mold or loaf pan, or a 9- by 13-inch pan. Let stand 5 to 10 minutes, then invert polenta out onto a platter and serve. If making

ahead, cool, cover, and chill up to 1 day. To reheat, place on a microwave-safe platter in a microwave oven. Heat, uncovered, on full power (100 percent) until polenta is hot in the center, about 10 minutes (or seal in foil and bake in a 350° oven until hot in the center, about 50 minutes). Slice polenta. Serves 6.

Per serving: 175 cal. (8 percent from fat); 3.9 g protein; 1.5 g fat (0.2 g sat.); 36 g carbo.; 1.4 mg sodium; 0 mg chol.

Polenta-Pesto Bites

For the fastest start, buy cooked polenta. You'll find it in logs or bars sealed in plastic in the refrigerator sections of well-stocked food markets. Or use cold molded polenta that you've made.

For a topping variation, replace pesto with purchased tapenade or a roasted red pepper spread.

1 package (about 2 lb.) ready-to-use polenta

½ cup prepared basil pesto

1 cup (¼ lb.) shredded parmesan cheese

Cut polenta into ⅓-inch-thick slices, then cut slices into about 50 equal pieces. Lay pieces slightly apart on

CHOOSE A FANCY MOLD *to give hot, firm polenta a bold shape, then surround it with grilled sausage chunks. You can slice polenta with a knife or do it the Italian way—push a taut string through it to cut off portions.*

Polenta with wheat germ

Polenta with buckwheat

Ready-to-eat polenta

Instant polenta

White polenta

Plain Polenta

POLENTA SPIN-OFFS

Instant polenta. Cooked polenta is dried, then dehydrated and pulverized to make instant mix. Just bring to a boil in liquid and it's ready. The texture is finer and a little gummier than that of regular polenta.

Ready-to-eat polenta. Firm, cooked polenta, plain or seasoned, is packed in airtight bags, ready to slice and heat. Or mash it flat in a casserole, cover with a saucy topping, and bake in the oven or heat in the microwave. How about inventing a new tamale pie?

Polenta with buckwheat. Tan bits of ground buckwheat add a nutty, slightly sweet flavor to regular or instant polenta. It's grand with earthy dishes like ratatouille or braised beef or pork.

Polenta with wheat germ. Wheat germ contributes its toasty flavor and a pleasant, chewy bite to regular or instant polenta. It's as adaptable as plain polenta.

White polenta. Dried white corn, finely ground, gives polenta a milder flavor than yellow corn. Our tasters felt it tasted like hominy grits. Serve it as a pleasant alternative to steamed rice or mashed potatoes.

lightly oiled 12- by 15-inch baking sheets. Broil polenta about 4 inches from heat to brown, about 5 minutes. Turn slices over, spread with pesto, and sprinkle with cheese. Broil until sizzling, about 5 minutes. Serve hot. Makes about 50.

Per piece: 37 cal. (46 percent from fat); 1.4 g protein; 1.9 g fat (0.6 g sat.); 3.4 g carbo.; 121 mg sodium; 2.2 mg chol.

POLENTA FOR A CROWD

When you ask Warren Petree of Mountain View, California, how to make polenta for a crowd, you get an expert opinion. He's in charge of the Italian Catholic Federation's annual Polenta Dinner and serves polenta to 350 people in one sitting. It takes a 15-person crew to tend polenta simmering in the 45-gallon pots, and according to Petree, the challenge is to locate cheerful volunteers who are willing to stir the required amount of time. The cooked polenta is served with beef stew or layered with cheese (see the facing page).

Although you probably don't anticipate cooking polenta on this scale, knowing how to multiply a polenta recipe can be helpful. You need spatter space; if your biggest pan is too small, use several smaller pans simultaneously. Allow 2 cups polenta for each 6 to 8 servings, and use liquid as suggested on page 50 to make polenta either soft or firm. Keep in mind that once the mixture is boiling, it takes no longer to cook than usual, about 15 minutes total. The extra time you need is at the beginning: the more liquid you use, the longer it takes to come to a boil.

Stir frequently as the mixture comes to a boil, then stir as the polenta simmers. Be especially careful to avoid sticking.

QUICK TREATS WITH POLENTA

• Sprinkle soft hot polenta with crumbled gorgonzola cheese and toasted walnuts.

• Accompany stews and other hearty dishes like braised lamb shanks, osso buco, and even chili with polenta instead of rice, pasta, or potatoes.

• Top bowls of soft polenta or slices of firm polenta with browned Italian sausages and a Mexican-style green or red tomato salsa.

• For breakfast or supper, pan-brown firm polenta slices in butter; top with powdered sugar and maple syrup.

• Brush firm polenta slices with olive oil, and brown on the grill over hot coals. Serve topped with chopped Roma-style tomatoes seasoned with capers, anchovies, and fresh basil leaves.

• Stir chopped dried tomatoes into polenta as it cooks.

• Spoon a cascade of sautéed mushrooms, broccoli, bell peppers, and asparagus over soft or firm polenta for an all-vegetable main dish. ∎

By Christine Weber Hale

PLUMP BUTTER-BROWNED BLINTZES *have sweetly spiced, light cheese filling. For the finishing touch, top with strawberry preserves and sour cream.*

PETER CHRISTIANSEN

Blintzes lighten up

And are suitable for any occasion if you use matzo meal

ALTHOUGH CHEESE blintzes are among the most popular of Jewish dishes, they are not part of the meals served in Jewish homes during the eight-day Passover celebration each spring. This is because the pancakes that enclose the filling for blintzes typically are made with flour, an ingredient excluded—by religious dietary laws—from Passover dishes. But Los Angeles food writer, restaurant critic, and Jewish food specialist Lorraine Shapiro offers a solution. She replaces the flour with matzo meal, which not only makes the pancakes acceptable under religious guidelines but also gives the thin pancakes a richer, toastier taste.

Shapiro's blintzes offer another plus: they are lighter than traditional versions. The filling is made with farmer's cheese or dry-curd cottage cheese, either of which is much leaner than the expected choice, cream cheese.

Enjoy blintzes for brunch or dessert with jam and sour cream or yogurt. Jams or pre-serves made with all-fruit ingredients are acceptable under Passover rules, but jams with corn syrup or other corn products are not.

If you don't have matzo meal on hand, and flour is appropriate for your use, use ½ cup all-purpose flour instead of the meal. The pancakes will be a little thinner and milder in flavor.

Cheese Blintzes

2 large eggs

6 tablespoons matzo meal

¾ cup low-fat or nonfat milk

About 3 tablespoons butter or margarine

Cheese filling (recipe follows)

Strawberry preserves (optional)

Sour cream or unflavored yogurt (optional)

In a blender or bowl, whirl or beat eggs, meal, and milk until thoroughly mixed. Melt ½ teaspoon butter in a 7- to 8-inch nonstick frying pan over medium heat. Pour about 2 tablespoons batter into hot pan; tip and swirl pan to cover bottom evenly with batter.

Cook until pancake top feels dry when lightly touched, about 1 minute. Turn cake over with a wide spatula (take care not to tear pancake). Cook until faintly speckled brown on bottom. Tip pancake out of pan and lay flat. Repeat to cook remaining batter; stir before you make each pancake, and add butter to pan as needed. Stack pancakes, separating them with waxed paper or plastic wrap; you should have 12 pancakes.

Divide filling into portions equal to the number of pancakes. Lay 1 pancake flat, darkest side down. Mound a portion of filling in the center. Fold opposite sides of pancake over the filling, then fold remaining sides over the filling to enclose; set seam side down and pat gently to make filling evenly thick. Repeat to fill remaining pancakes. If making ahead, lay filled blintzes in a 12- by 15-inch pan, cover airtight, and chill up to 4 hours.

Melt 2 teaspoons butter in an 11- to 12-inch nonstick frying pan over medium-high heat. When hot, fill pan with blintzes but do not crowd. Cook until golden brown on bottoms, about 1 minute. Turn with a spatula, and brown bottoms again. As blintzes brown, transfer them to a platter and keep warm in a 200° oven until all are cooked. Repeat to brown remaining blintzes.

Serve blintzes with preserves and sour cream to add to taste. Makes 4 servings.—*Lorraine Shapiro, Los Angeles*

Per serving: 294 cal. (37 percent from fat); 21 g protein; 12 g fat (6.9 g sat.); 23 g carbo.; 156 mg sodium; 139 mg chol.

Cheese filling. In a food processor or with a spoon, whirl or beat to blend well ¾ pound **farmer's cheese** (or dry-curd cottage cheese, sometimes called hoop cheese), 2½ tablespoons **sugar,** 1 tablespoon **unflavored nonfat yogurt** or nonfat milk, 2 teaspoons grated **lemon peel,** ¾ teaspoon **vanilla,** and ½ teaspoon **ground cinnamon.** ∎

By Christine Weber Hale

MOIST, TENDER *banana scones are full of plump blueberries.*

In search of the perfect scone

A baker turns inventor

WHEN *SUNSET MAGAZINE* recipe retester Linda Tebben ordered some delicious-sounding scones in a restaurant, she was disappointed when they turned out to be "the driest, most unappealing things" she'd ever eaten. However, they did inspire her to create scones to match her expectations.

As an avid, experienced home baker, Tebben was in the habit of following recipes exactly, just as her job at *Sunset* requires. But working alongside food writers as they developed recipes, she picked up some lessons in food science and basic proportions, particularly in the arena that intrigued her most—baking. Equipped with this newfound knowledge, she experimented with scones.

Not wanting all the butter and cream of the traditional scone, she substituted yogurt for some of the fat and discovered it produced an exceptionally moist and tender scone. Then she added the flavors of a favorite quick bread—blueberries, bananas, and whole-wheat flour. Her first creation, a fine success, inspired more invention. The next delicious scones included apples, pecans, lemon, and cinnamon.

In *Sunset*'s kitchen, Tebben still sticks to her precise ways in checking the workability of recipes, but at home she's turned into a nonstop recipe developer. And *Sunset*'s staff members have become taste testers for the treats she shares.

Blueberry Banana Scones

1¼ cups all-purpose flour

½ cup whole-wheat flour

¼ cup granulated sugar

1 teaspoon baking powder

½ teaspoon baking soda

¼ cup (⅛ lb.) butter or margarine, cut into chunks

½ cup lemon-flavor nonfat or low-fat yogurt

⅓ cup smoothly mashed banana

½ cup blueberries

¼ cup finely chopped walnuts

1 tablespoon brown or granulated sugar (optional)

In a food processor or bowl, whirl or stir together all-purpose flour, whole-wheat flour, ¼ cup granulated sugar, baking powder, and baking soda. Whirl or cut in butter until mixture becomes fine crumbs. Add yogurt, banana, blueberries, and nuts; stir until evenly moistened.

Mound dough on a lightly oiled 12- by 15-inch baking sheet. With lightly floured hands, pat mound into a smooth 7-inch round. With a sharp, floured knife, cut halfway through dough to make 8 wedges. Sprinkle top with brown sugar.

Bake in a 350° oven until scone is golden brown, about 25 minutes. Serve hot, or slide onto a rack and let cool until warm. Cut into wedges. Serves 8.

Per serving: 225 cal. (37 percent from fat); 4.6 g protein; 9.3 g fat (4.1 g sat.); 32 g carbo.; 213 mg sodium; 16 mg chol.

Apple Pecan Scones

1¾ cups all-purpose flour

¼ cup sugar

½ teaspoon baking powder

¼ teaspoon baking soda

1 teaspoon grated lemon peel

¼ cup (⅛ lb.) butter or margarine, cut into chunks

½ cup lemon-flavor nonfat or low-fat yogurt

¾ cup peeled, cored, and finely chopped tart apple, such as Granny Smith or Newtown Pippin

¼ cup finely chopped pecans

⅛ teaspoon ground cinnamon

In a food processor or bowl, whirl or stir together flour, 3 tablespoons sugar, baking powder, baking soda, and lemon peel. Add butter and whirl or cut in until mixture becomes fine crumbs. Stir in yogurt, apple, and pecans until dough is evenly moistened.

Mound dough on a lightly oiled 12- by 15-inch baking sheet. With lightly floured hands, pat mound into a smooth 7-inch round. With a sharp, floured knife, cut halfway through dough to make 8 wedges. Mix together the remaining sugar and the cinnamon; sprinkle over top of dough.

Bake in a 375° oven until scone is golden brown, about 20 minutes. Serve hot, or slide onto a rack and let cool until warm. Cut into wedges. Serves 8.

Per serving: 218 cal. (38 percent from fat); 4 g protein; 9.1 g fat (4 g sat.); 31 g carbo.; 141 mg sodium; 16 mg chol. ∎

By Christine Weber Hale

CUT COOKED *chayotes in half lengthwise through edible seeds. Scrape out and chop flesh to use for filling.*

It looks like a pear, tastes like a squash

Chayotes are easy to find and use

CENTRAL AMERICA IS the original home of the chayote, a pear-shaped vegetable (technically a fruit) that belongs to the squash family. Chayote is just as easy to cook as summer squash and is readily available in most markets, though it's often overlooked because of its unusual appearance. A chayote may be pale green or white, smooth or prickly with soft spines. Chayote tastes like patty pan squash, but it is a little firmer and less watery in texture. Stuffing this mild vegetable shows off its curved pear shape.

Select firm, unblemished chayotes. They will keep well in the refrigerator for about a week.

Stuffed Chayotes

3 large (about ¾ lb. each) chayotes

1 small (about 4 oz.) red or green bell pepper

1 tablespoon salad oil

1 pound mushrooms, finely chopped

1 medium-size (about 6 oz.) onion, finely chopped

1½ teaspoons *each* dried thyme leaves and dried basil leaves

½ teaspoon pepper

1 pound ground lean beef

⅔ cup regular-strength beef broth

⅓ cup prepared green taco sauce

1 tablespoon cornstarch

Salt

About 4 ounces thinly sliced Swiss cheese or Finnish lappi cheese

If chayote skin is tough (to test, pierce with your fingernail) or spiny, peel the chayotes. If the skin is tender when pierced, rinse but don't peel.

Place chayotes in a 4- to 5-quart pan; cover with water and bring to boiling over high heat. Cover and simmer until chayotes are tender when pierced, 20 to 30 minutes. Drain; let stand until cool enough to touch.

Cut each chayote in half lengthwise at its widest part, slicing through seed. With a grapefruit knife, cut away flesh from each half, leaving a shell about ¼ inch thick. Finely chop flesh and seed; set aside.

Quarter bell pepper; discard stem and seeds. Set aside 1 piece and finely chop the remainder. In a 10- to 12-inch frying pan over medium-high heat, combine the chopped bell pepper, oil, mushrooms, onion, thyme, basil, and pepper. Stir often until liquid evaporates and mushrooms and onion are lightly browned, 12 to 15 minutes. Remove mixture from pan and set aside.

In the same pan over high heat, crumble beef and stir often until meat is well browned, 10 to 15 minutes. Mix broth, taco sauce, and cornstarch. Add broth mixture, mushroom mixture, and chopped chayotes to pan. Stir over high heat until liquid evaporates and mixture is shiny-looking. Remove from the heat, and add salt to taste.

Set chayote shells, cup sides up, in a 9- by 13-inch casserole (oval or rectangular). Mound the filling into chayote shells, using all. If making ahead, let cool, cover, and chill up to 1 day.

Drape filled chayote halves equally with cheese slices. Bake, uncovered, in a 375° oven until hot in center and cheese is melted, about 15 minutes (30 minutes if chilled). Cut remaining pepper quarter into slivers and place on chayote halves. Serves 6.

Per serving: 369 cal. (59 percent from fat); 22 g protein; 24 g fat (10 g sat.); 18 g carbo.; 192 mg sodium; 74 mg chol. ■

By Rebecca Ramsing

DARROW M. WATT

BAKED, CHEESE-TOPPED *chayotes are filled with beef, vegetables, and herbs.*

Why?

*Why does salt cure or corn meat?
Why does it make yeast bread doughs
easier to handle?*

Health-conscious cooks who throw away the saltshaker may wonder why some foods don't turn out the way they expect.

Although salt for flavor is definitely a matter of taste, salt also alters the chemistry and structure of many foods, sometimes dramatically. To get the results you desire, it helps to understand what salt does.

Why do you cure meats with salt, or salt and sugar, before smoking them?

If you cure meat, fish, or poultry with a rub of salt—or let the food stand in a brine of water and salt—before smoking, the food will be moister and more succulent when cooked. Curiously, although salt is used to draw moisture out of the flesh, it also helps the flesh taste moister when the meat is cooked.

If you want seasonings to delicately penetrate the curing meat (or fish or poultry), you must add sugar to the salt; this also gives the meat a smoother texture. Salt can't transport flavors through protein membranes, but sugar can because it dissolves more completely. Sugar also keeps membranes more tender and flexible, and balances saltiness if the mixture is well proportioned.

Smoking contributes a mellow, rich flavor to cured foods. However, smoke also contains bitter components that taste unpleasantly acrid on uncured foods; they are masked by curing.

Why does salt make corned beef red?

It doesn't. Saltpeter combines with meat's color pigment and stabilizes the red.

Why do you use salt to corn meat?

Corning means preserving meat with salt. A corning brine is composed of salt, water, saltpeter (sodium or potassium nitrate), and, sometimes, spices.

The salt partially dehydrates the meat and inhibits the growth of many types of bacteria. The salt also allows selected growth of desired fermentation bacteria.

"Why is salt added to baked goods?"
—Shirley Goldstein, Livermore, California

Salt in wheat-flour yeast dough or batter decidedly affects the shape and texture of the finished product. Baked or griddle-cooked wheat-flour mixtures that contain salt are better able to rise to their full potential and hold their shape than those that have no salt. Even a tiny bit of salt strengthens and toughens gluten, the elastic protein in wheat flour that develops when the flour is wet and beaten or kneaded. Compared with one containing a little salt, a yeast dough made without salt is stickier, takes more kneading to become elastic, and never feels quite as satiny and smooth.

As the bread mixture cooks, tiny pockets of carbon dioxide and moisture, created by the yeast and trapped by the gluten, swell to stretch the gluten. The gluten firms as it is heated, and the trapped bubbles give the food its texture. If the gluten is not strong enough, the pockets collapse and the food becomes dense. If you made identical yeast loaves, putting even just a little salt in only one, that would be the one that was taller and shapelier.

Salt also controls and slows yeast fermentation so bubbles are more uniform in size. Without salt, the dough rises faster and is easy to overproof. Overproofed breads have coarse textures and sunken tops. But you can also go too far. Too much salt has a reverse effect because it seriously inhibits yeast activity. And the food will probably be too salty to enjoy.

Why is salt less important in other baked foods?

In baked foods leavened with baking powder, like muffins and cakes, gluten is deliberately not developed because it makes the product form tunnels or become tough and rubbery; therefore, salt, which strengthens gluten, doesn't play a vital role.

More questions?

Are there other kitchen mysteries you're curious about? What culinary puzzles would you like answered? We'd like to know. Send your questions to Why?, *Sunset Magazine,* 80 Willow Rd., Menlo Park, Calif. 94025.

With the help of George K. York, extension food technologist at UC Davis, *Sunset* food editors will try to find solutions to your problems. We'll answer the questions in the magazine. ∎

By Linda Lau Anusasananan

RUBBING A SALT-SUGAR MIXTURE *over pork loin starts the curing process. Salt firms the meat by drawing out liquid; sugar allows flavors to seep back in. Curing makes meat taste juicier when cooked.*

In a 10- to 12-inch frying pan, stir nuts over medium-high heat until golden, about 6 minutes. Pour from pan and set aside.

Meanwhile, finely chop the chard. Place the frying pan over medium-high heat; add oil, chard, and onion. Stir often until chard is limp and wilted, about 5 minutes. Let cool. Add feta cheese, 2 tablespoons parmesan, tomatoes, capers, oregano, and pepper, and stir to mix well.

Lay wrappers flat in a single layer. Divide filling equally and mound compactly in centers of wrappers. Working quickly, moisten edge of each wrapper with water, then fold over filling to make a triangle and press edges to seal. As shaped, cover triangles with plastic wrap (lay ravioli in a wide pan, separating layers with plastic wrap; cover airtight and chill up to 4 hours).

In an 8- to 10-quart pan over high heat, bring 4 to 5 quarts water to boiling. While water heats, make lemon sauce and keep warm.

To boiling water, add 4 ravioli, 1 at a time; adjust heat to keep boil gentle, and cook uncovered 2 minutes. With a slotted spoon, transfer cooked ravioli to an oiled 10- by 15-inch pan and keep warm; do not stack ravioli (they can overlap). Repeat.

When all ravioli are cooked, quickly pour lemon sauce equally onto 4 warm dinner plates. Put 2 ravioli on each plate, sprinkle with pine nuts, and top with additional cheese to taste. Makes 4 servings.

Per serving: 426 cal. (40 percent from fat); 16 g protein; 19 g fat (6 g sat.); 50 g carbo.; 891 mg sodium; 29 mg chol.

Lemon sauce. In a 1- to 2-quart pan, smoothly mix ½ cup **regular-strength chicken broth** with 1 tablespoon **cornstarch.** Add ½ cup **low-fat milk.** Stir over medium heat until boiling. Remove from heat and stir in 1 teaspoon grated **lemon peel** and 1 tablespoon **lemon juice.** Serve hot.

Lenore M. Klass

San Bruno, California

An even
faster
route
to ravioli

"OF MAKING MANY BOOKS THERE IS no end," saith Ecclesiastes, "and much study is a weariness of the flesh." A variation on this theme might be: "Of stuffing ravioli there is no end, and much consumption thereof is a joy to the spirit." In search of new filling and new sauce, Lenore Klass sends us a recipe that is neither wholly Italian (although it contains parmesan cheese and dried tomatoes) nor entirely Greek (although it contains feta cheese and a sauce reminiscent of *avgolemono*).

She calls it Mediterranean Ravioli, and we'll just overlook the Asian egg roll wrappers. After all, the remaining ingredients are Mediterranean—pine nuts, oregano, capers, and olive oil.

Mediterranean Ravioli with Lemon Sauce

    2   tablespoons pine nuts
    ½   pound Swiss chard, rinsed and
        ends trimmed
    1   teaspoon olive oil
    1   small (3 to 4 oz.) onion, chopped
    ½   cup crumbled feta cheese
        About 6 tablespoons shredded
        parmesan cheese
    ¼   cup drained and diced oil-
        packed dried tomatoes
    1   tablespoon prepared capers,
        drained
    ½   teaspoon dried oregano leaves
    ¼   teaspoon pepper
    8   egg roll wrappers (6 in. square)
        Lemon sauce (recipe follows)

"SIMPLIFY, SIMPLIFY!" THOREAU said. It is not likely that he would attract much of a following in India, where the national soul cries, "Enrich! Complicate!"—especially in matters of cuisine. There, a cornucopia of spices pours out its riches to flavor even the simplest vegetarian food. Even the most complex curry needs further garniture—pickled limes, yogurt, cucumber, and, of course, chutney.

Chutney has become popular with Western cooks as an accompaniment not only to curries but also to more convertional foods, especially mild flavored fish and fowl. Although the original Indian chutney is based on mango, you can use almost any fruit. Susan Kelso's recipe includes dried apricots, an apple, pears, raisins, and white grape juice—and only a modest 10 additional ingredients.

Dried Apricot Chutney

1 pound (2 to 2½ cups) dried apricots, finely chopped

2 medium-size (5 to 6 oz. each) firm-ripe pears, peeled, cored, and diced

1 medium-size (about 6 oz.) apple, peeled, cored, and diced

1 cup firmly packed brown sugar

1¼ cups golden raisins

⅓ cup lemon juice

1 tablespoon ground cinnamon

4 cinnamon sticks, each about 2 inches long

1 teaspoon ground nutmeg

½ teaspoon ground cloves

2½ cups white grape juice

½ cup white wine vinegar

½ teaspoon cayenne

1 teaspoon mustard seed

2 tablespoons diced candied ginger

In a 5- to 6-quart pan, stir together apricots, pears, apple, sugar, raisins, lemon juice, ground cinnamon, cinnamon sticks, nutmeg, cloves, grape juice, vinegar, cayenne, mustard seed, and ginger. Place over high heat, and stir until mixture begins to bubble. Reduce heat and boil gently, stirring as needed to prevent sticking, until mixture is thickened and reduced to about 5 cups, 1¾ to 2 hours.

Let chutney cool. Discard cinnamon sticks, and spoon chutney into 1- to 2-cup jars. Use, or cover airtight and chill up to 1 month; freeze to store longer. Makes about 5 cups.

Per ¼ cup: 165 cal. (1.6 percent from fat); 1.2 g protein; 0.3 g fat (0 g sat.); 42 g carbo.; 12 mg sodium; 0 mg chol.

Susan Kelso

Kensington, California

IT IS THE PORK CHOP THAT GAVE RISE to the phrase "eating high on the hog" to mean living well. Actually, the pig's ears are higher, and even though they have evoked little enthusiasm from gourmets, they would rise even farther if they caught word of Roger Fitzsimmons's plan for perking up the chops with fiery flavors.

Peppered Pork Chops

2 medium-size (about ¼ lb. total) green California (Anaheim) or New Mexico chilies

1 large (about 1 oz.) fresh jalapeño chili

1 small (about ¼ lb.) red or green bell pepper

6 boned pork chops, each 1 inch thick (about 2 lb. total)

1 small (3 oz.) onion, diced

2 cloves garlic, minced or pressed

½ teaspoon each paprika, dried thyme leaves, and ground cumin

¼ teaspoon pepper

⅛ teaspoon cayenne

⅓ cup dry white wine

1½ cups regular-strength chicken broth

1 tablespoon cornstarch mixed smoothly with 3 tablespoons water

Place green chilies, jalapeño, and bell pepper in a 9- by 13-inch pan. Broil 4 to 6 inches from heat, turning occasionally until vegetables are charred all over, 5 to 8 minutes. Cover and let cool. Wearing kitchen gloves, pull off and discard skins, stems, and seeds of vegetables. Finely chop vegetables.

Trim fat from chops. Place a 10- to 12-inch frying pan over medium-high heat and rub with a scrap of fat to lightly oil; discard fat. When pan is hot, add chops and arrange around them the chilies, bell pepper, onion, garlic, paprika, thyme, cumin, pepper, and cayenne. Stir vegetable mixture occasionally and turn chops to brown on both sides, cooking until meat is no longer pink in center (cut to test), 12 to 15 minutes total. Remove chops and keep warm in a rimmed dish. Add wine and broth to pan; turn heat to high and boil uncovered until mixture is reduced to about 1½ cups. Blend in the cornstarch mixture, and stir until sauce is boiling.

Drain any juices from chops into sauce, put chops on plates, and add sauce. Serves 6.

Per serving: 253 cal. (29 percent from fat); 35 g protein; 8.1 g fat (2.7 g sat.); 6.2 g carbo.; 116 mg sodium; 95 mg chol.

Roger Fitzsimmons

Hillsboro, Oregon
By Joan Griffiths, Richard Dunmire

Hot tips about chili powders

CHILIES, FROM SWEET AND MILD to fiery and hot, are sold in many forms. Even when fresh, they're confusing. But when these members of the capsicum family are dried, then ground or crushed and even blended, real confusion ensues. Here's what you can expect from products with the following labels:

Cayenne. Hot, pungent powder made from different varieties of small, slender, very hot, bright red dried chilies; it may be just one kind of chili or a blend. Apply cautiously.

Chili powder, American-style. Mild to medium-hot blend of ground dried chilies and other seasonings such as cumin, oregano, allspice, garlic, coriander, and cloves; mix varies with producer. The powder can be used to season any dish that's good with chilies.

Chili powder, Asian-style (also called red chili powder). This hot chili powder sold in Asian markets is ground or finely crushed dried hot red chilies of various kinds; because it's entirely chilies, it's much hotter than American-style chili powder.

Crushed dried hot red chilies (also called crushed red pepper or chili flakes; label may specify a variety such as caribe). A combination of small pod flakes and seeds of hot to moderately hot chilies.

Ground California chilies (or California chili powder). Mild Anaheim (Anaheim-type, also called California) chilies, used fresh, are also dried when ripe and ground to make a mellow, brick red powder; use liberally.

Ground chile de arbol. Made from this small, slender dried hot red chili. Use sparingly, like cayenne.

Ground New Mexico chili (or New Mexico chili powder). New Mexico chili is an Anaheim-type named for where it grows. It can be slightly hot. Dried and ground, it makes a mellow, brick red powder; use interchangeably with ground California chili.

Ground pasilla chili. Dried pasillas, long and blackish brown, make russet-colored powder. The mild to medium-hot flavor is rich and complex. ∎

By Linda Lau Anusasananan

SUNSET'S KITCHEN CABINET

Creative ways with everyday foods—submitted by *Sunset* readers, tested in *Sunset* kitchens

Carrot-speckled Corn Muffins

Holly D. Hufstetler, Clearfield, Utah

HONEY *sweetens moist carrot muffins; cornmeal and poppy seeds add crunch.*

1 cup all-purpose flour
¾ cup whole-wheat flour
1 cup cornmeal
¼ cup poppy seeds
1 tablespoon baking powder
½ teaspoon baking soda
1 cup apple juice
2 large eggs
½ cup honey
¼ cup salad oil
1 cup (about ¼ lb. or 2 medium-size) firmly packed grated carrots

In a bowl, mix together all-purpose flour, whole-wheat flour, cornmeal, poppy seeds, baking powder, and soda. Add apple juice, eggs, honey, and oil, and beat until well blended; stir in carrots.

Divide muffin batter equally among 12 paper-lined or oiled muffin cups (2½ in. wide). Bake in a 375° oven until muffins are golden brown, about 25 minutes. Serve muffins warm or at room temperature. Makes 12.

Per serving: 231 cal. (28 percent from fat); 4.8 g protein; 7.1 g fat (1 g sat.); 38 g carbo.; 191 mg sodium; 35 mg chol.

Oriental Osso Buco

Roxanne Chan, Albany, California

ASIAN SEASONINGS—*ginger, soy, and rice vinegar—flavor succulent veal shanks, braised Italian-style.*

4 pounds veal shanks, cut into 3-inch lengths
⅓ cup all-purpose flour
2 tablespoons salad oil
1½ cups regular-strength chicken broth
¾ cup dry sherry
3 cloves garlic, minced or pressed
2 tablespoons minced fresh ginger
2 tablespoons reduced-sodium or regular soy sauce
2 tablespoons rice vinegar
2 tablespoons cornstarch smoothly mixed with ¼ cup water
2 teaspoons Oriental sesame oil
   Gremolata (recipe follows)
   Steamed white rice

Coat veal with flour and shake off excess. Place a 5- to 6-quart pan on medium-high heat. Add oil and veal; turn meat often until browned. Add broth, sherry, garlic, ginger, soy sauce, and vinegar. Bring to a boil, cover, and simmer until meat is very tender when pierced, about 1½ hours.

With a slotted spoon, transfer meat to a platter; keep warm. Add cornstarch mixture to sauce and bring to a boil over high heat. Ladle a little sauce onto meat; serve remaining sauce to add to taste. Drizzle meat with sesame oil, sprinkle with gremolata, and serve with rice. Serves 4.

Per serving: 367 cal. (37 percent from fat); 36 g protein; 15 g fat (3.2 g sat.); 20 g carbo.; 428 mg sodium; 124 mg chol.

Gremolata. Mix together 2 minced **green onions,** 1 tablespoon grated **lemon peel,** and ¼ cup minced **fresh cilantro** (coriander).

Frisée Salad with Canadian Bacon

Pamela Faust, Sacramento

DELICATE, *curly frisée and butter lettuce get a hot dressing of sautéed Canadian bacon, shallots, and apples.*

1 small head (about ⅓ lb.) frisée—small curly endive, rinsed and crisped
1 small head (about ⅓ lb.) butter lettuce, rinsed and crisped
6 shallots, minced
2 tablespoon olive or salad oil
⅓ pound Canadian bacon, cut into ¼-inch cubes
1 large (about ½ lb.) tart green apple, cored and diced
3 tablespoons lemon juice

Tear frisée and butter lettuce into bite-size pieces and mix in a large salad bowl; cover and chill.

In a 10- to 12-inch frying pan over medium-high heat, stir shallots in oil until limp, about 5 minutes. Add bacon and stir until lightly browned, about 5 minutes. Add apple; stir often until apple pieces are slightly softened, 3 to 5 minutes. Pour hot mixture and lemon juice over greens. Mix well. Serves 4.

Per serving: 173 cal. (50 percent from fat); 9.1 g protein; 9.7 g fat (1.8 g sat.); 14 g carbo.; 542 mg sodium; 19 mg chol.

Black Beans with Peppers and Tomatoes

Marilou Robinson, Portland

½ cup oil-packed dried tomatoes, drained, and 1 tablespoon of the oil

1 small (about ¼ lb.) chopped red onion

½ cup canned roasted red peppers, drained and cut into thin strips

2 cans (15 oz. each) black beans, rinsed and drained

¼ cup minced fresh cilantro (coriander)

Fresh cilantro sprigs, lime wedges, and sour cream

Coarsely chop tomatoes; set aside. Combine tomato oil and onion in a 10- to 12-inch frying pan. Stir often over medium-high heat until onion is limp, about 5 minutes. Add tomatoes and peppers; stir often until hot. Add beans and minced cilantro; stir gently until beans are hot. Pour into a bowl and garnish with cilantro sprigs. Add juice from lime wedges and sour cream to taste. Serves 4 to 6.

Per serving: 218 cal. (54 percent from fat); 6.7 g protein; 13 g fat (0 g sat.); 20 g carbo.; 242 mg sodium; 0 mg chol.

BLACK BEANS, *dried tomatoes, and red peppers are canned ingredients that go together fast for a great vegetable dish.*

Microwave Risotto

Phyllis Mael, Northridge, California

1 small (¼ lb.) onion, chopped

1 teaspoon olive or salad oil

1 clove garlic, minced or pressed

1 hot or mild Italian turkey sausage (about ¼ lb.), casing removed

1½ cups regular-strength chicken broth, heated to boiling

2 large (about 10 oz. total) Roma-type tomatoes, cored and chopped

½ cup short- or medium-grain white rice

¼ cup dry white wine

About ¼ cup grated parmesan cheese

Minced parsley

In a 1- to 1½-quart microwave-safe casserole, combine onion, oil, and garlic. Cook in a microwave oven on full power (100 percent) until onion is very limp, about 3 minutes. Crumble sausage into casserole. Cook on full power until meat is no longer pink, about 3 minutes; stir mixture once after 2 minutes.

Add hot broth to casserole with tomatoes, rice, and wine. Cover casserole with plastic wrap. Cook on full power until liquid is absorbed and rice is tender to bite, about 15 minutes; stir every 5 minutes. Stir in ¼ cup cheese. Serve risotto sprinkled with parsley and extra cheese to taste. Serves 2.

Per serving: 432 cal. (27 percent from fat); 21 g protein; 13 g fat (4.6 g sat.); 53 g carbo.; 590 mg sodium; 51 mg chol.

RISOTTO *for two cooks in the microwave oven; it's seasoned with turkey sausage.*

Coffee Squares

Luci Bernhard, San Pablo, California

½ cup (¼ lb.) butter or margarine

1 cup sugar

2 large eggs

1½ cups all-purpose flour

1 teaspoon ground cinnamon

½ teaspoon baking powder

½ teaspoon baking soda

¼ cup instant coffee or espresso powder dissolved in ⅔ cup water

1 cup raisins

Coffee glaze (recipe follows)

In a large bowl, beat butter, sugar, and eggs with a mixer until fluffy. Mix together flour, cinnamon, baking powder, and baking soda; add to butter mixture and beat until well blended.

Add coffee and raisins; stir until well blended.

Spread batter evenly into an oiled 10- by 15-inch baking pan. Bake in a 350° oven until center springs back when lightly pressed, about 20 minutes. While hot, spread with glaze. Serve warm or, if making ahead, store airtight at room temperature up to 1 day. Cut into 25 squares.

Per piece: 145 cal. (26 percent from fat); 1.6 g protein; 4.2 g fat (2.5 g sat.); 26 g carbo.; 79 mg sodium; 27 mg chol.

Coffee glaze. Dissolve 3 tablespoons **instant coffee** or espresso **powder** in 3 tablespoons **milk.** Add 1½ cups **powdered sugar** and stir until smooth.

Compiled by Christine Weber Hale

MOIST, *cake-tender coffee cookies get a double dose of coffee—in the batter and in the dark glaze.*

Tangy avocado salad, hot walnuts, a word on weights, and wine-tasting secrets

By Jerry Anne Di Vecchio

Certain foods and flavors come together in perfect harmony. For some people, it's mint sauce with lamb; for others, it's cream cheese with lox—and certainly, if my mail reflects favorite recipes, there's a devoted following for chicken baked in canned mushroom soup.

Another noteworthy duo was discovered by my friend Janis de Halas. She's a cosmetologist, and each month, when I make a visit for personal restorations, we talk food because she's also a great cook and gardener.

One day she had a special tale to tell, and it started with squash blossoms. She had planned to gather a few blossoms to stuff with a goat cheese filling. Her own blooms had wilted, the market had none, but she still had the filling. Where to put it? There sat an avocado, ripe and beckoning. She cut it in half, replaced the pit with the goat cheese mixture, and took a historic bite. The cheese gave the avocado just the right tang, the avocado gave the cheese a velvety essence, and the next thing you know, they were mashed together to fill roasted red peppers to make this handsome salad. The cabbage and toast add crunch; the peppers add color.

Avocados are in peak supply this month, so make use of this salad for lunch or dinner.

Additional advice from practical Janis is in keeping with the speedy nature of this dish: if your garden's red bells aren't ready to roast and peel, use canned (often in jars) roasted peeled red peppers from the supermarket.

BACK TO BASICS
Putting the heat on walnuts

Maybe native black walnuts never made the commercial big time because they are tough to crack and the meat is almost impossible to pick out in large pieces—as my brother and I can testify. This chore usually fell to us. One of my mother's annual pet projects was gathering the windfall nuts because she loved their oily, distinctive character in divinity—the fluffy white candy that's a standard in old cookbooks.

Until I learned about genetics, I had always thought that those long, tedious hours of shelling black walnuts led to my distaste for them. To most, they are mellow, rich, and flavorful. To others, like me, who are born with flavor receptors that detect a glucoside in walnuts, they are bitter and irritating. But the good news is that heat destroys this compound, and at the same time crisps and enhances walnuts for any taste.

English walnuts also have glucoside, but they are blessed with pale, easy-to-crack shells, and nuts that aren't as oily (and are less inclined to become rancid). These traits make English walnuts big business, and California's great Central Valley is the largest source in the world for them. Both English

A TASTE OF THE WEST
Avocado and Chèvre Red Pepper Salad

- 2 large (about ¾ lb. each) firm-ripe avocados
- 3 tablespoons lime juice
- ½ cup firmly packed fresh chèvre (goat cheese)
- 1 teaspoon dried or 2 teaspoons chopped fresh tarragon leaves
  Salt
- 1 jar (12 oz.) roasted red peppers

2 to 3 cups finely shredded green cabbage

1 baguette (8 oz.), sliced and toasted

Chili balsamic dressing (directions follow)

Fresh cilantro (coriander) leaves

Cut avocados in halves lengthwise and twist apart. Leave pit in 1 avocado half and rub avocado with a little of the lime juice; set this half aside.

Peel remaining 3 avocado halves, discarding pit. On a rimmed plate, coarsely mash these avocados with remaining lime juice, chèvre, and tarragon. Add salt to taste.

Drain roasted peppers and separate into 4 equal portions, keeping large pieces intact (slit whole peppers open along 1 side). Group scrappiest pieces in centers of 4 salad plates, laying flat. On top of the peppers on each plate, mound ¼ of the cabbage, then top with ¼ of the avocado mixture. Drape the large, smooth portions of peppers over avocado and pat gently to shape neatly. (If making ahead, cover airtight and chill up to 6 hours.) Peel and pit remaining avocado half and cut into thin slices. Arrange slices equally on the 4 plates beside filled peppers. Accompany with toasted baguette slices, and drizzle salad and toast with chili balsamic dressing. Garnish with cilantro. Makes 4 servings.

Per serving: 554 cal. (57 percent from fat); 14 g protein; 35 g fat (8.7 g sat.); 51 g carbo.; 623 mg sodium; 13 mg chol.

Chili balsamic dressing. Break off stems and shake seeds out of 2 **mild dried red chilies** (California, New Mexico, or mulato). Coarsely crumble or chop chilies and put in a 6- to 8-inch frying pan over lowest heat with 2 to 3 tablespoons **olive oil.** Heat about 10 minutes to flavor oil with chilies, then let mixture stand until cool (if making ahead, cover when cool and let stand up to 1 day). Add 2 to 3 tablespoons **balsamic vinegar;** stir to serve.

and black walnuts respond well to toasting.

To oven-toast walnuts, arrange them in a single layer in a baking pan. Bake in a 350° oven until the meat under the thin skin turns a pale to rich gold color (to test, check a broken nut or break one), about 12 minutes. Shake pan frequently.

To pan-toast walnuts, arrange them in a single layer in a frying pan and stir frequently over medium heat until the meat is a pale to rich gold color (to test, check a broken nut or break one), 10 to 12 minutes.

If you fill the baking or frying pan with more than 1 layer of nuts, you need to watch them more closely and stir more often. Rub warm nuts in a towel to remove the loose brown skin, then lift nuts from towel.

Use, or store toasted walnuts airtight for a few days; freeze to store longer.

While pan-toasting, you can add a few ingredients to make glazed English walnuts for appetizers; their nooks and crannies capture the glaze very well.

Savory glazed walnuts. In a 10- to 12-inch frying pan, combine 1 cup toasted **walnut halves,** 1 teaspoon **butter** or margarine, 2 tablespoons **sugar,** 2 tablespoons **vinegar,** and 1 tablespoon **soy sauce.** Stir over high heat until liquid evaporates and most of the mixture sticks to nuts and not to the pan, about 3 minutes. Pour nuts onto a sheet of foil and push apart. Let cool briefly for surface to harden, then serve (you can store them airtight up to 4 days; they stick together, but you can break them apart). Makes 1 cup.

Per ¼ cup: 196 cal. (73 percent from fat); 3.8 g protein; 16 g fat (2 g sat.); 12 g carbo.; 270 mg sodium; 2.6 mg chol.

GREAT TOOL

Weights and measures

A cooking scale has real advantages. In baking, you get the most consistent results. Recipe nutritional values are more accurate. And a scale is fast and easy to use.

In *Sunset*'s test kitchen, the workhorse we've relied on for years is a commercial balance scale that accommodates as much as 10 pounds. Food sits on one side, weights on the other, and a 1-pound adjustable sliding weight in the center determines ounces. With no working parts, it never breaks down.

One summer not long ago, while browsing through a Sunday antiques market in southern France, I was drawn to an old, handsome balance scale with polished brass plates. The gleaming weights were in metric units, so for day-to-day home cooking I later bought a set of American standard weights. These turn up in a variety of places, and a good starting point for a search is the yellow pages under Scales or Restaurant Equipment and Supplies. I found my set in the Chantry catalog (Box 3039, Clearwater, Fla. 34630; 813/446-1960). Sets include seven weights graduated from ¼ ounce to 1 or 2 pounds and cost $69 in brass, $39 in a combination of brass and cast iron. Chantry also has a balance scale, without weights, in red, green, or black for $139 to $169, depending on the finish.

Since weights don't wear out, they can often be found in secondhand and antiques shops. The trick is to get a full set.

FINE FAST FOOD

A green Georgian pâté

Phkali (p-*kol*-y) is a refreshingly simple, light, and delicious vegetable pâté that hails from the Georgian republic via Seattle's Pirosmani Restaurant. Since the Iron Curtain was raised, the unique qualities of the countries behind it are reemerging. Pirosmani's chef and co-owner, Laura Dewell, knows Georgia firsthand because she has spent time cooking in this sunny country, which is nestled between the Black and Caspian seas with the Caucasus Mountains as a backdrop. The Georgian dishes on Pirosmani's menu speak of the Mediterranean character of the region.

Traditionally, phkali is served as small round cakes beside flatbread stuffed with fresh mozzarella and feta (Mexican panela and queso fresco are alternatives).

Phkali. You need 1½ cups dry-squeezed cooked **spinach leaves.** To get this amount, start with 2 pounds (6 qt., lightly packed) spinach leaves. Rinse and drain. Stir leaves (they have enough moisture on them for cooking) in a 6- to 8-quart pan over high heat until wilted. Drain spinach in a colander. When cool, put about ¼ of the leaves at a time in a square of cheesecloth and twist to squeeze out as much liquid as you can. (You can also start with 2 boxes, 10 oz. each, frozen spinach; thaw, drain, and squeeze.) Whirl the spinach in a food processor until it is coarsely chopped, then set it aside.

In food processor, make a smooth paste by whirling ¼

SINCE WEIGHTS DON'T WEAR OUT, *quaint old sets are as useful as new ones.*

KEVIN CANDLAND

friend. I cooked the pasta in clear broth soup so the shapes would show up well, then kept mum with others around the table and watched his reaction—puzzled, squinting to be sure, then a sheepish, tickled-pink smirk.

cup chopped **onion,** 2 cloves **garlic,** ½ cup packed **fresh cilantro** (coriander) **leaves,** ¼ cup packed **Italian parsley leaves,** and ½ cup **walnuts** (toasted, if desired; see Back to Basics). Scrape mixture into a bowl. Add spinach and mix well. Stir in, to taste, **salt** and about 1½ tablespoons **white wine vinegar.**

Pat mixture into 2-tablespoon-size thin round cakes, or pack pâté into a small dish and scoop out to serve. If making ahead, cover and chill up to 1 day. Makes 2 cups.

Per ¼ cup: 78 cal. (58 percent from fat); 4.5 g protein; 5 g fat (0.5 g sat.); 6.3 g carbo.; 92 mg sodium; 0 mg chol.

NEWS NOTE
Pasta doodling

A lot of folks are having fun with pasta shapes these days. You're apt to find bicycles, bunnies, hearts, stars, seasonal autumn leaves and Christmas trees, and many other nontraditional shapes,

plain or colored by food ingredients. But, believe it or not, there's more.

Buckeye Beans & Herbs in Spokane (800/449-2121) also offers sports shapes—footballs, soccer balls, and baseball bats, balls, and gloves. Canterbury Cuisine in Redmond, Washington (800/733-6663), has Western gear—cowboy hats and boots. Both have catalogs.

The Buckeye catalog provokes chuckles like the ones I got when I served baseball pasta to a baseball-freak

HOT TIP
Barbecue problems?

The kettle-shaped barbecue introduced by Weber about 30 years ago turned cooking over coals (and now gas) into a controllable, predictable art. Now Weber has established a barbecue hotline. From April 10 through Labor Day, its army of experts will be on call from 6 to 4 Mondays through Fridays to answer questions about charcoal or gas grilling. Just dial (800) 474-5568. ■

BOB THOMPSON ON WINE
Mesmerize by memorizing

Newcomers to wine hear stories about the expert who takes one sip of a mystery wine and tells all: who made it, in what year, from exactly which village. Most of us are torn between belief and suspicion.
There is a simple fact behind the feat. Differences in sun and soil will make any grape variety behave one way in one place, another way somewhere else. If you want to be an instant expert, here is the game (if you are a waste-not, want-not, as I am, get six to eight people together and go directly from tasting to dinner).

Assemble three wines, all of one type but from three different regions, each clearly identified on the label. Sauvignon Blanc is a good white for the purpose, Pinot Noir a useful red. Set out three glasses. Pour a different wine into each. As you taste each wine, focus on two separate questions. First, how does it feel—harsh, biting, smooth? Second, what do its flavors remind you of—cherries, vanilla, woody stems? Do this once, and the differences will be obvious to you. Do it several hundred times, and you will memorize those differences so well that you can amaze your friends.

Among Sauvignon Blancs, these teach the regional lesson well:

Napa Valley—Grgich Hills

Cellar, Robert Pepi Winery, Silverado Vineyards, Robert Mondavi Winery. (Look for juicy textures and sweet, juicy flavors like those in long grasses in the spring.)

Sonoma County—Kenwood Vineyards, Dry Creek Vineyard, Simi Winery, Clos du Bois Wines. (Look for crisp to drying textures and herblike flavors.)

Santa Barbara—Firestone Vineyard, the Gainey Vineyard. (Look for slightly juicy textures, and flavors vaguely reminiscent of asparagus.)

For the dinner entrée, consider rockfish (often called snapper), lingcod, or the smooth-textured sablefish (also called butterfish, black cod, or Alaska black cod).

Among Pinot Noirs, these clearly tell stories of their

regional origins:

Carneros—Saintsbury, Carneros Creek, Acacia Winery. (Think of middling-firm textures and the subtle smell of red cherries.)

Russian River Valley—Gary Farrell, Rochioli Vineyards & Winery, Dehlinger. (Think of outright juicy textures, plus the taste of soft-ripe black cherries.)

Santa Barbara—Byron Vineyards & Winery, Sanford, Santa Barbara Winery. (Think of fleshy textures and the aromas of the whole strawberry plant when you brush the leaves as you pick ripe berries.)

With Pinot Noir, just about any red meat will do, but game birds or tenderloin of pork can be especially appropriate.

CRUMBLED FETA, FRESH BASIL, *and barbecued onion garnish servings of wine-marinated boneless lamb. Serve with couscous.*

Lamb grilled, baked, or stir-fried

Four fresh ideas for a boned, butterflied leg and quick-cooking smaller cuts

I T'S TRADITIONAL. WITH SPRING comes lamb, especially for Easter dinner. Because lamb is in high demand now, markets have a plentiful supply. However, lamb is available year-round, some of it imported from New Zealand or Australia.

When you look for lamb at the meat counter, you'll probably be surprised by the choices. Many cuts are quite reasonable in price and take just a short time to cook. (The most common reasons given for passing up lamb at the meat counter are "I won't use a whole leg" and "Racks are too costly.")

Look for arm chops, loin chops, boneless sirloin roasts (perfect for four, or two meals for two), shoulder chops or blade steaks, or sirloin steaks (also labeled as lamb steaks or sirloin chops). Because a lamb is relatively small, few cuts are tough. Only the shank and leg require long cooking.

Markets carry both fresh and frozen lamb. In some areas you may be able to locate preseasoned lamb (seasonings often include garlic or onion plus herbs), either seasoned by the supermarket or sold as prepackaged, preseasoned roasts. The preseasoned products are convenient—ready to pop into the oven or onto the barbecue.

The following recipes use many of the convenient cuts mentioned above. The butterflied leg serves 8 to 10. The others are perfect for 4.

Grilled Butterflied Lamb Leg with Herbs and Feta

1 boned leg of lamb (4½ to 5 lb.)

¾ cup dry red wine

⅓ cup lemon juice

½ cup minced fresh basil leaves

2 tablespoons sugar

1 tablespoon minced fresh or 2 teaspoons crumbled dried rosemary leaves

1 tablespoon minced fresh or 2 teaspoons crumbled dried oregano leaves

1 large (about 10 oz.) onion

2 large garlic cloves, thinly sliced

½ cup crumbled feta cheese

Basil and oregano sprigs (optional)

Salt and pepper

Lay lamb boned side up. With a sharp knife, make lengthwise cuts through thickest parts about halfway through meat. Push cuts open and pat flat to make meat as evenly thick as possible. Trim off fat.

In a deep bowl or 2-gallon heavy plastic food bag, mix wine, lemon juice, ¼ cup minced basil leaves, sugar, rosemary leaves, and oregano leaves. Add lamb and turn to coat evenly. Cover or seal and chill, turning occasionally, at least 2 hours or up to 1 day.

Cut the onion into ½-inch-thick slices, then crosswise into half-rounds. Lift the meat from the marinade; reserve liquid. Lay meat flat, boned side up. Cut slits about ½ inch deep and as wide as onion all over meat. Lay garlic slices in the slits. Fit onion slices, rounded side out, into slits holding garlic.

Thread a long (at least 18 in.), sturdy meat skewer through the meat

THINLY SLICED BARBECUED *boneless sirloin roast is the centerpiece for an intimate Easter dinner. Spoon Asian-style sauce over meat and rice cubes.*

parallel to the longest side and about 2 inches from edge, securing the onion slices as much as possible with the skewer. Insert another skewer through the opposite side of the meat, securing any loose or uneven edges of meat to the main section of the roast.

To prepare barbecue, ignite 60 charcoal briquets in a barbecue with a lid. When coals are mostly covered with gray ash (about 30 minutes), divide in half and bank on opposite sides of firegrate; place a drip pan in center. To maintain temperature, add 6 briquets to each side now and after 30 minutes of cooking. Place grill 5 to 6 inches above coals.

Place meat on a lightly oiled grill, onion side up. Brush with half the reserved marinade. Cover with lid and open drafts. Cook until a thermometer inserted into the thickest part of meat (not against the skewer) registers 140°, about 1 hour. Halfway through cooking, brush with remaining marinade.

Supporting meat with skewers, transfer meat to a carving board. Sprinkle lamb with cheese and remaining ¼ cup minced basil. Garnish with basil and oregano sprigs, and season to taste with salt and pepper. Remove skewers to slice meat. Serves 8 to 10.

Per serving: 436 cal. (54 percent from fat); 40 g protein; 26 g fat (11 g sat.); 7.2 g carbo.; 179 mg sodium; 147 mg chol.

Barbecued Sirloin Roast with Asian Flavors

½ cup *each* chopped fresh ginger and chopped fresh mint leaves

⅓ cup *ketjap manis* (sweetened soy sauce), or ⅓ cup soy sauce with 2 tablespoons sugar

¼ cup chicken broth

6 cloves garlic, minced or pressed

1 tablespoon Oriental sesame oil

1 boneless sirloin lamb roast (also labeled London broil or butterball), about 1½ pounds

Mint sprigs (optional)

Rice cubes (recipe follows)

In a large bowl, mix ginger, mint, ketjap manis, broth, garlic, and sesame oil. Place roast in mixture, turn, and let marinate at least 1 hour or up to overnight. Turn frequently if marinating 1 hour, or every couple of hours as possible if holding overnight; reserve marinade when roast is removed to be cooked.

In a barbecue with cover, place roast on a grill 4 to 6 inches above a solid bed of medium-hot coals (you can hold your hand at grill level only 3 to 4 seconds). Cover and cook, turning every 5 minutes or as needed to brown evenly, until a thermometer inserted in thickest part of lamb reads 135° to 140°, 20 to 25 minutes. Transfer to platter; keep warm and let stand about 5 minutes. Meanwhile, bring

Easy-to-cook lamb cuts

You don't need to roast a whole leg of lamb to enjoy a lamb dinner. A boneless butterflied leg cooks in just an hour on the grill, and smaller cuts can be prepared in much less time.

LOIN CHOP
Cut from the loin (broil or grill)

ARM CHOP
Cut from top of shank next to shoulder (broil or grill)

SHOULDER CHOP
Also known as blade steak. Cut from the shoulder; more bone and fat than on sirloin steak (broil or grill)

SIRLOIN STEAK/CHOP
Cut from top of back leg (broil or grill)

BONELESS SIRLOIN ROAST
Also known as butterball roast or London broil. Cut from the sirloin (broil, grill, or roast)

BUTTERFLIED LEG
Bone removed; spread flat (broil or grill)

LUCY I. SARGENT

reserved marinade to a boil in a small pan over high heat; pour into a bowl. Garnish platter with mint sprigs and rice cubes. Thinly slice meat. Pass cooked marinade. Serves 4.

Per serving: 797 cal. (35 percent from fat); 40 g protein; 31 g fat (12 g sat.); 86 g carbo.; 1,459 mg sodium; 124 mg chol.

Rice cubes. In a 2- to 3-quart pan, combine 2 cups **long-grain white rice** and 3½ cups **water.** Cover and bring to a boil on high heat, then cook over low heat just until water is absorbed, about 20 minutes.

Spoon hot rice into a 9-inch square pan. With back of spoon, press firmly to form an even layer rinsing spoon frequently with water to prevent sticking. Cool. (If making ahead, cover and store at room temperature up to 4 hours.)

Run a knife around pan edge, then turn rice out onto a board. Cut into 1-inch squares, rinsing knife frequently.

Italian-style Stir-fried Lamb

1½   pounds lamb sirloin steaks, shoulder chops (blade steaks), arm chops, or stew meat

¼   cup minced parsley

2   tablespoons minced oil-packed sun-dried tomatoes

½   to 1 teaspoon crushed dried hot red chilies

3   tablespoons dry marsala

2   cans (15 oz. each) small white beans, rinsed and drained

2   large (about ½ lb.) Roma-type tomatoes, cored and diced

About 1 teaspoon olive oil

2   tablespoons *each* balsamic vinegar and chicken broth

Parsley sprigs (optional)

Salt and pepper

Trim fat and bone from steak; cut across grain into ⅛-inch-thick slices about ¼ inch wide and 3 inches long (you should have 1 lb.). Combine meat, parsley, sun-dried tomatoes, chilies, and marsala; let stand at least 15 minutes, or chill up to next day.

Meanwhile, to a 10- to 12-inch nonstick frying pan over medium-high heat, add beans and tomatoes; cook, stirring often, just until hot, about 3 minutes. Transfer from pan to a serving platter, and place in a 200° oven.

In the same pan, heat oil until hot. Add half of lamb mixture and stir-fry until meat is brown-tinged and just barely pink when cut, about 3 minutes. Remove meat; spoon over bean mixture in oven. Repeat to cook remaining meat; transfer to platter.

Add vinegar and broth to same pan; stir to release pan drippings. Boil until reduced to 2 tablespoons.

STIR-FRIED LAMB, *seasoned with chilies, sun-dried tomatoes, and marsala, is served over white beans and tomatoes.*

JOSHUA ETS-HOKIN

Spoon over meat and bean-tomato mixture. Garnish with parsley; offer salt and pepper to taste. Serves 4.

Per serving: 342 cal. (32 percent from fat); 32 g protein; 12 g fat (2.8 g sat.); 24 g carbo.; 430 mg sodium; 75 mg chol.

Quick Mustard-crusted Chops with Potatoes

About 2 tablespoons olive oil

4   large (about 2 lb.) thin-skinned potatoes, scrubbed and thickly sliced

¼   cup Dijon mustard

2   teaspoons mustard seed

½   to 1 teaspoon ground pepper

4   loin lamb chops (each 2 inches thick, about 1½ pounds total)

¼   cup Italian-seasoned bread crumbs

Parsley sprigs (optional)

Heat 2 tablespoons oil in a 10- by 15-inch baking pan about 30 seconds in a 450° oven. Remove and add potatoes; turn to coat all sides. Bake until golden and soft-crisp, about 45 minutes; turn every 15 minutes.

Meanwhile, combine mustard, mustard seed, and pepper. Trim fat from chops; place on a lightly oiled 10- by 15-inch baking pan.

When potatoes are almost done, move to bottom rack in oven and turn oven to broil. Place chops 4 to 6 inches beneath broiler; cook until tops are browned, about 6 minutes. Turn chops and top equally with mustard mixture, then bread crumbs; return to broiler until meat is just pink, about 6 minutes more (cut to test). Evenly divide potatoes among 4 plates; place chops alongside potatoes. Garnish with parsley. Serves 4.

Per serving: 405 cal. (29 percent from fat); 22 g protein; 13 g fat (2.9 g sat.); 47 g carbo.; 616 mg sodium; 50 mg chol. ■

By Betsy Reynolds Bateson, Christine Weber Hale

Food and Wine

A balloonist's-eye view of the Napa Valley between St. Helena and Calistoga shows its narrow confines packed wall-to-wall with vineyards. Mount St. Helena looms over its north end.

Heaven

CHARLES O'REAR

WINING AND DINING IN THE NAPA VALLEY JUST KEEPS GETTING BETTER. HERE'S A GUIDE TO THE VALLEY'S BEST FOOD AND WINE EXPERIENCES

ON A TYPICALLY BRILLIANT SPRING DAY, THE NAPA Valley Wine Train pulls out of the station and rolls northward through the valley. Passengers ease back into plush swivel chairs, wineglasses in hand, and gaze out over hillsides tinged with traces of blooming mustard.

Later, between bites of veal mousse in a light truffle cream sauce, passengers survey a checkerboard of fields: green and leafy vineyards adjoin blank areas scraped bare but for piles of dead vines, set ablaze and sending thick white smoke into the blue sky. These are the scars of phylloxera, the grapevine-killing insect that has traumatized the valley. But recovery is

Backed by French oak barrels at St. Clement Vineyards, winemaker Dennis Johns checks the ruby color of his Cabernet Sauvignon.

**By
Lora J. Finnegan, Elaine Johnson,
and
Bob Thompson**

Valley map shows seven sub-appellations that stake out distinctive vineyard districts.

just as apparent as the train passes vineyards replanted on phylloxera-resistant rootstock, the skinny young sprigs peeking from milk carton collars.

As the train proceeds north, the valley's compact dimensions become clear. Just 30 miles long and narrowing to about a mile across at its waist, the Napa Valley has about 35,000 acres in vineyard, about a fifth of what's planted in France's Bordeaux region.

In this valley, the best of California's natural attributes—perfect weather, rich soil, sheltering hills—blend in a miniature masterpiece of nature's artistry. But like a work in progress with which the artist is never satisfied, the brushstrokes of change are always visible.

The last 20 years have brought a ninefold increase in wineries. With almost every arable acre of the valley floor now planted to vines, grape growers have literally taken to the hills. New subappellations identify some of these upland districts, as well as marking out distinctive sections of the valley floor.

The winery boom has been accompanied by explosive growth in tourism and a soaring number of restaurants offering dining experiences that rival the best of any big city. Just savor the images of some menu selections we discovered: lobster sausage, house-smoked red trout fillet, and miyagi oysters in ponzu sauce. And those are only appetizers.

On a day trip or a long weekend in the Napa Valley, you can revel in hedonistic pleasures some folks fly to France for: world-class wines at châteaulike wineries, innovative meals in elegant settings, memorable lodges surrounded by vineyards. Of course, you'll miss the expense, jet lag, and language difficulties of a Gallic sojourn. *C'est la vie!*

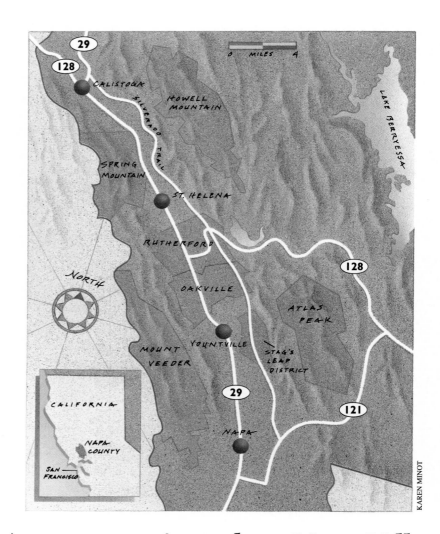

KAREN MINOT

A wine taster's guide to Napa Valley

THIRTY YEARS AGO, VISITORS TO THE Napa Valley saw more prunes and walnuts from State Highway 29 than they did grapevines (although some old Italian farmers did grow Carignane between the rows of prunes). With only 10 wineries to choose from, novices hit up each and every roadside tasting room for Chenin Blanc and Riesling, while the knowledgeable focused on Beaulieu, Inglenook, Charles Krug, and Louis M. Martini for Cabernet Sauvignons going back as many as 10 vintages. Real insiders sneaked up into the hills to Mayacmas for Cabernet, to Souverain for Zinfandel, and to Stony Hill for a newcomer called Chardonnay.

It was an easy time. It started to disappear when Robert Mondavi built his mission-style cellars in 1966, and was long gone by 1975. Now, with the winery count past 220, a satisfying tour takes advance planning and disciplined execution.

Some rules and cautions to keep in

mind: three wineries a day is the optimum, four a reasonable number. Expect to be jostled by crowds at the biggest, best-known places with organized tours. Plan on needing appointments to visit small, out-of-the-way properties. And don't be surprised when many proprietors charge a fee for tasting. For help with planning and directions to wineries, write or call the Napa Valley Vintners Association (Box 141, St. Helena 94574; 800/982-1371) and ask for its excellent (and free) winery touring map.

Comparative tastings of a particular varietal or two can provide purpose to a tasting tour. Cabernet Sauvignon and Chardonnay are the life and breath of today's Napa: rare is the winery that does not produce one or both, rarer still the visitor who turns away from them. Two alternative approaches to winery touring help make sense of this abundance of riches. One is to home in on the valley's federally recognized subappellations, which leaves you the option

A Domaine Chandon tour group pauses between rows of stainless steel fermentation tanks.

of concentrating on Cabernet Sauvignon and Chardonnay, but does not require it. The other is to focus on an offbeat varietal or two.

ONE APPROACH: DIVIDE AND CONQUER

Subappellations are a way of drawing ever-finer distinctions among regions of varying sun and soil within the Napa Valley, as the French have done with communes in Bordeaux and Burgundy. Trying them one against another is amusing at least, instructive at best.

Oakville and Rutherford. Side by side on the valley floor at its midpoint, these two towns-cum-appellations are the heart of Napa winemaking. Visitors will need to edit their options with greater firmness here than anywhere else, and be ready to face the crowds that go with well-organized public tours. A gamut of Cabernets for first-timers to try: Cakebread, Caymus, Franciscan, and Robert Pepi.

Stag's Leap District. Stag's Leap and

BEST WINERY TOURS

While wine tasting engages the senses, a good winery tour can stimulate the mind. Here are a handful of the best.

Robert Mondavi Winery. As a way to learn about winemaking, it's hard to beat Mondavi's extensive guided tour. The 1-hour tour begins with a walk out to the vineyards, leads you through the winemaking facilities and barrel room, and ends with a tasting.

St. Supéry Winery and Wine Discovery Center. A self-guided tour takes you through a display vineyard showing different vine trellising methods used on six grape varieties; inside, a relief map shows the valley's contours and a soil model shows a cutaway vine with its root structure.

Beringer Vineyards. At Napa's oldest continuously operated winery, 45-minute tours give you a good historical perspective on valley winemaking by taking you into caves hand-chiseled in the 1800s.

Domaine Chandon. Hourly guided tours give you a complete picture of the *méthode champenoise*—from vineyard to press to riddling rack. Afterward, you can celebrate the experience with a glass of bubbly ($2.50 to $5) in the tasting room.

TO LEARN MORE ABOUT WINE TASTING:

Robert Mondavi's 3½-hour tour and wine essence tasting lets you sample 24 fragrances associated with wines. It's offered free each Tuesday from June through October; for reservations, call (707) 226-1395, ext. 4312.

Merryvale Vineyards holds an excellent beginner's wine component tasting seminar in its cavernous cask room every Saturday morning. After a tour, participants train their palates to identify the flavors of tannins, tartaric acid, sugar, and alcohol. Cost is $5; for reservations, call (800) 326-6069.

BEST WINERY GARDENS

Vitis vinifera isn't the only plant of interest in the valley. These four wineries are each well worth a spring visit to see their showcase gardens in bloom.

Sutter Home Winery. Victoria's famed Butchart Gardens was the inspiration for a garden of more than 800 varieties surrounding a handsome 1884 Victorian home. Highlights include a rose garden with 150 varieties and dwarf Japanese maples. For hours, call (707) 963-3104.

Schramsberg Vineyards. Surrounding a vineyard founded by Jacob Schram in 1862, Schramsberg's gardens were sadly overgrown when owners Jack and Jamie Davies took over in the mid-1960s to make sparkling wines. Today the garden is a mix of modern and Victorian styles, including many specimens planted in the 1880s. Open by appointment only; call 942-4558.

Traulsen Vineyards. Rose fanciers will love this tiny Zinfandel-only winery, where the flower garden is half as big as the adjacent 2-acre vineyard. Look for antique and David Austin English roses. Open Fridays through Sundays and by appointment; call 942-0283.

Chateau Montelena. Below a castlelike château lies 3-acre Jade Lake, ringed with daffodils and roses. Paths wander past Chinese pagodas and plantings of calendulas, cyclamen, dogwood, irises, and poppies. To arrange for a guided tour, call 942-5105.

Roses are fragrant standouts among camellias, daylilies, and hundreds of other plant varieties in the Victorian-style garden at Sutter Home Winery in St. Helena.

Cabernet Sauvignon come close to being synonymous. Bisected by the Silverado Trail just northeast of the city of Napa, the district is compact, easy to explore, and notably photogenic because its towering rock wall contrasts so dramatically with the softer hills around it. Readily visitable within 1 mile: Clos du Val, Chimney Rock, Pine Ridge, Silverado, and Stag's Leap.

Mount Veeder. Unmatched panoramas can be found on the lonely roads winding up to this area in the west hills, almost purely Cabernet and Chardonnay country. Anchor a tour with the Hess Collection and Chateau Potelle. Mayacmas, Mount Veeder, and other small-to-minuscule neighboring wineries require appointments.

Howell Mountain. History says this is Zinfandel country, and that's still a good way to approach it, though modern focus has been more on Chardonnay. Only a few wineries are along these remote roads high in the hills east of St. Helena; none offers daily tours or tastings, so appointments are necessary. For Zinfandel, begin with Lamborn. (Burgess and Deer Park are other possibilities just outside the official subappellation boundaries.) For Chardonnay, Chateau Woltner is the starting point.

ANOTHER TACTIC: PICK A VARIETAL

Here are some of the most promising varietals around which to plan a tour. Wineries are listed from south to north.

Merlot. The rising red star in the wine market has a profusion of producers in Napa. Among the best regarded and most easily visited: Clos du Val, Stag's Leap, Rutherford Hill, Louis M. Martini, Freemark Abbey, Markham, and Clos Pegase.

Sauvignon Blanc. Bordeaux's great white variety does as well in Napa as Cabernet does, but to far less acclaim in the marketplace. Too bad, given its friendliness to fish, oysters, and, above all, Southwestern herbs and spices. To establish a baseline for it, try Robert

Pepi, Robert Mondavi, St. Supéry, Grgich Hills, St. Clement, and Sterling.

Pinot Noir. Most of Napa's Pinot Noir grapes now grow in or near the Carneros region, south of the valley proper, but several wineries in the valley itself focus on this wine. Notable among them: Newlan, Robert Sinskey, Robert Mondavi, ZD, and Cuvaison.

Sangiovese. The great variety of Tuscany and Umbria is in its early days in Napa, but shows great promise. For the pure article, explore Robert Pepi, Swanson (appointment required), and Flora Springs. Sangiovese-Cabernet blends are also intriguing, but the two current producers—Shafer and Atlas Peak—are difficult to visit.

Rhône varietals. Though rarer in Napa than elsewhere, red Syrah and white Viognier can make a day between them. Among wineries that welcome visitors, Joseph Phelps has both, Swanson (by appointment) has Syrah, and Beringer has Viognier.

On a slow train through the valley, you can drink in the view as you drink down a different vintage with each course of the vintners' luncheon.

The old and new converge gracefully at the Hess Collection. You can appraise wine poured in a tasting room flanked by a turn-of-the-century stone wall or contemporary art displayed in spacious galleries.

A MOVABLE FEAST

On its 36-mile round-trip excursions past wineries and through vineyards, the Napa Valley Wine Train lets you eat, drink, and sightsee your way through the valley in one comfortable chair. The speed is so deliberate (about 12 mph on average) that from window seats you can discern differences in the way vines are trellised in the vineyards.

The lunch train ($61) boards at 11 on weekdays and at noon on weekends. A champagne brunch trip ($57) boards at 8:30 on Sundays. The dinner train ($72) boards at 6 on weekdays, at 5:30 on weekends. During vintners' luncheons ($69), you can chat with a winemaker and enjoy his or her wine selections while you dine. You can also just go along for the ride ($24) on any of these trips and sample the fare in the deli car or wine tasting car ($5 for four tastes). You can't yet disembark during the 3-hour trip from Napa to St. Helena, though plans are afoot for whistle-stops. For reservations, call (800) 427-4124.

PHIL SCHERMEISTER

CHARLES O'REAR

Smoked squid and grilled endive salad (left) and Meyer lemon and mango meringue pie (center) at Catahoula Restaurant; saddle of rabbit in smoked bacon with rack of rabbit (right) at the French Laundry.

Tapioca brulée (left) at the French Laundry; sake-marinated sea bass in ginger broth with shrimp dumplings (center) at Terra: Asian noodle salad with grilled chicken (right; recipe on page 82) at Wappo Bar Bistro.

Napa's food scene heats up

LONG BEFORE HOSTS OF HAPPY PICNICKERS lolled beneath spreading oaks, before a single restaurant unfurled a white tablecloth, even before the first vine reached for the sky, the native Wappo people had a name for the valley. They called it Napa, which has been loosely translated as *bountiful supply of food.*

Only recently has the valley as we know it lived up to its culinary promise. Early winemakers who wanted to show off their wares had to entertain at home. "It was the wild West when I started in the valley," notes Philippe Jeanty, executive chef of Domaine Chandon Restaurant, who came to California in 1977 from the Champagne region of France. "The biggest obstacle was to bring the quality of raw ingredients up to what I was used to."

It took Domaine's classic French cuisine to demonstrate that great wine needs great food to be at its best. But the casual California grill approach

taken by many valley restaurants, and which Mustards has exemplified so well since 1983, has proved that great wine and food pairings can come in styles other than French.

The number of restaurants in the valley has mushroomed since the late 1980s. One reason is that the supply of superb ingredients has grown along with them. "The Napa Valley is one of few places that have such an abundance close by. Everything here shines," says Thomas Keller, chef at the French Laundry. Wild and farm-raised game, beef, pork, lamb, tender lettuces, wild mushrooms, goat cheeses, herbs, and orchard fruit all come from nearby.

Not only are there more players today in Napa's restaurant arena, but they play better. Increasing numbers of chefs and food professionals are moving here, bringing with them well-tuned palates and high expectations. And their clientele is ideal. If visitors don't already

know fine food and wine, they come because they want to. Chefs like Keller, who arrived last summer via Los Angeles and Manhattan, are finding they can live in the country but cook as if they were still in the city.

Diners in the valley can choose from any number of culinary styles—"Cal-Ital," California grill, classic French, bistro French, country French, even Cajun. But most restaurants share some distinctive features: a reliance on local ingredients, seating that looks to the beauty outdoors wherever possible, a come-as-you-are attitude toward dress, and the food's affinity for wine.

Just as with wine tasting, the biggest problem with dining in the Napa Valley is making up your mind where to start. (That and getting a reservation—the most popular restaurants can fill up as long as six weeks ahead for weekend dinners.) To help hone our list of Napa's quintessential experiences

Under a canopy of mulberry branches and striped umbrellas, diners relax in the summer heat at Tra Vigne. Terra-cotta-colored walls and granite tables contribute to the somewhere-in-Italy feeling.

ANDY FREEBERG

(listed here alphabetically), we leaned on the expertise of food professionals in the valley. But explore a little, and you may find other personal favorites.

THE TOP 10 RESTAURANTS

All Seasons Cafe & Wine Shop. Meals here, in an old-fashioned building on a corner in downtown Calistoga, have the warmth and casualness of dinner at a friend's. Fans come for the long and changing wine list—knowing they can also choose any bottle from the wine shop for a modest corkage fee—and for the bistro-style cooking.

Salads are excellent, especially warm spinach with smoked chicken, pancetta, and a lemony dressing. You can get a generous plate of penne pasta, or pizza with a tender-crisp crust. Among the entrées, look for grilled duck breast or beef tenderloin in changing guises, or a recent favorite, lightly crusted salmon on lentils with Indian spices. Dessert choices include memorable pies stuffed full of seasonal fruit.

Open for lunch and dinner daily ex-

cept Wednesdays, and for brunch Fridays through Sundays. 1400 Lincoln Ave., Calistoga; (707) 942-9111.

Bistro Don Giovanni. The backbone here is Italian: satisfying country fare with occasional touches of brilliance. To whet your appetite, try the grilled portobello mushrooms and sautéed bitter greens with balsamic vinegar au jus (see recipe on page 82). You might move on to the risotto of the day—perhaps snap peas and brown mushrooms with wood fire–roasted chicken—or a pasta selection like linguine with broccoli and Meyer lemon zest.

Be prepared for a generous hand with garlic in many of the dishes. And if you come when the bistro is in full swing, expect lively clatter and possibly erratic service.

Open for lunch and dinner daily. 4110 St. Helena Highway (State 29), Napa; 224-3300.

Catahoula Restaurant & Saloon. Chef and owner Jan Birnbaum's spicy Southern-inspired cooking and charismatic personality have attracted a dedi-

THE CIA COMES TO NAPA

The valley's ripening reputation as a center of culinary excellence comes into full fruit this July when the Culinary Institute of America at Greystone opens its doors in St. Helena. This is the first time that the CIA, the country's most prestigious school for professional chefs, will open a campus outside its headquarters in Hyde Park, New York. Inside the massive 1889 stone structure (the former Christian Brothers Greystone Cellars), chefs will continue their education in graduate-level courses. A 2-acre organic garden will be an extension of the classroom. Diners can test the institute's prowess at the campus's 125-seat restaurant, where Hyde Park graduates will prepare lunch and dinner with Mediterranean flavors. A small museum of culinary artifacts and a store with chefs' supplies and cookbooks will also be open to the public. For the opening date, call (707) 967-1100.

cated following to his restaurant in the 1917 Mount View Hotel and Spa.

The Southern theme comes through in photos of the Catahoula Cur, Louisiana's state dog, and in hearty (and decidedly nonspa) dishes: richly flavored rooster gumbo, pecan-crusted catfish, grilled hominy cakes, and spicy sausages. The wood-fired oven gives a delicious smokiness to squid for a mixed green salad, and even to a s'mores cake with a graham cracker flavor, warm marshmallow cream, and chocolate and caramel sauces.

Open for lunch and dinner daily except Tuesdays, and for brunch on weekends. 1457 Lincoln Ave., Calistoga; 942-2275.

Domaine Chandon Restaurant. Ask valley residents which restaurant consistently delivers exceptional food and service, and time and again, the votes go to Domaine Chandon. Chef Philippe Jeanty produces an elegant French meal

At Wappo Bar Bistro, eclectic fare takes you to far corners of the globe; the warm interior with redwood wainscoting and parchment lamps lands you back in casual Calistoga.

well worth a splurge. (Men are requested to wear jackets at dinner; at lunch, doors open to the terrace and dress is more casual.)

As might be expected at this sparkling wine house, a glass of bubbly goes especially well with starters like the dramatic tomato soup in a puff pastry bowl and fresh sardines on a basil potato purée. Entrées arrive beautifully presented. Try perfectly roasted sturgeon on a bed of sautéed mushrooms with richly flavored juices, or squab that changes with the season. Wine choices are extensive, with many good values.

Open for lunch and dinner Wednesdays through Sundays (lunch served daily from May through October). 1 California Dr., Yountville; 944-8844.

The French Laundry. First-timers to this country restaurant feel as if they've found a hidden gem; indeed, no sign gives away its location in a historic stone building that has served as laundry and bordello. Discoveries continue inside, or in the courtyard garden during summer.

Choose a four- or five-course prix fixe menu with options, or a five-course vegetarian menu. Chef Thomas Keller lightens the intellectual cooking and architectural presentations with many whimsical touches. A clothespin holds your napkin, the bill arrives on a laundry tag. "Tongue and cheek salad" is

Blueberry pancakes, fresh fruit, and plenty of coffee start the day in Scott Courtyard's checkered kitchen. Breakfast seating extends into the sunny living room overlooking the pool.

tender beef cheeks topped with sliced lamb tongue, vegetables, and a horseradish cream. Moist saddle of rabbit wrapped in smoked bacon arrives with a tiny "rack of rabbit" on top.

Some other dishes that hit the mark are *agnolotti* stuffed with sweet potatoes, roasted sea bass on white beans with preserved lemon, and, to close, flaky apple *pithiviers*.

Open for dinner daily except Mondays; lunch service is planned to begin this summer. 6640 Washington St., Yountville; 944-2380.

Mustards Grill. Convivial commotion, great food that you can relate to, and, as the sign outside says, "Way too many wines": that's Mustards's appeal in a nutshell.

Ribs come just the way they should, with a smoky flavor and plenty of sauce. Ultrathin onion rings, heaped in a veritable mountain, are lightly battered and addictive. Diners seeking something

NOEL BARNHURST

TASTEFUL LODGING

Today's Napa Valley travelers can choose from more than 100 lodges. If finding innovative food is a key goal of your valley exploration, then you should stay at a resort with a first-rate restaurant or a bed-and-breakfast that puts as much effort into its culinary offerings as it does into its bedroom decor.

Resort-and-restaurants

Meadowood, 900 Meadowood Lane, St. Helena; (707) 963-3646 or (800) 458-8080. Rates start at $270. Set on 250 forested acres above the Silverado Trail, Meadowood offers 85 rooms in secluded cottages. At The Restaurant, Chef Roy Breiman presents what he dubs Napa Provençale cuisine, featuring several seafood selections and lots of fresh local ingredients. The wine list includes a selection from nearly every producer in the valley.

Auberge du Soleil, 180 Rutherford Hill Rd., Rutherford; 963-1211. $250 to $600. Fifty stylish rooms with Southwestern decor are set into a hillside of oaks and olive trees. From private terraces, enjoy grand views of the nearby hills or the Mayacmas Mountains across the valley. The restaurant's California cuisine doesn't always measure up to the price tag, but the view certainly does. Many valley habitués count a glass of wine on the terrace at sunset among the best experiences Napa offers.

Bed-and-breakfasts

Country Garden Inn, 1815 Silverado Trail, Napa; 255-1197. $115 to $198. In keeping with its 1850 vintage, this 10-room inn is furnished with English pine antiques. Champagne breakfast begins with fruit, scones, and cinnamon coffee cake, continues with eggs Benedict, waffles, or a traditional English breakfast. Afternoon tea comes with a selection of cookies and rich chocolate cake; happy hour brings sherry or wine, tasty spreads for toast, cheeses, and a pickle tray. Lest you go to bed hungry, there are dainty evening desserts.

The Crossroads Inn, 6380 Silverado Trail, Yountville; 944-0646. $175 to $200. Each of the four rooms of this chaletlike retreat commands postcard views across the valley. Enjoy a glass of wine in a whirlpool tub or afternoon tea on a private deck. Breakfast in your room may include quiche, French toast, whole-wheat pancakes, or a ham- and asparagus-filled puff pastry with a rich tarragon sauce.

Zinfandel Inn, 800 Zinfandel Lane, St. Helena; 963-3512. $100 to $250. This imposing stone château sits on 2 acres. All three rooms, each with a whirlpool tub, fireplace, and balcony, are decorated in French provincial style. Truffles and champagne greet your arrival. The hearty breakfast may be eggs Benedict, Belgian waffles, or pancakes.

Foothill House, 3037 Foothill Blvd., Calistoga; (800) 942-6933. $135 to $250.

This former farmhouse has been remodeled into an inn with three guest rooms decorated in a cheery country style. (A private cottage retreat is also available.) Samples from the owner's 200-case wine cellar are often shared with guests, along with appetizers such as baked Brie with roasted garlic and chunky marinara, during an afternoon wine appreciation hour. Elaborate breakfasts may include baked French toast with cream cheese, walnuts, and edible flowers.

Scott Courtyard, 1443 Second St., Calistoga; (800) 945-1515. $110 to $140. Six suites, three with kitchens, surround a flower-bedecked courtyard with pool and hot tub (the suite above the social area can be noisy). Decor is an eclectic '40s and '50s mix with themes like Hollywood, tropical, and Philadelphia. In the afternoon, join fellow guests for wine and cheese. Breakfast, served buffet-style, may feature great blueberry pancakes, eggs pesto, or French toast.

For other lodging, call the Napa Valley Tourist Bureau at (800) 523-4353, the Yountville chamber at (707) 944-0904, the St. Helena chamber at 963-4456, or the Calistoga chamber at 942-6333.

The following local referral services can make lodging reservations: Accommodation Referral, (800) 240-8466; B & B Style, (800) 995-8884; Napa Valley Reservations, (707) 252-1985; and Wine Country Reservations, 257-7757.

BEST WINERY PICNICS

Picnicking is one of the sublime ways to enjoy wine and food pairings. The perfect spot should be quiet, set away from traffic, and a bit secluded, and should offer views of vines or the valley that are as heady as the wine. You'll find such spots at each of these three wineries.

Rutherford Hill Winery. In the hills off the Silverado Trail, on the east side of the valley, Rutherford Hill has tables under shady oaks for when it's hot; when it's not, go for the tables in the olive grove with sweeping views of the Rutherford Bench.

Joseph Phelps Vineyards. Just up the trail from Rutherford Hill is this peaceful winery. It has only three tables, but the setting—looking down into a tiny valley with a vineyard and lake—makes it worth the effort of calling ahead (707/963-2745) to reserve.

Vichon Winery. Perched in the Mayacmas Mountains on the valley's west side, Vichon has the best overall view of the valley. On Wednesdays from May through October, the winery also offers the option of a lavish catered picnic that begins with an in-depth tour of its parent facility, Robert Mondavi. Cost is $25 per person; to reserve, call (800) 842-4661.

WHERE TO FILL YOUR PICNIC BASKET

Options for picnic supplies are as glorious as the sites. Local goat cheeses, breads, olive oils, and, naturally, wines are widely available and make a good start to an alfresco meal. These stores, listed south to north, are particularly noteworthy.

Pometta's Deli & Catering Co., 7787 St. Helena Highway (State 29), Oakville; (707) 944-2365. This valley institution with chicken-shack decor has been barbecuing birds since the '40s. Other choices include sandwiches such as the piquant muffaletta—layered ham, cheese, and herbed black olives on a seeded roll.

Oakville Grocery Co., 7856 St. Helena Highway (State 29), Oakville; 944-8802. "Picnic heaven" is an apt description for this 1880 roadside landmark, recently added to the National Register of Historic Places. Fencing supplies and dog kibble have gone the way of the original general store; these days you'll find a chichi selection of artisan breads, countless cheeses, outstanding cookies, olives, local and imported gourmet

pantry items, salads, and sandwiches such as turkey, pesto, and smoked mozzarella on focaccia. Wine choices are numerous (winery chief Joe Phelps is a co-owner): look for limited bottlings from the valley and re-released wines from the grocery's cellar.

V. Sattui Winery, 1111 White Lane, St. Helena; 963-7774. Picnics at tables in the 2-acre grove next to the stone winery are a classic valley experience. In the tasting room shop, choose from a wide array of sandwich fixings and homemade salads and desserts (most prepackaged

and ready to go), plus fruit and gourmet products.

Cantinetta Tra Vigne; 1050 Charter Oak Ave., St. Helena; 963-8888. In this 19th-century sherry distillery turned Italian deli and market extraordinaire, sample Tra Vigne's own lines of oils and vinegars, and pick up pizzas, salads, sandwiches, and Italian cookies. You can spread out your purchases on granite tables in the adjacent courtyard.

The Model Bakery, 1357 Main St., St. Helena; 963-8192. Rustic breads from the 1920s brick oven include *pain du vin,*

The vine- and oak-covered folds of the Mayacmas Mountains set the stage for a sumptuous spread at Vichon Winery. The feast includes layered sandwiches, meat, cheeses, olives, fresh fruit, and biscotti from Oakville Grocery; calzone, bread, and condiments from Cantinetta Tra Vigne; and Chardonnay and Cabernet Blanc from Vichon.

a sourdough whole-wheat loaf made from a starter cultivated with wine grapes. Other offerings include individual pizzas and fruit tarts, big cookies, and sandwiches.
Palisades Market, 1506 Lincoln Ave., Calistoga; 942-9549. At this family-run gourmet food market and deli, look for fancy breads, cheeses, and olives, fennel pheasant-pork tureen, and sandwiches such as the chicken Caesar or the Palisades pesto—oven-roasted turkey on sun-dried tomato focaccia with pesto mayonnaise.

more unusual can turn to special fish or game offerings from the oak grill, or regular features like the Long Island duck—brined, air-cured, and smoked, with mango chutney.

Part of Mustards's success is its high turnover. You're not encouraged to linger, but you'll probably have such a good time you won't notice.

Open for lunch and dinner daily. 7399 St. Helena Highway (State 29), Yountville; 944-2424.

Showley's Restaurant. In their quiet restaurant nestled into a 135-year-old building, the Showleys and their staff radiate such warmth that they give new meaning to "family-run." Generous salads, handmade fettuccine, and braised meats command a loyal following. So outstanding are the lamb shanks with garlic mashed potatoes and rosemary–Pinot Noir glaze, it would be tempting to order them every time. A waitress, Nini, invented her namesake dessert: a fila cup with pistachio ice cream and intense chocolate sauce.

You can sit in the old-fashioned rooms or on the cozy patio beneath the branches of a century-old fig tree.

Open for lunch and dinner daily except Mondays. 1327 Railroad Ave., St. Helena; 963-1200.

Terra. In contrast to the sunny decor of neighboring Showley's, Terra, with its stone walls and subdued lighting, has the enchanting feel of a grotto. It's the setting for some of the most sophisticated and creative cooking in the valley. Chef Hiro Sone (formerly of Spago in Los Angeles) combines the flavors of France, northern Italy, and the Pacific Rim, particularly his native Japan, and it all works magically.

In the pure Asian vein, don't miss lacquered quail with crisp mahogany skin over thin Hong Kong noodles with a sweet-tart miso sauce. Richly flavored sweetbread ragout could be from a French bistro but for the Asian shiitake mushrooms.

Several other favorites are succulent sake-marinated sea bass, served in ginger broth with shrimp dumplings; lamb medaillons with an intense anchovy and black olive sauce; and *fromage blanc* tart with a crackling sugar topping and a texture between cheesecake and the creamiest custard.

Open for dinner daily except Tuesdays. 1345 Railroad Ave., St. Helena; 963-8931.

Tra Vigne. You can delight in some of Napa's most memorable spaces at this re-creation of an Italian villa, whether you're part of the see-and-be-seen crowd indoors or you dine alfresco beneath the mulberry trees glittering with lights.

Not every menu item deserves a blue ribbon, but there are a number of excellent options. For starters, try the roasted polenta triangles with a balsamic vinegar–game sauce, or the house-cured prosciutto. A mushroom pizza comes slathered with roasted garlic and melted teleme cheese. Classic greens-filled ravioli in sage butter has just the right bite. And regulars rave about the spice-rubbed chicken. The restaurant's version of tiramisu is a rich and boozy layered chocolate cake reminiscent of an adult Oreo cookie.

Open for lunch and dinner daily. 1050 Charter Oak Ave., St. Helena; 963-4444.

Wappo Bar Bistro. You can eat your way around the world at this charming hangout on a Calistoga side street. For lunch, try colorful cold Asian noodle salad with grilled chicken and a lively hoisin dressing (recipe on page 82). Central American masa cakes come loaded with black beans, duck carnitas, and tangy cheese. Middle Eastern pomegranate-glazed pork chunks are served over a delicious lentil-bulgur pilaf with lots of browned onions.

Pomegranate appears again at dinner in a walnut sauce for rice-filled chile rellenos. To quench your thirst, try the tall juice spritzer, sometimes made with Zinfandel grape juice. Save room for super-creamy ice cream.

You can enjoy your meal at copper-topped tables inside the narrow restaurant, but in summer, the vine-covered patio with fountain is the place to be.

Open for lunch and dinner daily except Tuesdays. 1226B Washington St., Calistoga; 942-4712. ■

ANDY FREEBERG

Bring Napa to your table

A taste of the valley to try at home

I N OUR QUEST TO DEFINE THE Napa Valley's premier eateries, we sampled some wonderful dishes, a few of which we've adapted for the home cook.

We lightened Bistro Don Giovanni's portobello mushrooms and greens. The Asian noodle salad from Wappo Bar Bistro features several make-ahead steps. And, although Mustards Grill makes its own bread for the cowboy toast, we've substituted purchased frozen bread dough with terrific results.

Grilled Portobello Mushrooms with Greens

1 cup balsamic vinegar

4 cups regular-strength beef broth

½ pound red Swiss chard

¾ pound broccoli rabe

4 large (4 to 5 in. diameter, 1 lb. total) portobello mushrooms

1½ tablespoons olive oil

Salt and pepper

2 cloves garlic, cut lengthwise into paper-thin slices

¾ pound spinach, stems removed

4 teaspoons chopped fresh chives

In a 10- to 12-inch frying pan over high heat, boil vinegar and broth, stirring occasionally, until reduced to ⅓ cup, 15 to 20 minutes; set aside.

Trim stem ends from chard and broccoli rabe, then cut stems into ½-inch slices up to base of leaves. Stack leaves, and cut into 1- to 2-inch strips. Set aside. Trim ends from mushrooms, rinse caps, and drain. Lightly brush with 1½ teaspoons of the oil; sprinkle with salt and pepper.

Lay mushrooms, skin side up, on a grill over medium coals (you can hold your hand at grill level only 4 to 5 seconds). Cook, turning to brown evenly, until mushrooms are just tender when pierced through centers of stems, 8 to 10 minutes. Set aside.

Heat remaining oil with garlic in an 8- to 10-quart pan over medium-high heat. When garlic begins to brown, add chard and broccoli rabe stems; stir until softened, about 3 minutes. Increase heat to high. Stir in sliced leaves and spinach, cover, and cook just until wilted, 2 to 3 minutes. Season to taste with salt and pepper.

With a slotted spoon, divide greens equally among 4 plates; top each with a mushroom. Spoon balsamic sauce on top; sprinkle with chives. Serves 4.

Per serving: 116 cal. (33 percent from fat); 7.9 g protein; 4.3 g fat (0.6 g sat.); 16 g carbo.; 204 mg sodium; 0 mg chol.

Asian Noodle Salad with Grilled Chicken

2 tablespoons *each* hoisin sauce and soy sauce

4 or 5 boned and skinned chicken breast halves (⅓ lb. each)

12 ounces fresh Chinese-style noodles (spaghetti-size)

½ cup thinly sliced green onions

1 large (4 oz.) carrot, cut into long, thin strands, or shredded

½ small (14 oz.) European cucumber, seeded and cut into thin strands, or shredded

½ cup finely shredded red cabbage

½ cup finely shredded napa or Savoy cabbage

1 can or jar (7 oz.) baby corn, drained

2 tablespoons chopped fresh cilantro (coriander)

Hoisin dressing (recipe follows)

2 tablespoons coarsely chopped salted peanuts

24 barely cooked edible-pod peas (¼ lb. total)

1 small (2 lb.) cantaloupe, seeded, peeled, and cut into 24 wedges

24 small red Belgian endive leaves or small radicchio leaves

In a wide bowl, combine hoisin sauce and soy sauce; add chicken and stir to coat. Cover and chill at least 2 hours or until next day.

In a 4- to 5-quart pan over high heat, bring 2½ quarts water to boiling. Add noodles and cook, uncovered, just until tender to bite, 2 to 3 minutes. Drain, immerse in cold water until cool, drain well, and put into a large bowl. Add onions, carrot, cucumber, red and napa cabbages, corn, and cilantro. Cover and chill up to 2 hours.

Place chicken on a lightly greased grill 4 to 6 inches above a solid bed of medium coals (you can hold your hand at grill level only 4 to 5 seconds). Cook until meat is no longer pink in thickest part (cut to test), about 10 minutes; turn once and baste with marinade. Lift meat to a board.

Add ¾ of the hoisin dressing to noodles; stir gently. Divide salad on 4 or 5 plates; sprinkle with peanuts. Arrange equal portions of edible-pod peas, cantaloupe, and endive alternately around rims of plates. Cut each breast half crosswise into ½-inch-thick slices; keep shape intact. Top each salad with 1 sliced breast half. Drizzle remaining dressing over chicken. Makes 4 or 5 servings.

Per serving: 577 cal. (19 percent from fat); 46 g protein; 12 g fat (2.2 g sat.); 68 g carbo.; 1,708 mg sodium; 142 mg chol.

Hoisin dressing. In a small bowl, whisk 1 clove minced **garlic,** 1 tablespoon minced **fresh ginger,** ½ cup **seasoned rice vinegar,** 2 tablespoons *each* **hoisin sauce** and **soy sauce,** 1 tablespoon **sesame oil,** and 1 tablespoon **chili oil.** If making ahead, cover and chill until next day.

Cowboy Toast

2 large heads (½ lb. total) garlic

About 3 tablespoons olive oil

All-purpose flour

1 loaf (1 lb.) frozen white bread dough, thawed

Goat cheese spread (recipe follows)

Cut garlic heads into halves horizontally, keeping each half intact as much as possible. Pour 2 tablespoons oil into an 8-inch-wide baking pan; swirl pan to coat bottom. Lay garlic, cut side down, in pan. Bake in a 375° oven until cloves are golden brown on bottom and oozing at edges, about 35 minutes. Let stand until cool. Using a fork or knife tip, pick out cloves.

On a lightly floured board, roll out dough to a 12- by 15-inch rectangle. Scatter garlic cloves on top. Starting with a long side, roll dough into a smooth, compact cylinder. Pinch seam and ends to seal. Place seam down on an oiled 12- by 17-inch baking sheet. Pat to flatten loaf slightly. Cover loosely with plastic wrap, and let stand in a warm place until almost double in size, 30 to 40 minutes.

Uncover and bake in a 350° oven until bread is a rich brown, about 30 minutes. Cool until only slightly warm, then cut into 1½-inch slices. Brush with remaining oil.

Lay slices on a grill 4 to 6 inches above a solid bed of medium coals (you can hold your hand at grill level only 4 to 5 seconds). Lightly toast, 2 to 3 minutes per side. Offer hot with goat cheese spread. Serves 6.

Per serving: 408 cal. (40 percent from fat); 13 g protein; 18 g fat (6.2 g sat.); 48 g carbo.; 477 mg sodium; 18 mg chol.

Goat cheese spread. In a small bowl, beat 6 ounces soft **goat cheese,** 2 tablespoons **milk,** and 2 tablespoons finely chopped **chives.** If making ahead, cover and chill up to next day. Serve at room temperature. ■

By Paula Smith Freschet

Dry-cured

Thasos

Nyons

Cured with herbs

SPANISH-STYLE *specialty olives are crisp and of generous size, with pungent flavorings.*

Know your olive options

A quick guide to identifying, buying, flavoring, and storing

PALE GREEN TO DEEP black, smooth to prunelike, tiny to huge, crisp to soft, fruity to bitter: olive choices are so numerous, it's difficult to know where to start.

At olive bars cropping up in specialty markets, you can start with a taste. But whether you sample one from bulk stock or take a chance on a whole jar, it's fun to know more about your choices.

Green olives are picked young; they're mild, fruity, and crisp. As olives mature on the tree, they turn purple, then black, and become softer and oilier. The fruit gets nuttier and more bitter.

Olive nomenclature is based on a hodgepodge of curing styles, geographic origins, and varieties of olive. But it's the curing method used to remove the astringent glucoside in raw olives that most influences the taste.

Lye-cured olives, also called Spanish-style, are mild green or black-ripe. After a lye soak, fruit is rinsed and stored in brine.

Specialty lye-cured olives are usually California-cured, green, and quite salty. They may have Cajun, Italian, or other flavorings, or be stuffed with jalapeños or almonds.

Dry-cured olives (also called salt-cured or oil-cured) are picked black, then layered with salt until wrinkled and chewy. They are quite salty, with concentrated, bitter to earthy flavors; most tasters either love them or hate them.

California, Morocco, and Europe produce this kind, which Greeks call *Thasos.* They may be coated in olive oil, or in oil and herbs, but have no brine; the exception is meaty French *Nyons,* which is sometimes brined after dry-curing.

Brine-cured olives vary the most within their category. Place of origin may differ from the sources noted here. *Ascolano:* mild, sweet, meaty, less salty than some. Italy. *Atalánti:* nutty and salty, soft, large. Greece.

Elitses: slightly bitter, meaty, tiny. Greece.
Farga Aragon: a bit acrid and smoky, soft. Spain.
Gaeta: sharp, slightly soft and chewy. Italy.
Ionian: mellow, nutty, rich, slightly crisp. Greece.
Kalamata: distinctive wine or vinegar flavor, firm. Greece.
Manzanillo: herbaceous, bitter, salty, firm. Spain.
Niçoise: mellow, nutty, rich, meaty. France.
Picholine: tart, slightly smoky, crisp. France.
Sicilian: tangy, bitter, salty, crunchy. California.

Buying and storing. You may also see these options: *low-sodium* olives have a mild taste; *cracked* olives allow the brine flavorings (including salt) to penetrate more; *pitted* olives are convenient, but they're softer, blander, and saltier than unpitted olives.

If you buy in bulk, ask for brine to cover lye- or brine-cured olives that will be stored longer than a few days (dry-cured olives need no storage liquid). Opened containers of olives keep up to several months when refrigerated airtight. Skim off any film that forms on brine; discard any olives if moldy.

Flavoring ideas. Maggie Blyth Klein, author of the newly updated *The Feast of the Olive* (Chronicle Books, San Francisco, 1994; $10.95), prefers a light hand with seasonings. She enhances all olives with a coating of quality olive oil (drain brine first). For mild green olives, Klein suggests adding bay, garlic, cloves, and cumin, or using lemon zest and juniper berries. Most kinds are good marinated in olive oil with fresh rosemary and garlic. ■

By Elaine Johnson

Brine-cured

Elitses

Kalamata

Gaeta

Ascolano

Manzanillo

Niçoise

Sicilian

Farga Aragon

Picholine

Ionian

Atalánti

NORMAN A. PLATE

MOLE, SPINACH, and cheese–topped corn tortillas bake in the oven with red bananas. A citrus salad and black beans complete the easy meal.

Open-faced enchilada supper

A complete meal in less than an hour for family or favored guests

A FEW EASY COOKING techniques and prepared foods from the supermarket create a super Mexican weeknight or party meal. The fabulous flavor combination—mole, red bananas, black beans, cilantro, and spices—comes from the Yucatán in southern Mexico.

Canned black beans and mole sauce from a jar, red bananas that bake in their jackets alongside open-faced enchiladas, and a simple citrus salad let you put the meal together in less than an hour—even faster with a little prep a day ahead. Serve with Mexican beer and tortilla chips.

Easy Yucatán Enchilada Supper

For dinner in less than 30 minutes, prepare the beans and salad ahead.

    Black beans (recipe follows)

    Citrus salad (recipe follows)

1 jar (8¼ oz.) mole paste

1½ cups regular-strength chicken broth

2 packages (10 oz. each) frozen spinach, thawed

6 medium-size (about 4 oz. each) red bananas or regular bananas

6 corn tortillas, about 6 inches in diameter

1 cup (5 oz.) crumbled cotija or feta cheese

1 cup (4 oz.) shredded jack cheese

6 large lettuce leaves or ti leaves (from a florist), rinsed and drained

    Cilantro sprigs, lime wedges, and salsa

Prepare black beans and citrus salad. In a 2- to 3-quart pan, mix together mole paste and broth. Cook over medium heat, stirring often, until mole mixture is smooth and hot; remove from heat. Place spinach in a colander; press all liquid from spinach.

In a 350° oven, bake bananas until very soft to touch, 20 to 30 minutes. Meanwhile, place 3 tortillas on each of 2 baking sheets (about 12 by 15 inches each). Spoon about 3 tablespoons mole over each tortilla, leaving bare the outer ¼-inch rim. Sprinkle ⅓ cup spinach over mole on each tortilla; top equally with cotija and jack cheeses.

Bake enchiladas in oven with bananas until hot and cheese is melted, about 10 minutes. (If oven is small, remove baked bananas before baking enchiladas; cover with foil to keep warm.)

If using ti leaves, arrange on 6 dinner plates. Place an enchilada, banana, portion of citrus salad, and portion of beans on each leaf. (Or serve beans on the side.) If using lettuce leaves, place enchilada, banana, and beans directly on each plate. Tuck a lettuce leaf next to beans; place salad on leaf. Garnish each plate with cilantro, lime wedges, and salsa; offer remaining mole sauce to add as desired. Serve immediately. Makes 6 servings.

Per serving: 500 cal. (29 percent from fat); 24 g protein; 16 g fat (4 g sat.); 71 g carbo.; 875 mg sodium; 39 mg chol.

Black beans. To a 10- to 12-inch frying pan over medium-high heat add 2 teaspoons **olive oil,** 1 medium-size (8 oz.) **onion,** chopped, and 4 cloves **garlic,** minced or pressed. Cook, stirring occasionally, until onion begins to brown and sticks to pan bottom. Add ¼ cup **regular-strength chicken broth** and scrape brown bits from pan bottom; cook until liquid evaporates. Repeat process, using ¼ cup more **broth.**

Add 2 cans (15 oz. each) **black beans,** drained and rinsed, 2 tablespoons **lime juice,** and ⅛ teaspoon **ground allspice.** Heat until beans are hot (for softer beans, mash about half the beans and stir). If making ahead, cool, cover, and chill up to overnight. To reheat, add ¼ cup broth and heat beans over medium heat, about 10 minutes. Makes 2 cups.

Citrus salad. Cut peel and white membrane from 2 large (2 lb. total) **grapefruit** and 4 medium-size (2 lb. total) **oranges.** Then cut segments free from inner membranes and place in a bowl. Gently stir in 2 tablespoons minced **fresh cilantro** (coriander), 1 tablespoon **lime juice,** and ⅛ teaspoon **ground cinnamon.** Cover and chill until ready to use, up to overnight. Makes 4 cups. ∎

By Betsy Reynolds Bateson

NORMAN A. PLATE

WIDE, SHALLOW PAELLA PAN *makes the ideal cooking and serving container for this delicious chicken and rice party dish. The inspiration is Spanish paella, but the seasonings are Chinese.*

A new pan, a new paella

Far Eastern flavors go into the pan with chicken and rice

THE PAN STARTED IT. I wanted to replace my beat-up 12-inch frying pan with something a little bigger. Browsing through a cookware store, I happened to spot a paella pan. It was a little deeper and a little wider than what I had in mind. It was better-looking, too, made of heavy aluminum with handles on opposite sides of the rim. Best of all, it was half of what I planned to pay. Not only did my investment pay off, but the pan inspired a new dish.

Traditional Spanish paella was my guide: rice and chicken are the foundation. And both are equally at home with some of my favorite ingredients: sweet Chinese sausage (instead of plain pork), pungent shiitake mushrooms, soy sauce, and fresh ginger. A flurry of fresh cilantro adds a shot of fresh color, and its flavorful zing replaces the earthy flavor of saffron. My Asian paella looks great and is a hit with family, guests, and me—especially—because it can be completely cooked ahead of time, then warmed while the party gets under way.

Which leads to a good question. Do you need a paella pan to make Chinese chicken paella? No, any shallow metal or ceramic baking dish that holds 4½ quarts works fine. You may have to visit an Asian grocer for some of the ingredients, but supermarket alternatives work well, too.

Chinese Chicken Paella

10 to 12 large chicken thighs (about 4 lb. total), skinned

    Soy marinade (recipe follows)

3 cups (3½ to 4 oz.) dried shiitake mushrooms

1 pound Chinese sausage (*lop cheong*) or frozen brown-and-serve pork link sausages, thinly sliced

3½ cups long-grain white rice

1 cup thinly sliced green onions

2 whole star anise (optional)

    About 5 cups regular-strength chicken broth

1 package (1 lb.) frozen petite peas, thawed

1 cup fresh cilantro (coriander) sprigs

Rinse chicken and mix in a deep bowl with ¼ cup of the soy marinade. Cover and chill 30 minutes or up to 1 day; mix occasionally.

Rinse mushrooms. Soak in about 3 cups hot water until soft, about 20 minutes. Lift mushrooms from water, squeezing liquid into bowl; reserve soaking liquid. Cut off and discard tough mushroom stems. Thinly slice caps and mix with ½ cup of the soy marinade. Let stand at least 30 minutes.

Drain and discard marinade from chicken. Place chicken pieces slightly apart in a 10- by 15-inch pan. Bake in a 450° oven until thighs are slightly browned and no longer pink at bone (cut to test), about 20 minutes. Reserve pan drippings.

In a 14-inch (at least 4½ qt.) paella pan, or 5- to 6-quart pan over medium-high heat, stir sausage slices often until browned, about 10 minutes. Lift out sausage with a slotted spoon. Discard all but 2 tablespoons fat. Add rice, onions, and star anise to pan. Stir over medium heat until rice turns opaque, about 10 minutes.

Carefully, to avoid sediment, pour mushroom soaking liquid into a glass measure; discard sediment. Add enough chicken broth to mushroom liquid to make a total of 6½ cups. Add to rice mixture along with mushrooms and their marinade; bring to a boil.

Cover paella pan tightly with a lid or foil, or pour mixture from the 5- to 6-quart pan into a shallow 4½- to 5-quart casserole (about 10 by 15 in.) and cover tightly with foil. Bake in a 350° oven for 20 minutes. Stir into rice the sausage, peas, and drippings from chicken; lay chicken pieces on rice. (If making ahead, cool, cover, and chill up to 1 day.) Cover tightly and continue to bake until chicken is hot and rice is tender to bite, 10 to 15 minutes longer (1½ to 1¾ hours, if chilled). Sprinkle with cilantro. Offer remaining marinade to add to taste. Serves 10 to 12.

Per serving: 475 cal. (25 percent from fat); 27 g protein; 13 g fat (4 g sat.); 58 g carbo.; 661 mg sodium; 85 mg chol.

Soy marinade. Mix ½ cup **dry sherry** with ½ cup **reduced-sodium soy sauce,** 2 tablespoons minced **fresh ginger,** 1½ tablespoons **sugar,** and 4 cloves **garlic,** minced. ∎

By Linda Lau Anusasananan

SCATTER TENDER ARUGULA *leaves over roasted vegetables, then top pizza with shaved parmesan cheese and balsamic-Dijon dressing.*

Roasted vegetable pizza

Topped with arugula, this pie is healthy and hearty

BISTRO-STYLE EATING is here. Or, to put it another way, wholesome, casual foods that require little last-minute preparation are the rage at smart restaurants.

This nutritious, salad-topped pizza features flavorful slow-roasted vegetables you make ahead (you can prepare the quick pizza crusts in advance as well). Shortly before serving, simply distribute the vegetables over the crusts and heat for 5 minutes in the oven. Top with arugula (thinly slice the leaves if they are large) and a few delicious shavings of parmesan, and drizzle a savory dressing over all.

The pizza crusts can be quickly prepared from thawed frozen bread dough. For an even speedier option, purchase prepared individual-size pizza shells.

Bistro Pizza Salad

1   pound mushrooms, rinsed

2   medium-size (about ¾ lb. total) onions

1   medium-size (about 1¼ lb.) eggplant, ends trimmed

¾   pound (about 4 medium-size) Roma-type tomatoes, cored

2   tablespoons olive or salad oil

1   loaf (1 lb.) frozen bread dough, thawed

½   cup chopped canned roasted red peppers

4   cups (about 3 oz.) lightly packed arugula leaves, tough stems removed, rinsed and drained

¾   cup (about 2 oz.) shaved parmesan cheese

Balsamic-Dijon dressing (recipe follows)

Slice mushrooms ½ inch thick. Cut onions into wedges about ½ inch thick in center and eggplant into about ½-inch cubes. Cut tomatoes crosswise into ¼-inch slices; set aside.

In a 450° oven, heat oil in a 10- by 15-inch baking pan just until hot. Remove pan and add mushrooms, onions, and eggplant; return to oven and cook until just golden, about 45 minutes, turning vegetables every 15 minutes. Add tomatoes; continue to cook until most liquid has evaporated, about 20 minutes more. If making ahead, chill, covered, up to 1 day.

Meanwhile, divide dough into 4 equal pieces. On a floured board, roll each piece of dough into a 7- to 8-inch round. As rolled, cover with plastic wrap to prevent drying.

Heat an 8- to 10-inch non-stick frying pan over medium heat until hot (or use 2 frying pans simultaneously); add 1 unwrapped dough round. Cook dough round until bottom looks dry and is covered with large brown spots, about 3 minutes. Turn bread over; cook until bottom is browned, for 2 or 3 more minutes.

If bread puffs, pierce bulges to release steam and gently press flat with a spatula. If making ahead, let crusts cool on racks; store airtight at room temperature up to 1 day.

Place crusts on baking sheets. Add red peppers to roasted vegetables and top cooked crusts with mixture, about 1 cup on each crust. Spread vegetables evenly over crusts, leaving about a ½-inch crust border. Bake in a 500° oven just until hot, about 5 minutes. Place on 4 dinner plates. Sprinkle arugula and parmesan equally over plates; drizzle dressing over all. Serves 4.

Per serving: 527 cal. (29 percent from fat); 20 g protein; 17 g fat (3.8 g sat.); 78 g carbo.; 995 mg sodium; 9.6 mg chol.

Balsamic-Dijon dressing. Combine 2 tablespoons **balsamic vinegar,** 1 tablespoon **olive** or salad **oil,** and 1 teaspoon **Dijon mustard;** mix until well blended. ∎

By Betsy Reynolds Bateson

MELTING BROILED *cheese flows down sandwich sides to flavorfully unite the three layers.*

With chilies, egg salad makes the ultimate sandwich

THIS SAVORY SANDWICH offers a creative solution to the post-Easter egg hunt dilemma. Chop the hard-cooked eggs and turn them into a piquant salad. Then layer the salad and chilies on toasted sourdough, and cap the stack with cheese. After a quick trip under the broiler, the sandwiches are ready to be the stellar attraction of a hearty lunch or light supper.

You can roast the chilies, but canned ones work just as well. The egg salad stays fresh-tasting if you make it a day ahead.

Hot Egg Salad and Mild Chili Sandwich

6   hard-cooked large eggs, peeled and finely chopped

¼   cup unflavored nonfat yogurt or reduced-fat mayonnaise

2   tablespoons minced fresh cilantro (coriander)

1   green onion, ends trimmed, thinly sliced

2   teaspoons lime juice

½   teaspoon ground cumin

Roasted chilies (directions follow) or 3 cans (4 oz. each) whole green chilies

4   slices (about ¾ lb. total) sourdough bread, each about 4 by 6 inches and ½ inch thick

1 ¼   cups (about 5 oz.) shredded jack cheese

Cilantro sprigs (optional)

Mix together eggs, yogurt, minced cilantro, onion, lime juice, and cumin until well blended. Use, or if making ahead, cover and chill up to 1 day.

Slit chilies open along 1 side; discard any seeds.

Lay bread in a single layer in a 10- by 15-inch pan. Bake at 450° until the tops

of the slices are lightly browned and crisp, about 7 minutes. Remove from oven and turn slices over, topping equally with chilies, egg mixture, and cheese. Broil sandwiches about 6 inches from heat until cheese melts and lightly browns, 3 to 4 minutes. Transfer to plates and garnish with cilantro sprigs. Serves 4.

Per serving: 542 cal. (37 percent from fat); 29 g protein; 22 g fat (9.3 g sat.); 59 g carbo.; 822 mg sodium; 357 mg chol.

Roasted chilies. In a 10- by 15-inch pan, lay 8 large (about 1½ lb. total) **poblano** (also called pasilla) or Anaheim (also called California or New Mexico) **chilies** in a single layer. Broil chilies 4 inches from heat, turning often, until skins are charred on all sides, 10 to 15 minutes. Set aside until cool enough to handle. Pull off and discard skins and stems. ∎

By Christine Weber Hale

HEAT MAKES A DIFFERENCE: *The cheesecake on the left, baked at 300°, is creamy, smooth, and delicate in flavor. The one on the right, baked at 400°, is cracked on top; its texture is denser, firmer, wetter, and slightly granular, and the flavor isn't as fresh and subtle. Cakes were baked the same length of time.*

Why?

Why do cheesecakes crack or sink?
Why does the filling look curdled?
Why bake the crust before filling it?

Want to make a prize-winning cheese-cake? That was the goal of Verna Wheeler of Placentia, California, but after dozens of unsuccessful attempts she was frustrated and puzzled. Every recipe was different and so were the results. She asked us to investigate.

Why do cheesecakes sometimes crack in the center?

One reason is the tension created by temperature differences as the cheesecake bakes. Most cakes are basically a blend of eggs, sugar, and cream cheese or fresh curd cheese such as cottage cheese—essentially a custard mixture, though not as tricky. Heat firms the protein in the eggs and cheese; that makes the cake firm first where it

gets hottest first—around the edge. As the edge firms, it tightens and pulls away from the softer, cooler center. When the cake is baked in a 400° oven, the temperature contrast between the edge and the center is great enough to create a tug of war, and one or more crevices form in the middle of the cake. This is more likely to happen in large cheesecakes, because smaller cakes have less mass to heat and therefore cook more evenly and quickly.

Cracks are easy to avoid. Bake cheesecake at a lower temperature—300° to 350° is a good range. Or equalize heat penetration with water. Set the cake pan in a larger pan and fill the larger pan with hot or boiling water up to the level of the cake, then bake. (If the pan has a removable rim, nest the pan in a cupped

sheet of foil that extends up to or above the rim.)

Overcooking also makes cheesecakes crack. As the cake bakes, its weblike protein structure of egg and cheese tightens. Cooked too long, the web begins to squeeze out the moisture it holds. The cake loses its smooth texture, gets grainy, and tastes weepy. And because the cake is shrinking, it cracks where it is softest.

The best test for deciding when a cheesecake has cooked enough to be firm and cut neatly when cool is to gently shake the pan in the oven. If the center of the cheesecake just barely jiggles, the cake is done. If it ripples, it's too soft, and if it doesn't move, it's overcooked.

However, most cheese-cakes still taste pretty good overcooked. Clever cooks camouflage cracks with sour cream or fruit toppings.

Why does cheesecake sometimes sink in the center?

Burst bubbles. As the cake mixture is beaten, bubbles of air are trapped. At a high oven temperature, the bubbles expand and push the cake up. But the cake doesn't have the strength to hold the bubbles, except at the rim where it is firmest. So, as in a soufflé, when the bubbles cool, they collapse in the softer cake center, creating a cupped or sunken surface.

To minimize bubbles, don't beat cheesecake batter at high speed with a mixer.

However, in some cheese-cake recipes, egg whites are whipped and folded into the cheese mixture. Whites that are whipped with even a little sugar are better able to hold bubbles as the cake cooks and cools.

To minimize bubble collapse, bake the cheesecake at a lower temperature (300° to 350°). The bubbles won't swell as fast or get as big, preserving the light texture and the flat, even surface.

Why does cheesecake batter sometimes look curdled or lumpy when you add the cheese?

Cream cheese is made from smooth particles of cream molded together. Liquid ingredients need to be added to the cheese in small portions to blend in smoothly. Lumps of cheese often form when eggs are added too quickly. This is why most recipes direct you to thoroughly mix in the eggs one at a time. If the mixture separates, whisking is the best way to make it smooth again. Reduced-fat cream cheese may take more time to blend smoothly with ingredients. If it's not smoothly mixed in, the cheesecake texture and flavor suffer.

Why are some cheesecake crusts baked before adding the filling?

Crusts made from graham cracker or cookie crumbs with butter and sugar don't need to be baked before adding the cheesecake filling because the starchy element is already cooked. However, if you bake these crusts a little before filling them, the heat forces the fat and sugar into the crumbs and bonds them more tightly to make a crust that is less crumbly, crisper, and toastier in flavor.

A crust made with uncooked flour dough needs more time to cook than the cheesecake does. If it's not baked before filling, it will be doughy, pale, and raw-tasting.

More questions?

We would like to know what kitchen mysteries you're curious about. Send your questions to Why?, *Sunset Magazine,* 80 Willow Rd., Menlo Park, Calif. 94025. With the help of George K. York, extension food technologist at UC Davis, *Sunset* food editors will try to find solutions. We'll publish the answers in the magazine. ■

By Linda Lau Anusasananan

BERRY SAUCE *and almond-flavored custard set off sliced pineapple and papaya; kiwi fruit triangles and berry sauce hearts garnish top.*

A fanciful light dessert for spring

Two make-ahead sauces show off fresh tropical fruits

ALTHOUGH THIS dessert looks as if it requires the talents of a professional chef, anyone can achieve the attractive arrangement. And its components can be prepared ahead—the berry sauce up to two days, custard up to 4 hours, and fruit up to 2 hours.

The trick to serving the dessert is to have the plates and ingredients prepared and waiting. Then slowly pour both sauces at the same time in the center of each dessert plate (surface tension keeps the sauces from blending); use a spoon to help spread the sauces. Gently arrange the fruit over the sauces, then garnish the perimeter of the almond custard with berry sauce hearts. Instructions follow.

Tropical Fruits with Two Sauces

You can purchase the syrups that flavor the custard at coffee bars, specialty food stores, and liquor stores.

Berry sauce (recipe follows)

Flavored soft custard (recipe follows)

1   medium-size (about 3 lb.) pineapple

1   small (about 1 lb.) firm-ripe papaya

3   medium-size (about ¾ lb. total) kiwi fruits

Prepare the berry sauce and custard; chill until serving time.

Cut and discard ends, peel, and eyes from pineapple. Slice into 8 equal rounds; remove core from each round. Peel and halve papaya; scoop out seeds. Cut each half lengthwise into 8 wedges. Peel kiwi fruits. Slice each lengthwise into ⅜-inch wedges, then cut each wedge into ⅜-inch-thick triangles. Cover and chill fruits up to 2 hours.

Reserve about 2 tablespoons of the berry sauce. Starting at the same time, pour remaining berry sauce and custard in center of a dessert plate, covering half of plate with sauce, half with custard; do the same with 7 more plates. Using a ½ teaspoon measure, position small drops of the reserved berry sauce on custard portion on each plate (see photo); pull a knife continuously through berry drops to form a string of hearts. Place a pineapple round in center of each plate, lay 2 papaya slices in berry sauce, and sprinkle kiwi fruit triangles down center. Serves 8.

Per serving: 177 cal. (2.2 percent from fat); 4.4 g protein; 4.3 g fat (1.6 g sat.); 32 g carbo.; 43 mg sodium; 111 mg chol.

Berry sauce. In a blender or food processor, whirl 1½ cups (12 oz.) thawed **frozen unsweetened raspberries** and 1 cup hulled **strawberries** until smooth. Pour berry purée through a wire strainer. Rub residue with a rubber spatula to push out more purée; discard seeds. Add about 2 tablespoons *each* **powdered sugar** and **fresh orange** or lemon **juice** to purée to taste. Cover and chill up to 2 days.

Flavored soft custard. In top of a double boiler placed over medium heat, scald 2 cups **low-fat milk;** remove from heat. In a small bowl, mix 4 **large egg yolks** and 2 tablespoons **sugar;** slowly stir in some of the hot milk, then pour mixture into pan.

Set pan in bottom of a double boiler filled with about 1 inch simmering water (water should not touch bottom of top pan). Stir until custard thickly coats the back of a metal spoon, 8 to 12 minutes. Stir in to taste 2 tablespoons to ¼ cup **flavored syrup** (almond, pistachio, caramel, or chocolate-mint); add ½ teaspoon **vanilla**. Cool, cover, and chill up to 4 hours. ∎

By Betsy Reynolds Bateson

Chefs well armed produce great ribs

Follow up with tuna and tequila, and spinach with mustard

BREATHES THERE THE man with soul so dead who never to his friends hath said, "I make the best barbecued ribs you have ever tasted"? If there is, he will remain unhonor'd and unsung, at least in these pages.

Steve Estvanik's formula for success started when he decided to base a sauce on ginger, a flavor to which he admits a craving. To this he added a half-dozen other aromatics to achieve the desired complexity.

Ginger Ribs

4 to 6 pounds beef ribs from the loin

½ cup catsup

½ cup reduced-sodium soy sauce

½ cup prepared salsa

½ cup chopped fresh cilantro (coriander)

¼ cup dry sherry

3 tablespoons minced fresh ginger

3 cloves garlic, minced or pressed

Trim large or loose chunks of fat from beef and discard. Do not cut ribs apart; rinse pieces and pat dry.

Mix catsup, soy sauce, salsa, cilantro, sherry, ginger, and garlic. In a large heavy plastic food bag, combine the seasoning and ribs. Seal. Rotate bag to mix. Or lay ribs flat or slightly overlapping in a large rimmed pan and pour seasoning mixture over the ribs, coating on all sides; cover.

Chill ribs at least 30 minutes or up to 2 hours. Turn ribs over occasionally or baste with the sauce.

Lift bones from sauce; reserve sauce. Lay ribs on a barbecue grill over a solid bed of medium-hot coals (you can hold your hand at grill level 3 to 4 seconds). Turn ribs to brown evenly, basting frequently with sauce up to the last 5 to 10 minutes of cooking. Cook until meat is done to your taste; allow 25 to 30 minutes for medium-rare, about 35 minutes for medium, and 40 to 45 minutes for well done (cut to bone to test). Cut between bones to serve. Makes 4 to 6 servings.

Per serving: 233 cal. (39 percent from fat); 21 g protein; 10 g fat (4.3 g sat.); 11 g carbo.; 1,317 mg sodium; 59 mg chol.

Seattle

THE SUCCULENT AHI tuna swims in the wide ocean; the succulent century plant *Agave tequilana* grows on the high, dry plateau of central Mexico. Never the twain shall meet, right? Well, actually, the meeting took place in Moscow, Idaho. The result is A. J. Marineau's Ahi Margarita, in which tequila (a distillation of the juice of the century plant), lime, salt, and other goodies form a marinade for the fish and later become the foundation for the sauce.

Ahi Margarita

4 tablespoons tequila

3 tablespoons lime juice

1 teaspoon olive oil

¼ teaspoon onion powder

¼ teaspoon paprika

½ teaspoon grated orange peel

2 ahi tuna steaks, about 1¾ inches thick (about ¾ lb. total)

2 tablespoons nonfat sour cream

Salt

In a bowl, stir together tequila, lime juice, olive oil, onion powder, paprika, and orange peel. Rinse fish, pat dry, and turn pieces over in tequila mixture. Cover and chill at least 10 minutes or up to 2 hours.

Lift fish from marinade, reserving liquid. Lay fish on a lightly oiled barbecue grill over a solid bed of medium-hot coals (you can hold your hand at grill level for only 3 to 4 seconds).

Cook until steaks brown lightly but are still rosy in center, and edges have turned white about ¼ to ⅓ inch in from the surface on top and bottom sides, 10 to 14 minutes total. Remove from grill and keep warm.

Quickly pour remainder of marinade into a 10- to 12-inch frying pan. Bring to a rolling boil on high heat until reduced to about ⅓ cup, 1 or 2 minutes. Remove from heat and whisk in the sour cream. Spoon sauce over fish and add salt to taste. Makes 2 servings.

Per serving: 271 cal. (13 percent from fat); 37 g protein; 3.8 g fat (0.7 g sat.); 3 g carbo.; 70 mg sodium; 68 mg chol.

Moscow, Idaho

By Joan Griffiths, Richard Dunmire

MEXICO'S MASA FLOUR, *cooked like soft polenta, is a creamy base for chili-chicken sauce.*

It tastes like a chicken tamale

But takes minutes instead of hours

TRADITIONAL TAMALES take tedious hours to make. But here's good news for tamale fans: there's a faster, thoroughly unorthodox way to bring good tamale tastes together.

The trick is to separate the elements. Instead of making masa dough and spreading it on corn husks to wrap around a filling, you cook masa flour like polenta—which is logical because both are made of ground corn. The result is a creamy mixture that is cooked by the time it comes to a boil.

In place of the filling, you make an authentic mellow chili sauce that simmers to full flavor in about a quarter of an hour, then add cooked chicken to it. Spoon the masa mixture into bowls and top with the sauce.

Look for the masa flour, chilies, and cotija cheese in well-supplied supermarkets or Latino grocery stores.

Sloppy Tamale

- 3 ounces (about 14 large) dried guajillo or New Mexico chilies
- 3 cloves garlic
- 1 can (15 oz.) tomato purée
- 3 cups shredded cooked and skinned chicken
  Salt
- 2 quarts regular-strength chicken broth
- 4 cups dehydrated masa flour (corn tortilla flour)
- ½ cup crumbled cotija or feta cheese
  Fresh cilantro (coriander) leaves

Remove stems and seeds from chilies. Rinse chilies and drain briefly. With scissors, cut chilies crosswise into ½-inch pieces; soak in 1½ cups hot water until soft, about 10 minutes.

In a blender or food processor, whirl chilies with garlic and enough soaking water to purée smoothly; add remaining soaking water.

In a 10- to 12-inch frying pan over medium heat, stir chili mixture often until thickened and fragrant, 10 to 15 minutes. Add tomato purée and stir over low heat, uncovered, until hot. Stir in chicken, and simmer gently until chicken is hot, about 3 minutes. Add salt to taste.

Meanwhile, in a 5- to 6-quart pan, stir chicken broth into masa flour until smoothly blended. Stirring, bring to a rolling boil over high heat.

Ladle creamy masa into wide bowls and top with equal amounts of the chili sauce and cheese; sprinkle with cilantro. Serves 6.

Per serving: 552 cal. (24 percent from fat); 35 g protein; 15 g fat (2.8 g sat.); 74 g carbo.; 586 mg sodium; 70 mg chol. ■

By Linda Lau Anusasananan

SUNSET'S KITCHEN CABINET
Creative ways with everyday foods—submitted by *Sunset* readers,
tested in *Sunset* kitchens, approved by *Sunset* taste panels

Halibut with Avocado Salsa

Rayna Roseman, Tucson

½ cup chopped fresh basil leaves
1 tablespoon olive oil
½ teaspoon grated lime peel
⅓ cup lime juice
6 equal-size halibut steaks (about 6 oz. each)
1 large (about 10 oz.) firm-ripe avocado
1 large (about ½ lb.) firm-ripe tomato, cored
2 tablespoons chopped green onion
    Salt and cayenne

In a small bowl, mix basil, oil, lime peel, and lime juice.

Rinse fish and pat dry. Coat fish with ¼ cup of the lime mixture; set in a bowl, cover, and chill 30 minutes to 1 hour.

Peel, pit, and dice avocado. Chop tomato; mix with avocado. Add remaining lime mixture, onion, salt, and cayenne to taste.

Set fish on a rack in a 12- by 15-inch broiler pan. Broil about 4 inches from heat, turning once, until just barely opaque but still moist-looking in thickest part (cut to test), 8 to 12 minutes. Transfer to platter and spoon avocado salsa over fish. Serves 6.

Per serving: 244 cal. (41 percent from fat); 30 g protein; 11 g fat (1.6 g sat.); 6.6 g carbo.; 82 mg sodium; 44 mg chol.

CHUNKY AVOCADO SALSA *dresses broiled basil-marinated halibut steaks.*

BLT Omelet

Mickey Strang, McKinleyville, California

2 or 3 large eggs
1 teaspoon butter or margarine (optional)
6 tablespoons chopped tomato
1 or 2 strips crisply cooked turkey or pork bacon, crumbled
¾ cup shredded iceberg lettuce
    Salt and pepper

In a small bowl, beat eggs to blend with 2 tablespoons water. Place a 7- to 8-inch nonstick frying pan on medium-high heat. When pan is hot, add butter (if used), and tilt pan to coat bottom and sides. Pour in egg mixture; when eggs firm on pan bottom, lift cooked portion to allow uncooked egg to flow underneath. Cook until omelet is firm but top still looks shiny and moist, or to your taste. Shake frequently to keep omelet moving freely. Over half the omelet, sprinkle ¼ cup tomato and the bacon; run a spatula around edge of omelet, then tip pan and slide spatula under omelet to release it from pan. Fold omelet in half, slide onto a plate, and mound lettuce beside it. Garnish omelet with remaining tomato. Add salt and pepper to taste. Serves 1.

Per serving: 203 cal. (58 percent from fat); 16 g protein; 13 g fat (3.9 g sat.); 6.1 g carbo.; 321 mg sodium; 435 mg chol.

SANDWICH CLASSIC *of bacon, lettuce, and tomato shifts gears when omelet replaces the bread.*

Les Leekettes

Paul Franson, Palo Alto, California

24 green onions
1 tablespoon extra-virgin olive oil
1 clove garlic, minced
½ cup dry white wine
½ cup regular-strength chicken broth
    Salt and pepper

Trim and discard root ends of onions. Cut tops off just above the point where they turn green; reserve for another use. Rinse white part of onions well and pat dry.

Place a 10- to 12-inch frying pan over medium-high heat and add oil. When oil is hot, add onions. Cook, turning often, until onions begin to brown, about 5 minutes. Add garlic and stir until it turns golden, about 30 seconds. Add wine and broth.

Simmer, uncovered, over low heat until onions are very tender when pierced, 3 to 5 minutes. Lift out onions with a slotted spatula; drain briefly and place on a warm platter. Boil pan juices, uncovered, over high heat until reduced to about 3 tablespoons, about 5 minutes. Pour juices over onions. Add salt and pepper to taste. Serves 4.

Per serving: 65 cal. (54 percent from fat); 2 g protein; 3.9 g fat (0.6 g sat.); 7.3 g carbo.; 23 mg sodium; 0 mg chol.

BRAISE GREEN ONIONS *in wine to achieve a quicker and less costly equivalent of braised leeks.*

Sherried Leg of Pork

Grace V. Stevens, San Mateo, California

¾ cup dry sherry

3 tablespoons soy sauce

1½ tablespoons minced fresh ginger

2 cloves garlic, pressed or minced

2 teaspoons sugar

1 fat-trimmed, boned, rolled, and tied leg of pork or lamb, 3½ to 4 pounds

About ¾ cup regular-strength chicken broth

1½ tablespoons cornstarch

In a large heavy plastic food bag, combine sherry, soy, ginger, garlic, and sugar. Add meat and seal bag; rotate to coat meat and set the bag in a bowl. Chill, turning occasionally, 2 hours or up to 1 day. Lift roast from marinade; set on a rack in an 8- by 12-inch pan. Reserve marinade.

Roast meat, uncovered, in a 350° oven until a thermometer in thickest part reads 150° to 155° for pork, 1¾ to 2 hours, or 135° to 140° for medium-rare lamb, about 1½ hours.

Transfer roast to a platter; keep warm. Skim and discard fat from pan drippings. Measure drippings and add reserved marinade and enough broth to make 1½ cups. Return mixture to pan over medium heat; stir to free browned bits. Mix cornstarch with 3 tablespoons water and stir into drippings; stir until boiling. Serve with meat. Serves 8 to 10.

Per serving: 258 cal. (30 percent from fat); 33 g protein; 8.7 g fat (3 g sat.); 4.9 g carbo.; 402 mg sodium; 108 mg chol.

PORK LEG *marinated in sherry and ginger makes a handsome roast with dark, rich gravy.*

Tradewinds Fruit Salad

Marilou Robinson, Portland

3 medium-size (about ¾ lb. total) kiwi fruit

2 cups strawberries, rinsed

1 can (20 oz.) lichees, drained

2 cups ¾-inch chunks fresh pineapple

1 can (8 oz.) sliced water chestnuts, rinsed and drained

Lime dressing (recipe follows)

6 to 8 large butter lettuce leaves, rinsed and crisped

Peel kiwi fruits; thinly slice crosswise. Hull strawberries and thinly slice. In a large bowl, combine kiwi slices, strawberries, lichees, pineapple, and water chestnuts. (If making ahead, cover and chill up to 4 hours.)

Pour lime dressing over fruit and mix gently. Place 1 lettuce leaf on each of 6 to 8 salad plates. Spoon fruit mixture onto lettuce. Serves 6 to 8.

Per serving: 133 cal. (5 percent from fat); 1.3 g protein; 0.8 g fat (0 g sat.); 34 g carbo.; 59 mg sodium; 0 mg chol.

Lime dressing. Mix 1 teaspoon grated **lime peel**, ¼ cup **lime juice**, 1½ tablespoons firmly packed **brown sugar**, 1½ teaspoons **Dijon mustard**, and 1 teaspoon **fish sauce** (*nam pla* or *nuoc mam*) or soy sauce.

COMBINE TROPICAL FRUITS, *berries, and an Asian dressing for a fresh, light salad.*

Toasted Walnut Pound Cake

Judith Burkholder, Littleton, Colorado

1½ cups coarsely chopped walnuts

1½ cups (¾ lb.) butter or margarine

2 cups granulated sugar

7 large eggs

1 teaspoon vanilla

3 cups all-purpose flour

Powdered sugar

Bake nuts in an 8- or 9-inch-wide pan in a 325° oven until golden under skin, about 20 minutes. Let cool. Pour warm nuts into a cloth towel and rub to remove as much of the skin as possible; discard skins.

In a large bowl, beat butter and sugar with a mixer until fluffy. Beat in eggs, 1 at a time, until fluffy. Beat in vanilla. Gradually mix in flour, then beat until blended. Mix in nuts. Scrape batter into a buttered and floured 10-inch (14-cup) decorative or plain tube cake pan.

Bake in a 325° oven until cake is well browned and springs back when pressed in center, about 1 hour and 10 minutes. Cool in pan about 15 minutes. Invert cake onto a plate; let cool, then dust with powdered sugar. Slice thinly. Serves 16 to 20.

Per serving: 360 cal. (55 percent from fat); 5.6 g protein; 22 g fat (9.9 g sat.); 37 g carbo.; 168 mg sodium; 113 mg chol.

Compiled by Linda Lau Anusasananan

TOASTED WALNUTS *generously stud this golden fine-textured pound cake.*

FOOD GUIDE

Fabulously fast fettuccine, herbs go to the freezer, a sweet onion sandwich, and bubbling wines

By Jerry Anne Di Vecchio

Surprisingly, most good cooks—even the most talented professionals—don't feel they cook much differently from anyone else. But as someone who has spent years watching all kinds of cooks at work, I know that decisions, often unspoken, at each step make the difference. I've learned to be very inquiring about look, smell, taste, and texture, all critical to recreating a dish in the image of the original.

Fettuccine alla Norcina is a perfect example.

It is served at L'Opera on Pine Avenue in Long Beach, California—a city that has regained vitality to match its waterfront setting after long years of stagnation.

The fettuccine was among several dishes on the menu that caught my eye one busy evening. I later called the team of chefs—Stefano Colaiacomo, Luis Lopes, and Donna Woo—and asked them to share a few recipes. Since restaurant dishes are usually designed to be made one serving at a time, recipes invariably need retooling for home kitchens. But first, the ingredients and steps must be reviewed.

The L'Opera chefs make their pastas fresh, so I asked how they would feel if I suggested purchased fresh pasta as an alternative. No problem, they said, but be sure not to overcook it.

I knew we had a dish that would be great for the harried home cooks among us when they said to put the pasta water on to boil before you start the sauce.

How do they make the sauce? Exact proportions aren't really important. It's the way in which the ingredients are treated. The sausages are browned just enough to develop flavor instead of being cooked through. Garlic is subtle in this dish. It's cooked just until golden; less time and the taste will be harsh, more and it will be bitter and scorched. How much mild red pepper to use? Enough to give a mellow taste, but be sure the peppers are skinned and cut in thin slivers. How much white wine? Enough to cover the pan bottom. And so it goes with each ingredient and each step. When it came to the cream—the recipe calls for at least a cup per person—I asked the chefs if they would mind if I also gave a less rich alternative. Of course not, they assured me, if it tastes good. I served the cream and the milk versions side by side in our test kitchen, and my cohorts had to taste each several times to decide which was which. Some

A TASTE OF THE WEST

L'Opera's Fettuccine alla Norcina

¾ pound hot Italian sausages

1 clove garlic, minced

2 teaspoons olive oil

½ cup thinly sliced peeled roasted red bell peppers (fresh or canned)

½ cup dry white wine

¼ teaspoon crushed dried hot red chilies (optional)

¼ cup tomato sauce

4 cups whipping cream or 4 cups milk mixed smoothly with 2 tablespoons all-purpose flour

   Salt and pepper

1 to 1⅛ pound fresh fettuccine (6 cups cooked)

¼ cup minced Italian parsley

   Thin shavings parmesan cheese (optional)

If you are going to make and serve this dish at one fell swoop, put a 5- to 6-quart pan with 3 to 4 quarts water over high heat; cover pan with a lid and bring water to a boil.

   Meanwhile, pierce sausages in several places with a fork. In a 10- to 12-inch frying pan over medium-high heat, lightly brown sausages, 5 to 8 minutes. Set sausages on a plate and cut into ½-inch-thick rounds. Wipe frying pan clean, return to heat, and add garlic and olive oil; stir until lightly browned, about 2 minutes. Return sausages and any juices to pan along with bell peppers, wine, chilies, and tomato sauce. On high heat, stir several times until liquid comes to a full rolling boil. Let boil about 2 minutes. Add cream (or milk and flour—scraping container to get all the flour) and stir until sauce returns to a full rolling boil. Stir and boil about 1 minute. If making ahead, set sauce aside up to 2 hours, then stir over high heat until boiling. Season to taste with salt and pepper.

   To boiling water, add pasta, and stir several times to prevent sticking. Cook, uncovered, until pasta is tender to bite, 2 to 3 minutes. Drain at once, then pour into a large bowl. Pour sauce onto pasta and mix, using 2 forks to lift pasta until some of the sauce is absorbed (mixture should be slightly soupy). Serve pasta and sauce in shallow bowls. Sprinkle with parsley and add cheese, salt, and pepper to taste. Makes 4 to 6 servings.

Per serving with cream: 914 cal. (69 percent from fat); 20 g protein; 70 g fat (38 g sat.); 48 g carbo.; 552 mg sodium; 275 mg chol.

Per serving with milk: 557 cal. (44 percent from fat); 23g protein; 27 g fat (10 g sat.); 53 g carbo.; 578 mg sodium; 121 mg chol.

tasters actually liked the milk-based sauce best.

So what is the secret to being a good cook? Knowing when enough is neither too much nor too little—and remembering that good cooking takes patience, practice, and an observing eye.

BACK TO BASICS
Freezing herb leaves

When fresh herbs wither before I've had time to use them, my wee bit of Scottish heritage comes to the fore and torments me about waste—especially since staff writer Christine Hale proved that a little forethought and the freezer can save them. She has explored the ways to preserve herbs for freshest flavor and found that freezing works best. In blind tastes of dishes using the herbs, most of us couldn't tell the difference between fresh and frozen. Here's how to freeze:

Step 1. Rinse herbs and let drain until dry.

Tough-leaf herbs such as rosemary and thyme change little when thawed. Freeze on the stem, or strip off leaves for more compact storage.

Hardy parsley and chives are best chopped or snipped before freezing. Thawed, they are a little limp but still have lots of flavor and color.

Moderately firm-leaf marjoram and oregano darken when thawed; freeze on the stem or freeze just the leaves.

Tender-leaf herbs such as basil, sage, summer savory, and tarragon get black and limp when they thaw—no problem if you're adding them to cooked mixtures (to measure, crumble frozen leaves). But if color is important (as in a pesto sauce), you can retain most of it—as well as the flavor—if you blanch the leaves before freezing: immerse them in boiling water just until they turn a brighter green, 2 to 3 seconds. Immediately plunge leaves into ice water and let stand until cold; drain. Spread leaves out on towels and blot to dry.

Step 2. Lay herbs in 1 layer on baking sheets, keeping pieces slightly apart (spread cut parsley or chives in a thin layer). Freeze on pans just until herbs are rigid, about an hour.

Step 3. Quickly pour frozen herbs into small freezer plastic bags, press out air, seal, and return to the freezer.

To use: Pour herbs you need from bag, reseal, and return the rest to the freezer immediately. You can freeze herbs up to a year, but flavor falls off with the duration of storage.

QUICKLY TRANSFER *frozen basil leaves to freezer bags and refreeze. Leaves keep their color if blanched before freezing.*

GREAT INGREDIENT
Fresh sweet onions

Fresh sweet onions are the province of spring and summer—and a joy to my onion-loving household. These onions taste sweet because they contain more water and sugar than the other ones. They are mild, too, because they have fewer sulfur compounds, which make other onions taste hot and also make your eyes sting and tear. And they're very juicy, which makes them quite perishable; refrigerate (separating with paper towels) if you don't plan to use them within a few days.

Domestic fresh sweet onions surface at the market in April and last into August. They're grown in many places—usually indicated by their name. Most are white fleshed—Maui, Walla Walla, Vidalia, Texas 1015 Super-Sweet, California Imperial, and New Mexico Carzalia—except for one red from Fresno County called Fresno Sweet Red.

It distresses me to see so many recipes call for cooking these lovely onions. All onions get mild and sweet when cooked, so less costly regular onions work as well in cooked dishes. But the pleasure of a sweet onion very lightly cooked and especially eaten raw, as in this sandwich, cannot be matched.

Sweet onion salad sandwich. Peel and thinly slice 1 large (about ¾ lb.) **sweet onion** and separate into rings. Mix with 1 tablespoon **white wine vinegar,** 1 tablespoon minced **parsley,** 1 tablespoon finely chopped drained **dried tomatoes packed in oil,** and 1 teaspoon drained **prepared capers.**

Set 1 **baked thin-crust Italian bread shell** (12 in. wide, 10 oz.) or a ½-pound focaccia piece in a 10- by 15-inch pan. Dot with 2 to 4 tablespoons **gorgonzola** or cambozola **cheese.** Bake in a 375° oven until bread is hot and cheese is soft, about 8 minutes. Smear cheese over bread and mound onion salad on bread. Cut into 2 to 4 pieces. Season to taste with **salt** and **freshly ground pepper.** Serves 2 to 4.

Per small serving: 252 cal. (27 percent from fat); 11 g protein; 7.5 g fat (2.2 g sat.); 37 g carbo.; 426 mg sodium; 9.4 mg chol.

NEWS NOTE
Beyond goat cheese

Chèvre (goat) cheese has become astonishingly popular these past few years, probably because its nippy flavor goes so well with salads. The boom means that other equally likable goat products are also more available. Goat-milk yogurt is being made by several companies, and it's found in health and specialty food stores. Like goat cheese, goat-milk yogurt has a wonderful bright, fresh tartness.

Naturally homogenized goat milk has long had a devoted albeit limited following (it's most popular among those allergic to cow's milk). But this is changing as the milk is found with greater frequency in supermarkets, where you can also find canned evaporated and powdered dried goat milk.

The biggest news may be that Meyenberg low-fat (1 percent) goat milk is now being produced by Jackson-Mitchell of Santa Barbara, California.

For drinking, the sharp edge of goat milk takes a little getting used to. But it works extremely well as a flavor element with other foods. Carol Jackson of Jackson-Mitchell whirls up breakfast smoothies of apricot nectar, bananas, and low-fat goat milk. The combination makes sense if you've already discovered what a terrific duo dried apricots and fresh goat cheese make as an appetizer.

For another combination, where the contrast is less dramatic though equally

KEVIN CANDLAND

PARSLEY GIVES *this cool, smooth potato soup its delicate hue, and low-fat goat milk adds a subtle tartness.*

refreshing, try this cool, pale green potato soup.

Chèvre vichyssoise. In a 1½- to 2-quart pan, mix 3 cups diced peeled **potatoes** and 3 cups **regular-strength chicken broth.** Cover and bring to a boil; simmer until potatoes mash easily, about 20 minutes.

Ladle about ½ the mixture at a time into a blender and whirl until smoothly puréed. Add to blender ½ cup packed chopped **parsley** and whirl with some of the potato mixture until very smoothly puréed; combine potato mixtures. Add 1 quart **low-fat** or regular **goat milk** and ¼ cup **lemon juice.** Cover and chill until cold, at least 2 hours or up to 1 day. Ladle into bowls and add about 2 tablespoons (¾ cup total) **goat-milk yogurt** to each. Season to taste with **salt** and **pepper.** Makes 6 servings.

Per serving: 152 cal. (22 percent from fat); 9 g protein; 3.7 g fat (2 g sat.); 23 g carbo.; 149 mg sodium; 10 mg chol.

SMART SNACK
Tantalizing, wholesome hummus

My slim, energetic friend Judy has modernized hummus to make a great, speedy, low-fat snack. She's replaced tahini (sesame seed paste) and olive oil in the recipe with just a few drops of Oriental sesame oil, and freshened the flavor and color of this garbanzo bean spread with lots of parsley.

Judy's hummus. Drain 1 can (about 1 lb.) **reduced-salt** or regular **garbanzos** and rinse with cool water; drain again. Combine in a blender or food processor with ½ cup packed **parsley,** ¼ cup **lemon juice,** 2 or 3 cloves **garlic,** and 1 teaspoon ground **cumin.** Whirl until smooth, scraping container sides as needed. Stir in to taste 1 to 2 teaspoons **Oriental sesame oil.** Serve with crisp **carrot sticks,** crusty bread, or water crackers. Covered and chilled, the hummus stays fresh 3 to 4 days. Makes 1⅓ cups.

Per tablespoon hummus: 19 cal. (28 percent from fat); 0.8 g protein; 0.6 g fat (0 g sat.); 2.6 g carbo.; 26 mg sodium; 0 mg chol.

GREAT SERVICE
Retinning copper pans

Tin linings of old copper pans are often worn away. Even new tin linings can be fragile. If an empty pan is set over heat, it doesn't take long for the tin to melt into puddles. When this neutral metal lining is gone, the taste of copper compounds intrudes unpleasantly, even unhealthfully, if the foods cooked in the pan are high in acid.

Retinning is a limited service not found in many communities. This I learned from readers who want to know whom to contact, and the hard way, when I ruined one of my own pans. One place to start looking is in the yellow pages under Plating. Also, inquire at good cookware shops, or ask antiques dealers who handle copper cookware.

Once you've found a retinner, be sure to establish cost (a 2½ qt. pan usually costs $35 to $45 plus shipping) and the time (usually 2 to 6 weeks) it will take up front. If the pan has any special stamps or markings you want to preserve, make sure the retinner understands and can do what you expect. These companies will accept pans shipped to them.

California
Costa Mesa. Normandy Refinishers, 1603 Superior Ave.; (714) 631-5555.
Palo Alto. Peninsula Plating Works, 232 Homer Ave.; (415) 326-7825.
Pasadena. Normandy Refinishers, 355 S. Rosemead Blvd.; (818) 792-9202.
San Francisco. Coleman B. Cook Silver Co., 101 Vicente St. at W. Portal Ave.; (415) 242-1812.

Oregon
Portland. Oregon Re-Tinners, 2712 N. Mississippi Ave.; (503) 287-7696.

Washington
Seattle. Zapffee Silversmiths Inc., 12004 Aurora Ave. N.; (800) 544-9313. ■

BOB THOMPSON ON WINE
A champagne toast to spring

Too many people think about champagne and the rest of the world's sparkling wines only once a year—New Year's Eve. Then is not a bad time for a bit of the bubbly, but now is always the best time, because sparkling wine tickles your nose when you inhale deeply, bubbles over with life, and smells as earthy and vital as a budding spring garden.

Champagne comes with all kinds of shadings, from *cuvées de prestige* that cost a king's ransom down to relatively affordable nonvintage Bruts. Californian bubblies made by the champagne method range similarly in prestige and price, but cost less all along the line.

To celebrate spring, think first of Californian nonvintage Bruts and Blanc de Noirs, especially the Blanc de Noirs.

The name Blanc de Noirs is close to a guarantee that the wine is made from Pinot Noir grapes, and almost a promise that it will taste like fruit and feel as light as air. Most cost between $11 and $15. To try: Chandon Carneros Blanc de Noirs, Gloria Ferrer Sonoma County Blanc de Noirs, Mumm Napa Napa Valley Blanc de Cuvée Noirs.

Bruts blend Pinot Noir and Chardonnay in variable amounts. Oddly, Chardonnay adds weight, and produces fuller flavors as well. That result may suit your taste better than Blanc de Noirs do. To the Bruts of the above list of producers, add those of Domaine Carneros, Codorniu Napa, and Maison Deutz.

Either type will make a good accompaniment to brunch or a light lunch. If strawberries are about, have some of those. Put a small one in each glass; the bubbles bounce them around until you can't help feeling jolly just about that.

Lastly, an old piece of advice worth repeating: If champagne and its closest kin taste too austere to you, do not go halfway. Plunge into an outright sweet, splendidly fruity, made-from-Muscat Asti Spumante (Mondodoro) or one of California's most skillful imitators of it (Ballatore). Asti Spumantes cost about $11 to $15, American counterparts less than half that.

Celebrating

Strawberry Sundae with Strawberry-Wine Syrup

Pastry chef and co-owner Nancy Silverton of Campanile restaurant in Los Angeles shared this grand recipe with us. You make a strawberry purée and freeze half for sherbet, then add cream to the other half and freeze it for ice cream. The syrup is intensely flavored with spiced wine and strawberries.

¾ cup plus ⅓ cup sugar

1 cinnamon stick (¾ in. long)

1 whole clove

2 peppercorns, cracked

¼ teaspoon ground nutmeg

¼ cup water

1¾ cups Beaujolais wine

2 cups sliced hulled strawberries (¼ in. thick) plus 1 quart whole hulled strawberries

2 tablespoons lemon juice

¼ cup light corn syrup

¾ cup whipping cream

Plain crisp cookies (optional)

To make syrup, in a 10- to 12-inch frying pan over medium-high heat, stir ¾ cup sugar, cinnamon, clove, peppercorns, nutmeg, and water often until sugar is deep amber and just begins to smoke, 6 to 8 minutes. Remove from heat. Protecting hands, stir in wine. Boil over high heat, stirring often, until sugar remelts and volume is reduced to 1 cup, 6 to 8 minutes.

Add sliced strawberries. Reduce heat and simmer, stirring occasionally, until mixture is reduced to 1¼ cups, 6 to 8 minutes. Remove cinnamon and clove. Use warm, or chill airtight up to 2 days, then reheat until warm.

In a food processor or blender, whirl the whole strawberries, remaining ⅓ cup sugar, lemon juice, and corn syrup into a smooth purée.

For sherbet, freeze half of purée in an ice cream maker as manufacturer directs. Transfer to an airtight container and freeze until firm, 1 hour or up to 1 week.

For ice cream, add cream to remaining purée and freeze as manufacturer directs. Freeze airtight as for sherbet.

To serve, place scoops of sherbet and ice cream into 4 to 6 large wineglasses. Spoon wine syrup on top. Offer with cookies. Serves 4 to 6.

Per serving: 364 cal. (24 percent from fat); 1.8 g protein; 9.9 g fat (5.8 g sat.); 60 g carbo.; 33 mg sodium; 33 mg chol.

Strawberries!

BY PETER FISH & ELAINE JOHNSON

Strawberry. Say the word and you conjure up a May afternoon when you feel spring warming into summer. You see a roadside stand where red ripe fruit gleams on a rickety wooden table.

The strawberry has certain powers of enchantment. It may be the most mutable of all fruits. Popped into the mouth whole, it offers a pleasure that is innocent yet sensual, as the sweet juice drips down your chin and onto your fingers. Stacked between cake and cream in a shortcake, it sparkles with the all-American appeal of a small-town Fourth of July. Blended with wine and spices into a sundae, the strawberry rises to heights of cosmopolitan elegance.

The West is the strawberry capital of the United States. California alone accounts for 80 percent of the nation's crop, and this month marks the peak of its strawberry season. These berries are triumphs of scientific research and technology mixed with plain old hard work, but it is hard to think of technology or hard work when you think of strawberries. Instead, your thoughts drift toward those short-cakes, those sundaes, those berries savored fresh from their green mesh boxes. You may find yourself remembering that most famous remark about the strawberry, attributed to William Butler by way of Izaak Walton: "Doubtless God could have made a better berry, but doubtless God never did."

Strawberry Shortcake with Lemon-Ginger Cream

In our test kitchens we tried many shortcakes to come up with this tender, rich, citrus-flavored version. If you use crème fraîche for the topping, it will be quite thick and sweet; with sour cream it will be thinner and more tart. Use berries as soon after purchase as possible. If you need to hold them a day or two, chill them in their containers, loosely covered and unwashed. To prevent sogginess and preserve flavor, rinse strawberries with their caps attached. Serve berries at room temperature for best flavor.

About 2 cups all-purpose flour

⅓ cup plus about 2 tablespoons sugar

2 teaspoons baking powder

2 teaspoons grated lemon peel (colored part only)

½ teaspoon baking soda

½ teaspoon salt

½ cup (¼ lb.) butter or margarine, cut into chunks

2 large egg yolks

⅔ cup buttermilk

2 quarts strawberries, rinsed and hulled, at room temperature

Lemon-ginger cream (recipe at right)

In a large bowl, combine 2 cups flour, ⅓ cup sugar, baking powder, lemon peel, soda, and salt. With a pastry blender or your fingers, cut in or rub in butter until mixture looks mealy. Combine yolks and buttermilk to blend, then add to flour mixture and stir with a fork until dough holds together.

On a floured board, knead dough with floured hands just until smooth, 15 to 20 turns. Reflour board and pat out dough 1 inch thick. Cut into 6 circles with a floured 2½- to 3-inch round cutter, gathering and repatting scraps as needed. Lift onto an ungreased 12- by 15-inch baking sheet and sprinkle with 1 teaspoon sugar.

Bake shortcakes in a 400° oven until deep golden, 12 to 14 minutes. Transfer to a rack until cool, at least 30 minutes.

Set aside 6 whole berries. Slice remaining berries, place in a bowl, and stir with 2 tablespoons sugar; let stand 10 minutes to 1 hour. Split shortcakes horizontally and place each bottom on a plate. Cover them with some lemon-ginger cream and sliced berries, then the shortcake tops. Garnish each with a whole berry. Offer with remaining cream and sliced berries. Serves 6.

Per serving: 656 cal. (45 percent from fat); 9.5 g protein; 33 g fat (19 g sat.); 85 g carbo.; 676 mg sodium; 152 mg chol.

Lemon-ginger cream. In a small bowl, combine 1 cup **crème fraîche** or sour cream, ⅓ cup chopped **crystallized ginger,** 2 tablespoons **sugar,** and 1½ teaspoons **grated lemon peel.** In the large bowl of a mixer, beat ½ cup **whipping cream** until thick. Fold in crème fraîche mixture.

California strawberries certainly have good breeding. But do they have good taste?

At 9 o'clock on a May morning in Ventura County, the coastal overcast has not yet decided whether to lift or hang around all day. On the Bob Jones Ranch, farm workers bend over rows of bushy green plants, picking strawberries and setting them into cardboard flats. Ranch foreman Doug Wagner reaches into one of the flats and picks up a strawberry for display. It is conical and ruby red, and it exudes a fragrance that makes you forget the fog. It is perfect.

People sometimes call California the Big Orange. It could be called the Big Strawberry. Even in a year like this one, when disastrous storms walloped most of its strawberry-growing regions, California produces more strawberries by far than any other state in the nation: 1 billion pounds, or 800 million pint baskets, by 1994's count.

Yet for all their preeminence in the nation's produce sections, California strawberries draw frequent abuse. They lack character, it is said. They are voluptuous yet vapid: if they were people they would be starlets lounging poolside, angling for bit parts on "Beverly Hills 90210." But their defenders maintain that California strawberries picked ripe in spring and summer can hold their own against berries from anywhere in the world.

THE QUESTION OF FLAVOR
The strawberry is hardly a new crop in California. It was cultivated by Franciscan mission fathers as early as the 1770s. But not until the 1950s did California become the nation's strawberry patch. Today California contains 23,000 acres of strawberries. The leading growing regions lie near the Pacific Ocean: coastal Santa Cruz, Monterey, and San Luis Obispo counties; Santa Maria; Ventura County's Oxnard Plain; and pockets of Orange and San Diego counties. "Strawberries are like people—they both like mild winters and mild summers," says Victor Voth, a short,

CHACO MOHLER

ANDY FREEBERG

Year-round berries: In spring, a grower plows fields in Shasta County in Northern California. Later, the berries' daughter plants are sent to Southern California (fruit production begins in January) and central California (peak production this month). Bottom, berries are picked near Watsonville.

peppery man whose decades of research have earned him the nickname Mr. Strawberry.

Voth and his fellow University of California researchers are probably the group most responsible for what California strawberries look and taste like today. During the past 40 years, they've developed strawberry varieties that bear abundant fruit in what used to be the off-season (fall and winter) and strawberries that withstand long-distance shipping—traits that are the key to California's current dominance of the market. (Other successful varieties have been developed by commercial outfits, notably Watsonville-based Driscoll Strawberries Associates.)

Although the results have been revolutionary, the breeding process itself is "tedious," says Voth. He explains that because a strawberry's chromosomes come in sets of eight (as opposed to a human's sets of two), isolating a single trait "is like going to Las Vegas, gambling with eight dice, and hoping it comes up snake eyes on all eight." For every new variety that holds some potential for farmers, researchers look at about 100,000 seedlings.

Genetic complexity is just one challenge of breeding. Another is that strawberry flavor is more than just sweetness: scientists have identified 300 aromatic compounds in the taste and smell of a strawberry. And flavor has to compete with those other priorities: namely, that the strawberry be big and red enough to appeal to consumers, tough enough to stand up to shipping, and hardy enough to ripen in cooler months. During his years of walking the test fields, Voth says, he wouldn't even taste a variety until he was sure it possessed these traits. "Why should you taste it if it doesn't have those other things? Without those, it's not going to make it."

At a UC research station in Watsonville, pomologist Doug Shaw hands out samples of varieties recently developed through the University of California. Not all seem promising. A variety called Selva is dry and bland, although Shaw says it can be tasty when picked at the peak of ripeness. One unnamed, still-experimental berry tastes more like passion fruit and mango than strawberry; another possesses a fine flavor but is audibly crunchy

NOEL BARNHURST

Strawberry-Rhubarb Mousse

Flo Braker, Bay Area baking columnist and author of "The Simple Art of Perfect Baking," created this soft, low-calorie mousse with its sweet-tangy fruit combination. The recipe contains raw egg whites; though the risk of salmonella contamination is quite low, exercise caution serving it to young children, the elderly, and those with deficient immune systems.

2 cups sliced rhubarb (¾ in. thick)

¾ cup plus 2 tablespoons sugar

1 tablespoon water

2 packages unflavored gelatin

½ cup orange juice (preferably freshly squeezed)

2 quarts strawberries, rinsed, hulled, and sliced lengthwise ¼ inch thick

2 teaspoons grated orange peel

3 large egg whites

½ cup whipping cream

Mint sprig

In a 2- to 3-quart pan, stir rhubarb, ¼ cup sugar, and water. Bring to simmering over high heat, then reduce heat and simmer, covered, until rhubarb is very tender when pierced, 8 to 10 minutes.

In a small bowl, stir gelatin into orange juice and let stand until softened, 4 to 5 minutes; set aside.

Meanwhile, place 2 cups strawberries and ½ cup sugar in a 10- to 12-inch frying pan over medium-low heat. Occasionally shake pan and gently stir until sugar dissolves, 5 to 8 minutes. Remove from heat; gently stir in rhubarb and gelatin mixtures and orange peel. Let cool, then chill until mixture is cold to touch and flows slowly when tilted, 30 to 40 minutes (do not overchill).

In the large bowl of an electric mixer, beat egg whites and remaining 2 tablespoons sugar until soft peaks form; transfer to another large bowl. In mixer bowl, beat cream until thick, then fold in rhubarb mixture. Gently fold in egg whites until no streaks remain. Chill airtight until slightly firm to touch, about 20 minutes.

Set aside about 6 of the prettiest berry slices. In a deep 2- to 2½-quart glass serving bowl, spread ¼ of mousse in an even layer. Using ½ of remaining strawberries, arrange them individually on top in a very even double layer. Spread with ½ of remaining mousse. Repeat layering, ending with small mounds of mousse. Chill airtight until mousse is slightly firm to touch, at least 1 hour or up to 1 day.

Garnish with reserved berries and mint, and spoon into bowls. Serves 10 to 12.

Per serving: 135 cal. (23 percent from fat); 3 g protein; 3.5 g fat (1.9 g sat.); 24 g carbo.; 21 mg sodium; 11 mg chol.

when you bite into it. Shaw is not impressed: "People don't want a strawberry that crunches like a carrot. I can't tell you how many 'almost' varieties I have—perfect except for color or softness."

But next come the winners. In Southern California the industry standard is Chandler. Victor Voth isn't keen on it. "A sack of sugar," he complains. "I like a little acid in my strawberry." But to Shaw and many others, Chandler's sweet taste is the essence of strawberry, its aroma seductive enough to lure a shopper from the far side of a supermarket (though most markets don't label strawberries by variety, so you might not know it's a Chandler). A newer variety, Camarosa, may give Chandler a run for its money. It tastes nearly as good and produces more reliably large berries. For Northern California growers, Shaw likes a variety called Seascape, although he worries that its naturally dark red color may lead consumers to reject it as overripe.

Come May or June, argues Shaw, any of these strawberries can compete with the best, present or past. "At our clone bank at UC Davis, we have samples of strawberries from earlier in the century," says Shaw. "To be honest, we have varieties now that are just as good as those we had in 1940."

OUT OF SEASON AND IN THE MONEY

Modern cultivation methods mean that strawberry farming today is a much more expensive proposition than it was in 1940. Then, growers kept plants in the ground for six or seven years. Today they replace their plants every year; they also lay down new drip-irrigation tape, fumigate the soil for pests and fungus, and use plastic mulch to warm the ground and speed up plant growth. All this can cost as much as $12,000 an acre before the first strawberry is harvested.

The one part of the business that hasn't changed much in 50 years is the actual harvesting. No one has developed a machine that can successfully pick strawberries, so it's still done by hand. It's tough, backache-producing work, usually performed by migrant and local laborers paid $5 to $8 an hour.

Once the berries are harvested, technology

At a Watsonville research station, pomologist Doug Shaw displays the fruit of UC research. Bottom, Jim Cochran, his wife, Christine Miller, and their son, Jimmy, enjoy a break at Swanton Berry Farms north of Santa Cruz.

ANDY FREEBERG

takes over again. Packaged strawberries are put on pallets and whisked to packing houses, where they're cooled to 33° and gassed with carbon dioxide to slow their metabolic processes. Then they're slapped into refrigerated trucks. "Say the grower picks midmorning on Monday," says Don De Armond of Statewide Cooling, a produce shipping company in Oxnard. "We can generally ship by midafternoon, and the strawberries will arrive in Boston or Philadelphia by Thursday or Friday."

California farmers depend on selling before and after the traditional May and June strawberry season because fruit fetches premium prices off-season. Says UC pomologist Kirk Larson, "In December, Southern California strawberries bring at least $20 a flat. Come April, it's $4 to $5. If you don't have fruit up front in Southern California, you've lost it."

Northern California growers stretch the berry season into late fall. Southern California growers try to get a jump on things, harvesting berries as early as December. To do that, growers employ some geographic trickery. In spring, they plant strawberry plants in extreme Northern California. The plants grow there, putting out runners—daughter plants— until fall, when cold temperatures and shorter days make the plants go dormant. Growers transport the daughter plants to Southern California, where warm temperatures and more sunlight signal that spring has come and it's time for the plants to bear fruit—even though the calendar reads December. "It's a sophisticated system," says Larson. "Luckily, strawberry plants are small enough to move around. Just try doing it with apple trees."

Growing strawberries nearly year-round has its drawbacks. Winter storms, like those that drenched California in January and March, can do costly damage. Strawberries are highly sensitive to their environment. (That's why if the berries you buy one week don't thrill you, the berries you buy the next probably will.) A few cold and rainy days can make the berries taste bland and waterlogged; more than a few bad days can destroy the plants.

GROWING STRAWBERRIES THE OLD WAY

Some small California strawberry growers try to steer a different course. Although they generally plant the same UC-developed varieties as larger commercial growers, they don't grow out of season or for long-distance shipping. In Healdsburg, Nancy and Malcolm Skall till Middleton Farm, which sells at local farmers' markets and to restaurants such as Berkeley's Chez Panisse. Nancy Skall aims to grow organic strawberries with the flavor she remembers from her youth. "When I was a little girl, we had a Victory garden that grew strawberries with a really intense flavor. My mother used to mash them with sugar and put them on white bread. I thought that flavor had disappeared. It hasn't. We have that flavor here."

In Davenport, in Santa Cruz County, Jim Cochran of Swanton Berry Farms grows berries on a spectacular plot of land wedged between the Santa Cruz Mountains and the Pacific. Cochran takes as his model the obsessive concern vineyard owners lavish on premium wine grapes.

"There are probably about 10 answers to why our berries taste so good," says Cochran. "What it boils down to is an attitude. I think about flavor a lot. Most people think about tonnage and shelf life. I pick them riper—that's common sense. I choose a variety that tastes good. I don't overirrigate or overfertilize. I grow them on rich soil so they have complex flavor. It's no real mystery; people just weren't putting their minds to it."

This care comes at a price, though. Cochran's yields are lower than those of conventional farms, his picking costs higher. That makes his berries more expensive: $1.50 to $2.50 a pint. Only a handful of Bay Area restaurants and supermarkets carry his berries, and because he doesn't use fungicides and picks the berries riper, they have a shorter shelf life. And you won't be able to find them in the markets at all come December or January.

"It's really hard to grow a good strawberry consistently," Cochran says. "You have to be on it not just every day, but every hour. That's where my gray hair comes from."

CHRISTOPHER GARDNER

Eat, drink, and be merry at California strawberry festivals

You've got your strawberry tamales, your strawberry pizza, your strawberry slushes and margaritas. You've got strawberries on skewers, in pies, and fresh by the carton and crate. You've got strawberry shortcake–eating contests and strawberry tart tosses. Sure, other things may lure you: arts and crafts, live music. But mostly California's 1995 strawberry festivals are great places to go to eat, drink, and live strawberries.

Arroyo Grande, May 27 and 28, Arroyo Grande Valley Strawberry Festival, Branch St.; (805) 489-1488.

Garden Grove, May 26–29, Garden Grove Strawberry Festival, Village Green, Stanford Ave. at Euclid St.; (714) 638-0981.

Monterey, June 24 and 25, Monterey County Strawberry Festival, Laguna Seca Raceway; (408) 663-4166.

Oxnard, May 20 and 21, California Strawberry Festival, College Park, 3250 S. Rose Ave.; (805) 385-7578.

Santa Maria, April 21, 22, and 23, Santa Maria Valley Strawberry Festival, Santa Barbara County Fairgrounds, 937 S. Thornburg St.; (800) 549-0036.

Walking and talking strawberries? Berries on a stick? Its all part of the fun at California strawberry festivals.

STRAWBERRY FIELDS FOREVER?

Most California strawberry growers have cause for at least a few gray hairs. In a state with 32 million people, perhaps the most remarkable thing about strawberries is that they're still being grown here at all. As Victor Voth says, strawberries and people tend to like the same places, and regions such as the Santa Clara Valley and the Los Angeles Basin have lost most of their strawberry farms to offices and homes. Many growers learn to leapfrog urban sprawl. Kuni Shinta's parents sharecropped strawberries in Palo Alto in the 1920s; in the '50s, Shinta himself farmed in Sunnyvale in the Santa Clara Valley. When development surrounded him, he recalls, "I played the real estate game," selling off land to acquire acreage near Watsonville.

Environmental concerns also pose problems for growers. Except for organic farmers like the Skalls and Jim Cochran, growers depend on a chemical called methyl bromide to fumigate the soil before planting. But the EPA suspects that methyl bromide depletes the ozone layer, and may ban it—a disastrous idea in many growers' view. Growers also worry about increased competition from Mexico and Chile. "Our climate still gives us a unique advantage," says California Strawberry Commission president David Riggs. "But we may be losing it."

Even under the best circumstances, strawberry growing can be risky. "Every year you worry about the weather, about the economy," says Cochran. Strawberry shipper Don De Armond agrees: "It's a gambler's way of life. A guy has to make a lot in a good year to survive the bad."

Back at the Bob Jones Ranch, it's nearing noon. The overcast has lifted, and the berry fields shine in the mild sun. Workers will be picking strawberries here all this month and into June. Farther north, the harvest will continue into November. And then it will be time to start all over again. Doug Wagner looks over his fields. "Strawberry growing is an art," he says. "It's a challenge. You learn every day. But I don't think I'd do anything else. I still like strawberries." ∎

CHICKEN BREAST *wears a formal jacket of black and white sesame seed. The roasted meat is served hot on radicchio leaves along with a sesame-seasoned slaw.*

All dressed up in sesame seed

It's more than just decoration in these two salads

BLACK AND WHITE sesame seed, combined, make a handsome, crunchy coating for meats and cheeses.

The two kinds of sesame seed have the same rich, nut-like flavor. Black sesame seed, which is a bit chewier, is found in well-stocked supermarkets or Asian groceries.

Black and White Chicken with Sesame Slaw

½ cup rice vinegar

¼ cup firmly packed fresh cilantro (coriander), minced

3 tablespoons Asian sesame oil

2 tablespoons soy sauce

2 teaspoons Dijon mustard

4 chicken breast halves (about 1½ lb. total), boned and skinned

⅓ cup black sesame seed

⅓ cup white sesame seed

8 large radicchio leaves, rinsed and crisped

8 cups (about ½ lb.) finely shredded cabbage

Fresh cilantro sprigs

Mix vinegar, minced cilantro, sesame oil, soy sauce, and mustard. Rinse chicken, pat dry; place in a deep bowl. Pour half the vinegar dressing over chicken and turn pieces to coat. Cover and chill at least 1 hour or up to 1 day, turning occasionally. Cover and chill remaining dressing.

Put black and white sesame seed in a 7- to 8-inch frying pan over medium-high heat. Shake pan often until seed begins to pop and white seed is lightly browned, 8 to 10 minutes. Pour seed from pan into a shallow bowl; let cool.

Lift chicken from dressing-marinade, draining briefly; discard marinade. Coat each chicken piece thickly with seed, then lay slightly apart in a 9- by 13-inch pan. Bake, uncovered, in a 425° oven until meat is no longer pink in the thickest part (cut to test), 12 to 15 minutes.

On each of 4 dinner plates, arrange 2 radicchio leaves to form a large cup. Cut chicken into ½-inch slices. Arrange 1 breast half in each radicchio cup. Mix cabbage with half the reserved dressing and mound beside radicchio cups. Spoon remaining dressing over chicken. Garnish with cilantro sprigs. Serves 4.

Per serving: 461 cal. (47 percent from fat); 47 g protein; 24 g fat (3.7 g sat.); 16 g carbo.; 742 mg sodium; 99 mg chol.

Sesame-dressed Greens with Sesame-crusted Goat Cheese

1 log (5½ oz.) unripened chèvre (goat) cheese, chilled

⅓ cup black or white sesame seed

1 large egg white

1 head (about 5 oz.) butter lettuce, rinsed and crisped

1 small head (about 5 oz.) radicchio, rinsed and crisped

Sesame dressing (recipe follows)

2 teaspoons butter or margarine

Baguette slices (optional)

Cut goat cheese into 6 equal rounds. Pour sesame seed into a small, shallow bowl. In another small bowl, beat egg white to blend.

Coat 1 cheese round at a time with egg white. Drain cheese briefly, then coat with seed. Set slice on a plate. Repeat to coat remaining pieces of cheese and set slightly apart. If making ahead, cover and chill up to 4 hours. Tear lettuce and radicchio into bite-size pieces. In a large bowl, mix leaves with dressing, then spoon equally onto 6 salad plates.

In an 8- to 10-inch nonstick frying pan, melt 1 teaspoon butter over medium-high heat. When butter sizzles, add half the cheese slices and cook until bottoms are crusty, about 1 minute. With a spatula, turn rounds over and brown bottoms again, about 1 minute longer. As cooked, return cheese to plate and keep warm. Add remaining butter to pan and brown remaining cheese. Place 1 cheese slice on each salad and serve at once. Accompany with baguette slices. Serves 6.

Per serving: 208 cal.; (78 percent from fat); 7.5 g protein; 18 g fat (3.3 g sat.); 6.1 g carbo.; 214 mg sodium; 34 mg chol.

Sesame dressing. Mix 3 tablespoons **seasoned rice vinegar** (or 3 tablespoons rice vinegar and ¾ teaspoon sugar), 1 tablespoon **Asian sesame oil,** and 2 teaspoons minced fresh **ginger.** ■

By Christine Weber Hale

Mastering the mango

Here's how to choose, prepare, and eat the world's most popular fruit

WESTERNERS WHO'VE enjoyed the sweet-tart flavor and intriguing perfume of a perfectly ripe mango are all members of the world's largest fruit fan club.

Unfortunately for many of these fans, the enjoyment of mangoes is limited to restaurant meals. They may savor the exotic fruit's flavor—frequently described, if inadequately, as a combination of peach, pineapple, and apricot—but the struggle to free the fruit from the pit keeps them from serving it at home.

But anyone can master a mango: simply follow our pointers for choosing, preparing, cooking, and eating one. With mangoes now available in Western markets almost year-round, you'll have plenty of opportunities to enjoy them.

A PERFECT PICK

To choose a mango, first make sure that it has a floral scent; unripe fruit has no odor. Look for firm fruit. Although a ripe mango will give slightly to the touch—much as a peach or nectarine does—

don't buy soft or bruised fruit.

The colors of a ripe mango often resemble the hues of fruit sherbets: orange, raspberry, lemon, and lime. But although many aficionados believe a perfectly ripe mango's skin must show at least three of these colors, some varieties ripen to a rich golden yellow, while others stay green. And depending on the variety, the flesh inside is golden yellow to rosy orange.

Although mangoes are available almost year-round, their peak season is May through August. That's when

HOW NOT TO MANGLE A MANGO

To a novice, locating a mango pit can be a true mystery. But once you learn some mango anatomy, removing the pit is easy. To locate the pit, simply hold the mango with its narrower profile facing you and with the two plumper sides (cheeks) in your hands. The long, ½- to ¾-inch-thick pit runs the length of the fruit between the cheeks. Once you determine its location, follow our step-by-step directions for peeling and cutting the fruit.

1. *Cup the mango in one palm, then peel the skin from the flesh with a small, sharp knife.*

2. *After determining the pit's location, and allowing for its ½- to ¾-inch thickness, slowly cut through mango lengthwise down side of pit until fleshy cheek is completely cut off. Repeat on other side.*

3. *Cut remaining fruit from pit in thin slices; use in recipes that call for diced fruit, or serve as an appetizer. (Or suck the juicy flesh directly from the pit.)*

MANGO SALSA *tops tuna steak that has a chili-cumin crust. Tomatoes and bell pepper color the mango sauce. Recipe on page 108.*

MANGOES AND BLACKBERRIES *combine in an open-top pie.*

you'll find the largest, sweetest, and juiciest fruit. Mangoes vary widely in size; some types fit in the palm of your hand, while others grow to the size of a miniature football. Although their taste is similar, the larger fruit has more flesh in relation to the size of the pit.

Tommy Atkins and Haden varieties (available early May through August) are prized for their fiberless fruit. They are usually quite large, ranging from ¾ to 1 pound. Kent and Keitt are two late-summer varieties. Kent is small, sometimes with fibers that cling to the pit, which make it stringier and more difficult to cut and eat; the skin may be green when ripe. Keitt is the largest and meatiest mango variety, weighing from 1 to 1¼ pounds. Its skin also may stay green when ripe; the orange flesh has little fiber.

Voodoo Tuna with Mango Salsa

Tim Sullivan, executive chef at Epazote in Del Mar, California, works magic with an ahi tuna and mango entrée.

Voodoo sauce (recipe follows)

Mango salsa (recipe follows)

1 medium-size (½ oz.) dried ancho chili

1 teaspoon ground cumin

¼ teaspoon *each* salt and pepper

6 fillets (about 6 oz. each) ahi tuna

About 1 tablespoon olive oil

Lime wedges and mint sprigs (optional)

Prepare sauce and salsa. Seed and stem chili; spread apart to lay flat in a 9-inch-square pan. Bake in a 350° oven until just toasted, 6

to 8 minutes; watch carefully, as it burns easily. In a blender, whirl cooled chili until finely ground. Add cumin, salt, and pepper.

In a barbecue with a lid, ignite 60 mounded charcoal briquets on firegrate. Let burn until coals are barely covered with gray ash, about 15 minutes. Push coals into a single layer and set grill 4 to 6 inches above coals.

Meanwhile, rub all sides of tuna steaks with chili mixture and drizzle with oil. Place steaks on hot grill (you can hold your hand at grill level only 2 to 3 seconds). When steaks start to brown, about 4 minutes, turn with spatula; cook until just opaque on outer edge and just pink in center (cut to test), about 8 minutes total. Distribute warm voodoo sauce equally among 6 dinner plates; spread in a smooth layer. Place hot tuna steaks on sauce; spoon salsa over fish. Garnish with lime and mint. Serve immediately. Serves 6.

Per serving: 323 cal. (17 percent from fat); 43 g protein; 6 g fat (1.1 g sat.); 26 g carbo.; 312 mg sodium; 77 mg chol.

Voodoo sauce. Stem, seed, and crumble 2 large (¾ oz. total) **dried California** or New Mexico **chilies** and stem, seed, and mince 2 large (2 oz. total) **fresh jalapeño chilies.** Add to a 5- to 6-quart pan over medium-high heat along with 2 teaspoons **sesame oil,** 1 cup chopped **red bell pepper,** 1⅓ cups chopped **red onion,** and 1 tablespoon minced **garlic.** Cook, stirring often, until

vegetables are just tinged golden, about 5 minutes. Add 1 cup *each* chopped **mango** and chopped **Roma-type tomatoes,** 1 tablespoon minced **fresh ginger,** ⅓ cup **fresh-squeezed orange juice,** and ⅓ cup *each* **regular-strength chicken broth** and **rice vinegar;** bring to a boil. Cover, reduce heat, and simmer until very soft and well blended, about 1½ hours. In a food processor or blender, whirl mixture until smooth. With a wooden spoon, rub sauce through a fine metal strainer; discard residue. Stir in 2 teaspoons **fish sauce** and 1 teaspoon **soy sauce.** Use, or cover airtight and refrigerate up to 1 week.

Mango salsa. Combine 1 cup diced **mango,** ⅓ cup diced **canned roasted red peppers,** ½ cup diced **red onion,** 1 medium-size (¾ oz.) fresh **jalapeño chili** (stemmed, seeded, and minced), 2 tablespoons minced **fresh mint leaves,** and 1 tablespoon **fresh lime juice.** Cover and chill until ready to use, up to 4 hours.

Kitty's Mango Blackberry Pie

5 cups sliced mangoes (about 3 medium-size, 2½ lb. total)

2 cups blackberries (or blackberries and raspberries), rinsed and drained

⅓ cup *each* granulated sugar and firmly packed brown sugar

5 tablespoons all-purpose flour

2 tablespoons lime juice

Pastry dough (recipe follows)

In a large bowl, combine mangoes and berries. Sprinkle with sugars, flour, and lime juice. Gently mix to coat fruit evenly; set aside.

On a lightly floured board, roll chilled pastry dough into a 14-inch round. Place in a 9- or 10-inch decorative pie pan, letting pastry drape over edge. Evenly spoon fruit mixture into pastry; fold draped pastry toward center over fruit, pinching up to form a rim around pie.

Bake in a 350° oven until

THE EASIEST WAY TO EAT A MANGO

1. *Do not peel. After cutting cheeks from pit (see page 130), score flesh into ½- to ¾-inch squares, cutting down to, but not through, skin.*

2. *From bottom, gently push mango cheek inside out; start at one side and slowly move toward the other, pushing fruit cubes up and apart.*

3. *Eat fruit out of hand or cut chunks from skin to serve.*

crust is golden brown and filling bubbles in center, about 1½ hours. Cool on a rack. Makes 8 servings. —*Kitty Sullivan, pastry chef at Cilantro's and Epazote in Del Mar, California.*

Per serving: 433 cal. (37 percent from fat); 4.5 g protein; 18 g fat (4.4 g sat.); 66 g carbo.; 213 mg sodium; 0 mg chol.

Pastry dough. Combine 2 cups **all-purpose flour** and ¾ teaspoon **salt.** Using a pastry blender, cut ⅔ cup chilled **vegetable shortening** into flour mixture until it resembles small peas. Drizzle with 4 to 6 tablespoons **ice water** and mix with a fork until mixture forms a ball. Wrap dough in plastic wrap, flatten into a 6-inch disk, and chill at least 20 minutes or until the next day.

Grilled Asian-spiced Mango and Chicken

Ken Oringer, Chef de Cuisine for Silks restaurant at the Mandarin Oriental Hotel in San Francisco, serves squab rather than chicken; use whichever you prefer.

4 boneless, skinless chicken breast halves (1½ lb. total) or 4 squabs (4 lb. total), halved

Soy marinade (recipe follows)

2 large (2 lb. total) firm, ripe mangoes

2 medium-size (1 lb. total) oranges

1 tablespoon *each* ground coriander and Chinese five spice

¼ teaspoon *each* salt and pepper

6 cups (½ lb.) frisée greens, root ends trimmed, rinsed and crisped

8 cups (1 lb.) bite-size pieces butter lettuce, rinsed and crisped

Mango vinaigrette (recipe follows)

½ cup raspberries

Marinate chicken in the soy marinade for at least 4 hours or until the next day; turn occasionally.

Meanwhile, with a sharp knife, cut skin from mangoes. Following directions on page 130, cut 2 rounded cheeks from each pit. Trim remaining ½ inch of flesh from edge of each mango; mince these trimmings and reserve for mango vinaigrette (recipe follows). Cut peel and white membrane from oranges and discard. Slice each orange crosswise into 6 rounds. Cover and chill orange rounds until used.

Combine coriander, five spice, salt, and pepper. Lift chicken from marinade; place on a baking sheet (reserve marinade for basting). Set mango cheeks next to chicken. Sprinkle and pat chicken and mangoes all over with spice blend.

In a barbecue with a lid, ignite 60 mounded charcoal briquets on firegrate. Let burn until coals are barely covered with gray ash, about 15 minutes. Push coals into a single layer; set grill 4 to 6 inches above coals.

Place chicken and mango cheeks on hot grill (you can hold your hand at grill level only 2 to 3 seconds); baste with reserved marinade. Us-

GRILLED MANGO *adds sweet, smoky flavor to an Asian-spiced chicken salad with mango vinaigrette.*

ing a spatula, turn chicken and mangoes when they start to brown, about 5 minutes. Baste again and cover barbecue. Let chicken and mangoes cook until no pink remains when chicken is cut in thickest part, about 20 minutes; turn and baste chicken and mangoes every 5 minutes (depending on mango ripeness, cooking time may be less than for the chicken; remove mangoes when soft and seared).

Meanwhile, combine frisée, lettuce, and vinaigrette. Evenly divide among 4 dinner plates. Lay mangoes cut side down; slice each into ⅜-inch-wide slices, starting ½ inch from the top down through the wide bottom end. With a wide spatula, transfer the slices to the dinner plates atop greens.

Gently fan slices apart. Lay chicken and orange rounds next to mangoes; sprinkle servings with raspberries. Serves 4.

Per serving: 493 cal. (29 percent from fat); 43 g protein; 16 g fat (2.8 g sat.); 47 g carbo.; 1,362 mg sodium; 104 mg chol.

Soy marinade. In a large bowl, combine ½ cup **soy sauce** with ¼ cup **olive oil,** and 1 tablespoon *each* minced **garlic,** minced **fresh ginger,** crushed **juniper berries,** and grated **orange peel.**

Mango vinaigrette. Stir together ½ cup of the diced **reserved mango** (from the mango trimmings), ¼ cup **balsamic vinegar,** and 1 tablespoon *each* **olive oil** and **Dijon mustard.** ■

By Betsy Reynolds Bateson

QUICK TREATS FROM RIPE MANGOES

Mango pasta salad. Peel and slice 1 large mango. Mix slices with 3 cups cooked pasta, ⅓ cup minced cilantro leaves, 2 tablespoons *each* seasoned rice vinegar and lime juice, and 2 teaspoons Asian sesame oil; add salt and pepper to taste. Serves 4.

Mango granita. Whirl together 2 cups chopped mango, 1 cup guava juice, and ¼ cup fresh lime juice in a food processor. Pour into ice cube trays and freeze at least 2 hours. In food processor with motor running, add slightly defrosted cubes and

process until smooth. Serve, or freeze up to 2 weeks. Makes about 3½ cups.

Frozen mango-yogurt shake. Whirl together 1 cup chopped mango, ¾ cup orange juice, and ½ cup cooked sweet potato in a blender. Add 1 cup nonfat vanilla frozen yogurt; whirl until smooth. Serves 2.—*Daily's Fit & Fresh Restaurant, San Diego*

Tropical pops. Push wooden ice cream sticks through peeled mango cheeks; dip into melted dark chocolate. Place on baking sheet and drizzle with

melted white chocolate (chips or chopped bar suitable for melting). Freeze on sheet in single layer at least 2 hours or up to 2 weeks; cover with plastic when chocolate is firm. (Allow ½ cup dark chips and ¼ cup white chips for 2 pops. To drizzle white chocolate, place in a small zip-lock plastic bag and melt in microwave. Cut off 1 corner of bag; squeeze over dark chocolate.)

NILOUFER ICHAPORIA *tests the doneness of soufflé-topped potatoes. Other aromatic dishes (at left) include pepper water soup, mung beans with cilantro and chilies, and rice with mustard seed.*

PETER CHRISTIANSEN

Vegetarian sampler from India

High-flavor, low-calorie dishes to try on their own or as a whole menu

NILOUFER ICHAPORIA'S appreciation for the artful use of seasonings began at an early age. She and her boarding school classmates in Bombay, India, would fight over spices in the bottom of the soup pot the way American kids tussle over Halloween candy.

Now in San Francisco, Ichaporia finds the food of her childhood has virtues beyond its complex, inviting flavors. Many favorite dishes are vegetarian and low-calorie, qualities more and more cooks are looking for. Her recipe sampler includes the pepper water soup from her school days.

For authentic renditions, you will need to shop at an Indian grocery store. (Tamarinds are also available in Latino markets.) But you can get good results with suggested supermarket alternatives.

Indian Frying Pan Potato Soufflé

Sautéed potatoes with garlic, ginger, and chilies have a puffy egg topping (see photo above right). The dish is good hot or cool at dinner, or for breakfast.

1   large (½ lb.) onion, chopped
2   tablespoons minced fresh hot green chilies (Asian, serrano, or jalapeño)
4   large cloves garlic, minced or pressed
3   tablespoons minced fresh ginger
½   teaspoon ground turmeric
¼   cup salad oil
6   medium-size (about 2¼ lb. total) thin-skinned potatoes
4   to 6 large eggs, separated
¾   cup coarsely chopped fresh cilantro (coriander)
     Salt

You'll need a 10- to 12-inch frying pan (nonstick, if possible) with a snug-fitting domed lid. In the pan over medium-high heat, frequently stir onion, chilies,

garlic, ginger, and turmeric in oil until onion is limp, 8 to 10 minutes.

Peel potatoes, quarter lengthwise, and slice crosswise ¼ inch thick. Add to onion and stir often, uncovered, until potatoes are tender to bite, about 15 minutes. If potatoes stick, loosen with a little water and cook until water evaporates.

Shortly before potatoes are done, beat egg whites with a mixer until stiff, moist peaks form. Beat yolks separately just to blend; fold into whites.

Stir most of the cilantro into potato mixture. Spoon eggs onto potatoes; pour 2 tablespoons water into pan at the edge. Cover and cook over medium heat until soufflé springs back when gently pressed in the center, 8 to 10 minutes; sprinkle with remaining cilantro. Serve hot or at room temperature; add salt to taste. Serves 6 to 8.

Per serving: 217 cal. (40 percent from fat); 6.1 g protein; 9.7 g fat (1.6 g sat.); 27 g carbo.; 43 mg sodium; 106 mg chol.

Pepper Water Soup

The tart, tamarind-based soup makes a fine first course. To honor its vegetarian spirit, use water; for richer flavor, use half chicken broth.

¾ pound (about 20) dried tamarind pods; or ⅔ cup (about 3¾ oz.) tamarind paste (or brick) with seeds; or ⅔ cup cider vinegar and 2 tablespoons sugar

7 to 8½ cups water

3 large cloves garlic, minced or pressed

2 tablespoons cumin seed

1 tablespoon black peppercorns

1 tablespoon coriander seed

1 large (½ lb.) onion, chopped

1 dried California or New Mexico chili (4 in. long), stemmed and rinsed, in 5 pieces

2 tablespoons fresh or dried curry leaves (optional)

2 teaspoons salad oil

1 tablespoon black or yellow mustard seed

¾ cup tiny cherry tomatoes or halved large cherry tomatoes (optional)

3 tablespoons coarsely chopped fresh cilantro (coriander)

Salt

If using tamarind pods, remove most of the brittle shells. Place tamarind with seeds in a small bowl; pour 2 cups steaming hot water over fruit. Let stand until tamarind is soft, about 15 minutes. Rub mixture with fingers to release pulp from seeds. Pour mixture into a fine strainer set over a 2- to 3-quart pan; rub mixture to extract moisture and pulp. Discard residue. (Omit this step if using vinegar.)

To pan, add 5 cups water (if using vinegar, add 6½ cups water) and garlic.

In a blender or mortar with pestle, coarsely grind cumin, peppercorns, and coriander. Add spices to tamarind mixture; bring to a boil on high heat. Cover and simmer 15 minutes.

Meanwhile, in an 8- to 10-inch frying pan over medium heat, frequently stir onion, chili, and curry leaves in oil until onion is very limp, 10 to 15 minutes. Add mustard seed, and stir about 2 minutes. Scrape mixture into

PALETTE OF INDIAN *ingredients features, counterclockwise from right, tiny Asian chilies, cilantro, tomatoes, yellow mung beans, onion, block of tamarind, ginger, garlic, lime, and spices: coriander, black mustard seed, turmeric, cumin, and curry leaves.*

tamarind water. Add tomatoes; simmer until hot, about 2 minutes. Sprinkle with cilantro. Serve hot or at room temperature. Season to taste with salt. Serves 8.

Per serving: 60 cal. (35 percent from fat); 1.4 g protein; 2.3 g fat (0.2 g sat.); 10 g carbo.; 5.1 mg sodium; 0 mg chol.

Moong Dal with Cilantro

Dal is a satisfying dried-bean stew. This version is especially good with the yogurt rice (recipe on facing page). Cook with water to be authentic, or with chicken broth for extra flavor.

2 cups split, skinned mung beans (*moong dal*) or lentils, sorted of debris and rinsed

1 quart water or regular-strength chicken broth

¼ teaspoon ground turmeric

About 1 ounce fresh hot green chilies (6 Asian, or 1 serrano or jalapeño)

1 medium-size (5 oz.) onion, slivered

2 tablespoons minced ginger

1 tablespoon fresh or dried curry leaves (optional)

2 tablespoons salad oil

2 cups coarsely chopped fresh cilantro (coriander)

3 tablespoons lime juice

1 tablespoon sugar

Cayenne (optional)

Salt

In a 3- to 4-quart pan over high heat, bring beans, water, turmeric, and 1 whole chili to a boil. Cover and simmer until beans are barely tender to bite, about 20 minutes (about 25 minutes for lentils).

Meanwhile, in an 8- to 10-inch frying pan over medium-high heat, frequently stir remaining chilies, onion, ginger, and curry in oil until onion is limp, 8 to 10 minutes.

Add onion mixture and cilantro to beans. Simmer, covered, about 2 minutes. Stir in lime juice and sugar.

Remove chilies, if desired. Pour into a bowl; sprinkle lightly with cayenne. Add salt to taste. Serves 6 to 8.

Per serving: 230 cal. (16 percent from fat); 13 g protein; 4.1 g fat (0.6 g sat.); 37 g carbo.; 11 mg sodium; 0 mg chol.

Rice with Yogurt and Spices

Rice is enhanced with a potpourri of seasonings including curry leaves, an aromatic herb that looks like tiny citrus leaves.

The dish is good hot or cool; if it stands until cool the rice will absorb yogurt, so

you might want to add ½ to 1 cup more yogurt just before serving.

1 tablespoon minced fresh ginger

2 tablespoons minced fresh small hot green chilies (Asian, serrano, or jalapeño)

1⅓ cups unflavored nonfat or low-fat yogurt

2 teaspoons salad oil

2 tablespoons fresh or dried curry leaves (optional)

2 tablespoons black or yellow mustard seed

3½ cups hot cooked long-grain white rice

Fresh cilantro (coriander) sprigs

Salt

In a bowl, mix ginger, chilies, and yogurt. Pour oil into a 6- to 8-inch frying pan over medium-high heat. When oil is hot, add curry leaves and mustard seed; stir until seeds pop, about 1 minute.

Scrape seed mixture into bowl; add rice and mix gently. Serve hot or at room temperature. Garnish with cilantro sprigs. Add salt to taste. Serves 6 to 8.

Per serving: 167 cal. (12 percent from fat); 5.9 g protein; 2.3 g fat (0.3 g sat.); 30 g carbo.; 38 mg sodium; 0.9 mg chol. ∎

By Elaine Johnson

AN HERB SAUCE *bathes poached eggs, thin slices of prosciutto, tender herb biscuits, and spinach. Serve sparkling wine with this exceptional brunch dish.*

A better (for you) eggs Benedict

Perfect poached eggs on tender herb biscuits, with a lightened hollandaise sauce

I F YOU SAVOR SINKING a fork into a perfectly poached egg bathed in lemony sauce atop a tender biscuit, you'll appreciate herbed eggs Benedict. And although this variation of the popular brunch entrée isn't low-fat, it has a third less fat than the traditional dish.

Some butter is used to achieve the tender herb biscuits, but we've lightened up the sauce, which is far easier to prepare than a true hollandaise. Because of the robust flavor of the prosciutto, which replaces the traditional Canadian bacon, you need less than half the normal amount of meat.

There are several make-ahead options. You can pre-pare the eggs up to two days ahead, and clean the spinach and prepare the sauce a day in advance.

Herbed Eggs Benedict

12 poached eggs (directions on facing page)

Light hollandaise sauce (recipe follows)

Buttermilk herb biscuits (recipe follows)

¼ cup regular-strength chicken broth

1½ pounds spinach, rinsed and drained, stems trimmed

¼ pound thinly sliced prosciutto

Basil and parsley sprigs (optional)

Poach eggs up to 2 days before serving, make sauce up to a day before serving, and prepare biscuits (best if made the day served).

In a covered 10- to 12-inch nonstick frying pan over medium-high heat, cook broth and spinach until spinach wilts and all liquid evaporates, about 5 minutes. Remove from heat, cover, and keep warm.

Heat sauce if made ahead. Halve biscuits and place 2 halves, cut side up, on each of 6 dinner plates. Arrange prosciutto over biscuits. Gently lift spinach from pan, and place equally on plates beside biscuits. Top prosciutto with hot poached eggs, and pour about ⅓ cup warm sauce over each serving. Garnish with herb sprigs; serve at once. Serves 6.

Per serving: 612 cal. (46 percent from fat); 29 g protein; 31 g fat (15 g sat.); 56 g carbo.; 1,405 mg sodium; 486 mg chol.

Light hollandaise sauce. To a 2- to 3-quart pan, add 1½ cups **regular-strength chicken broth**, 1 cup **low-fat milk**, 1 tablespoon **butter** or margarine, 2 teaspoons finely chopped **fresh basil leaves** (or 1 teaspoon dried basil leaves), 1 teaspoon **Dijon mustard**, and ⅛ teaspoon **pepper**. In a measuring cup, combine ¼ cup **lemon juice** and 2½ tablespoons **cornstarch;** stir until cornstarch is dissolved. Stirring broth mixture with a wire whisk over medium-high heat, slowly add cornstarch mixture. Stir

GENTLY PRESS BISCUIT DOUGH *into a 1-inch-thick round. Then cut 3-inch biscuits, pressing leftover bits of dough together to cut more biscuits.*

SLOWLY ADD *the cornstarch–lemon juice mixture to sauce of milk, broth, and herbs, stirring with a wire whisk.*

constantly until mixture comes to a boil. Set aside and keep warm, or chill, tightly covered, up to 1 day.

Buttermilk herb biscuits. In a large bowl, stir together until thoroughly blended 2½ cups **all-purpose flour,** 1 tablespoon *each* **sugar** and **baking powder,** 1 tablespoon *each* chopped **fresh basil leaves** and **fresh parsley** (or 1½ teaspoons *each* dried basil leaves and dried parsley), ½ teaspoon **baking soda,** and ¼ teaspoon **salt.** Cut 7 tablespoons firm **butter** (or margarine) into chunks; add to flour mixture. With pastry blender, cut in butter until particles resemble rice. Add 1 cup **buttermilk;** stir with a fork until most of the dough sticks together. Turn dough out onto a lightly floured board, and turn gently to coat all surfaces with flour. Knead, making about 8 turns, just until dough sticks together.

Gently pat dough into a 1-inch-thick round. With a

POACHED EGGS

To make perfect poached eggs. In a 5- to 6-quart pan, bring about 2 quarts water to a boil. Heat-treat 6 **eggs** in shells by gently lowering, one at a time, into constantly boiling water. After 8 seconds, remove eggs in the same order as they were placed in the water. Repeat with 6 more eggs. Poach eggs at once, or chill up to 2 days.

To poach. In a 5- to 6-quart pan over high heat, bring 2 quarts **water** and 2 tablespoons **distilled white vinegar** to a gentle boil. Reduce the heat, maintaining a temperature that causes bubbles to form on the pan

WITH SLOTTED SPOON, *lift and drain poached egg, then transfer to a storage dish. Chill up to 2 days; reheat in hot water.*

bottom (one may pop on top occasionally). Holding as close to the water as possible, break each egg di-

rectly into the water (do not crowd eggs in pan; 4 or 5 eggs at a time are manageable). Cook until the eggs have the firmness you desire, about 4 minutes for soft yolks and firm whites (test by poking egg gently with a spoon tip).

To store. Lay poached eggs in a single layer in a baking dish, about 9 by 13 inches; cover with plastic wrap. Chill up to 2 days.

To reheat. Heat 2 quarts water in a 5- to 6-quart pan until just hot to touch; remove from heat. Add eggs; let stand 5 to 10 minutes, or until eggs feel hot. Lift from water with a slotted spoon, drain, and use.

flour-dusted 3-inch round cutter, cut straight down through dough, then lift straight up. Push dough scraps together; repeat process to make a total of 6 rounds. Place on a lightly

buttered 10- by 12-inch baking sheet. Bake in a 400° oven until tops are golden, about 15 minutes. Use warm. (If you want to make ahead, cool completely and wrap airtight; store at room tem-

perature. Shortly before serving, halve biscuits. Place biscuit halves, cut sides up, on a baking sheet; heat in a 300° oven until warm, about 5 minutes.) ∎

By Betsy Reynolds Bateson

Onion rings with fire

This restaurant specialty is worth making at home

WHILE DINING recently in a Santa Fe restaurant, I half-heartedly sampled an onion ring. Nothing new, I'd thought before tasting. I was wrong. The crisp, thin onion slice's chili flavor made me take a new look at this menu standby.

To experience the unique chili flavor of the onion rings I tasted, it's worth tracking down dried ancho and California or New Mexico chilies. These chilies are available in Latino markets, gourmet shops, and the international sections of some supermarkets. Many mail-order food catalogs also carry them.

However, even if you skip these particular chilies, you can come up with tasty onion rings. Just substitute 2 tablespoons chili powder.

Chili Onion Rings

1 medium-size (about ½ oz.) dried ancho chili

1 medium-size (about ¼ oz.) dried California or New Mexico chili

3 large (about 1½ lb. total) red or yellow onions

1 cup all-purpose flour

About 1 quart salad oil for frying

Salt (optional)

Stem and seed chilies; spread chilies flat in an 8- to 9-inch square pan. Bake in a 300° oven until just toasted, 5 to 8 minutes; watch carefully, as they burn easily. Cool. In a blender, whirl chilies until finely ground; set aside.

Peel and thinly slice onions; separate into rings. Place half the flour and ground chilies in a plastic bag, add half the rings, and shake to coat rings evenly with flour-chili mixture. Re-

peat with remaining flour, ground chilies, and onions.

In a deep 5- to 6-quart pan over high heat, bring about 1 inch salad oil to 325° on a thermometer. Add flour-coated onions, about ¼ of them at a time; cook, stirring often, until golden brown, about 5 minutes. The temperature of the oil will drop at first, then rise again as onions brown; regulate heat accordingly.

With a slotted spoon, remove onions and drain on paper towels. Serve warm, piled in a paper napkin–lined basket or plate; sprinkle with salt as desired. Makes about 6 cups, 12 servings.

Per ½-cup serving: 135 cal. (63 percent from fat); 1.8 g protein; 9.5 g fat (1.2 g sat.); 12 g carbo.; 6.1 mg sodium; 0 mg chol. ∎

By Betsy Reynolds Bateson

GOLDEN CRISP, *slender onion rings glisten with powdered ancho and California chilies.*

PETER CHRISTIANSEN

VEGETABLE CANNELLONI *combines mellow eggplant and sweet carrots with savory seasonings. Serve with grilled lamb.*

PETER CHRISTIANSEN

Discover the eggplant wrap

Baked slices enclose pork or carrot filling

WOOD STRIPS *on a damp towel help guide knife to make even slices.*

SOFT AND CREAMY roasted eggplant slices replace traditional pasta wrappers in these cannelloni dishes. The key to success is evenly cut eggplant. If not uniformly thick, the slices brown unevenly. For even slices, use this technique.

To slice eggplant, you need two narrow, unfinished, untreated wood strips. Each should be straight and relatively smooth, and measure ¼ inch thick, about 2 inches wide, and about 1 foot long.

To keep strips from slipping, spread a damp towel on a flat counter. Set eggplant on the towel and put a wood strip on each long side of the eggplant (see photo at left). Hold eggplant in place with one hand (keep fingers well above the knife) and slide a long, sharp knife flat along the strips to slice. Remove slices as each is cut.

Baked Eggplant Slices

2   medium-size (about 2½ lb. total) eggplant, each about 6½ inches long, stems trimmed

2   to 3 tablespoons olive oil

Slice each eggplant lengthwise into uniform ¼-inch-thick pieces (see preceding). Rub bottom of a 10- by 15-inch pan with 1 tablespoon oil (cook eggplant in sequence or use several pans). Lay slices in pan, rub lightly, then turn oiled sides up. Pieces shouldn't overlap. Bake in a 375° oven until well browned and soft when pressed, 35 to 45 minutes; remove slices as they brown. Use as directed in the following recipes.

Spiced Pork Cannelloni with Eggplant

Chinese salted black beans are in Asian groceries and some supermarkets.

Baked eggplant slices (recipe precedes)

½   cup regular-strength chicken broth

1   tablespoon soy sauce

2   teaspoons cornstarch

½   pound ground lean pork

2   tablespoons salted black beans (optional)

1   tablespoon minced fresh ginger

2   tablespoons slivered green onion

Peanut sauce (recipe follows)

Set aside the 12 largest baked eggplant slices; finely chop remainder.

Smoothly mix broth and soy with cornstarch.

In an 8- to 10-inch frying pan over medium-high heat, stir pork often until crumbly and well browned, about 5 minutes; drain off fat. Sort black beans of debris; rinse and mash beans. To pan, add beans, ginger, and broth mixture. Stir on high heat until boiling. Mix in chopped eggplant; set aside.

Lay reserved eggplant slices flat. Spoon cooked mixture equally onto slices. Pat filling to cover slices, leaving bare ½ inch at ends and ¼ inch on long sides.

Roll from cut end of slice to enclose filling. Place seam down in a 9- by 13-inch casserole; if making ahead, cover and chill up to 1 day. Bake, uncovered, in a 400° oven until hot in center, 15 to 25 minutes (20 to 30 minutes if chilled). Top with onion and peanut sauce. Serves 6.

Per serving: 273 cal. (63 percent from fat); 11 g protein; 19 g fat (4.8 g sat.); 17 g carbo.; 495 mg sodium; 28 mg chol.

Peanut sauce. Mix well ¼ cup **smooth peanut butter,** 2 tablespoons **berry jelly,** 2 tablespoons **rice** or cider **vinegar,** 1 teaspoon **soy sauce,** and ⅛ teaspoon **crushed dried hot red chilies.**

Eggplant and Carrot Cannelloni

Follow steps for making **spiced pork cannelloni with eggplant,** preceding, but prepare this filling instead of the meat mixture.

In a 10- to 12-inch frying pan over medium-high heat, mix 1 large (about ½ lb.) chopped **onion,** 2½ cups finely chopped **carrots,** 2 chopped cloves **garlic,** 1 tablespoon **soy sauce,** 1 teaspoon **cumin seed,** 1 teaspoon **mustard seed,** and ½ cup **water.** Stir often until liquid evaporates and browned bits stick to pan, about 12 minutes. Add ¼ cup **water** and stir to release browned bits; repeat this step 2 or 3 times, until vegetables are richly browned. Stir into pan 2 tablespoons **water** and chopped **eggplant;** remove from heat. Fill reserved 12 eggplant slices, and bake as directed. Omit peanut sauce and add salt to taste. Serves 6.

Per serving: 130 cal. (35 percent from fat); 3.2 g protein; 5.1 g fat (0.7 g sat.); 20 g carbo.; 387 mg sodium; 0 mg chol. ■

By Karyn I. Lipman

A blast of flavor zips through tofu stir-fry

While rum and red beans bake together

Now a vegetarian, Mary Lee Gowland misses the chewiness of meat, especially in Chinese dishes where beef, pork, lamb, poultry, and fish lend their unique textures to vegetable mixtures. In fried, firm tofu she has found an admirable protein alternative, both in texture and in nutritional value.

Although mild in flavor, tofu soaks up seasonings that emphasize its meaty texture. In Gowland's recipe, bok choy, bell pepper, and tofu— all essentially quite mild-tasting— become lively with the addition of garlic, green onions, soy sauce, and liquid hot pepper seasoning.

Spicy Bok Choy with Fried Tofu

6   to 8 ounces firm tofu

    About ¾ pound baby bok choy, rinsed and drained

1   tablespoon salad oil

2   cloves garlic, minced or pressed

4   green onions, ends trimmed and thinly sliced

1   large (about ½ lb.) red bell pepper, stemmed, seeded, and cut into thin slivers

2   tablespoons water

3   tablespoons reduced-sodium soy sauce

2   teaspoons sugar

1   teaspoon liquid hot pepper seasoning

1   teaspoon cornstarch mixed smoothly with 1 tablespoon water

2   cups hot cooked rice

Cut tofu into 1-inch-thick slices. Lay slices on towels and cover with more towels. Set a flat pan on the top towels; put a 1-pound can (such as a can of beans or tomatoes) on the pan. Let tofu drain 10 to 15 minutes.

Meanwhile, discard bruised or yellowed bok choy leaves. Cut each head in half lengthwise; if bases of bok choy pieces are thicker than 1 inch, cut portions in half lengthwise.

Cut tofu into 1-inch cubes.

Pour oil into a 12-inch frying pan or a wok over medium-high heat. When oil is hot, add tofu. Turn pieces with a spatula as needed until tofu cubes are golden brown. Transfer to paper towels to drain.

In pan, mix garlic, onions, red pepper, bok choy, and 2 tablespoons water. Cover and cook, stirring often, until bok choy stems are just tender when pierced, 3 to 5 minutes. Uncover and stir in tofu, soy sauce, sugar, hot pepper seasoning, and cornstarch mixture. Stir until sauce is boiling. Spoon onto hot cooked rice. Makes 2 servings.

Per serving: 545 cal. (25 percent from fat); 24 g protein; 15 g fat (2.2 g sat.); 81 g carbo.; 1,100 mg sodium; 0 mg chol.

M Gowland

Oakhurst, California

In New England, baked beans are standard Saturday night fare, and frugal cooks often present the cold leftover beans for breakfast.

The regional favorite also stars in fund-raising suppers held by churches and grange halls. Recipes vary, but most begin with dried white beans (navy or Great Northern) and include salt pork, brown sugar, molasses, and mustard. In Oregon, far from New England traditionalists, Richard Bogdanski uses red kidney beans and rum (which is, after all, a distillation of molasses, with its dark, exotic flavor but without its sweetness).

Rum Baked Beans

8   thick slices bacon (10 to 12 oz. total), cut into ½-inch pieces

1   large (8 to 10 oz.) onion, chopped

2   large cans (27 oz. each) reduced-sodium dark red kidney beans

1   cup firmly packed brown sugar

1   cup catsup

1   tablespoon red wine vinegar

½   teaspoon crushed dried mint

    About ½ cup dark rum

1   tablespoon mustard seed

½   cup prepared mustard

½   teaspoon liquid hot pepper seasoning

In a 5- to 6-quart ovenproof pan, stir bacon occasionally over medium heat until brown and crisp, 8 to 10 minutes. With a slotted spoon, transfer bacon to paper towels to drain.

Discard all but 1 tablespoon bacon fat in pan. Add onion to pan and stir often until onion is limp and faintly browned, 8 to 10 minutes. Stir in beans and their liquid, sugar, catsup, vinegar, mint, ½ cup rum, mustard seed, prepared mustard, and hot pepper seasoning. Stir well and heat until bubbling. Stir in bacon and cover pan.

Bake beans in a 300° oven for about 2 hours. Stir well and continue to bake, uncovered, until beans are thick, about 30 minutes, or until they are the consistency you like. Add, to taste, 1 to 3 tablespoons more rum. Makes 6 to 8 servings.

Per serving: 426 cal. (16 percent from fat); 16 g protein; 7.4 g fat (2.3 g sat.); 76 g carbo.; 1,199 mg sodium; 9.6 mg chol.

Richard Bogdanski

Grants Pass, Oregon

By Joan Griffiths, Richard Dunmire

SUNSET'S KITCHEN CABINET
Creative ways with everyday foods—submitted by *Sunset* readers, tested in *Sunset* kitchens

Cinnamon Bran Dollar Cakes
Chris Whipple, Pioneer, California

DOLLAR-SIZE *cinnamon bran pancakes are topped with fresh berries and syrup.*

2 cups *each* 100 percent bran cereal and hot water

½ cup *each* all-purpose flour and sugar

1½ teaspoons baking powder

1 teaspoon ground cinnamon

¼ teaspoon ground allspice

2 large eggs

About 1½ tablespoons salad oil

1 teaspoon vanilla

Maple syrup

Freshly sliced strawberries

In bowl of an electric mixer, stir together cereal and hot water; let stand a few minutes until liquid is absorbed.

Combine flour, sugar, baking powder, cinnamon, and allspice; set aside.

To cereal, add eggs, 1 tablespoon oil, and vanilla. Gradually add flour mixture; beat until smooth.

Lightly rub a 10- to 12-inch nonstick frying pan with remaining oil (use 2 pans for faster cooking), and heat over medium heat. Add 1 heaping table-spoon batter for each cake; cook cakes until both sides are browned, about 2 minutes per side. Keep cakes warm on a rack set on a 10- by 15-inch baking pan in a 250° oven. Serve with warm syrup and berries. Serves 6.

Per serving: 228 cal. (28 percent from fat); 5.9 g protein; 7 g fat (1.2 g sat.); 42 g carbo.; 296 mg sodium; 71 mg chol.

Party Garden Slaw
Judy Wong, Oakland, California

EASY SLAW SALAD *for a crowd uses precut vegetables and marinated artichokes.*

1 large head (about 1 lb.) iceberg lettuce, cored and shredded

2 cups *each* broccoli flowerets, shredded carrots, and shredded purple cabbage (Take advantage of prepared vegetables from the market.)

2 cups thinly sliced mushrooms

1 cup sliced radishes

½ cup (about 8) sliced mild Greek peppers

2 jars (6 oz. each) marinated artichoke hearts, liquid reserved from 1 jar

Honey-Dijon dressing (recipe follows)

In a large bowl, combine lettuce, mushrooms, broccoli, cabbage, carrot, radishes, peppers, and artichoke hearts; gently fold to mix. If making ahead, cover and chill up to 4 hours. To serve, pour dressing over vegeta-bles; mix to coat evenly. Makes about 18 cups, 14 to 18 servings.

Honey-Dijon dressing. In an empty artichoke jar, combine **reserved liquid from marinated artichoke hearts** with ⅓ cup **red wine vinegar,** 1 tablespoon *each* **honey** and **Dijon mustard,** and ½ teaspoon **pepper;** shake to mix well.

Per cup: 43 cal. (33 percent from fat); 1.7 g protein; 1.6 g fat (0.2 g sat.); 6.6 g carbo.; 129 mg sodium; 0 mg chol.

Quick and Lean Kung Pao Chicken
Tracy L. Johnston, San Marcos, California

KUNG PAO CHICKEN *offers bold, rich flavors and is low-fat; serve with rice.*

¼ cup regular-strength chicken broth

2 tablespoons *each* soy sauce and dry sherry

1 teaspoon *each* cornstarch and Oriental sesame oil

¾ pound chicken meat, cut into ¼- by 2-inch pieces

3 cloves garlic, chopped or slivered

¼ to ¾ teaspoon crushed dried hot red chilies

About 1 tablespoon salad oil

10 green onions, ends trimmed (6 cut into 1½-inch pieces, 4 reserved for garnish)

⅓ cup unsalted dry-roasted peanuts

About 4 cups hot cooked rice

Mix broth, soy, sherry, cornstarch, and sesame oil to blend; set aside. Mix chicken with garlic and chilies.

In a wok or 12-inch frying pan over high heat, heat 2 teaspoons oil until hot. Add half the chicken mixture; stir-fry until chicken has golden brown tinge and is no longer pink in thickest part (cut to test), about 3 minutes; re-move to a dish. Repeat with remaining chicken, adding oil as needed.

Return cooked chicken to wok; stir in reserved sauce, onion pieces, and nuts. Cook, stirring, until sauce bubbles and thickens, about 1 minute. Serve with rice; add onion garnish. Serves 4.

Per serving: 510 cal. (25 percent from fat); 28 g protein; 14 g fat (2.3 g sat.); 65 g carbo.; 599 mg sodium; 60 mg chol.

Pine Nut Macaroons

Marie Bergamini, Walnut Creek, California

2 large egg whites
⅓ cup sugar
1 tablespoon instant coffee
1 teaspoon vanilla
1 cup pine nuts or slivered almonds

With an electric mixer, beat egg whites until soft peaks form. Add sugar, 1 tablespoon at a time, beating until thoroughly incorporated, about 30 seconds after each tablespoon. Add instant coffee and vanilla; beat until coffee is completely dissolved. Gently fold in nuts.

Drop rounded tablespoons of batter onto greased and floured baking sheets, each 12 by 15 inches (you'll need 3 sheets). Bake in a 325° oven until golden, about 20 minutes; switch pan positions after 10 minutes. Let macaroons cool 5 minutes on sheets; transfer to racks to cool completely. Serve, or store airtight up to 3 days; freeze for longer storage. Makes about 2½ dozen.

Per cookie: 40 cal. (65 percent from fat); 1.4 g protein; 2.9 g fat (0.5 g sat.); 3.2 g carbo.; 3.9 mg sodium; 0 mg chol.

COFFEE-SCENTED, *pine nut–laced meringue bakes into flavorful macaroons.*

Fruited Pepper Steak Salad

Kim Chew, Pleasanton, California

½ pound flank steak
¾ cup dry white wine
3 tablespoons soy sauce
2 teaspoons Oriental sesame oil
2 medium-size jalapeño chilies, deveined, seeded, and minced
2 medium-size (1 lb. total) oranges
1 medium-size (7 oz.) apple
1 medium-size (7 oz.) red bell pepper
1 large head (about 1 lb.) romaine lettuce, rinsed and crisped
2 teaspoons salad oil
1 lime, cut in 4 wedges

Slice steak across the grain into ¼- by 2-inch strips. In a bowl stir together wine, soy sauce, sesame oil, and jalapeños. Add meat and marinate at least 15 minutes, or up to 2 hours.

Meanwhile, cut peel and white membrane from oranges; slice each crosswise into 6 rounds. Core apple; slice into 16 wedges. Devein and seed bell pepper; cut into 16 wedges. Evenly divide oranges, apple, and bell pepper among 4 dinner plates. Cut romaine into 4 wedges; place next to fruit.

Heat oil in a wok over high heat. Lift meat from marinade, drain, and cook until brown-tinged, about 3 minutes; spoon into a bowl. Add marinade to wok; bring to a boil. Spoon warm meat and cooking sauce over lettuce. Add lime for garnish. Serves 4.

Per serving: 282 cal. (35 percent from fat); 15 g protein; 11 g fat (3.2g sat.); 26 g carbo.; 825 mg sodium; 30 mg chol.

FRESH FRUITS *surround romaine wedges topped with warm stir-fried beef.*

Whole-wheat Pizza Dough

Merry Beyeler, Ramah, New Mexico

1 package active dry yeast
1 tablespoon sugar
1¼ cups warm water (110°)
2 tablespoons olive or salad oil
¾ teaspoon garlic powder
½ teaspoon salt
1½ cups whole-wheat flour
    About 1½ cups all-purpose flour

In a large bowl, sprinkle yeast and sugar over warm water; let stand 5 minutes. Stir in oil, garlic powder, and salt. Add whole-wheat flour; stir to blend. Beat with mixer until dough is elastic and stretchy, 3 to 5 minutes. Stir in 1½ cups all-purpose flour.

To knead with a dough hook, beat until dough is stretchy and cleans side of bowl, about 5 minutes; if dough is sticky, add more all-purpose flour, 1 tablespoon at a time.

To knead by hand, place dough on a floured board; knead until smooth and springy, 5 to 10 minutes.

Place dough in a bowl; cover airtight with plastic wrap. Let rise until doubled, about 45 minutes. Knead on a lightly floured board to expel air.

To use for pizza, press into a 10- by 15-inch baking pan with rim or a 14-inch round pizza pan. Cover with favorite toppings; bake at 400° until browned, 35 to 45 minutes. Crust serves 8.

Per serving of crust (without topping): 216 cal. (21 percent from fat); 6 g protein; 5.2 g fat (0.7 g sat.); 37 g carbo.; 139 mg sodium; 0 mg chol.

Compiled by Betsy Reynolds Bateson

THIS WHOLE-WHEAT *dough makes a grand crust; you choose the toppings.*

FOOD GUIDE

A grand trifle, a lesson in meat, creams with Latin culture, and a good wine with a gray name

By Jerry Anne Di Vecchio

One warm June evening in Bologna, I was dining alone in a legendary restaurant. The host, attentive to the comfort of his guests, sat down to chat with me. As a result, I came away with the recipe for this marvelous dessert. It resembles a trifle, but outdoes the best of them. And the recipe is so simple, it stuck in my head—along with other pleasant memories.

In the beginning, I had to make my own mascarpone. Now you can buy it—or use crème fraîche, which works as well. And I have discovered that whipping cream does the job, too. I used to bake the pound cake, but it's much quicker to buy it fresh or frozen, and the results don't suffer.

The essence of this dessert—excellent even without the berries piled on top—is a combination of foams. (For an egg-safe variation, omit the eggs and sugar and whip up 1 package [4.4 oz.] pavlova meringue mix with sugar and water as directed; do not bake.) The foams, folded gently together, are sandwiched between cake slices saturated with the liqueur or juice of your choice. But if, like me, you can't decide which choice is ideal, just keep experimenting. It's a delicious task.

BACK TO BASICS

Butterfly meats for speed

A boned and butterflied leg of lamb is a great barbecue favorite, but it's not the only meat for butterflying. In last year's August Food Guide (1995 *Recipe Annual*, page 146), I butterflied a beef rib-eye roast to make a quick-cooking steak. And any hunk of boneless meat, from beef or pork roasts to a turkey breast, can be cut that way, too. Occasionally, there's a gasp from kitchen onlookers when I'm seen taking a knife to a gorgeous roast, laying it out flat with long cuts. But as I spread the cuts open to make the piece of meat wider and thinner, the benefit of such boldness is evident. Butterflying not only creates more area for sauces and marinades to stick to the meat, but also creates more surface to brown—and the thinner meat cooks

A TASTE OF THE WEST

Bolognese Berry Cream Dessert

1   pound cake (10¾ oz.), thawed if frozen

    About ⅓ cup liqueur, wine, or fruit juice (choices follow)

4   large eggs, separated

¼   teaspoon cream of tartar

½   cup granulated sugar

1   cup mascarpone, crème fraîche, or whipping cream

4 to 6 cups berries (blackberries, blueberries, boysenberries, olallieberries, raspberries, and strawberries, in any combination)

Powdered sugar

Cut cake into ⅛- to ¼-inch-thick slices. Choose a wide bowl (at least 10-cup size) and using ½ the cake, slightly overlap slices to cover bottom and evenly around bowl sides (slices won't reach the rim). Moisten the cake with about ½ the liqueur.

In a deep bowl using a mixer on high speed, whip egg whites with cream of tartar until foamy. Continue to beat at high speed, gradually adding ¼ cup granulated sugar, then whip until whites hold stiff peaks.

In another deep bowl (no need to wash beaters), whip yolks on high speed with remaining ¼ cup granulated sugar until they are about triple in volume. Scrape yolks into bowl with whites. In the bowl used for yolks, whip mascarpone, crème fraîche, or whipping cream at high speed until it holds distinct peaks. With a whisk, fold (do not beat) whipped cream into egg mixture until there are very few lumps. Scrape mixture into cake-lined bowl and gently spread to make level. Cover (as much as you can) with remaining cake slices. Sprinkle cake with remaining liqueur. Cover and chill at least 4 hours or up to 1 day (filling gets firmer as it stands).

Rinse and drain berries. Uncover dessert and mound berries on cake; dust with powdered sugar. Scoop portions onto individual plates.

Makes 8 to 10 servings.

Per serving: 322 cal. (53 percent from fat); 5.7 g protein; 19 g fat (4 g sat.); 33 g carbo.; 161 mg sodium; 184 mg chol.

Liqueur, wine, or fruit juice choices—pick one: **madeira; marsala; sherry; muscat dessert wine** such as Essensia (an orange muscat) or Muscat Canelli; **late-harvest wine** such as Johannisberg Riesling or Gewürztraminer; **flavored liqueur** such as orange, apricot, raspberry, hazelnut, or almond; or **fruit juice** such as orange or raspberry.

much, much faster.

Another advantage is that one big piece of meat is easier to manage on the grill than many little ones.

Butterflying sounds more complicated than it is. These step-by-step illustrations show you where to make butterflying cuts in a leg of lamb; a boned roast such as beef rib-eye, cross-rib, tenderloin, or New York strip, or a boned pork loin or tenderloin; and even a whole or half turkey breast.

To butterfly: The cut doesn't have to follow the grain of the meat (on a steak or chop, make the cut horizontally). Each cut should be made through the middle of a thick part of meat (be careful not to cut the piece apart). Push the cuts open and down to flatten the meat. Where you want the meat thinner, repeat the step, always dividing the thick parts equally. For easy handling on the grill, I usually run a couple of metal skewers parallel through the longest dimension of the meat.

Nice rice vinegar

Rice vinegar, plain or seasoned (salt and sugar added), has become a staple in my kitchen. Most rice vinegars have Japanese names, but many are made here and they're in most supermarkets. A characteristic common to all rice vinegars is a mild, slightly sweet flavor. Sugar makes the seasoned version even smoother. You know the taste if you've ever eaten sushi—rice vinegar gives the rice that subtle and distinctive tang.

Wine lovers, especially, have come to appreciate rice vinegar in salad dressings because it does not have the sharp acetic aroma present in wine, cider, and white distilled vinegars.

But my pleasure in rice vinegar goes beyond sushi and green salads. It has become one of my favorite no-fat seasonings.

A good splash of rice vinegar with some minced fresh ginger makes a baked potato or sweet potato taste even better than butter does. I also brush vinegar on ears of corn and sprinkle them with salt.

And I actually yearn for this no-fat rice vinegar salad dressing on all kinds of other foods—cold asparagus, shrimp and grapefruit, Belgian endive, sliced pears, sliced tomatoes, celery root, crab, tuna, and, yes, potatoes. Once made, the dressing can be chilled indefinitely.

Rice vinegar dressing. Mix **rice vinegar** (about ¼ cup) with enough **fish sauce** (*nuoc mam* or *nam pla*) or soy sauce (1 to 2 tablespoons) to make it a little salty, enough **sugar** (2 to 3 teaspoons) so it no longer stings your tongue, and a generous sprinkling of minced **fresh ginger** (at least 1 tablespoon). Makes about ⅓ cup.

Per tablespoon: 16 cal. (0 percent from fat); 0.5 g protein; 0 g fat; 2.9 g carbo.; 119 mg sodium; 0 mg chol.

Seasoned rice vinegar, with its sweet finish, makes this really hot mustard that goes extremely well with barbecued meats—butterflied, perhaps.

Cook the mustard to get rid of the raw taste and texture—it's easy in the microwave.

Sweet-hot rice vinegar mustard. In a glass measuring cup, mix ¼ cup **dry mustard,** 2 tablespoons **water,** and 1 tablespoon **honey.** Let stand 10 minutes to get rid of the mustard's natural bitterness. Stir in 3 to 4 tablespoons **seasoned rice vinegar** and cook on high (100 percent) in a microwave oven until mixture bubbles at edges, 1½ to 2 minutes; stir several times. Serve warm or cool. Store airtight up to 5 days and stir before using. Makes ⅓ cup.

Per tablespoon: 41 cal. (33 percent from fat); 1.2 g protein; 1.5 g fat (0 g sat.); 6 g carbo.; 179 mg sodium; 0 mg chol.

Delicious Latin creams

When I think of cream I think first of England. The food halls of London's Harrods department store have so many kinds of creams, the selection makes me dizzy. Clearly, cream is not a one-dimensional

BUTTERFLYING MEATS

Boned leg of lamb
Leg, boned, opens to make a heart shape. Butterflied, it gets much wider.

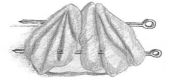

Boned roasts
Use any boned beef or pork roast. This rolled beef cross-rib is opened and butterflied, making a long rectangle.

Turkey breast
Use a boned whole breast with skin to hold halves together, or a boned half breast, skinned if you like. Butterfly meat to even out thickness.

LUCY I. SARGEANT

LATIN-STYLE CREAMS *can be sweet or sour, thick or thin. They make delicious alternatives to whipping or sour cream.*

food. Nor do the English have a monopoly on variety. I first enjoyed Latin-style creams in Mexico, and have since bought many domestically made products in the Los Angeles area, Arizona, and New Mexico. Now I find them in Mexican and other Latino markets in Central California, and producers tell me they are regularly shipping their products to other parts of the West where Latin foods are sold.

Latin-style creams are especially worth looking for at this time of year, when summer fruits beg for such good company. And understanding what you are buying is easier now because of nutrition labeling. Names kept me confused for a long time because they're not standardized (regulations, however, are in the works). Check labels for fat content: 30 to 40 percent, like whipping cream, is needed if you want to whip creams or cook them without having them curdle.

Creams range from sweet to tart and from thin to thick. They come unflavored or salted. Cultures are added to develop specific flavors and textures, as for regular buttermilk and sour cream.

You can expect to find some or all of the following creams in a well-stocked Latino market. They cost from $2.75 to $4.25 (or more where supply is limited) for 15 to 16 ounces, depending on the type of cream. When in doubt, shake the container gently to determine the cream's consistency.

Crema Mexicana has the same amount of butterfat (or more) as whipping cream. It can be sweet and pourable like whipping cream, or delicately tart and very thick like crème fraîche.

Crema Mexicana agria is as thick as sour cream, with similar fat content (15 to 20 percent), has a similar tartness, and is salted.

Crema fresca casera translates loosely as *home-style fresh cream.* It's a sweet, pourable whipping cream.

Crema Centroamericana is as rich as, or richer than, whipping cream. It can be liquid and sweet, or thick, rich, and tangy. Some brands are labeled soft-ripened cheese. To me, this version is much like mascarpone and can be used in its place—to make the Bolognese Berry Cream Dessert on page 118, for example.

Crema Centroamericana acida has the consistency, tang, and fat content of sour cream; it's also salted.

Jocoque is Mexican-style sour cream, but its fat content may be the same as, or less than, regular sour cream. Some labels describe it as salted buttermilk, but it's thicker; some call it a thin sour cream. The taste of this product ranges from mildly tart to refreshingly sharp.

Grigio or Gris with Pinot means more than gray

The way to make sure you fall in love with Pinot Grigio at first sip is to have a bottle with lemony veal at one of Il Cortile's courtyard tables on a warm evening in Venice.

But you need not go to all that trouble and expense. Pinot Grigio—Pinot Gris in France—is one of those wines that is right at home anywhere. All you need is a bucket of steamed clams, a bowl of spaghetti bolognese, a platter of chicken, or, to be sure, a plate of *la piccata di vitello.*

At the top of its form, Pinot Gris has a dusty perfume almost as reminiscent of flowers as of fruit. Pinot Gris is a paler-hued sport of Pinot Noir; those who have smelled one of the old roses in a fine old red Burgundy have some idea of what to expect.

In texture, Pinot Gris that lean toward a refreshing briskness come from cool places such as Alsace, the Alto Adige, and Oregon's Willamette Valley. Silkiness better describes those from sunnier zones such as Italy's Umbria or California's Temecula district.

From Umbria northward, Italians make Pinot Grigio as a varietal wine, adding a regional name as a further hint of its character. Most French Pinot Gris comes from Alsace under the varietal name, a recent replacement for the traditional Tokay d'Alsace.

In this country, grape and varietal wine go by either Pinot Gris or Pinot Grigio. Oregon's young wine industry launched Pinot Gris here, and remains the leader. California is catching up well enough that both states now produce worthy contenders.

An oaky style of winemaking insults this variety's airy delicacy, though a faint trace of wood does the wine no harm. But steering clear of oak makes the wine more companionable with food and helps keep the price down. Look for 1993s or 1994s, for their freshness.

Americans to try ($10 to $14):

Callaway Temecula Pinot Gris; King Estate Oregon Pinot Gris, Estate Reserve (not the pale-flavored basic bottling); Knudsen Erath Willamette Valley Pinot Gris.

Italians to seek, mostly at specialty wine shops ($8 to $14):

i Mesi Trentino Pinot; Pinot Grigio del Umbria; F. Peccorari Isonzo Pinot Grigio; Tiefenbrunner Alto Adige Pinot Grigio; Marco Felluga Collio Pinot Grigio.

Ambassadors from France ($14 to $23):

Hugel Pinot Gris Cuvée Traditionelle; Kuentz-Bas Pinot Gris Cuvée Tradition; Andre Ostertag Reserve; Trimbach Reserve. ■

Yakima Valley
BARBECUE

Winery owners celebrate their Merlot and their bountiful region with an easygoing dinner built around wine, lamb, and early-summer produce

GENTLE JUNE BREEZES, HINTING OF HOT, DRY DAYS TO COME, FLOAT seductive scents through Yakima Valley. And at Chinook Wines, in the southeast end of the valley outside Prosser, Washington, the tang of sagebrush from Horse Heaven Hills is also in the air, along with the musky perfume of young wine grapes.

Winery owners Kay Simon and Clay Mackey entertain at the winery and live nearby. For them, this season is a time of celebration. After two years in the barrel and six months in the bottle, their signature Merlot is ready for release. Yakima Valley's hot days, cool nights, extra sunshine (about 2 hours a day more in summer than California gets), loamy soil,

By Linda Lau Anusasananan
and Jena MacPherson

Photographs by
Rex Rystedt

fresh produce (left). Merlot tasting and barbecue feast prepared by Kay Simon and Clay Mackey (above) is at the couple's winery.

ON THE SHADED LAWN beside the tasting room, Clay Mackey bastes leg of lamb with Merlot marinade.

and—maybe—the latitude it shares with Burgundy and Bordeaux in France unite to produce fine varietal grapes. Wines made from them consistently receive domestic and international recognition. Valley conditions also have established the region's reputation as Washington's fruit and vegetable basket. In addition to grapes, about 100 other commercial crops grow here, including apples, asparagus, cherries, hops, mint, peaches, and peppers.

When Simon and Mackey invite family, friends, and their grape growers to the first official tasting of their Merlot—noted for its smooth, early drinkability and its aging potential—they serve dinner outdoors.

The winery is the perfect setting: tall evergreens shade the white clapboard wine-tasting cottage, the generous lawn where winery visitors picnic, the wine storage building, and the red barn where the wine is made.

The menu Simon and Mackey prepare reflects the bounty of the Northwest. To emphasize the purpose of the gathering, the winery's Merlot is blended into many of the dishes.

From Mackey's perspective, "long, warm days are meant for barbecuing." He butterflies a leg of lamb from Ellensburg, bathes it in a Chinook Merlot marinade, then grills it.

While guests mingle around the barbecue, they nibble on tender asparagus spears, so fresh they have the just-cut herbaceous scent.

When the lamb comes off the grill, the buffet is ready. Simon, the winemaker and a talented cook and gardener, has made salad with baby lettuce leaves gathered from two raised beds just a few steps from the house and the big red barn. Bing cherries, from the orchard thriving beside the wine-tasting cottage, are also part of the salad.

Lentils for the make-ahead casserole come from the Palouse region to the northeast—a world source for this legume. Nutty white Cougar Gold cheese, also made in the Palouse, tops the curried lentils and famous Walla Walla sweet onions.

Simon's hazelnut-laden biscotti also contain Merlot; more of the red wine is sipped with the cookies and used for dunking them.

MENU
for a Yakima Valley
BARBECUE

Asparagus and Mustard Vinaigrette

Cherry Cheese Salad

Grilled Merlot Lamb

Baked Curried Lentils

Hazelnut Merlot Biscotti

Chinook Wines Merlot

THE DINNER THAT KAY SIMON AND Clay Mackey present with their Merlot tasting may vary a little from year to year, but the focus is always on lamb and early-summer produce. The foods in this menu for 8 to 10 are available throughout the West—even if the ingredients don't come from your own backyard.

Most of the preparation can be started a day ahead. About an hour or less before serving, put the lentil casserole in the oven to bake or reheat, grill the butterflied lamb leg, and mix the salad.

Asparagus and Mustard Vinaigrette

4 pounds asparagus

　　Mustard vinaigrette (recipe follows)

Snap off and discard tough ends of asparagus. In a 6- to 8-quart pan, bring about 3 quarts water to a boil over high heat. Add asparagus and cook, uncovered, until just tender when pierced, 3 to 5 minutes. Drain and immediately immerse in ice water. When cool, drain well. (If making ahead, cover and chill up to 1 day.) Arrange spears on a platter and offer vinaigrette for dipping. Serves 8 to 10.

Per serving: 121 cal. (82 percent from fat); 3 g protein; 11 g fat (1.4 g sat.); 4.1 g carbo.; 38 mg sodium; 0 mg chol.

Mustard vinaigrette. In a blender or food processor, combine ¼ cup **red wine vinegar**, 1 clove **garlic**, 1 tablespoon **Dijon mustard**, ½ teaspoon **pepper**, and ½ teaspoon **sugar**; whirl until garlic is minced. With motor on, add ½ cup **salad** or olive **oil** in a slow, thin stream. Blend in **salt** to taste. (If making ahead, cover and chill up to 1 day.) Makes ¾ cup.

Cherry Cheese Salad

¾ cup thinly sliced mild red onion

2 tablespoons lemon juice

3 quarts bite-size pieces mixed salad greens or mesclun, rinsed and crisped

1 quart bite-size pieces radicchio, rinsed and crisped

1 pound dark sweet cherries such as Bing, pitted

　　Merlot dressing (recipe follows)

¾ cup (¼ lb.) packed blue cheese, coarsely crumbled

　　Salt and pepper

In a small bowl, combine onion with 2 cups water and lemon juice; chill 15 to 30 minutes. Drain well.

In a large bowl, combine onion, salad greens, radicchio, cherries, and dressing; mix lightly. Sprinkle salad with cheese and season with salt and pepper to taste. Serves 8 to 10.

Per serving: 135 cal. (54 percent from fat); 4.2 g protein; 8.1 g fat (2.8 g sat.); 12 g carbo.; 186 mg sodium; 8.5 mg chol.

Merlot dressing. Whisk together 3 tablespoons *each* **Merlot**, fruity **extra-virgin olive oil**, and **raspberry vinegar**, and 1½ teaspoons *each* **honey** and **Dijon mustard**.

Grilled Merlot Lamb

Mackey likes to lay a few soaked chunks of fruit wood from the couple's orchard on the coals for a sweet fragrance as the meat cooks.

½ cup soy sauce

½ cup Merlot

½ cup dry white wine

4 cloves garlic, pressed or minced

½ cup chopped fresh or 2 tablespoons dried oregano leaves

2 tablespoons coarsely chopped fresh or 1 tablespoon crumbled dried rosemary leaves

1 tablespoon coarsely ground pepper

1 leg of lamb (5 to 6 lb.), boned, butterflied, and fat trimmed

　　Oregano and rosemary sprigs (optional)

　　Salt

Combine soy sauce, Merlot, white wine, garlic, chopped oregano, chopped rosemary, and pepper in a 9- by 13-inch baking dish. Add lamb and turn to coat with marinade. Cover and chill at least 6 hours or up to 1 day, turning meat over several times.

Lift lamb from marinade and place on a barbecue grill 4 to 6 inches above a solid bed of medium-hot coals or gas heat (you can hold your hand at grill level only 3 to 4 seconds). Cook, turning as needed to brown meat evenly, until a thermometer inserted in thickest part of leg reaches 135° to 140° for rare (thinner portions will be well done), 30 to 45 minutes. Brush meat occasionally with marinade up until the last 10 minutes of cooking. Transfer meat to a platter; keep warm and let rest 5 to 15 minutes. Garnish with sprigs of fresh oregano and rosemary. Thinly slice meat. Add salt to taste. Serves 8 to 10.

Per serving: 216 cal. (35 percent from fat); 31 g protein; 8.5 g fat (3 g sat.); 1.5 g carbo.; 487 mg sodium; 97 mg chol.

(Continued on page 126)

REGIONAL INGREDIENTS are the theme for this meal: valley asparagus (left) for the appetizer, a casserole of lentils and Cougar Gold cheese from the Northwest's Palouse region, a salad of greens and cherries from the garden, and local lamb.

MERLOT TO THE LAST. With hazelnut biscotti and garden-warm strawberries, more wine to sip completes the dessert.

Hazelnut Merlot Biscotti

¾ cup hazelnuts

½ cup (¼ lb.) butter or margarine, at room temperature

¾ cup sugar

2 large eggs

2 tablespoons Merlot

1 teaspoon vanilla

2 cups all-purpose flour

1½ teaspoons baking powder

¼ teaspoon salt

Place nuts in a 9- to 10-inch-wide pan. Bake in a 325° oven until nuts are golden under the skin, 15 to 20 minutes. Pour nuts onto a towel and rub to remove loose skins. Let nuts cool, lift from towel, and discard brown skins. Coarsely chop nuts.

In a large bowl, beat butter and sugar until well blended. Beat in eggs until fluffy. Beat in Merlot and vanilla.

Mix flour, baking powder, and salt. Add flour mixture and nuts to butter mixture, stir, then beat until well blended.

With a spoon, drop ½ the dough in dollops down the length of an oiled 12- by 15-inch baking sheet, keeping dough at least 1 to 1½ inches from center of pan. Repeat with remaining dough on opposite side of pan. With floured hands, pat each portion into a flat log about ¾ inch thick. Bake in a 325° oven until logs are lightly browned on top, about 25 minutes. Remove from oven and let cool about 5 minutes.

On the pan, cut logs crosswise into ½-inch-thick slices. Tip slices over onto a cut side (it may take a little juggling to keep them all on the pan; the cookies touch).

Return cookies to oven and bake until the biscotti are browned, 20 to 25 more minutes. Transfer biscotti to racks until cool. Serve or store airtight up to 1 week. Makes about 4 dozen.

Per cookie: 63 cal. (47 percent from fat); 1 g protein; 3.3 g fat (1.3 g sat.); 7.5 g carbo.; 49 mg sodium; 14 mg chol. ■

Baked Curried Lentils

1 tablespoon olive oil

2 large (about 1 lb. total) Walla Walla or other onions, chopped

2 cloves garlic, pressed or minced

1 tablespoon Madras curry powder

5 cups regular-strength chicken broth

1 pound (about 2⅓ cups) lentils

1 cup (about ¼ lb.) shredded Cougar Gold or other white cheddar cheese

In a 5- to 6-quart pan, combine oil, onions, and garlic; stir over high heat until onions are tinged with brown, about 8 minutes. Stir in curry powder. Add broth and bring to a boil.

Sort and discard debris from lentils. Rinse lentils, drain, and add to broth. Cover and simmer until lentils are tender to bite, 30 to 35 minutes. If mixture is soupy, boil uncovered until liquid is just below surface of lentils; stir often. Pour lentils into a shallow 2½- to 3-quart casserole. (If making ahead, cool, cover, and chill up to 1 day.) Bake, covered, in a 350° oven until lentils absorb most of the liquid, about 30 minutes (if chilled, 1 to 1¼ hours). Uncover and sprinkle with cheese. Bake until cheese melts, about 5 minutes. Serves 8 to 10.

Per serving: 245 cal. (25 percent from fat); 18 g protein; 6.9 g fat (3 g sat.); 32 g carbo.; 137 mg sodium; 12 mg chol.

THE MERLOTS OF YAKIMA VALLEY

These wineries rank Merlot as one of their best wines, and they welcome visitors. You'll find some of these wineries' Merlots in good wine shops; others are in limited supply even at the winery. Area code is 509.

Blackwood Canyon Vintners, Route 3, Box 2169H, Benton City 99320; 588-6249. 10 to 6 daily.

Chateau Ste. Michelle, W. Fifth & Avenue "B," Grandview 98930; 882-3928. 10 to 4:30 daily.

Chinook Wines, Wine Country and Wittkopf roads, Prosser 99350; 786-2725. Noon to 5 Fridays through Sundays, or by appointment.

Columbia Crest Winery, Columbia Crest Rd., Box 231, Patterson 99345; 875-2061. 10 to 4:30 daily.

Covey Run Vintners, 1500 Vintage Rd., Zillah 98953; 829-6235. 10 to 5 daily.

The Hogue Cellars (across from Chinook Wines), Wine Country and Lee roads, Prosser 99350; 786-4557. 10 to 5 daily.

Hyatt Vineyards Winery, 2020 Gilbert Rd., Zillah 98953; 829-6333. 11 to 5 daily.

Kiona Vineyards Winery, Route 2, Box 2169E, Benton City 99320; 588-6716. Noon to 5 daily.

Oakwood Cellars, Route 2, 2321 Demoss Rd., Benton City 99320; 588-5332. Noon to 6 Saturdays and Sundays, or by appointment.

Portteus Vineyard & Winery, 5201 Highland Dr., Zillah 98953; 829-6970. Noon to 5 daily.

Seth Ryan Winery, Sunset Rd. and State Highway 224, Benton City 99320; 588-6780. 11 to 6 Saturdays and Sundays.

Staton Hills Winery, 71 Gangl Rd., Wapato 98951; 877-2112. 11 to 5:30 daily.

Tefft Cellars, 1320 Independence Rd., Outlook 98938; 837-7651. Noon to 5 Fridays through Mondays, or by appointment.

Washington Hills Cellars, 111 E. Lincoln Ave., Sunnyside 98944; 839-9463. 11 to 5:30 daily.

Yakima River Winery, 1657 N. River Rd., Prosser 99350; 786-2805. 10 to 5 daily.

A SAVORY FILLED FOCACCIA *paired with a salad makes a delicious casual meal.*

A new spin on focaccia

Entertain friends with this wonderful specialty bread from Napa

FOCACCIA, THE FLAT and tender Italian bread, has been turned on its side—and rolled up.

Like traditional focaccia, the base here is moist bread scented with olive oil. But the standard sprinkle of toppings is replaced with a savory treasure of fillings: sweet caramelized onions, smoky *pancetta*, and herbed cheeses and chard.

We discovered these individual meal–size breads at the Cantinetta at Tra Vigne restaurant in the Napa Valley, and enjoyed them on a picnic.

Prepare stuffed focaccia when you have a few hours to enjoy the process and a receptive audience to savor the results. They can also be made a day ahead, or frozen.

Spiral Stuffed Focaccia

This dough doesn't rise before baking.

1 pound pancetta or Canadian bacon, sliced ¼ inch thick

2 packages active dry yeast

1 cup warm water (110°)

1½ tablespoons sugar

3 tablespoons extra-virgin olive oil

1½ teaspoons salt

1 cup cold low-fat milk

5¼ to 5½ cups all-purpose flour

Cheese-chard filling (recipe follows)

Onion filling (recipe follows)

1 tablespoon cornmeal

About 3 tablespoons beaten egg

Place pancetta in a single layer in a 10- by 15-inch rimmed baking pan. Bake in a 350° oven until light brown but not crisp, 20 to 25 minutes. Discard fat; let cool.

In a bowl, sprinkle yeast over water; let stand until dissolved, about 5 minutes. Add sugar, oil, salt, and milk. Stir in 5 cups of the flour. Turn onto a lightly floured board and knead, adding flour as required to prevent sticking, until dough is smooth and no longer sticky, 8 to 10 minutes.

Let dough rest 10 minutes. On a lightly floured board, knead a few turns to expel air. Reflour board and roll dough into an evenly thick 12- by 24-inch rectangle. Spread cheese filling over dough, then arrange pancetta on top; scatter with onion filling.

Working from a long side, roll up dough. Pinch long seam closed. Cut into 8 equal pieces. For each, along 1 cut side gently stretch dough to enclose filling, pinching along center to form a seam.

Sprinkle 2 baking sheets, each 12 by 15 inches, with cornmeal. Evenly space focaccia seam side down on sheets, then press gently to flatten to about 2 inches high. Brush with egg.

Bake in a 350° oven until deep golden, 35 to 40 minutes; switch pan positions halfway through baking. Let cool on a rack at least 30 minutes; serve warm or at room temperature. If making ahead, chill airtight up to 1 day, or freeze. Makes 8.

Per focaccia: 673 cal. (29 percent from fat); 34 g protein; 22 g fat (7.5 g sat.); 85 g carbo.; 1,485 mg sodium; 76 mg chol.

Cheese-chard filling. Half-fill a 5- to 6-quart pan with water and bring to a boil over high heat. Put in ⅔ pound **Swiss chard.** Cook until stems are pliable, about 1½ minutes; drain, rinse with cool water, and pat very dry. Coarsely chop.

In a bowl, mix chard, 1½ cups **part-skim ricotta cheese,** 1 cup grated **parmesan cheese,** 1½ teaspoons chopped **fresh sage leaves** or ¼ teaspoon dried sage, ¾ teaspoon chopped **fresh thyme** or ¼ teaspoon dried thyme, ¼ teaspoon **ground nutmeg,** and **pepper** to taste.

Onion filling. In a 10- to 12-inch frying pan over medium heat, occasionally stir 6 cups thinly sliced **onions,** 2 tablespoons **extra-virgin olive oil,** and 2 teaspoons minced **garlic** until onions are very soft and deep golden, 30 to 35 minutes. Add 2 teaspoons chopped **fresh thyme** or ½ teaspoon dried thyme, and **pepper** to taste. ∎

By Elaine Johnson

GREAT DISHES for a
LOW-FAT
SUMMER

For a lean, lazy dinner, serve grilled turkey breast and apricots with hearty, make-ahead barley salad.

BY LINDA ANUSASANANAN • BETSY REYNOLDS BATESON • CHRISTINE WEBER HALE • ELAINE JOHNSON
PHOTOGRAPHS BY NOEL BARNHURST

S tay cool, eat light, take it easy. That's what everyone wants out of summer, right? Well, at *Sunset,* we decided you might like some help with the food part of the equation. We've put together 21 low-fat recipes to take you through a healthy summer—and one that certainly won't be dull. Salmon? Yes. Desserts? Sure. Pasta? Of course. The looks, taste, and satisfaction of these dishes don't even hint at their low fat content.

In fact, you might adapt a few of our trimming techniques to your own favorite dishes: use broth instead of butter to moisten pasta; use low-fat and nonfat yogurt instead of mayonnaise and sour cream (or at least use part yogurt) for creamy dressings and dips; grill or roast instead of sautéing; choose fat-trimmed lean cuts; season foods vividly with herbs, chilies, and citrus; and focus on fruit for dessert.

For more low-fat recipes, look to *The Best of Sunset Low-Fat Cook Book* (1994; $17.95) and two new *Sunset* cookbooks, *Low-Fat Stir-Fry* (1995; $9.99) and *Low-Fat Vegetarian* (1995; $9.99). And finally, a new column on everyday low-fat cooking begins next month (see page 163).

Slide hot grilled lamb balls or chicken chunks off skewers into pocket bread, then add the final seasonings.

LIGHT BITES BEFORE DINNER Simple spreads? Yes. And bolder ideas, too

THE IDEAL APPETIZER TAKES THE edge off hunger but doesn't make a significant dent in calories allocated for dinner. Two basics of a summer cook's repertoire—a hot grill and an abundant supply of produce—are all you need to turn out appetizers that meet these criteria.

Give fat-stripped chicken chunks or lean lamb-bulgur balls a quick turn on the barbecue for smoky enrichment. Load fresh fruit and shrimp salad into lettuce wrappers. And create creamy spreads and dips that depend on puréed roasted vegetables, not fat, for their rich texture and flavor.

And why not think beyond dinner? The chicken, lamb, and shrimp dishes all suit lunch for a light main dish, and the spreads are ideal for snacks anytime.

Skewered Lamb Balls with Lime Sauce

½ cup bulgur (cracked wheat)

1 cup boiling water

½ pound ground lean lamb

1 teaspoon ground coriander

1 clove garlic, minced

¼ teaspoon *each* salt and pepper

¼ cup lime juice

2 tablespoons *each* minced fresh cilantro (coriander) and basil leaves

6 small (4 in. wide) pocket breads, cut in half crosswise, or 3 (6 to 7 in. wide) pocket breads, quartered

In a bowl, mix bulgur and boiling water and let stand until bulgur is tender to bite, about 15 minutes. Drain and squeeze excess moisture from bulgur.

Mix bulgur with lamb, ground coriander, garlic, salt, and pepper. Divide into 24 equal portions and shape each into a ball. Thread 3 balls onto each of 8 metal skewers. Squeeze each ball into a 1½- to 2-inch oval.

Lightly oil a barbecue grill over a solid bed

of hot coals or gas grill on high heat (you can hold your hand at grill level only 2 to 3 seconds); lay skewers on hot grill. Close lid on gas grill. Cook to brown meat well, about 6 minutes total; turn skewers over once.

In a small dish, combine lime juice, minced cilantro, and basil. Transfer skewers to a tray. Pull hot meat off skewers and put into pocket bread, adding lime sauce. Makes 6 appetizer servings.

Per serving: 195 cal. (26 percent from fat); 11 g protein; 5.6 g fat (2.1 g sat.); 26 g carbo.; 265 mg sodium; 25 mg chol.

Orange-Cumin Chicken Pockets

Boned, skinned chicken thighs marinated in orange juice with cumin seed and chilies become flavorful barbecued nuggets.

About ⅔ pound boned, skinned chicken thighs (4 to 6 total)

2 teaspoons grated orange peel

⅔ cup orange juice

1 clove garlic, minced or pressed

1 teaspoon cumin seed, coarsely crushed

¼ teaspoon crushed hot dried red chilies

6 small (4 in. wide) pocket breads, cut in half crosswise or 3 (6 to 7 in.) pocket breads, quartered

1 cup shredded iceberg lettuce

Unflavored nonfat yogurt

Salt and lime wedges

Cut out and discard lumps of fat from thighs; rinse meat and pat dry. Cut meat into 24 equal pieces and combine in a bowl with orange peel and juice, garlic, cumin, and chilies; mix gently. Cover and chill at least 15 minutes or up to 1 day.

Thread 4 chicken chunks onto each of 6 metal skewers; reserve the marinade.

Lightly oil a barbecue grill over a solid bed of hot coals or gas grill on high heat (you can hold your hand at grill level only 2 to 3 seconds); lay skewers on hot grill. Close lid on gas grill. Cook, turning and basting several times, until chicken is browned and no longer pink in center (cut to test), 5 to 6 minutes total.

Slide chicken chunks into pocket bread halves. Add lettuce, yogurt, salt, and juice of lime wedges, to taste. Makes 6 appetizer servings.

Per serving: 151 cal. (14 percent from fat); 13 g protein; 2.4 g fat (0.5 g sat.); 19 g carbo.; 197 mg sodium; 42 mg chol.

Sweet Garlic Spread

Spread onto slices of crusty baguettes.

1 head garlic (about ¼ lb.)

½ teaspoon olive oil

¾ cup low-fat ricotta cheese

2 tablespoons gorgonzola cheese or other blue cheese, crumbled

¼ cup chopped fresh chives

Tiny shrimp and papaya chunks, seasoned and served Asian-style in tender lettuce leaves, can play double-duty in larger portions as a salad.

1 tablespoon *each* minced fresh basil leaves and parsley

½ teaspoon minced fresh rosemary leaves

Salt

Cut garlic head in half crosswise. In a square 8- to 9-inch pan, smear oil in a small area and set garlic halves, cut side down, on oiled section. Bake in a 375° oven until garlic is soft when pressed and cut sides are browned, about 40 minutes.

Let garlic cool. Use or, if making ahead, cover and chill up to 1 day. Squeeze garlic cloves from skin; discard skin. In a bowl, mash cloves smoothly, then add ricotta cheese, gorgonzola cheese, chives, basil, parsley, and rosemary, and mix well. Add salt to taste. Use, or chill airtight up to 1 day. Makes 1 cup.

Per 2 tablespoons spread: 47 cal. (17 percent from fat); 4.2 g protein; 0.9 g fat (0.4 g sat.); 5 g carbo.; 53 mg sodium; 1.6 mg chol.

Papaya Shrimp Tumble

⅓ cup lime juice

¼ cup chopped fresh cilantro (coriander)

¼ cup thinly sliced green onions

1 or 2 fresh jalapeño chilies, stemmed, seeded, and minced

1 teaspoon sugar

1 small (1 lb.) firm-ripe papaya, peeled, seeded, and cut in ½-inch cubes

½ pound tiny shelled cooked shrimp, rinsed and well drained

Fish sauce (*nuoc mam* or *nam pla*)

About 24 butter lettuce leaves, rinsed and crisped

In a bowl, mix lime juice, cilantro, onion, chili, and sugar. Stir in papaya, shrimp, and fish sauce to taste. Pour into shallow dish and surround with lettuce leaves. Scoop papaya mixture into lettuce cups and hold to eat. Makes 6 to 8 appetizer servings.

Per serving: 52 cal. (7 percent from fat); 6.6 g protein; 0.4 g fat (0.1 g sat.); 6.1 g carbo.; 67 mg sodium; 55 mg chol.

Spiced Eggplant Dip

For a mix of spices you can use instead of the Chinese five-spice powder, combine ¼ teaspoon *each* ground cinnamon, ground ginger, and crushed anise seed.

2 eggplant (about 1¼ lb. each)

2 cloves garlic, chopped

2 tablespoons chopped fresh ginger

¾ teaspoon Chinese five-spice powder

¼ teaspoon cayenne

3 to 4 tablespoons reduced-sodium soy sauce

2 tablespoons chopped fresh cilantro (coriander)

Cracker bread or water crackers, sliced cucumbers, and red bell peppers

Spread lean vegetable blend lavishly. Its bold flavor and underlying sweetness develop as the ingredients roast.

Set eggplant in a 9- to 10-inch square pan and pierce each eggplant deeply several times with a fork. Bake in a 425° oven until eggplant is very soft when pressed, about 45 minutes. Let cool. Pull off and discard skin, stem, and any large seed pockets. Put eggplant pulp in a colander and press gently to remove excess liquid. In a food processor or blender, whirl eggplant pulp, garlic, ginger, five-spice, and cayenne until smoothly puréed. Mix in soy sauce to taste. Mound mixture in a bowl and garnish with cilantro. Serve with cracker bread and vegetables. Makes about 2 cups.

Per ¼ cup: 37 cal. (2 percent from fat); 1.7 g protein; 0.1 g fat (0 g sat.); 8.4 g carbo.; 230 mg sodium; 0 mg chol.

Roasted Vegetable Spread

Slather this spread onto toast or over hot corn on the cob, use as a dip for fresh vegetables, or spoon generously onto baked potatoes or hot pasta.

½ teaspoon salad oil

2 large (about 1 lb. total) red onions, chopped

2 small (about ¾ lb. total) firm-ripe tomatoes, cored and chopped

4 cloves garlic, chopped

1 cup canned roasted red peppers, drained and chopped

2 tablespoons minced parsley

   Salt and pepper

Rub a 12- by 15-inch pan with oil and place onions, tomatoes, and garlic in it. Bake in a 450° oven until most of the liquid has evaporated and vegetable edges are tinged with brown, about 45 minutes; turn vegetables with a wide spatula every 15 minutes. Let cool.

In a blender or food processor, whirl roasted vegetables, red peppers, and parsley until smoothly puréed; scrape container sides as needed. Add salt and pepper to taste. Mound roasted vegetable spread in a small bowl. Serve or, if making ahead, cover airtight and chill up to 4 days. Makes 1½ cups.

Per 2 tablespoons: 28 cal. (10 percent from fat); 0.9 g protein; 0.3 g fat (0 g sat.); 5.8 g carbo.; 31 mg sodium; 0 mg chol.

FEASTS FROM THE GRILL...
SALMON, TURKEY, CHICKEN, AND MORE

Take your pick and match them with salads of potatoes, brown rice, barley, lentils, and quinoa

TIMING. IT'S ALWAYS A CHALLENGE, especially after a stressful day or when guests are expected. But here's an easy way to stay in control. Less than a half-hour before you plan to eat, fire up the barbecue—allow about 20 minutes for charcoal, 10 for gas. Then put the star of the meal on to grill. The moment it's perfectly cooked, bring forth a platter partially laden with a handsome, made-ahead salad—filling enough to complete the main part of the meal—and place the hot entrée alongside.

Such a presentation is even more appealing when it's seasonal and low in fat: brown sugar– and soy–glazed salmon, smoke-enriched corn and tomatoes, apricot-basted turkey breast, yogurt-marinated spicy chicken legs, and citrus-chutney pork tenderloin all meet these standards.

The salads—made with potatoes, brown rice, barley, lentils, or quinoa, and full of fresh summer produce—stand well on their own and can be prepared a day ahead.

Grilled Salmon with Potato and Watercress Salad

3 pounds small (each about 2 in. wide) red thin-skinned potatoes

1 cup thinly sliced red onion

1 cup seasoned rice vinegar

About ½ pound watercress, rinsed and crisped

1 salmon fillet, about 2 pounds

1 tablespoon soy sauce

1 tablespoon firmly packed brown sugar

2 cups alder or mesquite wood chips, soaked in water

Salt

In a 5- to 6-quart pan, bring about 2 quarts water to a boil over high heat; add

potatoes. Cover and simmer over low heat until potatoes are tender when pierced, 15 to 20 minutes. Drain and immerse in cold water. When potatoes are cool, drain well. Use or, if making ahead, cover and chill up to 1 day.

Soak the onions about 15 minutes in cold water to cover. Drain and mix onions with rice vinegar. Cut potatoes in quarters; add to onions.

Trim tender watercress sprigs from stems, then finely chop enough of the coarse stems to make ½ cup (discard extras or save for other uses). Mix chopped stems with potato salad. Mound watercress sprigs on a large oval platter with potato salad alongside; cover and keep cool.

Rinse salmon and pat dry. Place, skin side down, on a piece of heavy foil. Cut foil to follow outlines of fish, leaving a 1-inch border. Crimp edges of foil to fit up against edge of fish. Mix soy sauce with brown sugar and brush onto the salmon fillet.

On a charcoal barbecue. Mound and ignite 50 to 60 charcoal briquets on the firegrate of a barbecue with lid. When briquets are spotted with gray ash, about 20 minutes, bank ½ of the coals on each side of the firegrate. Drain wood chips and sprinkle equally onto mounds of coals. Place grill 4 to 6 inches above coals.

On a gas barbecue. Turn gas heat to high. Place wood chips in the barbecue's metal smoking box or in a small shallow foil pan, and set directly on the heat in a corner. Close lid until barbecue is hot, about 10 minutes. Adjust gas for indirect cooking (no heat down center).

Lay fish on center of grill, not over coals or flame. Cover barbecue (open vents for charcoal) and cook until fish is barely opaque in thickest part (cut to test), 15 to 20 minutes. Transfer fish to a platter with salad. Add salt to taste. Serve hot or cool. Makes 6 servings.

Per serving: 439 cal. (19 percent from fat); 34 g protein; 9.4 g fat (1.4 g sat.); 54 g carbo.; 1,062 mg sodium; 77 mg chol.

Lightly smoked salmon fillet, with glaze of

brown sugar and soy, slides onto platter with cool potato and watercress salad to make a whole meal.

Grilled corn and tomatoes, complemented by mushroom and rice salad with caper dressing, make an all-vegetable dinner.

Grilled Corn with Mushroom Pilaf

1 teaspoon olive oil

½ cup thinly slivered shallots

½ pound mushrooms, thinly sliced

3 cups packaged precooked long-grain brown rice

3½ cups vegetable broth or regular-strength chicken broth

½ cup lemon juice

3 tablespoons drained capers, chopped

3 tablespoons Dijon mustard

¾ teaspoon coarsely ground pepper

1 large (about ¾ lb.) red bell pepper, stemmed, seeded, and diced

½ cup chopped fresh basil leaves or parsley

Large romaine lettuce leaves, rinsed and crisped

6 medium-size (about 10 oz. each) ears of corn

6 large (about ¼ lb. each) Roma-style tomatoes, cut in half lengthwise

Salt

Pour oil into a 3- to 4-quart pan over high heat; add shallots and mushrooms, and stir until mushrooms begin to brown, about 5 minutes. Stir in rice and 2½ cups broth; bring to boiling over high heat. Cover and simmer over low heat until rice is tender to bite, 5 to 7 minutes. Let cool.

Combine 1 cup broth, lemon juice, capers, mustard, and ground pepper. If making ahead, cover and chill caper dressing and rice mixture separately up to 1 day.

Stir ¾ cup caper dressing, bell pepper, and basil into rice mixture. Line a large platter with lettuce leaves. Mound rice salad on lettuce; cover and keep salad cool.

Pull husks back from corn, leaving attached; discard silks, and rinse ears. Lay corn and tomatoes on a hot barbecue grill over a solid bed of hot coals or high heat on a gas grill (you can hold your hand at grill level 2 to 3 seconds); close lid on gas grill. Turn corn and tomatoes as needed to speckle with brown, 10 to 15 minutes. Place corn and tomatoes on platter beside rice salad. Spoon remaining dressing over corn, tomatoes, and mushroom pilaf. Add salt to taste. Makes 6 servings.

Per serving: 342 cal. (13 percent from fat); 9.9 g protein; 5.1 g fat (0.4 g sat.); 74 g carbo.; 927 mg sodium; 0 mg chol.

Barbecued Turkey Breast and Apricots

2 cups barley, rinsed and drained

4 cups regular-strength chicken broth

2 cups thinly sliced celery

1 cup thinly sliced green onions

1 can (5 oz.) sliced water chestnuts, drained

1 teaspoon grated orange peel

3/4 cup orange juice

2 tablespoons lemon juice

2 tablespoons sweet-hot mustard

1/4 teaspoon ground nutmeg

1 cup unflavored nonfat yogurt

2 boned turkey breast halves (about 3 lb. total), skinned

1/4 cup apricot jam

6 to 8 (about 1 1/2 lb. total) firm-ripe apricots

4 cups arugula leaves or baby lettuce greens, rinsed and crisped

In a 3- to 4-quart pan, bring barley and broth to a boil over high heat. Cover and simmer over low heat until barley is tender to bite, about 30 minutes. Let cool. Mix barley with celery, green onions, and water chestnuts. If making ahead, cover and chill up to 1 day.

Combine orange peel, orange juice, lemon juice, mustard, and nutmeg; stir 3/4 cup of this mixture into yogurt. Add yogurt dressing to barley and mix well. Mound barley salad on a platter; cover and keep cool.

On a charcoal barbecue. Mound and ignite 50 to 60 charcoal briquets on the firegrate of a barbecue with lid. When the briquets are spotted with gray ash, about 20 minutes, bank 1/2 of the coals on each side of the firegrate.

On a gas barbecue. Turn gas heat to high and close lid until barbecue is hot, about 10 minutes. Adjust gas for indirect cooking (no heat down center).

Set a foil drip pan in center of firegrate or between gas flames. Set turkey on grill over drip pan. Cover barbecue (open vents for charcoal) and cook 15 minutes.

Meanwhile, mix remaining 2 tablespoons of the orange mixture with apricot jam. Cut apricots in half and remove pits. Align fruits, cut sides up, and run a long metal skewer through sides of apricots.

When turkey has cooked 15 minutes, brush with apricot jam mixture. Lay apricots on grill directly over heat. Cover barbecue and continue to cook, turning apricots once, until the fruit is hot and a thermometer inserted in thickest part of turkey reaches 155°, about 10 minutes longer. Brush cut sides of apricots with jam mixture. Transfer turkey and fruit to platter beside barley salad. Garnish with arugula. Thinly slice turkey and serve hot or cool. Serves 6 to 8.

Per serving: 436 cal. (7 percent from fat); 43 g protein; 3.6 g fat (1 g sat.); 61 g carbo.; 182 mg sodium; 89 mg chol.

Barbecued Chicken Legs with Spiced Lentils

1 cup unflavored low-fat yogurt

2 teaspoons cumin seed

1 teaspoon *each* crushed dried hot red chilies, ground turmeric, and ground coriander

6 whole chicken legs (drumstick with thigh, about 4 lb. total)

3/4 pound (about 2 cups) lentils

5 cups regular-strength chicken broth or vegetable broth

1/4 cup lime juice

1 tablespoon minced fresh ginger

1 European cucumber (about 3/4 lb.)

1/2 cup thinly sliced green onions

1/2 cup chopped mint leaves

Lettuce leaves, rinsed and crisped

Mint sprigs

Salt

In a large bowl, mix 1/2 cup yogurt, 1 teaspoon cumin, and 1/2 teaspoon *each* dried chilies, turmeric, and coriander. Pull off and discard skin and fat from chicken. Rinse chicken, pat dry, and add to yogurt mixture; mix to coat well. Cover and chill at least 30 minutes or up to 1 day, turning chicken over occasionally.

Meanwhile, sort lentils and discard debris. Rinse lentils, drain, and place in a 3- to 4-quart pan. Add broth, remaining cumin, dried chilies, turmeric, and coriander. Bring to a boil, cover, and simmer until lentils are just tender to bite, 30 to 40 minutes. Drain, reserving liquid.

Set lentils aside and return liquid to pan; boil, uncovered, over high heat until reduced to 1/3 cup. Mix the cooking liquid, lime juice, and ginger with lentils. If making ahead, cover and chill up to 1 day.

Cut 1/2 the cucumber into 1/2-inch cubes. Stir cucumber cubes, green onions, and chopped mint into lentils. Line a platter with lettuce leaves. Mound lentil salad on lettuce. Thinly slice remaining cucumber. Cover salad and cucumber slices, and keep cool.

Lift chicken from marinade and place on a lightly oiled hot grill 4 to 6 inches above a solid bed of hot coals or use a gas grill on high heat (you can hold your hand at grill level only 2 to 3 seconds). Close lid on gas grill. Cook chicken, turning to brown evenly, until meat at bone is no longer pink (cut to test), 25 to 30 minutes. Transfer chicken to platter with lentils. Garnish with mint sprigs and cucumber slices. Add the salt and remaining yogurt to taste. Makes 6 servings.

Per serving: 485 cal. (26 percent from fat); 54 g protein; 14 g fat (3.9 g sat.); 40 g carbo.; 239 mg sodium; 118 mg chol.

Grilled Pork Tenderloins with Quinoa Salad

You'll find quinoa with the grains in well-stocked supermarkets.

2 pork tenderloins (3/4 to 1 lb. each)

1/4 cup *each* orange juice and lemon juice

2/3 cup chopped Major Grey chutney

1 tablespoon soy sauce

1 1/2 cups quinoa

1 teaspoon salad oil

1 large (1/2 lb.) onion, finely chopped

3 cups regular-strength chicken broth

2 cups seedless grapes, halved

2 large (1 lb. total) firm-ripe nectarines, pitted and diced

1/3 cup chopped fresh mint leaves

Salt

Large butter lettuce leaves, rinsed and crisped

Fresh mint sprigs

Trim fat and thin silvery membrane from tenderloins. Fold thin ends of meat under for uniform thickness. With cotton string, tie folded ends, and set meat in a bowl.

Stir together orange juice, lemon juice, and chutney. Combine 1/4 cup of the mixture with soy sauce and coat pork with it. Cover pork and chill, turning occasionally, at least 1 hour or up to 1 day. Cover and chill remaining chutney dressing up to 1 day.

Place quinoa in a fine strainer; rinse thoroughly under cold running water. Pour quinoa into a 5- to 6-quart pan over medium heat. Stir often until quinoa is golden brown, 10 to 12 minutes. Add oil and onion, and stir often, 2 to 3 minutes. Add broth and bring to a boil; cover and simmer until quinoa is tender to bite, 12 to 15 minutes. Let cool. If making ahead, cover and chill quinoa mixture up to 1 day. With a fork, stir 1 cup chutney dressing into quinoa salad. Mix grapes, nectarines, and mint with salad; season to taste with salt. Line a platter with lettuce leaves. Mound salad on lettuce; cover and keep cool.

Lift pork from marinade and save marinade. Place pork on a hot barbecue grill 4 to 6 inches above a solid bed of medium-hot coals or medium-high on a gas grill (you can hold your hand at grill level for only 3 to 4 seconds). Close lid on gas grill. Turn meat to brown evenly, brushing often with reserved marinade up until the last 5 minutes of cooking. Cook meat until a thermometer inserted in center of thickest part registers 150° to 155° and meat is no longer pink in thickest part (cut to test), 18 to 22 minutes. Lay pork beside salad and thinly slice. Garnish with mint sprigs. Serve pork, hot or cool, with salad. Serves 6.

Per serving: 485 cal. (18 percent from fat); 32 g protein; 9.8 g fat (2.5 g sat.); 72 g carbo.; 368 mg sodium; 69 mg chol.

Cold turkey, tomatoes, and capers are mixed into pasta salad seasoned with rice vinegar.

PASTA SALADS THAT FILL YOU UP

Vinegar and yogurt dressings keep them lean

OLD-FASHIONED MACARONI FOR salad has been replaced by pasta in dozens of shapes, sizes, colors, and flavors. And the newest combinations can be remarkably light, even as main dishes. With mayonnaise out and low-fat dressings in, most of the calories in these pasta salads, even with moderate additions of meat or fish, come from complex carbohydrates. The nutritional analysis completely contra-

dicts the old saw that rich ingredients and good taste are inseparable.

For summer meals, these pasta salads offer two pluses. They're fast. You can boil the pasta and cool it down in minutes, ready to season. Or you can make the salads well ahead and store them in the refrigerator—they are equally fresh tasting the next day. If you can't find pastas like orechiette or orzo, you can always substitute macaroni.

Orechiette Salad with Turkey

1   pound dried orechiette or radiatore (curled) pasta

6   tablespoons seasoned rice vinegar

    About ¼ cup regular-strength chicken broth

2   pounds firm-ripe Roma-type tomatoes, cored and chopped

3   tablespoons prepared, drained capers

¾   pound cooked skinned turkey breast or smoked turkey breast, cut in strips

½   cup minced fresh basil leaves

    Basil sprigs (optional)

    Salt

Cook pasta in 3 to 4 quarts boiling water until tender to bite, 12 to 14 minutes; drain. Immediately cover with cold water; change water several times until pasta is cool, then drain well. Mix pasta with vinegar and ¼ cup broth. Mix tomatoes and capers. If making ahead, cover and chill pasta and tomato mixtures separately up to 1 day.

Spoon pasta into a wide bowl. (If made ahead, you may need to stir a few tablespoons more broth into pasta to moisten.) Arrange turkey, tomatoes, and basil on pasta. Mix well and add salt to taste. Garnish with basil sprigs. Makes 7 to 9 servings.

Per serving: 302 cal. (5 percent from fat); 21 g protein; 1.7 g fat (0.3 g sat.); 50 g carbo.; 345 mg sodium; 35 mg chol.

Orzo Salad with Smoked Trout

2   tablespoons pine nuts

1   pound dried orzo or small seashell pasta

1¼ cups unflavored nonfat yogurt

    About ¼ cup regular-strength chicken broth

2   tablespoons lemon juice

1   tablespoon grated lemon peel

2   to 3 tablespoons minced fresh dill

¼   to ⅓ pound boned and skinned smoked trout, broken into large flakes

    Dill sprigs (optional)

    Salt

Pour nuts into a 6- to 8-inch frying pan. Stir often over medium-high heat until nuts are golden, 4 to 6 minutes. Pour nuts from pan; if making ahead, store airtight up to 3 days.

Cook pasta in 3 to 4 quarts boiling water until tender to bite, about 10 to 12 minutes; drain. Immediately cover with cold water; change water several times until pasta is cool, then drain well. Mix pasta with yogurt, ¼ cup broth, lemon juice, lemon peel, and minced dill. If making ahead, cover and chill up to 1 day. (If salad is made ahead, stir in a little more broth to moisten before serving.)

Mound salad on a platter and scatter trout over it. Sprinkle salad with pine nuts and gar-

Thin ham slivers, piled high, tumble over curry-flavored cold couscous with cucumbers and shredded romaine lettuce.

nish with dill sprigs; add salt to taste. Makes 6 to 8 servings.

Per serving: 260 cal. (8 percent from fat); 13 g protein; 2.3 g fat (0.4 g sat.); 46 g carbo.; 180 mg sodium; 5.4 mg chol.

Curried Couscous Salad

1½ cups regular-strength chicken broth

1 cup couscous

Curry dressing (recipe follows)

1 small (about ¼ lb.) green bell pepper, stemmed, seeded, and finely chopped

¼ cup chopped dried apricots

6 cups finely shredded romaine lettuce

1 small (about 6 oz.) cucumber, peeled, seeded, and cut into thin slivers

⅓ pound thinly sliced cooked ham, cut into thin slivers

Salt and pepper

In a 1½- to 2-quart pan, bring broth to a boil over high heat. Stir couscous into broth, cover, remove from heat, and let stand until liquid is absorbed, about 10 minutes. Stir hot couscous with a fork to fluff, then mix in ¾ cup curry dressing, bell pepper, and apricots. Use, or cover and chill up to 1 day. Stir with a fork just before serving; you may want to add a little more curry dressing if dry.

Mound shredded lettuce equally on 4 dinner plates. Spoon couscous salad onto lettuce, scatter with cucumber slivers, and top with ham. Accompany with remaining dressing and add salt and pepper to taste. Makes 4 servings.

Per serving: 377 cal. (13 percent from fat); 21 g protein; 5.3 g fat (1.7 g sat.); 62 g carbo.; 854 mg sodium; 23 mg chol.

Curry dressing. Stir together 1 cup **unfla-vored nonfat yogurt,** ½ cup **regular-strength chicken broth,** ¼ cup chopped **Major Grey chutney,** 1 tablespoon **lemon juice,** and 1 teaspoon **curry powder.** If making ahead, cover and chill up to 1 day. Makes about 1¾ cups.

Green and White Salad

¾ pound (about 5 cups) spiral-shape dried pasta

⅔ cup seasoned rice vinegar

About ⅔ cup regular-strength chicken broth

2 to 3 teaspoons soy sauce

1 teaspoon Asian sesame oil

½ teaspoon crushed dried hot chilies

½ teaspoon pepper

1 package (about 1 lb.) soft tofu, drained, cut into ½-inch cubes

4 cups bite-size broccoli flowerets

½ cup thinly sliced green onions

⅓ cup minced parsley

Butter lettuce leaves, rinsed and crisped

Cook pasta in 3 to 4 quarts boiling water just until tender to bite, about 10 minutes; drain. Immediately cover with cold water; change water several times until pasta is cool, then drain well.

Mix pasta with rice vinegar, ⅔ cup broth, 2 teaspoons soy sauce, sesame oil, chilies, pepper, and tofu. Cover and chill least 1 hour or up to 1 day. (If making ahead, you may need to moisten the salad with a little more broth.)

Meanwhile, in a 2- to 3-quart pan over high heat, bring 1 inch water to a boil. Add broccoli; cover, and cook until broccoli is tender-crisp when pierced, 4 to 5 minutes. Drain broccoli and immerse in ice water until cool, then drain well. If making ahead, wrap airtight and chill up to 1 day.

Mix broccoli, green onion, and parsley with pasta mixture. Line a wide bowl with butter lettuce and mound pasta salad onto leaves. Add soy sauce to taste. Makes 6 to 8 servings.

Per serving: 236 cal. (12 percent from fat); 11 g protein; 3.1 g fat (0.2 g sat.); 42 g carbo.; 518 mg sodium; 0 mg chol.

CHILLED SOUPS TEMPER HOT DAYS
Surprising ingredients produce simple, hearty fare

APPLES WITH POTATOES, MANGOES with black beans, peaches with rice—hardly run-of-the-mill soup combinations. But these low-fat, satisfying soups—with the refreshing tang of fresh fruit—may be just what you crave for lunch in order to save space for a special dinner, or savor for evening to balance that big business lunch.

For busy schedules, these soups offer considerable flexibility. All can be assembled in minutes. Two need to cook first, but you can chill them down in about 15 minutes by setting the pan in ice water and stirring frequently. Or you can make the soups the day before—even in the morning—and refrigerate until it's time to serve.

To complete these simple meals, consider sandwiches to go with the soups. To keep your nutritional edge, avoid rich spreads for the bread. Make use of leaner alternatives such as nonfat sour cream, Dijon mustard, or roasted vegetable purées (see page 131). If the filling is meat, be sure it is lean and fat is trimmed.

Black Bean Gazpacho

This soup keeps cool two ways. You refrigerate the basic ingredients—then whirl them smooth in a blender—and use chilly tasting cucumbers with mango for salsa that is spooned into the soup.

- 2 cans (14 or 15 oz. each) black beans, cool or chilled
- ¾ cup vegetable broth or regular-strength chicken broth, cool or chilled
- 1 teaspoon ground cumin
- ½ teaspoon ground coriander
- 1 cup ½-inch cubes European cucumber
- 3 tablespoons chopped red onion
- 3 tablespoons lime juice
- 1 medium-size (about ¾ lb.) firm-ripe mango
- ¼ to ½ teaspoon crushed dried hot red chilies
- 3 tablespoons unflavored nonfat yogurt
  Fresh cilantro (coriander) leaves
  Salt

Rinse and drain beans. In a blender, combine 1¼ cups beans, broth, cumin, and ground coriander; whirl until smoothly puréed. Pour soup into a bowl and stir in remaining beans. Use, or if making ahead, cover and chill up to 1 day.

Mix cucumber, red onion, and lime juice. Cut peel off mango and slice fruit from sides and edges of the flat pit; discard pit. Cut the mango pieces into ½-inch cubes and add to cucumber mixture; season to taste with chilies. Use, or if making ahead, cover and chill up to 6 hours. Ladle soup into shallow bowls and spoon cucumber-mango salsa into each. Garnish with yogurt and cilantro leaves. Add salt to taste. Serves 2 or 3.

Per serving: 225 cal. (8 percent from fat); 11 g protein; 1.9 g fat (0.2 g sat.); 43 g carbo.; 694 mg sodium; 0.3 mg chol.

Coconut Rice Soup with Peaches

Hot chicken broth, the base of this soup, keeps peaches from darkening and soaks into the precooked rice, making grains tender in about 5 minutes. Rich coconut flavor—without the fat of coconut milk—comes from coconut extract, found in the spice aisle at the supermarket.

- 4 cups regular-strength chicken broth
- ½ cup lime juice
- 3 tablespoons firmly packed brown sugar
- 1 teaspoon coconut extract
- ½ cup packaged precooked white rice or ¾ cup cooked white rice
- 2 cups peeled and sliced firm-ripe or ripe peaches
- 1 tablespoon minced fresh cilantro (coriander)
- 1 tablespoon finely chopped salted roasted peanuts
  Salt

In a 4- to 5-quart pan over high heat, bring broth, lime juice, brown sugar, and coconut extract to a boil. Add rice, cover pan, and remove from heat. After 5 minutes, stir in peaches. Cover and chill until cold, at least 1 hour or up to 4 hours.

Ladle soup into bowls; sprinkle with cilantro and peanuts. Add salt to taste. Makes 4 servings.

Per serving: 173 cal. (20 percent from fat); 5.6 g protein; 3.8 g fat (1 g sat.); 35 g carbo.; 138 mg sodium; 0 mg chol.

Apple-Potato Vichyssoise with Herbs

- 2 large (about 1 lb. total) tart apples such as Granny Smith or Newtown Pippin
- 1 pound thin-skinned potatoes, peeled and coarsely chopped
- 2½ cups regular-strength chicken broth
- 2 tablespoons lemon juice
- 2½ cups 1 percent fat milk
- 3 tablespoons minced fresh mint leaves
- 3 tablespoons chopped fresh chives
- 1 teaspoon minced fresh thyme leaves
  Chive spears and mint sprigs
  Salt

Set 1 apple aside. Peel, core, and coarsely chop the other.

In a 3- to 4-quart pan, combine chopped apple, potatoes, broth, and lemon juice. Bring to a boil, cover, and simmer until potatoes and apple are soft enough to mash easily, about 35 minutes. Cover and chill until cold, at least 4 hours or up to 1 day.

In a blender, smoothly purée potato-apple mixture, in portions if necessary. Pour soup into a bowl, and mix in milk, mint, chopped chives, and thyme. Serve, or if making ahead, cover and chill up to 4 hours. Just before serving, peel, core, and coarsely shred remaining apple; stir into soup. Ladle soup into individual bowls and garnish with chive spears and mint sprigs. Add salt to taste. Makes 4 to 6 servings.

Per serving: 147 cal. (15 percent from fat); 6.2 g protein; 2.4 g fat (1 g sat.); 28 g carbo.; 105 mg sodium; 4.1 mg chol.

This speedy gazpacho needs no cooking. It's a black bean soup, using canned beans, topped with a mango and vegetable salsa.

Crisp lattice for plum cobbler uses strips of fila dough. The strips, discreetly buttered, bake separately.

CREATIVE CRUSTS KEEP COBBLERS LEAN

Plums, cherries, and apricots bake with citrus and berries

I'S THE UPPER-CRUST APPROACH THAT makes juicy fruit cobblers natural candidates for low-fat desserts. Cobblers are basically pies baked without a bottom crust, which automatically reduces the fat calories from rich pie dough by half. And when a little imagination is put to work on alternative crusts, you can have your cobbler and eat it with a clear conscience, too.

These cobblers have different approaches: fila dough makes a shatteringly crisp lattice, a crumbled oatmeal-rich cookie dough bakes on the fruit to make a chewy-crisp streusel, and sweet biscuit dumplings that also bake on the fruit are made lighter and more tender by replacing part of the butter with yogurt.

Each cobbler teams at least two fruits to bring out the best in each. Their juices are thickened by quick-cooking tapioca or a little flour.

Think you can't enjoy cobbler without a scoop of ice cream? Give vanilla low-fat or nonfat frozen yogurt or vanilla ice milk a try.

Plum-Orange Cobbler with Fila Lattice

   8 fila sheets (each 12 by 16 in., about 5 oz.)
2 1/2 tablespoons melted butter or margarine
        About 1 cup sugar
3 1/2 tablespoons quick-cooking tapioca
   2 tablespoons grated orange peel
  1/2 teaspoon ground cinnamon
        About 3 pounds firm-ripe plums
        Vanilla low-fat frozen yogurt

Lightly butter and flour a 12- by 15-inch baking sheet. Place a 3- to 3 1/2-quart shallow casserole upside down on sheet. With the handle of a spoon, trace around casserole sides. Lift off casserole.

Lay 1 sheet of fila flat on a work surface. (Keep remaining fila tightly covered with plastic wrap to prevent drying.) Brush fila sparingly with butter. Top with a second fila sheet. Brush with more butter, then top with another sheet. Repeat to use all fila, brushing the top layer with butter; reserve about 1/2 tablespoon butter. Cut fila stack crosswise into 1-inch-wide strips.

Lay about half the strips diagonally across the outline traced on baking sheet, spacing strips about 1 inch apart. Trim ends of strips so they are about 1/3 inch inside the tracing. Lay remaining dough strips at an angle on top of the first layer, spacing about 1 inch apart. Trim ends of strips so they are about 1/3 inch inside the tracing. Sprinkle lattice evenly with 2 tablespoons sugar. Lay strip scraps beside the lattice if you want to bake them for snacks; sprinkle with sugar.

Bake fila lattice in a 350° oven until golden brown, 15 to 20 minutes. If making ahead, cool, cover airtight, and let stand at room temperature up to 1 day.

In the casserole, mix 3/4 cup plus 2 tablespoons sugar with tapioca, orange peel, and cinnamon. Pit plums and thinly slice fruit. Stir with dry ingredients in casserole and let stand at least 15 minutes or up to 1 hour to let tapioca soften; stir occasionally. Spread fruit out level. Bake in a 350° oven, stirring occasionally, until plum juice bubbles, 35 to 45 minutes (you may want to set the casserole on a rimmed pan in case juices bubble over rim).

Use fruit hot, warm, or at room temperature. With 2 spatulas, carefully set fila lattice on top of plums. Serve at once, scooping into bowls. Top with frozen yogurt. Serves 8.

Per serving: 287 cal. (18 percent from fat); 2.6 g protein; 5.6 g fat (2.5 g sat.); 60 g carbo.; 142 mg sodium; 9.7 mg chol.

Frozen yogurt melts into warm apricot cobbler saturated by blackberry juices.

Cherry-Blueberry Crisp

⅓ cup firmly packed brown sugar

2 tablespoons all-purpose flour

½ teaspoon ground cinnamon

3 cups pitted sweet dark cherries

2 cups blueberries, rinsed and drained

1 tablespoon lemon juice

   Oatmeal topping (recipe follows)

   Vanilla low-fat frozen yogurt

In a shallow round or square 8-inch casserole, stir brown sugar with flour and cinnamon. Add cherries, blueberries, and lemon juice; mix well. Spread fruit level and sprinkle evenly with oatmeal topping.

Bake in a 350° oven until fruit mixture bubbles and topping is golden brown, 35 to 40 minutes. Serve hot, warm, or cool. Scoop into bowls and serve with frozen yogurt. Makes 6 servings.

Per serving: 273 cal. (25 percent from fat); 3.7 g protein; 7.5 g fat (3.9 g sat.); 51 g carbo.; 71 mg sodium; 16 mg chol.

Oatmeal topping. In a bowl stir together 1 cup **quick-cooking rolled oats**, ¼ cup firmly packed **brown sugar**, ¼ teaspoon *each* **ground cinnamon** and **ground ginger**, and 3 tablespoons melted **butter** or margarine.

Apricot-Blackberry Cobbler

2 pounds firm-ripe apricots, pitted and quartered

2 cups blackberries, rinsed and drained

½ cup sugar

1½ tablespoons lemon juice

3 to 4 tablespoons quick-cooking tapioca

   Biscuit topping (recipe follows)

   Vanilla low-fat frozen yogurt

In a 2½- to 3-quart shallow casserole, mix apricots, blackberries, sugar, lemon juice, and tapioca. Let stand at least 15 minutes or up to 1 hour to soften tapioca; stir several times. Spread fruit level. Drop biscuit topping in 8 equal mounds over fruit.

Bake in a 350° oven until fruit mixture bubbles in center and biscuits are golden brown, about 45 minutes. Serve hot, warm, or cool. Spoon into bowls and serve with scoops of low-fat frozen yogurt. Makes 6 to 8 servings.

Per serving: 294 cal. (12 percent from fat); 5.7 g protein; 4 g fat (2.1 g sat.); 61 g carbo.; 203 mg sodium; 9 mg chol.

Biscuit topping. In a food processor or a bowl, whirl or stir together 1¾ cups **all-purpose flour**, ¼ cup **sugar**, 1 teaspoon **baking powder**, and ½ teaspoon **baking soda**. Whirl or cut in 2 tablespoons **butter** or margarine. Stir in ¾ cup **unflavored low-fat yogurt** and 1 teaspoon grated **lemon peel** just until evenly moistened. ■

Freeze bargain berries for winter desserts

It's surprisingly easy, and the payoff comes when berry prices soar

INDUSTRIALLY QUICK-FREEZE *soft berries, such as blackberries and raspberries, so they are easy to measure when you make luscious, economical winter treats.*

SUMMER BERRIES can't get much better or cheaper than they are in June and July, especially if you grow or pick your own, or buy in bulk at farm stands or farmers' markets. And if you'd like to keep the good deal going, freeze some of this fruit to use in pies and other treats later in the year, when berries are expensive.

Freezing without sugar works well for all berries, and the process is child's play. Of course, you should start with prime-quality fruit.

First, sort berries, discarding any that are bruised or have even a hint of mold.

Gently rinse berries to remove dust and any other debris. The most effective method is to dump several handfuls of berries at a time into cool water, then at once skim them out with your hands, a large strainer ladle, or even a colander. Do not let the berries stand in water (they'll get soggy) or run water over them full force (the pressure is enough to bruise). Lay berries in a single layer on several thicknesses of towels and let stand a few minutes until drained and mostly dry. Do not pat berries to dry; this also bruises them. Hull strawberries and gently pull currants from stems.

Individually quick-freeze juicy berries that crush easily—blackberries, boysenberries, olallieberries, loganberries, marionberries, raspberries, strawberries, and currants.

Arrange clean, dry berries in a single layer (they can touch slightly) in large rimmed pans. Freeze, uncovered, until berries are hard, 1 to 2 hours. Then quickly pour berries into freezer storage containers, seal, and return to freezer for as long as a year. Berries will not stick together; however, if a few do lump, tap to break apart. To use fruit, pour out the amount you want. Reseal remaining berries and return them at once to the freezer. Be sure to use freezer storage containers; otherwise the berries will get freezer burn as they lose moisture and dry out.

Just freeze blueberries and gooseberries. These berries, like cranberries, don't need to be individually frozen because they have tougher skins. Pour the clean, dry berries into freezer storage containers and freeze. You'll get best results if you pack them in 2- to 4-cup bags or boxes so they can freeze quickly. The frozen berries will pour out readily.

Out of the freezer, juicy berries thaw rapidly, leak juice, and get mushy. But when you cook or purée them, their flavors are difficult to distinguish from fresh. Blueberries and gooseberries leak less but soften more than fresh berries do when cooked.

Once your freezer is well stocked, file these ideas for cool-weather berry treats:

Instant sorbet. Whirl slightly thawed frozen berries in a blender or food processor to make a thick slush, flavoring to taste with sugar, honey, jam, or a sweet liqueur with orange, black raspberry, or cassis flavor. Serve at once.

Fruit floats. Make instant sorbet and scoop into tall glasses of fruit juice or nectar. Try blackberries or blueberries in orange juice, raspberries in apricot nectar or lemonade, or strawberries in a raspberry-cranberry beverage.

Berry pies. Measure frozen berries and mix with filling ingredients. Pour into pie crust and bake as recipe directs, allowing a few extra minutes for filling to heat enough to bubble. If crust browns before filling is done, drape it with foil. A delicious summer-winter team is blueberry pie with a handful of dried cranberries mixed in.

Berry ice cubes. Drop frozen berries into beverages like sparkling water, matching berries with berry-flavor sparkling water and fruit juice or juice-blend beverages. Stir to cool the beverage and crush the berries. ∎

By Maura Devlin

NOEL BARNHURST

A melody of Mexican flavor for potatoes

SCALLOPED POTATOES soothe the soul and nourish the body, but they usually lack drama. When Dean Forgaard adds cheddar cheese, canned corn with Mexican seasonings, green chilies, cayenne, and paprika, the potatoes come on as brightly as a mariachi band. Forgaard calls them Potatoes Plus. Leftovers reheat well in the microwave.

Potatoes Plus

- 6 medium-size (5 to 6 oz. each) russet potatoes, scrubbed
- 2 cups (½ lb.) shredded sharp cheddar cheese
- 2 cups nonfat or reduced-fat sour cream
- 1 can (11 oz.) corn with Mexican seasonings, drained
- 1 can (7 oz.) diced green chilies
- ¼ teaspoon cayenne
- Paprika
- Salt and pepper

Put potatoes in a 5- to 6-quart pan, and add water to cover them by at least ½ inch. Cover and bring to a boil over high heat; reduce heat, and simmer until potatoes are tender when pierced, about 30 minutes. Drain, and let stand until cool to touch.

Peel potatoes, then shred them using a hand shredder or shredding blade in a food processor.

Pour potatoes into a lightly oiled or buttered shallow 3-quart casserole and mix them with cheese, sour cream, corn, chilies, and cayenne. Swirl mixture evenly in casserole. Sprinkle with paprika. If making ahead, cover and chill up to 1 day. Bake, uncovered, in a 350° oven until lightly browned and hot in center, about 1 hour (if chilled, 1 hour and 20 minutes). Season to taste with salt and pepper. Makes 10 to 12 servings.

Per serving: 179 cal. (33 percent from fat); 9.4 g protein; 6.5 g fat (4 g sat.); 20 g carbo.; 340 mg sodium; 20 mg chol.

Dean M Forgaard MD

Stanwood, Washington

FREQUENT CONTRIBUTOR Sandy Szwarc devised the poetically named Strawberry Clouds as a low-calorie substitute for strawberry shortcake. The latter involves a rich biscuit (or, in these degenerate days, sponge cake rounds from the grocery) and whipped cream. For his base, Szwarc bakes a meringue bolstered and flavored by vanilla cookie crumbs, almonds, and almond extract. Instead of whipped cream to go with the berries, nonfat vanilla frozen yogurt is the choice.

Strawberry Clouds

- ⅛ cup slivered almonds
- 2 large egg whites
- About ⅔ cup sugar
- ¾ teaspoon almond extract
- ¾ cup finely crushed vanilla cookie wafer crumbs (about 24 cookies)
- 2 cups strawberries, rinsed, hulled, and sliced
- Nonfat vanilla frozen yogurt

Spread almonds in an 8- to 10-inch-wide pan. Bake in a 350° oven until golden, 5 to 8 minutes. Finely chop nuts.

In a deep bowl, whip egg whites with a mixer on high speed until they hold soft peaks. Beating at high speed, gradually add ⅔ cup of the sugar, 1 tablespoon at a time, until whites hold stiff peaks. Add extract and beat to blend, then fold in nuts and cookie crumbs.

Scrape meringue mixture into an oiled or buttered 8-inch-diameter cake pan with removable rim. Swirl mixture to make an even layer. Bake in a 350° oven until meringue feels dry and firm when touched and is a light golden brown, about 20 minutes.

Let meringue stand in pans to cool; if making ahead, package airtight and let stand up to 1 day. Remove pan rim and set meringue on a platter.

Mix strawberries with sugar to taste and spoon over the meringue. Cut dessert in wedges and serve with scoops of frozen yogurt. Makes 6 to 7 servings.

Per serving: 176 cal. (26 percent from fat); 3 g protein; 5 g fat (0.7 g sat.); 31 g carbo.; 49 mg sodium; 0 mg chol.

Sandy Szwarc

Albuquerque

LIFE WAS SIMPLER WHEN salsa was Mexican hot sauce and chutney was Major Grey's mango preserve, but it is more interesting now that both can be made out of a wide variety of ingredients and paired with a wider range of fish, flesh, and fowl. Distinctions are difficult and perilous, but these may roughly serve: chutneys are cooked, usually, and salsas are most often made of fresh ingredients.

Marjorie Ohrnstein's salsa for salmon is based on papaya and kiwi fruit, with citrus juices, green and yellow bell peppers, and jalapeño chilies. The salmon is dipped in a mixture of oil and cayenne before grilling; this is a kinder, gentler version of the fiery Cajun treatment.

Grilled Salmon with Papaya-Kiwi Salsa

1   small (about 1 lb.) firm-ripe papaya, peeled, seeded, and diced

1   large (about 5 oz.) kiwi fruit, peeled and diced

3   tablespoons lemon juice

2   tablespoons lime juice

1   medium-size (5 to 6 oz.) green bell pepper, stemmed, seeded, and diced

1   medium-size (5 to 6 oz.) yellow bell pepper, seeded and diced

2   large (about 2 oz. total) fresh jalapeño chilies, stemmed, seeded, and diced

1   to 2 tablespoons sugar

6   salmon steaks (same thickness, about 2½ lb. total)

1   tablespoon olive oil

¼   teaspoon cayenne

Cilantro (coriander) sprigs

Salt

In a bowl, gently mix papaya, kiwi, lemon juice, lime juice, green pepper, yellow pepper, jalapeños, and sugar to taste. Use, or cover and chill up to 4 hours.

Rinse salmon and pat dry. In a shallow pan, combine oil and cayenne. Dip salmon fillets in oil mixture to coat lightly. Place fillets on a hot oiled barbecue grill over a solid bed of hot coals or gas heat on high (you can hold your hand at grill level for only 2 or 3 seconds). Close lid on gas grill. Cook until fish is opaque but still moist-looking in center of thickest part (cut to test), about 5 minutes on each side. Serve fish garnished with cilantro and add the papaya salsa and salt to taste. Makes 6 servings.

Per serving: 315 cal. (37 percent from fat); 34 g protein; 13 g fat (1.2 g sat.); 14 g carbo.; 80 mg sodium; 92 mg chol.

Marjorie Ohrnstein

Los Angeles
By Joan Griffiths, Richard Dunmire

PETER CHRISTIANSEN

GOLDEN CHUNKS *of mango and grilled tuna steak soak up the same seasonings.*

One lively marinade does two jobs well

THE CARIBBEAN SIZZLE OF these tuna steaks, grilled rare, is complemented by the fresh, uncooked mango chutney served with them. Both fish and chutney are boldly flavored by a blend of citrus, chili, mint, and ginger that plays up the contrasts of sweet, sour, hot, cool, and sharp.

Tuna with Mint-Mango Chutney

¼   cup chopped fresh mint leaves

¼   cup orange juice

2   tablespoons lime juice

1   tablespoon minced fresh ginger

⅛   to ¼ teaspoon minced fresh habanero chili or 1 to 2 teaspoons minced fresh serrano chili

4   tuna (ahi) steaks, about 1 inch thick (4 to 6 oz. each)

1   large (about 1 lb.) firm-ripe mango

Fresh mint sprigs

Salt and pepper

Mix chopped mint, orange juice, lime juice, and minced ginger with chili to taste.

Rinse fish and pat dry. In a bowl, turn fish in ⅛ of the mint mixture, coating well. Let stand at least 15 minutes, or cover and chill up to 2 hours, turning fish over several times.

Meanwhile, cut peel off mango. Slice fruit off each side of the wide, flat pit. Cut remaining fruit from edges of pit. Dice fruit into ½-inch cubes. Add mango to reserved mint mixture; add more chili to taste, if desired.

Lift tuna from marinade and drain. Place fish on a barbecue grill 4 to 6 inches above a solid bed of hot coals or gas heat on high (you can hold your hand at grill level only 2 to 3 seconds). Close lid on gas grill. Cook, turning once, until fish is lightly browned but still red inside (cut to test), 6 to 8 minutes. Transfer fish to platter or plates, and spoon mango mixture over it; garnish with mint sprigs. Add salt and pepper to taste. Serves 4.

Per serving: 170 cal. (6.4 percent from fat); 24 g protein; 1.2 g fat (0.3 g sat.); 16 g carbo.; 40 mg sodium; 45 mg chol. ■

By Linda Lau Anusasananan

SUNSET'S KITCHEN CABINET

Creative ways with everyday foods—submitted by *Sunset* readers, tested in *Sunset* kitchens

Yogurt Waffles

Frances Gardner, Portland

1¼ cups all-purpose flour

1½ teaspoons baking powder

1 teaspoon baking soda

¼ teaspoon salt

2 large eggs

2 tablespoons honey

1¾ cups (16 oz.) unflavored low-fat yogurt

¼ cup melted butter or margarine, cooled

Sliced peaches or other fruit

Peach yogurt (optional, or another flavor)

Maple syrup

In a food processor or bowl, whirl or stir flour, baking powder, soda, and salt to blend. Add eggs, honey, unflavored yogurt, and butter; whirl until smooth (or in another bowl, beat wet ingredients to blend, then stir into flour mixture until smooth).

In an oiled waffle maker according to manufacturer's instructions, cook waffles until well browned. Waffles will be moist inside. For a drier texture, place waffles directly on racks in a 200° oven about 10 minutes. Serve with sliced peaches, peach yogurt, and syrup. Makes 4 waffles (8 in. square).

Per serving: 396 cal. (39 percent from fat); 13 g protein; 17 g fat (9.3 g sat.); 47 g carbo.; 862 mg sodium; 144 mg chol.

SERVE TANGY WAFFLES *with syrup, favorite fresh fruit, and more yogurt.*

Taco Zucchini Cups

Nancy Reed, Bremerton, Washington

2 large eggs

1 tablespoon chili powder

½ teaspoon dried oregano leaves

½ teaspoon salt

2 cups shredded zucchini

1 cup coarsely crushed taco-flavor or plain tortilla chips

1 cup (¼ lb.) shredded cheddar cheese

⅓ cup minced onion

½ cup minced green bell pepper

In a bowl, beat eggs to blend. Stir in chili powder, oregano, and salt, then zucchini, chips, half the cheese, onion, and all but 2 tablespoons pepper.

Spoon mixture into 24 nonstick miniature muffin cups (1¾ in. wide and ¾ in. deep). Top evenly with the remaining cheese. Bake in a 450° oven until taco cups are deep golden, 14 to 16 minutes.

Loosen taco cups with a knife; lift to a platter. Sprinkle with remaining bell pepper. Serve warm. Makes 24.

Per taco cup: 47 cal. (57 percent from fat); 2.1 g protein; 3 g fat (1.3 g sat.); 3.1 g carbo.; 102 mg sodium; 23 mg chol.

ZUCCHINI *combines with Mexican seasonings for appetizer-size frittatas.*

Chicken Español

Mrs. Scott Kemper, Sacramento

4 chicken legs with thighs (2 lb. total), skinned

1 tablespoon olive oil

¼ cup diced ham

1 cup sliced green onions

2 cloves garlic, minced or pressed

3 cups coarsely chopped tomatoes

1½ cups chopped celery

1 cup diced red bell pepper

2 tablespoons lime juice

1 dried bay leaf

1½ teaspoons chili powder

¼ teaspoon turmeric

¼ cup madeira

Hot couscous or rice

Parsley sprigs

Salt and pepper

In a 5- to 6-quart pan over high heat, brown chicken in oil, turning occasionally, about 8 minutes. Lift out chicken.

Reduce heat to medium-high. To pan add ham, onions, and garlic; stir often until garlic is golden, 1 to 2 minutes. Stir in tomatoes, celery, bell pepper, lime juice, bay leaf, chili powder, and turmeric, then tuck chicken pieces among vegetables.

Bring to simmering; reduce heat and simmer, covered, until meat is no longer pink in thickest part (cut to test), about 15 minutes. Stir in madeira and simmer 1 minute. Spoon over couscous in wide soup bowls. Garnish with parsley and season to taste with salt and pepper. Serves 4.

Per serving: 323 cal. (31 percent from fat); 37 g protein; 11 g fat (2.4 g sat.); 15 g carbo.; 325 mg sodium; 136 mg chol.

SERVE CHICKEN *and vegetables with couscous to soak up the juices.*

Asparagus-Prosciutto Rolls

Lynn Edman, San Francisco

32 medium-size asparagus spears (about 2 lb. total)

16 paper-thin slices provolone cheese (each about 4 by 5 in., ½ lb. total), at room temperature

About ⅓ cup homemade or purchased pesto

16 paper-thin slices prosciutto (each about 4 by 7 in., 3 oz. total)

Fresh basil sprigs (optional)

Trim tough ends from asparagus, then peel lower parts of stalks. In a 10- to 12-inch frying pan over high heat, bring 1 inch water to a boil. Add asparagus and simmer, covered, until tender-crisp to bite, 2 to 3 minutes. Drain, immerse in ice water until cold, and drain again.

Separate cheese slices; cut each in half crosswise. Spread each piece with ½ teaspoon pesto. Separate prosciutto slices; cut into halves lengthwise.

For each roll, wrap a cheese slice lengthwise around an asparagus stalk, then spiral a piece of prosciutto around cheese to hold it in place. Serve, or chill airtight up to 6 hours. Garnish with basil sprigs. Makes 32.

Per piece: 47 cal. (67 percent from fat); 3.3 g protein; 3.5 g fat (1.5 g sat.); 0.9 g carbo.; 130 mg sodium; 7.5 mg chol.

SLICED PROVOLONE *cheese, prosciutto, and pesto wrap around asparagus.*

Sushi Shrimp Salad

Roxanne Chan, Albany, California

4 cups cooked medium-grain white rice, at room temperature

2 cups diced seeded cucumber

1 cup thawed frozen peas

½ cup thinly sliced radishes

¼ cup sliced green onions

Sushi dressing (recipe follows)

1 pound cooked, peeled, and deveined large (31 to 35 per lb.) shrimp

1½ quarts rinsed, crisped fresh spinach leaves

Whole radishes

Salt

In a large bowl, combine cooked rice, cucumber, peas, sliced radishes, onions, and dressing. Gently mix in shrimp.

Arrange spinach leaves on a platter and spoon sushi salad into the center. Garnish with whole radishes. Season to taste with salt. Makes 4 entrée servings.

Per serving: 525 cal. (16 percent from fat); 34 g protein; 9.1 g fat (1.5 g sat.); 76 g carbo.; 968 mg sodium; 221 mg chol.

Sushi dressing. Combine ½ cup **seasoned rice vinegar** and 2 tablespoons *each* minced **fresh ginger, prepared horseradish,** and **Asian sesame oil.**

LOW-FAT SALAD *combines sushi-flavored rice, shrimp, and crisp vegetables.*

Low-fat Raspberry Custard Brulée

Victoria Martinez, West Hills, California

2 tablespoons cornstarch

¼ cup granulated sugar

1¼ cups nonfat milk

3 large eggs

¼ cup reduced-fat sour cream

1 teaspoon vanilla

2 cups raspberries, rinsed and patted dry

⅓ cup firmly packed brown sugar

In a 2- to 3-quart pan, mix cornstarch and granulated sugar. Add milk and eggs and whisk until smooth. Stir over medium-high heat until very thick and bubbling, 5 to 7 minutes. Remove from heat and whisk vigorously until smooth. Let cool completely, then whisk in sour cream and vanilla.

Divide berries among 6 ovenproof ramekins (¾- to 1-cup size). Spoon custard on top. Sprinkle evenly with brown sugar. Place ramekins in a rimmed 10- by 15-inch baking pan and broil 5 to 6 inches below heat until brown sugar melts, about 5 minutes. Serve warm. Makes 6 servings.

Per serving: 186 cal. (20 percent from fat); 5.9 g protein; 4.1 g fat (1.5 g sat.); 32 g carbo.; 63 mg sodium; 111 mg chol.

Compiled by Elaine Johnson

FILL RAMEKINS *with raspberries and top with cooked custard and sugar; broil.*

FOOD
Guide

BY JERRY ANNE DI VECCHIO

A TASTE OF THE WEST: Chinese chicken salad

Even best-liked dishes ride waves of popularity, and with each reincarnation come subtle differences. Right now, the star is Chinese chicken salad.

Curious, I looked through back issues of *Sunset* to see how this salad has evolved. The first recipe dates to 1957, and over the years we toyed with variations until publishing our most-requested version, from Ming's Restaurant in Palo Alto, California, in November 1970. It was distinguished by fried cellophane noodles that exploded into puffy wisps.

Then last summer, Fred Halpert of Brava Terrace in St. Helena, California, asked me to come and try the unusual tomato varieties he's been growing next to the restaurant. After our appetites were whetted by his crop, we sat down to lunch. There it was—Chinese chicken salad. It was so refreshing, it inspired this simpler, equally refreshing version. He's brought back cellophane noodles, but saturated them with flavor instead of with frying oil. Baby greens replace iceberg lettuce. The chicken is contemporary, too. You can roast it ahead, or quick-start the dish with a cooked bird from the market. Want another plus? This version is low in fat. Thanks, Fred.

Chinese Chicken Salad

Cooking time: 15 to 20 minutes

Prep time: 35 to 40 minutes

Notes: Look for cellophane noodles and Oriental sesame oil at well-stocked supermarkets and Asian grocery stores.

Makes: 6 servings

- 4 or 5 ounces cellophane noodles (*saifun,* made of bean or yam, not rice)
- ½ pound Chinese pea pods, strings removed
- ½ cup rice vinegar
- 3 tablespoons soy sauce
- 1½ tablespoons minced fresh ginger

NOEL BARNHURST

JULY '95

- A great chicken salad, revised, revitalized
- Fresh and fast cucumber pickles
- An auxiliary grill for the barbecue
- A breakfast of grapes and cheese toast
- Celebrate summer with free-spirited Zinfandels

A cool tangle of chicken, transparent noodles, pea pods, and peppers give Chinese chicken salad a new look.

1 tablespoon sugar

1 tablespoon dry mustard mixed until smooth with 1 tablespoon water

1 tablespoon Asian sesame oil

2½ to 3 cups boned and skinned cooked chicken

1 tablespoon salad oil

2 cloves garlic, thinly sliced

1 cup thinly slivered red onion

2 tablespoons lemon juice

2 large (½ lb. *each*) red or yellow bell peppers, stemmed, seeded, and diced

About 6 cups tender salad greens, rinsed and crisped

½ cup finely chopped fresh cilantro (coriander)

Cilantro leaves

1. In a 4- to 6-quart pan, bring about 2 quarts water to boiling. Add noodles and return to boiling, stirring once. Remove from heat and let stand until tender to bite, 10 to 15 minutes. Pour into a colander and, with scissors, snip noodles to make shorter strands. Drain at least 10 minutes.

2. In the same pan, bring 6 cups water to boiling on high heat. Add peas and cook just until bright green, about 1 minute. Drain, and at once immerse in ice water until cold; drain.

3. Mix rice vinegar, soy, ginger, sugar, mustard mixture, and sesame oil. Tear chicken into thin strips, discarding fat.

4. Pour 1 tablespoon oil into a wok or 12-inch frying pan over high heat. Add garlic and stir-fry until pale gold, about 1 minute. Add onion, lemon juice, and 2 tablespoons water. Stir-fry until liquid evaporates and onion is limp, about 3 minutes; scoop from pan with a slotted spoon; add to chicken.

5. To pan, add peppers and 2 tablespoons water; stir-fry over high heat just until peppers are barely limp, about 2 minutes. With a slotted spoon, scoop peppers into a small bowl. If making ahead, chill onion, chicken, and peppers up to 4 hours.

6. Shake noodles in colander to remove last drops of water, then pour into a bowl and mix with about ⅓ of the dressing.

7. Mix salad greens with all but 1 tablespoon of the chopped cilantro and arrange on a large platter. Mound noodles on greens. Arrange chicken mixture, peas, and peppers on and around noodles. Top with remaining dressing and sprinkle with remaining chopped cilantro. Mix well. Garnish with cilantro leaves.

Per serving: 301 cal. (85 cal., 28% from fat); 20 g protein; 9.4 g fat (1.8 g sat.); 33 g carbo.; 587 mg sodium; 52 mg chol.

BACK TO BASICS

A cucumber primer

A cucumber is cool. That's a fact. Its interior temperature may be up to 20° cooler than the surrounding air, and it's 96 percent water, so its chilly, thirst-quenching character is not just imagined. I grew up with the dark green so-called market cucumber that produced progeny at a furious rate in our summer garden. Because our cucumbers came right off the vine, we peeled them only when the skin was bitter or a little leathery (a bite told us), and scooped out the seeds when they got hard enough to notice. One of my first kitchen jobs was scoring the sides of cucumbers with a fork so they would have what I considered a chic variegated edge when sliced.

In today's markets, most dark green cucumbers have a thin edible film on them to keep them fresh longer. If the film isn't the old-fashioned heavier wax, it won't be noticeable after rinsing, so there's no need to peel cucumbers unless the skin is bitter.

Other cucumber choices include the long, tender-skinned dark green English (also called burpless or European), which is usually hothouse grown and sealed in a plastic sleeve (instead of coated), and its pale green counterpart, the Armenian cucumber. Both are very mild-tasting. Also suited to salads is the skinny Japanese cucumber, the stubby Sfran (a shorter, fatter version of market cukes), and the lemon (in color and shape) cucumber. The pickling cucumber is firmer.

But all respond well to my great-grandmother Gibson's standard quick-brining. Taste the cucumber skin, and peel if necessary. If the cucumber itself is just a little bitter, go ahead and use it. Check the seeds, and if they are even slightly hard, scoop them out with a teaspoon.

Salted cucumbers. **1.** Thinly slice **cucumbers** into a bowl and cover with water. Add enough **vinegar** to make the water sour, then enough **sugar** to balance it (roughly 3 tablespoons vinegar and 2 to 3 teaspoons sugar to each 2 cups water), and **salt** to taste.

2. Squeeze the slices with your hands to bruise them lightly so the solution will penetrate. (Sometimes my great-grandmother would slice an **onion** in with the cucumbers and squeeze it, too.) Let stand 5 to 10 minutes, or cover and keep in the refrigerator up to 3 days.

3. Lift out with a slotted spoon to eat as a salad, to add to salads, or to eat in sandwiches.

For breakfast, try Black Corinth grapes with gorgonzola toast.

GREAT TOOL
Another kind of grill

When my daughter was young, she loved Japanese restaurants with chefs who juggled cleavers and cooked on the tabletop. But I saw something more—another way to barbecue. The tool you need is a supplemental grill with tiny gaps, which is designed to sit on or replace the regular barbecue grill. Hardware and cookware stores sell them in many designs for as little as $10 to $30. The grill keeps tiny pieces of food from falling into the fire, so I use it to barbecue stir-fry, emulating the Japanese chef's tabletop showmanship.

The main rule is the pieces of food must be bigger than the grill gaps (even as the food cooks and shrinks).

The other rule is that the grill must be very, very hot. Mound coals up to within an inch or so of the grill. Turn gas to the highest setting.

Rub a little salad oil over whatever you plan to cook—sliced (or chunked) vegetables and thinly sliced meats. Grill vegetables first (they stick less). To control the pieces, use a wide spatula in each hand. One spatula becomes a barricade to keep the pieces on the grill. Then use both spatulas to scoop vegetables off.

Stir-fry the meat, add to the vegetables, and season to taste with salt and pepper. Or try some of the seasoning sauces that are flooding market shelves. One combination I like uses an **Asian peanut sauce** (sometimes called satay sauce): stir-fry chunks of **green onion,** some firm **tomato** wedges, then **beef strips.** Mix the foods with chopped fresh **cilantro,** and moisten to taste with the peanut sauce.

SEASONAL NOTE
It's minigrape time

Grape clusters tiny enough to nest in the palm of your hand may look too pretty to be real. But they are real, and they make their fresh appearance about mid-July.

Their romanticized name is champagne grapes, even though they are actually Black Corinth, a seedless grape variety that has been grown for many years in the West.

Before the "fresh" movement, they were mostly dried and sold in boxes as Zante currants. In those days, the only place I could find them on their delicate stems was in the fancy produce stands in the Los Angeles Farmers Market, at Third Street and Fairfax Avenue— where I willingly paid a premium for their novelty.

The clusters invite nibbling, and the ideal way is to munch the little grapes right off the bunch. Any stems that you get are tender enough to swallow.

The grapes also make a delightful dessert with a bit of cheese like a sharp cheddar or a Stilton.

For something grander, they are naturals sitting atop a cake or cheesecake or draped over scoops of ice cream. Frosting heightens their glamour. To do this, rinse the grape clusters and let stand until dry. Then whip egg white until foamy, brush over the clusters, dust with granulated sugar, and let stand until white dries, about 15 minutes, before serving.

Champagne grapes also make a grandly uncomplicated breakfast to carry outside and enjoy with gorgonzola bruschetta. Toast slices of crusty bread under the broiler, then spread gorgonzola cheese thickly on one side of each piece and return to broiler until cheese melts. As your beverage, consider strong coffee with hot milk or an aromatic tea such as Darjeeling.

BOB THOMPSON ON WINE: Independent Zinfandels

One satisfying way to celebrate the Fourth of July is by making small declarations of independence. Put Zinfandel on the holiday menu instead of anything imported.

Like most of us, Zinfandel comes from immigrant stock but the family has been here for so many years it has become completely Americanized. You can tell how much so by how well it goes with catsup and how thoroughly it confuses Europeans. One Frenchman, faced with his first glass of it, said: "I don't like it, you can't drink it, you have to eat it." Homage to a stout heart, that.

While the grape variety has relatives in Italy today—the resemblance is only passing—both the Mediterranean and American branches of the family probably came from central Europe. Nobody knows exactly where—the ancestors died out without leaving a trace. It was, no doubt, some region with a great tomato sauce. In any case, Zinfandel had landed in New York under its own name by the 1840s and moved west by the 1860s. (The cousin who became Primitivo did not show up in southern Italy until sometime after 1850.)

Now, as then, Zinfandel makes wispy little Beaujolais-like reds, goes into wines as heady as port, and fills all the gaps between. For Fourth of July purposes, stick with the welter- and mid-dleweights. In these classes, Zinfandel has plenty of blackberry flavor and enough tannin to cut grilled steak, but not so much that it dries out chicken.

For picnic weather, one of the fresh-fruity Zins fits the bill. Think about ($5.75 to $7) Charles Krug Napa Valley, Mirassou Central Coast, Robert Mondavi–Woodbridge California. For a starlit barbecue, a slightly heartier model may serve better. Consider ($6 to $12) Beringer North Coast, Franciscan Oakville Estate Napa Valley, Kenwood Sonoma Valley, Louis M. Martini North Coast, Round Hill Napa Valley, Sebastiani Sonoma County, Seghesio Sonoma County. ■

LONG, CRUSTY BATONS *are biscotti flavored with basil and pine nuts. They make harmonious partners for soup and salad.*

KEVIN CANDLAND

Savory biscotti

They're Italian cookies, but they're not for dessert

BISCOTTI, OR TWICE-baked cookies, are an Italian favorite that has taken the West by storm. No place that serves espresso or cappuccino is without them, and even supermarkets have them by the bag. The Italians favor biscotti for dunking in coffee or sweet wine, or to go with desserts. We think this concept translates well to other parts of the meal and propose biscotti as a savory stand-in for toast.

Here are two crunchy choices that are meant to be dipped into soup or munched with salad, but that are equally satisfying as a snack, or with a soft cheese as an appetizer.

Basil–Pine Nut Biscotti

¾ cup pine nuts

6 tablespoons butter or margarine, at room temperature

½ cup grated parmesan cheese

2 teaspoons crumbled dried basil leaves

1 teaspoon grated lemon peel

2 large eggs

¼ cup nonfat milk

2 cups all-purpose flour

2 teaspoons baking powder

In an 8- or 9-inch-wide pan, bake pine nuts in a 350° oven until lightly browned, 8 to 10 minutes.

In a large bowl, beat butter, parmesan, basil, lemon peel, and eggs until well blended. Stir in milk and nuts.

Mix flour and baking powder; add to butter mixture and stir to moisten thoroughly.

On a lightly oiled 12- by 15-inch baking sheet, shape dough into a rectangle about 15 inches long and ½ inch thick. Bake in a 350° oven 15 minutes. Remove from oven and, on pan, cut rectangle into about ½-inch-wide slices (crosswise for short biscotti, on a diagonal for longer pieces). Lay slices cut side down; edges can touch.

Reduce oven temperature to 325°. Bake biscotti until lightly browned and dry and firm to touch, 40 to 50 minutes. Transfer biscotti to racks to cool. Serve, or if making ahead, store cooled biscotti airtight up to 5 days; freeze to store longer. Makes about 3 dozen cross-cut pieces, about 2 dozen diagonal-cut pieces.

Per cross-cut piece: 69 cal. (55 percent from fat); 2.3 g protein; 4.2 g fat (1.7 g sat.); 6 g carbo.; 72 mg sodium; 18 mg chol.

Rosemary Walnut Biscotti

1 cup walnuts

6 tablespoons butter or margarine, at room temperature

1 tablespoon minced fresh or 1 teaspoon crumbled dried rosemary leaves

2 large eggs

¼ cup nonfat milk

1¾ cups all-purpose flour

¼ cup whole-wheat flour

2 teaspoons baking powder

¼ teaspoon salt

In an 8- or 9-inch-wide pan, bake walnuts in a 350° oven until they are browned and smell toasted, 8 to 10 minutes. Let cool, then coarsely chop.

In a large bowl, beat butter, rosemary, and eggs until well mixed. Stir in milk and nuts. Mix all-purpose flour, whole-wheat flour, baking powder, and salt; add to butter mixture and stir until thoroughly moistened.

On a lightly oiled 12- by 15-inch baking sheet, shape dough into a rectangle about 15 inches long and ½ inch thick. Bake in a 350° oven 15 minutes. Remove from oven and, on pan, cut rectangle into about ½-inch-wide slices (crosswise for short biscotti, on a diagonal for longer pieces). Lay slices cut side down; edges can touch.

Reduce oven temperature to 325°. Bake biscotti until lightly browned and dry and firm to touch, 40 to 50 minutes. Transfer biscotti to racks to cool. Serve, or if making ahead, store cooled biscotti airtight up to 5 days; freeze to store longer. Makes about 3 dozen cross-cut pieces, about 2 dozen diagonal-cut pieces.

Per cross-cut piece: 69 cal. (57 percent from fat); 1.6 g protein; 4.4 g fat (1.5 g sat.); 6 g carbo.; 67 mg sodium; 17 mg chol. ∎

By Christine Weber Hale

Great

COOKS SHARE THEIR FAVORITE

Western

PICNIC FOODS AND SPOTS

Picnics

FROM SAN DIEGO TO PORTLAND

The West is blessed with all the elements of a great summer picnic. We have close to 600 million acres of public lands to roam, some of the best scenery in the country, and weather that's noticeably drier than the rest of the nation's at this time of year. And the preeminence of our agriculture and the culinary influences of our multiethnic population mean we have especially fresh and varied choices to fill our picnic baskets.

How do experts on the West's regional foods celebrate this abundance? We spoke with three to learn about the ingredients, recipes, and places that make their picnics memorable. Their recipes for items marked with an * on the menus begin on page 153.

KITTY MORSE

IF YOU ADDED A FEW GOATS AND CAMELS, laughs Kitty Morse, the hills of north San Diego County would be indistinguishable from those of her homeland in Morocco. Palm trees with shaggy turbans, citrus groves, an agricultural region near the coast with desert beyond, plus glorious beaches—these similarities to Casablanca lured Morse to the North County 20 years ago.

One of Morse's favorite North County haunts is the Vista farmers' market, where her preparations for our picnic begin. With a basket on her arm, she

By Elaine Johnson • Photographs by Gary Moss

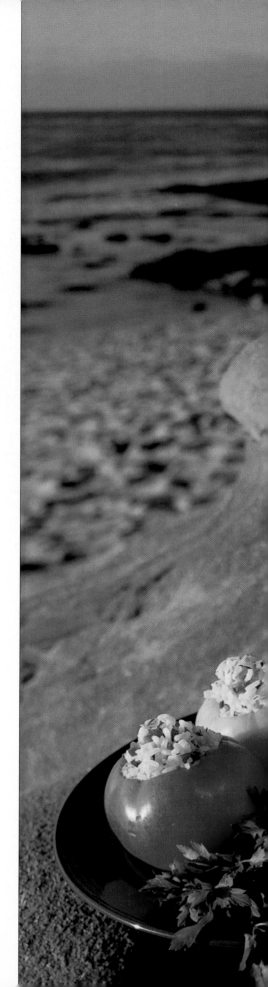

A TASTE OF MOROCCO IN
SAN DIEGO COUNTY

Tomatoes Casablanca*

Hummus • Pocket Bread

Marinated Olives • Feta Cheese

Skewered Lamb*

Date-Almond Truffles*

Sapotes

Fragrant Watermelon Drink

FOR FOUR

JOHN PHILLIP CARROLL

A SALUTE TO NORTHERN CALIFORNIA

California Chili Chicken*

Parsley and Herb Salad*

Orange–Red Onion Salad*

Guacamole Artichokes

San Francisco Sourdough Bread

California Microbrewery Beer

FOR SIX TO EIGHT

FOURTH-GENERATION CALIFORNIAN John Phillip Carroll enjoys picnics in the golden grasses of the East Bay hills and simple city park repasts near his home in San Francisco. But his most vivid picnicking memories are from Oregon in the early '80s, when he worked with food maven James Beard.

Beard loved to picnic, though when he became elderly, a meal in the car was more feasible than an outdoor ramble. Carroll and Beard would often drive to Tillamook Head, a special place from Beard's childhood, and park at a spot overlooking the water. What was on the menu? Frequently Kentucky Fried Chicken, one of Beard's favorites, Carroll wryly admits.

Carroll's own cooking is more likely to draw inspiration from Beard's classes—a celebration of food and wine—than from his fast-food cravings. In his years with Beard, and later while researching recipes for *California the Beautiful Cook Book* (Collins Publishers, 1991), Carroll developed an appreciation for the heritage and agricultural abundance that have shaped California cuisine.

Carroll's chili chicken is an adaptation of an old San Joaquin Valley recipe, from the days when meals at ranchos were cooked with Mexican flavors and foods at hand. Chicken simmers in a thick sauce of chili powder, white wine, and *(Continued on page 154)*

greets the rare-fruit growers whose farms dot the nearby hills and chooses among their offerings: creamy sapotes and cherimoyas, blood oranges, passion fruit, bananas, and guavas. She also picks up dates grown in the Coachella Valley, 2 hours away.

Morse is the author of a cookbook featuring recipes from California farms, and of *The Vegetarian Table: North Africa,* due out next year from Chronicle Books. Back at her Moroccan-style home, she puts together her picnic, explaining how Morocco and California cuisines are as similar as their topography. They share seasonings—cilantro, oregano, cumin, lemons, and olive oil—plus plenty of fresh produce and grilled foods.

Morse loves salads made with season-al ingredients; her rice-lemon salad in tomato shells is not only delicious, but also easy to transport. Her skewered lamb and vegetables, in an intriguing paprika-cumin marinade, can be cooked ahead at home or grilled at the picnic.

After so many years in California, Morse happily adds nontraditional—and deli-prepared—foods to her menu: pocket bread, feta cheese, and hummus (North Africa's *bessara* is thinner, with no sesame butter). But the fragrant orange blossom water that flavors the watermelon drink and the date-almond truffles are pure Morocco.

We're tempted to spread the feast beside the fountain in the cool tiled courtyard of Morse's home, but the roar of the ocean calls.

RECIPES FOR YOUR GRAND PICNIC

These dishes can be made a day ahead unless otherwise noted. When packing your picnic, keep foods cold and hold no more than 2 hours at room temperature.

For the San Diego menu (page 151), make the watermelon drink by puréeing seedless watermelon chunks in a blender, then strain and chill. Serve over ice and add orange blossom water to taste. (You'll find orange blossom water in the gourmet food section or with cocktail preparations.) If you can't find sapotes—a green-skinned, creamy fruit— substitute another fruit favorite.

Tomatoes Casablanca

Cooking time: About 20 minutes
Prep time: About 20 minutes
Makes: 4 servings

    4 large (2½ lb. total) ripe tomatoes
      Salt
 1½ tablespoons extra-virgin olive oil
    ½ cup diced carrot
    ½ cup minced onion
    1 cup cooked long-grain rice
    ¼ cup diced jicama
    3 tablespoons coarsely chopped Italian parsley
    1 teaspoon grated lemon peel
 1½ tablespoons lemon juice
      Pepper

1. Slice off tomato tops; set aside. Hollow centers with a spoon, leaving a thin wall; reserve flesh. Generously sprinkle hollows with salt, turn upside down, and set aside.

2. In an 8- to 10-inch frying pan over medium heat, stir oil, carrot, and onion until vegetables are golden, about 8 minutes.

3. Chop enough tomato flesh to make ¼ cup (save remainder for other uses); add to vegetables with rice, jicama, parsley, lemon peel, and juice. Season with salt and pepper. Spoon into tomatoes; cover with tops.

Per serving: 147 cal. (54 cal., 37% from fat); 3 g protein; 6 g fat (0.9 g sat.); 22 g carbo.; 159 mg sodium; 0 mg chol.

Skewered Lamb

Cooking time: About 25 minutes
Prep time: About 25 minutes, plus at least 1 hour for marinating
Makes: 4 servings

    8 small (1½ in., ½ lb. total) thin-skinned potatoes
    8 diagonal slices carrot, each ½ inch thick and about 2½ in. long
    8 pattypan or sunburst squash (1½ in.) or 8 1-inch chunks of larger squash
    ⅓ cup extra-virgin olive oil
    ⅓ cup chopped fresh cilantro
    2 large cloves garlic, minced
    2 tablespoons lemon juice
      About 1 tablespoon ground cumin
    1 tablespoon sweet Hungarian paprika or regular paprika
    1 teaspoon ground ginger
      Salt and pepper
    8 squares (1½ in.) red bell pepper
    ½ pound boneless leg of lamb, cut in 8 chunks (each 1½ in. wide)

1. Half-fill a 4-quart pan with water; bring to boil over high heat. Add potatoes; simmer 5 minutes. Add carrots; cook 4 minutes more. Add squash; simmer until all vegetables are barely tender to bite, about 3 more minutes. Drain; let cool.

2. In large bowl, mix oil, cilantro, garlic, juice, 1 tablespoon cumin, paprika, and ginger. Season to taste with salt and pepper. Add cooked vegetables, bell pepper, and lamb. Cover; chill 1 hour or up to 1 day.

3. Alternately thread vegetables and meat on 4 metal skewers (16 in. long), reserving marinade. Grill over a bed of hot coals (you can hold your hand at grill level 2 to 3 seconds), or broil 3 inches below heat, turning often, until done, 8 to 10 minutes for medium-rare. Baste often with marinade.

4. Serve hot or at room temperature with dishes of salt and cumin for dunking.

Per serving: 296 cal. (153 cal., 52% from fat); 14 g protein; 17 g fat (4.3 g sat.); 23 g carbo.; 45 mg sodium; 39 mg chol.

Date-Almond Truffles

Prep time: About 15 minutes
Makes: 28

 1¼ cups toasted slivered almonds
    1 cup pitted dates
    1 tablespoon orange blossom water
    1 tablespoon honey
    ½ teaspoon ground cinnamon
    ½ cup sweetened shredded coconut

1. In food processor, whirl almonds, dates, orange blossom water, honey, and cinnamon until finely chopped. (Or finely chop nuts and dates; mix with other ingredients.)

2. Form into 1-inch balls; roll in coconut, pressing to coat lightly.

Per truffle: 62 cal. (32 cal., 52% from fat); 1.4 g protein; 3.6 g fat (0.7 g sat.); 7.2 g carbo.; 4.3 mg sodium; 0 mg chol.

For the Northern California menu, buy the biggest artichokes you can find. Steam, hollow out, and let cool. Fill with your favorite guacamole and chill. Allow one half per person.

California Chili Chicken

Cooking time: About 40 minutes
Prep time: About 20 minutes
Notes: If you don't have a nonstick 5- to 6-quart pan, brown chicken in a nonstick frying pan, then transfer to a regular 5- to 6-quart pan for simmering.
Makes: 8 servings

    ½ cup cornmeal
      Salt and pepper
    8 chicken pieces (breast halves or legs with thighs, 4 lb. total), skinned
    3 tablespoons olive oil
    1 onion (6 oz.), minced
    3 cloves garlic, minced or pressed
    3 tablespoons chili powder
    1 teaspoon ground cumin
    ½ cup dry white wine
    ½ cup chicken broth
    ¼ cup toasted slivered almonds
    1 cup large ripe pitted black olives
      Fresh cilantro or parsley sprigs

1. In a bag, combine cornmeal and 1 teaspoon *each* salt and pepper. Shake a few chicken pieces at a time in mixture to coat.

2. In a nonstick 5- to 6-quart pan over medium-high heat, brown half of chicken in half of oil, turning as needed, about 6 minutes. Lower heat if coating begins to scorch. Repeat with second batch. Remove chicken.

3. To pan, add onion and garlic; stir often until golden, about 5 minutes. Add chili powder and cumin; stir 1 minute. Mix in wine, broth, and almonds. Return chicken to pan. Slice enough olives to make ½ cup; sprinkle over chicken. Set whole ones aside.

4. Cover chicken; simmer until no longer pink in thickest part (cut to test), about 15 minutes, turning occasionally. Cook uncovered on medium-high heat, stirring, until sauce is very thick, 2 to 3 minutes.

5. Skim fat from sauce. Serve chicken hot or cold. Garnish with whole olives and cilantro; season to taste with salt and pepper.

Per serving: 282 cal. (117 cal., 41% from fat); 26 g protein; 13 g fat (2 g sat.); 13 g carbo.; 545 mg sodium; 76 mg chol.

(Continued on page 155)

cornmeal with olives and almonds. It's delicious cold, and just messy enough to be perfect outdoor food.

Three vegetable dishes underscore California's role as produce bowl for the nation. A feathery herb salad is a good complement to the spicy chili chicken. So is the classic orange–red onion salad, which harks back to the citrus and olive trees planted by mission fathers. Cold artichokes filled with guacamole decadently combine two more recent California crops.

SINCE CHILDHOOD, JANIE HIBLER HAS loved to picnic. Growing up, she'd spend mornings with friends making graham cracker sandwiches, then tote the snacks to a local meadow or creek. For Hibler's 19th birthday, her dad gave her an English picnic basket, complete with place settings and matching tin boxes, that she still uses.

Hibler's picnics now take her to Portland's rose garden, or to trails near the family's cabin near Mount St. Helens. From her kitchen the day of our picnic, we see that the only patch of sun is down the Willamette River on Sauvie Island.

We spend the morning visiting while Hibler prepares a repast of the Northwest foods she loves and has described in cookbooks such as *Dungeness Crabs and Blackberry Cobblers* (Alfred A. Knopf, 1991). Sweet Oregon spot prawns, which make a brief appearance in summer, are a special treat, and Hibler makes a quick mayonnaise to go with them, incorporating tart sorrel leaves from her backyard.

The mayonnaise also goes well with Walla Walla onions and her fresh herb bread in sandwiches made at the picnic. Dessert is dense peach-almond cake, a good traveler.

With the basket packed to the brim, we head for Sauvie Island and the elusive patch of sun. Clouds close in as Hibler explains that the island is a favorite place in winter for viewing bald eagles, in summer for hiking and visiting peach orchards.

The sky is now black. Ignoring it, we arrange our meal, wrestling with the tablecloth in a fierce wind. A fine Oregon Pinot Gris in hand, we raise our glasses to good food, good times, and a (nearly) idyllic setting. Fat raindrops fall. Undaunted, we keep eating. Finally, the skies open. In a mad jumble of cloths, dishes, and tumbling hazelnuts, we make a run for it. Dessert tastes just as good in the car. We've had a great adventure, as authentic a Northwest picnic as one could ask for.

NORTHWEST FLAVORS

Chilled Oregon Spot Prawns

*Sorrel Mayonnaise**

*Walla Walla Sweet Onion Sandwiches on Herb Bread**

Local Goat Cheese

Cherry Tomatoes

Roasted Hazelnuts • Seasonal Fruits

*Peach-Almond Cake**

Oregon Pinot Gris

FOR SIX TO EIGHT

JANIE HIBLER

Parsley and Herb Salad

Prep time: About 25 minutes

Notes: For milder flavor, substitute ⅓ cup watercress for the tarragon, marjoram, and sage.

Makes: 6 to 8 servings

1 ½ cups tender 1-inch curly-leaf parsley sprigs

⅔ cup tender 1-inch Italian parsley sprigs, or more curly-leaf parsley

1 cup chopped fresh basil leaves

⅔ cup 1-inch watercress sprigs

2 tablespoons *each* minced fresh tarragon and marjoram leaves

1 tablespoon minced fresh sage leaves

3 tablespoons freshly grated parmesan cheese

1 small clove garlic, minced

2 tablespoons extra-virgin olive oil

1 ½ tablespoons water

1 tablespoon lemon juice

Salt and pepper

1. Mix parsleys, basil, watercress, tarragon, marjoram, sage, and parmesan. In capped jar, shake garlic, oil, water, and juice to blend. Season with salt and pepper to taste.

2. If making salad and dressing ahead, chill separately, airtight, up to 4 hours. To serve, shake dressing; mix gently with herbs.

Per serving: 54 cal. (39 cal., 72% from fat); 1.8 g protein; 4.3 g fat (0.9 g sat.); 3 g carbo.; 52 mg sodium; 1.8 mg chol.

Orange–Red Onion Salad

Cooking time: 15 minutes

Prep time: 30 minutes, plus chilling

Makes: 8 servings

1 red onion (¾ lb.), cut in thin rings

4 large oranges (2¾ lb. total)

3 quarts inner leaves (8 in. or smaller) from 2 heads romaine lettuce (save large leaves for other uses)

4 large radishes, finely shredded

Whole radishes and orange slices

¼ cup extra-virgin olive oil

3 tablespoons red wine vinegar

Salt and pepper

1. In a large bowl, cover onion with boiling water; let stand 15 minutes. Drain, rinse with cold water, then pat dry. Chill airtight until very cold, about 2 hours.

2. With a sharp knife, cut peel and white membrane from outside of oranges. Cut between inner membranes to free segments; discard membranes and peel.

3. Place romaine in a transportable container; add onion and orange segments on top; scatter shredded radishes over all. Garnish with whole radishes and orange slices. Serve, or chill airtight up to 4 hours.

4. In a tightly capped jar, shake oil and vinegar to blend; season with salt and pepper. Shake again before serving; pour over salad.

Per serving: 142 cal. (68 cal., 48% from fat); 2.6 g protein; 7.5 g fat (1 g sat.); 19 g carbo.; 11 mg sodium; 0 mg chol.

For the Northwest menu, buy 1 ½ to 2 pounds spot prawns (or good-size shrimp) cooked in the shell, or simmer in white wine, and chill. Use sorrel mayonnaise to dip prawns, and to spread on bread for onion sandwiches. If Walla Wallas aren't available, use other sweet onions such as Maui or Vidalia. For mildest flavor, slice at the picnic.

Sorrel Mayonnaise

Prep time: About 10 minutes

Notes: Substitute spinach if sorrel is unavailable. For an egg-safe version, prepare mayonnaise as directed but omit the vinegar and egg. Instead, mix 1 large egg white with 2 tablespoons lemon juice. Chill airtight at least 48 hours or up to 4 days. Stir in 2 tablespoons water; proceed.

Makes: About 1 cup

1 tablespoon chopped shallot

1 tablespoon champagne or white wine vinegar

1 large egg

½ teaspoon salt

1 cup packed sorrel leaves (or spinach leaves plus 2 tablespoons lemon juice)

¾ cup salad oil

Freshly ground pepper

In a blender, whirl shallot, vinegar, egg, salt, and sorrel until smooth. With motor running, gradually add oil, whirling until thick. Season with pepper; use, or chill airtight up to 1 week.

Per tablespoon: 98 cal. (95 cal., 97% from fat); 0.6 g protein; 10.6 g fat (1.4 g sat.); 0.5 g carbo.; 73 mg sodium; 13 mg chol.

Janie's Herb Bread

Baking time: About 40 minutes

Prep time: About 15 minutes, plus 1 to 2 hours thawing and 40 minutes rising

Notes: We've simplified the original recipe by substituting frozen bread dough.

Makes: 1 loaf, about 2 pounds

All-purpose flour

2 loaves (1 lb. each) frozen white bread dough, thawed according to package directions

¾ cup minced fresh basil leaves

2 tablespoons minced chives

1 tablespoon minced fresh rosemary leaves

1 teaspoon grated lemon peel

Whole basil leaves and chives

1 tablespoon well-beaten egg

1. On lightly floured board, gather dough together; knead in minced herbs and peel until evenly mixed, adding flour as needed to prevent sticking. Shape into a smooth ball; place in oiled ½-quart soufflé dish. Cover; let rise in warm place until doubled, about 40 minutes.

2. Bake in a 375° oven until deep golden, 35 to 40 minutes. Brush bread and whole basil leaves and chives all over with egg, then arrange herbs attractively on loaf. Bake until glaze is just set, 1 to 2 minutes more.

3. Let cool in dish 15 minutes. Loosen from dish; cool completely on rack.

Per ounce: 70 cal. (8.1 cal., 12% from fat); 2.3 g protein; 0.9 g fat (0 g sat.); 13 g carbo.; 165 mg sodium; 2 mg chol.

Peach-Almond Cake

Baking time: About 1 hour

Prep time: About 15 minutes

Makes: 8 servings

⅓ cup (3½ oz.) almond paste

½ cup plus 1 tablespoon sugar

¾ cup (⅜ lb.) butter, softened

4 large eggs

1 ¼ cups all-purpose flour

1 medium-size ripe, juicy peach

1. In food processor or mixer bowl, whirl or beat paste, ½ cup sugar, and butter until fluffy. Add eggs 1 at a time, mixing well after each addition; whirl or beat in flour.

2. Spread batter in buttered, floured 8-inch-diameter cake pan with removable rim. Peel, pit, and slice peach ¼ inch thick. Slightly overlap slices on cake; sprinkle with 1 tablespoon sugar.

3. Bake in a 375° oven until a toothpick inserted in cake comes out clean, 55 to 60 minutes. Cool on rack; loosen from sides. To serve, push cake from rim.

Per serving: 389 cal. (216 cal., 56% from fat); 7 g protein; 24 g fat (12 g sat.); 38 g carbo.; 216 mg sodium; 155 mg chol. ∎

Berry bounty from
Northwest country inns

Raspberry muffins, boysenberry cobbler, and a mixed berry cake keep guests coming back for more

If you inhale deeply in the Pacific Northwest, you smell the sweet, unmistakable scent of berries. The soft climate is so ideal for them that you can't go far without catching their aroma. And this time of year, when vines and bushes are loaded with fruit, you can't go far without catching a taste.

Few know more about enjoying berries than berry-country innkeepers. At their inns, hospitality and pride in local products converge in particularly delicious ways.

You can try these dishes at four memorable places, or sample them at home and take advantage of the bounty of berries hitting markets all over the West.

Besides familiar raspberries and blueberries, more unusual choices in the blackberry family are making their brief seasonal appearance now. Two true blackberries are Marion—richly flavored and tender—and Olallie—long, slender, and sweetest when deep purple. Tay and Logan, blackberry-raspberry crosses, are red with an elongated shape and distinct perfumed flavor (Tays are particularly aromatic). Boysen, which is likely a Logan-blackberry cross, is the queen of berries—fat, sweet, and luscious.

All berries have a short shelf life. Chill them up to a day or two if necessary, but consume them as soon as possible. Wait to rinse them until just before using.

Hanson Country Inn, 795 S.W. Hanson St., Corvallis, OR (503) 752-2919. Rates start at $65; 4 rooms and a cottage. On a knoll above the Willamette Valley, the Northwest's biggest berry-growing area, is a white clapboard-and-brick building that looks just as you dreamed a country B & B would.

Patricia Covey has restored the grand Dutch colonial, once the home of poultry breeders, to its original 1928 charm.

Outdoors, a rose garden, gazebo, and brick pathways give the inn a genteel air. Inside, New Zealand gum paneling, floral prints, and vintage china set the stage for some old-fashioned berry treats.

Covey's cobbler (for dessert, or a decadent breakfast) is worth every calorie: cream-rich dough puffs up around big, soft boysenberries. Her frosty is a refreshing, low-fat drink that's great for a quick breakfast or light dessert.

Boysenberry Cobbler

Baking time: About 45 minutes
Prep time: About 20 minutes
Makes: 6 servings

- ¼ cup (⅛ lb.) melted butter or margarine
- 1¼ cups all-purpose flour
- 1 cup plus 1½ tablespoons granulated sugar
- 2½ teaspoons baking powder
- 1 cup whipping cream
- 1 teaspoon vanilla
- 1 quart boysenberries or blackberries

   About 1 tablespoon powdered sugar

   Mint sprigs (optional)

1. Evenly divide butter among 6 ramekins or deep ovenproof bowls (1⅓- or 1½-cup size); place slightly apart in a rimmed 10- by 15-inch baking pan.

2. In a bowl, combine flour, 1 cup granulated sugar, and baking powder. Add cream and vanilla and stir just until evenly moistened. Drop equal spoonfuls of dough into ramekins.

3. In bowl, gently mix berries with remaining 1½ tablespoons granulated sugar; set aside ⅔ cup, then spoon remaining berries over dough.

4. Bake in a 350° oven until cake portion is deep golden and springs back slightly when gently pressed, 40 to 45 minutes. Scatter remaining berries on top, sift powdered sugar over. Offer warm; garnish with mint.

Per serving: 475 cal. (189 cal., 40% from fat); 4.6 g protein; 21 g fat (13 g sat.); 70 g carbo.; 300 mg sodium; 66 mg chol.

BREAKFAST BENEATH THE GAZEBO *at Hanson Country Inn in Corvallis starts with warm, golden boysenberry cobbler.*

Raspberry Frosty

Prep time: About 10 minutes
Notes: The frosty is good with most flavors of fruit sherbet or sorbet.
Makes: 6 cups, 6 servings

    2½ cups raspberries
     2 cups low-fat milk
    1½ cups ice cubes
     ½ cup pineapple (or other flavor) sherbet or sorbet
     3 tablespoons sugar

In a blender, whirl berries, milk, ice, sherbet, and sugar until ingredients are smoothly puréed.

Per cup: 112 cal. (20 cal., 18% from fat); 3.3 g protein; 2.2 g fat (1.2 g sat.); 21 g carbo.; 48 mg sodium; 7.3 mg chol.

THIS FROSTY, *tinted with sweet Willamette Valley raspberries, is good for breakfast or dessert.*

Steamboat Inn, Steamboat, OR; (503) 498-2411. Rates start at $90; 15 units. About 40 miles east of Roseburg is a stretch of the North Umpqua River known for some of the most challenging steelhead fishing in the world. Steamboat Inn, built in the '50s, traces its roots to local camps that served fly-fishermen such as Zane Grey in the '20s.

Today, visitors still seek the superb angling opportunities, but they're as likely to come for hiking in the Douglas fir forests, for the comfortable cabins on the riverbank, or for the candlelit family-style dinners at the sugar pine slab table.

The cooks make a memorable breakfast, too. One of their guests' favorite

157

4. Spoon batter into 14 buttered 2¾-inch muffin cups or 8 buttered ramekins (about 1-cup size). Top evenly with streusel; press slightly into batter. Bake in a 400° oven until deep golden, about 25 minutes.

5. Loosen muffins from containers (if using ramekins, let cool completely first) and turn out onto a rack.

Per regular muffin: 253 cal. (99 cal., 39% from fat); 3.6 g protein; 11 g fat (5.8 g sat.); 35 g carbo.; 238 mg sodium; 39 mg chol.

Sylvia Beach Hotel, 267 N.W. Cliff St., Newport, OR; (503) 265-5428. Rates start at $63; 20 rooms. The draw of good books and good conversation is so strong at this creaky turn-of-the-century hotel on the ocean that one could easily forget about meals. But that would be a mistake, for the restaurant, Tables of Content, is the setting for some darned good eating.

Rooms are decorated in an author motif (the Alice Walker is painted with an African village scene; the Colette has filmy gauze over the bed.) The library stretches to the rafters.

Conversations begin at dinner, when each guest tells two truths and a lie about herself and others must guess the lie. By breakfast everyone seems like old friends.

Imaginative cooking, served family-style, includes blueberries from a farm just inland, and other berries from near Portland. Head breakfast cook Renée Scott frequently prepares a recipe from her St. Louis childhood: it's like a cross between a rich butter cake and a cheese-cake, with berries on top.

*A **STREAMSIDE BREAKFAST** features raspberry-hazelnut muffins from Steamboat Inn.*

recipes is streusel muffins with berries from small farms just west of Roseburg.

Raspberry Streusel Muffins

Baking time: About 40 minutes
Prep time: About 40 minutes
Notes: If cooking giant muffins in ramekins, be sure to let them cool before turning out so they won't fall apart.
Makes: 14 regular or 8 giant muffins

- ⅓ cup hazelnuts
- 1¼ cups sugar
- 3 tablespoons plus 1½ cups all-purpose flour
- 2 tablespoons butter or margarine, plus ⅓ cup melted
- ¼ teaspoon ground nutmeg
- ½ cup whole-wheat pastry flour (or ¼ cup regular whole-wheat flour plus ¼ cup all-purpose flour)
- 2 teaspoons baking powder
- ½ teaspoon baking soda
- ¼ teaspoon salt
- 1 large egg
- ½ cup *each* milk and sour cream
- 1½ cups raspberries

1. To toast nuts, place in an 8- to 9-inch baking pan; bake in a 350° oven until golden beneath skins, about 15 minutes. Rub in a towel to remove loose skins.

2. Chop nuts. In a bowl, combine with fingers until crumbly the nuts, ¼ cup sugar, 3 tablespoons all-purpose flour, 2 tablespoons butter, and nutmeg. Set streusel aside.

3. In a bowl, combine remaining 1½ cups all-purpose flour, 1 cup sugar, whole-wheat flour, baking powder, soda, and salt. In another bowl, whisk egg, milk, sour cream, and ⅓ cup melted butter until smooth. Add flour mixture and stir just until evenly moistened. Gently fold in raspberries.

St. Louie Ooey-Gooey Berry Butter Cake

Baking time: About 55 minutes
Prep time: About 20 minutes
Notes: If you make the cake a day ahead, bring it to room temperature to serve.
Makes: 10 servings

- 5 tablespoons melted butter or margarine
- ½ cup granulated sugar
- 2 large eggs
- ⅔ cup sour cream
- 1 cup all-purpose flour
- ½ teaspoon baking powder
- ½ teaspoon baking soda
- 4 ounces (½ of a large package) softened cream cheese
- 1½ cups powdered sugar
- 1 cup blackberries such as Marion
- ½ cup blueberries

1. In a mixer bowl, beat butter, granulated sugar, and 1 egg until pale and thickened. Beat in sour cream. Combine flour, baking powder, and soda, then beat into butter mixture until smooth. Spread evenly in a buttered and floured 9-inch cake pan with a removable rim.

2. Bake in a 350° oven until cake is pale golden and springs back slightly when gently pressed, 20 to 25 minutes.

3. Meanwhile, in bowl beat cream cheese, powdered sugar, and remaining egg until smooth. Spread over cake and arrange blackberries and blueberries on top. Bake until edges of topping are set and lightly browned but center still jiggles when pan is gently shaken, 25 to 30 minutes.

4. Let cake cool completely on a rack. Loosen from rim with a knife, then push out. Serve or, if making ahead, chill airtight up to 1 day.

Per serving: 313 cal. (135 cal., 43% from fat); 4.1 g protein; 15 g fat (8.9 g sat.); 42 g carbo; 209 mg sodium; 79 mg chol.

Inn at Swifts Bay, Route 2, Box 3402, Lopez Island, WA; (360) 468-3636. Rates begin at $75; 5 rooms and a house. Guests literally dash for their cameras when breakfast is served at this comfortable English country–style B & B.

Owners Christopher Brandmeir and Robert Herrmann serve thick Belgian waffles with flecks of ground hazelnuts; the waffles are loaded with berries grown nearby, and a big dollop of crème fraîche

LUSCIOUS BERRIES *picked minutes away from the Inn at Swifts Bay on Lopez Island tumble over the bed-and-breakfast's toasted hazelnut Belgian waffles.*

(similar to sour cream) on top. Plates are garnished with edible flowers from their garden and more fresh fruit.

Breakfast more than fortifies guests for a day of biking, sailing, or exploring the island's grassy fields and old orchards.

Hazelnut Waffles with Berries and Crème Fraîche

Cooking time: About 1 hour

Prep time: About 15 minutes

Notes: A food processor makes the batter easy to prepare. Look for crème fraîche in your market's dairy case, or substitute

sour cream to spoon over the waffles.

Makes: 18 regular waffle squares (4-in. size), 6 servings

- 1½ cups toasted hazelnuts (see directions on page 114)
- 2 cups all-purpose flour
- ¼ cup sugar
- 2 teaspoons baking powder
- ½ teaspoon baking soda
- ½ teaspoon salt
- 2 cups buttermilk
- 3 large eggs
- ⅓ cup salad oil
- 1 cup crème fraîche or sour cream
- 5 to 6 cups mixed berries (raspberry, blueberry, Tay, Logan, or Marion)

   Edible flowers (optional) such as Johnny-jump-ups or nasturtiums

   Berry syrup

1. Whirl nuts in a food processor (or part at a time in a blender) until very finely ground (if overprocessed, nuts will turn to butter). If using blender, transfer nuts to a large bowl.

2. To nuts add flour, sugar, baking powder, soda, and salt; whirl or stir to blend. Add buttermilk, eggs, and oil; whirl or whisk just until evenly moistened.

3. Bake batter in an oiled regular or Belgian waffle iron according to manufacturer's directions until well browned. Serve as cooked, or keep warm directly on rack of a 200° oven while making remaining waffles.

4. Place waffles on plates and spoon crème fraîche and berries on top. Garnish with flowers and offer with berry syrup.

Per serving: 717 cal. (405 cal., 56% from fat); 16 g protein; 45 g fat (9.5 g sat.); 67 g carbo.; 592 mg sodium; 126 mg chol. ■

By Elaine Johnson

OREGON BLACKBERRIES *and blueberries, with a cream cheese topping, bake atop butter cake at the Sylvia Beach Hotel in Newport.*

A **SUMMER SUPPER** *by Nancy Oakes and Bruce Aidells includes grilled sausages with capellini, sliced tomatoes, parmesan crisps, and a peach-ginger cobbler. Below, Nancy works on the cobbler and chats with Bruce before he prepares the entrée.*

PETER CHRISTIANSEN

Dinner with Nancy and Bruce

What does a duo of professional chefs cook up for guests? Quick, easy, delicious foods

E VER WONDER WHAT CHEFS COOK AT home? After long hours of professional cooking, it hardly seems possible they'd want to prepare a meal—let alone entertain. But Nancy Oakes, co-owner and chef of Boulevard restaurant in San Francisco, and her husband, Bruce Aidells, owner of Aidells Sausage Company, enjoy having friends over, especially since a home remodel gave them a dining room with windows facing San Francisco Bay, and a kitchen just an arm's reach away.

Their easy menu features fresh summer flavors and, of course, Aidells's fabulous sausages. Oakes looks for specialty tomatoes in season, such as Marvel Stripe, Brandywine, and Green Zebra. She drizzles them with olive oil and balsamic vinegar, then sprinkles them with slivered fresh basil.

Grilled Lemon-Chicken Sausages with Capellini

Cooking time: About 30 minutes
Prep time: About 30 minutes
Notes: For julienne lemon peel, use a vegetable peeler to cut strips of peel, then slice with a sharp knife into about 1/8- by 1 1/2-inch strips. If sausages are not cooked, cook before grilling. Bring 4 quarts water to a boil, add sausages, turn off heat, and let sausages steep 10 minutes. Remove sausages; cool to room temperature.

Makes: 8 servings

2 tablespoons olive oil
3 tablespoons minced garlic
1/2 to 1 teaspoon dried hot chili flakes
2/3 cup regular-strength chicken broth
1/2 cup fresh lemon juice
1 pound dried capellini or other thin spaghetti
1/2 cup loosely packed julienne lemon peel, yellow part only (from about 2 lemons)
8 lemon-chicken sausages (about 2 lb. total)

1 pound arugula leaves, tough stems removed, rinsed, drained, and coarsely chopped
Salt and pepper

1. Ignite about 60 charcoal briquets in a barbecue with dampers open.

2. Meanwhile, in a 6- to 8-quart pan, bring 4 quarts water to a boil over high heat.

3. While water is heating, add 1 tablespoon of the oil to a 10- to 12-inch frying pan over medium heat. When oil is hot, add garlic and chili flakes; cook, stirring often, until garlic is just golden brown, about 1 minute. Add broth and lemon juice; cook 1 minute longer. Remove from heat.

4. Add pasta to boiling water; cook until just tender to bite, about 2 minutes. Drain pasta and rinse with cold water. In a large bowl, mix pasta with remaining oil and lemon peel; set aside.

5. When briquets are covered with gray ash, spread into a single layer; let burn until you can hold your hand at grill level only about 4 seconds. Place sausages on grill. Turn as needed to brown all sides, 10 to 15 minutes. Remove sausages, and slice each diagonally into 3 pieces; cover with foil to keep warm.

6. Just before serving, bring broth mixture to a boil over high heat; add arugula. Cook, stirring, just until hot, about 1 minute. Pour over pasta and mix; spoon onto a large, shallow serving platter. Arrange sausages over pasta. Add salt and pepper to taste.

Per serving: 483 cal. (198 cal., 40% from fat); 24 g protein; 22 g fat (5.7 g sat.); 48 g carbo.; 738 mg sodium; 35 mg chol.

Parmesan Crisps

Baking time: About 10 minutes
Prep time: About 10 minutes
Notes: For a shortcut, buy shredded parmesan from the deli case.
Makes: 16 crisps, 8 servings

2 cups (about 6 oz.) shredded parmesan cheese, such as grana or reggiano

3 tablespoons all-purpose flour

1. Stir together cheese and flour.

2. Lightly oil and flour 2 baking sheets, each about 12 by 15 inches. Place portions containing 2 tablespoons cheese mixture each about 2 inches apart on baking sheets; with the back of a spoon, spread into 3- to 3 1/2-inch rounds.

3. Bake in a 375° oven until edges are golden brown, 8 to 10 minutes (check often to avoid overbrowning). Cool 10 minutes; transfer to rack to cool completely. You can make them a day ahead; store airtight.

Per crisp: 55 cal. (32 cal., 59% from fat); 3.6 g protein; 3.6 g fat (2.3 g sat.); 1.9 g carbo.; 68 mg sodium; 9.4 mg chol.

Peach and Ginger Cobbler

Baking time: About 1 hour
Prep time: About 1 hour
Notes: To speed prep time, or when good, fresh peaches are hard to find, substitute 4 pounds thawed frozen sliced peaches for fresh peaches.
Makes: 8 servings

10 large (about 4 1/2 lb. total) firm-ripe peaches

About 1 cup sugar

3 tablespoons cornstarch

1/3 cup orange juice

2 teaspoons vanilla

2 cups all-purpose flour

1/2 cup finely chopped crystallized ginger

1 tablespoon baking powder

1/2 teaspoon salt

1 cup heavy cream

4 tablespoons butter or margarine, melted

1 quart vanilla ice cream (optional)

1. Peel, pit, and thickly slice peaches into a large bowl. Combine 1/2 cup of the sugar with cornstarch; sprinkle over peaches. Gently stir to evenly coat slices. Add orange juice and vanilla; stir gently. Spoon into a buttered 3- to 3 1/2-quart baking dish (about 9 by 13 in.); set aside.

2. In a large bowl, combine flour, ginger, 2 tablespoons of the remaining sugar, baking powder, and salt. Stirring with a fork, slowly add cream until mixture is just combined; batter will resemble cookie dough.

3. Scoop about 1/3 cup batter into a 2-inch ball. Roll in melted butter, then in remaining sugar. Place atop fruit. Repeat to make a total of 8 balls, spacing 1 inch apart over fruit.

4. Place in a 350° oven; bake until center bubbles and top is golden brown, about 1 hour. Let cool at least 15 minutes; serve with ice cream as desired.

Per serving: 523 cal. (153 cal., 29% from fat); 5.3 g protein; 17 g fat (10 g sat.); 90 g carbo.; 400 mg sodium; 56 mg chol. ∎

By Betsy Reynolds Bateson

Tea-smoking moves outdoors

Classic Chinese wok technique works on the barbecue, and it's easier

IN TINY CHINESE KITCHENS, A COVERED wok is used to smoke poultry with tea, sugar, and rice in the dry pan. After the poultry is lightly smoked, a smelly process for indoors, it's steamed or fried.

But we have a simpler, quicker way: use the barbecue to smoke and cook the birds simultaneously.

Here we start with split game hens. They are delicately permeated by the smoky perfume of smoldering damp tea leaves, orange peel, anise, and soaked wood chips.

The presentation of the tea-smoked birds is similar to that of Peking duck.

Skin and meat are sliced from the warm birds and wrapped in flour tortillas with pungent hoisin sauce, fresh cilantro, and green onions. A slaw of napa cabbage with pickled ginger makes a refreshing companion.

Tea-smoked Hens

Cooking time: About 30 minutes
Prep time: About 20 minutes
Notes: Marinate the hens just before cooking or up to 1 day ahead. Instead of hens, you can use a 3- to 4-pound chicken, quartered.

Hoisin sauce is found in the Asian food section of most well-stocked supermarkets, but you may have to go to an Asian market for the star anise, or use anise seed. Look for the wood chips at a supermarket or hardware store.
Makes: 8 servings

4 Cornish game hens (1 1/2 to 2 lb. each)

1/3 cup dry sherry

1 teaspoon salt

1/2 teaspoon ground white pepper

Pared peel (orange part only) from 1 large orange

1 cup fruit wood or mesquite wood chips

1/2 cup (about 1 3/4 oz.) loose black tea leaves

2 star anise or 1 teaspoon anise seed

2 cinnamon sticks (each about 3 in.)

16 green onions with tops, ends trimmed

Fresh cilantro (coriander) leaves

16 warm flour tortillas (6 to 7 in. wide)

Hoisin sauce (optional)

1. Remove neck and giblets from game hens; reserve for another use. Cut game hens in half lengthwise; rinse and pat dry.

2. Mix sherry, salt, and pepper. Rub sherry mixture all over hens; if making ahead, cover and chill up to 1 day.

3. Cut orange peel into 1-inch pieces and put in a 2- to 3-quart pan with 3 cups water, wood chips, tea, anise, and cinnamon. Cover and let stand 10 to 30 minutes.

(Continued on page 162)

4. Stack 2 sheets of foil, each about 12 by 15 inches, then fold edges up to make a shallow pan about 4 by 8 inches.

5. Pour tea mixture into a fine strainer set over a bowl; reserve liquid and pour mixture into foil pan.

6. *In a charcoal barbecue with a lid,* prepare a solid bed of medium coals (you can hold your hand at grill level only 4 to 5 seconds). Set pan with chips onto coals close to a side of the barbecue; set grill in place.

In a gas barbecue, set pan with chips on heat in a corner of the barbecue; set grill in place. Turn heat to medium-high, put lid on, and let barbecue heat 10 to 15 minutes.

7. Lay hens, skin down, on grill but not over smoking chips. Cover barbecue (open vents for coals) and cook until hens brown on 1 side, about 15 minutes. Turn hens over, and if smoking has slowed, drizzle 2 tablespoons of the reserved liquid over chips. Cover barbecue and cook until meat at thigh bone is no longer pink (cut to test), about 10 minutes.

8. Transfer hens to a platter and garnish with green onions and cilantro. Wrap tortillas in a thick napkin to keep warm, and set in a basket. To eat, slice skin and meat from birds, put in tortillas, and season with hoisin sauce; add onions and cilantro, and fold tortillas to enclose filling.

Per serving: 494 cal. (207 cal., 42% from fat); 45 g protein; 23 g fat (6.1 g sat.); 24 g carbo.; 453 mg sodium; 132 mg chol.

Cabbage and Ginger Slaw

Prep time: About 30 minutes

Notes: Look for pickled ginger in the Asian section or refrigerator case at the supermarket or in Japanese grocery stores.

Makes: 6 servings

- 6 cups finely shredded napa cabbage
- 2 cups shredded carrots
- 1 large (about ½ lb.) red bell pepper, stemmed, seeded, and cut into thin slivers
- ½ cup finely slivered pickled ginger
- ½ cup seasoned rice vinegar

Mix cabbage, carrots, bell pepper, ginger, and vinegar. If making ahead, cover and chill up to 6 hours.

Per serving: 44 cal. (2 cal., 4% from fat); 1.3 g protein; 0.2 g fat (0 g sat.); 10 g carbo.; 358 mg sodium; 0 mg chol. ∎

By Linda Lau Anusasananan

KEVIN CANDLAND

TEA-SMOKED HEN, *warm from the barbecue and ready to sliver, rests on crisp napa slaw with carrots and pickled ginger.*

Everyday Low-fat Cooking

By Elaine Johnson

PHILIP SALAVERRY

Rethinking pesto: Red peppers instead of oil

When my husband, Patrick, and I get home late from work, neither of us having stopped at the store, we invariably turn to each other and say, "Pasta." In summer, standard provisions include basil. With some parmesan and olive oil, that used to translate easily into pesto.

The past year or two, though, I've become more aware of fat in my diet and, like many cooks, no longer use it blithely. As you will see in this monthly column, I'm looking for ways to enjoy the flavors I love while using fat more wisely.

My sister confirmed my misgivings about pesto by reading me the label on some she purchased: nearly 8 grams of fat in only a tablespoon (and I'd use much more). Maybe there was a way to rethink pesto.

First came the oil. What about substituting a jar of roasted red peppers (a favorite pantry staple)? Puréed in the blender with the basil and garlic, they made a thick sauce that coats pasta nicely.

Next came the parmesan. I found I could get good flavor with only an ounce, a third of what a traditional recipe calls for. I used a little more for topping the pasta, where it can really be appreciated.

Now all dinner needed was more vegetables. Thinking of French ratatouille,

but wanting something faster and lighter, I steamed eggplant, then browned it with zucchini in a nonstick pan using only 2 teaspoons olive oil.

My new pesto is multicolored instead of green, and tastes closer to ratatouille than true pesto, but still has many of my favorite flavors. I hope you'll join me at my table in the months ahead as I explore many other low-fat cooking possibilities.

Pasta with Red Pepper Pesto

Cooking time: About 20 minutes
Prep time: About 20 minutes
Makes: 4 servings

1 ½ cups (12 oz. jar or can) drained prepared roasted red bell peppers or pimientos in water

1 cup firmly packed fresh basil leaves, plus a few basil sprigs

1 clove minced garlic

⅓ cup freshly grated parmesan plus ⅓ cup thin shavings (2 oz. total)

¾ pound Asian eggplant, sliced crosswise ¾ inch thick

¼ cup water

1 pound zucchini (yellow and green), sliced diagonally ½ inch thick

2 teaspoons olive oil

2 cups coarsely chopped tomatoes

¾ pound dried fusilli or penne pasta

Salt and freshly ground pepper

1. In a blender, whirl red peppers, basil leaves, garlic, and grated parmesan until basil is finely chopped.

2. Place eggplant and water in a 10-inch nonstick frying pan. Cover tightly and bring to boil over high heat. Reduce heat; simmer until eggplant is tender when pierced, about 5 minutes. Uncover.

3. Add half the zucchini and half the oil. Over high heat, turn vegetables often until well browned, 8 to 10 minutes. Brown remaining zucchini in remaining oil; off the heat, add reserved vegetables and the tomatoes.

4. Meanwhile, fill a 6-quart pan ¾ full of water; bring to boil. Add pasta; boil until barely tender to bite, 8 to 12 minutes. Drain and return to pan, and mix in pesto.

5. Mound pasta and vegetables in a dish. Garnish with basil sprigs; top with cheese shavings. Mix at the table. Add salt and pepper.

Per serving: 496 cal. (72 cal., 15 % from fat); 20 g protein; 8 g fat (2.9 g sat.); 87 g carbo.; 430 mg sodium; 9.6 mg chol. ∎

KEVIN CANDLAND

PLAYFUL SWIRLS *of puréed basil contrast boldly with golden soup.*

Corn and basil take the heat

And make an exceptionally fresh soup

I T'S HEAT, NOT A LONG LIST OF ingredients, that brings out the lush flavors of corn and basil in this elegantly simple soup. If your corn is exceptionally sweet, a splash of lime juice rounds out the balance of tastes.

Sweet Corn and Basil Soup

Cooking time: About 45 minutes

Prep time: About 15 minutes

Notes: You can make the soup a day ahead and reheat to serve. You can make basil purée a few hours ahead.

Makes: 4 to 6 servings

8 medium-size ears (each about 8 in. long) corn, husks and silks removed

1 large (about ½ lb.) onion, chopped

2 tablespoons extra-virgin olive oil or salad oil

5 cups plus 2 tablespoons regular-strength chicken broth

2 tablespoons cornstarch mixed smooth with 2 tablespoons water

1 cup packed (about 2 oz.) fresh basil leaves

Lime wedges (optional)

Salt

1. With a sharp knife, cut corn kernels from cobs; discard cobs. Combine corn, onion, and 1 tablespoon oil in a 5- to 6-quart pan. Stir often over medium-low heat about 20 minutes; do not let mixture brown.

2. Transfer about half the corn and onion mixture to a blender or food processor. Whirl, adding 2 cups broth, until smoothly puréed. Pour soup back into pan; add 3 cups broth and cornstarch mixture. Over high heat, bring soup to a boil, stirring often.

3. Meanwhile, in a 10- to 12-inch frying pan, bring about 3 cups water to boiling over high heat. Immerse basil in water; as soon as it turns bright green, in about 2 seconds, scoop out and immediately immerse in ice water. When basil is cold, drain and pat gently between towels to dry. In a blender or food processor, combine basil with the remaining 1 tablespoon oil and 2 tablespoons broth. Whirl until smoothly puréed. Use, or if making ahead, protect purée from darkening by pouring into a close-fitting container (or cover surface with plastic wrap), cover, and chill up to 2 hours.

4. Ladle hot soup into 4 to 6 wide bowls. Spoon an equal amount of the basil purée into each bowl. Draw the tip of a spoon or knife through purée to swirl decoratively. Serve with salt and with lime wedges to squeeze into soup.

Per serving: 190 cal. (67 cal., 35% from fat); 6.2 g protein; 7.4 g fat (1.2 g sat.); 29 g carbo.; 64 mg sodium; 0 mg chol. ■

By Christine Weber Hale

Cool dips for sweet fruit

D IPS ARE NOTORIOUS FOR BEING rich, but here are two exceptions. Lemon curd and caramel sauce taste lavish but are based on lean versions of yogurt and sour cream. Each dip makes enough for about 3 dozen fruit bites.

Lemon Curd Dip

Prep time: 5 to 10 minutes

Makes: About 2½ cups

2 cups nonfat or low-fat vanilla-flavor yogurt

⅓ cup purchased or homemade lemon curd

1 teaspoon grated lemon peel

Mix yogurt, lemon curd, and peel. Serve, or if making ahead, cover and chill up to 1 day.

Per tablespoon: 20 cal. (4.5 cal., 23% from fat); 0.7 g protein; 0.5 g fat (0.3 g sat.); 3.2 g carbo.; 14 mg sodium; 4 mg chol.

Caramel Dip

Prep time: 5 to 10 minutes

Makes: About 2½ cups

2 cups nonfat, reduced-calorie, or regular sour cream

⅓ cup purchased or homemade caramel sauce

1 tablespoon minced fresh ginger

Mix cream, caramel, and ginger. Use, or if making ahead, cover and chill up to 1 day.

Per tablespoon: 16 cal. (0 cal. from fat); 0.9 g protein; 0 g fat; 2.8 g carbo.; 19 mg sodium; 0 mg chol. ■

By Christine Weber Hale

NORMAN A. PLATE

LEMON CURD *dip enhances strawberries.*

SUNSET'S KITCHEN CABINET

Creative ways with everyday foods—submitted by *Sunset* readers, tested in *Sunset* kitchens

Steak and Black Bean Salad

Frank and Jan Hickey, Olympia, Washington

   1/3 cup lemon juice

   1/4 cup minced fresh cilantro (coriander)

   1 1/2 teaspoons sugar

   1 clove garlic, minced

   1 fresh jalapeño chili, stemmed, seeded, and minced

   2 green onions, ends trimmed

   1 can (15 oz.) black beans, drained

   1 large (1/2 lb.) red bell pepper, stemmed, seeded, and chopped

   1 cup cooked corn

   5 cups mixed salad greens

   About 1/2 pound barbecued beef steak

   1 large (10 oz.) firm-ripe avocado

   Salt

1. Mix lemon juice, cilantro, sugar, garlic, jalapeño, and 2 tablespoons water.

2. Thinly slice onions and mix with beans, bell pepper, corn, and half the dressing.

3. Place greens in a wide bowl; mound bean salad alongside. Thinly slice meat, and peel, pit, and slice avocado. Arrange meat and avocado on salad; add remaining dressing. Mix, and add salt to taste. Makes 4 servings.

Per serving: 401 cal. (144 cal., 36% from fat); 27 g protein; 16 g fat (4.7 g sat.); 41 g carbo.; 473 mg sodium; 51 mg chol.

LEFTOVER BARBECUED *steak becomes a quick entrée salad.*

Curried Turkey Burgers

Kathleen B. Coggins, Sacramento

   1/2 cup reduced-fat mayonnaise

   1 1/2 tablespoons curry powder

   2 pounds ground turkey

   1 large (1/2 lb.) onion, minced

   1 large egg white

   1/4 pound jack cheese, thinly sliced

   6 hamburger buns, split and toasted

   Salt

1. Mix mayonnaise and 1 1/2 teaspoons curry powder to blend.

2. Mix remaining curry, turkey, onion, and egg white. Make 6 equal patties, each 3/4 inch thick.

3. Place patties on a hot oiled grill over a solid bed of very hot coals or highest gas heat (you can hold your hand at grill level only 1 to 2 seconds). Close lid on gas grill. Cook, turning once, until meat is browned and no longer pink in the center (cut to test), about 10 minutes total. Lay cheese on patties after turning.

4. Spread buns with seasoned mayonnaise, add patties; add salt to taste. Makes 6 servings.

Per serving: 523 cal. (252 cal., 48% from fat); 36 g protein; 28 g fat (7.7 g sat.); 30 g carbo.; 605 mg sodium; 96 mg chol.

CURRY ADDS FLAVOR *to turkey burgers and to the spread on the buns.*

White Chocolate–Blueberry Torte

Jeanne Ryan, Portland

   1 1/4 cups graham cracker crumbs

   1/4 cup (1/8 lb.) melted butter or margarine

   2 tablespoons sugar

   1/2 cup plus 2 tablespoons sugar

   3 tablespoons cornstarch

   2 cups blueberries

   1 cup (6 oz.) white chocolate chips (suitable for melting)

   1 package (1/2 lb.) neufchâtel (light cream) cheese

   1/4 cup nonfat sour cream

1. Mix crumbs, butter, and 2 tablespoons sugar; press evenly into a 9-inch cake pan with removable rim. Bake in a 350° oven until slightly browner, about 15 minutes. Use cool.

2. In a 2- to 3-quart pan, mix remaining 1/2 cup sugar and cornstarch; stir in 1/4 cup water and blueberries. Stir over high heat until mixture boils and thickens, about 2 minutes. Let cool to room temperature.

3. Set aside 1 tablespoon chocolate chips; put remainder in metal bowl nested over hot (not boiling) water. Stir often until smoothly melted. Remove from heat and add cheese and sour cream; beat to blend smooth with a mixer or a whisk. Scrape into crust and spread evenly. Spoon blueberry mixture onto torte. Cover and chill until cold up to 1 day.

4. Finely grind remaining chocolate in a blender or food processor. Sprinkle chocolate over torte. Makes 10 to 12 servings.

Per serving: 275 cal. (126 cal., 46% from fat); 4.1 g protein; 14 g fat (7.8 g sat.); 34 g carbo.; 209 mg sodium; 25 mg chol.

Compiled by Christine Weber Hale

SHIMMERING BLUEBERRIES *are the final touch for white chocolate–cheese torte.*

FOOD
Guide

BY JERRY ANNE DI VECCHIO

A TASTE OF THE WEST: Tangy ribs and corn

When we plan to serve beef back ribs, we choose our guests with care. They shouldn't fuss about messy faces and greasy hands, and they have to be washable—because there's absolutely no way to adequately enjoy ribs except by gnawing away. Once up to our elbows in bones, it's only practical to use our hands for the rest of the meal, which makes corn on the cob the perfect partner.

Barbecuing is the easiest way to cook bulky back ribs (not to be confused with beef short ribs) and corn. The dry heat of the grill browns them appetizingly and quickly, and the wafting smoke infuses them with flavor. Salt and pepper are perfectly adequate seasonings, but a sweet-sour glaze I tasted in a Thai restaurant is truly sensational.

Part of the glaze is used to shine up the meat and vegetables as they finish cooking, part is thinned with lime juice and fresh herbs to make a tangy sauce that is spooned onto the foods as you eat. A crusty loaf, warmed with butter and sprinkled with chopped green onions and fresh cilantro, goes well with this meal. You might even split the bread in half and toast it on the grill. And what could be more appropriate for dessert than scoops of a favorite ice cream or sorbet on sugar cones?

After we finish the meal, I always volunteer to hose down anyone who wants to freshen up.

Thai Beef Ribs and Corn

Cooking time: 40 to 50 minutes

Prep time: 30 to 40 minutes

Notes: You can make the basting-seasoning sauce a day ahead. Cook corn first if barbecue grill is too small for the ears and the ribs.

Makes: 6 servings

  1 tablespoon cornstarch

  ½ cup sugar

NOEL BARNHURST

AUGUST '95

- Make a tasty mess with ribs and corn on the grill

- Brighten up hash with vegetables

- Bake a tart with plums and apricots

- Solutions when food and wine disagree

This ultimate finger food is flavored with a sweet-sour glaze.

1 cup chicken broth

1 teaspoon grated lemon peel

1/4 cup *each* lemon juice and rice vinegar

2 tablespoons minced fresh ginger

About 3 tablespoons fish sauce (*nam pla* or *nuoc mam*) or soy sauce

1/2 teaspoon crushed dried hot red chilies

6 ears corn (about 4 lb. total)

12 beef back ribs (5 1/2 to 6 lb. total), cut apart and fat trimmed

1/4 cup lime juice

1/4 cup *each* chopped fresh cilantro and green onions

1. In a 4- to 5-quart pan, mix cornstarch with sugar. Stir in broth, lemon peel, lemon juice, vinegar, ginger, 2 tablespoons fish sauce, and chilies. Stir over high heat until boiling, then stir often until Thai sauce is reduced to about 1 1/4 cups (if you boil away too much, just add water). Use sauce hot or cool. If made ahead, cover and chill up to 5 days.

2. Pull corn husks back but do not break off. To make a decorative handle, tie husks together on each ear with a thin husk strip. Discard corn silk and rinse ears.

3. In a barbecue with a lid, cover firegrate with a solid layer of hot coals or heat gas grill to high (you can hold your hand at grill level only 2 to 3 seconds). Lay corn on grill (husks can hang over edge outside lid). Cover barbecue and open vents on lid. Cook corn until lightly browned, about 10 minutes, turning to keep color even. Push corn to a cool area of grill (or remove and keep warm). Lay ribs on grill. Cover and cook until meat is lightly browned, turning as needed, about 10 minutes (if flame-ups occur, immediately cover grill with lid).

4. Measure 1/4 cup Thai sauce and season it to taste with remaining fish sauce. Stir in lime juice, cilantro, and green onions; set herb-flavored Thai sauce aside.

5. Use remaining sauce to baste corn and ribs. After meat has cooked 10 minutes, brush again generously with sauce. When meat is richly browned, transfer ribs and corn to a platter and brush pieces with any remaining sauce.

6. As you eat ribs and corn, moisten to taste with herb-flavored Thai sauce.

Per serving: approx. 359 cal., 30% (108 cal.) from fat; 23 g protein; 12 g fat (4.6 g sat.); 43 g carbo.; 400 mg sodium; 56 mg chol.

BACK TO BASICS

Haute hash

When a visit with a friend is interrupted by pangs of hunger, hash is one of my favorite emergency meals. Even a relatively empty refrigerator, freezer, and cupboard can be squeezed to produce hash ingredients. But what kind of hash? Technically, hash as a noun refers to foods that are chopped—usually leftover potatoes and meat, but it might be anything—then browned.

At John O'Groats restaurant in West Los Angeles, hash is not merely the repository for remains of a previous meal. The menu describes it as vegetarian hash with two eggs, any style, on top. I spotted a plateful being slid onto the counter between a customer and his morning news, and immediately placed my order. Potatoes and onions are the foundation. Instead of meat, more vegetables are added for color, and apple—the surprise—brings just enough sweetness to pull all the elements together.

John O'Groats vegetarian hash. For 2 servings, use 1 boiled or baked **potato** (2 to 2 1/2 in. wide), sliced or diced. You can use any kind of potato, but I like unpeeled red-skinned ones. You also need about 1/2 cup chopped **onion**, red if you want more color; about 1/2 cup sliced, diced, or chopped **carrot,** raw or cooked; about 1/2 cup **corn kernels,** fresh, canned, or frozen; about 1/2 **apple** (red is prettiest), cored and sliced or diced; a big handful of fresh **spinach leaves** (or other greens such as arugula, mustard, or watercress); and 2 or 3 **red cabbage** or radicchio **leaves,** torn into pieces or chopped.

Use just enough **butter** or olive oil to coat the bottom of a 10- to 12-inch nonstick frying pan. Brown the potato, onion, and carrot. Mix corn into the hash, then lay apple slices around the edges. When apple slices are brown, turn them over, but don't mix into the rest of the hash until the second apple side browns. Then scatter the spinach and cabbage over the hash and turn with a wide spatula to mix. Cook until spinach leaves are bright green and limp. Add **salt** and **pepper** to taste.

Trade tricks: Use a pan that gives the hash plenty of space for fast, even browning. Don't nervously poke at the hash; let the ingredients cook undisturbed until they form a crusty brown surface. Also, beware of smacking the hash down with the spatula, as many cooks are tempted to do. This will rupture all those nice browned surfaces. Do I serve **eggs** on top? Soft fried, if I have any.

KEVIN CANDLAND

Fresh apricots make this a one-time-of-the-year dessert.

SEASONAL NOTE

The two-fruit tart

Nature has a way of bringing certain flavors together briefly for the better of both—new potatoes with shad roe, or rhubarb with strawberries, for example. Right now, it's apricots with plums. Plums go on for months, but only during these few weeks can you pair them with fresh apricots in this tart. The fruit gets very juicy as it bakes. If you want the tart wedges to hold their shape, be sure to let the dessert cool completely before cutting. Otherwise, scoop the tart warm into bowls.

Last year I tasted a new-to-me plum called a plumcot. It is slightly golden and has a hint of apricot flavor, but it just doesn't match the taste of apricots and plums together.

Apricot Plum Tart

Cooking time: About 1½ hours

Prep time: 25 to 30 minutes; allow at least 4 hours to cool

Notes: You can make the tart, or just the crust dough, a day ahead.

Makes: 6 servings

2 pounds ripe to firm-ripe apricots

1 pound ripe to firm-ripe red-skinned plums

About 1 cup sugar

6 tablespoons instant tapioca

1 teaspoon grated orange peel

½ teaspoon grated lemon peel

¼ cup orange muscat wine such as Essencia or 2 tablespoons orange-flavor liqueur such as Cointreau (optional)

1½ cups all-purpose flour

½ teaspoon baking powder

10 tablespoons butter or margarine, cut in small pieces

1 large egg

Sweetened, softly whipped cream, vanilla ice cream, or sweetened sour cream (optional)

1. Rinse apricots and plums and slice fruit from pits into a bowl; discard pits. Mix ½ cup sugar (add ¼ cup more sugar if fruit is firm and less ripe) and tapioca; add to sliced fruit along with orange peel, lemon peel, and wine. Stir to mix well; set aside.

2. In a food processor or bowl, combine all-purpose flour, ¼ cup sugar, and baking powder. Add butter. Whirl or rub until mixture is very fine crumbs. Add egg and whirl or mix until dough is evenly moistened and sticks together. (If making more than 4 hours ahead, cover and chill; use at room temperature.)

3. With floured fingers, press dough evenly over bottom and sides of a 9- or 10-inch cheesecake pan with removable rim. Make dough sides about 1¾ inches high in a 9-inch pan, about 1¼ inches high in a 10-inch pan.

4. Pour fruit mixture into pastry and shake to level.

5. Bake in a 350° oven until fruit bubbles in center, about 1½ hours. As tart bakes, use a fork to push fruit speckled with tapioca into filling occasionally so it will cook.

6. Let tart stand until cool in center, at least 4 hours or up to 1 day; cover when cool. Run knife between crust and pan rim; remove rim. Cut tart into wedges and accompany with whipped cream to taste.

Per serving: 267 cal., 37% (99 cal.) from fat; 3.5 g protein; 11 g fat (6.2 g sat.); 41 g carbo.; 147 mg sodium; 44 mg chol.

BOB THOMPSON ON WINE: How a wine changes its taste

When M. F. K. Fisher taught a food and wine pairings class in the early years of the Napa Valley Wine Library Wine Appreciation Course, she would trot out four little plates of food and four glasses of red wine for each student.

The first plate contained cheese, the second an artichoke heart, the third a vegetable salad. I forget the fourth. The game was to identify the four wines by type, with help from the food. Some students, emboldened by successes at earlier, simpler tasks, would hazard wonderful guesses. "Glass 1 is a young Pinot Noir with just a hint of sulfur, Glass 2 is a Cabernet, probably from a vineyard at Rutherford." Glass 3 usually stumped the boldest and the brightest, or made them claim they had gotten a bad bottle.

Louis P. Martini, waiting to do his turn on red winemaking, would sit in the back of the room muttering, "Smell the wine, smell the wine!"

All four glasses always held the same wine, usually a Zinfandel. A couple of people would overhear Martini and figure it out, but the redoubtable Mrs. Fisher would outshout him long enough for some of her scholars to bewilder themselves, setting the stage for her to explain how the chemistry of the foods would alter that of the wine until each glass tasted quite unlike the rest.

Cheese flatters every wine by softening both acids and tannins, as all wise wine sellers know. Less widely understood is that the faintly alkaline artichoke flattens them both. As for the salad turning its accompanying wine horrible, it was the vinegar in the dressing as done the deed, traditional vinegar being nothing more or less than spoiled wine. When wine books forbid people to have wine with salad, vinegar is the reason, not poor, innocent lettuce. Wine judges even use lettuce as a palate cleanser at competitions.

The moral of the story: now, in the warmth of summer, when a cool, refreshing salad is a welcome main dish almost as often as it is a side issue, use a nonthreatening dressing and have your wine in peace.

A little lemon juice will do well on its own or with oil. A colleague says rice vinegar works just fine. A blue cheese dressing is the best help of all for wine. The lumpier the blue the better. ∎

KEVIN CANDLAND

MANGO SORBET *in a citrus bowl is a stunning dessert. Serve quickly—in about 15 minutes, the bowl softens and comes unglued.*

Frozen citrus bowls

Sugar-water syrup glues fruit slices together—make or buy sorbet to fill them

A T ALL SEASONS CAFE IN CALISTOGA, California, sorbet arrives at the table in semitransparent frozen bowls made entirely from citrus slices. It's a dramatic close to a meal—a special touch that's easy to re-create at home.

All you need is a sharp knife to make thin, even slices of citrus fruits. (The recipe has enough extra for you to use the prettiest slices and save the rest for lemonade.) Bowls hold well in the freezer if you want to make them days ahead.

All Seasons varies its sorbet flavors with the changing availability of fruit. Three favorites that might appear on August menus are intensely flavored mango, raspberry, and blackberry, all based on the same simple recipe.

Frozen Citrus Bowls

Cooking time: About 10 minutes
Prep time: About 45 minutes, plus at least 2½ hours in freezer

Notes: The citrus slices must be thin to hold together. To chill the syrup faster, set pan in a bowl of ice water.

Makes: 6 citrus bowls

- ½ cup *each* sugar and water
- 2 lemons (¾ lb. total)
- 2 limes (½ lb. total)
- 2 oranges (1 lb. total)
  Scoops of sorbet (recipes follow, or use purchased)
  Mint sprigs

1. In a 1- to 2-quart pan over high heat, bring sugar and water to a boil, stirring occasionally. Let cool; chill until cold.

2. Meanwhile, with a sharp knife, cut lemons, limes, and oranges into even, paper-thin (1⁄16 to 1⁄8 in. thick) slices.

3. Line 6 bowls (2 to 2½ in. deep, 1½- to 2-cup size) with plastic wrap. Using the prettiest pieces, dip the citrus slices in syrup, lift to drain, and overlap to snugly line bottoms and sides of bowls. Save any leftover syrup and citrus slices for other uses.

4. Wrap citrus bowls airtight, then freeze until firm, at least 2½ hours or up to 1 week. Working quickly, gently lift frozen citrus bowls from molds, peel off plastic wrap, place each on a dessert plate, and fill with your favorite sorbet.

5. Serve filled bowls immediately (they keep their shape only about 15 minutes), or return to freezer for up to 1 hour, then serve. Garnish with mint.

Mango Sorbet

Cooking time: About 10 minutes
Prep time: About 40 minutes, plus 3 to 4 hours in freezer
Makes: 1 quart, 8 servings

- 1¼ cups sugar
- 1 cup water
- 2 ripe mangoes (2 lb. total)
- 2 tablespoons lime juice

1. In a 1- to 2-quart pan over high heat, bring sugar and water to a boil, stirring occasionally. Let cool, then chill until cold.

2. Peel mangoes with a small, sharp knife, cut flesh from pits, then cut into chunks. In a blender or food processor, whirl flesh and lime juice into a smooth purée. Blend in sugar syrup.

3. Freeze mango mixture in ice cream maker according to manufacturer's directions until softly frozen. Place in freezer, airtight, until firm enough to scoop, 3 to 4 hours or as long as 1 week. If the sorbet is too hard to scoop, let it soften briefly at room temperature.

Per serving: 173 cal., 1% (1.8 cal.) from fat; 0.4 g protein; 0.2 g fat (0.1 g sat.); 45 g carbo.; 2.5 mg sodium; 0 mg chol.

Raspberry Sorbet

Follow directions for **mango sorbet** (preceding), but omit mangoes and lime and substitute 1 quart **raspberries.** Purée as directed, then press through a fine strainer set over a bowl, rubbing to extract all liquid; discard seeds. Sorbet takes 2 to 3 hours to firm in freezer.

Per serving: 151 cal., 1.8% (2.7 cal.) from fat; 0.6 g protein; 0.3 g fat (0 g sat.); 38 g carbo.; 0.3 mg sodium; 0 mg chol.

Blackberry Sorbet

Follow directions for **mango sorbet** (preceding), but instead of mangoes and lime juice, use 1 quart **blackberries.** Purée as directed, then press through a fine strainer set over a bowl, rubbing to extract all liquid; discard seeds. Sorbet takes 2 to 3 hours to firm in freezer.

Per serving: 158 cal., 1.7% (2.7 cal.) from fat; 0.5 g protein; 0.3 g fat (0 g sat.); 40 g carbo.; 0.3 mg sodium; 0 mg chol. ∎

By Elaine Johnson

I

It's 6:17 A.M. Bill Williams zips up his windbreaker, pulls his baseball cap down a little lower over his eyes, and steps into a blustering wind. Williams's crop needs his attention. He and his crew must harvest the day's orders before the tide retreats and strands his barge. *Tide? Barge?* Williams grows Pacific oysters, and Williams's Shellfish Farms covers about 760 intertidal acres in Morro Bay, California. After daily harvesting, Williams's oysters are iced and shipped to such places as Galley Restaurant in Morro Bay and Finicky Fish Market and Fat Cats in Port San Luis. There, Williams's oysters join salmon from Washington and British Columbia, trout from Idaho, and, from California, Mediterranean bay mussels from Carlsbad and Santa Barbara, tilapia and hybrid striped bass from Palm Springs, and sturgeon produced near Sacramento. Bill Williams is just one example in a new and expanding breed of Western farmers who practice aquaculture.

Aquaculture began in the United States in the last century with oyster and trout farming, but Asian countries have farmed fish for thousands of years. What's new is aquaculture's skyrocketing growth. It is now the fastest-growing sector of U.S. mainstream agriculture. Last year, 12 percent of all seafood consumed in this country had been domestically farmed. Experts predict that the percentage will rise to 25 during the next five years.

A phenomenal jump in global seafood demand at a time of declining wild harvests—down 7 percent in the last three years—has galvanized fish farming. World demand is expected to increase by 70 percent in the next 35 years. With human populations growing, wild fish resources shrinking, and nutritionists telling us to eat more fish, aquaculture is the way to fill the gap.

What does aquaculture mean to consumers? You can buy farmed fish and shellfish from all over the world, and your choices are no longer limited by the season or

Who grew that fish on your plate?

SALMON EVERYWHERE, OYSTERS ALL YEAR, NEW NAMES AT THE MARKET AND ON MENUS... THANKS TO TODAY'S FISH FARMERS

BY

CHRISTINE WEBER HALE

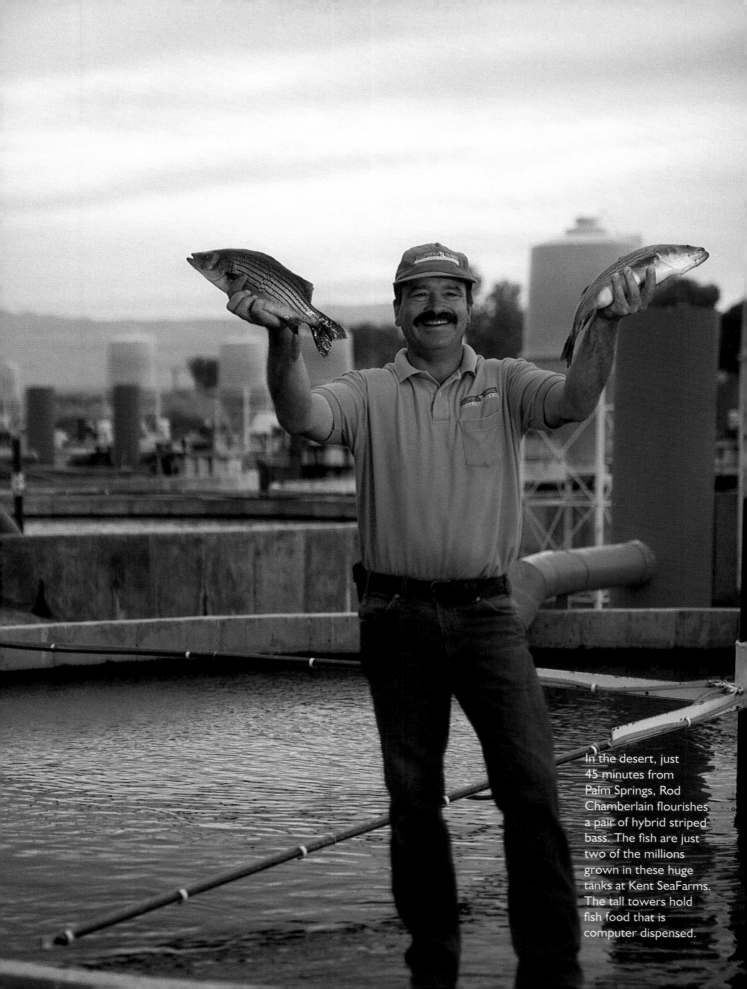

In the desert, just 45 minutes from Palm Springs, Rod Chamberlain flourishes a pair of hybrid striped bass. The fish are just two of the millions grown in these huge tanks at Kent SeaFarms. The tall towers hold fish food that is computer dispensed.

Down on the mollusk farm

Hundreds of oyster, clam, and mussel farms thrive along the Pacific coast. Farmers either purchase their mollusk larvae (seed) from laboratory nurseries or gather wild larvae from spawning adults. Once the larvae are a specific size, they are placed in sheltered growing areas to feed on natural food sources until they reach market-size in nine months to five years, depending on species, food supply, and water temperature. Generally, mollusks grow faster in warmer water.

You can visit many Western oyster farms that have their own retail stores and sell oysters shucked or in the shell. Here are a few, listed north to south.

Westcott Bay Sea Farms: 4071 Westcott Dr., Friday Harbor, WA; (360) 378-2489.

JKT Oyster Farm: 1033 Old Blyn Highway, Sequim, WA; (360) 683-1028.

Taylor United: S.E. 130 Lynch Rd., Shelton, WA; (360) 426-6178.

Brady's Oysters: 3714 Oyster Place E., Aberdeen, WA; (360) 268-0077.

Qualman Oyster Farm: 4898 Crown Point Rd., Coos Bay, OR; (503) 888-3145.

Clausen Oysters: 4215 U.S. Highway 101 S., Coos Bay, OR; (503) 267-3704.

Coast Seafoods: 25 Waterfront Dr., Eureka, CA 95501; (707) 442-2947.

Hog Island Oyster Company: 20215 Shoreline Highway, Suite 1, Marshall, CA; (415) 663-9218.

Tomales Bay Oyster Company: 15479 State Highway 1, Marshall, CA; (415) 663-1242.

At the Abalone Farm (right) on the California coast, about 6 million abalone make their home in 560 grow-out tanks. Honeycombs of plastic or fiberglass sheets fill tanks, giving abalone surfaces to cling to.

Harvested Pacific oysters (above) grown for the half-shell trade rest in holding tanks at California's Tomales Bay Oyster Company until they are shipped. Drew Alden (right) hauls up oysters growing in mesh bags to check their size.

concerns about conservation. In the West, abalone, catfish, clams, crayfish, mussels, oysters, salmon, hybrid striped bass, sturgeon, tilapia, and trout are farmed. Cultivated products such as blue lobsters and caviar are in the works. The safety and quality of farmed fish can be monitored. But even as aquaculture is reshaping future resources, it is one of the most hotly debated issues in the food industry.

What is aquaculture?

Aquaculture, which simply means *cultivating in water,* can be divided into two basic types: extensive and intensive. Extensive aquaculturists "plant" their "crops" in a natural environment and let them develop on their own until they reach harvest-size. (Saltwater aquaculture is often called mariculture, indicating that the species are grown in a bay or the ocean instead of in manmade freshwater tanks or ponds.) Mollusks, specifically oysters, mussels, and clams, are mostly farmed in this way.

Intensive aquaculturists create a completely controlled environment. Often, water is pumped in and must be constantly cleaned as it recirculates. Machines dispense food at regular intervals—a full-time job if you have a million fish.

Abalone, some crayfish, hybrid striped bass, sturgeon, tilapia, and trout are raised in densely populated tanks (sometimes called raceways if they're long and narrow). Water moves continuously through these tanks. As fish and shellfish grow, they are kept in same-size batches to reach market-size simultaneously.

Some intensive farms utilize technology almost as complex as that used in space exploration. Solar AquaFarms in Sun City, California, for example, raises tilapia in a big way—5 million pounds annually. And it does it smack-dab in the middle of the desert. The farm, covered by huge greenhouses, sprawls across an area equal to 26 football fields. Inside the greenhouses, enormous solar-heated tanks create the steamy, tropical environment in which tilapia thrive—not unlike the Nile of ancient Egypt, where these fish are thought to have evolved. Each 60- by 500-foot raceway holds half a million gallons and about 200,000 fish. Efficiency is vital. Every drop of water must be reused. A patented treatment and recycling system purifies the water and converts fish waste to organic fertilizers. Computers monitor and control feeding, water temperature, and oxygen and nitrogen levels; they also keep growth and population statistics. And if the computers fail, attendants are on-site 24 hours a day, ready to take over.

Markets and menus are changing

Tilapia comes from Solar AquaFarms 365 days of the year. Salmon floods the market—430 million pounds are farmed annually worldwide. Five years ago, you might have paid as much as $14.99 a pound for salmon. Today farmed specials at $2.99 a pound aren't unusual. The old adage about avoiding months with the letter *r* no longer applies to shellfish safety. Sturgeon and striped bass, disappearing in the wild, are enjoying a revival because of aquaculture.

The food service industry values the convenience, steady supply, and relatively constant price that aquaculture brings to fish. Restaurants can plan menus with assurance that fish and shellfish will arrive. Some farms even offer customized fish. Kent SeaFarms, near Palm Springs, sells its hybrid striped bass in 10 sizes. Chefs praise the consistent quality and portion sizes of farmed fish, which help them standardize preparation.

But what if you're a consumer outside the food industry? How do you know if fish at a restaurant or at the market is farmed? Even if you're curious, don't expect to find signs. Currently, restaurants and retailers are not required to label fish or shellfish as farmed—except in Washington, where a 1992 state law requires that farmed salmon be labeled.

Wild abalone, salmon, and sturgeon are seasonal. So when you see these fish featured as seasonal specialties, they are usually wild.

Even if fish is labeled as farmed, this information is frequently ignored when the fish is marketed through wholesale brokers. The salesperson or server may have no clue as to the source. Mollusks, however, are certified as to where and when they were harvested, and the seller must make the information available if you ask.

Is it safe?

The safety of fish and shellfish, whether farmed or wild, is the biggest concern of both consumers and people in the aquaculture and fishing industries. Water quality often determines safety. Since wild fish swim where they want, waters they visit can't often be monitored. And even waters that are monitored aren't always places you'd want your dinner to hail from.

But farmed fish are another matter. Commercially grown clams, mussels, and oysters are raised in waters whose safety must be tested under the FDA's National Shellfish Sanitation Program (NSSP), administered by state health departments. Under NSSP, farmers must sample water from several sites in the

173

What's that salmon on you

Salmon is one of the most popular eating fish, and it's farmed worldwide in greater volume than any other. This is why you see salmon bargains in the market at the same time that headlines prophesy the demise of salmon in the wild. What's more, salmon offer a sometimes confusing lesson in geography.

Norway, which pioneered salmon farming in the 1970s, produces more than half the world's supply—more than 550 million pounds a year. Other major players include Chile, the United Kingdom, and Canada.

In the West, 10 million pounds of salmon are pulled from Washington's Puget Sound each year. Four large companies—Global Aqua U.S.A., Scan Am, Stolt Sea Farm, and Birting Salmon L.P.—dominate the business. Each has several farms near Bainbridge Island, Port Orchard, Anacortes, Port Townsend, Port Angeles, and Hartstene Island. About 70 percent of Washington's salmon goes to Californ-

It could be Atlantic or Pacific, farmed or wild, red or pink, foreign or domestic

ia; the rest ends up in the Midwest and Southwest and in Japan and other Asian countries—about 70 percent in food service, 30 percent in markets.

But the salmon that is farmed in the West is not one that grows naturally here: farmers prefer Atlantic salmon because it is the hardiest, so far, and most efficient to farm.

Most fish-farming controversy is directed at salmon producers, particularly in the Northwest, where salmon fishing, part of the region's economy, suffered when farmed salmon brought prices down. Allegations of medicated fish and water pollution persist. Responding to concerns, Pete Granger,

executive director of the Washington Farmed Salmon Commission, says that farmed salmon receive fewer antibiotics than other farmed creatures such as cows, hogs, or poultry. And when antibiotics are used, they are FDA-approved ones, such as amoxicillin, given to the smolt (baby fish) just before they are moved from freshwater to salt, when they are most susceptible to disease. The fish are given no more medication, and when they reach market-size, the FDA agrees they've had ample time to purge any drugs.

As for pollution, Granger cites an EPA study that determined that water currents under Puget Sound pens are strong enough to flush the area.

Life for farmed salmon begins as eggs in a freshwater hatchery. As smolt, they are transferred to floating-net pens to grow for 10 to 18 months, until they are 6 to 10 pounds. On large farms, feeding is monitored by computers. Floating pens can be towed to a safe location if algae bloom (which

An Atlantic salmon in Washington wrestles with Lorenzo Weise-Hansen as he lifts it from its watery pen at Scan Am's Cypress Island Farm.

DAVID S. ROBBINS

plate?

suffocates the fish) develops.

Comparing the flavor and texture of wild salmon with those of farmed isn't simple. There are distinct differences among species. A pale amber gold wild Atlantic and an intensely red wild sockeye salmon will be decidedly unalike in looks and taste. Unquestionably, what salmon eat affects their flavor, and some feed mixes produce superior results. Because farmed salmon eat more regularly and don't have to work as hard for their grub, they tend to be a little fattier and softer than their wild counterparts. Fattier salmon, like the Atlantic (wild or farmed) and king, are quite moist because of their oil content. When we surveyed leading fish chefs in the West about their preference for farmed or wild salmon, it was a toss-up.

Visiting a farm. While most Puget Sound salmon farms aren't usually open to the public, it is often possible to arrange a special group tour by calling the Washington Farmed Salmon Commission at (360) 671-1997.

harvest area each month, testing for biotoxins and bacteria. Shellfish are tested for natural biotoxins such as paralytic shellfish poisoning and domoic acid.

Only mollusks, often consumed whole and raw, are federally regulated as they grow because they are filter feeders—they ingest algae filtered from the water. If harmful bacteria are present, they concentrate in the meat and can cause illness or worse. Because other fish and shellfish aren't filter feeders, and don't ingest the toxins directly, they are slower to accumulate harmful bacteria. Monthly water checks around farmed mollusks spot pollution well before it reaches dangerous levels. If water and shellfish tests don't meet NSSP standards, the shellfish cannot legally be harvested or sold.

But no farmer wants to get to that point. John Davis, owner of Carlsbad AquaFarms in Carlsbad, California, raises Mediterranean bay mussels. He speaks for many aquaculturists when he says, "The last thing in the world I want is for someone to get sick from my product." Because Davis's mussels grow in a restricted area—the FDA has designated the water quality unpredictable—they must be cleansed before being sold. Davis has developed and built his own "depuration" system. After harvest, his mussels get a spa treatment, reposing as long as 48 hours in trays of purified water, which purges their meat of any impurities.

The FDA works with the state to inspect the handling, processing, and packing of all shellfish, including mollusks, and fish—but only sporadically unless there is a consumer problem. Within a year, the FDA hopes to introduce a new mandatory regulatory program, Hazard Analysis and Critical Control Point (HACCP).

Under the program, inspection focus shifts from after-the-fact correction to problem prevention. Fish processors will be required to police their own sites through a detailed system of record keeping and safety checks. The FDA will review the records and continue conducting on-site inspections. However, an FDA spokesperson says the number of inspectors will drop because of government downsizing; some people question how this change will affect the program, particularly as penalties for violations have yet to be established.

HACCP rules will apply to all domestic seafood processors, distributors, and importers, and also to foreign processors that export fish and shellfish into the United States. Retail sales and food preparation are not covered by the program.

Salmon with Citrus-Mint Gremolata

Cooking time: About 12 minutes
Prep time: About 10 minutes
Notes: Use a frying pan with an ovenproof handle. Brown fish on one side over direct heat, then finish under the broiler.
Makes: 4 servings

- 4 oranges (about 2 lb. total)
- 2 lemons (½ lb. total)
- ¼ cup minced fresh mint leaves
- ½ cup thawed frozen orange juice concentrate
- 1 tablespoon butter or margarine
- 4 salmon fillets (6 to 7 oz. each) with skin, 1 to 1¼ inches thick

Mint sprigs (optional)

1. Finely shred enough orange peel to make 1 tablespoon; reserve. Then, with a knife, cut peel and white membrane from oranges. Cut between fruit and inner membrane to release segments. Put fruit in a colander to drain (save juice, if desired).

2. Finely shred enough lemon peel to make 1 tablespoon, then ream lemons for ¼ cup juice.

3. Mince orange peel and lemon peel, then mix with minced mint.

4. Combine orange juice concentrate and lemon juice.

5. In a 12- to 14-inch ovenproof frying pan, melt butter over medium-high heat. When butter sizzles, add salmon fillets, skin down. Cook until skin is well browned and crisp, about 7 minutes. Gently slide a spatula under skin of each fillet to release from pan but leave fish in place.

6. Brush salmon with about ¼ of the orange juice concentrate mixture. Broil about 4 inches from heat until salmon is just barely opaque but still moist-looking in center of the thickest part (cut to test), 3 to 4 minutes.

7. Transfer fish to plates or a platter and keep warm. Stir remaining orange juice concentrate mixture into frying pan and return to broiler just until sauce bubbles, about 4 minutes. Pour sauce over salmon, then sprinkle with mint-peel mixture. Arrange orange segments decoratively around fish and garnish with mint sprigs.

Per serving: 351 cal., 36% (126 cal.) from fat; 35 g protein; 14 g fat (2.2 g sat.); 35 g carbo.; 109 mg sodium; 94 mg chol.

Wild vs. farmed, and other fights

Aquaculture's most vocal critics include commercial fishermen. For years, fishermen and fish farmers have traded insults and accusations—some legitimate, many unsubstantiated—in something of a range war. Farmers have been accused of dosing fish with antibiotics and steroids, and of producing mushier, less flavorful fish. Fishermen, in turn, have been blamed for depleting wild stock, and for careless and rough handling of their catches.

Although the infighting has undermined consumer confidence, it has shaken up questionable fishing and fish-farming practices. Now the collective chorus is a variation on Rodgers and Hammerstein's *Oklahoma!*: "The farmer and the cowman should be friends." The California Seafood Council works, when feasible, with the state Fish and Game Department and with individual fisheries in assessing and replenishing wild stock. And the California Aquaculture Association and California Seafood Council recently took another cooperative step when they signed a joint marketing agreement to promote California sturgeon.

But opposition to aquaculture goes beyond economics. For some, it's aesthetics. Saltwater farms along the coast are usually in sheltered waters or bays, and homeowners with views of the water generally don't want to look at fish farms.

Other critics have environmental concerns. Tom Worthington and Paul Johnson, owners of the San Francisco–based Monterey Fish company, acknowledge that aquaculture has increased the variety of fish they can sell year-round, but worry that this convenience masks a larger issue. Johnson says, "The constant supply that aquaculture provides blinds people to problems in the environment, such as the decline in wild fish populations." Worthington and Johnson also voice a fear, held by many, that genetically manipulated hybrids might escape and breed with their wild counterparts, leading to a decline in true wild species.

A bright future

Controversy aside, aquaculture is having its day in the sun. The greatest expansion is expected where land, labor, and water cost less, in South America and Mexico.

Western universities, marine laboratories, and other experimental sites are on the fast track to finding ways to farm more kinds of fish. And geneticists are researching ways to help fish mature faster. With so many breakthroughs, it now seems that the only factor limiting aquaculture is the same one hampering wild fish—the need for clean water.

The Western farm
Clams

WESTERN CLAM FARMING, CONCENTRATED in the Pacific Northwest, began by accident. In the 1920s, the poisonous effluent of pulp mills in Shelton, Washington, wiped out downstream native Olympia oyster beds. Puget Sound farmers replanted the beds with Pacific oyster seed from Japan, which also included Manila clam seed. After a few years, farmers noticed the Manila clams and how well they grew, and began farming them, too.

Today the Manila is the first choice for Western clam farming, and the biggest grower is Taylor United, which harvests 2½ million pounds a year from numerous sites in southern Puget Sound. Taylor United, a family firm founded in the 1890s, is also a major grower of oysters and mussels. Brothers Bill and Paul Taylor are the fourth generation to head the business.

Taylor's clams are farmed intertidally, as are most oysters, but the clams grow in the seabed rather than on anything constructed. Seed, tended in a nursery until they're about ¼ inch long, are planted by hand in the intertidal beds—about 1 million per acre. After three years, it's harvest time.

As clams grow, they must be protected from predators. Netting over the beds fends off ducks and crabs. Another enemy, the moon snail, has to be individually weeded out.

Harvesting, like planting, is done by hand. Clams are dug up, the big ones gathered and the undersize returned to the bed to continue growing. Gathered clams go into submerged pens for one to five days, where they purge themselves of any sand as they wait to be shipped. The bulk of clams goes to California and New York, mostly to restaurants.

Taylor United is also working with geoduck (say *gooey duck*). This mollusk can reach a gargantuan 12 pounds. Farmed geoducks will be marketed at about 2 pounds, and sold in Asian markets and restaurants in the West.

Hybrid Striped Bass

FARMED HYBRID STRIPED BASS HAS BEEN AN insider secret for too long. Already an established favorite with Asians and highly regarded by Italians who recognize its kinship to European sea bass, popular in Italy, this cross of Atlantic striped bass and freshwater white bass is finally moving into upscale restaurants and markets. Farming began in the 1970s when the Atlantic bass catch dropped drastically.

Farmed striped bass is a freshwater fish. The biggest farmer is in a most unlikely spot—the California desert, near Palm Springs. Here, Kent SeaFarms produces 3½ million pounds a year, 60 percent of the national supply. The fish thrive in 80° water fed from a geothermal aquifer into 96 huge circular, computer-monitored concrete tanks. The bass take about 10 months to grow to their market-size of 1½ to 3 pounds. In the wild, bass take three years to get this big. Almost all the fish are sold whole (in the round, with innards), but some are also sold live in West Coast Asian markets and restaurants. The majority go to the East Coast and Canada, the balance to Los Angeles, the San Francisco Bay Area, Asia, and Europe.

fish glossary
Crayfish

CRAYFISH, CRAWFISH, OR CRAWDAD. CALL them what you like, these freshwater crustaceans aren't nearly as popular here in the West as they are in Louisiana. In that state, cultivated crayfish—33,000 tons a year, used in Cajun cooking—is king. By comparison, Western-farmed crayfish production is limited; most crayfish sold in the West are wild, trapped in the Sacramento Delta and in Oregon rivers and lakes.

John Young raises about 50,000 crayfish a year, along with catfish, at J & J Aquafarms in Sanger, California. He finds the crayfish market in the West too slow to make the crustacean his principal crop. Local restaurants buy some of his crayfish, but he

sells most as pets or bait.

Mike Jenkins, who owns California Lobster in Red Bluff, California, raises Australian crayfish, which he calls California lobster (below left). It's bigger and has much stonger claws than a crayfish. It's smaller than a Maine lobster, and has a sweet, delicate flavor and tender texture.

Jenkins is currently at work on 6,800 square feet of greenhouse with solar-heated tanks to accommodate production, and he plans to distribute to Asian markets in the West, where the California lobster should retail for about $17 a pound. Your first opportunity to taste it will be this summer, probably in upscale San Francisco Bay Area restaurants.

Catfish

CATFISH FARMING IS BIG IN THE SOUTH. Mississippi produces about 80 percent of the farmed catfish in this country—a whopping 500 million pounds a year. Most of the catfish in mainstream supermarkets and restaurants comes from the South.

In the West, farmed catfish is a small industry serving a different market. Nearly all of California's production—about 5 million pounds a year—is sold live to Asian and Latino markets, or is used to stock recreational fishing ponds.

California's largest catfish farm, in Niland, is owned by siblings George and Fern Ray. They started Fish Producers in 1969, when there were just a few catfish farms in the

Sacramento Valley rice-growing region and all the fish were used for sportfishing bait. But in 1976, Ray started selling live fish to ethnic markets. Now at least three dozen catfish producers are doing the same, and the Rays annually harvest about 1 million pounds. Live fish are trucked in tanks three times a week to Los Angeles, Orange, and San Diego counties.

The majority of Western catfish are reared in still-water earthen ponds and take about three years to reach the favored 3-pound market-size.

Whether wild or farmed, catfish can taste muddy or swampy when they have eaten a specific algae. Farmers can avoid this and keep their fish fresh-tasting by draining their ponds frequently or by scraping the algae from the water's surface.

Curried Catfish and Chips

Cooking time: 35 to 40 minutes
Prep time: About 20 minutes
Notes: If contact with taro makes your hands sting, wash them at once with soapy water. Then wear waterproof gloves when handling taro.
Makes: 4 servings

- 1¼ to 1½ pounds catfish fillets
- 1 large egg
- ¾ cup ice water
- 2 teaspoons *each* soy sauce and curry powder
- ½ teaspoon *each* cayenne, ground cumin, ground ginger, and coconut extract
- ¾ cup all-purpose flour
- 1 to 1½ quarts salad oil
- About ¾ pound taro (2 to 3 in. long) or ¾ pound russet potatoes
- About ¾ pound sweet potatoes
- Salt
- Rice vinegar

1. Rinse fish, pat dry, and cut into pieces about 1½ by 3 inches.

2. In a bowl, beat egg to blend with water, soy sauce, curry powder, cayenne, ground cumin, ground ginger, and coconut extract. Add flour, and mix with a fork—batter should be lumpy.

3. Pour 1½ to 2 inches oil into a 14-inch wok or a deep 10- to 12-inch pan. Place on high heat until oil reaches 375°.

4. Meanwhile, peel taro and sweet potatoes and cut into thin rounds by pushing across blade of a food slicer. Fry taro and sweet potatoes, separately in about 4 batches, in hot oil until brown and crisp, 4 to 8 minutes, turning slices over as needed. Transfer with a slotted spoon onto a paper towel–lined 10- by 15-inch pan. Sprinkle with salt. Keep warm in a 250° oven as fish cooks.

5. Coat fish, 1 piece at a time, with curry tempura batter; drain briefly and gently slip 4 or 5 pieces at a time into oil. Cook until golden brown and fish is opaque but still moist-looking in center (cut to test), 4 to 5 minutes. As cooked, transfer with slotted spoon to towel-lined pan in oven; do not stack. Scoop out bits of batter in oil before adding more fish. Serve fish and chips when all are cooked, seasoning with salt and rice vinegar.

Per serving: 570 cal., 41% (234 cal.) from fat; 29 g protein; 26 g fat (4.3 g sat.); 55 g carbo.; 253 mg sodium; 100 mg chol.

The freshest choice is live

Buying live takes a little know-how. Here are some tips.

• **Make a lively choice.** Fish should swim vigorously, abalone shrink back or wiggle a little when the flesh is touched; clams and mussels close when tapped, and crabs and lobsters kick energetically.

• **Have the store do the cleaning.** Unless you say otherwise, the live fish you purchase gets popped into a bag as is. If you aren't prepared to deal with this, ask to have the fish bled, gutted, and scaled—or whatever is needed.

• **Fish can be too fresh.** Freshly killed fish cooked before it passes through rigor mortis can be grainy, mushy, or incredibly tough. Icing the fish as soon as it is killed and dressed minimizes the effects of rigor mortis. When rigor mortis is over, the fish gets limber and flesh feels normal.

• **Choose bivalves with care.** The shells of live oysters should be tightly closed. Clam, mussel, or scallop shells can be open, but should begin to close when you tap them. Reject any shellfish with broken shells.

• **Buy from a reputable dealer.** The seller must be able to verify, with certification, that bivalves came from safe water.

• **Transport and store properly.** Unless you can get your fish or shellfish into the refrigerator in less than an hour, keep it cold in an ice chest on the trip home. Live shellfish need air; if they are sealed in plastic bags, open the bags at once. Store at 32° to 38° as long as 24 hours in containers covered lightly with damp towels. Holding longer is risky. Do not put shellfish in fresh water; it kills them. They can sit on ice if the melt can drain away from them.

• **Clean thoroughly.** Scrub shells under running water or immerse briefly in water to rinse, but don't let them stand in water.

• **Debeard mussels.** Pull the stringy beard off shortly before cooking. The mussel dies soon after.

• **Shellfish open on the grill.** A no-fuss way to prepare bivalves is on a grill over medium-hot coals. (If heat is too high, juices evaporate and shellfish can scorch.) When shellfish pop open, 3 to 5 minutes, eat them with lemon, a little horseradish or hot sauce, or a drizzle of butter.

Sturgeon

THESE RIVER AND COASTAL WATER dwellers once flourished in the West, relatively unchanged for 100 million to 200 million years. The lifespan of a sturgeon is estimated at 100 years or more, giving it time to grow to monstrous size. The largest on record was caught in 1912 in British Columbia and weighed 1,800 pounds.

In 1892, a record 5½ million pounds were landed—from the Columbia, Sacramento, Snake, and Fraser rivers. Then, in only seven years of unrestricted fishing, sturgeon were almost wiped out. By 1899, the take had dropped to 73,000 pounds. The few that survived are now strictly regulated; most wild ones taken commercially come from the Columbia River.

Today, 90 percent of the sturgeon farmed is from the Sacramento Valley, produced by three companies—Sierra AquaFarms, Stolt Sea Farm, and The Fishery. Collectively, they market about 1½ million pounds a year. Most goes to restaurants; the rest goes to retailers and smokers. A few fish are sold live, mostly in West Coast Asian markets.

Sierra AquaFarms is responsible for about 70 percent of the sturgeon farmed. Here, high technology coddles this prehistoric relic. Sturgeon dwell in huge indoor tanks holding 110,000 gallons of water. Computers monitor water temperature and oxygen and nitrogen levels.

NOEL BARNHURST

Every 20 minutes, a programmed robot travels from tank to tank, distributing the exact amount of feed for optimum growth. At age 3½ to 4 years, the fish reach 20 pounds and most are sold.

Sturgeon is delicious, but it is best known for its eggs, which make the finest caviar. And caviar is part of the farmed sturgeon vision. In the wild, a female sturgeon takes about 18 years to produce eggs. Farmed females can produce in eight years, when they weigh about 100 pounds. The cost of feed and care makes this an expensive investment, but lucrative for the farmers.

Although the fish is killed to remove the eggs, the meat is excellent eating.

Oysters

IN 1850, GOLD RUSH WEALTH DEMANDED luxury, and that included oysters. Overharvesting quickly depleted the wild beds of native Olympia oysters, and oyster culture began. The Pacific Northwest grows more species of oysters—including Pacific, European flat, Kumamoto, and Olympia, the only surviving native—than any equivalent area in the world. Market names are historically taken from where the oysters are grown. You're likely to see names like Hama Hama, Hood Canal, Samish Bay (all in Washington), or Hog Island (California). Even when oysters are the same species, growing conditions influence flavor, texture, and sometimes appearance.

Today, Washington leads the nation in farmed oyster production. About 300 farms, from Samish Bay near the

Canadian border to Willapa Bay, yield between 10 million and 12 million pounds a year. Oregon harvests 300,000 to 500,000 pounds yearly. And California's oysters come from Humboldt Bay, Drakes Estero in Drakes Bay, Tomales Bay, Morro Bay, and the Santa Barbara Channel. How oysters are sold—shucked or for the half-shell trade—determines how they are farmed. Oysters for shucking are primarily grown by bottom culture. Since consumers see only the shucked oyster meat, it doesn't matter if the shells cluster together.

Oysters to be served on the half-shell must be kept from clustering as they grow. Some are bottom-cultured, but most are grown in a variety of off-bottom methods, including longline, stake, rack and bag, and suspended bag culture.

Trout

IDAHO PRODUCES MORE THAN TWO-thirds of the 60 million pounds of farmed trout sold annually. It can do so because an underground aquifer provides a generous supply of the pure, cold spring water that trout require.

Trout farming in Idaho probably began just before the turn of the century. By 1909, trout farmed in Devil's Corral fed local miners. The Snake River Trout Company, the first large commercial producer, was founded in 1928. A few more farms began operating during the next 30 years; production was a steady 2 million pounds per year.

Change came in the 1960s. Better information about the trout's life cycle, nutrition needs, and genetics generated exponential growth. Currently, the state harvests about 40 million pounds of trout annually.

Clear Springs Foods, Idaho's largest trout farm, produces about half of Idaho's trout. Fertilized trout eggs, shipped weekly from the brood station in Soda Springs, go to four locations in Snake River Canyon. The eggs hatch in indoor nurseries of flowing water. As trout grow, they continually sort themselves into same-size lots as they swim against the current. Metal comb or bar graders are placed across the raceways. Fish small enough to pass through move along, leaving larger siblings trapped behind. After about eight months in the raceways and another two months in the nursery, trout are market-size.

Clear Springs, which sells to restaurants in the United States and Canada, offers trout gutted, with or without heads and tails. It also has trout fillets, guaranteed boneless.

Abalone

MANY CENTURIES AGO, THE OHLONE, THE native inhabitants of California's central coast, made plentiful abalone a staple of their diet and used the pearlescent shells for tools and jewelry.

The days of boundless abalone are long gone. Overfishing and a resurgence of the abalone-loving sea otter have cut the commercial abalone harvest by 90 percent in less than 40 years—from 5 million pounds in 1957 to barely half a million pounds last year.

Of the dozen abalone farms and research sites on California's coast, only a few produce significant crops. The oldest, the Abalone Farm in Cayucos (started in 1968), sells about 1 million abalone annually. It sells most live abalone under the Ocean Rose label. A few go to U.S. restaurants, but the bulk of the crop goes to Japan and other Pacific Rim countries where abalone is a popular, though expensive, delicacy.

The outlandish prices are not easily earned. One adult female produces as many as 2 million eggs, but the harvest rate is only 2 percent—beating the rate in the wild, which is far less than 1 percent. Baby abalone grow in raceway tanks with pumped-in ocean water, or in cages placed in sheltered coastal waters. Abalone must cling to a surface, so tanks and cages are filled with honeycombs of plastic or fiberglass sheets they can attach themselves to. Like most snails, abalone have voracious appetites. Abalone Farm's crop wolfs down as much as 60 tons of kelp a week. But even when well fed, abalone grow slowly—an inch a year at best—and don't reach market-size for three to four years.

According to experts, California's coastal waters are the perfect temperature for maximum abalone growth, and also provide a replenishable supply of kelp. And abalone meat isn't the only prize. Growers may soon be selling abalone pearls, too.

Grilled Sturgeon with Black Bean Salsa

Cooking time: 10 to 12 minutes
Prep time: About 45 minutes
Notes: To get a head start, marinate fish and let salsa chill up to 2 hours.
Makes: 4 servings

- 3 tablespoons orange juice
- 1½ teaspoons grated lime peel (green part only)
- 3 tablespoons lime juice
- 1 fresh jalapeño chili, stemmed, seeded, and minced
- 1 tablespoon minced fresh cilantro
- 2 to 2½ pounds sturgeon, cut into 4 portions, each 1 inch thick
- 1 Roma-type tomato (2 to 3 oz.), diced
- 1 can (15 oz.) black beans, rinsed and drained well
- 1 orange (about ¾ lb.)
- 1 firm-ripe papaya (about 1 lb.), peeled, cut lengthwise into quarters, and seeded
- Fresh cilantro sprigs
- Salt and pepper

1. Combine orange juice, lime peel, lime juice, jalapeño, and minced cilantro. Rinse fish, pat dry, and place in a 9- by 13-inch pan. Spoon half the juice mixture evenly over fish. Cover; chill at least 15 minutes or up to 2 hours, turning once.

2. To remaining orange juice mixture, add tomato and beans. With a sharp knife, cut peel and white membrane from orange. Holding orange over bean mixture, cut between membrane and fruit to release segments. Break each segment into 2 or 3 pieces and add to bean salsa. Mix salsa gently and serve, or cover and chill up to 2 hours.

3. Lift fish from marinade and lay on a hot, lightly oiled grill above a solid bed of medium coals or over medium heat on a gas grill (you can hold your hand at grill level only 4 to 5 seconds). Cover gas grill. Cook 5 minutes; turn steaks over and continue to cook until fish is opaque but still moist-looking in thickest part (cut to test), about 6 minutes longer.

4. Arrange equal portions of fish, salsa, and papaya on plates; garnish with cilantro sprigs. Season to taste with salt and pepper.

Per serving: 368 cal., 24% (90 cal.) from fat; 42 g protein; 10 g fat (2.2 g sat.); 28 g carbo.; 252 mg sodium; 75 mg chol.

Oven-fried Tilapia with Tomato Relish

Cooking time: About 50 minutes

Prep time: About 25 minutes

Notes: Look for *panko*—Japanese-style coarse dried bread crumbs—with ethnic foods in well-stocked supermarkets or in Japanese markets. Or use coarsely crushed dried bread crumbs.

Makes: 4 servings

4 Roma-type tomatoes (about 1 lb. total), cut into halves

2 zucchini (about ¾ lb. total), ends trimmed and sliced into 1-inch chunks

1 red onion (5 to 6 oz.), cut into 8 wedges

6 cloves garlic, peeled

3 tablespoons salad oil

¾ cup panko

¼ cup grated parmesan

1 large egg white

4 tilapia fillets (3 to 4 oz. each), rinsed

Salt and pepper

1. In a 10- by 15-inch baking pan, mix tomatoes, zucchini, onion, and garlic with 1 tablespoon oil. Spread vegetables out in a single layer. Bake in a 500° oven, occasionally turning vegetables with a wide spatula, until garlic is soft when pressed and lightly browned, 20 to 25 minutes. Spoon garlic from pan and bake remaining vegetables until edges get very dark and browned bits stick, 5 to 10 minutes longer. Let vegetables cool briefly. Coarsely chop with garlic. Scoop relish into a dish. Rinse pan and dry.

2. Meanwhile, in a shallow pan, mix panko and parmesan. In another shallow pan, beat egg white until slightly frothy. Dip each fillet in egg white, drain briefly, then coat well with panko.

3. Pour remaining oil into the 10- by 15-inch pan and swirl to coat bottom. Place pan in a 500° oven for 5 minutes. Supporting with a wide spatula, set panko-coated fillets well apart in a hot pan. Bake 5 minutes; turn fillets over with spatula and bake until crumbs are lightly browned and fish is opaque but still moist-looking in thickest part (cut to test), 3 to 5 minutes more. Serve fish with relish; add salt and pepper to taste.

Per serving: 335 cal., 40% (135 cal.) from fat; 24 g protein; 15 g fat (2.6 g sat.); 27 g carbo.; 342 mg sodium; 40 mg chol.

Recipes by Paula Smith Freschet, Christine Weber Hale

FARMED TILAPIA HAS A LONG HISTORY. A native of Africa and the Middle East, tilapia was probably cultivated by the ancient Egyptians. Some biblical scholars suggest that the tilapia was a fish St. Peter caught, since another name for it is St. Peter's fish.

Today, major production areas include Taiwan, Costa Rica, Columbia, Ecuador, Mexico, the Middle East, Indonesia, and the United States.

Tilapia is a hardy, adaptable fish, and a natural to farm. It lives in salt, fresh, or brackish water, even with very little oxygen, and thrives in dense populations. It can even nourish itself from algae in the water. However, it can't get too cold: a temperature of 55° or warmer is essential.

Farmed tilapia is a staple of Asian and Latino markets in the United States, and is also making its way into mainstream supermarkets. Solar AquaFarms in Sun City, California (page 173), a subsidiary of Chiquita Brands International, is the Western Hemisphere's largest tilapia grower. The farm raises two tilapia species, *Tilapia mossambica* and *T. nilotica*. Both reach market-size, about 1½ pounds, in 10 months, and are certified organic. Tilapia has one weakness. It's like a sponge, absorbing flavors from its environment. If grown in clean water and fed a diet of fishmeal and grain, tilapia is mild and sweet. If a specific alga grows in the water, the fish eat it and will develop an undesirable strong muddy, musky flavor.

NOEL BARNHURST

TWO NATIVE SPECIES OF MUSSELS GROW wild along the Pacific coast. The large mussels commonly found on coastal rocks, *Mytilus californianus,* are not used commercially. *Mytilus trossulus,* a native blue mussel, is grown by three farms on Puget Sound. Penn Cove Mussel Company, on Whidbey Island, was the first mussel farm on the West Coast—it now harvests as much as 500,000 pounds annually.

Pacific blue mussels are difficult to grow in Puget Sound. They tend to die after their first year of spawning before reaching a desired market-size. Recently, several new farms in the sound and along the coast have begun raising the hardier Mediterranean mussel, *Mytilus gallo-provincialis.* This mussel, though not a native, was discovered growing voluntarily in several locations along the West Coast. No one knows for sure how it got here, but one theory speculates that it was carried over on the bottoms of Spanish explorers' galleons.

Typically, mussels are cultivated in long tubular mesh bags or on ropes suspended from floats. The submerged bags hang from floats or floating platforms until the mussels mature, in six months to two years, depending on water temperature and food supply.

Most mussel farms are in coastal bays and inlets, but a few have popped up in surprising places. At Carlsbad Aqua-Farms (page 175), John Davis raises mussels in Outer Agua Heonda Lagoon of the San Diego Gas & Electric Company's power plant. Much of the 200,000 pounds he produces each year goes to Los Angeles, Chicago, and New York. Ecomar, another producer, has moved mussel farming into the ocean. At a number of sites 3 to 12 miles offshore in the Santa Barbara Channel, it uses two different techniques. In one, it plants mussels on the legs of offshore oil platforms (14 rigs in all; the water around them is quite pure, confirmed by regular testing).

The other technique is an ocean-modified rope culture. Ecomar harvests half a million pounds of mussels each year. Harvested mussels are cleaned, sorted, and on their way to restaurants within 24 hours. At least half go to Los Angeles and Orange counties. ■

PETER CHRISTIANSEN

GENEROUS AMOUNTS *of cilantro and ginger with seasoned rice vinegar and mirin (sweetened rice wine) add Asian flavor to a fat-free marinade.*

Fresh-flavored, oil-free marinades

Season grilled foods without adding fat

OIL-FREE MARINADES ARE EASIER TO make than you might think. And they don't have to be as expensive as those in the market. Asian seasonings give one marinade its punch. Balsamic vinegar is the base for a basil baste with rosemary, oregano, and honey. And the chili power of the sweet chili barbecue sauce can be adjusted to suit your family's taste.

Barbecuing and broiling are great cooking techniques for marinated foods. To barbecue, use an even layer of medium-hot coals (you can hold your hand at grill level 3 to 4 seconds) or heat a gas grill to medium-high and cook with lid closed. Turn and baste foods frequently until cooked to your liking. Basic grilling times are about 10 minutes for 1-inch-thick fish steaks or fillets; 15 to 20 minutes for flank steak, cut vegetables (skewers or a fish basket make vegetables manageable), or boneless chicken breasts; and 25 minutes for large chicken pieces or beef or pork ribs.

Ginger-Soy Marinade

Cooking time: 10 to 25 minutes
Prep time: 15 minutes, plus marinating time
Makes: 1⅓ cups

- ⅓ cup *each* seasoned rice vinegar and mirin (sweetened rice wine)
- ⅓ cup *each* minced fresh ginger and fresh cilantro
- ¼ cup reduced-sodium soy sauce
- 2 cloves garlic, minced

1. Combine seasoned rice vinegar, mirin, ginger, cilantro, soy sauce, and garlic.

2. Use to marinate 1 to 2 pounds firm-fleshed fish, chicken, or pork tenderloin at least 15 minutes or up until the next day.

3. Grill over a solid bed of medium-hot coals or a medium-hot gas grill; baste frequently with remaining sauce.

Per tablespoon: 16 cal., 0% (0 cal.) from fat; 0.2 g protein; 0 g fat; 2.7 g carbo.; 189 mg sodium; 0 mg chol.

Balsamic Basil Baste

Cooking time: 10 to 25 minutes
Prep time: 10 minutes, plus marinating time
Makes: About 1 cup

- ⅔ cup balsamic vinegar
- ⅔ cup minced fresh basil leaves
- ¼ cup honey
- 2 tablespoons lemon juice
- ½ teaspoon *each* dried rosemary and dried oregano

1. Combine balsamic vinegar, fresh basil leaves, honey, lemon juice, rosemary, and oregano.

2. Use to marinate 1 to 2 pounds cut vegetables, lamb chops, or chicken at least 15 minutes or up until the next day.

3. Barbecue over a solid bed of medium-hot coals or a medium-hot gas grill; baste frequently with remaining sauce.

Per tablespoon: 20 cal., 0% (0 cal.) from fat; 0.1 g protein; 0 g fat; 5.3 g carbo.; 1.4 mg sodium; 0 mg chol.

Sweet Chili Barbecue Sauce

Cooking time: 10 to 25 minutes
Prep time: 5 minutes, plus marinating time
Makes: About 1½ cups

- ½ cup cider vinegar
- ⅓ cup light or dark molasses
- ⅓ cup Dijon mustard
- 2 tablespoons *each* tomato paste and soy sauce
- 3 to 4 teaspoons liquid hot pepper seasoning

1. Combine cider vinegar, molasses, mustard, tomato paste, soy sauce, and liquid hot pepper seasoning.

2. Use to marinate 1 to 2 pounds pork or beef ribs, flank steak, or chicken at least 15 minutes or up until the next day.

3. Barbecue over a solid bed of medium-hot coals or a medium-hot gas grill; baste frequently with remaining sauce.

Per tablespoon: 21 cal., 0% (0 cal.) from fat; 0.1 g protein; 0 g fat; 4.3 g carbo.; 222 mg sodium; 0 mg chol. ∎

By Betsy Reynolds Bateson

Melon Mania

At 9 A.M. on a blazing Saturday at San Francisco's Ferry Plaza farmers' market, the sun is already turning noses red. Shoppers linger beneath canvas umbrellas, avoiding the glare between stands. It's going to be a thirsty day, the kind melons are made for.

Customers at Nick Atallah's stand eagerly sample a juicy green-striped melon with deep orange flesh. It looks beautiful enough to be in a still-life painting. Some mistake it for cantaloupe, but not many cantaloupes achieve such a heady aroma and sweetly musky taste.

"This is French Charentais," Atallah explains. "The French are devils for flavor." He has Asian melons, too—Emerald Jewel and Sprite. Their chartreuse flesh is crisper and candy sweet, with less complex flavors.

Around the corner, grower Dave Fredericks likens the smooth texture and flavor of a Sharlyn melon to vanilla Häagen-Dazs. Then he exhorts passersby to try a melon claimed to be an aphrodisiac in Persia. *Kharboozeh mashedi,* he calls it, slicing into the squiggly striped, torpedo-shaped fruit. "That rhymes with 'hard to say, my chérie.' "

The growing crowd is intrigued, if skeptical. The melon is crisp like an Asian pear, with an intensely sweet floral taste. The juice practically pours out. Whether or not this exotic specimen awakens appetites of another nature, it couldn't be more satisfying to an overheated shopper.

At farmers' markets and specialty stores throughout the West, getting passionate about melons is especially easy to do this month. Hot days and nights produce the

Tired of your everyday cantaloupe? Here's how to shop for and cook with some of the more exotic melons in the marketplace. Recipes begin on page 184.

PHOTOGRAPHS BY PETER CHRISTIANSEN

Ha-Ogen

Charentais

Ananas

Santa Claus

Juan Canary

Ambrosia

Persian

Galia

Frozen Melon-Mint Bombe

Cooking time: About 10 minutes

Prep time: About 2¼ hours, plus at least 4½ hours freezing

Notes: For the most dramatic effect, make this in a melon-shaped mold, sold at cookware stores such as Sur La Table in Seattle (800/243-0852; $14.95 plus shipping). Or use a plain metal bowl.

Makes: 6 to 8 servings

- 1   envelope unflavored gelatin
- ½   cup water
- 3½ cups 1-inch chunks peeled, seeded aromatic green-flesh melon such as Galia, Santa Claus, or honeydew
- ⅓   cup plus ½ cup light corn syrup
- 5   tablespoons lemon juice
- 1   tablespoon minced fresh mint leaves
- 5   cups 1-inch chunks peeled, seeded aromatic orange-flesh melon such as Ambrosia, Charentais, or cantaloupe
- 3   tablespoons whipping cream
- 1   teaspoon grated lemon peel
     Melon or fig leaves (optional)

1. In a 1- to 1½-quart pan, sprinkle gelatin over ½ cup water. Let stand until softened, about 5 minutes. Stir over medium heat until steaming, 2 to 3 minutes; let cool.

2. Meanwhile, place a deep 6- to 7-cup melon-shaped metal mold (about 7 in. long) or round metal bowl in the freezer. In a food processor or blender, whirl green melon, ⅓ cup corn syrup, 2 tablespoons lemon juice, and half of the gelatin mixture into a smooth purée. Whirl in mint.

3. Freeze mixture in an ice cream maker as manufacturer directs. (Or freeze in ice cube trays until firm to touch, about 3 hours. Then whirl in a food processor until very smooth, stopping often to scrape bowl; this takes several minutes.)

4. Spread softly frozen sorbet in an even layer over inside of cold mold, forming a flat, wide rim around top. Freeze upright and airtight for 15 minutes. Check sorbet; if it has slipped a little from sides, respread flush with rim. Freeze until firm, 45 minutes to 1½ hours.

5. Remelt remaining gelatin in pan. Rinse food processor or blender, then add gelatin, orange melon, ½ cup corn syrup, 3 tablespoons lemon juice, cream, and lemon peel; whirl into a smooth purée. Freeze in ice cream maker or ice cube trays as directed above. Pack into mold and spread flush with green rim. Freeze leftover sorbet for later use. Freeze bombe airtight until firm in center, at least 3 hours or up to 2 weeks.

6. To serve, let stand at room temperature until you can insert a knife tip into center of sorbet, 5 to 15 minutes. Meanwhile, chill dessert plates in freezer.

7. Dip mold into a bowl of hot water until green layer softens very slightly, 10 to 15 seconds. Place a chilled plate on top and invert, giving a strong shake. Remove mold; garnish bombe with leaves. With a long knife, cut in half lengthwise, then cut into wedges. Serve on chilled plates.

Per serving: 179 cal., 11% (19 cal.) from fat; 2.1 g protein; 2.1 g fat (1.1 g sat.); 42 g carbo; 63 mg sodium; 6.2 mg chol.

Smoked Chicken and Melon

Cooking time: About 1 hour

Prep time: About 1 hour, plus at least 2 hours marinating

Notes: Chicken and firmer melon slices marinate in a spicy syrup. Barbecuing the meat and fruit over wood chips adds a delicious smokiness.

Makes: 4 servings

- 6   stalks (¼ lb.) fresh lemon grass
- 1   teaspoon hot red chili flakes
- 1¼ cups water
- ⅔   cup sugar
- ⅓   cup distilled white vinegar
- 2   to 2½ pounds firm or crisp melon such as Persian, Charentais, or cantaloupe
- 1   chicken (about 3 lb.), quartered, fat removed
- 2   cups hickory or alder wood chips
- 2   tablespoons chopped fresh cilantro, plus sprigs
     Salt

1. Discard dried tops, tough outer layers, and discolored root ends from lemon grass. Bruise stalks with a mallet; coarsely chop.

2. In a 1- to 1½-quart pan, bring lemon grass, chili flakes, water, sugar, and vinegar to a boil. Reduce heat; simmer, covered, 15 minutes. Uncover; simmer until syrup mixture is reduced to 1½ cups, about 12 minutes. Strain, pressing to extract liquid. Let cool. Set aside ¼ cup syrup; chill airtight.

3. Meanwhile, cut melon crosswise into ¾-inch slices. Cut each slice into 5- to 6-inch pieces; remove seeds but not rind.

4. Place melon in 1-gallon zip-lock plastic bag, chicken in another. Add half of remaining syrup to each. Seal; turn to coat. Chill at least 2 or up to 24 hours; turn 2 or 3 times.

5. About 25 minutes before cooking, place wood chips in a bowl with water to cover.

---

most flavorful examples of the season.

And we have more melons than ever to enjoy. They hail from close by and as far away as Europe, Asia, and the Middle East. Some are new hybrids developed for qualities such as sweetness. Many are old varieties that backyard seed savers and immigrants have recently introduced to farmers.

It's small-scale growers like Atallah and Fredericks, selling at farmers' markets, who make enjoying these melons possible. Most varieties wouldn't survive mass production. Some need coddling as they grow, and require expertise to pick ripe. Often fruit is too fragile to ship. It has taken farmers' markets' adventurous clientele to appreciate the unusual melons and pay their higher prices.

We found nine melons that are most readily available, but keep your eyes open for others, particularly if you live in the hot, dry climates that melons love best.

To get a good melon, you have to know what to look for (see descriptions that follow). Some will soften a little after picking, but none will develop more flavor. In general, avoid melons with dents or bruises, and those that indicate overripeness with a lot of give, sloshing seeds, or a fermented scent. Hard-rind melons keep longer than soft-rind ones (some of these last only a day or two). Chill melons if storing them longer than a day, and wait to remove seeds until just before using, as they help keep the melon moist.

Ambrosia. This extra-sweet cantaloupe hybrid has fine netting (the mesh pattern on the rind), fairly soft flesh, and a mildly floral, musky fragrance. A ripe melon has raised netting on a creamy background color, and its blossom end yields to gentle pressure.

Ananas and Sharlyn. These melons are tough to tell apart.

(cut to check), 20 to 25 minutes. About 5 minutes before chicken is done, place melon on grill over coals; discard marinade (if grill is small, finish cooking chicken, keep warm, then heat melon). Cook melon just until hot, turning once, 5 to 8 minutes.

8. Sprinkle with chopped cilantro and garnish with cilantro sprigs. Season to taste with salt and reserved syrup.

Per serving: 434 cal., 44% (189 cal.) from fat; 42 g protein; 21 g fat (5.7 g sat.); 19 g carbo; 134 mg sodium; 132 mg chol.

Melon, Basil, and Bacon Salad

Cooking time: About 20 minutes

Prep time: About 25 minutes

Notes: Any soft, aromatic melon works well, but the salad is especially attractive with 3 colors, such as green Ha-Ogen or Galia, creamy Ananas, and orange Charentais.

Makes: 4 servings

     6 slices (5 oz.) bacon
 1 ½ tablespoons firmly packed brown sugar
     2 quarts peeled, seeded melon wedges (¾ in. by 2 in.)
   ¼ cup lime juice
   ⅓ cup finely slivered fresh basil leaves, plus basil sprigs

1. Line a 10- by 15-inch baking pan with foil. Arrange bacon in single layer; bake in a 350° oven 10 minutes. Spoon off drippings. Evenly pat sugar onto bacon. Bake until deep golden, about 10 minutes.

2. Lift bacon to a board; let cool slightly, then cut into ½-inch diagonal slices. In a shallow bowl, combine melon, juice, and slivered basil. Top with bacon; garnish with basil sprigs.

Per serving: 199 cal., 25% (50 cal.) from fat; 5.4 g protein; 5.6 g fat (1.7 g sat.); 36 g carbo; 195 mg sodium; 8.4 mg chol.

6. *In a charcoal-fueled barbecue with a lid,* ignite 70 mounded charcoal briquets on firegrate. Let burn until barely covered with ash. Bank coals on opposite sides of firegrate; place drip pan between coals. Drain chips; sprinkle equally over coals.

On a gas barbecue, adjust controls for indirect heat, and set a drip pan between heat sources (if manufacturer recommends).

Turn heat to high; place chips in barbecue's metal smoking box or in a small shallow foil pan and set directly on the heat in a corner. Close lid; allow 5 to 10 minutes to reach temperature.

7. Place chicken on oiled grill over drip pan; discard marinade. Open vents, cover barbecue, and cook, turning every 5 minutes, until meat is no longer pink in thickest part

Both taste exceptionally sweet and perfumed. A true Ananas has a chewier texture and multicolored flesh (pale orange to cream and pale green). Sharlyn's uniform cream-color flesh nearly dissolves in the mouth. When fruits are ripe, rinds of both melons begin to turn orange.

Charentais. Also sold by variety names such as Alienor, Charmel, and Savor, Charentais is very sweet and aromatic, with firm, juicy flesh. When fruit is ripe, the gray background under the green vertical stripes begins to turn cream. Look for a clean, fresh perfume and a blossom end that yields to gentle pressure.

Galia. This finely netted melon is very juicy and sweet, with an intense floral nose and succulent flesh. When fruit is ripe, the rind has a light green to gold background color.

Ha-Ogen. The intoxicating perfume is what people first notice about green-striped Ha-Ogen. Flesh is velvety, sweet,

and tropical-tasting, though lacking acidic balance. Ripe melons have a mottled green-orange background (sometimes with a sparse net). The almost skinlike rind bruises easily.

Juan Canary. Its flavor is medium sweet, mildly tropical, and musky. Flesh of ripe fruit is soft and juicy. The smooth, hard rind has little aroma; to determine ripeness, look for deep yellow color and a bit of give at the blossom end.

Persian. These melons need a lot of heat to ripen; most are picked too green. A nice melon has some yellow background color beneath the fine netting. Also, check for a bit of give at the blossom end. The flesh is firm and slightly musky.

Santa Claus. Christmas is another name for this green- and yellow-striped melon with a smooth, hard rind. The flesh is soft and juicy, fairly sweet, and a bit bland. The brighter the yellow stripes, the riper the melon. ∎

Our new no-fry, low-fat taco salad

Bake the tortilla shell to make this Mexican favorite lighter, fresher, and easier

Huge, crackling flour tortilla shells filled with crisp green salad make a lively parade as they stream out of Mexican restaurants' kitchens. But for most home cooks, the vat of bubbling oil needed to fry the shells keeps the dish off-limits.

Until now, that is. The popularity of the taco salad demands an easier way to make it. In *Sunset*'s kitchens we borrowed a technique from the recipe we invented for low-fat tortilla chips: bake, don't fry. The tortillas, dunked in water that has a few drops of oil floating on its surface, become limber for shaping and gather a faint oil film that helps them bake crisp.

Obviously, fat calories drop significantly when you bake tortillas instead of frying them, turning the taco salad into an exceptionally wholesome dish.

The tool you need to make the bowls is ultrasimple—an empty food can (the big size used for juice and broth). The shape of the bowl varies with the size of the flour tortilla you use. Bigger tortillas, readily found in Latino markets, make bigger ruffles for the taco bowl rim.

The salad that fills these taco bowls is seasoned with citrus and chilies, a combination popular in Yucatán. The dressing has no oil, which gives the recipe more lean merits. The same seasonings soak into onions and chicken breasts that are grilled, then served hot or cold on the salad.

CRISP TORTILLA holds shredded lettuce and black bean salad topped with barbecued chicken breasts, pink onion rings, and a citrus dressing.

For a refreshing companion that's also light, serve an authentic *agua fresca;* this one is made from watermelon.

To keep last-minute details minimal, take advantage of the make-ahead steps that are integral to the salad and to the beverage.

Taco Bowl Salad with Grilled Chicken

Cooking time: 25 to 50 minutes to bake tortilla shells, 10 to 12 minutes for salad

Prep time: About 25 minutes for shells, about 55 minutes for salad, plus 1 hour for marinating

Notes: You can store cool tortilla shells airtight up to 1 week. If some of the shells don't shape nicely, break them into chips, and make a few more shells.

You can marinate chicken and onions up to 1 day; if you do, also cover and chill remaining orange dressing.

Makes: 6 servings

TORTILLA BAKES *crisp because you dip it first in water mixed with a few drops of salad oil. Only a little oil clings to tortilla.*

DRAPE DAMP *tortilla over a foil-covered can. Bake until firm and able to hold a cup shape, about 5 minutes. Invert and bake until crisp.*

6	flour tortillas (10- to 13-in. size)
1½	teaspoons salad oil
1½	cups fresh orange juice
1¼	cups fresh lime juice
⅓	cup minced shallot
1¾	teaspoons sugar
½	cup chopped fresh cilantro
1½	teaspoons dried hot chili flakes
1½	teaspoons cumin seed, crushed
2	cloves garlic, pressed or minced
6	boned and skinned chicken breast halves (about 5 oz. each)
1	red onion (about ½ lb.)
2	cans black beans (15 oz. each), rinsed and drained
1	red bell pepper (about ½ lb.), stemmed, seeded, and chopped
3	quarts finely shredded iceberg lettuce
1	firm-ripe avocado (about 10 oz.), peeled, pitted, and thinly sliced
	Fresh cilantro sprigs
	Reduced-fat sour cream or Mexican sour cream (crema Mexicana, crema Mexicana agria, or jocoque)
	Salt

1. To make taco bowls. If using 10-inch tortillas, set 2 empty food cans (4 in. wide) 3 to 4 inches apart on a 14- by 17-inch foil-lined baking sheet. If using 12- or 13-inch tortillas, set 1 food can on baking sheet. Drape a 12-inch foil square over top of each can.

2. Fill a 12- to 14-inch pizza pan (about ¾ in. deep) or another rimmed container with about ½ inch water, and add ¼ teaspoon of the oil. Quickly immerse 1 tortilla in water; lift out, and drain.

3. Drape damp tortilla over can. If you place the tortilla slightly off-center, the finished bowl will have a tall, dramatic ruffle on 1 side. If you have room for another tortilla on pan, add another ¼ teaspoon oil to water, dip, and drape.

4. Bake tortillas in a 450° oven until lightly browned and firm enough to hold their shape, 4 to 5 minutes.

5. Carefully lift hot tortillas off cans (use pot holders), set cans aside, and place tortillas, cup sides up, on pan. The ruffles on larger tortillas may need support when the shells are inverted; loosely crumple foil into balls (about 4 in. wide) and push them against areas that sag. Return to oven and bake until tortillas feel crisp, 2 to 3 minutes longer. Cool on rack. Repeat steps until all taco bowls are made. Use warm or cool.

6. To make salad. Mix orange juice, lime juice, shallot, sugar, chopped cilantro, chili flakes, cumin, and garlic.

7. In a zip-lock plastic bag, combine chicken and ⅓ cup of the orange juice dressing. Seal bag and rotate to mix; set bag in a bowl.

8. Cut onion crosswise into ½-inch-thick slices, and place in another zip-lock bag with ⅓ cup of the orange dressing. Seal bag and rotate to mix; set in bowl with chicken.

9. Chill chicken and onion at least 1 hour; turn bags over occasionally.

10. Drain dressing from onion into a measuring cup and add enough of the remaining dressing to make ½ cup, then mix this dressing with beans and red pepper. Let bean salad stand as chicken cooks.

11. Drain and discard dressing from chicken. Place chicken and onion slices on a grill over a solid bed of hot coals (you can hold your hand at grill level only 2 to 3 seconds). Cook, turning pieces once, until chicken is white in thickest part (cut to test) and onion slices are lightly browned, 10 to 12 minutes. Transfer meat and onion to a platter. Slice breasts, and separate onion slices into rings. If making ahead, let stand up to 1 hour.

12. In each tortilla bowl, mound ⅙ of the lettuce and top equally with bean salad, then lay chicken and onion rings on top. Garnish salads with avocado slices and cilantro sprigs. Accompany with remaining orange dressing, sour cream, and salt to add to taste.

Per serving with 10-inch tortillas: 581 cal., 22% (126 cal.) from fat; 47 g protein; 14 g fat (2.2 g sat.); 70 g carbo.; 606 mg sodium; 82 mg chol.

Watermelon Agua Fresca

Prep time: 10 to 15 minutes

Notes: You can chill until the next day.

Makes: About 2 quarts, 6 servings

1	watermelon (7 lb.) or a 7-pound piece
⅓	cup lime juice
3	to 5 tablespoons sugar
1¼	cups cold water
	Ice cubes
	Lime wedges (optional)

Cut rind off melon and discard. Cut flesh into about 1-inch cubes. Purée melon, a portion at a time, in a blender or food processor. Pour through a strainer into a 2- to 3-quart pitcher or bowl to remove seeds. Mix melon purée with lime juice, sugar to taste, and water. Pour into glasses over ice cubes. Garnish with lime wedges.

Per serving: 115 cal., 9% (11 cal.) from fat; 1.7 g protein; 1.2 g fat (0 g sat.); 27 g carbo.; 7.7 mg sodium; 0 mg chol. ■

By Linda Lau Anusasananan

Everyday Low~fat Cooking
BY ELAINE JOHNSON

KEVIN CANDLAND

Chicken gets a healthy trim

Imagine: a quick nip and tuck, and away go those fat deposits. Liposuction for chicken sure is easy. If you eat a lot of chicken (and who doesn't?) pulling off skin and trimming lumps of fat before cooking can make a significant difference in its fat content—and yours.

For a chicken breast half, this simple surgery reduces the percentage of calories from fat from 36 to only 19. There's just one hitch. Without the skin, the meat can dry out. To get around this, you need a moist cooking technique.

Steeping is a variation on poaching I learned at *Sunset* and rely on often to cook slimmed-down chicken pieces. I just add chicken to a pan of water, bring it to a boil, then let it stand off the heat. With no vigorous bubbling during cooking, the meat is smooth and tender.

Steeped chicken chunks are handy for quick meals: wrapped fajita-style in a tortilla with vegetables and salsa; on toasted country bread with mustard, cracked pepper, and arugula; or with yogurt, tarragon, and lemon peel to dress cannellini beans.

In hot weather, steeped chicken is refreshing served cold over Asian rice noodles with crisp vegetables—and preparing it won't heat up the house.

I used to buy the noodles (they look like bundles of fishing line) at an Asian market, but now they've made their way into the supermarket. So have two flavorings for the meal: fish sauce and seasoned rice vinegar. Along with the steeped, liposuctioned chicken, they've become staples of my low-fat repertoire.

Cool Summer Chicken

Cooking time: About 25 minutes
Prep time: About 30 minutes
Makes: 4 servings

- 4 boned, skinned chicken breast halves (1⅓ lb. total), fat trimmed
- 8 ounces dried thin rice noodles (also called rice sticks) or angel hair pasta
- 1 cup finely shredded carrot
- ¾ cup cucumber crescents (peel a cucumber, quarter lengthwise, seed, and thinly slice crosswise)
- 1 to 2 tablespoons minced fresh jalapeño chilies, plus about 12 paper-thin crosswise slices
- 2 tablespoons finely shredded fresh mint leaves
- 1 cup seasoned rice vinegar
- 4 teaspoons fish sauce (*nuoc mam* or *nam pla*) or soy sauce
- 1½ teaspoons sugar
  Mint sprigs and lime wedges

1. Fill a 3- to 4-quart pan ½ full with water; add chicken and bring just to boiling over high heat. Remove from heat; cover tightly. Let stand undisturbed 18 minutes. Cut chicken in thickest part; if still pink, let stand a few more minutes. Lift from pan and immerse in ice water until cold. Drain, then use or chill airtight up to 1 day.

2. Meanwhile, bring 3 quarts water to a boil in a 4- to 5-quart pan. Add noodles, remove from heat, and soak until just tender to bite, 4 to 7 minutes (for angel hair, break up any clumps with a long fork). Drain, rinse with cool water, and drain again. Place in 4 wide, shallow bowls.

3. Slice chicken diagonally into ½-inch pieces, keeping each breast half together. Place a portion on each bowl of noodles; arrange carrot and cucumber alongside. Scatter with minced chilies and shredded mint.

4. Combine vinegar, fish sauce, and sugar; spoon over portions. Garnish with sliced chilies and mint sprigs. Squeeze lime on top.

Per serving: 456 cal., 5.1% (23 cal.) from fat; 39 g protein; 2.6 g fat (0.6 g sat.); 66 g carbo.; 1,503 mg sodium; 88 mg chol. ■

CHILEAN SEA BASS *with snap peas and pasta has a honey-mustard sauce.*

PETER CHRISTIANSEN

When you grill in a bag

You can capture a delicate, smoky flavor in sauces with the help of homemade foil containers

SMOKING HUNKS OF MEAT OR SLABS of fish on the barbecue is no trick, but luring smoke flavor into a sauce on the grill is. To do so, take a tip from wilderness cooking. When foods are sealed in foil and cooked over the campfire, they stay especially moist. But if you put ingredients in foil bags that aren't sealed and set the bags on a grill over smoldering wood chips, the sauce picks up a discreet and delicate amount of smoke in a very few minutes. At the same time, the foods stay moist and need no turning or tending.

This technique works especially well with quick-cooking fish and shellfish, such as Chilean sea bass and shrimp, that

have a natural compatibility with smokiness. For a complete main course, serve with pasta or rice to soak up the sauce.

Where do you get foil bags? You make them in just a few minutes from sheets of foil pressed around a simple form (see recipe notes). Make bags for individual portions because they are easier to handle on the grill than one large bag. Why not use foil pans? The tall cuff on a foil bag gives you a better grip and holds more sauce than the shallower pans, which are inclined to buckle and spill.

Bag-smoked Chilean Sea Bass

Cooking time: About 20 minutes

Prep time: About 30 minutes. You can complete most steps while charcoal ignites (about 25 minutes). Allow 10 minutes to heat a gas grill.

Notes: Make 4 foil bags. To make each bag, stack 2 sheets of heavy-duty foil, each 12 by 14 inches. In the center of the foil, sit a flat-bottomed, 3¾- to 4¼-inch-wide straight-sided dish (such as a soufflé dish) or food can (about 28-oz. size). Fold foil up and press smoothly against dish or can sides, then lift out the form without distorting foil. Fold rim of foil down to make bag about 5 inches tall.

Makes: 4 servings

> 2 cups hickory or apple wood chips
> 1½ cups chicken broth
> ⅓ cup honey
> 5 tablespoons Dijon mustard
> 2 tablespoons cornstarch
> About ½ teaspoon pepper
> 1⅓ pounds Chilean sea bass, cut into 4 equal pieces
> 4 foil bags (see notes, preceding)
> ⅓ pound sugar snap peas, ends and strings removed
> About 4 cups hot cooked fettuccine or linguine
> Salt

1. Soak wood chips in water at least 20 minutes or up to 1 hour.

2. Smoothly mix broth with honey, mustard, cornstarch, and ½ teaspoon pepper. Rinse fish and drain.

3. Drain wood chips. In a barbecue with a lid, scatter chips over a solid bed of very hot coals (you can hold your hand at grill level only 1 to 2 seconds). For gas barbecue, turn on high, put chips in a foil pan, and set directly on flame in a corner of the gas barbecue; close lid and heat 10 minutes.

4. Put 1 piece of fish in each foil bag and set bags on center of grill. Pour an equal portion of broth mixture into each bag. Cover barbecue, open vents for charcoal, and cook until fish is opaque in center of the thickest part but still moist-looking (cut to test, but be careful not to pierce bottom of bag), about 15 minutes. Add equal amounts of peas to each bag, cover barbecue, and cook just until peas turn bright green, about 2 minutes.

5. To serve, put pasta in rimmed plates or shallow bowls, set fish on pasta, and pour sauce and peas over fish. Season to taste with salt and pepper.

Per serving: 509 cal., 11% (57 cal.) from fat; 38 g protein; 6.3 g fat (1.6 g sat.); 71 g carbo.; 648 mg sodium; 115 mg chol.

Bag-smoked Shrimp with Capers

Cooking time: About 20 minutes

Prep time: About 30 minutes. You can complete most steps while charcoal ignites (about 25 minutes). Allow 10 minutes to heat gas grill.

Notes: To make bags, see notes with Chilean sea bass recipe, preceding.

Makes: 4 servings

> 2 cups hickory or apple wood chips
> 1 cup chicken broth
> ½ cup dry white wine

3 tablespoons drained and minced oil-packed dried tomatoes

3 cloves garlic, minced or pressed

2 tablespoon drained prepared capers

1 tablespoon grated lemon peel

2 tablespoons lemon juice

1 pound (30 to 35 per lb.) shrimp, shelled and deveined

4 foil bags (see notes, preceding)

4 cups hot cooked white rice

¼ cup minced fresh basil leaves

Basil sprigs (optional)

Salt and pepper

1. Soak hickory chips in water at least 20 minutes or up to 1 hour.

2. Mix broth with wine, tomatoes, garlic, capers, lemon peel, and lemon juice.

3. Drain wood chips. In a barbecue with a lid, over a solid bed of very hot coals (you can hold your hand at grill level only 1 to 2 seconds), scatter chips onto coals. For gas barbecue, turn heat to highest setting, put chips in a foil pan, and set directly on flame in a corner of the gas barbecue; close lid and heat 10 minutes.

4. Divide shrimp among foil bags and set on center of grill; add broth mixture equally to each bag. Cover barbecue, open vents for charcoal, and cook until shrimp turn pink and sauce is boiling, about 5 minutes.

5. To serve, pour shrimp and juices from bags into rimmed plates or shallow bowls, add rice, sprinkle with minced basil, and garnish with basil sprigs. Season to taste with salt and pepper.

Per serving: 458 cal., 17% (77 cal.) from fat; 26 g protein; 8.5 g fat (1.4 g sat.); 64 g carbo.; 288 mg sodium; 140 mg chol. ■

By Christine Weber Hale

INDIVIDUAL-SERVING CONTAINERS *are set right on the grill. They work especially well for fish and shellfish.*

BROWN-SUGAR PRALINE *holds coconut in candies from the West Indies.*

Sweet bites of coconut

THE NIP OF FRESH GINGER BALANCES the sweet intensity of these simple, quick-to-make Caribbean-style pralines from Jamaica. Chewy bits of coconut are bound in brown-sugar candy.

Jamaican Coconut Pralines

Cooking time: About 30 minutes, plus cooling time

Prep time: About 10 minutes

Makes: About 3 dozen

1 pound (2⅓ cups) firmly packed brown sugar

½ cup whipping cream

2 tablespoons light corn syrup

1 tablespoon minced fresh ginger

3½ cups sweetened flaked dried coconut

1. In a 3- to 4-quart pan, combine sugar, cream, syrup, and ginger. Bring to a boil over medium-high heat. Boil, uncovered, stirring until 234° on a thermometer.

2. Let cool 20 minutes. Beat vigorously with a spoon until candy begins to look creamy, about 5 minutes. Let stand 5 minutes, then stir in coconut.

3. Drop candy in rounded tablespoon-size portions, slightly apart, onto foil or waxed paper. Let stand until cool. Serve, or store airtight at room temperature up to 1 week.

Per piece: 94 cal., 32% (30 cal.) from fat; 0.3 g protein; 3.3 g fat (2.7 g sat.); 17 g carbo.; 25 mg sodium; 3.7 mg chol. ■

By Christine Weber Hale

Hot or cold, a drink that refreshes

THE REFRESHING COMBINATION OF lemon grass and mint in this tea comes to the West by way of India, brought to us by reader Niloufer Ichaporia of San Francisco. You can enjoy it hot or cold.

Lemon Grass–Mint Tea

Prep time: About 10 minutes

Makes: 5½ cups

2 stalks (3 oz. total) lemon grass, rinsed

2 cups (1½ oz.) lightly packed mint sprigs

1½ tablespoons black tea leaves (optional)

6 cups boiling water

Sugar and milk (optional)

1. Split lemon grass lengthwise; crush with a mallet or hammer. Cut into 2-inch lengths. Place lemon grass, mint, and tea in a teapot that holds at least 7 cups. Add boiling water; cover. Let stand 3 to 4 minutes; stir.

2. To serve hot, pour through a fine strainer into cups; to serve cold, pour over ice. Add sugar and milk to taste. ■

By Elaine Johnson

GOLDEN TEA *is a brew of fragrant lemon grass, black tea leaves, and fresh mint.*

The kindest cut for flank steak

*Plus, artichokes on a
sandwich and shrimp with
a strong sauce*

BREAD CAN BE COMBINED WITH
other foods in thousands of inge-
nious ways. Just consider meat
pies, pasties, Welsh rabbit, and that
perennial Army favorite, creamed
chipped beef on toast. Eggs Benedict is
another such combination that rises to the
level of art. And for those who simply
love artichokes, Ted Rosenbaum's colorful and richly flavored Artichoke Open
Face is a true high point.

Artichoke Open Face

Cooking time: About 20 minutes
Prep time: About 25 minutes
Makes: 12 pieces, 6 servings

2 tablespoons pine nuts
2 jars (6½ oz. each) marinated
   artichoke hearts
1½ cups (6 oz.) shredded mozzarella
   cheese
⅓ cup diced red bell pepper
½ cup diced seeded tomato
3 tablespoons grated parmesan
   cheese
6 English muffins, split and toasted

1. Frequently shake nuts in a 6- to 8-inch
frying pan over medium heat until nuts are
toasted, about 5 minutes. Pour from pan.

2. Drain artichokes; reserve marinade for
another use, if desired. Cut artichokes into
½-inch-wide pieces. Mix pieces well with
pine nuts, mozzarella, bell pepper, tomato,
and 1 tablespoon parmesan.

3. Set muffins, toasted sides up, in a 10- by
15-inch pan. Top equally with artichoke
mixture, then sprinkle muffins with remaining parmesan. Bake in a 350° oven
until mixture is hot in the center, about 15
minutes.

Per serving: 304 cal., 41% (126 cal.) from
fat; 13 g protein; 14 g fat (5.2 g sat.); 33 g
carbo.; 735 mg sodium; 24 mg chol.

Ted Rosenbaum

Bainbridge Island, Washington

LARRY HERSCHER'S MARINATED FLANK
Steak, cooked over hot coals, is
well suited to any warm evening.
This cut is not notable for its tenderness, but it has a rich, beefy flavor.
Cutting the meat into thin, slanting slices
across the grain makes it easier to manage with knife and fork.

Marinated Flank Steak

Cooking time: 15 to 20 minutes
Prep time: 10 to 15 minutes, plus 4
hours for marinating
Notes: The meat can marinate overnight.
Makes: 5 to 7 servings

⅓ cup red wine vinegar
1 tablespoon salad oil
1 teaspoon prepared mustard
1 tablespoon Worcestershire
¼ cup catsup
2 tablespoons soy sauce
1 teaspoon minced garlic
¼ teaspoon pepper
1 flank steak (1½ to 2 lb.), fat
   trimmed

1. In a 1-gallon zip-lock plastic freezer bag
or deep bowl, mix vinegar, oil, mustard,
Worcestershire, catsup, soy sauce, garlic,
and pepper. Add steak, seal bag or cover
bowl, and chill at least 4 hours, turning meat
occasionally.

2. Lift steak from marinade and drain briefly; reserve marinade.

3. Place meat on a grill over medium-hot coals or gas grill on medium-high (you can hold your hand at grill level only 3 to 4 seconds). Close lid on gas grill. Cook meat, turning to brown evenly; baste several times with marinade. Allow 12 to 15 minutes for medium-rare steak.

4. Transfer meat to a platter and keep warm; pour remaining marinade into a 6- to 8-inch frying pan and bring to a boil over high heat. Cut meat across the grain into thin, slanting slices, and accompany with the marinade.

Per serving: 186 cal., 45% (85 cal.) from fat; 20 g protein; 9.4 g fat (3.4 g sat.); 3.8 g carbo.; 489 mg sodium; 49 mg chol.

Glendora, California

J AMES FRENCH'S SHRIMP WITH PASTA combines delicacy with strength— not the brute strength of lazily bubbling, long-simmering red meat sauce, but the subtle strength of harmonizing.

Shrimp with Pasta

Cooking time: About 25 minutes
Prep time: 20 to 25 minutes
Notes: You can season the shrimp and let them chill up to 4 hours.
Makes: 6 servings

- 4 cloves garlic
- 2 tablespoons olive oil
- 1 teaspoon dried oregano leaves
  About ½ teaspoon pepper
- 1 tablespoon lemon juice
- 1 pound shrimp (about 40 per lb.), shelled, deveined, and rinsed
- ¼ cup pine nuts
- ½ cup drained dried tomatoes packed in oil, slivered
- 2 to 2½ teaspoons grated lemon peel
- 6 tablespoons chopped Italian parsley
- ½ cup chicken broth
- 12 ounces dried vermicelli, cooked
- ½ cup packed feta cheese, crumbled
  Salt

1. Mince 1 clove garlic; thinly slice remaining cloves.

2. Mix minced garlic, 1 tablespoon oil, oregano, ¼ teaspoon pepper and lemon juice, and shrimp. Cover; chill at least 15 minutes.

3. Meanwhile, in an 8- to 10-inch frying pan over medium heat, shake pine nuts often until lightly toasted, 3 to 5 minutes. Pour from pan. Add remaining 1 tablespoon oil to pan along with sliced garlic. Stir until garlic is golden (take care not to scorch), about 3 minutes. Return nuts to pan and remove from heat; stir in ¼ teaspoon remaining pepper, tomatoes, lemon peel, and parsley, then scrape into a bowl.

4. In a 10- to 12-inch frying pan over high heat, stir shrimp mixture just until shrimp turn pink, about 3 minutes. Add broth and remove from heat.

5. Add hot pasta to seasonings in bowl; mix well. Pour shrimp mixture over pasta and sprinkle with feta. Mix and serve, adding salt and pepper to taste.

Per serving: 502 cal. 41% (207 cal.) from fat; 25 g protein; 23 g fat (5 g sat.); 51 g carbo.; 284 mg sodium; 106 mg chol.

Boise

By Joan Griffiths, Richard Dunmire

Thin, crisp slice-and-bake croutons

C ROUTONS DON'T HAVE TO BE CUBES. These thin rounds are made mostly with goat cheese, soft and fresh or ripened, and lightly crusted with black pepper. They make delectable, buttery, crisp nibbles as an appetizer and are an especially delightful topping for greens.

Peppered Chèvre Crouton Wafers

Cooking time: 20 minutes per pan
Prep time: About 10 minutes, plus 4 hours for chilling
Notes: You make and shape the dough at least several hours or up to days ahead; it needs to be cold to slice neatly. Cut off a

few slices to bake, and serve them warm. Or bake up the whole batch and store croutons airtight. You can hold them at room temperature up to 3 days, or in the freezer for several months, ready to pull out as needed.

Makes: About 7 dozen

- 5 ounces (about ½ cup) chèvre (goat) cheese, cut into chunks
- 3 tablespoons butter or margarine
- ⅔ cup all-purpose flour
- 1 teaspoon coarsely ground pepper

1. In a bowl or a food processor, beat or whirl cheese and butter until blended. Add flour, and beat or whirl until smoothly blended. Place dough on a 12- by 16-inch piece of plastic wrap; roll dough in wrap and shape into a log about 11 inches long. Unwrap log and sprinkle evenly with pepper; press gently to make pepper stick. Again, roll log in plastic wrap to enclose. Chill log until firm, at least 4 hours or up to 3 days.

2. Unwrap log and slice crosswise into ⅛-inch-thick rounds. Place rounds about 1½ inches apart on ungreased 12- by 15-inch

SCATTER TANGY GOAT CHEESE *wafers over crisp greens to dress up salad.*

baking sheets. Bake in a 325° oven until lightly browned, 18 to 20 minutes. Transfer to racks. Serve croutons warm or cool.
—*Mary Robins, Menlo Park, California*

Per piece: 12 cal., 60% (7.2 cal.) from fat; 0.4 g protein; 0.8 g fat (0.5 g sat.); 0.8 g carbo.; 10 mg sodium; 1.9 mg chol. ■

By Linda Lau Anusasananan

SWORDFISH STEAK, *draped with cheese melted over prosciutto strips, is topped with a shimmering lemon sauce and nippy capers.*

For a fast dinner party...

Grill swordfish, make a sauce with lemon and white wine

W HEN GUESTS ARE COMING AND time is tight, a dish that lands on the table in a half-hour or less can be a lifesaver. Here's a real catch for such a situation: grilled swordfish with the sophisticated touches of prosciutto and fontina cheese. Pick up these ingredients when you buy the fish—most likely on the way home from work.

Once the grill is hot, the fish cooks with one flip. Waiting in the wings, ready to come to a boil, is a tangy lemon sauce made with a few simple seasonings most cooks keep on hand. While the grill heats, you'll have time to steam potatoes and sugar snap peas to round out the menu.

Grilled Swordfish with Prosciutto and Fontina

Cooking time: About 10 minutes

Prep time: About 15 minutes; allow at least 30 minutes for coals or 10 minutes for gas grill to heat.

Notes: Broiling is another way to cook the fish.

Makes: 4 servings

⅓ cup chicken broth

¼ cup dry white wine

1½ teaspoons cornstarch mixed with 1 tablespoon water

1 teaspoon grated lemon peel

1 teaspoon sugar

4 swordfish steaks (each about 6 oz. and ¾ in. thick)

2 very thin slices (½ to 1 oz. total) prosciutto, cut into strips

4 thin slices (about 1 oz. total) fontina cheese

1½ tablespoons drained prepared capers

2 tablespoons lemon juice

Coarsely ground pepper (optional)

1. In a 1- to 1½-quart pan, combine broth, wine, cornstarch mixture, lemon peel, and sugar; set aside.

2. Rinse fish, pat dry, and lay on a lightly oiled barbecue grill 4 to 6 inches above a solid bed of very hot coals or gas grill on high (you can hold your hand at grill level only 1 to 2 seconds). Cover gas grill.

3. Cook until fish is lightly browned on bottom, 3 to 4 minutes. Turn steaks over and top each equally with prosciutto strips, then lay cheese on prosciutto. Cover grill, open vents, and cook until fish is no longer translucent but is still moist-looking in the center of the thickest part (cut to test), about 4 minutes longer. Transfer swordfish to a platter and keep warm.

4. Quickly stir broth mixture over high heat until boiling. Add capers and lemon juice, and pour sauce over fish; sprinkle with pepper.

Per serving: 241 cal., 33% (80 cal.) from fat; 33 g protein; 8.9 g fat (3.2 g sat.); 2.9 g carbo.; 348 mg sodium; 70 mg chol. ∎

By Christine Weber Hale

SUNSET'S KITCHEN CABINET
Creative ways with everyday foods—submitted by *Sunset* readers, tested in *Sunset* kitchens

Quick Chicken Chili Verde
Renee Noble, Scottsdale, Arizona

- 1 teaspoon salad oil
- 1 onion (about ½ lb.), chopped
- 1 pound ground chicken or turkey
- 1 teaspoon ground cumin
- 1 can (14½ oz.) diced tomatoes
- 1 can (7 oz.) diced green chilies
-    Salt
- 8 to 12 large iceberg lettuce leaves, rinsed and crisped
-    Prepared salsa
-    Low-fat sour cream (optional)

1. Pour oil into a 10- to 12-inch frying pan. Add onion, chicken, and cumin. Stir often over medium-high heat until onion begins to brown, about 8 minutes.

2. Add tomatoes, including liquid, and chilies. Simmer, uncovered, over medium heat until most of the liquid evaporates, 10 to 15 minutes. Add salt to taste.

3. Spoon chicken mixture into lettuce leaves, add salsa and sour cream to taste, and roll up to eat. Serves 4.

Per serving (no condiments): 245 cal., 44% (108 cal.) from fat; 22 g protein; 12 g fat (2.7 g sat.); 13 g carbo.; 567 mg sodium; 94 mg chol.

SCOOP SPEEDY *version of chicken chili verde into cool iceberg lettuce cups; season with salsa and sour cream.*

Roasted Tomato Pasta Salad
Dawn Horner, Los Angeles

- ½ cup chopped fresh basil leaves
- ½ cup red wine vinegar
- ¼ cup olive oil
- 1 tablespoon firmly packed brown sugar
- 1 tablespoon Dijon mustard
- 1 clove garlic, pressed or minced
- 10 Roma-type tomatoes (1¾ lb. total)
- ¾ pound dried rotelle pasta
- 2 ounces string cheese, torn into fine strands
-    Salt

1. Mix basil, vinegar, oil, sugar, mustard, and garlic; pour 3 tablespoons of mixture into a 10- by 15-inch pan.

2. Cut each tomato lengthwise into 3 equal slices; turn to coat with dressing. Bake in a single layer in pan, in a 425° oven until edges brown, 40 to 50 minutes.

3. Meanwhile, in a 5- to 6-quart pan, bring 3 quarts water to a boil. Add pasta, and cook, uncovered, until tender to bite, 7 to 9 minutes; drain. Cool in cold water; drain. Mix pasta with ⅔ cup remaining dressing.

4. Pour pasta into a shallow bowl with tomatoes, rest of dressing, and cheese. Mix; add salt to taste. Serves 4 to 6.

Per serving: 361 cal., 30% (108 cal.) from fat; 11 g protein; 12 g fat (2.6 g sat.); 52 g carbo.; 143 mg sodium; 5 mg chol.

ROAST ROMA *tomato slices with basil, then add to curly pasta and top with strands of cheese for a hearty salad.*

Summer Fruit Soup
Clare B. Le Brun, San Anselmo, California

- ⅓ cup sugar
- 1 firm-ripe peach (about ½ lb.)
- 2 cups blueberries, rinsed
- 3 cups strawberries, hulled and rinsed
- 1 cup raspberries, rinsed
- 3 tablespoons lemon juice
- 2 tablespoons raspberry liqueur or raspberry-flavor syrup (optional)
- 2 to 2½ cups lemon sorbet

1. In a 2½- to 3-quart pan, mix sugar and ¾ cup water. Bring to a rolling boil over high heat. Peel peach; thinly slice it into boiling syrup and cook 1 minute. Add blueberries and cook 1 minute. Let cool.

2. In a blender, smoothly purée ½ the peach-blueberry mixture, ½ the strawberries, and ½ the raspberries. Return purée to pan, and add lemon juice and liqueur. Cover and chill until cold, at least 2 hours or up to 1 day.

3. Slice remaining strawberries and add to soup with remaining raspberries. Ladle into shallow bowls; add 1 scoop sorbet to each. Serves 6 or 7.

Per serving: 164 cal., 3.3% (5.4 cal.) from fat; 1.3 g protein; 0.6 g fat (0 g sat.); 41 g carbo.; 11 mg sodium; 0 mg chol.

Compiled by Linda Lau Anusasananan

LEMON SORBET *is a cool accent in this refreshing dessert soup made with summer peaches and berries.*

FOOD
Guide

BY JERRY ANNE DI VECCHIO

A TASTE OF THE WEST: Seasonal, lean lasagne

A fantasy I've never had time to indulge is a spa visit that lasts long enough to produce serious change. Once, though, I spent a day behind the shining red doors of one of San Francisco's venerated, now deceased, salons. It was perfect, to the last moment.

The pampering paused only briefly, and that was for a light lunch. It was appetizing, attractive, and nutritionally thoughtful, relying on complex carbohydrates and vegetables to provide satisfying volume. This approach is the mantra of today's low-fat gurus, but Deborah Szekely has pursued this tack for decades at Rancho La Puerta, the spa she founded in 1939 in Tecate, just south of the border.

And now chef Michel Stroot carries on the lean-eating concept. I like his lasagne for several reasons: It uses lots of vegetables that are exceptional in quality and in value this month. Portions can be generous because fat and calories are well balanced, yet there's ample cheese. The sauce, made with mellow dried ancho chilies, has a bit of backbone. And the lasagne can be made ahead.

Like most casseroles, it's easy to make but time consuming. When pressed, I save about a half-hour by omitting the ancho chili sauce and using 5 cups of canned mild enchilada sauce instead.

La Puerta Lasagne

Cooking time: About 50 minutes, plus 10 if refrigerated

Prep time: 30 to 40 minutes and 10 minutes standing time

Notes: If making ahead, cover and chill up to 1 day.

Makes: 6 servings

Ancho chili sauce (recipe follows)

About 1 pound Swiss chard

PETER CHRISTIANSEN

Generous portions won't hurt. Deceptively rich tasting, this lasagne—filled with savory vegetables and cheese—is low in fat and calories. The sauce has a mellow chili nip.

196

- Vegetable lasagne with chili flavors
- Try turkey confit, then put it on a sandwich
- A flat bread with warm grapes
- Getting a handle on hot pasta
- Washington Merlots for a gamy repast

1 cup chopped onion

1 teaspoon dried oregano leaves

2 teaspoons salad oil

About ½ pound zucchini

1 cup low-fat ricotta cheese

1 cup thinly sliced green onions, including tops

Salt

½ pound dried lasagne pasta, cooked and drained

1½ cups corn kernels, fresh cut or frozen

2 to 3 ounces queso quesadilla or low-fat jarlsberg cheese, shredded

1 tablespoon crumbled cotija or shredded parmesan cheese

1. Make ancho chili sauce, and as it is under way, trim and discard discolored stem ends from Swiss chard. Chop chard and put in a 4- to 6-quart nonstick pan. Add chopped onion, ½ teaspoon oregano, salad oil, and ⅓ cup water. Cover and cook on medium heat, stirring often, for 8 minutes. Uncover and stir often until liquid evaporates and vegetables start to sizzle, about 25 minutes. Pour from pan.

2. Trim ends from zucchini and thinly slice; put in pan with 1 tablespoon water. Stir often over medium-high heat until slices are tinged with brown, about 5 minutes. Pour from pan.

3. Mix ricotta cheese, ½ cup green onions, remaining ½ teaspoon oregano, and salt to taste.

4. Spread about 1 cup ancho chili sauce over bottom of a 9- by 12- or 13-inch casserole (at least 2 in. deep), then cover sauce neatly with ¼ of the lasagne noodles. Scatter ⅓ of the chard, zucchini, and corn over pasta. Drizzle with 1 cup chili sauce. Top neatly with another ¼ of the lasagne noodles, another ⅓ of the chard, zucchini, and corn, then dot evenly with the ricotta, gently spreading to cover filling. Cover ricotta with about ¾ cup sauce and

neatly layer ¼ of the noodles on top. Scatter remaining chard, zucchini, and corn onto noodles, moisten with another ¾ cup sauce, and cover neatly with remaining noodles. Spread remaining sauce over noodles to cover.

5. Bake, covered, in a 350° oven until sauce bubbles at casserole edge, about 30 minutes (40 if chilled). Uncover lasagne and sprinkle with quesadilla cheese, then cotija. Bake, uncovered, until quesadilla cheese melts, 5 to 8 minutes. Let stand at least 10 minutes. Cut lasagne into rectangles with a knife and lift out with a wide spatula; sprinkle with remaining green onions for garnish.

Per serving: 338 cal., 22% (73 cal.) from fat; 17 g protein; 8.1 g fat (3.3 g sat.); 54 g carbo.; 311 mg sodium; 17 mg chol.

Ancho chili sauce. Discard stems and seeds from 2 **dried ancho chilies** (about 3 in. long, 1 oz. total). Pour 1½ cups boiling **water** over chilies and let stand at least 5 minutes or up to 6 hours.

Core 1 pound **tomatoes** (about equal size). Set tomatoes and 1 **fresh jalapeño chili** in a 10- by 15-inch pan. Broil 3 to 4 inches from heat until vegetable skins are charred, about 10 minutes, turning pieces over as needed. Discard chili stem and seeds. Put unpeeled tomatoes and chili in a blender; add ancho chilies and ½ cup of the soaking water.

In a 4- to 6-quart nonstick pan, combine 1 (about 5 oz.) finely chopped **onion**, 2 (½ lb. total) finely chopped **carrots**, 2 teaspoons **ground cumin**, 1 teaspoon **dried oregano leaves**, and ½ cup **water**. Cook over high heat, stirring occasionally, until liquid evaporates, then stir often until vegetables are browned, about 10 minutes. Stir 1 cup **vegetable** or chicken **broth** into pan, then pour mixture into blender. Holding blender lid down with a towel, turn motor to low speed, then to high and smoothly purée mixture. Return sauce to pan. Add another 1 cup vegetable or chicken broth. Simmer rapidly, stirring often until reduced to about 5 cups, about 10 minutes. Salt to taste.

KITCHEN DISCOVERY

You can make confit— with turkey

I love duck confit—the salt-cured meat has such succulence—but I don't like the fat. And because most duck at the market is frozen, I have to plan ahead to make the dish. Somehow, the planning part keeps getting lost. So once, when in a great hurry to produce confit, I turned to turkey thighs, reasoning that the dark, moist meat might work some-

thing the way duck does.

It was a good move, and one I've made many times since. Turkey confit is as good as duck and a ton leaner, the way I make it. I bone and skin the thighs myself, or have this done at the market. The salt-and-sugar cure does its work in 2 hours or less. Then—to stop the salt penetration—I rinse the meat right away, saving the spices. Instead of boiling or frying, I put the meat, spices, and a little water in a casserole, seal it tightly, and bake slowly until the meat is very moist and tender. Turkey confit

der. Turkey confit is delicious hot as a main dish. Or let the meat cool in the juices so the liquid thickens to become cold meat jelly. Then you can make confit sandwiches—big ones for lunch, little open-face ones for appetizers.

Turkey Confit

Cooking time: 1 1/4 to 1 1/2 hours

Prep time: 55 minutes to 2 hours

Notes: After salt is rinsed from turkey, you can wrap meat and spices airtight and chill up to 1 day. Confit keeps well, refrigerated, up to 1 week.

Makes: 8 to 10 servings

> About 4 pounds turkey thighs (any size), boned and skinned
>
> 6 tablespoons kosher salt
>
> 1/4 cup firmly packed brown sugar
>
> 1 teaspoon dried thyme leaves
>
> 2 teaspoons allspice
>
> 1 tablespoon *each* mustard seed and coriander seed

1. Trim and discard all fat on turkey thighs. Rinse and drain meat.

For a fine sandwich, put thinly sliced baked turkey confit on toasted bread with mustard, roasted red peppers, and arugula.

2. Combine salt, sugar, thyme, allspice, mustard seed, and coriander seed. Rub mixture all over turkey. Cover and chill 45 minutes to no more than 2 hours.

3. Put turkey and spices in a fine-mesh colander and rinse meat well with cool running water, rubbing to release as much salt as possible. Let drain.

4. Spread meat flat, with spices, in a single layer (edges can overlap) in a close-fitting pan. Add about 1/8 inch water to pan and cover tightly with foil.

5. Bake in a 375° oven until meat is very tender when pierced, 1 1/4 to 1 1/2 hours. Serve hot, warm, or chilled in juices. Thinly slice meat; serve with warm or jellied juices.

Per serving: 147 cal., 29% (43 cal.) from fat; 23 g protein; 4.8 g fat (1.6 g sat.); 1.6 g carbo.; 239 mg sodium; 85 mg chol.

SEASONAL NOTE

Hot grapes, made simple

Crisp green or red seedless grapes briefly swirled over high heat in a dry pan or with a little butter almost instantly become juicy, tart-sweet bubbles that dress up the simplest foods. If you think of these hot grapes as a relish, you get the gist of their adaptability.

Pour them over grilled sausages, especially Italian or Polish ones. Or place them beside a roasted or grilled chicken or turkey. Spoon alongside cold or hot salmon—or sautéed sole, as a fresh twist on sole Véronique.

When my associate, Linda Anusasananan, was on a food tour of Italy, she came across hot grapes on focaccia. This recipe is as simple as it is surprising, and frozen dough makes it easy. Serve the bread for breakfast or brunch, or with chicken salad for lunch.

Grape Focaccia

Cooking time: About 25 minutes

Prep time: 5 minutes to shape dough, 20 minutes for rising

Notes: For breakfast, thaw dough overnight in the refrigerator.

Makes: About 1 1/4 pounds, 6 servings

Thaw 1 loaf (1 lb.) **frozen white bread dough.** Pour 2 teaspoons **olive oil** into a 9- by 13-inch pan. Turn dough in oil to coat, then press firmly to cover pan bottom (if dough wants to spring back, let stand 10 minutes, then continue). Scatter 1 1/2 cups **seedless grapes** over dough and press fruit into it without crushing. Sprinkle with 1 to 1 1/4 teaspoons **kosher salt,** 1 teaspoon **anise seed,** and 1 to 1 1/2 tablespoons **sugar.** Cover airtight and let stand in a warm place until puffy, about 20 minutes. Bake, uncovered, on bottom rack of a 375° oven until bread is well browned on bottom, about 25 minutes.

Per serving: 221 cal., 14% (30 cal.) from fat; 6.1 g protein; 3.3 g fat (0.3 g sat.); 43 g carbo.; 686 mg sodium; 0 mg chol.

BACK TO BASICS

What is pesto?

Pesto means, in Italian, *pounded.* Although the usual implication is that basil is being pulverized in a mortar with a pestle—more likely in a blender or food processor—there are now all kinds of pesto sauces to make or buy. An herb or green is essential—even spinach has taken a whirl. And like basil pesto, these pestos do well on pasta (hot or cold as salads) with vegetables, or on toast.

I like this departure using green pistachio nuts and parsley—the nuts impart a delicate sweetness. The pesto is great on September's prime, ripe tomatoes, sliced or roasted.

Pistachio pesto

Prep time: 3 to 5 minutes

Notes: If making ahead, cover and chill up to 1 day.

Makes: 3/4 cup

In a blender or a food processor, combine 1/4 cup **salted pistachios,** 1 cup packed **parsley,** 1/4 cup **white wine vinegar,** 1/4 cup **chicken broth,** and 2 tablespoons **extra-virgin olive oil.** Whirl until mixture is smoothly puréed.

Per tablespoon: 39 cal., 85% (33 cal.) from fat; 0.8 g protein; 3.7 g fat (0.5 g sat.); 1.4 g carbo.; 17 mg sodium; 0 mg chol.

No strain to drain

Quickly separating hot pasta—or ears of corn or sugar snap peas—from boiling water is less of a struggle if you can lift the foods out with a helpful utensil.

There are two solutions: One is to use a pan with a perforated liner that you can lift out of the water. Pans with perforated liners or inserts, typically 8- to 12-quart size, are available in most stores that sell cookware. Prices range dramatically, based on material, size, and workmanship, from $30 to $300.

A cheaper solution to the problem is a separately purchased perforated or mesh metal basket that you place in the pan beneath the food. You'll find them where pans with liners are sold, but your options may be fewer. Select one that fits easily in your pan—if the basket is narrower or taller, no problem. If it's shorter, just don't fill above it in the cooking pan. Expect to pay from $10 to $35.

To improvise, you can nest a large bowl-shaped metal strainer with a handle, available in grocery stores, in the cooking pan. Or use a really big skimmer to scoop foods from the hot water. You'll find skimmers in regular and Asian cookware stores. These gadgets start at about $3.

PETER CHRISTIANSEN

Several ways to get pasta out of boiling water fast: If cooking a large quantity, use pans with perforated inserts. For small portions, nest wire strainer in a pan. Or scoop pasta with large ladles made of wire or perforated metal.

BOB THOMPSON ON WINE: Yearning for Merlot

To have somebody sitting in front of a pretty good breast of duck in a better-than-average Paris restaurant start longing for a bottle of Washington Merlot could be taken as a serious compliment to Washington Merlot. Or you could dismiss the party in question as a nut. Inasmuch as the somebody was me, please call the notion a compliment.

The Merlot came to mind for one reason. Dense, rich, gamy-tasting meats want one of two wine styles that are polar opposites. They either take to a velvety old red with gamy tones of its own, or to a brisk, even edgy young wine with flavors firmly focused on fruit. A mature, velvet-smooth Burgundy—say an Echézeaux—echoes the taste and feel of rich, gamy meat and costs the earth wherever you find

it. A young Washington Merlot provides ringing counterpoints of both flavor and texture, and costs a modest price, maybe not in Paris, but in our part of the world. Thus my moment of longing.

The duck happened to have been roasted, but it might have been grilled or could have appeared as that ultra-French, ultra-rich idea, the confit. A briskly refreshing Washington Merlot would have been the ticket in any case.

The grape variety is hard to grow in central and eastern Washington, being especially tender in the extreme winter cold that can come to the Columbia River basin. However, the wines have been so distinctive during the past several vintages that growers there have made it the most-planted red wine variety in the state.

A majority of producers favor a style that concentrates on Merlot's varietal flavors, which sometimes hint at cassis, sometimes at herbs such as dill or anise. Some winemakers prefer to soften and sweeten it slightly with time in new French oak barrels. Prices range from $9 to $15 for all but the luxury lots, which top out at about $30.

Among the leanest, crispest, most focused on Merlot flavors: Chateau Ste. Michelle, Columbia Winery, Washington Hills, and Waterbrook.

Slightly richer or fuller, with a more overt touch of oak, but still true to Merlot and to Washington's crisp textures: Gordon Brothers, the Hogue Cellars, the Hogue Cellars Reserve, Andrew Will, and Columbia Winery "Milestone." ■

'MARVEL STRIPE'

'BRANDYWINE'

'GREAT WHITE'

'CHEROKEE PURPLE'

'GOLDIE'

'EVERGREEN'

'AMISH PASTE'

'COSTOLUTO GENOVESE'

'ORANGE CHERRY'

'GREEN GRAPE'

'STUPICE'

'RED CURRANT'

'YELLOW CURRANT'

HEIRLOOM

Ruby color, round shape, and rich, herbaceous flavor once defined that glory of summer, the ripe tomato. These days, the color may be vibrant green, near white, or chocolate. The size can be that of a pea or a baseball, and the form can be lumpy, pear-shaped, or ruffled. And the taste? Intensely sweet to tangy, tropical, or earthy. Yet despite such novel qualities, these "new" tomatoes go back centuries.

Where have they been all our lives? Until recently, they were only in home gardens and specialty seed catalogs. Now they're popping up at farmers' markets, top restaurants, even supermarkets.

Heirloom is the term given to many of the tomatoes, an appropriate term for something that connects us to earlier times. They're varieties that have passed from generation to generation among families and friends. Today they're locally grown, picked ripe, and raised commercially by small specialty farms.

By buying and growing heirlooms we keep their heritage alive, encourage a diverse selection of tomatoes in the marketplace, and enjoy the excitement of discovery.

THE NEWEST TOMATOES IN THE MARKETPLACE ARE SEVERAL GENERATIONS OLD. HERE ARE THE TOP 12 FOR GROWING AND COOKING

This is peak harvest season, the best time to discover heirloom tomatoes. Of hundreds of varieties, the ones pictured at left get the most votes from our survey of expert growers for memorable flavor, good looks, and adaptation to the West's climates.

ENJOYING TOMATOES AT THEIR BEST

For best flavor, select or harvest tomatoes fully colored. Choose while still firm (they will last several days on the counter), or pick or buy them slightly soft to use in a day or two. But don't wait until they turn extra-soft with translucent flesh, or you'll get an off-taste.

Never refrigerate a tomato that isn't completely ripe (fully colored); flavor development will stop, though color may continue to change. As for chilling fully ripe tomatoes, some experts say flavor declines; some insist it doesn't. All agree that tomatoes are tastiest at room temperature.

With tomatoes this good, you don't need to do much to get great results. Jan Blüm, owner of Seeds Blüm (an heirloom seed company near Boise), suggests the simplest recipe of all. "They're best if

ROASTED TOMATO SOUP
For intensely flavored orange soup, purée roasted 'Goldie' tomatoes with broth; add sour cream swirls.

TOMATOES

BY ELAINE JOHNSON & LAUREN BONAR SWEZEY

NOEL BARNHURST

eaten right off the bush, with tomato juice running down your wrist. I keep a salt-shaker on a post in the garden."

THE EXPERTS' PICKS

Look for their selections at farmers' and specialty markets. Kinds vary by area, and some sources label tomatoes more by color than name. A few tomatoes are more difficult to find, but you can grow these at home.

Diverse flavors are one of the charms of heirloom tomatoes. Partly, differences are a matter of perception; some palates are more tuned to sweet or acidic tastes. But climate, soil, and growing methods also affect flavor.

Unless noted, plants are indeterminate (vinelike, need support, and generally bear over a longer period than determinate plants, which are compact and bushy).

'AMISH PASTE'. Dates to the turn of the century. Oblong, paste-type fruit with solid flesh, few seeds, sweet flavor; also used for slicing. Large for a paste tomato. Less available in markets than some.

'BRANDYWINE'. An Amish Beefsteak with pink-red color "like Gamay Beaujolais," says Jeff Dawson, garden director of Fetzer Vineyards Valley Oaks Garden Project in Hopland, California. Large; rich flavor, firm-soft texture, thin skin.

'CHEROKEE PURPLE'. Said to have originated with the Cherokee. Pink-chocolate with handsome green stripes on shoulders, round to oblong, medium size. Sweet, earthy, complex flavor; soft texture. Big producer; disease tolerant.

'COSTOLUTO GENOVESE'. An Italian variety with an unusual fluted profile. Deep red color; intense, full, sweet flavor; meaty texture. Size varies. Good fresh or cooked. Vigorous, heavy yield.

'EVERGREEN'. Yellow-green with vivid green interior. Medium to large, with irregular shape; sweet-tart flavor; firm texture; delicate skin. Vigorous plant.

'GOLDIE'. May have been around for 150 years. Large, with beautiful golden orange color, sweet flavor, good acid balance. Vigorous plant.

'GREAT WHITE'. Actually a light yellow. Large Beefsteak with mild, melonlike flavor, low acidity. Vigorous plant.

'GREEN GRAPE'. Cherry-type tomato. Yellow-green when ripe. Very sweet and juicy taste with some acidity; seeds are

Fireworks Tomato Salad

Cooking time: About 10 minutes

Prep time: About 30 minutes

Notes: This rainbow-colored salad with the lively flavor of salsa shows off the smaller tomatoes' shapes. Serve on its own, spooned over slices of larger tomatoes, or with steak or chicken.

Makes: 4 servings

- ¾ pound (3 to 4) fresh pasilla or Anaheim chilies
- 1 large fresh jalapeño chili
- 5 cups small, ripe, multicolored heirloom tomatoes (or 1-inch chunks of larger tomatoes)
- 2 tablespoons lime juice
- ⅓ cup coarsely chopped fresh cilantro, plus sprigs
-   Salt and pepper

1. Place pasilla and jalapeño chilies on a 10- by 15-inch baking sheet. Broil 2 to 3 inches from heat until black and blistered all over, turning as needed, 6 to 10 minutes.

2. Let chilies cool, then peel, seed, and rinse. Coarsely chop pasillas and mince jalapeño.

3. For small tomatoes, leave any tiny ones whole; quarter or halve somewhat bigger ones. In a bowl, combine tomatoes, chilies, lime juice, and chopped cilantro. Season to taste with salt and pepper. Garnish with cilantro sprigs.

Per serving: 76 cal., 11% (8 cal.) from fat; 3.3 g protein; 0.9 g fat (0.1 g sat.); 17 g carbo.; 27 mg sodium; 0 mg chol.

Four-in-One Roasted Tomatoes

Cooking time: About 1½ hours

Prep time: About 15 minutes

Notes: Baking intensifies tomatoes' flavor and sweetness. Use this basic recipe to roast tomato halves to go with meats (as noted here) or to turn into marinara sauce, a richly flavored appetizer spread, or a deceptively simple soup (directions are on page 204).

For plain roasted tomatoes, large slicing kinds taste very good but hold their shape less well than smaller slicers or paste or currant types.

Makes: 8 servings plain roasted tomatoes

- 1 onion (6 oz.), peeled and cut into lengthwise slivers
- 2 tablespoons extra-virgin olive oil
-   Salt and pepper
- 4 to 5 pounds ripe tomatoes
- 1 tablespoon minced garlic

1. In an 11- by 17-inch roasting pan, combine onion and 1 tablespoon oil. Sprinkle generously with salt and pepper, then stir. Cut enough tomatoes in half horizontally to fill pan, placing cut side up over onions. (If using tiny cherry tomatoes, don't cut; simply scatter over onions.)

2. Brush tomatoes with remaining oil, sprinkle generously with salt and pepper, and pat garlic on top. Bake, uncovered, in a 450° oven until juices in pan have evaporated and onions just begin to caramelize, 1¼ to 1½ hours; as needed for even cooking, move tomatoes and onions gently with a spatula from edges to center of pan. Do not let mixture scorch.

3. Serve tomatoes and onions hot to accompany grilled meats, polenta, or other foods. Or use as directed in one of the ways outlined on page 204.

Per serving plain roasted: 88 cal., 44% (39 cal.) from fat; 2.2 g protein; 4.3 g fat (0.6 g sat.); 13 g carbo.; 21 mg sodium; 0 mg chol.

NOEL BARNHURST

FIREWORKS TOMATO SALAD
*Low-calorie, salsa-flavored salad
combines roasted chilies with
small, multicolored tomatoes.*

Roasted Tomato Soup

Cooking time: About 5 minutes
Prep time: About 15 minutes
Makes: 5 to 6 cups, 4 servings

1. To pan with **roasted tomatoes and onions** (from Four-in-One Roasted Tomatoes, page 202), add 1 cup boiling **chicken broth**, and stir to loosen browned bits.

2. Whirl half of mixture in a blender into a smooth purée, then add ¾ cup more boiling broth. Repeat with remaining tomato mixture and ¾ cup more boiling broth. If a thinner texture is desired, add additional broth. Pour into wide bowls.

3. Combine ¼ cup **reduced-fat sour cream** and ⅛ teaspoon **salt.** Drop several small spoonfuls into each bowl, then pull a knife tip through sour cream into soup to form designs.

Per serving: 206 cal., 48% (99 cal.) from fat; 6.3 g protein; 11 g fat (2.4 g sat.); 27 g carbo.; 140 mg sodium; 5 mg chol.

Roasted Tomato Marinara

Cooking time: About 20 minutes
Prep time: About 15 minutes
Notes: If desired, add warm chunks of cooked Italian sausage (¾ lb.) to cooked sauce.
Makes: 3 to 3¾ cups, 8 servings; enough for 2 packages (12 oz. each) dried pasta, cooked

1. Coarsely chop **roasted tomatoes and onions** (from Four-in-One Roasted Tomatoes, page 202), then return to pan.

2. Stir in ¾ cup **dry red wine** such as Zinfandel if using red tomatoes (use dry white wine with other tomato colors), ¾ cup **vegetable broth,** and ½ cup chopped **fresh basil.**

3. Bake in a 450° oven, stirring occasionally, until slightly thickened, about 20 minutes. Add 1 teaspoon **sugar** if sauce is too tart. If sauce gets too thick, add more broth.

4. Use sauce hot or let cool, then chill airtight up to 2 days or freeze.

Per serving (sauce only): 108 cal., 37% (40 cal.) from fat; 2.4 g protein; 4.4 g fat (0.6 g sat.); 14 g carbo.; 116 mg sodium; 0 mg chol.

Roasted Tomato Spread

Cooking time: About 10 minutes
Prep time: About 10 minutes
Notes: Serve at room temperature with raw vegetables such as red bell peppers, cucumbers, or carrots; slender baguettes; or crackers.
Makes: About 3 cups, 12 servings

1. Coarsely chop **roasted tomatoes and onions** (from Four-in-One Roasted Tomatoes, page 202). Mixture should equal about 3 cups and be thick and fairly dry; if it's too wet, return to roasting pan and bake in a 450° oven 10 to 20 minutes longer, stirring often.

2. In a bowl, combine tomato mixture with 2 teaspoons minced **fresh marjoram leaves** or ½ teaspoon dried marjoram leaves. Garnish with **fresh marjoram sprigs.**

Per serving (spread only): 58 cal., 43% (25 cal.) from fat; 1.5 g protein; 2.8 g fat (0.4 g sat.); 8.5 g carbo.; 14 mg sodium; 0 mg chol.

NOEL BARNHURST

Grilled Pesto-Tomato Sandwiches

Cooking time: About 5 minutes
Prep time: About 20 minutes
Notes: Grower Stuart Dickson of Stone Free Farm in Watsonville, California, contributed this sandwich idea. His favorite tomato choice is 'Marvel Stripe', but fluted 'Costoluto Genovese', as well as deeply colored 'Evergreen' and 'Goldie' look beautiful, too.
Makes: 4 servings

1. You'll need 8 to 10 ounces **bread** cut into ½-inch-thick diagonal slices about 6 inches long. Use a flat loaf like francese or ciabatta and cut 12 slices; or cut 8 slices of French bread (not a skinny baguette). Cut enough slices of your favorite **heirloom tomatoes** (about 1 lb.) to cover bread. Rinse and crisp 2 cups lightly packed **arugula leaves.**

2. Place bread (without tomatoes) on a 12- by 15-inch baking sheet and broil 2 to 3 inches below heat until golden, about 3 minutes. Turn bread over and spread with ⅔ cup homemade or purchased **pesto.** Broil until bread edges are golden, about 2 minutes.

3. Arrange arugula and tomatoes on bread. Season generously with **salt and pepper;** serve open-face.

Per serving: 389 cal., 51% (198 cal.) from fat; 10 g protein; 22 g fat (3.8 g sat.); 38 g carbo.; 658 mg sodium; 6.7 mg chol.

---

small. Often sold as an heirloom, though is a more recent open-pollinated variety. Compact, determinate plant; a prolific producer.

'MARVEL STRIPE'. Originally from Oaxaca, Mexico, from seed saved for five generations. Large bicolored Beefsteak-type yellow tomato with red stripes. Mildly sweet, good tomato flavor, low acidity. Vigorous plant; a prolific producer.

'ORANGE CHERRY'. Large (1½ inches) for a cherry-type tomato, with intense orange color and exceptionally sweet tomato taste. Rarely available in markets.

'RED CURRANT'. A species from South America with clusters of pea-size fruits. Sweet-tart, fruity flavor. Vigorous, prolific plant. 'Yellow Currant' is similar. (Some tomatoes sold as currants aren't the true species and may be larger.)

'STUPICE'. All-around favorite, from Czechoslovakia. Small; rich red color; sweet, nicely balanced, regular tomato taste. Slightly tough skin. Excellent fresh or roasted. Occasionally available in markets. Early, heavy producer; easy to grow.

HOW TO SAVE YOUR OWN SEEDS

If you've discovered an heirloom tomato you'd love to grow next season, you can save the seed. In most cases, the seeds will produce exactly the same kind of tomato. (By contrast, seed from a hybrid tomato— a cross of two varieties—will never produce the same tomato.) Even though tomatoes are self-pollinating, a few kinds few kinds cross-pollinate with other tomatoes nearby. If the grower didn't isolate the plants or protect the flowers, you may not get the same tomatoes next season. You won't know until you grow the seeds.

Tomato seeds are encased in a gel sac. Allowing seeds to go through a fermentation process that removes the sac helps destroy seed-borne diseases.

1. Choose thoroughly ripe, soft fruit. Wash, and cut open across the middle (not through the stem end).

2. Into a labeled container, gently squeeze tomatoes to extract seed, pulp, and juice. Cover with plastic wrap.

3. Set the container at room temperature out of sun. Stir twice a day until covered with mold; it will smell foul. This takes about three days (less in warmer weather). Don't let fermentation go beyond this point or seeds may germinate.

4. Pour everything into a fine strainer; rinse clean with water. Blot seeds dry and finish drying on a dish (seeds stick to paper or cloth) out of sun; stir twice a day. This takes one to three days, depending on the temperature.

5. Store seeds in an airtight container, and set in a dark spot that's cool and dry.

A good reference for learning more about seed saving is Suzanne Ashworth's *Seed to Seed: Seed Saving Techniques for the Vegetable Gardener* (Seed Saver Publications, Decorah, IA, 1991; $19.95).

HOW TO GROW HEIRLOOMS NEXT SPRING

Sow seeds in flats or containers six to eight weeks before danger of last frost is past; set them on a water heater or use a heating coil to keep between 75° and 90°. Keep soil moist. Right after germination,

set plants in bright, indirect light.

After several sets of leaves form, transplant into 4-inch pots. Water only enough to keep roots from drying out; fertilize weekly with fish emulsion or half-strength liquid fertilizer.

A week or so before transplanting into the ground, set tomatoes outside in partial shade (protect from frost), and gradually introduce them into full sun.

Plant in full sun in well-amended soil. Growers prefer compost, manure, or an organic fertilizer (such as 7-10-7) plus kelp, and cover crops (such as fava beans) planted in fall. Soils high in phosphorus are important for fruit production.

In cool or short-season climates, cover planting bed with black plastic, plant through it, and then cover with row covers. Set determinate types about 2 feet apart, indeterminate types 3 feet apart.

Water regularly to get plants established, then water deeply but less frequently to develop deep rooting. Stuart Dickson of Stone Free Farm in Watsonville, California, says, "Don't pamper them—make them work for their water." This is especially important when they are fruiting. Most growers prefer drip irrigation.

Diseases and insects don't seem to be a major hindrance to growing heirlooms. David Cavagnaro, a writer and photographer who works with Seed Savers Exchange, says most heirlooms are vigorous plants that often outgrow foliage diseases. To avoid soil-borne diseases, rotate crops so they don't grow in the same bed for three to four years. Small tomato hornworms can be controlled with *Bacillus thuringiensis* (BT); handpick large ones. ∎

German-style berry pudding

Just bring to boiling, then cool to enjoy its fresh flavors

A TRADITIONAL GERMAN SWEET, this pudding can be made with almost any red fruit. Custard sauce highlights its intense berry flavors.

Rote Grütze

Cooking time: 25 to 30 minutes
Prep notes: Allow 15 minutes for pudding, 5 for custard. To cool, set pans in ice water and stir often.

Makes: 6 servings

- 6 cups strawberries
- 6 cups raspberries
- 1¼ cups sugar
- 6 tablespoons quick-cooking tapioca
- 1 cup fresh currants, *fraises des bois* (wild strawberries), or raspberries
- 1 cup milk
- 2 large eggs
- 1 teaspoon vanilla
- 1 cinnamon stick (about 3 in.)

1. Rinse strawberries and hull. Rinse raspberries and drain on towels.

2. In a blender or food processor, smoothly purée strawberries and 4 cups raspberries, a portion at a time. Rub purée through a fine strainer into a 3- to 4-quart pan. Discard residue.

3. Mix ¾ cup sugar with tapioca and stir into berry purée. Stir often over medium-high heat until mixture comes to a boil, 10 to 12 minutes. Let pudding cool to room temperature, stirring occasionally.

4. Gently stir remaining raspberries and currants into pudding, then spoon into 6 dishes. When pudding is cool, serve or cover and chill until cold, about 2 hours.

5. Meanwhile, in the top of a double boiler, mix milk, eggs, ½ cup sugar, vanilla, and cinnamon. Set pan over simmering water and stir until custard coats spoon in a smooth, velvety layer, 10 to 15 minutes.

6. At once, set top of double boiler in ice water; stir frequently until custard is cool. Use, or cover and chill up to 1 day. Discard cinnamon stick. Offer custard sauce to pour over pudding.

Per serving: 365 cal., 11% (39 cal.) from fat; 5.7 g protein; 4.3 g fat (1.5 g sat.); 81 g carbo.; 88 mg sodium; 77 mg chol. ∎

By Christine Weber Hale

65 years of Kitchen Cabinet

It all began in 1929 with five recipes from our readers. And now Sunset's newest book preserves the best. This excerpt samples it by the decade **By Jerry Anne Di Vecchio**

L IKE SO MANY FAMILIES WHO MOVED West, we received a housewarming gift of *Sunset* from the resident relative. An incredible gardener who had become Westernized through its pages, my cousin was almost evangelical in her enthusiasm for both the West and the magazine. It was at her home that I tasted my first rare hamburger—prepared from a *Sunset* recipe, grilled on a built-in brick barbecue made from a *Sunset* design, and served at a table-and-chair set built from barrels according to *Sunset* instructions. On her patio, I ate my first avocado, persimmon, and pomegranate—all enormously exotic to my Midwestern palate, but treated with comfort and familiarity in *Sunset* recipes.

This was just after World War II, and although still in grade school, I had already developed a burning passion for food and cooking. With the arrival of *Sunset* each month, I found myself turning to a feature called Kitchen Cabinet. The recipes weren't scary because they were short and looked easy, even to a 10-year-old. There was usually a little story about the contributor or the recipe, and there were endearing sketches that bridged my jump from comic books to cookbooks.

Time went on, and I became a *Sunset* food writer in 1959. One of my first tasks was to retest recipes for Kitchen Cabinet. I was thrilled to have such an old friend help me find my way as a journalist.

When we planned the *Kitchen Cabinet* book, leafing back through the years of this feature was particularly nostalgic for me. It has mirrored our lives and our ways of entertaining, eating, and cooking through almost seven decades—a lifetime for many.

Kitchen Cabinet came into being as a result of the travels of Genevieve Callahan and Lou Richardson. Gen, a home economist, was *Sunset*'s food editor. Lou was the magazine's editor. They told tales of motoring up and down the coast, through the valleys, over the mountains, and across the desert—pausing at every opportunity to attend church luncheons and socials, bridge parties, school teas, pancake breakfasts, crab feeds, local festivals. Everywhere they went, they invited cooks—good, great, any kind at all—to participate in a recipe exchange. Called Kitchen Cabinet, it first appeared in February 1929. You got $1 if your recipe was published.

Readers are still invited to share their favorite recipes. The recipes are still tested and must meet taste panel approval. They're still short and direct, and they still reflect the kinds of foods that West-

1929
J U N E
Lemon Cake Pie

As this dessert bakes, a cakelike topping forms over the sweet-tart lemon filling.

      Pastry for a single-crust 9-inch pie
1 1/2 cups sugar
    2 tablespoons butter or margarine, melted and cooled
  1/3 cup all-purpose flour
  1/4 teaspoon salt
  1/2 teaspoon grated lemon peel
    5 tablespoons lemon juice
    3 large eggs, separated
1 1/4 cups milk

On a lightly floured board, roll pastry into an 11 1/2-inch round; fit into a 9-inch pie pan. Trim and flute edge.

In a large bowl, stir together sugar and butter; blend in flour, salt, lemon peel, and lemon juice. In a small bowl, beat egg yolks to blend; stir in milk. Stir egg mixture into lemon mixture. In a medium-size bowl, beat egg whites with an electric mixer on high speed until they hold stiff, moist peaks; gently fold egg whites into lemon mixture.

Pour filling into pastry shell. Bake on lowest rack of a 375° oven until filling is richly browned on top and center feels set when lightly pressed (45 to 55 minutes). Let cool on a rack. Serve at room temperature. If made ahead, refrigerate for up to 6 hours. Makes 6 to 8 servings.—*E. J. S., Vancouver, WA*

Per serving: 412 calories, 61 g carbohydrates, 6 g protein, 16 g total fat (6 g saturated), 114 mg cholesterol, 243 mg sodium.

Cheese-frosted Biscuits.
Prepare biscuit dough, turn onto board, knead lightly.

Roll out the dough, cut into rounds, and place rounds close together in the pan.

Melt cheese and butter in double boiler; blend well; pour mixture over biscuits.

Bake in a hot oven (450°) about 15 minutes. Serve hot. Makes 24 small biscuits.

1939
J U N E

Spinach Salad Armenian

You'll need only half a cup of the dressing for this recipe; cover and chill the remainder to serve over other vegetable salads. (The egg-safe dressing is a 1995 modification.)

Spicy tomato dressing or egg-safe spicy tomato dressing (recipes follow)
1 pound fresh spinach, stems removed, leaves rinsed and crisped
Salt and pepper
2 hard-cooked large eggs, chopped

Prepare spicy tomato dressing. To serve, tear spinach into bite-size pieces and place in a large bowl. Add ½ cup of the dressing; mix gently, then season to taste with salt and pepper. Garnish with eggs. Makes 6 to 8 servings.—*Mrs. J. B., Elkton, OR*

Spicy tomato dressing. In a blender or food processor, combine 1 **large egg yolk**, ½ teaspoon grated **lemon peel**, ¼ teaspoon **dry mustard**, 1½ teaspoons *each* **paprika** and **Worcestershire**, 1 tablespoon **sugar**, ½ cup **canned tomato sauce**, and ¼ cup *each* **red wine vinegar** and **lemon juice**. Whirl until well blended. With motor running, add 1 cup **salad oil** in thin, slow, steady stream; continue to whirl until dressing is thickened. If made ahead, cover and refrigerate for up to 3 weeks. Makes about 2¼ cups.

Egg-safe spicy tomato dressing. In a small bowl, mix 1 **large egg white** with 2 tablespoons **lemon juice**. Cover airtight and refrigerate for at least 48 hours or up to 4 days (upon longer standing, egg will begin to solidify). Follow directions for dressing above, omitting egg yolk and blending egg white mixture with the remaining 2 tablespoons lemon juice and the rest of the ingredients.

Per serving of salad without dressing: 32 calories, 2 g carbohydrates, 3 g protein, 2 g total fat (0.5 g saturated), 61 mg cholesterol, 55 mg sodium.

Per tablespoon spicy tomato dressing: 59 calories, 1 g carbohydrates, 0.1 g protein, 6 g total fat (1 g saturated), 61 mg cholesterol, 23 mg sodium.

Per tablespoon egg-safe spicy tomato dressing: 57 calories, 1 g carbohydrates, 0.2 g protein, 6 g total fat (1 g saturated), 0 mg cholesterol, 25 mg sodium.

1945
J U N E

Cheese-frosted Biscuits

At first glance, these biscuits may seem a bit extravagant as to ration points, but you won't need to serve any butter or margarine with them.

2 cups sifted all-purpose flour
3 teaspoons baking powder
½ teaspoon salt
¼ cup shortening
⅔ to ¾ cup milk
¼ pound cold-pack sharp cheddar cheese food
½ cup butter or margarine

Mix and sift dry ingredients; cut in shortening until well mixed. With a fork, quickly stir in enough milk to make a soft but not sticky dough. Knead dough 16 to 18 strokes on a lightly floured board. Roll dough about ⅓ inch thick and cut into rounds with a floured 1½-inch biscuit cutter. Place the rounds close together in a greased 7- by 11-inch baking pan.

In the top of a double boiler, slowly melt cheese food and butter over hot water, stirring often. Pour cheese mixture evenly over biscuits. Bake in a hot oven (450°) about 15 minutes, or until biscuits are well browned. Serve hot. These take kindly to reheating, in case there are any left over. Makes about 24 small biscuits.—*J. R. J., Los Angeles*

Per serving: 110 calories, 8.5 g carbohydrates, 2.1 g protein, 7.6 g total fat (3.7 g saturated), 15 mg cholesterol, 194 mg sodium.

erners like to cook. In 1983, we began acknowledging Kitchen Cabinet cooks by full name rather than by initials alone—and that June, Fred Henchell of Eureka, California, was the first male contributor to be identified by name. The very first man in Kitchen Cabinet,

though, was an invited guest in the late 1930s and early 1940s: George Mardikian, a celebrity chef and legendary San Francisco and Fresno restaurateur, owner of Omar Khayyam's.

Ethnic flavors and ingredients often appear in Kitchen Cabinet on their way into mainstream Western cooking. Examples include tofu, cilantro, fresh chilies, soy sauce, and coconut milk. Cooking tools, too, have made debuts in our pages. Blenders, food processors, pasta machines, microwave ovens—readers bought them, experimented, and shared the results in Kitchen Cabinet.

Perhaps the best way to appreciate the changes that Kitchen Cabinet illustrates is to glance through the recipes and art from past decades. In the 1930s, the feature depicted an insular existence, with women pictured as nurturing homebodies socializing over dainty luncheons, playing bridge, and cooking the pièce de résistance for dinner.

The 1940s brought war—and advice for "doing without." Kitchen Cabinet offered tips for saving everything from bacon fat to string, for getting by without a maid, for cooking creatively within the limits imposed by rationing.

The 1950s were golden years. With wartime austerities at an end, our kitchens were white and shiny and full of gadgets. Television invaded and began to compete for the family's attention. We reveled in the convenience of frozen and packaged foods. And as we sampled the ideas our "boys" had brought home, foreign influences began to appear in our cooking.

The thirst for new ideas increased in the late 1950s and early '60s. Air travel made exploring abroad easier than ever, so we saw the world—then re-created our adventures back home with authentic dinners that had us combing ethnic markets.

The 1960s brought rebellion against prevailing social values and an emphasis on "natural" foods and meatless diets. Both represented a commitment to purer bodies and freer spirits.

By the early 1970s, Western cooking had begun to combine the changes of the past two decades, developing a style that

1956
FEBRUARY
Water Chestnut Appetizers

Salty, smoky, and sweet, these bacon-wrapped bites are longtime favorites. They taste best when made ahead, then reheated.

- ¼ cup soy sauce
- 16 canned whole water chestnuts (from 1 can, 8 oz.), drained
- 4 slices bacon
- ¼ cup sugar

Pour soy sauce into a small bowl; add water chestnuts and let stand for 30 minutes. Cut each slice of bacon in half crosswise, then cut each piece in half again lengthwise.

Drain water chestnuts briefly. Roll each one in sugar, then wrap in a piece of bacon and secure with a wooden pick. Arrange bacon-wrapped chestnuts on a wire rack in a shallow baking pan lined with foil. Bake in a 400° oven until bacon is browned and crisp (20 to 25 minutes). Drain on paper towels. Serve hot. If made ahead, let cool; then cover and refrigerate for up to 8 hours To reheat, arrange in a shallow baking pan and heat in a 350° oven for about 5 minutes. Makes 16 appetizers.—*E. S. E., Palo Alto, CA*

Per serving: 26 calories, 4 g carbohydrates, 1 g protein, 1 g total fat (0 g saturated), 1 mg cholesterol, 91 mg sodium.

1960
JANUARY
Milk Chocolate Pie

One rainy day, this recipe's contributor devised a pie from the memory of one she'd tasted 10 years before. We're glad!

- 1 bar (about 10 oz.) milk chocolate, at room temperature
- 2¼ cups milk
- 2 tablespoons *each* cornstarch and flour
- 2 egg yolks, well beaten
- 1 teaspoon vanilla
- 1 tablespoon butter
- Baked 9-inch pie shell
- Sweetened whipped cream

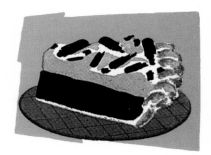

Using a vegetable peeler, pare down the long side of the milk chocolate bar to make a few long curls to use for garnish; set these aside. Scald 2 cups of the milk in the top of a double boiler over gently boiling water. Chop the remaining chocolate; stir it into the scalded milk until melted.

Blend the remaining ¼ cup milk with the cornstarch and flour until smooth. Gradually add flour mixture to chocolate mixture; stir until thickened. Add some of the hot mixture to the egg yolks, then slowly blend this back into the hot mixture. Cook, stirring, until thickened; remove from heat, stir in vanilla and butter, and let cool slightly. Spread in pie shell; chill. Top with whipped cream and chocolate curls.—*G. H., Berkeley, CA*

Per serving, 9 pieces: 343 calories, 34 g carbohydrates, 6.3 g protein, 21 g total fat (9.9 g saturated), 179 mg cholesterol, 66 mg sodium.

1970
J U L Y

Barbecued Salmon Fillets

You can use this method to barbecue one large salmon fillet or two smaller ones. If you like, substitute orange juice for the wine in the basting sauce and increase the lemon juice to 5 tablespoons.

1 or 2 large salmon fillets (3 to 4 lb. total)

¼ cup butter or margarine, melted; or ¼ cup salad oil

½ cup rosé or dry white wine

¼ cup *each* lemon juice and soy sauce

Parsley sprigs and lemon wedges

Rinse salmon and pat dry. Cut heavy-duty foil to the same size as salmon; place fish on foil, skin side down.

In a small bowl, stir together butter, wine, lemon juice, and soy sauce. In a barbecue with a lid, place fish, foil side down, on a grill 4 to 6 inches above a solid bed of low coals. Brush fish generously with butter mixture. Cover barbecue and open vents. Cook, basting with butter mixture about every 5 minutes, until fish is just opaque but still moist in thickest part; cut to test (15 to 20 minutes).

To serve, slide fish, still on foil, onto a board. Garnish with parsley sprigs and lemon wedges, if desired. Slice fish down to skin and lift each serving away from skin. Reheat butter mixture and offer to spoon over fish. Makes 8 to 10 servings.—*J. B., Lake Oswego, OR*

Per serving: 296 calories, 1 g carbohydrates, 35 g protein, 15 g total fat (4 g saturated), 108 mg cholesterol, 466 mg sodium.

1985
M A Y

Jicama-Pea Salad

Just four ingredients—jicama, green peas, seasoned vinegar, and mint—go into this refreshing salad.

1½ cups peeled, diced jicama

¾ cup seasoned rice vinegar (or ¾ cup unseasoned rice vinegar plus 2 tablespoons sugar)

About 1½ pounds unshelled peas; or 1 package (about 10 oz.) frozen tiny peas, thawed

¼ cup finely chopped fresh mint

8 to 16 large butter lettuce leaves, rinsed and crisped

Mint sprigs

In a bowl, combine jicama and vinegar; let stand for at least 15 minutes or up to 5 hours.

If using fresh peas, shell them; you need 2 cups. In a 2- to 3-quart pan, cook shelled peas in about 1 inch boiling water, uncovered, stirring occasionally, just until peas are bright green and heated through (2 to 3 minutes). Drain, immerse in cold water until cool, and drain again. (Don't cook frozen peas.)

Mix peas and chopped mint into jicama mixture. To serve, use a slotted spoon to ladle salad equally onto 8 lettuce-lined plates. Garnish with mint sprigs. Spoon any extra dressing over salads, if desired. Makes 8 servings.—*Gloria Thomasson, Tucson*

Per serving: 54 calories, 11 g carbohydrates, 2 g protein, 0.2 g total fat (0 g saturated), 0 mg cholesterol, 448 mg sodium.

emphasized freshness and experimentation. Supermarkets were bursting with choices. In Kitchen Cabinet, recipes had names from farther-flung places. Mexican ingredients were treated like everyday foods, and readers had come to enjoy tofu.

As the years went on, Westerners rejoiced in local, seasonal ingredients. Restaurants changed. French dominance slipped; the upstart California cuisine came into its own.

In the 1980s, the focus on fitness extended to food as well as exercise, stressing the importance of a well-balanced diet. At *Sunset*, we began offering nutritional information and revising cooking methods. Simpler, fresher ways to develop flavor became basic techniques. By the end of the decade, every recipe in *Sunset* included a nutritional breakdown.

This decade, the art of balance reigns, and Kitchen Cabinet marches on. Now it's my daughter and her friends who tell me how much confidence they gain from the success these dishes bring.

This book collection has all the old favorites adjusted for today's equipment and ingredients and tested for reliability. When we could trim fat, sugar, or salt to improve or update a dish, we've done so. All told, the book contains nearly 600 recipes—you'll even find the Milk Chocolate Pie I made when my in-laws first came to dinner.

There have been three other Kitchen Cabinet books—1931, 1938, and 1944. The 1944 collection notes that Kitchen Cabinet, then just 15 years old, had already received over 35,000 submissions. I blink when I think how many thousands more have been reviewed these past 50 years. ■

Old recipes and new

Kitchen Cabinet (224 pages, $29.95 hardback or $17.95 softcover—in major bookstores or call 800/759-0190 to order) was assembled by Sunset Books Senior Editor Cornelia Fogle with Cynthia Scheer. All recipes published prior to 1970 have been retested. And all recipes in the book have current nutritional data, except for those in the Kitchen Cabinet samplers that end each chapter. In this excerpt, we include two sampler recipes, Cheese-frosted Biscuits and Milk Chocolate Pie, and have added nutritional breakdowns.

Basic Baked Quesadillas

Cooking time: About 5 minutes

Prep time: About 15 minutes for all but the spinach filling, which takes about 10 minutes longer

Makes: 4 servings

4 flour tortillas (about 10 in. wide)
Filling (choices follow)
Salsa and salt

1. Lightly brush tortillas with water. Arrange ¼ of the filling ingredients on each tortilla, covering ½ of it. Fold tortilla over to cover filling. Place quesadillas slightly apart in 2 pans, each 12 by 15 inches.

2. Bake in a 500° oven until tortillas are crisp and golden, and filling is hot, about 5 minutes. Transfer to plates. Offer salsa and salt to add to taste.

Brie, ham, and papaya filling. Use ½ pound thinly sliced **cooked ham,** ¼ pound sliced **brie cheese,** and 1 firm-ripe **papaya** (1 lb.), seeded, peeled, and sliced.

Per quesadilla: 404 cal., 38% (153 cal.) from fat; 24 g protein; 17 g fat (2.4 g sat.); 38 g carbo.; 1,295 mg sodium; 62 mg chol.

Lamb and mango filling. Use ¾ pound thinly sliced barbecued **lamb** or beef; ⅓ pound sliced **teleme cheese;** 1 firm-ripe **mango** (1¼ lb.), peeled, pitted, and thinly sliced; and 2 tablespoons minced **fresh cilantro.**

Per quesadilla: 613 cal., 47% (288 cal.) from fat); 33 g protein; 32 g fat (9 g sat.); 49 g carbo.; 529 mg sodium; 92 mg chol.

Spinach and bacon filling. In a 10- to 12-inch frying pan, combine 1 pound stemmed and thinly sliced **shiitake mushrooms** (or regular mushrooms) with 4 slices chopped **bacon** and 3 cloves minced **garlic.** Stir often over medium-high heat until mushrooms and bacon are browned, about 15 minutes. If making ahead, cover and chill up to 1 day; reheat to use.

Divide mixture among tortillas, then sprinkle equally with 1 cup (4 oz.) shredded **jack cheese.** Top equally with ⅓ pound rinsed and drained **spinach leaves.**

Per quesadilla: 451 cal., 52% (234 cal.) from fat; 17 g protein; 26 g fat (11 g sat.); 38 g carbo.; 605 mg sodium; 45 mg chol.

Smoked salmon and chèvre filling. Spread 5 ounces unripened **chèvre** (goat) **cheese** onto tortillas; top with ¼ pound thinly sliced **smoked salmon;** ¼ cup minced **green onions;** and 1½ tablespoons minced **fresh dill.**

Per quesadilla: 310 cal., 38% (117 cal.) from fat; 17 g protein; 13 g fat (6 g sat.); 32 g carbo.; 617 mg sodium; 23 mg chol. ■

By Christine Weber Hale

KEVIN CANDLAND

FLOUR TORTILLA *wrapper gets crusty, cheese gets soft, and lamb and mango filling heats to become dinner quesadilla.*

In 20 minutes or less, make quesadillas for company

Four very contemporary main dishes filled with surprise ingredients

Toasty tortillas, oozing with melted cheese and savory bits, are the essence of a quesadilla. It's one of the West's most popular foods—as a snack, appetizer, or even as a main course. Because the quesadilla structure is so simple and the basic recipe is so easy, the temptation is to experiment.

For low-pressure weeknight entertaining, these big baked quesadillas are a quick solution. On the surface the fillings seem typical—meat or fish, cheese, and fruit or vegetables—but the choices— ham, brie, papaya, and other unexpected ingredients—push convention aside in a tasteful way. Once ingredients are gathered, the quesadillas can be filled, baked, and ready to serve in minutes. With a leafy green salad and a cool beverage, the meal is complete.

PAUL HAMMOND

Trim toppings for salads

Did you know there are about 9 grams of fat in 2 teaspoons of oil, or in a tablespoon of vinaigrette? Translate that to a big salad. Dress it with even a meager tablespoon of classic vinaigrette, and there goes a seventh of your day's recommended fat intake.

(Government guidelines suggest that you consume 30 percent or less of your total calories in the form of fat. If you take in 2,000 calories per day, that allows you about 65 grams of fat.)

Oil is a traditional ingredient in salad dressings because it coats greens nicely and balances the sharpness of vinegar. You can buy commercial no-oil dressings, but for me, too many are strangely flavored and lacking in freshness. The challenge in low-fat cooking is to use fresh ingredients that mimic oil's attributes but have no fat.

Here are two options.

For a nonfat vinaigrette, delicious with mixed greens, I was inspired by the flavors of an Italian carrot salad. This dressing has only 8 calories per tablespoon. In a saucepan, stir 1 cup **fresh carrot juice** and 2 teaspoons **cornstarch** over high heat until bubbling; let cool. Add 2 tablespoons **red wine vinegar,** 1 teaspoon minced bottled **green peppercorns,** ½ teaspoon minced **fresh tarragon,** and ¼ teaspoon **salt.** Use, or chill airtight up to 1 week.

Puréed mangoes have a clingy texture and fantastic flavor, especially with lime juice and vinegar to balance their sweetness. This mango dressing is refreshing on a shrimp salad, and since it has no fat, you can use ½ cup per entrée serving.

No-fat Mango Dressing

Prep time: About 25 minutes

Notes: You'll need 1½ pounds very ripe fruit. Underripe mangoes can occasionally be so high in pectin that the dressing will gel (if this happens, thin with water).

Makes: about 2⅓ cups

In a blender, whirl until very smooth: 1¾ cups ripe **mango** chunks, ⅓ cup fresh **lime juice,** ¼ cup fresh **orange juice,** ¼ cup **cider vinegar,** 1 tablespoon minced **fresh ginger,** 1½ teaspoons grated **orange peel,** and ¼ teaspoon **salt.** Use, or chill airtight up to 1 week.

Per tablespoon: 7 cal., 0% (0 cal.) from fat; 0 g protein; 0 g fat (0 g sat.); 1.8 g carbo.; 15 mg sodium; 0 mg chol.

Spinach-Shrimp Salad

Cooking time: About 15 minutes
Prep time: About 30 minutes

Notes: Complete the meal with good bread and Sauvignon blanc or Gewürztraminer.

Makes: 4 entrée servings

- ½ pound Belgian endive
- 3 quarts lightly packed spinach leaves (stems removed), torn into pieces if large
- 2 cups ½-inch cubes firm-textured sourdough bread
- 1 pound cooked shelled tiny shrimp
- 2 cups No-fat Mango Dressing (at left)
- Salt and pepper

1. Separate endive leaves. Rinse endive and spinach, drain, wrap in towels, and chill to crisp while preparing rest of salad.

2. Place bread cubes in an 8- or 9-inch baking pan. Bake in a 400° oven until golden and very firm, 12 to 14 minutes. Let cool.

3. Arrange spinach, endive, shrimp, and croutons on plates or in a large salad bowl. Add dressing, and salt and pepper to taste.

Per serving: 280 cal., 9% (25 cal.) from fat; 33 g protein; 2.8 g fat (0.6 g sat.); 35 g carbo.; 675 mg sodium; 221 mg chol.

WE'D LIKE TO HEAR FROM YOU!

Do you have tips or recipes for low-fat cooking? Write to Everyday Low-fat Cooking, Sunset Magazine, 80 Willow Rd., Menlo Park, CA 94025, or send e-mail (including your full name and street address) to lowfat@sunsetpub.com.

Soup is an adventure for mushrooms

Pineapple permeates waffles, and smoke meets chicken at the grill

Commercial mushroom soups tend to be bland and rather anonymous. The mushrooms are reduced to a few morsels, and the ambient liquid owes more to white sauce than to cream. These tinned mixtures are fine for making tuna-and-noodle casserole, but for a robust mushroom flavor pleasantly complicated by aromatic herbs and vegetables, try Norine Hanson's Mushroom Vegetable Soup.

Contrary to the Mock Turtle's song in *Alice's Adventures in Wonderland,* soup is rarely beautiful. Still, if handsome is as handsome does, this one is a beauty, and except for the optional cheese, it is totally vegetarian.

Mushroom Vegetable Soup

Cooking time: About 55 minutes
Prep time: About 25 minutes
Notes: The soup reheats well. Cool, cover, and chill up to 2 days.
Makes: 3½ to 4 quarts, 8 to 10 servings

- 1 pound mushrooms, rinsed and sliced
- 2 onions (1 lb. total), chopped
- 1 tablespoon salad oil
- 2 pounds thin-skinned potatoes, peeled and cubed
- 2 carrots (about ½ lb. total), sliced
- 1½ cups sliced celery
- 3 dried bay leaves
- 2 tablespoons chopped parsley
- 1 tablespoon dried oregano
- 1 teaspoon dried basil
- 1 can (6 oz.) tomato paste
- ½ cup dry red wine
- ½ cup reduced-sodium soy sauce
- Salt and pepper
- Grated parmesan cheese (optional)

1. In a 5- to 6-quart pan, combine mushrooms, onions, and oil. Stir often over medium-high heat until mushroom liquid evaporates and onions are slightly browned, about 15 minutes.

2. Add potatoes, carrots, and celery. Stir often until vegetables are lightly browned, about 10 minutes. Add 7 cups water, bay leaves, parsley, oregano, basil, tomato paste, wine, and soy sauce.

3. Bring soup to a boil, cover, reduce heat, and simmer until vegetables are tender when pierced and flavors have blended, about 30 minutes. Ladle into bowls and add salt, pepper, and cheese to taste.

Per serving: 145 cal., 13% (19 cal.) from fat; 4.9 g protein; 2.1 g fat (0.2 g sat.); 29 g carbo.; 648 mg sodium; 0 mg chol.

Norine Hanson
Las Vegas

As a verb, *waffle* carries a negative connotation—indecision, or fence straddling—but as a noun it has only the sweetest associations. Usually served with butter and syrup, the waffle (especially the thick Belgian kind) is increasingly offered with fruit and whipped cream. One associate recalls waffles being used as an underlay for rich creamed chicken back in Pennsylvania Dutch territory.

Alfred Fritz of Arroyo Grande, California, reveres the waffle as one of the great breakfast foods, especially when enhanced with fruit or nuts. His crowning achievement is Pineapple–Pine Nut Waffles, a true champion of breakfasts.

Pineapple–Pine Nut Waffles

Cooking time: 5 minutes, plus about 10 minutes per waffle
Prep time: 10 to 15 minutes
Notes: Toast nuts and measure dry ingredients the night before to speed breakfast preparation.
Makes: 3 waffles, each 8 inches square

1/4 cup pine nuts

1/2 cup all-purpose flour

1/2 cup whole-wheat flour

1/2 cup toasted wheat germ

1/4 cup unprocessed bran

1/4 teaspoon salt

1 1/2 teaspoons baking powder

1/4 teaspoon baking soda

1 large egg, separated

About 2 tablespoons salad oil

1 3/4 cups buttermilk

1 can (8 oz.) crushed pineapple, drained

Butter or margarine

Maple syrup or brown sugar

1. Stir nuts in a 6- to 8-inch frying pan over medium heat until toasted, 5 to 6 minutes.

2. Pour nuts into a bowl and add all-purpose flour, whole-wheat flour, wheat germ, bran, salt, baking powder, and baking soda; stir to mix.

3. In another bowl, beat egg yolk to blend with 2 tablespoons oil, then stir in buttermilk. Pour mixture into dry ingredients, add pineapple, and stir until the stiff batter is evenly moistened.

4. In another bowl, whip egg white on high speed just until it holds short, distinct, but moist peaks. Stir into waffle batter.

5. Heat an electric waffle iron to medium-high (or waffle setting), or place a waffle iron over medium-high heat. When iron is hot, brush grids lightly with oil. Spoon batter onto grids and bake until well browned and crisp, about 10 minutes. Repeat to cook remaining waffles. Serve hot with butter and maple syrup added to taste.

Per waffle: 539 cal., 42% (225 cal.) from fat; 22 g protein; 25 g fat (6.3 g sat.); 66 g carbo.; 741 mg sodium; 87 mg chol.

Arroyo Grande, California

CHICKEN LEGS GET A LEG UP IN flavor in Tom Capranica's Grill-smoked Citrus and Herb Chicken. First they luxuriate in a bath of citrus juices and wine scented by bay, garlic, ginger, and rosemary. Then they are grilled over coals with mesquite chips. An occasional brushing with the marinade helps intensify the flavor.

Grill-smoked Citrus and Herb Chicken

Cooking time: 30 to 35 minutes

Prep time: About 15 minutes, plus 2 hours to marinate chicken

Notes: To reduce fat and likelihood of grill flare-ups, discard chicken skin. While chicken marinates, soak wood chips and heat barbecue. Marinate chicken up to 1 day ahead.

Makes: 4 servings

4 whole chicken legs (drumsticks and thighs attached, 6 to 8 oz. each)

1 lemon

1 lime

1 orange (5 to 6 oz.)

1/4 cup dry white wine

3/4 teaspoon minced fresh ginger

3 cloves garlic, minced or pressed

1 fresh jalapeño chili, stemmed, seeded, and cut into thin slivers

1/2 teaspoon dried rosemary

2 dried bay leaves

1/4 teaspoon pepper

About 1 cup mesquite wood chips

Salt

1. Pull off and discard any lumps of fat on chicken. Rinse legs, pat dry, and put in a large, heavy plastic food bag.

2. Squeeze juices from lemon, lime, and orange and add to bag along with wine, ginger, garlic, jalapeño, rosemary, bay leaves, and pepper. Seal bag and turn over several times to mix ingredients and to coat chicken with marinade. Chill at least 2 hours. Turn bag over several times.

3. Mix chips with 2 cups water, and let stand at least 30 minutes.

4. Drain chips and distribute in a barbecue over a solid bed of medium-hot coals (you can hold your hand at grill level only 4 to 5 seconds).

5. Lift chicken from marinade, reserving marinade. Lay chicken on barbecue grill and cook, turning as needed to brown evenly, until meat at bone is no longer pink (cut to test), 30 to 35 minutes. Baste chicken frequently with marinade until the last 10 minutes of cooking. Add salt to taste.

Per serving: 216 cal., 46% (99 cal.) from fat; 22 g protein; 11 g fat (3.1 g sat.); 5.3 g carbo.; 75 mg sodium; 77 mg chol.

Phoenix

EVERY NOW AND THEN A TOQUE goes out to a chef who has a really new concept. Chuck Allen is such a chef, and Spinach Balls with Mustard Sauce is his concept. To a world grown weary of spinach dips, he offers relief in the form of crisp, deeply flavored baked spinach balls to deck the appetizer tray. They give the same sort of satisfaction that deep-fried appetizers give, without the accompanying guilt.

Spinach Balls with Mustard Sauce

Cooking time: About 20 minutes

Prep time: 20 to 25 minutes, plus thawing time for spinach

Notes: First prepare Mustard Sauce; cover and chill until serving time. Stir well before using.

Makes: 60 appetizers; allow 4 or 5 per serving

2 packages (10 oz. each) frozen chopped spinach, thawed and squeezed dry

2 cups herb-seasoned stuffing mix, finely crushed

1 cup (about 5 oz.) freshly grated parmesan cheese

2 tablespoons melted butter or margarine

5 green onions, ends trimmed and finely chopped, including tops

3 large eggs

1 teaspoon poultry seasoning mix

1/4 teaspoon cayenne

Mustard sauce (recipe follows)

1. In a large bowl, combine spinach, stuffing mix, cheese, butter, onions, eggs, poultry seasoning, and cayenne; mix well. If making ahead, cover and chill up to 1 day.

2. Shape spinach mixture into compact 1-inch balls. Arrange balls slightly apart on 2 ungreased 12- by 15-inch baking sheets. Bake in a 350° oven until golden brown, about 20 minutes.

3. Spear balls with toothpicks and dip into mustard sauce.

Per serving: 399 cal. (36 percent from fat); 24 g protein; 16 g fat (8.5 g sat.); 33 g carbo.; 1,638 mg sodium; 159 mg chol.

Mustard sauce. Stir together 1/2 cup Dijon mustard, 1 cup nonfat sour cream, 1 tablespoon dry white wine, and 3/4 teaspoon sugar.

Dana Point, California
By Joan Griffiths, Richard Dunmire

FOOD Guide

BY JERRY ANNE DI VECCHIO

A TASTE OF THE WEST: A simple, splendid baked soup

Have you ever noticed? When people talk about foods they loved most as children, gentle smiles and peaceful, faraway looks appear on their faces. Then they describe a dish that usually sounds pretty plain. They hasten to add that it may not seem like much, but oh my, how good it tasted. Then they sigh. That's just what Gianni Audieri, chef at San Francisco's Fior d'Italia Restaurant, did when we visited.

Something triggered the memory of a bread soup his mother used to make when he was a boy. In my mind, he created the image of a soggy cheese sandwich made even more bizarre by adding cabbage. But the caressing tone of his voice and his professional stature made it clear that this soup was more than the sum of its ingredients. I tried it out of curiosity, and thank heavens I'm curious. The soup is truly a wonder and so easy it's embarrassing. It does look humble, but it smells grand. The bread gets creamy, almost as silky as cooked bone marrow. The cabbage wilts until sweet and subtle; the cheese just flows. After my tasting panel had its enthusiastic fill, I put the soup to the real test. I set it out for staff stragglers who regularly check to see if there's any snacking to be had in *Sunset*'s kitchen. Within minutes the big soup pot was scraped bare.

Gianni's Bread and Cabbage Soup

Cooking time: 1½ hours

Prep time: 15 to 20 minutes

Notes: To get a head start, fill pan with all ingredients except the broth, cover and chill up to 1 day, then pour in boiling broth and bake.

Makes: 10 servings

1 loaf French bread (1 lb.)

1 head savoy or green cabbage (2 to 2½ lb.)

The rusticity of Gianni's Bread and Cabbage Soup is as appealing as its simplicity.

NOEL BARNHURST

214

OCTOBER '95

- Bread, cheese, and cabbage—in a soup?

- Pork tenderloins with a tuna sauce

- Red lentils from Palouse in a fast salad

- Slick little stoves for lots of big jobs

- With wine, the old should come last

1 pound fontina cheese, thinly sliced

1 cup (4 oz.) grated parmesan cheese

4 to 5 ounces pancetta or bacon, chopped

2 quarts beef broth

1. Cut bread into 1/4-inch-thick slices. Core cabbage and thinly slice. In a 6- to 8-quart pan, layer 1/3 each bread, cabbage, fontina, and, finally, parmesan. Repeat, making 2 more layers. With your palms, press ingredients firmly to level.

2. In a 3- to 4-quart pan over medium-high heat, stir pancetta frequently until slightly crisp, about 5 minutes; discard fat. Scatter meat over cheese in soup pan. In pancetta pan, bring broth to boiling and pour over layered ingredients.

3. Cover soup pan tightly with a domed lid (or domed lid made of foil); mixture puffs up and cheese sticks if it touches lid.

4. Set soup pan in a rimmed pan to catch any overflow. Bake in a 400° oven until a crusty crown forms, about 1 1/2 hours. Dip down through ingredients and ladle soup into bowls.

Per serving: 409 cal., 46% (189 cal.) from fat; 27 g protein; 21 g fat (12 g sat.); 30 g carbo.; 980 mg sodium; 64 mg chol.

TIMELY NOTE

Even faster fast-cooking lentils

Lentils and beans get lumped together as foods that take several hours to cook. That's wrong. The domestic everyday brown lentils are creamy smooth in 25 to 30 minutes, and falling apart in the hour it takes for a potato to bake and for most beans to be only half-done.

If you use hulled lentils, they can be ready to eat in about 5 minutes. Hulling is a chore the processor does for you, and there are plenty of them in the Northwest's Palouse area, which overlaps Washington and Idaho and where 150,000 to 200,000 acres are devoted to growing lentils, supplying 90 to 95 percent of the U.S. crop.

You can tell that Red Chief lentils (grown in the Palouse) are decorticated (hulled) because they are a bright orange coral (brown lentils are golden underneath). Red Chief is a relatively new variety, and I first found it in natural-food and specialty stores. Now it's in many independent markets in the West. You often see Red Chief lentils in soup mixes with beans and split peas.

Another orange lentil, tinier and brighter, is imported and sold in Middle Eastern food markets and specialty stores. You have to sort the imported lentils with care to pick out tooth-cracking bits of rock. They also cook so fast that they start to fall apart by the time the liquid is boiling—not a problem in soups.

Red Chiefs, however, will hold their shape as they cook tender, so I especially like them for salads. If you can't find them, order from Meacham Mills, Box 144, Clarkston, WA 99403; call (509)758-0412 for details.

Red Chief Lentil Salad

Cooking time: About 5 minutes

Prep time: About 15 minutes

Notes: You can serve the salad hot or cold, and if you want to make it ahead, cover and chill up to 2 days.

Makes: About 4 cups, 4 to 6 servings

2 cups Red Chief lentils

4 cups chicken broth

1/2 teaspoon dried rosemary leaves

1/2 cup minced parsley

1/4 cup sherry vinegar

1/4 cup minced shallots

1 tablespoon Dijon mustard

2 teaspoons minced fresh ginger

1/2 teaspoon grated lemon peel (yellow part only)

1/2 teaspoon hot chili flakes

Salt

1. Sort debris from lentils. Rinse and drain lentils.

2. In a 3- to 4-quart pan over high heat, bring broth and rosemary to boiling. Add lentils and cook, uncovered, just until they turn a lighter color and are tender enough to bite but not soft, about 5 minutes. Drain lentils, saving broth.

3. Mix parsley, vinegar, shallots, mustard, ginger, lemon peel, chili flakes, and 1/2 cup of the reserved broth. If serving lentils warm, add dressing and mix.

If presenting lentils cool, add dressing just before serving the salad. If lentils stand, they soak up the dressing; you can use some of the reserved broth to moisten them. Reserve the rest of the broth for other dishes. Season salad with salt to taste.

Per serving: 244 cal., 9% (21 cal.) from fat; 20 g protein; 2.3 g fat (0.6 g sat.); 40 g carbo.; 146 mg sodium; 0 mg chol.

Pork tenderloins in a tuna sauce look rich but are low in fat.

cold poached veal with tuna sauce. I add a big handful of parsley to make the sauce green and fresher tasting, too.

Pork Tenderloins with Tuna Sauce

Steeping time: 25 to 30 minutes
Prep time: About 25 minutes
Notes: If making ahead, cover and chill up to 1 day.
Makes: 6 servings

- 1 onion (½ lb.), sliced
- 1 lemon, sliced
- 2 pork tenderloins, each about ¾ pound, fat trimmed
- 1 small can (3 oz.) drained water-packed tuna
- ½ cup chopped green onions (including tops)
- ¼ cup packed chopped parsley
- 2 drained canned anchovy fillets
- ½ teaspoon dried tarragon leaves
- 2 teaspoons Dijon mustard
- 2 tablespoons lemon juice
- 6 tablespoons unflavored nonfat yogurt or sour cream
- 2 teaspoons drained prepared capers

1. In a 6- to 8-quart pan, combine 5 quarts water, sliced onion, and sliced lemon. Bring to a full rolling boil.

2. Drop pork into boiling water, cover tightly, and remove from heat at once. Let stand, undisturbed, for 20 minutes. Lift out pork and check center temperature; 150° to 155° is ideal. If pork is below 150°, return to pan, cover and let stand 10 minutes, and check again. (It's okay if temperature reaches 160°.) If the water gets cooler than 160°, take out pork, return water to boiling, remove from heat, and put pork back into pan. Even when the pork is done, the juices are a clear red and the meat looks faintly pink in center.

3. Use pork hot, cool, or chilled; to chill fast, immerse in ice water for 10 minutes.

4. As pork steeps, make sauce. Put tuna, green onions, parsley, anchovies, tarragon, mustard, lemon juice, and 2 tablespoons of the yogurt in a blender or food processor. Whirl until smoothly puréed; scrape container sides often. Stir in remaining yogurt. Serve, or cover and chill if making ahead.

5. Slice pork, garnish with capers, and accompany with the tuna sauce.

Per serving: 175 cal., 21% (37 cal.) from fat; 29 g protein; 4.1 g fat (1.4 g sat.); 3.6 g carbo.; 230 mg sodium; 80 mg chol.

PETER CHRISTIANSEN

BACK TO BASICS

A Chinese way to poach

The most succulent shrimp I have ever tasted were steeped, Chinese-style.

You dump shrimp into boiling water, cover the pan, and immediately remove it from the heat. As the water temperature slowly drops, gentle heat penetrates the food, poaching it with less stress than boiling, which toughens shrimp. It's the volume of water that controls the rate of cooking. Steeping is ideal for other relatively small pieces of meat or fish that are easily overcooked and, as a result, become dry: lean pork tenderloins and chicken breasts, in particular.

How do you know when these foods are done? You take out a piece and check. If it's not cooked, return it to the water for more steeping. If you misjudge, you can take the food out, return the water to boiling, then put the food back in the water to cook some more. Steeped foods are good hot or cold.

Poached pork, like chicken or veal, is pale, so a bright sauce is a good partner. The inspiration for this one comes from the Italian classic *vitello tonnato*,

GREAT TOOL
Tabletop stoves

Portable stoves took a big leap forward when the one-burner gas unit appeared.

I bought one of the early models and have used it for years to keep a soup simmering on the buffet, to sauté a quick main dish in front of guests—such as shrimp with sugar snap peas finished with a flame of brandy—or for cooking at picnics and tailgates.

Recently, on a cooking demonstration tour, I tried one of the newest models and was impressed with the improvements. One click and the automatic starter produced a leaping blue flame that I could adjust from very low to really hot. I had water boiling as fast as in my own kitchen. Widely available gas cassettes give several hours of intense cooking.

Current models from several companies are sleeker, available in more colors, and cheaper than the one I have. On checking with a number of stores, I found that the price range for a stove is $35 to $40; gas cassettes cost $2 to $3 each.

Usually you can find these stoves in housewares in department stores, but also check restaurant supply stores and even drugstores.

PETER CHRISTIANSEN

The new tabletop stoves are easy to use and much more handsome than their predecessors.

BOB THOMPSON ON WINE: Wine rules that make sense

Not all of the rules about drinking wine are the pipe dreams of gouty colonels whiling away their retirements in London clubrooms. Some are outright practical.

A particularly useful one is young wine before old, light wine before full-bodied. A workmate on the magazine provided one proof not long ago when he and his wife gave a dinner for friends.

The intended wine of the evening was one of California's richer, riper Zinfandels with some time in the bottle behind it. It was so tasty that the diners finished it long before they ran out of food. The ad-lib successor was a new Merlot from Washington State. "Not the way to go," the chap reported, rue-

fully. "Talk about sharp!"

In that comment was the validation of the rule. Young wines show both tartness and astringency more than older ones do. Lighter-bodied wines are more apt to be lean and tart than full ones in any case. He had grabbed the wrong end of the stick on both counts. Hardly a catastrophe, but it ended a companionable dinner on a note of disappointment, and minimized the value of his $15 investment in an excellent Merlot.

Had he started out with the young wine, its crackling vitality would not have seemed out of place, assuming the meal could have used a refreshing wine. Then the older, fuller-bodied Zinfandel would have seemed even

richer and silkier than it did alone, a cosseting luxury of an ending.

Serving dry wines before sweeter ones works on the same basic idea.

Oddly, in judging wines you leave the dry-before-sweet rule alone, but turn the young-before-old one upside down. Judges gather more accurate impressions if they start with older wines that have traded strength for the wiles of experience, then finish with brash young ones. The subtler wines take closer attention, so should be sorted out while the taster is at his or her freshest. Further, mature wines are less wearing on the palate than sharp-edged youngsters, so a taster is not as wearied physically on coming to the young wines. ∎

A

S MEXICAN FOODS GROW EVER more popular in the West, the pressure is on for authentic ingredients. One of the most important is *queso*—cheese, domestically made—which is moving beyond Latin enclaves into mainstream supermarkets. ✢ At least a dozen kinds of Mexican quesos (see chart on pages 220-221) are now being produced in the West. About half of them are widely distributed; the rest you have to search out. They have Spanish names, some more than one, and are made from cow's milk. Most are white or cream color with a mild, fresh taste. A few are sharp and intensely flavored. All are enjoyable just for eating, but it's how they behave in cooking that divides them into three categories—those fresh mild cheeses that hold their shape even when heated, those that melt, and the aged ones that make pungent seasoners. ✢ Fresh and melting-type cheeses spoil quickly, so use them before they pass the pull date stamped on the packages. Once packages are opened (or if the cheese is cut from a large wheel at the market), eat fresh cheeses within a few days, melting ones within a week or so; keep unused portions airtight in the refrigerator. A sour smell and taste, liquid in the package, and yellow to orange discoloration or mold are all signs of spoilage. If a little surface mold develops, trim it off and use the remaining cheese. But if the mold is pervasive, discard the whole piece. ✢ The saltier, pungent, aged cheeses contain less moisture and keep longer in the refrigerator. Discoloration and a sour smell also indicate spoilage. ✢ The recipes on the following pages make the most of the special qualities of Mexican cheeses.

A Cook's Guide to Mexican

MELLOW OR SHARP, smooth or crumbly, the numerous Mexican cheese options can be overwhelming. Counterclockwise from center: two coiled Oaxaca cheeses, a basket-textured panela, the football-shaped cuajada, crumbled cotija, and a wedge of mild queso fresco.

cheeses

At least a dozen products are now sold in many mainstream markets. Here's what to look for and how to use them. By Linda Lau Anusasananan

Caesar Salad with Cotija Croutons

Cooking time: About 5 minutes
Prep time: About 10 minutes
Makes: 8 servings

- 1/2 cup olive oil
- 3 tablespoons lemon juice
- 1 1/2 tablespoons red wine vinegar
- 3/4 teaspoon anchovy paste
- 2 cloves garlic
- 1 teaspoon Dijon mustard
- 1 cup (about 4 oz.) 1/2-inch cubes cotija or enchilado cheese
- 4 quarts bite-size pieces romaine lettuce, rinsed and crisped
- 2 tablespoons crumbled cotija cheese
  Salt and pepper

1. In a blender, whirl oil, lemon juice, vinegar, anchovy paste, garlic, and mustard until smooth and slightly thickened.

2. In an 8- to 10-inch nonstick frying pan over medium heat, brown cheese cubes, about 4 minutes; turn as needed. Set cubes in a 275° oven to keep warm.

3. In a large bowl, combine dressing, lettuce, and crumbled cotija; mix to coat leaves. Add warm cheese cubes, and salt and pepper to taste.

Per serving: 195 cal., 82% (162 cal.) from fat; 5.9 g protein; 18 g fat (1.9 g sat.); 3.6 g carbo.; 315 mg sodium; 12 mg chol.

Vermicelli with Fresh Cheese

Cooking time: 30 minutes
Prep time: 10 minutes
Notes: In Mexico, a starchy food like this pasta, cooked in a generous amount of broth until the liquid is mostly absorbed, is called dry soup or *sopa seca.* Mexican cream is cultured much like sour cream; it's available where Mexican cheeses are sold.
Makes: 4 to 6 servings

- 1 tablespoon salad oil
- 7 ounces dried angel hair pasta or vermicelli fideo
- 1/3 cup chopped onion
- 1 clove garlic, minced
- 1 can (14 1/2 oz.) diced tomatoes
- 2 cups chicken broth
- 1/3 cup 1/2-inch cubes queso fresco
- 2 tablespoons Mexican cream or sour cream (optional)
  Chopped parsley
  Salt and pepper

1. Pour oil into a 10- to 12-inch frying pan over medium heat. Break pasta into short pieces, and drop into pan. Stir often until golden, about 10 minutes. Add onion and garlic, and stir often until onion is limp, about 2 minutes.

2. Add tomatoes and liquid to pan along with broth; stir and bring to a boil. Reduce heat to low, cover, and simmer until noodles are tender to bite and broth is partially absorbed, about 10 minutes. Drop in the queso fresco. Simmer, covered, until cheese is hot, about 5 minutes. Ladle into shallow bowls. Drizzle with cream, and sprinkle with chopped parsley. Add salt and pepper to taste.

Per serving: 189 cal., 25% (48 cal.) from fat; 7.2 g protein; 5.3 g fat (1.7 g sat.); 29 g carbo.; 197 mg sodium; 4.4 mg chol.

SHOPPING FOR QUESO

YOU'LL FIND THESE CHEESES, vacuum-packed in small portions in plastic bags, in most Latino markets and some supermarkets. Latino markets also have them in big wheels or blocks in the meat counter or deli case; you can ask for a taste to decide which to buy. Because the names for these cheeses are not standardized, different makers often call the same cheese by slightly or totally different names. And some makers will give a basic cheese a proprietary name. Many of those names are given in this chart.

CHEESE	DESCRIPTION	USE
Cuajada	Fresh cheese. Curds are finely ground and formed into football-shaped ovals. Mild, clean flavor. Tender, moist texture.	Softens but doesn't melt when heated. Cube, crumble, or slice to use as a topping or filling. Good with fruit and herbs.
Panela	Very fresh cheese. Made from clotted curds drained in a basket. Tastes like cottage cheese. Squeaky texture—similar to that of a fresh Italian buffalo mozzarella.	Softens but doesn't melt when heated. Cube, crumble, or slice. Especially good in sandwiches, salads, soups. Good with fruit. Slices can also be pan-browned in a nonstick frying pan over medium heat or grilled.
Queso blanco fresco (also called *queso para freir*—cheese for frying)	Fresh cheese. Curds are finely ground and pressed into blocks. Mild flavor, firm texture.	Softens and holds shape when heated. Can be pan-fried; slice cheese and cook in a nonstick frying pan over medium heat until golden.
Queso crema	Fresh cheese. Curds are finely ground, mixed with cream, and shaped into big blocks. Sold by the piece from block. Mild flavor; tender, creamy, smooth texture, sometimes soft enough to spread.	Softens but doesn't melt when heated. Cube or slice to use in salads and soups, or as a filling. Good with fruit and fruit pastes.
Queso fresco (also called ranchero, estilo casero, or, in 5-lb. blocks, adobera)	Fresh cheese. Drained, clotted curds are ground, kneaded, and pressed into round molds. Slightly salty, it tastes like farmer's cheese or ricotta. Soft, crumbly, slightly grainy.	Softens but doesn't melt when heated. Cube, crumble, or slice to use as a topping or filling in tacos, tostadas, chile rellenos, enchiladas, burritos, quesadillas, beans, salads, soups.

Chile Rellenos in Spiced Broth

Cooking time: About 50 minutes
Prep time: About 20 minutes
Notes: Fresh, and relatively mild, dark green poblano chilies are sometimes mislabeled as pasillas.
Makes: 6 servings

- 2 cans (14½ oz. each) tomatoes
- 1 onion (about ½ lb.), coarsely chopped
- 2 cloves garlic
- 2 cups chicken broth
- 2 dried bay leaves
- 1 cinnamon stick (about 3 in.)
- 4 sprigs (about 4 in.) fresh thyme or ¾ teaspoon dried thyme
- 6 fresh poblano chilies (about 1½ lb. total)
- 7 ounces queso fresco, crumbled
- ½ cup crumbled cotija cheese
- ½ cup corn kernels, fresh-cut or thawed frozen

- ¼ cup chopped cilantro
- Salt and pepper

1. In a blender or food processor, smoothly purée tomatoes with their juice, onion, and garlic. Pour into 5- to 6-quart pan. Add broth, bay leaves, cinnamon, and thyme. Bring to a boil, then simmer, uncovered, over low heat for about 15 minutes to blend flavors.

2. Meanwhile, place chilies in a 10- by 15-inch pan. Broil about 4 inches from heat, turning until well browned (some portions will char), 10 to 15 minutes. Let chilies stand until cool to touch, then gently pull off and discard skins. Cut a slit down 1 side of each chili and carefully pull out and discard seeds. Rinse chilies and pat dry.

3. Mix queso fresco, 2 tablespoons of the cotija, corn, and 3 tablespoons chopped cilantro.

4. Carefully fill each chili with the cheese mixture, using all. Lay chilies, slit side up, in hot tomato sauce. Cover and simmer over low heat until filled chilies are hot in the center, 15 to 20 minutes.

5. With a slotted spoon, transfer each stuffed chili to a shallow bowl. Spoon tomato sauce around chilies, and sprinkle with remaining crumbled cotija cheese and chopped cilantro. Add salt and pepper to taste.

Per serving: 226 cal., 44% (99 cal.) from fat; 12 g protein; 11 g fat (6 g sat.); 21 g carbo.; 621 mg sodium; 29 mg chol. ∎

Requeson	Fresh cheese. Ricotta-like cheese with soft, spreadable, grainy texture, fresh milky taste.	Use like ricotta. Spread on crackers with jam; use in enchiladas and lasagne.
Asadero (also called *quesadilla*, a proprietary name)	Drained curds are heated and stirred, then shaped into a long log; it's sold sliced. Often processed for easy melting, it has a buttery, slighty tangy taste. Some types are similar to provolone. Firm and smooth.	Melts readily. Wonderful for quesadillas, nachos, fondues. Can get stretchy like mozzarella.
Chihuahua (also called *queso Menomita* or *queso blanco*)	Drained, salted curds are heated and stirred, then formed into creamy smooth white rounds—small or large. Flavor is like that of a tangy jack or a mild cheddar cheese. Texture ranges from that of creamy münster to that of soft jack cheese.	Melts readily; use like jack or cheddar cheese. Shred or slice and use in quesadillas, on enchiladas, or anyplace a melting cheese works. Can get stringy like mozzarella when overheated.
Manchego	Curds are cooked and stirred, then formed into golden rounds. Has a medium cheddar taste, smooth texture.	Melts readily. Use in sandwiches, quesadillas, nachos, fondues.
Oaxaca	Cooked asadero cheese is stretched and rolled into balls. Acts like string cheese, pulling apart in strands. Buttery and smooth.	Melts readily. Use in quesadillas, nachos, fondues.
Cotija (also called *queso añejado*—aged cheese)	Curds are shaped in small rounds or big blocks. It's a crumbly, salty, pungent cheese. Depending on maker, cotija can be soft and similar to feta, or it can be firm, with more complex flavors, like parmesan.	Salty enough to season foods. Use like feta or parmesan cheese. Grate or crumble, and sprinkle over tacos, pizzas, enchiladas, salads, soups, beans, pasta.
Enchilado	Curds, pressed firmly into round or rectangular molds, are dried until cheese is quite firm. May be cured and aged (añejado) like cotija for a harder texture and stronger flavor. Surface is coated with a mild red chili paste or paprika.	Holds shape when heated. Añejado-style can be used as seasoning, much like a parmesan. Slice, cube, or crumble; grate hard aged types. Use on salads, beans, tacos, enchiladas, quesadillas, soups, pasta.

The new party food?

Sausages

*Who can resist when the options include smoked chicken
with apple, Burmese curry turkey, turkey chorizo, and salmon?
And they're leaner than ever*

THE EASIEST *entertaining begins
when you throw an assortment of
sausages and whole bell peppers on
the grill (left). Add red potato salad
and a selection of mustards, and
it's time to eat.*

WHILE SAVORING LEMON-ROASTED chicken in a Chinese restaurant, Skip Lott, owner of Montibella Sausage Company, was seized by a wonderfully obvious idea. Why not put these ingredients in sausage? And so he did, joining the ranks of sausage makers who have made a major leap beyond bratwurst as they help rewrite the script for easy entertaining.

The new sausages are bursting with flavors from every cuisine. They start with a leaner meat—chicken, turkey, buffalo, even fish—or meat that's well trimmed. The succulence of fat is replaced by ingredients that hold moisture such as potatoes or apples, as in Lott's best-selling lemon chicken with potato or Silva Sausage Co.'s chicken apple sausages.

Today's sausages offer something for every taste—mild to wild, even slimmed-down traditional styles. And few foods take so little skill or time to prepare. For a truly simple, enjoyable party, pull together a sausage sampler or invite guests to bring their sausage discoveries to share. Roll them onto the grill to brown, then serve them with the following make-ahead menu that gives a nod to Oktoberfest.

HOW DO HIGH- AND LOW-FAT SAUSAGES COMPARE?

At *Sunset,* our taste panel put 40 sausages to the test. Some were traditional, many were part of the new lean wave. Ingredients included beef, buffalo, chicken, duck, lamb, salmon, and turkey, and seasonings ranged from plain or smoked to Thai and Yucatán. Here's what we found:
• The top four favorites were Aidells's lemon chicken with tarragon, Denver Buffalo's bratwurst (with buffalo), Montibella's smoked lemon chicken with potato, and Saag's *rojo grande* turkey.
• The taste and texture of fresh low-fat sausages vary greatly. Some are tender and juicy, others dry and crumbly. Those containing vegetables, fruits, or other moisture-holding ingredients were juicier.
• Smoked low-fat sausages tended to be moist and firm.
• Using a lot of seasonings to enhance lean sausages, if done skillfully, can yield delicious results. Or it can overwhelm. Fat smooths out flavors, and when you cut back, balancing seasonings gets trickier.
• Casings are changing. Some can be tough, others are almost unnoticeable. Saag's and Montibella Sausage Company are experimenting with skinless sausages that form a skinlike surface as they cook—and are very tender.

Oktoberfest for 10 to 12

- **Grilled Sausages**   - **Grilled Red Bell Peppers**   - **Red Onion Slivers**
- **Sauerkraut**   - **Honey-Mustard Potato Salad**
- **Mustards: Dijon, Coarse-grain, Yellow, Herb-flavored**
- **Breads: Pumpernickel, Baguettes, Olive, Sourdough, Crusty Rolls**
- **Beer**   - **Grapes, Pears, and Gingersnaps**

- Sausages need gentle heat to keep them from splitting.
- Lean sausages are more inclined to get firm and dry if overcooked, cooked at high heat, or microwaved.
- Lower-fat sausage links tend to be smaller and weigh less than their old-fashioned counterparts.

- A 3½-ounce (about 100 g) sausage with only about 1 tablespoon (10 to 11 g) fat can taste as juicy as one that contains three times as much fat.
- A very lean 3½-ounce sausage may have as little as 1½ teaspoons (6 g) fat.

SAUSAGE SAMPLING, SAUSALITO-STYLE

At Munich's grandest beer bash, sausages and tall steins of beer are essentials. But at one Sausalito family's own Oktoberfest, lower-fat sausages are used in this easily managed menu. Their selection includes pork and turkey Italian, Yucatán chicken and duck, Burmese chicken curry, and *rojo grande* turkey. If your market lacks such variety, call upon sausage makers that ship (see page 224).

Offer a selection of mustards, breads, and beers. To reduce saltiness of the sauerkraut, rinse it and drain well.

Grilled Sausages

Cooking time: 8 to 25 minutes
Prep time: 5 to 10 minutes
Notes: Cook raw (fresh) sausages, then cover and chill up to 1 day before grilling.
Makes: 10 to 12 servings

10 to 12 raw or smoked (cooked) sausages (about 4 oz. each)

1. *To bake or simmer raw sausages.* Lay sausages slightly apart in a single layer in a 9- by 13-inch pan. Bake in a 350° oven, uncovered, until sausages feel firm (not squishy) when pressed, about 15 minutes. Or bring about 1 inch water to simmering in a 10- to 12-inch frying pan. Add sausages, cover, and keep water just under active simmer until sausages feel firm (not squishy) when pressed, 8 to 10 minutes. Drain.

2. *To barbecue cooked sausages,* lay sausages, whole or split lengthwise, on a grill over a solid bed of medium-hot coals or gas grill on medium-high heat (you can hold your hand at grill level 3 to 4 seconds). Close lid on gas grill. Cook, turning, until sausages are browned, 8 to 10 minutes.

Estimated per 100 g (about 3½ oz.) low-fat sausage: 120 cal., 45% (54 cal.) from fat; 14 g protein; 6 g fat (2 g sat.); 1 g carbo.; 870 mg sodium; 45 mg chol.

Estimated per 100 g (about 3½ oz.) moderate-fat sausage: 220 cal., 65% (144 cal.) from fat ; 15 g protein; 16 g fat (5 g sat.); 2 g carbo.; 600 mg sodium; 40 mg chol.

Grilled Red Peppers

Cooking time: About 15 minutes
Prep time: 10 minutes
Notes: Char the peppers on the grill as it heats for the sausages.
Makes: 10 to 12 servings

5 or 6 red bell peppers (½ lb. each)

Place peppers on a barbecue over a solid bed of hot coals or gas grill on high (you can hold your hand at grill level only 2 to 3 seconds). Close lid on gas grill. Cook, turning, until peppers are charred on all sides, about 15 minutes. Let peppers cool slightly, then peel, stem, seed, and cut into quarters lengthwise. Place in serving dish.

Per serving: 21 cal., 4% (1 cal.) from fat; 0.7 g protein; 0.1 g fat (0 g sat.); 5 g carbo.; 1.5 mg sodium; 0 mg chol.

Honey-Mustard Potato Salad

Cooking time: 25 to 35 minutes
Prep time: 40 minutes
Notes: If making ahead, cover and chill up to 1 day.
Makes: 10 to 12 servings

5 pounds thin red-skinned potatoes, scrubbed

1 cup chopped red onion

3 cups thinly sliced celery

1 cup cider vinegar

⅓ cup honey

¼ cup Dijon mustard

4 teaspoons cumin seed

Salt and pepper

1. Bring about 4 quarts water to a boil in a 8- to 10-quart pan. Add potatoes, cover, and simmer over low heat until potatoes are tender when pierced, 20 to 30 minutes. Drain and immerse in cold water. When cool, cut into about 1½-inch chunks. Rinse onion with cool running water; drain well. In a large bowl, combine onion, celery, and potatoes.

2. Mix vinegar, honey, mustard, and cumin; pour over salad. Mix and season to taste with salt and pepper.

Per serving: 202 cal., 2% (5 cal.) from fat; 4.2 g protein; 0.5 g fat (0 g sat.); 45 g carbo.; 164 mg sodium; 0 mg chol. ∎

By Linda Lau Anusasananan

BUFFALO-BEEF *bratwurst tucked into a roll makes a wild variation on a hot dog.*

NOEL BARNHURST

NOEL BARNHURST

Yes, you can eat meat

IT ALWAYS SURPRISES ME WHEN A friend's diet resolutions include cutting out red meat, because meat is a very nutritious food, full of high-quality protein, iron, and B vitamins. While you may want to reserve slabs of steak for special occasions, meat can fit nicely into a low-fat diet if you know how to choose and prepare it.

This version of *pozole,* a Southwestern soup-stew richly flavored with chilies, hominy, and pork, illustrates these points.

Choose lean cuts. When my brother Bruce, who lives outside Santa Fe, makes his traditional pozole for me, he uses pork shoulder. But switching to pork loin cuts the fat in half.

When shopping for other recipes, select pork and beef cuts with "loin" and "round" in their names. Ham is another lean choice. For lamb, try arm chop, cuts from the loin, and leg (including top round, sirloin, and shank). A fat-trimmed roasted or broiled 3-ounce serving of any of these cuts has no more than 180 calories, 80 milligrams cholesterol, and 9 grams fat.

Use meat as a seasoning. Like a stir-fry, this pozole stretches meat with lots of vegetables. Cooking this way steers you toward moderate portions of meat: 2 to 3 ounces per person (3 ounces cooked is the size of a deck of cards).

Trim visible fat before cooking, and use a lean cooking method. Rather than browning meat and onions in oil, try the "sweating" technique (simmering briefly, then browning) used in the pozole.

Don't overcook. While the pork shoulder in my brother's pozole takes hours to get tender, many leaner cuts are tender to begin with and dry out if overcooked. Cooking with lean meat lets you streamline time as well as fat.

Streamlined Southwest Stew

Cooking time: About 35 minutes

Prep time: About 15 minutes

Notes: If your market sells these pork options only as bone-in chops, buy about 1⅛ pounds, then remove bones.

Makes: About 8 cups, 4 servings

¾	pound boned pork center loin, top loin, or sirloin (fat trimmed), cut into ¾-inch chunks
2	cups chopped yellow onions
4	cloves garlic, minced
5	cups low-sodium chicken broth, fat skimmed
1	teaspoon dried oregano leaves
1½	tablespoons New Mexico, California, or regular chili powder
3	cans (14½ oz. each) hominy, rinsed and drained
1	can (7 oz.) diced green chilies
	Sliced green onions and lime wedges

1. In a 5- to 6-quart pan, stir pork, yellow onions, garlic, and ⅓ cup broth. Cover tightly, bring to a boil over high heat, then simmer over medium heat for 10 minutes.

2. Uncover and stir over medium-high heat until juices mostly stick to pan and turn deep brown, about 4 minutes. Add 2 tablespoons of the remaining broth; stir until juices are well browned, about 4 minutes longer. Add oregano and chili powder; stir for 15 seconds.

3. Stir in remaining broth, hominy, and green chilies. Bring to a boil, then reduce heat and simmer, covered, until flavors are blended, about 10 minutes. Season to taste with green onions and lime.

Per serving: 401 cal., 17% (69 cal.) from fat; 29 g protein; 7.7 g fat (2.7 g sat.); 59 g carbo.; 1,181 mg sodium; 54 mg chol. ■

Tastes from Main Street America and beyond

Sunset's newest cookbook series is inspired by the down-to-earth cooking found in America's diners, France's bistros, and Italy's trattorias

PETER JOHNSON

SAUTÉED SHRIMP *tumbled over baked tomatoes, as served in a bistro, typifies the simply prepared dishes in Sunset's new, around-the-world cookbook series.*

WHEN WE TRAVEL, MOST OF US don't want to be onlookers—we want to be part of the scene. Nowhere is this desire more easily gratified than in comfortable neighborhood restaurants. It's here local folk gather to eat, gossip, sip a little wine or coffee, and linger—and they seldom hesitate to direct a few opening questions at a stranger like yourself. You rarely find these places in guidebooks among the three-star dining meccas, and seldom are they in the chic part of a city. Often they look a little worn, although welcoming.

These are the bistros of France, the trattorias of Italy, and the diners of America—and they are also the inspiration behind Sunset Books's newest series, Casual Cuisines of the World. The first three volumes, now available in major bookstores ($19.95 each), pay respect to the comfort foods of France, Italy, and the United States. The authors have both professional credentials and firsthand involvement with their topics. Gerald Hirigoyen, who wrote *Bistro, The Best of Casual French Cooking,* is French-born and the classically trained chef and owner of San Francisco's highly acclaimed Fringale. Mary Beth Clark, author of *Trattoria, The Best of Casual Italian Cooking,* has a cooking school in Milan and divides her time between there and this country. And Southern California author Diane Rossen Worthington, with many cookbooks to her credit, wrote *Diner, The Best of Casual American Cooking.* Those who live in or near Los Angeles know her well as the host of KABC's talk show "California Foods."

Each 128-page book provides you with basics geared to the country's cuisine, recipe names in the native language and English, beverage suggestions ranging from wines to malted milks, and measurements in both American standard and metric.

As for the recipes, here's a sampling.

From Chef Gerald Hirigoyen's *Bistro:*
Sautéed Shrimp with Fried Garlic and Baked Tomato

Gambas Sautées à L'ail, Tomates au Four

Fresh shrimp, sautéed in butter, garlic, and herbs, is a classic bistro standby. In this recipe, baked tomatoes give the dish still more substance and bright color. Vine-ripened tomatoes provide the best flavor. If they are difficult to find, you might consider substituting a bed of steamed spinach in their place. Serve a crusty baguette alongside for sopping up all the delicious juices.

Cooking time: 15 to 20 minutes
Prep time: About 25 minutes
Makes: 4 servings

- 4 tomatoes (about 1 ½ lb. total)
  Salt and freshly ground pepper
- 6 tablespoons olive oil
- 1 pound (30 to 35 per lb.) shrimp, peeled and deveined
- 1 tablespoon finely chopped garlic
- 1 tablespoon sherry vinegar
- 2 tablespoons chopped fresh parsley
  Dash of cayenne

1. Cut tomatoes in half crosswise and place them, cut side up, in a close-fitting ovenproof dish. Season tomatoes to taste with salt and pepper, and drizzle with 2 tablespoons of the olive oil. Bake in a 450° oven until heated through but still firm, about 15 minutes.

2. About 3 minutes before the tomatoes are done, pour 1 tablespoon oil into a wide frying pan and place over high heat. When oil is hot, add the shrimp and stir often until they are pink and firm, 2 to 3 minutes. Add salt and pepper to taste.

3. Transfer the baked tomatoes to individual serving dishes. Place the sautéed shrimp on top of the tomatoes, dividing them evenly. Keep warm.

4. In a small pan over high heat, combine the garlic and the remaining 3 tablespoons olive oil. Stir often until the garlic turns golden brown, about 1 minute.

5. Add vinegar to pan, and stir to dislodge any browned bits, about 30 seconds. Immediately pour mixture over the tomatoes and sautéed shrimp. Sprinkle parsley and cayenne evenly over the shrimp mixture, and serve at once.

Per serving: 317 cal., 62% (198 cal.) from fat; 20 g protein; 22 g fat (3.1 g sat.); 9.8 g carbo.; 153 mg sodium; 140 mg chol.

From Mary Beth Clark's *Trattoria:*

Orecchiette with Broccoli Rabe, Garlic, and Pine Nuts

Orecchiette con Cime di Rabe, Aglio, e Pinoli

A variety of small, round pasta shaped like little ears, orecchiette is typically found in southern Italian trattorias, especially those in Apulia.

Cooking time: About 30 minutes
Prep time: 30 to 40 minutes
Notes: Broccoli rabe has longer stems, smaller flower heads, and a somewhat more bitter flavor than regular broccoli, which can be substituted.
Makes: 4 servings

    1   pound broccoli rabe
    ¾   pound dried orecchiette pasta
    1   tablespoon unsalted butter
    2   tablespoons extra-virgin olive oil
    ½   cup finely chopped yellow onion
    ½   cup (2½ oz.) pine nuts
    1   or 2 fresh small red chilies, stemmed, seeded, and sliced into thin rings
    4   teaspoons chopped garlic
    1½ cups vegetable or meat broth
    2   tablespoons chopped fresh parsley

THE TRATTORIA *cookbook includes this pasta dish from Italy's Adriatic side.*

    1   cup fresh cilantro leaves (optional)
        Salt and freshly ground pepper
        Freshly grated Italian parmesan or pecorino romano cheese

1. Trim any tough portions from the broccoli rabe, then cut the stems and leaves into 1-inch lengths; leave the florets whole. Place the stems on a steamer rack over (not touching) gently boiling water. Cover and steam 2 to 3 minutes. Add the leaves and florets, and steam until cooked through yet firm when pierced, 2 to 3 minutes longer. Remove from the rack and set aside.

2. Fill a deep pan ¾ full of salted water and bring to a rolling boil. Add the pasta, and stir gently to prevent pieces from sticking. Cook until just tender to bite, 10 to 12 minutes or according to package directions.

3. Meanwhile, in a large frying pan over medium heat, melt the butter in the olive oil. Add the onion and pine nuts, and stir often until the onion is translucent and the pine nuts are lightly golden, about 3 minutes; do not allow the onion to brown. Add the chilies and garlic, and stir often for a few seconds until very fragrant. Add the broccoli rabe, and stir often for 2 minutes. Add the broth, bring to a boil on high heat, then reduce the heat to low and simmer for 1 minute.

4. Drain orecchiette briefly in a colander, and immediately add it to the frying pan. Mix well. Add parsley and cilantro, and mix again. Season to taste with salt and pepper. Transfer to a warmed serving bowl and sprinkle with cheese.

Per serving: 540 cal., 35% (189 cal.) from fat; 19 g protein; 21 g fat (4.4 g sat.); 75 g carbo.; 437 mg sodium; 7.8 mg chol.

From Diane Rossen Worthington's *Diner:*

Buttermilk Biscuits

Flaky biscuits like these are a grand diner tradition. Using shortening—as in this recipe—or lard produces a flakier biscuit. For a slightly softer crust, lightly brush the hot biscuits with melted butter when they come out of the oven.

Cooking time: 10 to 12 minutes
Prep time: 15 to 20 minutes
Makes: 12 to 14 biscuits

        About 2 cups all-purpose flour
    2½ teaspoons baking powder
    ½   teaspoon salt
    ½   teaspoon baking soda
    ½   cup cold solid shortening
    ¾   cup cold buttermilk

1. In a bowl, stir together 2 cups flour, baking powder, salt, and baking soda until well mixed. Add the shortening, and stir to coat with the flour mixture. Using a pastry blender, 2 knives, or your fingertips, and working quickly, cut or rub the shortening into dry ingredients until the mixture is the consistency of coarse meal.

2. Make a well in the center of the flour mixture. Add buttermilk, then stir with a fork just until a soft dough forms that pulls from the sides of the bowl.

3. Gather dough into a ball, and dust with flour on a lightly floured board. Knead very gently 5 or 6 times just until the dough holds together. Gently pat or roll the dough about ½ inch thick. Using a round 2- to 2½-inch biscuit cutter, cut as many dough rounds as possible, pressing straight down and lifting the cutter straight up without twisting. Place rounds about 1½ inches apart on an ungreased baking sheet. Very gently knead the scraps together 2 or 3 times, and cut as before. Do not reroll any additional scraps.

4. Bake in a 450° oven until evenly browned, 10 to 12 minutes. Serve hot.

Per biscuit: 139 cal., 49% (68 cal.) from fat; 2.4 g protein; 7.6 g fat (1.9 g sat.); 15 g carbo.; 224 mg sodium; 0.5 mg chol. ■

By Jerry Anne Di Vecchio

TENDER BUTTERMILK *biscuits from the Diner cookbook are an easy tradition.*

ALLAN ROSENBERG

PETER JOHNSON

A SIMPLE PLEASURE: *A generous cup of coffee topped with foamed milk.*

PHILIP SALAVERRY

Frothed milk options for cappuccino fans

Four ways to foam milk without a cappuccino machine

AH, THE DELICATE, CREAMY FROTH of a cappuccino, produced with a flourish at one of the West's burgeoning coffee bars. Have you wanted to create that foam at home, but shied from the complex (and often expensive) gadgetry involved? We tried out four low-tech solutions for frothing milk. You can add frothed milk to strong coffee for results that are similar to a true cappuccino but a lot easier to produce.

Each method introduces air into milk, doubling or tripling the milk's volume. We outline the basic processes at right; purchased devices come with more detailed instructions.

FROTHER CHOICES *include (clockwise from right) saucepan and wire whisk, rangetop steamer, manual frothing wand with pitcher, and electric frother (to use with metal pitcher or other container).*

Most options work best with small amounts of milk. Use about ½ cup for 2 servings. To prevent scorching, heat milk only until steaming (about 150°—you can test it with an instant-read thermometer).

Nonfat milk froths more easily than low-fat and whole, but foam is smoother and creamier with a little fat.

Once you've created the froth, pour the hot milk layer that forms beneath it into coffee, and spoon foam on top.

Saucepan plus wire whisk. Just pour cold milk into a small saucepan over medium-high heat, and whisk until milk is frothy and steaming. Foam will be fairly fine-textured with good volume.

Frothing wand. If you can rub your hands together, you can use the Swizzler. Place the ring end in steaming milk (heated in the microwave or on the range), vigorously roll the wand between your hands, and in about 30 seconds you'll have a good volume of smooth, long-lasting foam.

The Swizzler and recipe booklet are sold with or without a microwave-safe pitcher ($16 versus $10). If you don't buy the pitcher, you'll need another tall, narrow, heatproof container for frothing.

Buy it from department and discount home stores, or from the manufacturer; call (800) 669-1718. Shipping is extra.

Electric frother. Cappuccino Crazy is easy to use, but the vigorous frothing action can create uneven foam—sometimes bubbles so big they deflate easily.

Fill the reservoir with water; plug in. When the indicator light goes off, about 5 minutes, dunk the wand in a narrow, heatproof pitcher (not included) about a quarter full of cold milk. Pressing the steam-release button, heat and froth milk while you rotate the pitcher.

Look for Cappuccino Crazy in department and discount stores, or order it from the manufacturer; call (800) 233-9054. Cost is $50 plus $6 shipping.

Rangetop steamer. The Italian sports car of frothers, the Graziella, rates high on looks but requires practice to operate. Those who use it regularly swear by it. As neophytes, we stalled at the starting block with only meager foam.

Fill the inner reservoir with water to just beneath the safety valve, and heat on the range until steam escapes from under the valve cover. Fill a narrow, heatproof pitcher (not included) a third of the way with cold milk. Dip the frothing wand beneath the surface of the milk, and open the steam knob. Rotate the pitcher, slowly lowering it as bubbles raise the level of the liquid. The Graziella sells in coffee stores for $40 to $50. ∎

By Elaine Johnson

A DEEP-DISH PIZZA PAN *makes an ideal container for a super-scale pie.*

Ten-pound apple pie

Dessert for two dozen comes under a single crust

WHEN ASKED TO BRING PIES TO A beach party, Kathie Cooper of Palo Alto, California, responded in heroic style. She decided that trekking through the sand with just one big pie would be easier than juggling several smaller ones. Searching through her baking supplies, she spotted the perfect container: a deep-dish pizza pan. It held 10 pounds of apples, ample to satisfy an anticipated two dozen well-honed appetites, and the scale was dramatic.

Peeling this amount of apples does take time, but Cooper put to use an old-fashioned gadget that you can still buy in hardware and cookware stores: an apple peeler. Her model peels, cores, and slices in one ongoing operation. If you have to hand-peel the fruit, you can certainly speed up slicing with a food processor.

Cooper makes a double-crust pie, but our taste panel was equally satisfied with the top crust–only pie, which is faster and easier to manage with the soft dough. An extra-long rolling pin is helpful but not necessary. A 14- by 17-inch roasting pan can be substituted for the big pizza pan.

Apple Pie for a Crowd

Cooking time: 2 to 2½ hours

Prep time: About 3 hours

Notes: Deep, wide pizza or cake pans are found in cookware or cake-decorating supply stores. Make 2 batches of pastry for a double-crust pie. You can make the pie a day ahead and reheat, if you like.

Makes: 24 servings

- ¼ cup lemon juice
- 10 pounds Granny Smith apples
  About 3½ cups granulated sugar
  About 4½ cups all-purpose flour
- 2 teaspoons ground cinnamon
- 1 teaspoon ground ginger
- ½ teaspoon ground nutmeg
- ½ teaspoon ground allspice
- 2½ tablespoons powdered sugar
- 1½ cups (¾ lb.) cold butter or margarine
- 2 tablespoons solid shortening
- 5 to 7 tablespoons ice water
- 1 large egg yolk beaten with 2 teaspoons water

1. Make filling. In an 8-quart or larger bowl, mix lemon juice and 4 cups water. Peel, core, and slice apples about ¼ inch thick. As cut, put apples in bowl and mix to slow browning. Drain and discard liquid. Mix 3½ cups granulated sugar (or to taste), 1¼ cups flour, cinnamon, ginger, nutmeg, and allspice; add to apples. Gently mix until all slices are coated.

Pour the apple slices and juices into a 2-inch-deep, 14-inch-wide round pan, and spread the fruit level.

2. Make pastry. In a food processor or bowl, combine 3¼ cups flour and powdered sugar. Cut butter and shortening into small pieces and add to flour mixture. Whirl or cut with a pastry cutter until mixture is coarse crumbs. Add ice water a little at a time, stirring with a fork, just until dough holds together. Pat pastry into a ball. If making ahead, flatten ball to make a ¼-inch-thick round (or shape of baking pan), wrap airtight, and chill up to 1 day.

Lightly dust both sides of pastry with flour, then roll out on a well-floured board to make a round 3 to 5 inches wider than pan. As you roll, occasionally check under pastry to make sure it's not sticking; dust with flour if it is. Moisten edges of any tears, overlap slightly, and press together. Slide a long spatula under pastry to release if it sticks to the board. Gently fold pastry into quarters. Support pastry with both hands to lift off board. Place on apple filling with the tip of the triangle in the center of the pan. Unfold carefully to cover fruit. Trim pastry, leaving 1½ inches overhanging pan rim. Fold edge of pastry under so it extends only about ½ inch beyond rim, then press pastry firmly against pan rim, fluting the edge. Slash pastry top decoratively.

3. Make decorations. Gather pastry scraps into a ball and roll ⅛ inch thick on a lightly floured board. Cut decorative pieces, such as leaves or apples; brush 1 side with egg yolk mixture. Arrange pieces, egg side down, on pie. Brush top of pie with egg yolk mixture; sprinkle with 1 tablespoon sugar.

4. On a baking sheet without sides, lay a piece of foil several inches larger all around than the apple pie pan (you may need to fold together 2 strips of foil to make a piece that's large enough). Set pie on foil, and cup foil very loosely up around pan to catch any juices that boil over. Set stacked pans on bottom oven rack.

5. Bake pie in a 375° oven until crust is well browned, juices are bubbling, and apples in center are tender when pierced, 2 to 2½ hours. Check occasionally after 1 hour, and cover with foil any parts of the crust that are browned.

6. Set pie on a rack and let cool at least 2 hours; it will still be warm. If making ahead, let cool, then cover and chill. To reheat, lightly cover pie with foil and bake in a 350° oven until warm in the center, about 1 hour.

7. Serve pie warm or cool. Cut into about 2-inch squares and use a large spoon to scoop out portions. Store leftovers, covered, in the refrigerator up to 2 days.

Per serving: 410 cal., 29% (117 cal.) from fat; 3 g protein; 13 g fat (7.6 g sat.); 73 g carbo.; 119 mg sodium; 40 mg chol. ∎

By Linda Lau Anusasananan

Per serving: 83 cal., 25% (21 cal.) from fat; 2.3 g protein; 2.3 g fat (0.8 g sat.); 14 g carbo.; 64 mg sodium; 2.6 mg chol.

Bob Robinson

Riverside, California

The first law of meat is that the most expensive cuts come from loin and leg, the least expensive from those portions of the animal nearer the ground. Lamb shanks (the front legs) have a lot of bone encased in well-flavored but relatively lean, tough meat.

Braising (long, slow cooking in moist heat) preserves the flavor while breaking down the tough connective tissue. Conventional braising calls for browning the meat before adding liquid. James Kircher does not brown the shanks, but puts them on a bed of vegetables and seasonings to simmer. Then he browns the meat briefly in the oven while turning the cooking juices into a refined sauce.

Idaho Lamb Shanks

Cooking time: About 2¾ hours
Prep time: 35 to 40 minutes
Makes: 4 servings

- 1½   pounds carrots, thinly sliced
- 4   stalks celery, thinly sliced
- 1   onion (5 or 6 oz.), thinly sliced
- 2   cloves garlic, minced or pressed
- 1   firm-ripe tomato (5 or 6 oz.), cored and diced
- 1   tablespoon dried Italian herb seasoning mix
- ¼   teaspoon pepper
- 4   lamb shanks, about 1 pound each, bones cracked
- ¼   cup marsala or dry sherry
    Salt

1. In a 5- to 6-quart pan, combine carrots, celery, onion, garlic, tomato, herb seasoning, pepper, and 1 cup water.

2. Trim and discard fat from shanks. Add shanks to vegetable mixture, and bring to a boil over high heat. Cover and simmer until lamb is very tender and pulls easily from bone, about 2½ hours.

3. With a slotted spoon, carefully transfer shanks to a shallow casserole (about 8 by 12 in.) and place in a 375° oven to brown lightly, 10 to 15 minutes.

4. Meanwhile, pour pan juices through a fine strainer into a bowl; press liquid from vegetables, then discard vegetable residue. Skim fat from juices, then return juices to

Elevate crunch with pine nuts

There are many ways to put a crunch in the crust of a bread, but Robert Robinson likes a crunch that lurks in the soft interior as well. He finds that toasted pine nuts and wheat-barley cereal do the job admirably.

Crunchy Whole-Wheat Bread

Cooking time: About 35 minutes
Prep time: 45 to 50 minutes, plus about 2 hours for proofing and cooling
Notes: For less effort, mix and knead dough with a mixer and dough hook.
Makes: 2 loaves, each about 1½ pounds

- ⅔   cup pine nuts
- 1   package active dry yeast
- 2   cups warm (about 110°) water
- ⅓   cup honey
- ¼   cup (⅛ lb.) melted butter or margarine
- 1   teaspoon salt
- 2½   cups whole-wheat flour
- ½   cup wheat and barley cereal
    About 3 cups all-purpose flour

1. Place pine nuts in an 8- to 10-inch frying pan over medium heat and shake frequently until pale gold color, about 4 minutes. Pour from pan.

2. In a large bowl, combine yeast, ½ cup water, and 1 tablespoon honey; let stand until bubbly, 10 to 15 minutes. Stir in remaining 1½ cups water, remaining honey, butter, and salt. Add whole-wheat flour, cereal, and 1 cup all-purpose flour; beat until dough is shiny and stretchy, about 5 minutes. Add 1½ cups all-purpose flour and pine nuts, and stir until flour is moistened.

3. Scrape dough onto a board well coated with all-purpose flour; dust dough with flour to cover sticky surface. Knead until dough is velvety smooth and elastic, about 10 minutes; as pine nuts pop out, poke them back into dough. Add flour as required to prevent sticking.

4. Rinse, dry, and lightly oil mixing bowl; place dough in it. Cover airtight and let dough rise in a warm place until doubled, about 1½ hours.

5. Knead dough on lightly floured board to expel air, then cut dough in half. Knead each piece to make a smooth ball. Set balls, smooth side up, well apart on an oiled 12-by 15-inch baking sheet. Invert a large bowl over each ball to keep airtight. Let stand until slightly puffy, about 20 minutes.

6. Bake, uncovered, in a 375° oven until loaves are well browned, about 30 minutes. Put on a rack. Serve warm or cool.

7. To store, keep airtight at room temperature up to 1 day; freeze to store longer.

pan and add wine. Boil on high heat until reduced to about ¾ cup. Pour juices over shanks, and serve with salt to taste.

Per serving: 494 cal., 26% (126 cal.) from fat; 66 g protein; 14 g fat (4.7 g sat.); 20 g carbo.; 280 mg sodium; 200 mg chol.

Burley, Idaho

One of the outstanding items in the Western chef's bag of tricks is cross-cultural cooking, combining one nation's wrapping with another nation's stuffing, using Asian seasonings where they are least expected, and—in general—playing hob with conventional wisdom. The results, always surprising, are often surprisingly good, as are Gerald Gardner's Chinese Cheese Blintzes.

Chinese Cheese Blintzes

Cooking time: About 45 minutes
Prep time: 40 to 50 minutes
Makes: 5 servings, 10 blintzes

10 flour tortillas (8 in. wide)

¼ pound Chinese pea pods, strings removed, cut into 1-inch lengths

1 can (8 oz.) sliced bamboo shoots, drained and cut into matchstick-size pieces

2 green onions, ends trimmed and thinly sliced

1 small red bell pepper (3 to 4 oz.), stemmed, seeded, and cut into matchstick-size pieces

1 teaspoon Asian sesame oil
   Reduced-sodium soy sauce

1 pint (2 cups) low-fat large-curd cottage cheese

1 large egg

1 tablespoon minced fresh ginger

½ cup chopped fresh cilantro
   Nonfat sour cream or plain nonfat yogurt
   Chopped firm-ripe tomato

1. Dip your hands in water and rub over each tortilla to moisten; stack tortillas and seal in foil. Place in a 350° oven until hot in center, 10 to 15 minutes.

2. Meanwhile, in a 10- to 12-inch frying pan over high heat, stir-fry peas, bamboo shoots, green onions, and red bell pepper with oil for 1 minute, then stir in 1 tablespoon water. Continue stir-frying just until tender-crisp to bite, 2 to 4 minutes. Remove vegetables from heat, and season to taste with soy sauce.

3. In a bowl, blend cheese, egg, and ginger.

4. Spoon down center of each tortilla 1/10 of the vegetable mixture, 1/10 of the cheese mixture, and equal amounts of cilantro. Roll tortillas to enclose filling snugly, and place seam side down and slightly apart in a lightly oiled 10- by 15-inch pan.

5. Bake on lowest rack in a 350° oven until tortillas are crisp to touch and lightly browned, about 25 minutes. Transfer tortillas to plates, and accompany with soy sauce, sour cream, tomato, and cilantro to add to taste.

Per serving: 173 cal., 23% (40 cal.) from fat; 10 g protein; 4.4 g fat (1 g sat.); 23 g carbo.; 360 mg sodium; 23 mg chol.

Bellevue, Washington
By Joan Griffiths, Richard Dunmire

Why?

Why scald milk for custard? Why does it curdle? Why do you have to be so careful when cooking it?

WHEN HEAT BONDS EGGS AND MILK to make custards (stirred or baked) such as flan, crème brûlée, or quiche, the resulting liaison can be as smooth as velvet. But this changes dramatically if a custard overcooks, which can happen quickly. This is why custards have a reputation for being difficult. If you know what to look for, however, success is assured.

"Why do you need to scald milk when making custard?" asks Annamarie Khoury of Flagstaff, Arizona.

When you heat the milk (usually to scalding, which is just before boiling—tiny bubbles form at pan edge) before you mix it with the eggs, two results are predictable.

One, the custard cooks much faster than if you start with cold milk. You can't heat cold milk with the eggs quickly without cooking the eggs too much and curdling the custard. Two, scalding milk alters some of its proteins, which would otherwise form a thicker "skin" on the surface of cold custard.

Why do most custard recipes direct you to mix a little of the hot liquid with the eggs, then stir this mixture back into the rest of the hot liquid?

Eggs start to thicken, or firm, at very low heat, about 100°. The liquid doesn't have to be much hotter to start cooking the eggs if you drop them in whole or even if they are beaten together. You end up with curdled shreds of cooked egg and no thickening.

But if you first mix the beaten eggs with about an equal amount of hot liquid, the eggs' protein structure is diluted and becomes much more tolerant of heat. Then you can stir this mixture into the rest of the hot liquid without overcooking the eggs.

When custard cooks, egg and milk proteins form an invisible spongy web that holds the liquid in suspension—in other words, thickens it. If stirred, the mixture stays fluid. If baked, it forms a single mass.

Why is a custard sauce sometimes velvety thick, other times thin?

The same factors affect the texture of all custards, stirred or baked. A custard's thickness depends on a number of things: the ratio of eggs to liquid, which part of the egg you use (whole, yolk, white), the amount of fat in the milk or cream. If you use sugar, how much. And how fast the custard cooks.

The standard proportions for a velvety stirred custard or delicately firm and tender baked custard are 2 or 3 whole eggs

(4 to 6 yolks, or 4 to 6 whites) for each 2 cups milk or cream. Yolks thicken the most, whites the least, and whites break or curdle at a lower temperature. If eggs are further diluted, the custard will be thinner and also will need to get a little hotter for the eggs to thicken it. If the egg ratio is higher, the custard will be thicker and take less heat to cook.

Sugar raises the temperature that the custard has to reach to thicken; some Latin desserts contain so much sugar you can almost boil the mixture without curdling it. Acid, such as lemon juice, has the reverse effect. It causes the custard to thicken at a lower temperature.

Whipping cream makes the smoothest, softest, thickest custards. Nonfat milk makes the most delicate baked custards and the most fragile stirred ones.

The rate of the heat inversely affects how much a custard thickens. A custard cooked longer at lower temperatures will be thicker and smoother than the same mixture cooked at a higher heat.

Why is custard sometimes watery and grainy?

Heating too much and cooking too long both make custard curdle. The spongy protein web of eggs and milk loses its elasticity and then hardens, shrinks, and squeezes out the liquid it holds. The custard tastes watery and flat, and the toughened, oversolidified egg-milk protein feels and looks grainy. Overcooked baked custards get bubbles and start to leak clear liquid. The weeping is called syneresis.

Once a custard curdles, there is no way back. It's wiser to undercook slightly when in doubt.

The rate of heating is very important. With only a few degrees' difference between when a custard is as thick as it can get and when it curdles, the faster the heat is climbing the more difficult it is to stop at the optimum point.

This is why many recipes have you set the pan of stirred custard in cold water and stir to cool it enough to stop the cooking, and why it is vital to remove baked custards from the oven as soon as they test done.

Why stir custard over hot water or bake it in a hot-water bath?

The water controls the rate of heating. You can cook stirred custards over low heat, but you have to be vigilant. Gently simmering water has a constant temperature, but you still have to be attentive to the custard.

PULL YOUR FINGER *through stirred custard clinging to the back of a spoon, and the trail left behind shows whether, and how much, the custard has cooked.*

PETER CHRISTIANSEN

In the oven, water moderates the heat better than air does, and keeps the custard from overcooking at the edges before it is done in the center.

How can I tell when a custard is done?

A stirred custard clings in an even layer to the spoon, and the density of this coating is easiest to see on a metal spoon. Custards made with cream or whole milk and more eggs and sugar make a thicker, more opaque coating than a nonfat-milk custard.

To test, pull your fingertip through the coating on the spoon; if it leaves a clean path, the custard is done. The best way to test a baked custard is to shake it gently. The custard is done when it barely jiggles in the center. The old-fashioned test of inserting a knife tip is completely unreliable. The knife comes out clean only when the custard is overcooked or on the verge of being overcooked, and the cut leaves a gaping hole.

More questions?

What kitchen mysteries are you curious about? Send your questions to Why?, *Sunset Magazine,* 80 Willow Rd., Menlo Park, CA 94025; send e-mail (including full name and street address) to why@sunsetpub.com. With the help of George K. York, extension food technologist at UC Davis, *Sunset* food editors will try to find solutions. We'll publish the answers in the magazine. ■

By Linda Lau Anusasananan

Gruesome foods for a gory Halloween

Fun with worms, melting fingers, and bloody punch. Surprise: they taste good

SOME MAY SAY "YUCK," BUT THESE easy, gruesome recipes are guaranteed to yield delighted shrieks from others. You'll need a large bowl for the punch. If you don't have a glass punch bowl, stop at a party store for an inexpensive plastic one, or wrap the outside of your largest kitchen pan with black plastic for a cauldron effect.

Finger Pizzas

Cooking time: 8 minutes
Prep time: About 30 minutes
Makes: 8 pizzas

- 1 red bell pepper (4 oz.)
- 12 sticks (1 oz. each) mozzarella cheese
- 8 small (about 5 in. diameter) baked pizza crusts
- 1 cup purchased pizza sauce

1. Core, stem, and seed pepper; cut lengthwise into 1-inch-wide strips. Cut each strip crosswise into ½-inch pieces (fingernails). Round corners on one end of each piece.

2. Cut each cheese stick in half crosswise. On rounded end of each stick (finger), cut out a ½-inch-square notch into which a pepper piece will fit to make a nail.

3. Lay crusts slightly apart on 3 baking sheets, each 12 by 15 inches. Spread 2 tablespoons sauce evenly over each crust. Lay 3 cheese fingers well apart on each crust; fit a red pepper nail onto each. Bake in a 450° oven until cheese just begins to melt, about 8 minutes.

Per pizza: 338 cal., 40% (135 cal.) from fat; 10 g protein; 15 g fat (6.9 g sat.); 36 g carbo.; 422 mg sodium; 33 mg chol.

Worms!

Cooking time: About 5 minutes
Prep time: About 15 minutes, plus overnight chilling
Notes: Use a cleaned 1-quart milk or orange juice carton to hold straws.
Makes: About 100, including a few casualties

- 1 package (6 oz.) raspberry- or grape-flavor gelatin
- 3 envelopes unflavored gelatin
- 3 cups boiling water
- ¾ cup whipping cream
- 12 to 15 drops green food coloring
- 100 flexible plastic straws
- 1 tall (same height as extended straws), slender 4-cup container

1. In a bowl, combine gelatins. Add boiling water; stir until gelatins completely dissolve. Chill until lukewarm, about 20 minutes.

2. Meanwhile, gently pull straws to extend to full length; place in tall container. Blend cream and food coloring with the lukewarm gelatin mixture. Pour into container, filling

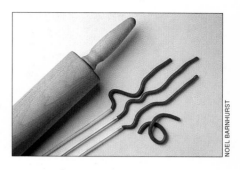

straws. Chill until gelatin is firm, at least 8 hours, or cover and chill up to 2 days.

3. Pull straws from container (if using a carton, tear carton away from straws). Pull straws apart; run hot tap water for about 2 seconds over 3 to 4 straws at a time. Starting at the empty ends, push worms from straws with rolling pin, or use your fingers; lay worms on waxed paper–lined baking sheets. Cover and chill until ready to use, at least 1 hour or up to 2 days. Worms will hold at room temperature up to 2 hours. —*Carol Peterson, Glendale, California*

Per worm: 17 cal., 42% (7.2 cal.) from fat; 0.4 g protein; 0.8 g fat (0.5 g sat.); 2 g carbo.; 6.8 mg sodium; 3 mg chol.

Plasma Punch

Cooking time: None
Prep time: About 20 minutes
Notes: For easy serving, scoop yogurt and sorbet ahead; freeze in a single layer on a cookie sheet. Add just before serving.
Makes: 30 servings, about 8 ounces each

- 1 bag (40 oz.) slightly thawed frozen strawberries
- 1 can (12 oz.) thawed frozen cranberry juice concentrate
- 1 can (12 oz.) thawed frozen raspberry juice concentrate
- 1 quart strawberry frozen yogurt
- 2 pints raspberry sorbet
- 2 bottles (1 liter each) cold sparkling mineral water
- 2 bottles (1 liter each) cold ginger ale

1. In a blender or food processor, smoothly purée half the slightly thawed strawberries with cranberry juice concentrate. Pour purée into a large (8 to 12 qt.) punch bowl. Repeat with remaining berries and raspberry juice concentrate. Mix in bowl.

2. Scoop yogurt and sorbet into punch; add mineral water and ginger ale. Serve.

Per 1-cup serving: 138 cal., 3.3% (4.5 cal.) from fat; 1.2 g protein; 0.5 g fat (0.3 g sat.); 34 g carbo.; 40 mg sodium; 1.3 mg chol. ■

By Betsy Reynolds Bateson, Mo Devlin

WORMS SLITHER *across the party table; Plasma Punch makes a great chaser.*

Black Bean and Broccoli Frittata

Roxanne Chan, Albany, California

FOR A PUFFY FRITTATA, *cook vegetables on the range, add beaten eggs, and bake.*

⅓ cup sliced green onions

1 clove garlic, minced

2 teaspoons salad oil

2 teaspoons chili powder

½ teaspoon ground cumin

1½ cups 1-inch broccoli florets

⅔ cup drained canned black beans

6 large eggs, separated

½ cup shredded sharp cheddar cheese

¼ cup fresh cilantro leaves

Chopped tomato

Salt and salsa

1. In a 10- to 12-inch nonstick frying pan over medium heat, stir onions and garlic in oil until limp, about 4 minutes. Add chili powder and cumin, and stir for 30 seconds. Add broccoli and 2 tablespoons water; stir until tender-crisp to bite, 3 to 4 minutes longer. Remove from heat, and stir in beans and egg yolks.

2. In a large bowl, beat egg whites until soft peaks form. Stir a spoonful of whites into broccoli mixture to soften, then fold mixture into remaining whites.

3. Return mixture to frying pan if ovenproof, or spoon into an oiled shallow 2-quart baking dish. Sprinkle with cheese. Bake in a 350° oven until set in center (cut to check), 15 to 17 minutes. Garnish with cilantro and tomato. Offer wedges with salt and salsa. Serves 6.

Per serving: 166 cal., 54% (90 cal.) from fat; 12 g protein; 10 g fat (3.8 g sat.); 8.1 g carbo.; 242 mg sodium; 222 mg chol.

Endive-Pear Salad with Anise Dressing

J. Hill, Sacramento

THIS ELEGANT *endive and pear salad has nuts and an anise-lemon dressing.*

1 teaspoon anise seed

1 small clove garlic

6 tablespoons olive oil

5 tablespoons lemon juice

¾ teaspoon dry mustard

Salt and pepper

1¼ pounds (2 large) firm-ripe pears

⅔ pound Oak Leaf or butter lettuce

⅔ pound (2 to 3 heads) Belgian endive, separated into leaves

3 cups coarsely chopped watercress sprigs

½ cup toasted walnut halves

1 tablespoon chopped chives

¼ cup freshly grated parmesan cheese (optional)

1. In a blender, whirl anise seed until coarsely ground. With motor running, add garlic; whirl to mince. Mix in oil, ¼ cup lemon juice, and mustard. Add salt and pepper to taste.

2. Core pears, thinly slice, mix with 1 tablespoon lemon juice. Line 6 salad plates with lettuce; arrange pears, endive, and watercress on top. Add nuts, chives, cheese, and dressing. Serves 6.

Per serving: 248 cal., 69% (171 cal.) from fat; 3.2 g protein; 19 g fat (2.3 g sat.); 19 g carbo.; 18 mg sodium; 0 mg chol.

Arizona Beef and Jalapeño Chili

Dorothy Norman, Parker, Arizona

ALL-MEAT CHILI *gets its heat from jalapeños, chili powder, and mole.*

2 pounds ground extra-lean beef

2½ cups chopped yellow onions

3 cloves garlic, minced or pressed

½ cup minced fresh jalapeño chilies (about 4 chilies)

¼ cup chili powder

3 tablespoons prepared brown or green mole paste

1 teaspoon *each* ground cumin and dried oregano leaves

1¾ cups beef broth

¾ cup beer

1 can (8 oz.) tomatoes

⅓ cup dehydrated masa flour (corn tortilla flour), or 2 corn tortillas (6- to 7-in. size), in pieces

Salt and sour cream

Sliced green onions

Warm corn tortillas (optional)

1. In a 5- to 6-quart pan over high heat, occasionally stir beef, yellow onions, garlic, and jalapeños, keeping meat in chunks, until onion is limp, about 15 minutes. Add chili powder, mole, cumin, and oregano; stir for 1 minute, breaking up mole. Stir in broth and beer. Bring to a boil; simmer, covered, about 50 minutes to blend flavors. Skim off fat.

2. In a blender, whirl tomatoes and masa until smooth. Stir into chili and simmer, stirring occasionally, for 5 minutes. Season to taste with salt and sour cream. Sprinkle with green onions. Serve with tortillas. Serves 4 or 5.

Per serving: 452 cal., 48% (216 cal.) from fat; 39 g protein; 24 g fat (8.8 g sat.); 21 g carbo.; 281 mg sodium; 110 mg chol.

Nutty Squash Soup

George F. Kossler, Palm Springs, California

 1   acorn squash (2½ lb.)

 3   tablespoons creamy old-fashioned
     peanut butter

 ¼   teaspoon ground nutmeg

 1½ cups low-fat milk

 2   cups chicken broth

     Chopped parsley

     Salt and pepper

1. Cut squash in half. Scoop out and discard seeds. Place skin up in a microwave-safe container with 1 tablespoon water. Cover with plastic wrap, and microwave on full power (100 percent) until tender when pierced, 15 to 20 minutes. (Or place squash skin up in a 9-by 13-inch baking dish, and bake tightly covered in a 400° oven until tender when pierced, about 1 hour.) Let stand until cool enough to handle.

2. Scoop squash from skin. In a blender, whirl squash, peanut butter, nutmeg, and milk into a smooth purée. Pour into a 3-quart pan, and add broth.

3. Stir soup over medium-high heat until it begins to bubble, 8 to 9 minutes. Ladle into 4 soup bowls. Scatter parsley over servings, and season to taste with salt and pepper. Makes 6 to 7 cups, 4 servings.

Per serving: 217 cal., 39% (85 cal.) from fat; 9.8 g protein; 9.4 g fat (2.6 g sat.); 30 g carbo.; 166 mg sodium; 7.3 mg chol.

ACORN SQUASH *and peanut butter give soup a creamy texture and mellow flavor.*

Pepper and Eggplant Focaccia Sandwiches

Louise K. Ross, Elk Grove, California

 8   round eggplant slices, about ½ inch
     thick and 3 inches wide

 2   tablespoons olive oil

 1½ pounds (2 large) red bell peppers

 8   squares (¾ in. thick, 4 in. wide, 1½ lb.
     total) plain or flavored focaccia bread;
     or use 4 sandwich-size English muffins
     (¾ lb. total), split and toasted

 3   tablespoons minced fresh basil leaves

 24 large (4 to 5 in.) spinach leaves,
     rinsed, stems removed

 1   cup thinly sliced red onion

 8   ounces mozzarella cheese, thinly
     sliced

     Salt and pepper

1. Brush eggplant on both sides with 1 tablespoon of the oil. Place eggplant and peppers on a rack in a 12- by 15-inch broiler pan. Broil with pan 6 inches beneath heat, turning foods as needed, until eggplant is deep brown (14 min. total) and peppers are black all over (20 min. total). Let cool. Peel and seed peppers, pat dry, and cut into 8 pieces.

2. Place focaccia on pan rack. Combine basil and remaining tablespoon oil; spread evenly over bread. On top place spinach, eggplant, peppers, onion, and cheese.

3. Broil 6 inches from heat until cheese is brown, about 4 minutes. Season to taste with salt and pepper. Serves 4 to 8.

Per serving: 394 cal., 32% (126 cal.) from fat; 18 g protein; 14 g fat (5.7 g sat.); 49 g carbo.; 570 mg sodium; 30 mg chol.

BROIL *layered open-face sandwiches on focaccia bread or English muffins.*

Chocolate-Raspberry Brownies

Kristie Lundstrom, Bellingham, Washington

 2   ounces unsweetened chocolate

 6   tablespoons butter or margarine

 1   cup sugar

 2   large eggs

 7   tablespoons seedless raspberry jam

 2   tablespoons raspberry vinegar

 ½   teaspoon vanilla

 ½   cup all-purpose flour

 ¼   teaspoon salt

 ½   cup toasted sliced almonds, coarsely
     chopped

 ¾   cup semisweet chocolate baking chips

1. In a 2- to 3-quart pan over low heat, stir unsweetened chocolate and butter until melt-ed. Remove from heat and stir in sugar, then eggs until glossy. Stir in ¼ cup of the jam, 1 tablespoon of the vinegar, and vanilla, then mix in flour, salt, and almonds. Spread in a buttered and floured 9-inch cake pan with a removable rim.

2. Bake in a 350° oven until brownies begin to pull from sides of pan, about 30 minutes. Let cool on a rack for 10 minutes.

3. In a 1- to 2-quart pan over low heat, stir chocolate chips, remaining 3 tablespoons jam, and remaining vinegar until melted. Swirl over brownies. Let cool on a rack. Loosen from rim, then push out. Serves 12 to 16.

Per serving: 209 cal., 47% (99 cal.) from fat; 2.6 g protein; 11 g fat (5.6 g sat.); 28 g carbo.; 93 mg sodium; 39 mg chol.

Compiled by Elaine Johnson

DECADENT FROSTED BROWNIES *contain raspberry jam and vinegar.*

FOOD
Guide

BY JERRY ANNE DI VECCHIO

A TASTE OF THE WEST: A sharp and luscious fruit salad

Overindulgence and holiday entertaining are, unfortunately, a
forged bond. Most of us struggle
through with good intentions and unreliable discipline, finishing with a few
extra pounds. So when I find a dish
that is not only seasonally attuned but
also delicious, quick, and lean, I'm
happy—and I serve it often. This salad
fits every criterion, putting to use the
fall harvest of Fuyu persimmons,
pomegranates, Asian pears, and ruby
grapefruit with a fat-free dressing.

The salad is a handsome starter for
any special meal, including Thanksgiving dinner. Presented on a tray or in
a bowl, it also suits buffet menus. You
can make lunch or a light supper of the
salad with a bit of toast and a little
cheese. And you can serve it with
frisée—its mild bitterness balances the
sweet fruit—or without.

Fall Fruit Salad

Cooking time: 2 to 3 minutes
Prep time: 20 to 25 minutes
Notes: As an alternative to frisée, use
the tender inner leaves of curly endive.
Makes: 6 servings

  1   to 2 tablespoons pine nuts
  2   firm-ripe Fuyu persimmons
      (½ lb. each)
  2   ruby grapefruit (1 lb. each)
  1   Asian pear (about ¾ lb.)
  3   tablespoons lime juice
  3   tablespoons rice vinegar
  2   tablespoons honey
  2   to 3 cups frisée, rinsed and
      drained
  ¾   cup pomegranate seed
      Salt

1. In a 6- to 8-inch frying pan over medium heat, frequently stir pine nuts until pale
gold, 2 to 3 minutes. Pour from pan.

2. Rinse persimmons, then trim off and

KEVIN CANDLAND

236

With its rice vinegar dressing and eccentric fruit combination, this probably isn't your mother's fruit salad.

discard leaf tops. Slice persimmons crosswise into thin rounds.

3. With a knife, cut peel and white membrane from grapefruit. Holding fruit over a bowl, cut between segments and inner membrane to release fruit into bowl. Also squeeze juice from membrane into bowl, then discard membrane.

4. Rinse pear and discard stem. Cut fruit crosswise into thin rounds, right through center seeds. Coat pear slices with grapefruit juice.

5. Mix 3 tablespoons grapefruit juice (reserve remainder for other uses) with lime juice, rice vinegar, and honey.

6. Line a salad bowl or individual plates with the frisée. Arrange pieces of persimmon, pear, and grapefruit on the greens; sprinkle fruit with pomegranate seed and pine nuts, then moisten with the grapefruit-lime dressing. Add salt to taste.

Per serving: 190 cal., 6.8% (13 cal.) from fat; 2 g protein; 1.4 g fat (0.1 g sat.); 47 g carbo.; 8.1 mg sodium; 0 mg chol.

NEW DIMENSIONS

Roast carrots for a sweet relish

Some of the most interesting dishes depend upon the plainest ingredients. This I've learned from cooks the world around who have worked with limited larders. One memorable result is this relish of carrots, onions, and ginger. Baking the diced vegetables first partially dehydrates them, intensifying their inherent sweetness and making them chewier, like dried fruit. Then the sugar and vinegar syrup saturates the vegetables as they simmer.

This is a relish to serve as you would any sweet-sour relish or chutney—with meat, poultry, or fish; in hamburgers or ham sandwiches; or spooned onto a bagel covered with cream cheese.

Carrot and Ginger Relish

Cooking time: About 1 hour and 15 minutes (1 hour to roast vegetables)

Prep time: About 35 minutes

Notes: The balsamic vinegar makes a darker relish; rice vinegar preserves the carrot color. Refrigerated, the relish keeps at least 1 month; stir occasionally to mix vegetables with syrup. Freeze to store longer.

Makes: About 2½ cups

- 4 cups ⅛- to ¼-inch cubed carrots
- 2 cups diced onions
- ¼ cup minced fresh ginger
- 1½ cups balsamic or rice vinegar
- ¾ cup sugar

1. Combine carrots, onions, and ginger in a 10- by 15-inch pan. Bake in a 400° oven, mixing occasionally with a wide spatula, until vegetables have shrunk to 2 to 2½ cups total, about 1 hour.

2. Scrape vegetables into a 4- to 5-quart pan; add 1½ cups water, vinegar, and sugar. Boil, uncovered, on high heat, stirring occasionally, until only about ½ cup liquid is left (tilt pan to check). Watch closely to avoid scorching, and stir more frequently as liquid is reduced.

3. Let relish cool, then chill at least 1 day for flavors to mellow. Serve, or store airtight in the refrigerator.

Per ¼ cup: 95 cal., 1.9% (1.8 cal.) from fat; 0.9 g protein; 0.2 g fat (0 g sat.); 24 g carbo.; 19 mg sodium; 0 mg chol.

NEWS NOTE

The other turkey

The first wild turkey I ever cooked was for Thanksgiving last year. It took no more effort than roasting a chicken, and I learned that I would've made a good Pilgrim. The darker, firmer, less sweet wild turkey meat suits my taste. It's more like the mild, lean dark meat of young pheasant, but without any gaminess.

However, size and cost may be problems for some folks. About the biggest dressed wild turkey you can buy is 14 pounds, and the average is 7 to 8 pounds (including giblets). Wild turkeys (actually, they are farm-bred) have a lot more bone to meat, proportionately, than domestic birds. Wild turkey is also more expensive—about $5 a pound.

Around the holidays, you can often buy them fresh, and any market that takes game orders should be able to get you a bird. Or you can order directly from Polarica/Game Exchange, 105 Quint St., San Francisco, CA 94124; (800) 426-3872.

Roast Wild Turkey

Cooking time: About 1¼ hours

Prep time: About 10 minutes

Notes: The soy sauce and the dry

sherry give the quick-cooking bird a good brown color.

Makes: 8 to 10 servings

1. Remove giblets from a 7- to 8-pound **wild turkey,** thawed if frozen. For gravy, use your favorite turkey gravy recipe. Most likely you'll need to start the gravy well ahead, because the turkey doesn't take long to roast.

2. Rinse turkey and pat dry. Combine 2 tablespoons *each* **soy sauce** and **dry sherry.** Rub this mixture over bird, inside and out. Set bird, breast down, on an oiled rack in a 10- by 15-inch pan.

3. Bake in a 375° oven until turkey back is slightly browned, about 20 minutes. Turn turkey breast up, and insert a thermometer to the bone in thickest part of breast.

Bake turkey until thermometer reaches 160°, 55 to 65 minutes, brushing several times with pan drippings.

4. Remove from oven, and let rest at least 10 minutes. Carve and serve.

Per serving, approximately 3 ounces cooked, skinned meat: 144 cal., 26% (38 cal.) from fat; 25 g protein; 4.2 g fat (1.4 g sat.); 0 g carbo.; 64 mg sodium; 67 mg chol.

An eau-de-vie (foreground) is always clear and intensely flavored by a fruit. Brandy in glass at left is amber color.

KEVIN CANDLAND

GREAT PRODUCTS

Western eaux-de-vie and more

For many years, I used Western brandy for cooking but rarely for sipping. About 10 years ago, Alsatian-born Jörg Rupf of St. George Spirits in Alameda, California, introduced me to the clear eau-de-vie—fruit brandy—he was distilling from pears. I saved it for cooking, too.

But now I sip with pleasure. These distilled liquors and liqueurs, including grappa and marc, have developed a level of refinement and variety that is attracting a great deal of attention. More than half a dozen producers are behind this evolution. And their wares, which have outranked their European counterparts in blind tastings, are found in good bottle shops.

Intensely fruity eaux-de-vie and experimental liqueurs that bridge wine-making and distillation are made by Bonny Doon Vineyard (also Ca' del Solo), Santa Cruz, California; Clear Creek Distillery, Portland; and Domaine Charbay Winery & Distillery, St. Helena, California; as well as St. George Spirits.

Most make a pear eau-de-vie. And they make other liqueurs as fruit supplies and inspiration dictate—from apricot, black walnut, marionberry, nectarine, orange muscat, persimmon, a prune-apricot-cherry blend, quince, raspberry, sour cherry, and Jerusalem artichokes (sunflower roots).

These liquids aren't inexpensive, and an occasional special issue or special decanter adds to the cost. Most eaux-de-vie and related liqueurs are available in half-bottles (375 ml.) for $15 to $45.

California wine brandies, also developing with admirable smoothness and complexity, are made by Carneros Alambic Distillery (Napa Valley), Domaine Charbay, Germain-Robin (Mendocino County), and St. George Spirits. Expect to pay $30 to $125 a bottle.

Candying citus peel

One reliable way to finish dishes with a twist of fresh elegance makes use of a very ordinary ingredient: orange peel. When you candy it yourself, the result is totally unlike the commercial candied peel used in fruitcakes, and candying is easy to do.

The peels of other orange- and yellow-skin citrus fruits also candy well, but lime peel doesn't—it turns brown and bitter.

Orange peel is my favorite, and I always keep a little jar of it in the refrigerator and dip out the glossy, translucent strands and liquid to scatter over tarts (fruit or chocolate), cheesecake, or cakes; over scoops of ice cream, bowls of berries, or fruit salads; onto segments of grapefruit and oranges; and even to embellish roasted chicken and other poultry, from turkey to quail.

Fresh Candied Peel

Cooking time: 25 to 30 minutes (includes blanching)

Prep time: About 10 minutes

Notes: Blanching gets rid of the bitterness in the peel. Use only the colored part of the peel, removing it with a vegetable peeler or using a food shredder for long strands. For a sauce, add the full amount of liqueur.

Makes: About ½ cup peel, 1 cup with liqueur

1. Using a vegetable peeler, pare ½ cup loosely packed peel (colored part only) from **oranges**, grapefruit, lemons, tangerines, or mandarins.

2. Stack several slices of peel at a time, and cut slices lengthwise into slivers ¹⁄₁₆ to ⅛ inch wide (or wider, depending upon how you want to use). Drop peel into boiling **water** to cover generously, and let boil about 1 minute. Drain. Repeat boiling step.

3. Ream 1 cup **juice** from pared fruit (use all or part orange juice with lemon peel—lemon juice alone is very sharp), and combine with 1 cup water in a 3- to 4-quart pan. Add peel and ½ cup sugar.

4. Boil on high heat, uncovered, until liquid has almost evaporated (to check, pull pan off the heat and let bubbles subside) and strands of peel look translucent and slightly darker in color, about 20 minutes. Watch carefully to avoid scorching.

5. With the pan off the heat (to avoid igniting fumes), add ½ cup **orange-flavor liqueur** such as Cointreau or curaçao to turn the mixture into a sauce and keep the peel from clumping. Or add just enough liqueur or additional citrus juice, 3 to 4 tablespoons, to keep strands from sticking together—the mixture thickens as it cools.

6. Use, or cover airtight and refrigerate up to 1 month.

Per tablespoon (with maximum liqueur): 37 cal., 0% (0 cal.) from fat; 0.1 g protein; 0 g fat (0 g sat) ; 7.2 g carbo.; 0.2 mg sodium; 0 mg chol.

Send letters to Food Guide, Sunset Magazine, 80 Willow Rd., Menlo Park, CA 94025; send e-mail to divecchioj@sunsetpub.com.

Raspberries, ice cream, and whipped cream are topped here with homemade candied orange peel.

BOB THOMPSON ON WINE: Something for everyone to celebrate

The French do not celebrate Thanksgiving with our exactitude, but their deep emotional attachment to the soil causes them to celebrate the harvest with banquets at least as grand as ours.

And so it is that one of the greatest Thanksgiving meals of my life unfolded there, not here. It happened a few days early, but not out of season. The food was worth a sonnet, but we must cut to the chase: the lessons that meal taught me about wine linger to this day.

The family that my wife and I were visiting lived in a fine old stone farmhouse near Cahors, well to the east of Bordeaux. The guest list was a Thanksgiving kind of guest list. It included Grandma, who lived at the top of the tower, our hosts, their adult son and daughter, the in-laws, a neighbor whose very important husband was marooned in Paris giving voice lessons, a retired diplomat and his wife, and two or three others whose exact connections remain obscure but who were just as companionable as the rest.

As the meal approached perfection in the kitchen, Papa began putting wine on the table: a local red made in part from his patch of Malbec, an obscure white Burgundy, a middling fancy claret, a California white in our honor, a rosé from the Midi, and the stunner, a Monbazillac, which is a sort of poor man's Sauternes, not quite as sweet and rich as the latter, but almost.

"Why the Monbazillac?" It seemed a legitimate question at the moment, prompted as it was by aromas of lamb filling every corner of a large house.

"Because," answered the host, looking around at the assembled company, "someone will like it."

Ah! It has been a lot of years since we sat down at that table, and I still give thanks for M. de Monpezat's honest wisdom. We live by it even when the crowd at our table is smaller and the meal simpler than that one.

In the Thanksgiving season, or any other time you are in the midst of putting on a rambling feast for family and friends, the ironclad, foolproof rule for choosing wine is Don't worry about the menu, study the guest list.

Incidentally, the Monbazillac was, Grandma conceded, quite acceptable with lamb, though she much preferred the claret. ∎

SPECIAL *Sunset* HOLIDAY SECTION

A GRAND THANKSGIVING OUT —OR IN

Let Western restaurants prepare your feast—or try their distinctly regional recipes at home

MARK RICHARDS

To family, friends, and a clean kitchen! Thanksgiving diners enjoy a traditional meal at the Lark Creek Inn, just north of San Francisco.

*T*HE FAMILY HAS GATHERED, DINNER LOOKS magnificent, and you haven't cooked a thing. What's more, nobody gets left with the dirty dishes.

If this is your idea of a perfect Thanksgiving, you're not alone. An increasing number of hotels, resorts, and restaurants are preparing dinner for home cooks who want a break. We joined their ranks last year and discovered innovative menu choices, regional twists on traditional favorites, and destinations worth planning a weekend around.

Because Thanksgiving away from home is growing in popularity, you need to make reservations as far ahead as possible (see page 251). If your top choices are already booked, start planning for next year. In the meantime, enjoy these restaurants' memorable regional recipes at home.

BY BETSY REYNOLDS BATESON • CHRISTINE WEBER HALE • ELAINE JOHNSON
FOOD PHOTOGRAPHY BY NOEL BARNHURST

240

Shiny yams are glazed in a reduction of apple juice, maple syrup, and molasses.

layer of syrup remains in bottom of pan, about 5 minutes longer.

4. Arrange yams on a serving dish; scrape syrup from pan and drizzle over yams. Season to taste with salt and pepper.

Per serving: 228 cal., 1.2% (2.7 cal.) from fat; 2.2 g protein; 0.3 g fat (0.1 g sat.); 55 g carbo.; 19 mg sodium; 0 mg chol.

Overnight Soft Herb Rolls

Cooking time: About 30 minutes

Prep time: About 30 minutes, plus about 45 minutes rising

Notes: Start these rolls 24 hours ahead, or knead and bake them all in one day.

Makes: 12 rolls

- 1 package active dry yeast
- ¼ cup cool (70°) water
- 3 tablespoons sugar
- 1 teaspoon salt
- 1 tablespoon *each* minced fresh parsley, dill, chives, and rosemary leaves (or use fresh parsley and substitute 1 teaspoon dried herb for each of the others)
- 2 tablespoons melted butter or margarine
- 1 large egg
- 1 cup milk or half-and-half
- 3½ to 3¾ cups bread flour or all-purpose flour
- 1 tablespoon lightly beaten egg

1. In a large bowl, sprinkle yeast over water. Let stand until dissolved, about 5 minutes. Stir in sugar, salt, parsley, dill, chives, rosemary, butter, whole egg, and milk, then stir in 3¼ cups flour until moistened.

2. Scrape dough onto a lightly floured board; knead until smooth, elastic, and no longer sticky, 12 to 15 minutes. Add flour as required to prevent sticking.

3. Shape dough into 12 equal balls; evenly space in a buttered 9- by 13-inch pan. Let rise as directed in next step, or if making

Herb-flecked golden rolls have a tender texture and rich flavor.

THE LARK CREEK INN
Larkspur, California

Imagine you have a grandmother who's a wonderful cook and lives in an elegant Victorian house with a huge dining room tucked into a redwood grove. That almost describes Thanksgiving at the Lark Creek Inn, except that chef Bradley Ogden's homestyle cooking seems modern. One other difference: most grandmothers don't serve 600 people.

The four-course dinner begins with a basket of fresh-baked rolls at your table and an American-style antipasto. For an entrée, most diners choose turkey from the oak-burning oven, with traditional trimmings like cranberry sauce and candied yams. But you can try an entrée like cedar-planked salmon with corn soufflé spoon bread or steak with skillet cheddar potatoes. Dessert offers multiple choices, too, from pumpkin pie with vanilla bean whipped cream to lighter fruit ices. —*E. J.*

Cranberry Sauce

Cooking time: About 15 minutes

Prep time: About 5 minutes

Makes: 3½ cups, 14 servings

- 6 cups (2 bags, 12 oz. each) fresh or frozen cranberries
- ⅔ cup granulated sugar
- ⅔ cup firmly packed brown sugar
- ½ cup orange juice
- 1 tablespoon lemon juice
- ⅛ teaspoon ground cinnamon
- 1 tablespoon vanilla

1. In a 2- to 3-quart pan over high heat, bring cranberries, granulated and brown sugars, orange and lemon juices, and cinnamon to simmering. Simmer uncovered, stirring occasionally, until cranberries are tender when pierced, 8 to 10 minutes.

2. Stir in vanilla; let cool. Serve, or chill airtight up to 1 week.

Per serving: 108 cal., 0.8% (0.9 cal.) from fat; 0.2 g protein; 0.1 g fat (0 g sat.); 27 g carbo.; 5 mg sodium; 0 mg chol.

Candied Yams

Cooking time: About 65 minutes

Prep time: About 20 minutes

Makes: 8 servings

- ⅓ cup apple juice
- 3 tablespoons firmly packed brown sugar
- 3 tablespoons maple syrup
- 2 tablespoons dark molasses
- ⅛ teaspoon *each* ground cinnamon and allspice
- 3 pounds yams or sweet potatoes, peeled and cut into ½-inch-thick diagonal slices
  Salt and pepper

1. In a rimmed 10- by 15-inch baking pan, combine apple juice, brown sugar, syrup, molasses, cinnamon, and allspice. Turn yams in mixture to coat, then arrange in a single layer, overlapping slightly.

2. Cover tightly and bake in a 375° oven 20 minutes. Turn yams over, then continue to bake, covered, until very tender when pierced, about 25 minutes longer.

3. Uncover yams and bake 15 minutes. Turn yams over and bake until only a thin

ahead, wrap airtight and chill up to 24 hours, then let rise.

4. Place pan in a warm place; let dough rise until double, 45 to 60 minutes. Brush with beaten egg; bake in a 350° oven until deep golden, 25 to 30 minutes.

Per roll: 199 cal., 19% (37 cal.) from fat; 6.4 g protein; 4.1 g fat (2 g sat.); 33 g carbo.; 224 mg sodium; 32 mg chol.

Apple Cider Sherbet

Prep time: About 35 minutes, plus at least 3 hours to firm in freezer

Notes: The Lark Creek Inn makes its sherbet with tart apple juice, part of which is boiled to concentrate. We've substituted, with good results, sweet apple juice and a little lemon. For the juice, reconstituted frozen gives a smoother texture; fresh provides a livelier flavor.

Makes: About 1½ quarts, 12 servings

 1 cup thawed frozen apple juice concentrate

 2 cups apple juice (fresh, or reconstituted from frozen concentrate)

 2 cups low-fat milk

 3 tablespoons lemon juice

1. In an ice cream maker, combine concentrate, apple juice, milk, and lemon juice. Freeze according to manufacturer's directions until softly frozen.

2. Wrap airtight and place in a freezer until firm enough to scoop, at least 3 hours.

3. Serve sherbet, or freeze airtight up to 1 week. If frozen solid, let stand at room temperature until softened, about 30 minutes.

Per serving: 76 cal., 7.1% (5.4 cal.) from fat; 1.5 g protein; 0.6 g fat (0.3 g sat.); 17 g carbo.; 28 mg sodium; 1.6 mg chol.

Pomegranate Ice

Cooking time: About 5 minutes
Prep time: About 40 minutes, plus at least 3 hours to firm in freezer

Notes: Look for unsweetened pomegranate juice in health-food stores. This beautiful ice with its vibrant flavor is especially good served with the apple sherbet (preceding).

Makes: About 1½ quarts, 12 servings

 2 cups sugar

 1 quart unsweetened pomegranate juice

1. In a 2- to 3-quart pan over high heat, stir sugar and 1 cup juice until sugar dissolves, about 5 minutes. Let cool, then combine with remaining juice and chill until cold (set pan in ice water to speed chilling).

2. Freeze mixture in an ice cream maker according to manufacturer's directions. Wrap airtight and place in freezer until firm enough to scoop, at least 3 hours or up to 1 week.

Per serving: 182 cal., 0% from fat; 0 g protein; 0 g fat; 47 g carbo.; 0.3 mg sodium; 0 mg chol.

TIMBERLINE LODGE
Timberline, Oregon

Since opening on Mount Hood in 1937, Timberline has served as the quintessential ski lodge and a monument to the skill of the Works Progress Administration craftspeople who created it. This national historic landmark is distinguished by hand-hewn beams, a 92-foot-high, 400-ton central stone chimney with walk-in-size fireplaces on two floors, and Native American and animal motifs in wood and iron.

Chef Leif Eric Benson is known for his regional expressions. Local fruits, salmon, and other Northwest ingredients figure prominently in his cooking. Diners might try roasted pork with berry demiglace, duckling with dried cherry sauce, or a traditional turkey dinner. To accommodate the 700 diners who come for Thanksgiving, tables spill out of the rustic Cascade Dining Room into the central fireplace area and the newer east wing. —*E. J.*

Fennel-Chestnut Soup

Cooking time: About 30 minutes
Prep time: About 15 minutes
Notes: You can substitute milk for the cream. The soup's texture will be lighter, so you won't be able to make decorative swirls on top.
Makes: 8 to 9 cups, 6 to 8 servings

 ½ cup *each* chopped onion and celery

 1½ cups chopped fresh fennel bulb

 (tops removed, a few tiny sprigs reserved)

 2 tablespoons butter or margarine

 ¼ cup all-purpose flour

 6 cups chicken broth

 1 can (about 1 lb.) unsweetened chestnut purée

 ¾ cup whipping cream or whole milk

 2 tablespoons dry sherry

 Salt and pepper

1. In a 3- to 4-quart pan over medium heat, frequently stir onion, celery, fennel bulb, and butter until vegetables are limp, 8 to 10 minutes. Add flour and stir 1 minute.

2. Stir in broth and purée, breaking up purée somewhat with a spoon. Bring to simmering; simmer, covered, 10 minutes to blend flavors.

3. Whirl mixture, part at a time, in a blender until smooth; return to pan. If making ahead, let cool, then chill airtight up to 2 days.

4. If using cream, set aside 1 tablespoon. Add remaining cream or all of milk to pan, along with sherry; whisk over medium-high heat just until simmering, 5 to 8 minutes.

5. Ladle soup into bowls. Drop remaining cream from spoon onto soup in patterns. Garnish with fennel sprigs; season to taste with salt and pepper.

Per serving: 192 cal., 56% (108 cal.) from

Light from the iron lamps and Columbia River basalt fireplace casts a golden glow over Thanksgiving tables in Timberline Lodge.

RICH IWASAKI

Fresh fennel and a swirl of cream decorate mellow-tasting chestnut soup.

fat; 4.6 g protein; 12 g fat (6.8 g sat.); 19 g carbo.; 162 mg sodium; 33 mg chol.

Roasted Pork Loin with Blackberry Demiglace

Cooking time: About 1¼ hours
Prep time: About 25 minutes
Makes: 8 servings

- ⅓ cup chopped onion
- ¼ cup chopped celery
- ¼ cup chopped carrot
- 1 tablespoon plus 2 teaspoons butter or margarine
- 2½ cups chicken broth
- 2 tablespoons tomato paste
- 1½ cups frozen blackberries, thawed (or use fresh berries)
- 2 tablespoons cornstarch
- 1 tablespoon raspberry vinegar
  Salt and pepper
- 4 cloves garlic, minced or pressed
- 1 tablespoon minced shallot
- 1 tablespoon chopped fresh rosemary leaves or 1 teaspoon dried rosemary
- 2 tablespoons red wine vinegar
- 1 tablespoon honey
- 1 teaspoon coarsely ground pepper
- 1 boned and tied pork loin (about 3 lb.), most of fat trimmed
  Fresh rosemary sprigs (optional)

1. Blackberry demiglace. In a 1- to 2-quart pan over medium heat, frequently stir onion, celery, carrot, and 1 tablespoon of the butter until vegetables are golden, 10 to 12 minutes.

2. Stir in 1¾ cups of the chicken broth and ½ tablespoon of the tomato paste. Simmer, covered, for 1 hour to blend flavors. Pour broth mixture through a fine strainer and return to pan.

3. Meanwhile, whirl blackberries in a blender until a smooth purée. Set a fine strainer over a bowl, and press berries through strainer to remove seeds.

4. To berries, stir in cornstarch and raspberry vinegar until smooth. Add berry mixture to broth mixture, and stir over high heat until bubbling. Season to taste with salt and pepper. If making ahead, chill airtight up to 2 days. Use hot.

5. Herb coating. In a 6- to 8-inch frying pan over medium-high heat, frequently stir garlic, shallot, and remaining 2 teaspoons butter until vegetables are golden, about 1 minute. Add remaining ¾ cup broth, and boil over high heat until reduced to ¼ cup, 5 to 7 minutes. Stir in chopped rosemary, red wine vinegar, honey, remaining 1½ tablespoons tomato paste, and coarsely ground pepper; then remove from heat.

6. Roasting. Place pork, fat side up, in a 9-by 13-inch pan and coat top, sides, and ends with herb coating. Roast in a 375° oven until a meat thermometer inserted in center of the thickest part reaches 150°, 50 to 60 minutes.

7. Serving. Transfer pork loin to a serving platter and let stand, lightly covered, for 10 minutes. Garnish pork roast with rosemary sprigs and serve with blackberry demiglace. Season roast to taste with salt and pepper.

Per serving: 341 cal., 45% (153 cal.) from fat; 36 g protein; 17 g fat (6.7 g sat.); 11 g carbo.; 173 mg sodium; 105 mg chol.

KASPAR'S RESTAURANT
Seattle

Thanksgiving dinner at Kaspar's Restaurant in the lower Queen Anne district offers relaxed dining, views of Puget Sound and the mountains, and superb Northwest regional cooking.

Chef-owner Kaspar Donier's starter choices for the buffet meal might be a squash tempura salad with sesame dressing, or roasted balsamic onions with prosciutto, dried tomatoes, and pine nuts.

Turkey will be the centerpiece, but you also might find salmon, duck, maple- and stout-glazed ham, and juniper-grilled beef with a trio of aïolis. Side dishes range from a roasted root salad to honey-glazed yams and country-style mashed potatoes.

Dessert choices are numerous. They might include ginger caramel custard, lemon mousse in almond lace cups, caramelized upside-down apple tart, and sour cream–poppy seed ice cream. —*C. W. H.*

Duck Breasts with Orange-Cranberry Sauce

Cooking time: About 35 minutes
Prep time: About 20 minutes
Notes: Duck smokes during browning; your kitchen should be well ventilated.
Makes: 6 servings

- 3 seedless oranges (1½ lb. total)
- 6 boneless duck breast halves (3 lb. total)

1 cup sake or dry Riesling

⅓ cup seasoned rice vinegar

⅓ cup chicken broth

⅓ cup dried cranberries

3 tablespoons honey

2 teaspoons minced fresh ginger

1 tablespoon cornstarch

1 tablespoon minced Italian parsley

Italian parsley sprigs (optional)

1. With a sharp knife, cut peels and outer white membranes from oranges. Cut between membranes to release segments; set segments aside.

2. Heat a 12- to 14-inch heavy frying pan over high heat. Add as many breast halves, skin side down, as will fit without crowding. Cook until skin is well browned and crispy, about 7 minutes. Turn over; brown other sides about 3 minutes, until just slightly pink in thickest part (cut to test).

3. Transfer browned breasts to a baking sheet. Cover with foil; keep warm in a 250° oven while browning remaining duck. Transfer remaining breasts to oven as browned to keep warm while preparing the sauce.

4. Pour off and discard fat from pan. To pan, add sake, rice vinegar, chicken broth, dried cranberries, honey, ginger, and cornstarch. Bring mixture to a boil over high heat, stirring occasionally, until sauce is reduced to 1½ cups, about 5 minutes. Stir in the minced parsley and reserved oranges.

5. If desired, cut duck crosswise into ½-inch slices and fan decoratively on individual plates, or serve duck breast halves on a large platter. Top with sauce; garnish with parsley sprigs.

Per serving: 384 cal., 33% (126 cal.) from fat; 30 g protein; 14 g fat (5.2 g sat.); 28 g carbo.; 351 mg sodium; 110 mg chol.

Roasted Root Vegetable Salad

Cooking time: About 1½ hours
Prep time: About 20 minutes
Notes: The fried horseradish topping is optional; make it on the day you serve.
Makes: 6 to 8 servings

    3 parsnips (1½ lb. total), peeled

    3 carrots (¾ lb. total), peeled

    3 beets (1½ lb. without greens), peeled

    1 celery root (¾ lb. without top), peeled

    3 onions (1½ lb. total), peeled

 2¼ cups olive or salad oil

    ¾ cup carrot juice

    1 teaspoon ground curry powder

    1 teaspoon Dijon mustard

    1 tablespoon seasoned rice vinegar

    ¼ pound peeled fresh horseradish, very thinly shredded (optional)

    Salt and pepper

1. Halve parsnips and carrots by cutting crosswise, then cut each half lengthwise in half. (Cut any large pieces in half again lengthwise.) Cut beets, celery root, and onions into 1½-inch-thick wedges.

2. Place all vegetables in an 11- by 17-inch roasting pan. Add ¼ cup of the oil and mix well. Bake in a 400° oven until vegetables are well browned and tender when pierced, about 1½ hours; stir occasionally. Cool to room temperature. If making ahead, cover and chill up to 1 day. Bring to room temperature before serving.

3. Carrot vinaigrette. Mix together 1 tablespoon of remaining oil, carrot juice, curry powder, mustard, and rice vinegar. If making ahead, cover and chill up to 1 day.

4. Fried horseradish. Heat remaining oil to 350° in a 2- to 3-quart pan on medium-high heat; maintain heat. Add ⅓ of the horseradish shreds; cook until golden brown and crispy, 25 to 35 seconds. Remove with a slotted spoon; drain on paper towels. Repeat to cook remaining horseradish. Season to taste with salt and pepper. If making ahead, cool completely, wrap airtight, and store at room temperature up to 6 hours.

5. To assemble the salad, pour vinaigrette onto a large, flat serving platter or into a large bowl. Arrange roasted vegetables decoratively over it. Sprinkle with horseradish.

Per serving: 228 cal., 36% (82 cal.) from fat; 3.8 g protein; 9.1 g fat (1.2 g sat.); 36 g carbo.; 163 mg sodium; 0 mg chol.

Kaspar's duck with cranberries, oranges, and sake sauce (top left) and roasted vegetables with fried horseradish wisps (above) give a new twist to the traditional meal.

Baked King Salmon with Corn and Sage Stuffing

Cooking time: About 1 hour and 10 minutes

Prep time: About 25 minutes

Notes: The baked cornhusks are optional; the salmon looks splendid with or without them.

Makes: 8 servings

- ⅔ pound very thinly sliced pancetta
- 6 cups chicken broth
- 1¾ cups polenta or cornmeal
- 3 cloves garlic, minced
- 1 tablespoon minced fresh sage leaves
- 4 ears of corn (about 2 lb. total), with husks
- 1 whole salmon (about 5 lb.), cleaned and boned, head and tail removed

Vegetable oil

Sage sprigs (optional)

1. Arrange pancetta slices in a single layer on 2 rimmed baking sheets. Bake in a 400° oven until lightly browned and slightly crisp, about 10 minutes. Coarsely chop half the slices; set pancetta aside. If making ahead, wrap airtight and chill up to 1 day.

2. In a 3- to 4-quart pan, combine broth, polenta, garlic, and minced sage. Bring to a boil over high heat, stirring often. Simmer, stirring often, until polenta thickens and tastes creamy and smooth, about 15 minutes (10 minutes for cornmeal).

3. Meanwhile, husk corn; reserve husks but discard silk. Cut kernels from corn; stir corn into polenta.

4. Lay salmon diagonally on a lightly oiled 10- by 15-inch baking sheet. Open fish so both cut sides face up. On one side, spread 3 cups of the polenta filling in an even layer. Overlap the whole pancetta slices on top of polenta filling. Fold opposite side of salmon over filling to cover.

5. Lightly brush top of fish with oil and lay cornhusks on top.

6. Stir chopped pancetta into remaining polenta, and spoon into a 2- to 3-quart baking dish; cover with foil.

7. Bake salmon and extra polenta in a 400° oven until salmon is 135° in the center of the thickest part, 15 to 20 minutes per inch of thickness (about 35 minutes total). Remove salmon from oven.

8. Uncover polenta in baking dish and broil 4 to 6 inches from heat until lightly browned, about 5 minutes.

9. To serve, gently remove cornhusks from salmon and line a serving platter with them. Gently slide fish onto platter. Garnish salmon and polenta with sage sprigs.

Per serving: 487 cal., 33% (162 cal.) from fat; 48 g protein; 18 g fat (3.9 g sat.); 33 g carbo.; 522 mg sodium; 115 mg chol.

STONEHOUSE
Montecito, California

Where do residents and visitors to the Santa Barbara area go for a stunning Thanksgiving dinner out? Almost unquestionably they head to the picturesque town of Montecito and the Stonehouse restaurant at the San Ysidro Ranch. Nestled in the foothills of the Santa Ynez Mountains, the 102-year-old ranch-turned-hotel offers the ultimate in rustic Western elegance. About 400 people enjoy their Thanksgiving feast in the restaurant's cozy wood- and stone-accented dining rooms.

Executive chef Gerard Thompson's innovative dishes might include butternut squash soup with berry-lentil fritters or a barbecued duck tamale on black bean sauce. The star, of course, is roasted turkey with all the trimmings. And with advance notice, you can order a whole turkey to carve at your table. Other options might include prime rib with smoked tomato-horseradish sauce, pork chops with cornbread stuffing, and vegetarian entrées.

For dessert, there's always a delicious version of pumpkin pie. Or you might enjoy chocolate semolina cake with mocha sorbet and chocolate sauce, or crêpes filled with fruit and honey-ginger mascarpone. —*C. W. H.*

Autumn Vegetables in Filo

Cooking time: About 1 hour

Prep time: About 30 minutes

Notes: The restaurant serves this as a meatless entrée with a truffle cream sauce. For home cooks, we've omitted the sauce and brushed a whiff of truffle-scented oil between filo layers.

Makes: 8 appetizer or 4 entrée servings

- 6 leeks (2¼ lb. total), root ends and tough parts trimmed, thinly sliced crosswise, and thoroughly rinsed
- 1 pound mushrooms, sliced
- ⅓ cup truffle or olive oil
- 1 jar (12 oz.) prepared roasted red peppers, drained and cut into ½-inch strips
- ¼ cup grated parmesan cheese
- 16 sheets (each 12 by 17 in., about 10 oz. total) filo

Italian parsley, for garnish (optional)

1. In a 12- to 14-inch frying pan, combine leeks, mushrooms, and 2 tablespoons of the oil over medium-high heat. Stir often until vegetables are golden brown, 20 to 25 minutes. Stir in red pepper strips and cheese. If making ahead, cool, cover, and chill up to 1 day. Drain off any excess liquid, and bring vegetables to room temperature before using.

2. Lay one sheet of filo on a flat surface; keep remaining filo tightly covered when not in use to prevent drying. Brush lightly with some of the remaining oil. Lay another sheet on top of the first; brush lightly with a little more oil.

Truffle-scented vegetables stuff a crisp, flaky filo wrapping.

3. Spoon ⅛ of the vegetable mixture on center of filo 3 inches in from a short edge. Fold short side of filo closest to filling over vegetables, then fold two longer sides over filling. Fold wrapped filling section over itself, and continue to do so until extending dough is completely wrapped around filling in a tight packet.

4. Repeat to make 7 more packets, using up all but 1 tablespoon oil.

5. Place packets, seam sides down, on a lightly oiled 12- by 15-inch baking sheet. Cut an X in the center of each packet, and gently bend back triangles of dough. Brush each packet lightly with remaining oil.

6. Bake in a 350° oven until golden brown, 30 to 35 minutes. Transfer to individual plates. Garnish with Italian parsley, if desired. Serve 1 packet for an appetizer, 2 for an entrée.

Per appetizer serving: 262 cal., 41% (108 cal.) from fat; 5.8 g protein; 12 g fat (2.1 g sat.); 32 g carbo.; 331 mg sodium; 2.4 mg chol.

Wild Green Salad with Pomegranate Vinaigrette

Cooking time: 10 minutes to toast nuts
Prep time: 20 minutes
Makes: 6 to 8 servings

- ¼ cup pomegranate juice concentrate (or ¾ cup pomegranate juice boiled until reduced to ¼ cup)
- ¼ cup olive or salad oil
- ¼ cup orange juice
- 3 tablespoons balsamic or red wine vinegar
- ½ teaspoon shredded lemon peel
- ¾ cup walnut halves
- 8 ounces salad mix, rinsed and crisped
- ½ cup (2¼ oz.) crumbled blue cheese
- ½ cup pomegranate seeds

  Salt and pepper

1. Whisk together pomegranate juice concentrate, oil, orange juice, vinegar, and lemon peel. If making ahead, cover and chill up to 2 days.

2. Spread nuts out in an 8- to 9-inch baking pan. Bake in a 350° oven until lightly toasted, about 10 minutes. Pour from pan; cool. If making ahead, package airtight and store at room temperature up to 1 day.

3. In a large bowl, gently mix salad greens with vinaigrette, then divide greens among 6 to 8 plates. Sprinkle equally with nuts, cheese, and pomegranate seeds. Add salt and pepper to taste.

Per serving: 182 cal., 74% (135 cal.) from fat; 3.6 g protein; 15 g fat (3 g sat.); 9.3 g carbo.; 125 mg sodium; 6.3 mg chol.

PATINA RESTAURANT
Los Angeles

Understatedly refined and quiet, Patina offers one of Los Angeles's most sophisticated Thanksgiving menus. This cornerstone of restaurateurs Christine and Joachim Splichal's culinary empire is just down the street from Paramount Studios and is popular in celebrity and movie circles.

Thanksgiving dinner might begin with a corn, acorn, and rock shrimp chowder, then move on to salmon and potato lasagne with shallot sauce or an autumn vegetable salad with chestnut dressing. Last Thanksgiving, entrées included roasted turkey with gingered yams—and for a change of pace, braised ham with caramelized mango, and whitefish with polenta and chanterelles. You'll savor the crumbleberry pie or roasted pears featured for dessert. If you can't decide on one dessert, a trilogy of pumpkin, apple, and pecan pies might fit the bill. —*C. W. H.*

Crumbleberry Pie

Cooking time: About 55 minutes
Prep time: About 45 minutes
Notes: Prepare the almond filling just before baking.
Makes: 12 servings

- 2¾ cups all-purpose flour
- 1⅓ cups sugar
- ⅛ teaspoon baking powder
- 1 cup plus 7 tablespoons butter or margarine
- 3 large eggs
- ½ teaspoon vanilla
- 1 cup finely ground blanched almonds
- 1 cup *each* blackberries, raspberries, and blueberries, rinsed and drained

  Vanilla ice cream (optional)

1. Sugar pastry. In a food processor or a bowl, whirl or stir together 1½ cups of the flour, ¼ cup of the sugar, and the baking powder. Whirl or cut in ½ cup (¼ lb.) of the butter until fine crumbs form. Whirl or mix in 1 egg until dough sticks together. Squeeze dough between fingers until it holds together. If making ahead, wrap airtight and chill up to 1 day.

2. Crumble topping. In a small bowl, mix 1 cup of the remaining flour and ½ cup of the remaining sugar. Using a pastry blender or your fingers, cut or rub 7 tablespoons butter and the vanilla into flour mixture until it resembles coarse crumbs. Squeeze dough together between fingers to make it stick together. If making ahead, wrap airtight and chill up to 1 day.

3. Almond filling. With an electric mixer, beat together remaining butter and sugar on high speed until blended. Beat in remaining 2 eggs, 1 at a time, until fluffy and well blended. Stir in remaining flour and the almonds just until evenly mixed.

4. To assemble pie, press sugar pastry onto bottom and up sides of a 9-inch pie pan; bring edges of crust flush with pan rim, and flute edges decoratively. Spread almond filling in pastry. Bake in a 350° oven until crust is lightly browned and filling is puffy, about 20 minutes.

5. Mix together berries and sprinkle over almond filling; press berries gently down into filling if necessary to anchor them. Break crumble topping into small chunks over berries. Return pie to oven and bake until crumble topping is lightly browned, about 35 more minutes. Serve warm or at room temperature with ice cream, if desired.

Per serving: 469 cal., 54% (252 cal.) from fat; 6.6 g protein; 28 g fat (15 g sat.); 50 g carbo.; 248 mg sodium; 113 mg chol.

Honey-roasted Pears with Armagnac Ice Cream

Cooking time: About 45 minutes
Prep time: About 35 minutes
Notes: Roast the pears so that they're done just before you sit down to dinner—they'll still be warm for dessert.
Makes: 8 servings

Streusel and a trio of berries top a rich almond filling and sweet pastry crust.

1 quart vanilla ice cream, softened

¼ cup armagnac or other brandy

4 firm-ripe pears (2 lb.), such as Bartlett, Bosc, or d'Anjou

¼ cup lemon juice

¼ cup (⅛ lb.) butter, melted

¼ cup honey

½ vanilla bean (about 3 inches long)

1 tablespoon *each* grated lemon and orange peel

¼ teaspoon *each* ground cinnamon, allspice, and nutmeg

Orange and lemon slices and mint leaves, for garnish

1. Armagnac ice cream. Stir together ice cream and armagnac until well blended. Cover and freeze until serving time, up to 3 days ahead.

2. Pears. Halve, peel, and core pears. Immediately sprinkle with 2 tablespoons lemon juice to prevent browning.

3. In a 9- by 13-inch baking pan, mix together remaining juice, butter, and honey. Slit vanilla bean lengthwise, and scrape seeds into butter mixture. Stir in grated lemon and orange peels, cinnamon, allspice, and nutmeg.

A glistening pear half, roasted with honey and spices, is the perfect foil for brandy-spiked ice cream.

4. With a small, sharp knife, score the rounded portion of each pear half diagonally ⅛ inch deep in one direction, then in opposite direction, to create a diamond pattern. Place pears cut side down in baking pan. Spoon some of the butter mixture over them.

5. Bake in a 350° oven, basting often with pan juices, until very tender when pierced, 40 to 45 minutes. Arrange warm pears on individual plates; garnish with orange and lemon slices and mint. Serve with armagnac ice cream.

Per serving: 302 cal., 42% (126 cal.) from fat; 2.9 g protein; 14 g fat (8.2 g sat.); 41 g carbo.; 116 mg sodium; 45 mg chol.

THE ARIZONA KITCHEN
The Wigwam Resort, Litchfield Park, Arizona

Imagine a setting of adobe buildings connected by walkways lined with palms, orange trees, and flowers, and you'll begin to visualize the Wigwam Resort, which is located about 17 miles west of downtown Phoenix. An open kitchen warms the Arizona Kitchen restaurant, where tables are laid with colorful woven place mats, pottery dinnerware, and blue-tinted Mexican glassware. Sonoran Desert foods have been integrated into the menu.

Turkey medallions with cranberry–ancho chili sauce is a menu favorite. Other entrées include roasted pheasant stuffed with wild rice and quinoa and glazed with chipotle-pomegranate honey; filet mignon in a prickly pear–Merlot sauce; and buffalo sirloin in a chili negro sauce. —*B. R. B.*

Turkey Medallions with Cranberry–Ancho Chili Sauce

Cooking time: About 40 minutes

Prep time: About 30 minutes, plus at least 1 hour for moistening cranberries

Makes: 4 servings

1 cup dried cranberries

3 tablespoons tequila

2 tablespoons olive or salad oil

1 onion (6 oz.), minced

3 cloves garlic, minced

¾ cup dry sherry

1 dried ancho chili, chopped, with stem removed

2 teaspoons minced fresh parsley

1½ teaspoons pepper

1 teaspoon minced fresh thyme leaves

½ teaspoon minced fresh rosemary leaves

1 quart chicken broth

1 tablespoon cornstarch

4 turkey tenderloins (each 6 oz.)

¼ cup all-purpose flour

About ½ teaspoon salt

1 cup (¼ lb.) shredded jalapeño jack cheese

½ cup (2 oz.) shredded parmesan cheese

Fresh cilantro sprigs (optional)

Tequila-laced dried cranberries top turkey medallions with cranberry-chili sauce.

1. Mince ½ cup of the cranberries; set aside. In a small jar with lid, combine the tequila and remaining cranberries; shake jar, and let cranberries moisten at least 1 hour or up to 2 days.

2. To a 5- to 6-quart pan over high heat, add 1 tablespoon of the oil. When hot, add onion and garlic. Cook, stirring, until golden brown, about 5 minutes.

3. Add reserved minced cranberries, ½ cup of the sherry, chili, parsley, 1 teaspoon of the pepper, thyme, and rosemary; stir until liquid evaporates. Add chicken broth; simmer over medium heat until reduced to 3 cups, about 20 minutes.

4. Mix cornstarch with 1 tablespoon water. Slowly whisk mixture into cranberry sauce, and bring sauce to a boil; boil 1 minute.

Strain sauce through a fine wire strainer. Keep sauce warm in a double boiler. (Or if making ahead, cool, cover, and chill up to 2 days. Reheat before serving.)

5. Cut each tenderloin in half crosswise. In a gallon-size plastic bag, combine flour, ½ teaspoon salt, and remaining ½ teaspoon pepper. Add turkey pieces to bag; shake to coat all sides. Remove from bag, shaking off excess flour.

6. Heat remaining tablespoon oil in a 10- to 12-inch frying pan over high heat. When hot, add turkey; sauté until well browned on all sides, 6 to 8 minutes. Set browned turkey pieces in a 10- by 15-inch baking pan. Discard excess fat from frying pan, then deglaze drippings with remaining sherry; reduce to 1 tablespoon over high heat. Add pan drippings to cranberry–ancho chili sauce.

7. Sprinkle jack and parmesan cheeses equally on top of browned turkey medallions. Broil 6 inches from heat until slightly pink when cut in thickest portion and cheese begins to bubble, 3 to 4 minutes.

8. Add salt to taste to cranberry–ancho chili sauce. Pour ⅓ cup warm sauce into the center of each of 4 warm dinner plates. Place 2 turkey medallions on sauce on each plate. Sprinkle tequila-soaked cranberries equally over servings. Garnish with cilantro sprigs; offer remaining sauce to add as desired.

Per serving: 637 cal., 34% (216 cal.) from fat; 59 g protein; 24 g fat (9.6 g sat.); 42 g carbo.; 897 mg sodium; 145 mg chol.

THE FORT
Morrison, Colorado

The Fort, perched atop red rock about 20 miles southwest of Denver, is a step back in time to the early 19th century. Here, owner Sam Arnold has constructed a full-size adobe replica of Bent's Fort, the state's first fur-trading post in southeastern Colorado. Upon arrival, you step through massive wooden doors into a courtyard with adobe beehive fireplaces before entering the restaurant area, which is divided into cozy seating areas in which about 900 people enjoy Thanksgiving dinner each year.

You might want to start with one of the mountain-inspired appetizers: roasted buffalo marrow bones, Rocky Mountain oysters, or buffalo tongue. Then there's turkey with all the fixings, or you can order from the regular menu, which offers buffalo and other game in addition to more conventional entrées. —*B. R. B.*

Zuni Pueblo–style Succotash

Cooking time: About 10 minutes
Prep time: 5 minutes
Makes: 8 servings

- 1 pound thawed frozen white or yellow corn kernels
- 2 packages (10 oz. each) thawed frozen baby or regular lima beans
- ¼ cup chicken broth or dry white wine
- 1 cup (about 4½ oz.) hulled, roasted, and salted sunflower seeds
- 1 cup (7 oz. can) diced green chilies
- ½ cup chopped prepared roasted red peppers

Sunflower seeds, chilies, and roasted red peppers flavor Southwestern succotash.

Fresh Italian parsley sprigs (optional)

Salt and pepper

1. To a 10- to 12-inch nonstick frying pan over medium-high heat, add corn, lima beans, and broth. Cover, and cook until hot and most liquid has evaporated, about 10 minutes. Stir in sunflower seeds, green chilies, and red peppers.

2. Spoon succotash onto a serving platter and garnish with parsley. Offer salt and pepper to add to taste.

Per serving: 244 cal., 32% (78 cal.) from fat; 11 g protein; 8.7 g fat (0.9 g sat.); 35 g carbo.; 212 mg sodium; 0 mg chol.

The Anasazi Restaurant in Santa Fe serves more than 550 meals on Thanksgiving, and you don't have to have turkey.

DOUG MILNER

THE ANASAZI RESTAURANT
Inn of the Anasazi, Santa Fe

Desert-colored walls, carved timbers, and locally woven fabrics reflect the Southwestern focus of the inn's comfortable dining room. And Southwestern flavors dominate the imaginative menu, known for an inspired combination of Native American, New Mexican, and cowboy fare.

Your first-course Thanksgiving choices might include a savory pumpkin soup with swirled cinnamon-maple cream topping. Roasted young turkey with acorn squash and chorizo-cornbread stuffing or

A savory chorizo-cornbread dressing is baked in acorn squash.

Taos honey-glazed salmon with fennel mashed potatoes could be among the entrées. Look for desserts like chocolate torte with raspberry sauce, light-as-air custard, and apple crisp, all dusted with tiny, edible flower petals. —*B. R. B.*

Chorizo-Cornbread Dressing in Acorn Squash

Cooking time: About 1½ hours
Prep time: About 45 minutes
Notes: If only smoked chorizo is available, peel off casings and mince.
Makes: 12 servings

½ pound raw chorizo or hot Italian sausage

1 pound baked cornbread, cut into 1-inch chunks

6 cups (about ½ lb.) coarsely chopped day-old white bread

1 red onion (¾ lb.), diced

1 cup chopped parsley

½ cup chopped celery

1 jalapeño chili (1 oz.), stemmed and minced

1 tablespoon minced fresh sage leaves, plus whole leaves for garnish

1 tablespoon grated lime peel

4 cups chicken broth

3 large eggs

½ teaspoon *each* salt and pepper

3 acorn squash (each about 2 lb.), cut into halves, seeds removed (optional)

1. Remove chorizo casings; crumble sausage into an 8- to 10-inch nonstick frying pan. Over medium-high heat, cook chorizo, using a spoon to break into small pieces; drain on paper towels.

2. In a large bowl, combine cooked chorizo, cornbread, white bread, onion, parsley, celery, jalapeño, minced sage, and lime peel. Whisk together broth, eggs, salt, and pepper. Pour broth mixture over chorizo-bread mixture; gently mix just until ingredients are moistened and combined.

3. Spoon about 1 cup of the chorizo-cornbread dressing into each squash half. Place stuffed squash in a 10- by 15-inch baking pan. Add ½ cup water to pan; cover pan with foil. Place remaining dressing in a lightly buttered 1½- to 2-quart baking dish; cover with foil. Bake both dishes in a 400° oven, about 45 minutes for dressing in dish, about 1 hour and 15 minutes for dressing-stuffed squash, until squash are tender when pierced with a fork. Remove foil from each dish; continue to bake until dressing is golden on top, about 15 more minutes.

(If you'd prefer, omit squash and spoon all of the dressing into a lightly buttered 3- to 3½-quart baking dish; cover with foil and bake until hot throughout, about 1 hour. Uncover and continue baking until golden on top, about 20 minutes longer.)

4. To serve squash, cut cooked filled halves in half again; arrange on a serving platter. Serve additional dressing as desired from baking dish. Garnish with sage leaves.

Per ¼ stuffed squash: 197 cal., 24% (47 cal.) from fat; 6.5 g protein; 5.2 g fat (1.6 g sat.); 34 g carbo.; 344 mg sodium; 44 mg chol.

Per 1 cup dressing without squash: 256 cal., 35% (90 cal.) from fat; 10 g protein; 10 g fat (3.1 g sat.); 32 g carbo.; 678 mg sodium; 87 mg chol.

Pumpkin-Chili Soup

Cooking time: About 40 minutes

Prep time: About 25 minutes

Notes: We've adapted this recipe for home cooks.

Makes: 8 servings

    1   leek (¾ lb.)
    1   fresh poblano chili (3 oz.)
    1   dried ancho chili (¾ oz.)
    1   tablespoon olive or salad oil
    6   cups chicken or vegetable broth
    ½   cup sour cream
    1½ teaspoons *each* fresh lime juice
        and maple syrup
    ¼   teaspoon ground cinnamon
    1   can (16 oz.) pumpkin
    ¼   cup honey
    1   tablespoon *each* minced fresh
        sage and thyme leaves
        Salt and pepper
        Cilantro sprigs

1. Trim root end of leek and tough parts of green tops, and discard; use only very tender green section. Slice leek crosswise into 1-inch pieces; pull layers apart and rinse away grit. Rinse poblano and ancho chilies; remove and discard stems. Cut both chilies open; rinse out seeds. Chop separately.

2. To a 5- to 6-quart pan over high heat, add oil. When hot, add leek and poblano chili. Sauté vegetables until tinged brown, about 5 minutes; add ancho chili during the last minute. Add broth, cover, and simmer to blend flavors, about 30 minutes.

3. In a small bowl, combine sour cream, lime juice, maple syrup, and cinnamon; chill until ready to use, up to 4 hours.

4. In a food processor or blender, purée vegetables and broth, pumpkin, honey, sage, and thyme until smooth. (If making ahead, chill covered up to 2 days.) Return purée to pan; heat over medium-high heat until hot. Season to taste with salt and pepper. Ladle equally into 8 soup bowls; garnish with a swirl of cinnamon-maple cream and cilantro.

Per serving: 143 cal., 45% (65 cal.) from fat; 4.3 g protein; 7.2 g fat (2.9 g sat.); 21 g carbo.; 102 mg sodium; 6.3 mg chol.

Planning your THANKSGIVING OUT

At MOST OF THESE PLACES YOU'LL NEED TO ACT QUICKLY TO SECURE A reservation for this year—or start thinking now about next year. Prices are exclusive of wine, tax, and tip unless noted.

Arizona

The Arizona Kitchen, the Wigwam Resort, 300 E. Indian School Rd., Litchfield Park (17 miles west of downtown Phoenix); (602) 935-3811. Dinner is served from 5 to 10:30; entrées $17 to $26, appetizers and salads $5 to $13. In addition to the Arizona Kitchen, the Terrace Dining Room serves Thanksgiving dinner (fixed price) from noon to 10; $28.50, $15 ages 6 through 11. Also available, a Thanksgiving package (four nights) at $783 per person, double occupancy. Nightly rates are $230 to $360.

California

The Lark Creek Inn, 234 Magnolia Ave., Larkspur (15 miles north of San Francisco); (415) 924-7766. A four-course Thanksgiving dinner is served from noon to 8; $60, $27.50 ages 10 and under. The restaurant began taking Thanksgiving reservations October 1. It is usually booked within a week. If you can't get in on Thanksgiving Day, a dinner with traditional Thanksgiving flavors is a menu option ($27.50) the Monday, Tuesday, and Wednesday of that week.

Patina Restaurant, 5955 Melrose Ave., Los Angeles; (213) 467-1108. Dinner is served from 3 to 9; about $45. Reservations for prime hours (6 to 8) begin to book up at least a month in advance.

Stonehouse at the San Ysidro Ranch, 900 San Ysidro Lane, Montecito (10 minutes south of Santa Barbara); (800) 368-6788. Dinner is served from 11 to 3; about $48 for a three-course menu. Reservations are accepted as early as six months ahead. The San Ysidro Ranch offers 21 cottages with 44 guest rooms and suites, each with a wood-burning fireplace or stove, a minibar, a video player, coffee service, and a private sun deck. Thirteen cottages have private outdoor whirlpool baths. Nightly rates are $235 to $750.

Colorado

The Fort, 19192 State Highway 8, just off W. Hampden Ave. (U.S. 285S), Morrison (20 miles southwest of Denver); (303) 697-4771, or fax (303) 697-4786. Dinner is served from noon to 7:30. The special Thanksgiving dinner costs $16.95, $8.95 ages 11 and under. You can also order from the regular à la carte menu. Entrées cost $14 to $29.

New Mexico

The Anasazi Restaurant, Inn of the Anasazi, 113 Washington Ave. (in downtown Santa Fe); (505) 988-3236. Dinner is served from 11 to 9:30; $44.95 for a four-course meal, $18 ages 12 and under. Dinner hours are booked months ahead, but there's the chance of a spot before 3 or after 8:30 as late as three weeks ahead. Rooms at the inn range from $239 to $399 per night.

Oregon

Timberline Lodge, Timberline (about 60 miles east of Portland). Dinner is served from 1 to 8; $27.95 (gratuity included), $11.95 ages 3 through 11. Priority for dinner reservations goes to lodge guests. Timberline began taking reservations from nonguests September 15. Peak dining times (4 to 7) begin to fill two months ahead. To spend Thanksgiving at Timberline, start planning now for next year; all 70 rooms are generally booked by early summer. Decor is mountain rustic; eight rooms have fireplaces. Rates range from $60 to $160. Amenities include a swimming pool, spa, and sauna. Call (800) 547-1406 for room reservations. For dinner reservations and other information, call (503) 272-3311, or write to Timberline Lodge, Timberline Ski Area, Timberline, OR 97028.

Washington

Kaspar's Restaurant, 19 W. Harrison St., Seattle; (206) 298-0123. Thanksgiving dinner is served from 1 to 6; the buffet dinner costs about $28, about $14 ages 4 through 12. Reservations can be made as early as three months ahead. ■

A Home-Cooked Feast in 5 Hours

Shopping and preparation are easier with our grocery list and step-by-step countdown to dinner

IF A HECTIC SCHEDULE ALLOWS THANKSGIVING to sneak up on you this year, or if you've been dreading the time it takes to plan and cook the holiday meal, don't worry. This menu is designed for just such situations. It's impressive enough to dazzle guests, but one person can prepare this dinner for 6 to 8 (at a relatively relaxed pace) in only 5 hours with no advance cooking.

Just think—on Thanksgiving Day you can sleep until 10 and still have your meal on the table by midafternoon. Simply decide what time you want to eat, count back 5 hours, and follow the timetable on page 254. You need to do only two things ahead of time: read recipes thoroughly, and shop two or three days in advance.

BY CHRISTINE WEBER HALE AND LINDA LAU ANUSASANANAN

KEVIN CANDLAND

Thanksgiving Dinner

- Honey-basted Turkey with Roasted Vegetables
- Giblet Gravy
- Herb and Garlic Mashed Potatoes
- Brown Rice and Sausage Dressing
- Spinach Salad with Pears and Cranberries
- Pumpkin Sundaes (pictured on page 256)

How to do it: *step-by-step*

MEAT:
- 1 **turkey** (13 to 15 lb.), fresh or frozen
- ¾ pound **mild Italian sausage**

PRODUCE:
- 6 **yellow onions** (2¾ lb. total)
- 3 **red onions** (1½ lb. total)
- 4 **red bell peppers** (2 lb. total), or 2 red plus 2 yellow or orange
- 1½ pounds **peeled carrots**, 2 to 3 inches long
- 3 bunches **Italian parsley**
- 2 **carrots** (½ lb. total)
- 1 head **celery**
- 2 heads **garlic**
- 3½ pounds **russet potatoes**
- 2 bunches **chives**
- Fresh herbs—1 bunch *each* **rosemary, thyme,** and **oregano** (optional)
- 1 pound **mushrooms**

- 2 to 3 **oranges** (1½ lb. total), for peel and juice
- 2 firm-ripe (¾ lb. total) **pears**
- 1 pound (4 qt.) packaged rinsed **baby spinach** leaves, or regular spinach

CANNED GOODS AND MISCELLANEOUS:
- 1 large (49½ oz.) and 2 small (14½ oz.) cans **chicken broth**
- 4⅔ cups (14 oz. package) **dried precooked brown rice**
- ⅓ cup **dried cranberries**
- 1 can (16 oz.) **pumpkin**
- **Caramel ice cream topping** (about ¾ cup)
- ¼ cup **pecans**

DAIRY PRODUCTS:
- 2 packages (4 to 5 oz. each) **reduced-fat garlic and herb–flavor Boursin** or Rondelé **cheese**

FROZEN FOODS:
- 2 packages (10 oz. each) **frozen chopped Swiss chard**
- 1½ quarts **vanilla reduced-fat ice cream** or frozen yogurt

ITEMS YOU MAY HAVE ON HAND:
- 2 tablespoons **olive** or salad **oil**
- ¼ cup **honey**
- ¼ cup **balsamic** or red wine **vinegar**
- ½ teaspoon ground **cinnamon**
- ½ cup **dry white wine**
- ½ teaspoon **pepper**
- ⅓ cup **cornstarch**
- **Salt**
- ½ cup **seasoned rice vinegar**
- 1 tablespoon **pumpkin pie spice**
- 2 tablespoons **rum** or brandy
- ½ cup **sugar**

AS LONG AS 3 DAYS AHEAD:
- **Shop for all ingredients.** (Buy a frozen turkey at least 2 days ahead and begin thawing in refrigerator, or **purchase a fresh turkey** 1 to 2 days ahead.)

THANKSGIVING DAY: 5 HOURS BEFORE SERVING
- **Prepare sundaes;** freeze in glasses.
- **Make pecan brittle** for sundaes.

4 HOURS AHEAD:
- **Remove** turkey giblets. **Rinse** turkey, pat dry, and return to refrigerator. **Cook** giblets and vegetables in broth.

3½ HOURS AHEAD:
- **Prepare and cook sausages and vegetables for dressing.** Cover and chill until ready to use.
- **Thaw Swiss chard** in a microwave oven, or place in colander and pour hot water over chard; reserve until ready to use.

2¾ HOURS AHEAD:
- **Place turkey** in roasting pan, **insert** meat thermometer, and brush with oil. **Prepare vegetables;** arrange around turkey.

2½ HOURS AHEAD:
- **Begin roasting turkey and garlic** for mashed potatoes.

1¾ HOURS AHEAD:
- **Remove garlic** from oven; let cool.
- **Strain** broth and chop giblets. **Measure broth;** if necessary, add water to make 4 cups.
- **Make gravy;** keep warm over very low heat.

1½ HOURS AHEAD:
- **Peel and chop potatoes;** begin steaming.

1 HOUR AHEAD:
- **Prepare salad dressing.**

50 MINUTES AHEAD:
- **Brush turkey** with honey glaze.
- **Bring broth-mushroom mixture for dressing to a boil.** Add chard and rice; simmer until tender. Remove from heat; cover to keep warm.

30 MINUTES AHEAD:
- **Mash potatoes** in pan with cheese and garlic. Remove from heat; cover to keep warm.

20 MINUTES AHEAD:
- **Remove turkey from oven;** place on platter. Let stand.
- **Brown vegetables under broiler;** arrange decoratively around turkey.
- **Skim fat** from pan juices; broil juices down if necessary. Brush half over turkey and vegetables; stir rest into gravy.

IMMEDIATELY BEFORE SERVING:
- **Bring gravy back to a boil** and transfer to serving container.
- **Transfer potatoes and dressing** to serving dishes, and garnish; garnish turkey platter.
- **Mix salad dressing with spinach.**

15 TO 20 MINUTES BEFORE SERVING DESSERT:
- **Remove sundaes from freezer.** Just before serving, garnish with pecan brittle.

Recipes

Oven-roasted Turkey

Turkey weight with giblets	Oven temp.	Internal temp.*	Cooking time**
10 to 13 lb.	350°	160°	1½ to 2¼ hr.
14 to 23 lb.	325°	160°	2 to 3 hr.
24 to 27 lb.	325°	160°	3 to 3¾ hr.
28 to 30 lb.	325°	160°	3½ to 4½ hr.

* Insert thermometer through thickest part of breast to bone.

** Add 30 to 50 minutes to cooking time for a stuffed, oven-roasted turkey.

Honey-basted Turkey with Roasted Vegetables

Cooking time: About 2½ hours
Prep time: About 30 minutes
Makes: 6 to 8 servings with leftovers

- 1 turkey, 13 to 15 pounds
- 1 tablespoon olive or salad oil
- 2 unpeeled yellow onions (1 lb. total), halved lengthwise
- 2 unpeeled red onions (1 lb. total), halved lengthwise
- 4 red bell peppers (2 lb. total) or 2 red plus 2 yellow or orange bell peppers, stemmed, seeded, and halved lengthwise
- 1½ pounds peeled carrots (2 to 3 in. long)
- ¼ cup honey
- ¼ cup balsamic or red wine vinegar
- ½ teaspoon ground cinnamon
- Italian parsley sprigs (optional)

1. Remove and discard leg truss from turkey; pull off and discard lumps of fat. Remove giblets and neck; reserve for Giblet Gravy (recipe follows). Rinse bird inside and out; pat dry, wrap airtight, and return to refrigerator until ready to roast. Start preparing Giblet Gravy.

2. When ready to roast, place turkey, breast up, on a V-shaped rack in a 12- by 17-inch roasting pan. Insert a meat thermometer straight down through thickest part of breast to touch bone. Brush turkey with oil.

3. Tuck onions, peppers, and carrots around and under turkey. Place pan on lowest oven rack. Roast in a 325° oven until vegetables are very tender when pierced and thermometer registers 160°, 1¾ to 2½ hours; occasionally baste turkey and vegetables with pan juices (and juices inside bird cavity).

4. Mix together honey, vinegar, and cinnamon. When turkey reaches 150°, 20 to 30 minutes before estimated finish time, brush honey mixture over turkey and vegetables.

5. Transfer turkey to a serving board or platter; let stand 20 minutes. Remove V-shaped rack; spread vegetables out in pan. Return pan to oven; broil vegetables 6 to 8 inches from heat until well browned in spots. Drain pan juices from vegetables; arrange decoratively around turkey.

6. Skim off and discard fat from pan juices. (If more than ⅓ cup juices, return juices to pan and broil in oven until reduced to ⅓ cup.) Brush half of pan juices over turkey and vegetables; stir remainder into gravy (recipe follows). Garnish turkey and vegetables with parsley.

Per serving: 503 cal., 32% (162 cal.) from fat; 52 g protein; 18 g fat (4.9 g sat.); 33 g carbo.; 162 mg sodium; 140 mg chol.

Giblet Gravy

Cooking time: About 2¼ hours
Prep time: About 20 minutes
Makes: 4 to 5 cups

- Giblets and neck from a 13- to 15-pound turkey
- 2 yellow onions (¾ lb. total), quartered
- 2 carrots (½ lb. total), cut into chunks
- ¾ cup sliced celery
- 5 cups chicken broth
- ½ cup dry white wine
- ½ teaspoon pepper
- ⅓ cup cornstarch
- Salt

1. Rinse giblets, and cut neck into 3 or 4 sections; chill liver airtight to add later, or discard. Combine remaining giblets, neck pieces, onions, carrots, celery, and 1 cup of the broth in a 5- to 6-quart pan over high heat. Boil, uncovered, stirring often as liquid evaporates; cook until giblets and vegetables are browned and browned bits stick to pan, about 20 minutes.

2. Add remaining broth, wine, and pepper to pan; stir to scrape browned bits free. Cover pan; simmer gently until gizzard is tender when pierced, about 1½ hours. If desired, add liver and cook 10 minutes.

3. Pour broth through a fine strainer into a bowl. Discard vegetables; save giblets for gravy. Pull meat off neck; finely chop neck meat and giblets. Measure broth. If needed, add water to make 4 cups.

4. To make gravy, mix cornstarch with ¼ cup water in the pan until smooth. Add broth and finely chopped giblets. Stir over high heat until boiling, about 5 minutes. Add salt to taste. Cover pan. Keep gravy warm over low heat until serving time; stir in remaining pan juices from turkey. Return to a boil just before serving.

Per ½-cup serving: 107 cal., 30% (32 cal.) from fat; 11 g protein; 3.5 g fat (1.1 g sat.); 8 g carbo.; 105 mg sodium; 75 mg chol.

Herb and Garlic Mashed Potatoes

Cooking time: About 40 minutes, plus 40 minutes roasting time for garlic
Prep time: About 25 minutes
Makes: 6 to 8 servings

- 2 heads garlic, cut in half crosswise through cloves
- 1 tablespoon oil
- 3½ pounds russet potatoes
- 2 packages (4 to 5 oz. each) reduced-fat garlic and herb–flavor Boursin or Rondelé cheese
- About ½ cup hot chicken broth or low-fat milk
- ⅓ cup minced chives
- Whole chives (optional)
- Mixed fresh herb sprigs such as rosemary, thyme, and oregano (optional)

1. Brush cut sides of garlic with oil; place garlic, cut sides down, on a 4- by 10-inch sheet of doubled heavy foil. Fold up edges of foil to form a shallow pan. Place garlic in oven alongside turkey; bake until golden brown on bottom and very soft when squeezed, 40 to 45 minutes.

2. Remove roasted garlic from oven; let cool. Squeeze or pluck cloves from 3 head halves. Leave other half-head whole; set garlic aside.

3. Peel potatoes; cut into chunks. Place on a rack set over ¾ to 1 inch water in a 5- to 6-quart pan. Cover pan; bring water to a boil over high heat. Boil gently until potatoes mash very easily, about 30 minutes.

4. Drain potatoes; remove rack from pan. Add loose garlic cloves and cheese to potatoes in pan. Mash with a masher or an electric mixer. Add as much broth as needed while mashing to make mixture smooth and creamy.

5. Stir in minced chives; cover to keep warm. Immediately before serving, spoon into a large serving bowl. Garnish with remaining half-head of roasted garlic, whole chives, and herb sprigs.

Per serving: 254 cal., 23% (59 cal.) from fat; 9.2 g protein; 6.6 g fat (3 g sat.); 40 g carbo.; 231 mg sodium; 11 mg chol.

Brown Rice and Sausage Dressing

Cooking time: About 30 minutes
Prep time: About 15 minutes
Makes: 12 cups, about 12 servings

¾ pound mild Italian sausage

1 pound mushrooms, thinly sliced

2 yellow onions (1 lb. total), thinly sliced

3¼ cups chicken broth

2 packages (10 oz. each) frozen chopped Swiss chard, thawed

4⅔ cups (14 oz. package) dried precooked brown rice

Chopped parsley

1. Remove and discard sausage casings.

Crumble sausage into a 5- to 6-quart pan; stir often over high heat until it browns, about 5 minutes. Drain off and discard fat. Add mushrooms and onions; stir often until mushrooms begin to brown, 15 to 20 minutes. Cover and chill until ready to use.

2. To finish preparing dressing, add broth to mushroom mixture; bring to a boil. Press excess liquid from thawed chard; add chard and rice to broth. Return to boil, cover, and simmer over low heat until rice is tender, about 5 minutes. Remove from heat; cover to keep warm. Just before serving, spoon into a serving dish and sprinkle with parsley.

KEVIN CANDLAND

Pumpkin sundaes are made with vanilla ice cream, canned pumpkin, and sweet spices. Rum-spiked caramel sauce and shards of pecan brittle are the toppings.

Spinach Salad with Pears and Cranberries

Prep time: About 20 minutes

Notes: For a shortcut, use packaged rinsed baby spinach.

Makes: 6 to 8 servings

- 1 teaspoon finely shredded orange peel
- ½ cup orange juice
- ½ cup seasoned rice vinegar
- ⅓ cup dried cranberries
- 2 firm-ripe (¾ lb. total) pears
- ¾ cup thinly sliced red onion, rinsed
- 1 pound (4 quarts) packaged rinsed baby spinach leaves or regular spinach leaves, rinsed and crisped, in bite-size pieces

To make salad dressing, combine orange peel, orange juice, seasoned rice vinegar, and dried cranberries. Core and thinly slice pears; add pears and onion to dressing. Just before serving, pour dressing over spinach; gently mix.

Pumpkin Sundaes

Cooking time: About 8 minutes

Prep time: About 15 minutes, plus at least 2 hours for freezing

Notes: Use purchased nut brittle as a shortcut. If you prefer, brittle can be made up to 2 days ahead. You can assemble and freeze sundaes up to 1 day in advance.

Makes: 6 to 8 servings

- 1½ quarts vanilla reduced-fat ice cream or frozen yogurt, softened
- 1 can (16 oz.) pumpkin
- 1 tablespoon pumpkin pie spice
- About ¾ cup caramel topping
- 2 tablespoons rum or brandy (optional)
- ½ cup sugar
- ¼ cup pecans

1. In a large bowl, mix ice cream, pumpkin, pumpkin pie spice, and 4 to 6 tablespoons caramel topping to taste. Scoop mixture equally into 6 to 8 tall stemmed glasses. Mix ½ cup caramel topping with the rum; spoon equally over ice cream. Place filled glasses in freezer. Cover and freeze until firm, at least

2 hours or up until next day.

2. To make brittle, pour sugar into a 10- to 12-inch frying pan over medium-high heat. Shake pan often until sugar liquefies and turns golden, 5 to 8 minutes. Stir in nuts and immediately pour onto a piece of buttered foil set on baking sheet. Tilt pan so syrup spreads into a thin layer. Let cool until firm, at least 10 minutes. With a knife, break into large pieces; reserve 6 to 8 pieces. Place remaining pieces in a plastic bag; coarsely crush with a rolling pin or mallet. Store airtight up to 2 days.

3. About 15 to 20 minutes before serving, remove sundaes from freezer. To serve, stick a large piece of brittle into each sundae; sprinkle sundae with crushed brittle.

A Real Thanksgiving for REAL people

By Christine Weber Hale

After putting this menu and timetable through stringent *Sunset* testing, we went one step further. We tested it with a time-pressed family.

Cindy and David Kuga of San Mateo, California, definitely fit our "busy" requirement. In addition to caring for their 2-year-old daughter, Mariko, both have demanding full-time jobs and long commutes.

After they agreed to be our "Thanksgiving guinea pigs," we set a dinner date and gave them the recipes, shopping list, and timetable in advance. It was agreed that a *Sunset* writer could come and watch, but no help was allowed.

As I knocked on the Kugas' door at 10:30 the morning of the test, I was more than a little nervous. What if, despite our careful checking, something was wrong? What if the menu left them frazzled and frustrated? We had a photographer arriving at 1—what if the food wasn't ready until 4?

Fortunately, most worries were dispelled by the sight of Cindy's calm demeanor as she opened the door. She invited me in, offered me fresh orange juice that she had squeezed that morning, then chatted with me as she continued cooking.

While we talked, she got the gravy going, started the brown rice dressing, put the turkey in the oven, and made the salad dressing. David returned home from an errand with Mariko around noon. Cindy finished preparing the meal, in between feeding Mariko lunch and putting her down for a nap (David helped a little with the final touches), and was ready for the photo by 1:45.

PETER CHRISTIANSEN

Cindy and David Kuga put the finishing touches on our menu. Cindy cooked it from start to finish in less than 5 hours.

As David nervously assembled the vegetables on the turkey platter, he asked if I wanted to take over so that the bird would look "professional." I declined, explaining that the point of the test was to make sure someone who wasn't a *Sunset* food staff member could get the same results we did. As you can see above, the Kugas' turkey was impressive. They didn't need my help at all. ■

Taking it Easy with Takeout

Everything you need to know to order the best Thanksgiving takeout, from a whole meal to pumpkin pie

URKEY TO GO. TIMES CERTAINLY HAVE changed. As much as we'd like to create lavish home-cooked feasts, busy schedules and demanding jobs sometimes make turkey with all the trimmings seem more like a nightmare than a celebration.

But now food businesses are helping to make the Thanksgiving feast easy for everyone. In many areas, with just a phone call you can arrange to pick up a fully cooked holiday dinner. And a few establishments even deliver to your door.

A takeout feast for six from the Ritz-Carlton at Laguna Niguel, California, includes a hot roasted turkey, chestnut stuffing, cranberry relish, vegetables, candied yams, mashed potatoes, and pumpkin pie. Check other large hotels for similar offerings.

JULIE DENNIS

BY LINDA LAU ANUSASANANAN • BETSY REYNOLDS BATESON • ELAINE JOHNSON

258

Businesses that have lots of ovens, like supermarket delis and big-city hotels, are most likely to cook Thanksgiving dinner for takeout. Some bakeries, caterers, delicatessens with rotisseries, and restaurants also cook a limited number of holiday dinners to go. Check newspaper and radio ads in November; many of these businesses advertise. Or call probable candidates and ask.

What can you expect?

There's a meal to fit every taste and budget. We sampled takeout Thanksgiving dinners priced from $30 to $140 for six to eight servings. All were satisfactory, and some rivaled home-cooked meals in quality.

Our $30 meal from a supermarket chain provided the basics—a fully cooked 11-pound turkey, bread stuffing, a dozen rolls, gravy, mashed potatoes, cranberry sauce, and pumpkin pie. The

meal had been precooked, frozen, and thawed. When reheated in its roasting bag, the turkey was extremely juicy but lacked crisp skin. Side dishes tasted a bit packaged, but many people would find this meal totally acceptable.

At almost five times the cost of the supermarket meal, our takeout dinner from a hotel might meet a gourmet's standards. The turkey was freshly roasted, and the side dishes were cooked from scratch. In addition to the basics provided by the supermarket meal, the hotel takeout dinner included a soup, two sal-

ads, and green vegetables. And at about $20 per serving, the takeout cost considerably less than eating in the posh hotel dining room. Other takeout options we sampled ranged between these two extremes in cost and quality of execution.

Thanksgiving takeout tactics

Q. When should I order?

A. Check in late October. Restaurants and smaller facilities sell a limited number of takeout meals, so it's wise to order a couple of weeks in advance. If you're

MEMORABLE TAKEOUT CHOICES

Carolyn Weil, owner of the Bake Shop in Berkeley, sells more than 300 pies baked from organic sugar pie pumpkins each Thanksgiving.

Alder-smoked turkey, a bread centerpiece, pie from organically grown pumpkins: a number of the takeout places we encountered offer noteworthy choices for your holiday meal. In addition to our sampling from around the West, you may find many more options in your neighborhood. Chinese restaurants, for example, may offer turkey cooked like a crisp roasted duck. Some natural-food stores sell range-fed turkeys. Many bakeries make special pies and other desserts just for Thanksgiving.

Northern California

San Francisco. Fournou's Ovens at the Renaissance

Stouffer Stanford Court Hotel, **905 California St., (415) 989-1910.** In addition to its regular four-course Thanksgiving dinners to go ($95 to serve four to six), the restaurant will prepare customized dinners using its recipes or yours. It will customize service, too; you can request delivery, china, linens, white-glove service, and cleanup. Prices vary.
La Nouvelle Patisserie, 2184 Union St., (415) 931-7655, and 865 Market St., 979-0553. Because this bakery specializes in desserts, its multicourse turkey dinner ($120 to serve six) includes both pumpkin pie and chestnut cake, plus a dozen chocolates. You can

also order special desserts such as pumpkin soufflé and marzipan pumpkins; a 10-inch chocolate turkey with multicolored feathers costs about $15.
Berkeley. The Bake Shop, 1926 Shattuck Ave., (510) 841-0773. Choose from five pies—pumpkin, apple, bourbon pecan, apple cranberry, and sweet potato. The one made from organic sugar pie pumpkins is a best-seller—more than 300 go out the door the day before Thanksgiving. A 9-inch pie costs $11 to $14. Place your order at least two days before pickup; the bakery is closed Thanksgiving Day.
Emeryville. Doug's Barbecue, 3600 San Pablo

Ave., (510) 655-9048. Try the Cajun turkey, a smoked whole turkey fried until crisp, with an order of spicy barbecue sauce and sweet baked beans. The deep-fried 14-pound turkey costs about $48. Order by the Friday before Thanksgiving. Convenient parking is available in front.
Sacramento. Freeport Bakery, 2966 Freeport Blvd., (916) 442-4256. A truly wonderful neighborhood bakery that bakes everything on-site: pumpkin, mincemeat, and olallieberry pies, pumpkin cheesecake, linzer torte, and more. The bakery also has many breads and rolls—try its rustic breadsticks and the fabulous

picking up a hot dinner, call early to get the pickup time you want. Some supermarkets can accommodate you almost until the last minute, but most ask for at least two days' notice.

Also check on the cancellation policy. Hotels often secure orders with credit card numbers and may charge if you don't pick up your dinner.

Q. How much will it cost?

A. Supermarket delis offer bargain prices for their complete precooked meals, ranging from $30 to $60 for six to eight servings. Most offer

only cold meals; a few will provide hot food for an additional charge. Sometimes all parts of the meal are cooked by outside vendors, and the supermarket just assembles them in a box.

Pick up a hot fresh-cooked dinner at a hotel and the price goes up—to about $90 to $140 for six to eight servings. Dinners from small delis, restaurants, and bak-

eries generally cost slightly less. The lower-priced dinners include the basics—a roasted whole 10- to 12-pound turkey (or whole breast or slices), a casserole of dressing, mashed potatoes and/or candied yams, rolls, gravy, cranberry sauce, and dessert. The higher-priced dinners generally contain higher-quality natural ingredients, and dishes may be cooked in-house. They may also include more courses, such as appetizers, soup, salad, vegetables, or extra desserts.

Q. Can I pick up dinner on Thanksgiving Day?

A. Most hotels and some restau-

grapevine loaf, which doubles as a centerpiece. Prices are $11 to $15 for pies, about $13 for cheesecakes, and $8 for the grapevine-shaped loaf. You can order as late as the Monday before Thanksgiving.
David Berkley's Fine Wines & Specialty Foods, 515 Pavilions Lane, (916) 929-4422. A complete food shop to answer every need for a Thanksgiving meal; remember to place your order at least a week ahead. The kitchen supplies cooked and prepared appetizers, soups, side dishes, and stuffings, as well as turkeys. Prices vary, but expect to pay about $40 for side dishes and appetizers to serve six to eight.

Southern California

Koo Koo Roo California Kitchen. Locations in Beverly Hills, Brentwood, Encino, Los Angeles, Manhattan Beach, Marina del Rey, Santa Monica, and West Los Angeles, (310) 479-2080 for catering information. You can dine on turkey or get turkey to go year-round at each location. Turkey for takeout on Thanksgiving Day must be ordered by the last week in October. A 24- to 26-pound bird is about $70; basic trimmings, which include gravy, stuffing, mashed potatoes, and cranberry sauce, cost $3 more per person. About 20 side dishes are available for pickup a day ahead. A catering department

Walter Goetzeler, owner of Freeport Bakery, Sacramento, displays his handsome grapevine-shaped loaves. Use one as a centerpiece, then pull off pieces for dinner.

offers delivery, service, and cleanup for additional charge.
Top-Valu Market. Locations in Santa Ana at 1120 S. Bristol St., (714) 957-2529, and in Long Beach at 2038 E. 10th St., (310) 434-1941. This large, well-stocked market offers Thanksgiving with a Mexican flair to its predominantly Latino clientele. Turkey comes with Spanish rice, cornbread dressing, refried beans, *bolillos*, and salsa. (A traditional turkey dinner with mashed

potatoes, bread dressing, rolls, and gravy is also available.) Dinner to serve six to eight costs about $30 (it costs about $36 if ordered after November 19; you must order at least 48 hours ahead). Flan costs an additional $2.99 per pound. The market will also roast your turkey for a nominal fee per pound.
Santa Monica. Border Grill, 1445 Fourth St., (310) 451-1655. This popular restaurant makes turkey tamales with

mole, about $2 apiece. Order 24 hours ahead. Closed Thanksgiving; pick up the day before.

Colorado

Denver. Cucina Leone, 763 S. University Blvd., (303) 722-5466. This European market cafe-deli uses quality ingredients to prepare food that tastes home-cooked. Options include spit-roasted stuffed turkey starting at $60 (serves 6 to 10), whole boned and stuffed turkey (16 pounds for 10 to 14 people, $95), bone-in turkey breast (10 pounds for 6 to 8, $60), and choice of about four kinds of stuffing, which might include bread with fresh sage; apple, onion, and Italian sausage; cornbread and apple; or prune, walnut, and armagnac. If you don't feel like turkey, you can try leg of lamb, beef tenderloin, prime rib, smoked loin of pork, rack of lamb, or four-peppercorn salmon. Order at least two days in advance.

Oregon

Ashland. Ciao Main, 272 E. Main St., (503) 482-8435. Jean Kowacki, chef-owner, makes great foods with rich flavors, such as savory mushroom bread pudding with sage, Cuban sweet potato salad, and polenta with squash, goat cheese, and eggplant salsa (from $4.50 to $6 per pound).

rants are open and cooking on Thanksgiving. They'll roast your bird that day, so you can arrange to pick it up hot at a reserved time.

Other facilities offer the dinner the day before, cold and ready to reheat. The meal is usually packed compactly in one or two boxes with reheating directions. Make sure that you'll have room in your refrigerator to store the meal overnight.

Q. How many will the meal serve?

A. Most meals with set menus serve six to eight and typically feature a 10- to 12-pound turkey with the trimmings. Bigger birds, some as large as 24 pounds, can sometimes be ordered for large gatherings. Side-dish portions we sampled were adequate for the number of servings suggested, and meals usually provided enough turkey for leftovers.

If you're buying the turkey à la carte, allow about ¾-pound bone-in turkey per person—more if you want leftovers. You'll usually need ½ to ¾ cup each of stuffing, potatoes, and vegetables per person.

If your family favors a certain dish, such as stuffing or mashed potatoes, or likes lots

FROM REFRIGERATOR TO TABLE

Reheating directions come with the dinner. If directions are vague, use the following guidelines to reheat your Thanksgiving meal:

We found that a cooked 10- to 12-pound **cold turkey**, in a roasting bag or lightly covered, takes about 1½ hours in a 325° oven to reheat to a nice hot serving temperature (a thermometer inserted through the thickest part of the breast, and touching the breastbone, should reach 140° to 145°). **To crisp the skin,** uncover the bird the last 15 to 20 minutes.

A quart of **cold stuffing or mashed potatoes,** baked, uncovered, in the same 325° oven, takes 35 to 45 minutes to reheat. **Reheat gravy, vegetables, and soup** in a microwave oven or on top of the range. **To refresh bread or pies,** bake, uncovered, in a 325° to 350° oven until warm, 10 to 15 minutes.

Food safety: The simple rule is to **keep food either hot or cold,** not in between. If foods that are normally served cold or hot are left at room temperature more than 3 hours, they can reach a temperature range (60° to 120°) in which bacteria can grow. Moist mixtures such as stuffing, mashed potatoes, and pumpkin pie are especially good mediums for bacterial growth, as is the turkey cavity. Keep food cold before heating, and refrigerate leftovers promptly. Remove any remaining stuffing from the turkey cavity soon after serving.

of gravy, order extra portions. You also might consider making a batch of one holiday family favorite to supplement the takeout menu.

Q. Where do you pick up? Do they deliver?

A. Traffic the day before Thanksgiving can be a nightmare. When you order, ask about pickup. Is easy parking available, or will you need to carry the dinner six blocks to your car? If parking is tight, ask about the best hours for pickup. Some businesses offer delivery service for a fee. Many hotels have drive-through service, and the doorman or concierge will help load your car. —*L. A.* ∎

"King of Smoke" is what some fans call Cyril Miller of Seattle Super Smoke because of his alder wood–flavor birds.

And the takeout roasted turkey is cured with Southwestern spices and stuffed with root vegetables and wild rice ($45 for a 10-pound turkey). Breads, rolls, and desserts are also available. Order your turkey by the Monday before Thanksgiving; other dishes can be ordered ahead or are available on a drop-in basis. Open until noon Thanksgiving Day.
Portland. Elephants Delicatessen, 13 N.W. 23rd Place, (503) 224-3955. "The food tastes like I might have made it myself—and if no one asks, I don't tell!" says one customer. Really good versions of traditional recipes have been a hallmark of Elephants's Thanksgiving takeout for 16 years. In addition to roasted turkey ($3.50 per pound), favorites include savory sage stuffing made with Elephants's breads

($2.95 per pint), giblet gravy made with turkey pan drippings ($3.50 per pint), buttermilk rolls (40 cents each), cranberry-orange relish ($4.40 per pint),

and pies ($9.95). Last day to order turkey is Monday of Thanksgiving week; other items are available until Wednesday. Closed Thanksgiving Day.

Washington

Seattle. Seattle Super Smoke, 2454 Occidental Ave. S., Suite 3A, (206) 625-1339. These smoking experts offer whole turkeys, turkey parts, and many other items year-round, but between Thanksgiving and Christmas alone, they sell 25,000 to 30,000 pounds of turkey. Super Smoke fans (who include managers of local restaurants, hotels, and markets) rave about the birds' moist meat and mild alder-smoke flavor. The 8- to 25-pound birds cost $3.25 per pound and are available at the store and by mail. At Thanksgiving, store customers can also buy trimmings to go with the birds: roasted turkey neck gravy, cornbread stuffing, cranberry-orange relish, and sweet potato pie.

BARELY A MINUTE *in the microwave heats brie enough to melt. Serve it with apricot sauce and baguette slices.*

When time is short, think brie

These two appetizers make the most of this popular cheese

IT'S THE STANDARD SEASONAL CRISIS. Barely home from an exhaustive shopping expedition and the phone rings. Friends are in town for the holidays. They want to drop by in about half an hour. Of course, you toss out the welcome mat—then head for the refrigerator to see what you can whip together in short order for nibbling.

Fortunately, there's a piece of brie cheese.

With brie and a few other easy-to-keep-on-hand ingredients, you can quickly create fresh, imaginative appetizers.

Spirited Apricot Brie

Cooking time: About 3 minutes
Prep time: About 15 minutes
Makes: 6 appetizer servings

- ½ cup apricot jam
- 1 tablespoon grated orange peel
- 1 tablespoon brandy or orange juice
- 1 tablespoon lemon juice
- ⅛ teaspoon ground cinnamon
- 1 piece brie cheese (about ½ lb.)
  Thin baguette slices or water crackers

1. Mix jam, orange peel, brandy, lemon juice, and cinnamon in a shallow microwave-safe serving dish just large enough to also hold the brie.

2. Cover apricot sauce and heat in a microwave oven at full power until sauce begins to bubble, 1 to 1½ minutes.

3. Set brie in apricot sauce. Return to microwave oven and cook, uncovered, until the cheese is hot and slightly melted, about 1 minute; check at 20-second intervals.

4. Scoop cheese and apricot sauce onto baguette slices.

Per serving without bread: 199 cal. 50% (99 cal.) from fat; 8.1 g protein; 11 g fat (5.6 g sat.); 18 g carbo.; 249 mg sodium; 38 mg chol.

Brie and Blue Torte

Prep time: 10 minutes
Notes: If making ahead, chill cheese airtight up to 4 days. Sprinkle apple and pear wedges with lemon juice, as cut, to slow browning.
Makes: 1 pound cheese, 8 to 10 appetizer servings

- 1 piece brie cheese (about ½ lb.), ripe enough to be creamy but not runny
- ½ pound soft blue cheese such as cambozola or gorgonzola
  Apple and pear wedges
  Thin baguette slices or water crackers

1. Cut brie in half horizontally.

2. Mash blue cheese with a fork to soften.

3. Place bottom half of brie, cut side up, on a small platter. Spread blue cheese evenly onto cut side of brie, making level and flush with brie sides. Fit remaining piece of brie, cut side down, on the blue cheese. Serve at room temperature.

4. Slice through cheeses and serve on fruit or baguette slices.

Per ounce cheese: 97 cal., 74% (72 cal.) from fat; 6 g protein; 8 g fat (7 g sat.); 0.4 g carbo.; 287 mg sodium; 25 mg chol. ∎

By Christine Weber Hale

STUFF BRIE *with blue cheese for a fast, tangy option.*

NORMAN A. PLATE

PAUL HAMMOND

Pound cake adventures with nonfat sour cream

PEOPLE KID MY FRIEND SUSAN BRYAN that she's a walking clipping service. No matter what the topic, she reaches into her handbag and pulls out an informative article. But the last time we got together, her "clipping" consisted of a sliver of pound cake, and she pronounced herself stumped.

The problem was her mother's recipe for sour cream pound cake. Susan felt she could no longer justify its weighty ingredients. She had tried substituting nonfat sour cream for the regular sour cream and for three-quarters of the butter, but the result was less than ideal: a dense cake with a strange, gummy layer. Would I help her remodel the recipe? She didn't expect a dessert exactly like her mother's, just closer.

A little sleuthing with sour cream manufacturers brought some good news: her substitution of nonfat sour cream for regular is something they recommend—and something you can try with your own holiday baking. But replacing the butter

with nonfat sour cream is another matter.

Susan wondered if the addition of a little baking powder would make the cake lighter. It helped, but as I worked with the recipe, I realized that fixing this cake was going to be complicated.

First, the extra sour cream was throwing off the cake's chemical balance. A little extra baking soda neutralized the sour cream's acidity, getting rid of part—but not all—of the gummy layer.

The mixing technique was another catch. The original recipe called for beating the butter and sugar together, then beating in whole eggs, to trap air and lighten the cake. In the absence of most of the butter, the beating was only partially effective. To compensate, I tried beating the sugar and egg whites into an airy foam. To cut down the cholesterol and fat I substituted egg whites for three of the original whole eggs.

A dozen cakes and some additional experiments later, the gummy layer was gone and the cake had a tender texture,

nearly like that of a true pound cake—with only 3.5 grams fat, 39 milligrams cholesterol, and 214 calories per slice. (Compare that with the original's 14 g fat, 95 mg chol., and 311 cal.) Though fat and cholesterol are significantly lower in the new cake, you still don't want to munch it like popcorn.

"I knew there was a reason I asked you to do this," laughed Susan, glad she hadn't had to bake the 12 cakes. But would she like the results? I brought her a slice. She says she's going to clip the recipe for her family reunion.

Svelte Sour Cream Pound Cake

Cooking time: 1½ hours
Prep time: About 20 minutes
Notes: This cake has a classic almond and vanilla flavor. To make a *spice cake*, substitute 2 teaspoons rum extract for the almond extract; also, add to the flour 2 teaspoons ground ginger, 1 teaspoon

ground cinnamon, and ½ teaspoon ground nutmeg.

Makes: 16 to 20 servings

- 6 large egg whites, at room temperature
- 2½ cups sugar
- ¼ cup (⅛ lb.) butter or margarine, softened
- 3 large eggs
- 1 carton (16 oz.) nonfat sour cream
- 1 teaspoon almond extract
- 1 teaspoon vanilla
- 3 cups cake flour
- 1 teaspoon baking powder
- ¾ teaspoon baking soda

1. In a large mixer bowl, beat egg whites on high speed until frothy. Gradually add ½ cup of the sugar, beating until whites hold soft peaks when beaters are lifted.

2. In another bowl, beat remaining 2 cups sugar and butter until very fluffy. Scraping side of bowl occasionally, add whole eggs 1 at a time, beating until incorporated. Then beat in sour cream, almond extract, and vanilla.

3. Combine flour, baking powder, and baking soda; beat into the butter mixture 1 cup at a time until blended, scraping side of bowl. Fold ¼ of egg whites into butter mixture to lighten it, then fold in remaining whites until no streaks remain.

4. Evenly spread batter in a buttered and floured plain or decorative 10-inch tube pan. Bake in a 300° oven until cake springs back at edge when lightly pressed, about 1½ hours. Let cool on a rack 10 minutes. Loosen cake from pan sides, turn onto rack, turn upright onto another rack, and let cool completely.

Per serving: 214 cal., 15% (32 cal.) from fat; 5 g protein; 3.5 g fat (1.8 g sat.); 40 g carbo.; 140 mg sodium; 39 mg chol.

Citrus Sour Cream Pound Cake

Recipe is pictured on preceding page.

1. Prepare recipe as directed for **Svelte Sour Cream Pound Cake** (preceding), omitting almond extract. With sour cream, add 1 tablespoon grated **orange peel** and 2 teaspoons grated **lemon peel**.

2. Stir until smooth 1⅓ cups sifted **powdered sugar**, 2 tablespoons **lemon juice**, and 1 tablespoon finely shredded lemon peel. Drizzle glaze over cooled cake. If desired, garnish cake with large curls of lemon peel, a **mint sprig**, and a **strawberry**.

Per serving: 240 cal., 13% (32 cal.) from fat; 5 g protein; 3.5 g fat (1.8 g sat.); 47 g carbo.; 141 mg sodium; 39 mg chol. ■

A French sandwich changes shape

Skinny baguette replaces round rolls and brings a crusty bonus

SETTLING IN FOR OUR PICNIC UNDER A cool canopy of trees on a sun-parched hillside in the south of France, Françoise Kirkman pops baton-shaped packets into our hands. *"Pan bagnat,"* she says. "The sandwiches you saw yesterday in Nice." Then she adds that *pan* means *bread* and *bagnat* is *bath*. Traditionally, you split open a round crusty roll, bathe it with an olive oil and herb dressing, and fill it with niçoise salad ingredients. "But the baker had no rolls, so I used baguettes."

No harm done, we concurred as we relished the baguettes. Even though the loaves were saturated by the essences of tuna, tomato, anchovy, egg, and garlic, the bread stayed firm and the length of the baguettes gave us a bonus of crisp crust. Kirkman had applied the oil with a lighter hand than the French typically do, but her version was equal in flavor. Nor did she stop with just one filling: her options are well worth trying.

Baguette Bagnat

Prep time: About 25 minutes
Notes: Choose from fillings that follow.
Makes: 2 servings

- 2 tablespoons extra-virgin olive oil
- 1½ tablespoons red wine vinegar
- 2 tablespoons chopped parsley
- ¼ teaspoon coarsely ground pepper
- ¼ teaspoon dried thyme leaves
- 1 clove garlic, minced
- 1 baguette (8 oz.)
  Niçoise, tomato, or Greek salad (recipes follow)
  Salt

1. Mix oil, vinegar, parsley, pepper, thyme, and garlic. Cut baguette in half crosswise, then cut each portion in half lengthwise, making the bottom of the baguette slightly thicker. Pull out soft interior (save for another use) to make bread shells about ½ inch thick.

HOLLOWED BAGUETTES, *brushed with an herb dressing, hold a generous amount of filling to make picnic sandwiches.*

Brush interior of shells with ½ the dressing.

2. Line each bottom section of baguette with ½ the leaves from the salad. Mound salad mixture onto leaves; drizzle equally with remaining dressing. Add salt to taste.

3. Cover filling with baguette tops. Serve, or wrap airtight and chill up to 6 hours.

Niçoise Salad

Line baguette bottom with ¾ cup lightly packed rinsed **arugula**. Mound onto leaves 1 can (6 to 7 oz.) drained **water-packed** or oil-packed **tuna**, ¼ cup thinly sliced **red onion**, ½ cup thinly sliced firm-ripe **tomato**, 2 thinly sliced hard-cooked **large eggs**, and 4 drained **canned flat anchovy fillets**.

Per serving: 650 cal., 33% (216 cal.) from fat; 42 g protein; 24 g fat (5.7 g sat.); 65 g carbo.; 1,330 mg sodium; 249 mg chol.

Tomato Salad

Line baguette bottom with ½ cup lightly packed rinsed **fresh basil leaves**. Mound onto leaves ½ pound thinly sliced **fresh mozzarella** or panela **cheese**, ¼ cup thinly sliced **red onion**, and ½ cup thinly sliced firm-ripe **tomato**.

Per serving: 790 cal., 48% (378 cal.) from fat; 32 g protein; 42 g fat (3.7 g sat.); 72 g carbo.; 781 mg sodium; 80 mg chol.

Greek Salad

Line baguette bottom with ½ cup lightly packed rinsed and drained **spinach leaves**. Top with ½ cup thinly sliced **English cucumber**, ¼ cup thinly sliced **red onion**, and ½ cup thinly sliced firm-ripe **tomato**. Sprinkle with 2 teaspoons **fresh** or 1 teaspoon dried **oregano leaves**, ¼ cup crumbled **feta cheese**, and 12 pitted **calamata olives**.

Per serving: 599 cal., 44% (261 cal.) from fat; 14 g protein; 29 g fat (7.3 g sat.); 71 g carbo.; 1,442 mg sodium; 15 mg chol. ■

By Linda Lau Anusasananan

Creative ways with everyday foods—submitted by *Sunset* readers, tested in *Sunset* kitchens

Blueberry–Coconut Crunch Muffins

Cathy Margulies, Los Angeles

CRUNCHY TOP *on moist blueberry muffins is a mix of brown sugar and coconut.*

2 cups all-purpose flour

1 cup granulated sugar

1 tablespoon baking powder

1/2 teaspoon baking soda

3 large eggs

3/4 cup milk

1/4 cup lime juice

3 tablespoons salad oil

2 teaspoons vanilla

1 1/4 cups fresh or frozen blueberries

1/3 cup finely chopped pecans

1/3 cup shredded sweetened dried coconut

3 tablespoons firmly packed brown sugar

1. Mix flour, granulated sugar, baking powder, and soda.

2. In bowl, beat eggs to blend with milk, lime juice, oil, and vanilla; add to dry ingredients. Stir just until evenly moistened. Gently stir in berries. Divide mixture equally among 12 oiled or paper-lined muffin cups (2 1/2 in. wide).

3. Mix pecans, coconut, and brown sugar; sprinkle evenly over muffins.

4. Bake in a 425° oven until golden brown, about 20 minutes. Cool 5 minutes; remove from pan. Serve warm or cool. Makes 12.

Per muffin: 263 cal., 32% (83 cal.) from fat; 4.6 g protein; 9.2 g fat (2 g sat.); 41 g carbo.; 206 mg sodium; 55 mg chol.

Salad with Nuts, Apple, and Toast

Christina Fredericks, Cardiff, California

SALAD FOR TWO *includes apple slices, toasted walnuts, and blue cheese toast.*

3 tablespoons raspberry vinegar

1 tablespoon minced shallots

1 tablespoon walnut or salad oil

1 teaspoon minced fresh or 1/4 teaspoon dried tarragon leaves

1 teaspoon honey

2 tablespoons gorgonzola or other soft blue cheese

6 baguette slices (about 1/2 in. wide, about 3 oz. total)

2 tablespoons chopped walnuts

4 cups butter lettuce, rinsed and crisped

1 red apple (about 1/4 lb.)

1. Mix vinegar, shallots, oil, tarragon, and honey to make dressing.

2. Spread cheese equally on 1 side of each baguette slice; set slices, cheese side up, in 1 end of a 10- by 15-inch pan. Spread walnuts in other end of pan. Bake in a 400° oven until cheese is brown and bubbling and walnuts are toasted, about 7 minutes. (If nuts brown sooner, remove from pan.)

3. Meanwhile, tear lettuce into bite-size pieces into a bowl and add dressing. Core and thinly slice apple into salad and mix. Spoon salad onto plates, sprinkle with nuts, and accompany with toast. Serves 2.

Per serving: 313 cal., 43% (135 cal.) from fat; 8 g protein; 15 g fat (2.9 g sat.); 39 g carbo.; 364 mg sodium; 6.3 mg chol.

Pumpkin Risotto

Jennifer A. Kirkgaard, Burbank, California

RED-GOLD RISOTTO, *tinted and flavored by pumpkin, is sweetened by parsnips.*

1 tablespoon olive or salad oil

1 onion (1/2 lb.), chopped

2 cups arborio or medium-grain rice

6 cups chicken broth

2 cups 1/2-inch cubes parsnips

1 cup dry white wine

1 cup canned pumpkin

1/2 cup shredded parmesan cheese

Italian parsley sprigs and parmesan curls (optional)

1. In a 4- to 5-quart pan, combine oil and onion. Stir often over medium-high heat until onion is lightly browned, about 8 minutes. Add rice and stir until opaque, 2 to 3 minutes. Stir in broth, parsnips, wine, and pumpkin; bring to a boil over high heat.

2. Simmer, stirring often, until rice is tender to bite, 20 to 25 minutes. Remove from heat and stir in shredded cheese. Spoon into a bowl; garnish with parsley and parmesan curls. Serves 4 to 6.

Per serving: 399 cal., 17% (67 cal.) from fat; 12 g protein; 7.4 g fat (2.6 g sat.); 69 g carbo.; 249 mg sodium; 5.3 mg chol.

Aunt Diane's Kielbasa Stew

Nancy Rowley, San Jose

1   pound turkey or regular kielbasa (Polish) sausages, cut into ½-inch-thick slices

3   cups chicken or beef broth

    About 1 pound onions, coarsely chopped

3   cloves garlic, minced or pressed

2   cans (15 oz. each) cannellini (white kidney) beans, rinsed and drained

½   pound escarole, rinsed and coarsely chopped

1. In a 4- to 5-quart pan over medium-high heat, frequently stir sausage until well browned, about 7 minutes. Pour from pan and set aside.

2. To pan, add 1 cup broth, onions, and garlic. Boil over high heat until liquid is almost gone, then stir often until onion bits are lightly browned, 10 to 12 minutes. Stir remaining broth into pan, scraping browned bits free, then add sausages and beans.

3. Cover pan and cook over high heat until boiling. Stir in escarole and cook just until it wilts, about 2 minutes. Ladle into wide bowls. Serves 4 to 6.

Per serving: 271 cal., 30% (81 cal.) from fat; 21 g protein; 9 g fat (3.9 g sat.); 29 g carbo.; 1,055 mg sodium; 41 mg chol.

SAUSAGE AND BEAN *stew for a busy night takes less than 30 minutes.*

Turkey Enchiladas

Judy Ewald, Mesilla, New Mexico

    Green sauce (recipe follows)

8   corn tortillas (6 to 7 in.)

2⅔ cups cooked, skinned turkey, torn into small pieces

1   cup *each* (½ lb. total) shredded cheddar and jack cheese

    Fresh cilantro sprigs

1. Make green sauce; if making ahead, cover and chill up to 1 day.

2. Dip 1 tortilla in very hot water until pliable and softened, 5 to 10 seconds; drain briefly. Spoon ⅓ cup turkey on an edge of the tortilla. Add ⅛ of the cheddar cheese. Roll tortilla to enclose filling; place seam side down in a shallow, lightly oiled 9- by 13-inch casserole. Repeat to fill remaining tortillas.

3. Spoon green sauce over filled enchiladas, moistening tortilla surfaces; sprinkle with jack cheese. Bake in a 350° oven until cheese melts and enchiladas are hot in center, about 30 minutes. Garnish with cilantro sprigs. Serves 4.

Per serving: 553 cal., 41% (225 cal.) from fat; 47 g protein; 25 g fat (13 g sat.); 32 g carbo.; 835 mg sodium; 132 mg chol.

Green sauce. In an 8- to 10-inch frying pan, combine 1 cup chopped **onion**, ½ cup **chicken broth,** and 2 cloves minced **garlic.** Stir often over high heat until broth evaporates and browned bits stick to pan. Add another ¼ cup chicken broth, and stir to free browned bits. Purée mixture in a blender or food processor with 1 cup firmly packed **fresh cilantro,** 1 can (7 oz.) **diced green chilies,** 1 stemmed and seeded **fresh jalapeño chili,** and ½ teaspoon **ground cumin;** add 1 more cup chicken broth as mixture is whirling.

TURKEY LEFTOVERS *bow out in enchiladas blanketed by cumin-spiked chili sauce.*

Chocolate Shortbread with Mint Glaze

Lynne Schaefer, Novato, California

1   cup (½ lb.) butter or margarine, at room temperature

½   cup sugar

1   teaspoon vanilla

1½   cups all-purpose flour

¾   cup cornstarch

½   cup unsweetened cocoa

½   cup semisweet chocolate baking chips

3   tablespoons whipping cream

½   teaspoon peppermint extract

1. Beat butter with sugar and vanilla until fluffy. Mix flour, cornstarch, and cocoa. Stir into butter mixture, then beat to blend well. Press dough in an even layer in a 9- by 13-inch pan.

2. Bake in a 325° oven until shortbread is dry and firm when lightly pressed, about 40 minutes. Cut into 48 squares, but leave in pan until cool.

3. In a 1- to 1½-quart pan over low heat, stir chocolate, cream, and peppermint extract just until chocolate is smoothly melted. Drizzle mixture from a spoon onto cookies. Let stand until glaze is firm, about 2 hours. Serve, or if making ahead, store airtight up to 2 days. Makes 4 dozen.

Per cookie: 77 cal., 55% (42 cal.) from fat; 0.7 g protein; 4.7 g fat (2.9 g sat.); 8.6 g carbo.; 40 mg sodium; 11 mg chol.

Compiled by Christine Weber Hale

CHOCOLATE SHORTBREAD *cookies make a thoughtful gift for the holidays.*

FOOD Guide

BY JERRY ANNE DI VECCHIO

A TASTE OF THE WEST: Roast goose with ease

Mrs. Cratchit put up with Scrooge, but she drew the line at roasting the Christmas goose in her own kitchen. She let the baker do it.

Nowadays, bakers rarely provide such service. This makes it even more amazing that in days long past, my own mother, who viewed cooking as a boring nuisance, often tackled goose for a holiday meal. She did it, she said, because dark, firm goose meat tastes so good, and the crisp skin makes it all the more worthwhile. Valid points. However, the first time I cooked goose, the house caught fire. There was no relationship between the two incidents (the clothes dryer malfunctioned), but it was a night to remember.

If this preamble suggests that I'm a bit tentative about urging you to cook your own goose, I admit that this was once the case. But no more. By accident, I made a great discovery. We were photographing a goose for a story and got a late start. By the time we were done, everyone else had gone home. So I stuck the bird in the refrigerator. When I reheated the goose the next day for tasting, I was amazed at the results. The skin got crisper than it had been originally, the meat was just as moist and flavorful as anticipated, and best of all, dealing with the vats of fat a goose renders (easily a quart or more) was yesterday's chore.

In defense of the fat, it is delicately flavored and has cooking merits. It doesn't scorch readily, and is great for roast potatoes (as follows). If kept airtight and chilled, goose fat stays fresh for several weeks.

Crisp Roast Goose with Giblet Gravy

Cooking time: 2 to 3 hours
Prep time: About 30 minutes, if thawed

- A crisper, less messy cooked goose
- Getting to the heart of marrow bones
- Secrets for crusty roasted potatoes
- How to make wine a memorable gift
- A blissful union of hazelnuts and chocolate

This crispy-skinned goose was cooked a day ahead. Potatoes are roasted crusty and brown in the bird's drippings, and cranberries add tang to the sweet-sour red cabbage rolls (recipes on page 270)

Notes: 8- to 10-pound geese tend to be proportionately meatier than larger ones. Be sure to order ahead.

Makes: 8 to 10 servings

1 goose, 8 to 12 pounds, thawed if frozen

1 lemon, cut in half

2 onions (each about 1/2 lb.), cut into chunks

4 cups chicken broth

1/4 cup cornstarch mixed smoothly with 1/3 cup water

2 tablespoons brandy or sherry

Salt and pepper

1. Remove giblets from goose and reserve for gravy. Pull off and discard fat lumps. Rinse bird inside and out.

2. With a fork, pierce goose skin all over, especially around thigh joints. Thinly slice 1/2 of the lemon and tuck slices in the goose cavity along with 1 chopped onion.

3. Set a V-shaped rack in a roasting pan at least 2 inches deep and about 12 by 17 inches. Place goose, breast down, in rack.

4. Put neck, heart, gizzard, and remaining chopped onion in a 9- to 10-inch-wide pan. Cover and chill goose liver.

5. Tent goose loosely with a solid sheet of foil (you may need to fold edges of several sheets together, making a tight seal), then crimp foil tightly to pan rim. Roast in a 375° oven for 1 hour.

6. At the same time, also put pan of giblets in oven to roast until well browned, about 2 hours; stir occasionally.

7. After goose has cooked for 1 hour, remove from oven carefully (to avoid spilling hot fat). Ladle or siphon fat from pan, leaving brown drippings. Save fat. (For one use, see roasted potatoes recipe on page 270). Taking care not to tear skin, turn goose breast up and squeeze juice from remaining lemon half over the bird.

8. Return goose to oven, uncovered, and roast until skin is well browned, 1 to 1 1/2 hours longer. A thermometer pushed to the bone in the thigh joint should register at least 175° to 180°. Siphon or ladle fat from pan 1 or 2 times.

9. When giblet mixture is browned, remove from oven and pour some of the chicken broth into pan. Let stand until browned bits in pan soften, then scrape mixture into a 3- to 4-quart pan and add remaining broth. Cover and simmer until neck meat is tender enough to pull from bone, 40 to 50 minutes. Let cool.

10. When goose is done, leave on the rack, but transfer to another rimmed pan, at least 12 by 15 inches. Let bird cool to warm, then cover and chill until cold, at least 6 hours or up to 1 day.

11. Pour fat from roasting pan and save. To pan, add about 1/2 cup water and scrape browned drippings free. Add drippings to simmered giblets. Pull meat from neck, discard bones, and finely chop neck and roasted giblets. Return meat to broth. Cover and chill until cold, at least 4 hours or overnight. Lift off and discard fat.

12. To reheat goose and crisp skin, set bird on rack in pan in a 375° oven until skin feels crisp when touched and meat is hot and sizzling, about 1 hour.

13. As goose heats, rinse reserved liver and pat dry. Put 1 tablespoon goose fat in 6- to 7-inch frying pan over medium-high heat. When hot, add liver, cover and brown lightly, turning once (interior should be pink), about 2 minutes. Lift liver from pan, discard fat, and thinly slice liver.

14. Measure giblet gravy and add enough water to make 4 cups. Bring gravy to boiling. Stirring, add cornstarch mixture and cook until boil resumes. Flavor gravy with brandy and salt and pepper to taste; add liver, if desired, or serve liver with goose.

15. Transfer goose to a platter. Slice off crisp breast skin in large pieces, then cut breast halves from bone. Cut breasts in portions across the grain and serve with sections of the skin. Cut legs from carcass (joint is almost at the center of the back), and slice meat from legs. Cut wings free, and slice crisp skin from carcass. Accompany goose with giblet gravy and salt and pepper to taste.

Per serving: 630 cal., 60% (378 cal.) from fat; 51 g protein; 42 g fat (13 g sat.); 8.7 g carbo.; 201 mg sodium; 221 mg chol.

BACK TO BASICS

Getting to the heart of marrow bones

Marrow is a passion of mine. And when I want something really earthy and easy for good-eating friends, I roast beef bones, trimmed bare of meat, that are full of marrow. This also gives me a reason to use the antique marrow spoons I found in a dusty shop in London's Beauchamp Place. The slender spoons do a masterful job of scooping out soft melting marrow—an act so indulgent it brings to mind the lustful gluttony

Dig into the hollows of roasted beef bones to retrieve the hot, flavorful marrow.

in the old film *Tom Jones.*

Marrow is a puzzle to many. Most assume this pale, waxy matter in the hollow of bones is fat. It does taste divinely rich. But marrow—composed of protein, carbohydrates, fat, and enzymes—is the nutritious factory where blood is produced, and it's not nearly so fatty as it appears.

Roasted Marrow Bones

I. Select meat-trimmed **beef leg bones with marrow** exposed on at least 1 end. Have bones cut into 3- to 4-inch lengths, and allow 1 or 2 bones for a serving.

2. Rinse bones and arrange in a single layer, slightly apart, in a shallow casserole. For each 3 to 5 pounds of bones, mix 1 teaspoon **dried thyme** with ½ teaspoon **dried hot chili flakes** and sprinkle over the bones.

3. Bake in a 450° oven until scraps on bones brown and marrow looks soft and melting, about 30 minutes. Turn bones over at least once for even color. About 5 minutes before removing from oven, sprinkle bones with minced **shallots**, minced **parsley** (for 3 to 5 lb. bones, 2 to 3 tablespoons each), and **freshly ground pepper.**

4. Serve bones from casserole or on warmed plates, and provide marrow scoops, slender bladed knives, demitasse spoons, or a similar tool. Thickly spread marrow on thin toasted **baguette** slices, and season to taste with **salt.**

No accurate nutritional data available.

Roasting potatoes right

Regardless of which hunk of meat you choose as the cornerstone of a special menu, potatoes will fit right in. And one of the most appetizing, least demanding ways to prepare them is peeled and roasted crusty brown. Any potato will work—waxy thin-skinned potatoes, mealy russets, big ones, small ones. The secrets are to have plenty of fat in the roasting pan and to leave the potatoes alone until the crusty surface gets thick enough to stick to the potatoes, not the pan, at which time you turn them over for even coloring.

Can I justify all the fat? Yes, because so little sinks in—as long as you don't rip the crust, which seals out the fat.

Roasted potatoes. Peel 1 or 2 **potatoes** (5 to 6 oz. each) for each serving.

Use a pan at least 1½ inches deep; the potatoes shouldn't be crowded or stacked.

For 8 to 10 servings (16 to 20 potatoes), put about 2 cups **goose fat** or olive oil in pan and place in a 375° oven until fat is heated, about 15 minutes.

Add potatoes to hot fat, rolling to coat. Then bake undisturbed until potatoes begin to get brown spots, basting occasionally. If you turn potatoes before a brown skin forms where they touch the pan, the thinner pale crust will stick. Ease a wide spatula under each potato and roll it over, then turn more often until potatoes are richly browned, 1¼ to 1½ hours. (Potatoes for 8 to 10 absorb only 3 to 4 tablespoons fat.) Serve with **salt** to taste.

Per potato: 107 cal., 22% (24 cal.) from fat; 2.2 g protein; 2.7 g fat (0.7 g sat.); 19 g carbo.; 6.4 mg sodium; 2.6 mg chol.

Cranberries with a bright bite

Several fruits have the distinction of being basically inedible without some help. One is olives, another cranberries. Cranberries have the advantage because they can be used raw. My favorite way is in a relish much like the one that used to be printed on the plastic bag they came in—grind a bag of cranberries and 1 or 2 seeded oranges (with peel on), adding just enough sugar to reduce the pucker factor. No roast turkey should ever appear without it.

I also like to add cranberries to other dishes, including meat, where their color and tang is a plus. This old favorite, sweet and sour braised red cabbage, gets new life with cranberries, and it certainly complements roast pork, ham—or goose.

Red Cabbage with Cranberries

Cooking time: 1¼ to 1½ hours
Prep time: 20 to 25 minutes
Notes: To get a head start, assemble cabbage rolls in casserole, then cover and chill up to 1 day.
Makes: 8 servings

- 2 heads red cabbage (about 2 lb. total)
- About ¾ cup red wine vinegar
- ½ cup firmly packed brown sugar
- 1 cup cranberries
- 3½ cups apple juice
- ½ teaspoon caraway seed
- Salt

I. To make cabbage rolls, cut 8 to 10 outer cabbage leaves free at stem base and pull off gently to avoid tearing. Bring 5 quarts water and ¼ cup vinegar to boiling in a 6- to 8-quart pan. Push leaves under in boiling water, 3 or 4 at a time, until limp, about 30 seconds. Lift out with a slotted spoon; let drain. Discard water.

2. Finely shred remaining cabbage, using a food processor with slicing blade, or a knife. Put cabbage in drained pan and add remaining ½ cup vinegar, brown sugar, cranberries, apple juice, and caraway seed.

3. Cover and bring mixture to a boil over high heat. Stir several times until cabbage is limp, then uncover and simmer until liquid is almost cooked away, 1 to 1¼ hours.

4. Spoon about ½ cup cabbage into

center of each blanched cabbage leaf, fold sides over filling, then roll to enclose and set seam down. Spoon remaining cabbage into a shallow casserole, about 9 by 13 inches, and set cabbage rolls on top. Cover.

5. Bake in a 375° oven until hot, about 20 minutes (30 to 35, if chilled); add salt to taste.

Per serving: 144 cal., 2.5% (3.6 cal.) from fat; 1.7 g protein; 0.4 g fat (0.1 g sat.); 36 g carbo.; 21 mg sodium; 0 mg chol.

KEVIN CANDLAND

Chocolate's perfect partner in this velvety mousse is smoothly ground toasted hazelnuts.

GREAT INGREDIENTS

A sweet blend

Nestled on the southern slopes of the Italian Alps is the city of Turin. Here they make the best chocolate I have ever tasted. Actually it was *gianduia* that brought me to euphoria—hazelnuts and chocolate, a combination so harmonious that it has a name all its own. All this was news to me—back when. Now I can buy truffles filled with gianduia, even at the grocery store. But there is more to life than truffles, and another delicious manifestation of gianduia is in this creamy mousse.

Gianduia Mousse

Cooking time: 35 to 40 minutes

Prep time: 45 to 50 minutes (including chilling)

Notes: Toast hazelnuts in a single layer in a rimmed pan in a 350° oven, shaking occasionally, until golden under the skin, about 15 minutes. Pour hot nuts onto a towel, and rub with cloth to remove the loose brown skin (some sticks). Lift nuts from cloth. For garnish, roast a few extra nuts and scatter them whole or coarsely chopped onto the mousse.

Makes: About 5 cups, 8 to 10 servings

- 1 cup toasted and skinned hazelnuts
- 1 package (3 oz., or ⅓ cup) cream cheese
- ½ cup hazelnut-flavor liqueur such as frangelico
- 1½ cups (9 oz.) semisweet chocolate bits or chunks
- 1 cup milk
- ½ cup sugar
- 2 large eggs
- 1 cup crème fraîche or whipping cream

1. Whirl nuts to a smooth paste in a blender, 3 to 5 minutes. Scrape container sides frequently.

2. In a bowl, mash cream cheese, then gradually whisk in the liqueur until smoothly blended. Add chocolate.

3. In a 10- to 12-inch frying pan, heat milk with nut paste and sugar until steaming. In a small bowl, whisk eggs to blend, add some of the hot liquid, then return mixture to the pan. Stir over low heat until mixture is thick enough to mound, about 8 minutes.

4. At once, remove from heat and add to chocolate mixture. Stir until chocolate melts. Cover and chill until cool but still easy to stir, about 45 minutes. Or nest bowl in ice water and stir often until cool, 5 to 8 minutes.

5. Whip crème fraîche until it holds distinct peaks, then fold smoothly into nut mixture. Pour into individual dishes and serve, or cover and chill up to 1 day.

Per serving: 406 cal., 62% (252 cal.) from fat; 5.7 g protein; 28 g fat (13 g sat.); 34 g carbo.; 60 mg sodium; 88 mg chol.

Let nostalgia guide your choice

For a moment, think of wine in the spirit of Christmas Past, Christmas Present, and Christmas Future. Do that, and it can play a small but useful role in building and burnishing holiday traditions.

The trick is to allow yourself to be sentimental. Start with Christmas Past. With any luck at all, somewhere in the history of family or friendship is a wine that brings back warm feelings from earlier holidays. Rarity and price should have little to do with the choice. Indeed, chances are pretty good that some of our warmest memories date from years when money was in such short supply that a bargain-bin Chianti was a splurge. In any case, what matters is that the sight of the label and the taste of the wine, like old snapshots, trigger some feelings you would like to keep alive.

Because bottles of the same wine can be shared across any distance, it can rouse the spirit of a Christmas Past for people who cannot be together. With a little luck and some planning, you can even sit down to an agreed-upon menu at the same hour as family or friends far away, and raise a toast at an agreed-upon minute.

As for Christmas Present, it offers two opportunities. The first is to start building a new tradition with a wine chosen to taste good with whatever you plan to eat. The second chance is to look ahead to Christmas Future with a wine chosen as a durable gift, to be opened in years to come.

Durable does not mean immortal, only that the wine stays in good form for at least three years. Almost all red wines will last that long with no trouble at all. Many made from Cabernet Sauvignon will last 10 or more. Whites are dicier, but many will last three years. A relative few—mostly French Chablis and American Sauvignon Blancs—will wait for a decade. As the number of bottles dwindles, you can build on tradition by giving the same wine again, from some later vintage.

As in choosing to celebrate holidays past, sentiment should rule. Pick something that already has been part of a memorable occasion. Write a note right on the label, so opening it will be sure to cause a small celebration, in the holiday season or out. ■

Unwrap cornhusks to reveal soft, chili-flavored masa filled with pork in chili sauce, green olives, and slices of potato and jalapeño.

THE PERFECT TAMALE

The Coronel family's holiday tradition is a
prizewinning solution for festive entertaining

BY ELAINE JOHNSON

Every Christmas season, Lupe Coronel's family celebrates with tamales.
They've always considered her version—mildly spicy pork with red chilies,
potatoes, green olives, and jalapeños—the best around. The family confirmed just
how good the tamales are when they captured a first-prize trophy at the 1994 Indio
International Tamale Festival near Palm Springs, California.

Tamales have long been a Latino Christmas tradition. For Indio's predominantly Latino population, the annual fair (December 2 this year) is a natural kickoff to
the season. The town turns out for a parade, music and dance performances, a car-
nival, and plenty of tamales: 34,000 were sold last year with earlygoers getting the
best selection; call (619) 347-0676 for information.

Families, as well as civic and professional groups, sell tamales that range from
chichi chicken with mango-habanero sauce to banana leaf–wrapped Salvadoran
ones with peas and garbanzos. Yet it's the deftly blended flavors of Coronel's traditional recipe from Durango, Mexico, that catch my attention as a judge for the
festival. At their home in nearby La Quinta, the Coronels teach me their secrets.

Right away, I learn the first point of tamale making: it's a group effort, enough
work that no one tackles it alone, and enough fun to make a good party.

Lupe's daughter, Liz, and son Zeke are there to lend a hand. So is Lupe's sister-
in-law, also Lupe; the two Lupes have been making tamales together for 30 years.

Sometimes the Coronels prepare the tamale components a day before assembly,
but today they're doing everything in one fell swoop. Mother Lupe starts simmering the pork. Aunt Lupe soaks cornhusks and cleans dried chilies for the purée that
seasons the meat and fresh masa.

Liz begins mixing the masa with the chili purée, lard, and salt. How do you
know when it's mixed enough? "When my mother tells me to stop, I stop," Liz
laughs. She stirs, kneads, and squeezes the masa until no lumps remain.

I follow the family around the kitchen, eyeballing quantities as they cook.
"Where I grew up, they didn't have measuring cups. You used your eyes and

MICHAEL GARLAND

To keep up with family and friends' demand, Lupe Coronel (left) and her family make 100 dozen tamales during the holiday season.

hands," mother Lupe says. (Later, when I try cutting back on the lard and salt in the masa and filling—and results don't taste nearly as good—I learn a couple more points about making the best tamales.)

Assembly is where extra hands really help. Lupe Coronel spreads masa on the husks, then passes them on to her sister-in-law, who fills them with meat, potatoes, pickled jalapeños, and olives, and rolls them up.

Then Liz and Zeke tie them (more authentic than folding them closed, insists their mother).

My first attempts at spreading the masa are pathetic, but I improve with coaching: spread masa on the husk's smooth side, they instruct, making quick flicks with a spoon from the center out.

At last we have a tidy mountain of stacked tamales. Many go into the freezer, ready for holiday meals and for spontaneous visits from friends and relatives. But they won't let me leave without a sample.

Liz and Zeke's brother, father, and uncle seem to have a sixth sense for mealtime, arriving just as the tamales come out of the steamer. We dive in. The tamales taste even more delicious than I remember from the festival.

Lupe's Pork Tamales

Cooking time: About 3 hours during preparation, plus 1 hour to heat finished tamales (1¾ hours if frozen)

Prep time: About 4 hours with 3 people doing assembly

Notes: Cooking and preparation can happen simultaneously; allow about 6 hours to do everything in one day. (Or make meat filling, chili purée, and masa a day ahead.) Buy fresh masa at a Mexican market or tortilla company, or substitute masa flour from the supermarket.

Makes: 4 to 4½ dozen

- 4 pounds boned pork shoulder (butt), most fat trimmed
- 3 ounces dried California or New Mexico chilies
- 1½ ounces dried pasilla chilies
- ¼ cup all-purpose flour
- 2 large cloves garlic
- 2 teaspoons coriander seed
- 2 teaspoons dried oregano leaves
- 1 teaspoon cumin seed
- ⅔ cup chopped tomato
- ⅔ cup chopped yellow onion
- ½ cup chopped green bell pepper
- ½ cup chopped seeded fresh Anaheim chilies
- 3 cups (1⅓ lb.) lard or solid vegetable shortening

- 2 tablespoons instant beef bouillon
- 2 teaspoons garlic salt
- ½ cup chopped fresh cilantro sprigs
- ½ cup sliced green onion
- 5 pounds plain prepared masa (without lard or salt; also called *masa fresca* and masa for tortillas) or use 8 cups dehydrated masa flour (corn tortilla flour) mixed until smooth with 5¼ cups warm water
- 2 teaspoons baking powder
- 2 tablespoons salt
- 1½ pounds russet potatoes
- 96 small drained, pimiento-stuffed green olives (from 1 jar, 10 oz.)
- 48 slices pickled canned jalapeño chilies (from 2 cans, each 7 oz.; save extra chilies plus carrot and onion seasonings for other uses)
- 1 pound dried cornhusks
- Salsa

1. Pork filling. Place pork in a 5- to 6-quart pan with 3 quarts water; bring to a boil over high heat. Reduce heat; simmer, covered, until meat is tender when pierced, about 2 hours. Drain broth, skim and discard fat, and reserve broth. Let meat stand until cool enough to handle; tear into chunks, discarding fat. Return meat to pan.

2. Meanwhile, discard stems and seeds from California and pasilla chilies. Place chilies in a 3- to 4-quart pan. Rinse well with water and drain. Add 1 quart water, and bring to a boil over high heat. Cover, reduce heat, and simmer, stirring often, until chilies are soft when pressed, 20 to 25 minutes. Drain chilies, reserving 2 cups liquid. Whirl chilies and reserved liquid in a blender until very smooth; set aside.

3. In a 1- to 2-quart pan over medium heat, stir flour until deep tan, 5 to 6 minutes; pour into a bowl. When pork is cooked, stir ½ cup reserved pork broth into flour; scrape into pan with meat.

4. In blender, whirl garlic, coriander, oregano, cumin, and 1½ cups pork broth until seasonings are very finely ground. Pour through a fine strainer into pan with meat, pressing to extract liquid. Discard seasonings.

5. To meat add 1½ cups chili purée, tomato, yellow onion, bell pepper, Anaheim chilies, ¼ cup lard, bouillon, and garlic salt. Bring to simmering over medium-high heat, stirring. Cook, stirring often, for 10 minutes to blend flavors. Stir in cilantro and green onion. With a fork, break any meat chunks into shreds. If making ahead, let cool, then chill airtight up to 2 days.

6. Masa. In a large bowl, break up masa with your hands. Add baking powder and salt; mix well. Place remaining 2¾ cups lard in a 2- to 3-quart pan over medium-high heat until melted; let stand until cool enough to touch. Pour into masa, add remaining chili purée, and mix until blended with your hands or a heavy spoon. Then, with spoon (or half at a time with a heavy-duty mixer) beat until very smooth and no lumps of masa remain. If making ahead, cover airtight and let stand up to 4 hours, or chill up to 2 days; bring to room temperature before using (takes 4 to 5 hours).

7. Remaining fillings. Peel potatoes and cut into 48 sticks, each 4 to 5 inches long and ¼ to ⅓ inch thick (save scraps for other uses). Place sticks in a 3- to 4-quart pan with water to cover. Bring to a boil over high heat, then simmer, covered, until tender-crisp to bite, about 3 minutes. Drain and set aside. Drain olives and jalapeños.

8. Cornhusks. Separate husks and discard silk. Select 5½ dozen large outer husks (5 to 6 in. wide across the middle and 7 to 8 in. long); trim larger husks to be this size, and save smaller ones for other uses. Soak husks in a sink with hot tap water to cover until pliable, about 20 minutes. Rinse, removing any grit; drain, and place in a large bowl. Tear about 12 husks into long, thin

Top: Set up an assembly line to speed tamale preparation. First spread an even layer of masa on cornhusks (steadied directly on masa or on counter). **Center:** Fill with flavorful shredded pork, potato sticks, green olives, and slivered jalapeños, then roll up to close. **Bottom:** Tie snugly with husk strips. Steam tamales, or stash them in the freezer to cook later.

strips. (If assembly takes more than a few hours and husks dry out, briefly resoak.)

9. Assembly. Work on a large counter or on a table lined with plastic. Set up masa and whole husks at 1 end; then fillings: meat, potatoes, olives, and jalapeños; then husk strips with space for tying tamales and containers to stack them in.

10. For each tamale, lay a husk fairly flat with smooth side up. Spoon ¼ cup masa in center. Hold husk with 1 hand; using quick flicks of the back of a soup spoon or a small spatula, evenly spread half of masa from center flush to 1 long edge (leave a 1-inch margin clear at top and bottom of husk; see top photo at left). Repeat process on other half of husk.

11. Spread 2 to 3 tablespoons filling in a band 1 inch from 1 long edge of masa. Place a potato piece, 2 olives, and a jalapeño piece over meat. Fold long edge of husk closest to fillings over them, then roll up snugly. If husk doesn't quite meet to enclose filling, patch with a piece of another husk.

12. Using husk strips, tie tamale as tightly as possible at both ends, then just to hold in place in center. If necessary, knot 2 strips together to make a longer tie. Repeat to make remaining tamales. Snip ties to neaten, if desired.

13. Cooking. Cook tamales as described below, or freeze airtight up to 3 months, then cook frozen. To cook 2 dozen tamales, you'll need an 8- to 10-quart pan. Set a rack on supports at least 1 inch from bottom of pan. Fill pan with 1 inch reserved pork broth or water (1 to 1½ qts.). Arrange tamales lengthwise over rack or foil, changing direction of tamales 90° every layer.

14. Cover and bring to a boil over high heat, then simmer over medium heat until masa no longer sticks to husks, and potatoes are tender to bite, 1 to 1¼ hours for freshly made tamales, 1½ to 1¾ hours for frozen; occasionally add boiling water to maintain level of liquid. Serve with salsa.

Per tamale: 245 cal., 59% (144 cal.) from fat; 8.9 g protein; 16 g fat (5.5 g sat.); 18 g carbo.; 673 mg sodium; 33 mg chol. ∎

MAIL-ORDER GOURMET TAMALES

Fired up about tamales but have no time to make them? Corn Maiden Company specializes in frozen tamales by mail: 16 flavors in appetizer or regular sizes. Black bean–jalapeño jack and green chili–smoked gouda are among the most popular. High marks also go to the pumpkin-brandy dessert tamales. Prices range from $18 to $30 per dozen for regular size, and shipping is extra; (310) 202-6180.

Everything you need to know for the perfect holiday sweets

Recipes for every cookie desire, from simple to fancy, chewy to crunchy. And we didn't forget about chocolate

DECEMBER SKEWS THE BAKING curve dramatically. Even if you never bake during the rest of the year, the urge to make cookies swells. But occasionally even the simplest cookies go wrong. Often you don't have enough time. And sometimes you want a cookie that doesn't look like all the others.

Where to start?

Questions you may have about cookies are apt to be answered in the Why? section of this guide. When you're pressed for time, bar cookies fill the bill, and a superb version follows. When you want cookies that create murmurs of admiration before they disappear, our pine nut pralines are the answer.

A praline wafer that's elegant, versatile

These delicate caramelized pine nut wafers, when hot from the oven, are flexible enough to fold and shape like pieces of paper. As they cool, they become rigid and hold their new form. Consequently, this single cookie is a one-man show in five acts—when all the various shapes and fillings are presented together. Unadorned, the shiny wafers are handsome on their own. As sandwiches, the cookies cling together with a filling of spicy dark chocolate or white chocolate studded with dried cranberries. The cones and tubes hold a whipped cream filling.

Pine Nut Praline Wafers

Cooking time: About 7 minutes per pan

Prep time: About 15 minutes

Notes: Measure cookie batter exactly to get uniform-size cookies. Store in rigid, airtight containers, separating layers with plastic wrap to prevent sticking and breakage. Hold at room temperature up to 1 week; freeze to store longer.

Makes: 30 cookies

> About ¼ cup (⅛ lb.) butter or margarine
>
> ¼ cup *each* light corn syrup and firmly packed brown sugar
>
> ¼ cup all-purpose flour
>
> ¼ cup pine nuts

1. In a 1- to 2-quart pan, melt ¼ cup butter over low heat. Add corn syrup and brown sugar. Stir over high heat until boiling. Remove pan from heat, and stir in flour until smooth. Mix in nuts.

2. Coat 12- by 15-inch nonstick baking sheets (they must be flat, not warped) with a nonstick cooking spray or additional butter, then lightly flour pans. For each cookie, place 1 level teaspoon batter on the baking sheet, allowing about 3 inches between cookies.

3. Bake in a 350° oven until cookies are evenly colored a rich golden brown, 5 to 7 minutes. If using 2 pans in 1 oven, alternate positions at half-time.

4. Let cookies cool on pan until they firm slightly, 1½ to 2 minutes. To test, slide a thin

PINE NUT PRALINE WAFERS *(left), shaped as cones, hold whipped cream laced with chocolate chunks. The praline wafer sandwiches (right) are held together by chili-flavored chocolate or white chocolate with dried cranberry filling. The iced apricot bars (top) are the cookie for cooks in a rush.*

PAUL HAMMOND

spatula under an edge. If the cookie is stretchy, wait just a few seconds longer. When cookies are barely firm, slide a spatula under them carefully and transfer to racks to cool in a single layer. If cookies stick to pan, return to oven until they soften slightly, then remove from pan.

5. As soon as the cookies are cool, package airtight.

Per cookie: 39 cal., 54% (21 cal.) from fat; 0.4 g protein; 2.3 g fat (1.1 g sat.); 4.8 g carbo.; 20 mg sodium; 4.3 mg chol.

Pine Nut Praline Sandwiches

Cooking time: About 7 minutes per pan

Prep time: About 15 minutes to assemble, 30 minutes for fillings to cool

Notes: Use 1 batch of filling—chili chocolate or white-chocolate cranberry—to make sandwiches from 1 batch of cookies. Fill cookies when baked, or store plain cookies and fill when convenient.

Makes: 15 sandwiches

1. Make the **pine nut praline wafers**, preceding.

2. Turn ½ the cookies flat side up on a sheet of waxed paper.

3. Gently swirl about 1½ teaspoons filling (choices follow) onto each inverted cookie and immediately sandwich the flat side of another cookie against it. Let stand until chocolate is slightly set and cool, about 30 minutes. Because these cookies are particularly prone to picking up moisture from the air (getting sticky and soft), package airtight in rigid container if you do not serve them at once.

Chili chocolate filling. Melt (in a microwave oven or over very low heat) 1 cup chopped **bittersweet** or semisweet **chocolate**, stirring until smooth. Add ⅛ to ¼ teaspoon **cayenne** to taste—enough for a faint touch of heat. Use warm.

Per sandwich: 134 cal., 57% (77 cal.) from fat; 1.6 g protein; 8.5 g fat (4.3 g sat.); 16 g carbo.; 41 mg sodium; 8.6 mg chol.

White chocolate–cranberry filling. Melt (in a microwave oven or over hot water) 1 cup chopped **white chocolate**, stirring until smooth. Add 2 tablespoons minced **dried cranberries**, and stir to mix. Use warm.

Per sandwich: 142 cal., 51% (72 cal.) from fat; 1.5 g protein; 8 g fat (4.2 g sat.); 17 g carbo.; 51 mg sodium; 8.6 mg chol.

Cream-filled Pine Nut Praline Cones

Cooking time: About 35 minutes

Prep time: 30 to 40 minutes to assemble, shape, and fill

Notes: Shape cookies while still pliable on metal cone-shaped pastry forms, avail-

WHILE WARM, *pine nut praline wafers are soft enough to wrap around metal forms. They harden quickly. Store cookies empty; fill to serve.*

able at specialty cookware shops. Or make cones 3 to 4 inches long, using lightweight cardboard, then wrap cones with foil.

Makes: 30 cookies

1. Make the **pine nut praline wafers**, preceding, but bake only 4 to 6 cookies at a time.

2. Shape each cookie around a cone, holding briefly until cookie is rigid—almost at once. Slip cookie from form and set on rack to cool. Repeat to shape and bake remaining cookies, warming as directed if they get hard. As soon as cookies are cool, store airtight as directed.

3. Up to 1 day before serving, beat 1½ cups **whipping cream** until it holds distinct peaks. Fold in ⅓ cup chopped **bittersweet** or semisweet **chocolate**, 3 tablespoons **powdered sugar**, and 1 tablespoon finely shredded **orange peel**. Spoon mixture into a pastry bag fitted with a ¾-inch plain tip. Cover and chill until cold, at least 15 minutes or up to 1 day.

4. Up to 1 hour before serving, pipe cream filling into cones. If desired, garnish cream with additional shredded orange peel and/or chopped chocolate. Serve, or cover and chill airtight no longer than 1 hour.

Per cookie: 86 cal., 69% (59 cal.) from fat; 0.8 g protein; 6.6 g fat (3.7 g sat.); 7 g carbo.; 24 mg sodium; 18 mg chol.

Cream-filled Pine Nut Praline Rolls

Make the **pine nut praline wafers**, preceding, and bake as directed for the pine nut praline cones, above, but shape warm cookies into tubes around cannoli tubes or a foil-wrapped ½- to ¾-inch-diameter round wood dowel or wooden spoon handle. Fill as directed for cones.

Nutritional information is the same as for cream-filled pine nut praline cones.

By Linda Lau Anusasananan

A simple, but not dull, brandied apricot bar

With a few strokes of a knife, one cookie becomes dozens. This alone, from the cook's perspective, could explain the popularity of bar cookies. But there's more to be told. Bar cookies can be firm and crisp, or cakelike. They can be plain and simple, or seasoned with a sophisticated hand like these tender apricot bars moistened with apricot syrup—with or without brandy. Because you can have the cookies mixed and baked in considerably less than an hour, they just might make the right gift to bring by the panful to a family, by the plateful to a single friend, or to pull out of the oven when carolers pause for refreshments.

PAUL HAMMOND

Brandied Apricot Bars

Baking time: About 20 minutes
Prep Time: About 20 minutes
Notes: Ice cookies or leave plain, as desired.
Makes: 3 dozen

- 1 cup (½ lb.) butter or margarine
- 1 cup granulated sugar
- ½ cup firmly packed brown sugar
- 4 large eggs
- 1 tablespoon grated orange peel
- 1 tablespoon vanilla
- 1¼ cups all-purpose flour
- 1 teaspoon baking powder
- ½ teaspoon baking soda
- ½ teaspoon ground cinnamon
- 2 cups chopped dried apricots
- 1 cup golden raisins
- ¼ cup apricot-flavor brandy or liqueur, or orange juice
- 7 teaspoons lemon juice
- ⅔ cup powdered sugar

1. In a large bowl, beat butter, ½ cup granulated sugar, and brown sugar with a mixer

until fluffy. Beat in eggs, 1 at a time, mixing well after each addition. Beat in orange peel and vanilla.

2. In another bowl, mix flour, baking powder, soda, and cinnamon. Stir into butter mixture along with apricots and raisins.

3. Pour batter into a lightly buttered 10- by 15-inch pan. Bake at 350° until cookie is browned and center springs back when lightly pressed, about 20 minutes.

4. *Apricot syrup.* While cookie bakes, combine remaining ½ cup granulated sugar, brandy, and 3 teaspoons lemon juice in a 1- to 1½-quart pan. Bring to a boil over high heat. Remove from heat, and when cookie comes from the oven, spoon warm syrup evenly over it. Let cool, then cut into 3 dozen equal pieces and leave in pan.

5. *Lemon icing.* Mix remaining lemon juice and powdered sugar until smooth. Drizzle or pipe icing over the cookies and then remove from pan.

6. Serve, or store cookies airtight up to 2 days; freeze to store longer.

Per piece: 148 cal., 35% (52 cal.) from fat; 1.6 g protein; 5.8 g fat (3.4 g sat.); 23 g carbo.; 94 mg sodium; 38 mg chol.

By Christine Weber Hale

Chocolate chips: attention to details

Turning the classic chocolate chip cookie into one that's thick and chewy or crisp and thin takes only subtle recipe manipulations. In fact, these differences often happen by surprise. But when you know what makes the cookie work, you can get exactly what you want—chewy, cakey, soft, crisp, thick, thin, even chewy-crisp. It's all in how you control the principals—ingredients, proportions, cookie size, and baking temperature.

Thick, Soft, and Chewy Chocolate Chip Cookies

Cooking time: About 7 minutes
Prep time: About 10 minutes
Makes: About 18

- 1¼ cups all-purpose flour
- ½ teaspoon baking soda
- ¼ teaspoon salt
- ½ cup (¼ lb.) butter or margarine, at room temperature
- ¾ cup firmly packed brown sugar
- ½ teaspoon vanilla
- 1 large egg
- 1 package (6 oz.) or 1 cup semisweet chocolate chips
- ½ cup chopped nuts (optional)

1. Mix flour, baking soda, and salt.

2. Beat butter, sugar, and vanilla with a mixer on medium speed until well blended. Beat in egg, mixing well. Add flour mixture, and beat slowly to incorporate, then beat to blend well. Stir in chocolate bits and nuts.

3. Drop batter in 2-tablespoon portions about 2 inches apart on baking sheets.

4. Bake in a 400° oven until cookies are brown at edges but about 1 inch in the center is still pale, 6 to 7 minutes. If using 2 pans in 1 oven, switch positions at half-time.

5. Let cookies cool on pan about 5 minutes, then transfer to racks with a spatula. Serve warm or cool. Store airtight up to 8 hours, or freeze for longer storage.

Per cookie: 160 cal., 46% (73 cal.) from fat; 1.7 g protein; 8.1 g fat (4.8 g sat.); 22 g carbo.; 124 mg sodium; 26 mg chol.

Soft, Thick, Cakey Chocolate Chip Cookies

Make **thick, soft, and chewy chocolate chip cookies,** preceding, reducing the butter to ⅓ cup and adding 3 tablespoons **milk** along with the egg.

Per cookie: 146 cal., 40% (58 cal.) from fat; 1.7 g protein; 6.4 g fat (3.8 g sat.); 22 g carbo.; 108 mg sodium; 21 mg chol.

Thin, Crisp Chocolate Chip Cookies

Cooking time: About 20 minutes
Prep time: About 10 minutes
Makes: About 32

- 1 cup all-purpose flour
- ¾ teaspoon baking soda
- ¼ teaspoon salt
- ½ cup (¼ lb.) melted butter or margarine
- ½ cup firmly packed brown sugar
- ⅓ cup granulated sugar
- ½ teaspoon vanilla
- 1 package (6 oz.) or 1 cup semisweet chocolate chips
- ½ cup chopped nuts (optional)

1. Mix flour, baking soda, and salt.

2. With a mixer on medium speed, blend butter, brown sugar, granulated sugar, 3 tablespoons water, and vanilla. Stir flour mixture into butter mixture, then beat until blended. Stir in chocolate chips and nuts.

3. Drop batter in 1-tablespoon portions about 2 inches apart on baking sheets.

4. Bake in 300° oven until an even golden brown color all over, 18 to 20 minutes. If using 2 pans in 1 oven, switch positions at half-time.

LITTLE CHANGES *make a big difference. The chocolate chip cookie at left is soft, thick, and chewy. With only minor ingredient adjustments, the same cookie, on the right, is thin and crisp.*

NORMAN A. PLATE

5. Let cookies cool on pan about 3 minutes, then transfer to racks with a spatula. Serve warm or cool. Store airtight up to 1 day, or freeze for longer storage.

Per cookie: 86 cal., 47% (40 cal.) from fat; 0.6 g protein; 4.4 g fat (2.6 g sat.); 12 g carbo.; 77 mg sodium; 7.8 mg chol.

Thin, Crisp, and Chewy Chocolate Chip Cookies

Make **thin, crisp chocolate chip cookies,** preceding, baking until the cookies are browned at edges but an area about 1 inch wide in the center is still pale, about 14 minutes.

Per cookie: 86 cal., 47% (40 cal.) from fat; 0.6 g protein; 4.4 g fat (2.6 g sat.); 12 g carbo.; 77 mg sodium; 7.8 mg chol.

Thick, Crunchy Chocolate Chip Cookies

Make **thin, crisp chocolate chip cookies,** preceding, increasing butter to ⅔ cup and omitting water.

Dough will be dry and crumbly; pinch into 1-tablespoon-size lumps. Bake cookies until they are an even golden brown color, 18 to 20 minutes.

Per cookie: 94 cal., 51% (48 cal.) from fat; 0.7 g protein; 5.3 g fat (3.2 g sat.); 12 g carbo.; 87 mg sodium; 10 mg chol. ∎

By Linda Lau Anusasananan, Andrew Baker

Why?

Why are chocolate chip cookies soft and chewy one time, thin and crisp another? Why do soft cookies get hard, and crisp cookies get soft?

Soft and chewy, dense and thick, thin and crisp are adjectives often used in pairs— even trios—to describe the ideal cookie. Clearly, perfection in a cookie is a matter of individual preference. And no cookie is judged more closely and more frequently than the chocolate chip, if our mail and the reactions of our own tasters are indicative.

The burning issue is how to make the cookie turn out the way you want, every time. Curiously, most cooks who asked for help use the same recipe—the one on the back of the Nestlé chocolate chip bag. It's a reliable recipe, but subtle changes produce surprising differences. To determine which factors influence the final cookie, we used the wrapper recipe and baked more than 25 variations. Each batch was slightly different, and changes in proportions, mixing methods, and baking were carefully controlled. The goal: to learn how to make the cookie that matches your favorite adjectives.

What makes cookies soft and chewy?

High moisture content does; so the recipe, baking time, and temperature must be adjusted to retain moisture. Binding the water in butter, eggs, and brown sugar (it contains molasses, which is 10 percent water) with flour slows its evaporation. The dough needs a little extra flour, which makes it stiffer. The stiff dough spreads less, less liquid evaporates, and the cookies are thicker. Mass also helps cookies stay moist—big dollops of dough make softer and chewier cookies than tiny spoonfuls of dough. Bake these thick cookies for a shorter time at high temperatures to firm them quickly and minimize spreading. Most importantly, don't bake them too long—remove from the oven when the cookie rim is brown and at least ⅓ of the center top remains pale. The centers will be just cooked and still soft.

Why are some cookies cakelike instead of chewy?

A little extra liquid in the cookie dough from water, egg, or milk makes the dough more elastic and adds steam as the cookies bake, making them puff more.

What makes a cookie crisp or crunchy?

Reducing the amount of ingredients that hold moisture—flour, egg, and brown sugar—makes it easy for liquid to evaporate, producing crisp cookies. The fat, which goes up proportionally when other ingredients

are cut back, gets hotter than the water in the dough and drives out the moisture. Fat also makes the dough softer and melts when hot, making the cookies spread. For crispness, bake cookies longer at lower temperatures to give them more time to spread before they firm. Then bake long enough to dry and brown them evenly to develop the maximum toasty flavor and crisp texture throughout.

What else makes cookies spread as they bake?

We've had many calls and letters from cooks having trouble with favorite recipes. All of a sudden, their cookies are spreading excessively. Most often the culprit is low-fat butter or margarine spread, which has about 20 percent more water, used in place of regular butter or margarine. It's this extra liquid that's causing the problem. Low-fat products can't be used interchangeably with regular fats for baking without other recipe adjustments.

Cookies also spread when you drop high-fat dough onto a hot baking sheet; the heat starts the dough melting and spreading before cookies can bake enough to hold their shape.

"When others follow my recipe for chocolate chip cookies, they turn out crunchy. Mine turn out chewy. Why?" asks Bobbie Barrett of San Carlos, California.

The way they measure ingredients and the real temperature of their ovens are the usual reasons cooks get different results from the same recipe. Flour should be stirred to loosen and fluff it, then spooned gently into a dry-measure cup (the kind you fill to the rim), and the top scraped level. If you tap the cup or scoop flour from the bag, the flour gets packed down and you can easily add 2 to 4 extra tablespoons flour per cup—enough to make a big difference in cookies.

You can scoop up white sugar; it doesn't pack. But you should firmly pack brown sugar into a dry-measure cup and scrape the top level.

Dry ingredients should never be measured in heaped-up cups or spoons; scrape dry ingredients level with the surface of the measuring tool. Measure liquid ingredients with liquid-measuring (usually glass or plastic) cups.

If your cookies seem to be baking faster than the recipe indicates they should, chances are your oven is hotter than the thermostat says. Or your oven may actually be running cooler if cookies aren't browning in a timely way. It's a good idea to double-check oven temperature with a thermometer and have the oven setting adjusted as needed.

What does a good party need?

Caterers know. Here they share their favorite recipes, quality shortcuts, and sensible advice. One basic rule: keep it simple

"MY CLIENT WANTS A NICE—BUT instant—lunch for 250 guests. A typical problem," says Joann Roth at Someone's in the Kitchen. Her solution: a menu that's ready and waiting—cold poached salmon, room-temperature salads, and a beautiful arrangement of individual desserts in the center of the tables.

Roth and the rest of the dozen-plus party planners whom we quizzed for entertaining advice have a plan for success. Foremost, they all favor their not-so-secret dishes that consistently win raves from a broad audience. These dishes have qualities that are as important to home cooks as to caterers. Many are surprisingly simple, and most have make-ahead steps that can be crammed into holiday schedules.

Two other hardworking caterer homilies: be flexible, and be prepared to adapt. If you don't have time to make a dish or an element of it, can you buy it? Will purchased pesto fill in for homemade? No time to make dessert? Buy one. If you're a baker, bake breads ahead and store them in the freezer. Otherwise, take advantage of handsome loaves at the market.

But perhaps the most valuable professional advice for a good party is: keep it simple. Avoid foods that take a lot of last-minute attention and detailed handling. When in doubt, serve a nice big roast. Meat as a centerpiece may sound tame, but, say the caterers, it works, especially for a crowd of guests with a wide range of tastes.

Contributing to this roundup: In Arizona, Alan M. Hause, Continental Catering, Phoenix; Carolyn Ellis, Arcadia Farms Cafe & Catering Company, Scottsdale. In California: Joann Roth and Robbie O'Brien, Someone's in the Kitchen, Tarzana; Lisa Wilson, Blue Heron Catering, Oakland; Marsha Polk-Townsend, RSVP Catering, Alameda; Paula LeDuc, Paula LeDuc Fine Catering, Emeryville; Zov Karamardian, Zov's Bistro, Tustin. In Portland, Nancy Briggs, Briggs & Crampton; Ron Paul, Ron Paul Charcuterie. In Seattle, Russell Lowell and Jonathan Hunt, Lowell-Thompson Catering; Phyllis Rosen, Catering by Phyllis.

NOEL BARNHURST

MICHAEL SKOTT

PROFESSIONAL PARTY GIVERS: *Russell Lowell, Jonathan Hunt, and Jeremy Bryant (front to back, at left) at Lowell-Thompson Catering, and Marsha Polk-Townsend, RSVP Catering.*

Handy tips, fast bites,

• *Freshen pesto.* To brighten color and flavor of purchased pesto, whirl in fresh parsley, cilantro, arugula, or more basil.

• *Buy instant flavor.* Start with quality prepared seasonings such as curry pastes, salsas, chutneys, and tapenades.

• *Choose wiltproof garnishes.* Best bets are fresh rosemary and parsley, kale (green or purple), cabbage (red, green, or napa), radicchio, and Belgian endive.

• *Think light.* Offer no-fat salsas instead of creamy dips. Serve turkey breast instead of beef tenderloin. Supplement smaller meat portions with generous amounts of grain or vegetables.

• *Use flaky filo pastry.* Lightly butter and stack sheets of filo dough to make lavish wrappers and crusts for baked foods.

TANTALIZING BITES *in wrappers: grapefruit and mint tuck into steak strip (center), and prosciutto cloaks shrimp with basil.*

and hardworking ingredients from the experts

• *Pick vegetables for color stability*. If they are to be kept hot for more than a few minutes, choose yellow, orange, red, and white vegetables such as corn, carrots, crookneck squash, golden squash, sweet potatoes, cauliflower, potatoes, and red cabbage. To set color of green vegetables, cook and immediately chill in ice water. Serve at room temperature or warm just before serving.

• *Make easy shrimp bites*. Lay a few basil or cilantro leaves on each shelled shrimp and enclose in a thin prosciutto slice. If raw, grill or broil. Serve hot or cold, a few for appetizers, more for a main dish.

• *Stuff potatoes*. Slash open tiny roasted red potatoes and fill with sour cream and caviar (from sturgeon or flying fish) for an easy appetizer.

• *Crisp-fry filled pasta*. In enough hot oil to cover, fry fresh filled pasta (homemade or purchased) such as wontons, tortellini, or ravioli until crisp. Serve with a spicy marinara sauce, chili salsa, or minced mango chutney.

• *Use big round cracker bread*. Roll slightly dampened cracker bread around grilled eggplant, tomatoes, feta cheese; slice for sandwiches; make smaller pieces for appetizers.

• *Personalize purchased desserts*. Top cheesecake with fresh fruit and a jelly glaze. Drizzle hot melted sugar over fruit tarts (only if glaze is not gelatin based). Swirl purchased caramel sauce or lemon curd through whipped cream or yogurt to top portions of pies or cakes.

• *Serve enough appetizers*. For an open house or similar reception, have five to six kinds. Allow two to three portions of each per guest.

• *Serve enough food*. For a dinner party, if meat (poultry or fish) is the main course, start with the equivalent of 4 to 6 ounces boned, uncooked meat per person, at least 4 ounces complex carbohydrates (potatoes, pasta, grains), and at least 3 ounces salad or vegetables. If serving less meat, increase the other two menu elements proportionally.

• *Serve enough wine*. Allow 1 bottle for 5 to 6 servings and, conservatively, at least 1½ to 2 servings per person. Increase wine by 25 percent if it's the only beverage. If serving several courses and several wines, have ½ to 1 bottle total per person.

• *Be beverage-savvy*. If there's an open bar, expect 50 percent of the guests to choose wine. Provide nonalcoholic options such as mineral water and fruit juice, at least a 2-glass serving per person.

Spiced Flank Steak and Grapefruit Appetizers
Lisa Wilson, Blue Heron Catering

Cooking time: About 8 minutes
Prep time: About 30 minutes
Notes: If preferred, grill steak instead of broiling it. Meat can be cooked and grapefruit segmented a day ahead.
Makes: 30 to 34 pieces, 15 to 17 appetizer servings

    1   flank steak (1 1/4 to 1 1/2 lb.)
    2   teaspoons ground cumin
    1   teaspoon dry mustard
    1   teaspoon ground cinnamon
    1/2 teaspoon cayenne
    1/2 teaspoon ground cloves
         About 1/2 teaspoon salt
    3   to 4 pink grapefruit (about 3/4 lb. each)
    30   to 34 fresh mint leaves (optional)

1. Trim fat and silvery membrane from steak. Mix cumin, mustard, cinnamon, cayenne, cloves, and 1/2 teaspoon salt, then rub mixture all over steak. Cover and chill at least 15 minutes or up to 2 days.

2. Cut peel and white membrane from grapefruit. Over a bowl, cut between inner membranes and fruit to release segments. If making ahead, cover and chill up to 1 day.

3. Broil steak on a rack in a pan about 4 inches from heat until rare in thickest part (cut to test), about 7 minutes, or medium-rare, about 9 minutes; turn once to cook evenly. Let meat stand at least 15 minutes. If making ahead, cover and chill up to 1 day.

4. Up to 1 hour before serving, drain grapefruit and save juice for another use. Select 30 to 34 of the most attractive grapefruit segments and lay on towels to drain; lightly blot tops to dry. Save remaining fruit for other uses.

5. Slice meat very thinly across the grain into 30 to 34 equal pieces. Wrap each grapefruit segment with a steak slice and set, seam down, on a platter. Tuck a mint leaf into each bundle. Serve, or wrap airtight and chill up to 1 hour. Add salt to taste.

Per 2 pieces: 49 cal., 37% (18 cal.) from fat; 5.1 g protein; 2 g fat (0.8 g sat.); 2.6 g carbo.; 80 mg sodium; 12 mg chol.

Date and Chorizo Rumaki
Alan M. Hause, Continental Catering

Cooking time: About 35 minutes
Prep time: About 30 minutes

Notes: To make a day ahead, assemble rumaki, put in cooking pan, cover and chill, then uncover and bake to serve.
Makes: 32 pieces, 16 appetizer servings

    16   slices thin-cut bacon (about 3/4 lb.)
    1/2 pound raw chorizo sausage
    1/4 pound (1/3 cup) cream cheese
    32   whole dates, pitted
    3   tablespoons chopped fresh cilantro

1. Arrange bacon slices in a single layer in a 10- by 15-inch pan. Bake in a 350° oven for 5 minutes. Discard fat and blot bacon with paper towels.

2. Remove chorizo from casing and crumble into an 8- to 10-inch frying pan. Stir often over medium-high heat until meat is lightly browned, about 7 minutes. Let drain in a fine strainer to remove fat.

3. Mix chorizo with cream cheese.

4. Cut halfway through dates on 1 side to make a pocket in each. Fill dates equally with the cheese mixture.

5. Cut bacon slices in half. Wrap each date with a piece of bacon and secure with a toothpick. Place dates on a rack in the 10- by 15-inch pan.

6. Bake in a 350° oven until bacon is brown and crisp, 25 to 30 minutes. Sprinkle with cilantro, and serve hot.

Per 2 pieces: 130 cal., 52% (68 cal.) from fat; 4 g protein; 7.6 g fat (3.3 g sat.); 12 g carbo.; 205 mg sodium; 19 mg chol.

Mussels with Thai Broth
Marsha Polk-Townsend, RSVP Catering

Cooking time: About 10 minutes
Prep time: About 20 minutes

Notes: For a fast but elegant meal, serve mussels with green salad and crusty bread, with mango sorbet for dessert. If curry paste isn't available, use all of this mixture: 1 tablespoon minced **fresh ginger**, 1 teaspoon **curry powder**, 1 teaspoon **chili powder**, and 1/4 teaspoon **cayenne**.

Makes: 4 main-dish servings

    1   cup dry white wine
    1/2 cup thinly slivered onion
    1   teaspoon minced garlic
    32   mussels (beards pulled off) or clams, suitable for steaming, scrubbed
    1   can (about 14 oz.) unsweetened regular or low-fat coconut milk
    3   to 4 teaspoons Thai red curry paste
    1/4 cup slivered fresh basil leaves

1. In a 5- to 6-quart pan, bring wine with

The big, beautiful roast

Roasting a piece of meat for a crowd is a no-brainer. Most caterers favor a boneless piece, such as a New York beef strip (boned loin) or tenderloin, that is a cinch to carve into slices, thick or thin.

Just slip the meat into the oven; sprinkling with salt and pepper is adequate, but extra seasoning adds character. Large roasts get a rich brown in the time they take to cook. But smaller, thinner cuts, such as pork tenderloin or venison loin, need more help. Before roasting, brown meat on a very hot grill or in a frying pan. If you do this ahead, you get a messy step out of the way. Chill the meat, then finish roasting to serve.

Beef Loin Roast

Cooking time: About 1 1/4 hours for rare, longer to cook more
Prep time: About 5 minutes

Notes: Suggestions for simple seasonings follow the recipe. Use an instant-read thermometer to check internal temperature of roast. Let hot roast rest before carving so juices settle back into the meat.

Makes: 22 to 28 servings

    1   fat-trimmed New York strip beef roast (boned loin), 8 to 10 pounds
         Salt and pepper
         Seasonings plus (optional)

1. Trim remaining surface fat from beef. Set meat on a rack in a 12- by 17-inch roasting pan. Leave meat plain, season with salt and

pepper, or rub with a seasoning option.

2. Roast meat in a 375° oven until a thermometer inserted in thickest part reaches 115° to 120° for very rare, 1 1/4 to 1 1/2 hours; 125° to 130° for medium rare, 1 3/4 to 2 hours; 135° to 140° for medium, 2 1/4 to 2 1/2 hours.

3. Let roast rest in a warm place, lightly covered, for 15 to 20 minutes. Serve hot, warm, or cool. If making ahead, cover and chill up to 1 day. Slice roast across the grain into thick or thin slices (easiest if meat is cold). Add salt and pepper to taste.

Seasonings plus:

Rub beef with olive oil, crushed garlic, and rosemary leaves.

Rub beef with olive oil, Cajun spice mix, and white and black pepper.

Rub beef with aromatic spices used to season the flank steak and grapefruit appetizer (above).

MARSHA POLK-TOWNSEND'S *mussels in coconut broth is a fast appetizer or main course for a dinner party. The dish is seasoned with purchased Thai curry paste.*

onion and garlic to a boil. Add shellfish. Cover and cook over medium heat until shells open, 5 to 7 minutes for mussels, 8 to 10 minutes for clams.

2. Mix coconut milk smoothly with 3 teaspoons curry paste, or more to taste.

3. Transfer shellfish to 4 wide soup bowls. Stir coconut milk mixture into pan; add basil and heat to simmering. Ladle into bowls.

Per serving: 337 cal., 59% (198 cal.) from fat; 18 g protein; 22 g fat (19 g sat.); 9 g carbo.; 84 mg sodium; 41 mg chol.

Pork Loin with Romesco Sauce
Ron Paul, Ron Paul Charcuterie

Cooking time: About 1 1/2 hours

Prep time: About 20 minutes

Notes: Meat can be roasted and sauce made a day ahead. Paul prefers pork at an internal temperature of 135°, but we suggest the food-safe temperature of 140° for meat that is quite pink in the center. Any extra romesco sauce is excellent with other meats or as a vegetable dip.

Makes: 8 to 10 main-dish, 16 to 20 appetizer servings

1 1/2 cups blanched almonds

1 boned, rolled, and tied center-cut pork loin (3 1/2 to 4 lb.), fat trimmed

About 1/2 cup olive oil

1 tablespoon fresh or dried rosemary leaves

Salt

About 1 1/2 teaspoons pepper

1 1/2 tablespoons chopped garlic

1 3/4 cups canned roasted red peppers, rinsed and drained

4 teaspoons drained prepared capers

2 teaspoons ground coriander

1/2 teaspoon *each* dried marjoram, thyme, basil, and oregano

1/2 teaspoon ground cumin

1. Place almonds in a 10- by 15-inch pan. Bake in a 400° oven until nuts are golden, about 15 minutes. Remove from pan and let cool.

2. Place a rack in the pan. Rub pork with 1 tablespoon oil and rosemary. Lightly sprinkle with salt and pepper. Set meat on rack.

3. Roast pork in a 400° oven until a thermometer inserted in thickest part reaches 140° for pink center, about 50 minutes; 150° for pale pink center, about 1 hour; or 155° for an evenly white center, 1 hour and 5 to 15 minutes. Let roast cool. If making ahead, cover and chill up to 1 day. Remove strings and thinly slice pork, arranging meat on a platter.

4. Meanwhile, in a 6- to 8-inch frying pan over medium-high heat, stir garlic and 1 tablespoon olive oil until garlic becomes golden and soft when pressed, about 5 minutes. Pour garlic mixture into a blender or food processor and add almonds, 1 1/4 teaspoons pepper, 1/3 cup olive oil, red peppers, capers, coriander, marjoram, thyme, basil, oregano, and cumin. Smoothly purée romesco sauce, then add salt to taste. Makes about 1 1/2 cups. Spoon sauce into a serving dish. If making ahead, cover and chill up to 1 day.

5. Accompany pork with sauce.

Per serving pork: 230 cal., 43% (99 cal.) from fat; 30 g protein; 11 g fat (3.8 g sat.); 0.2 g carbo.; 72 mg sodium; 86 mg chol.

Per 1 tablespoon sauce: 85 cal., 81% (69 cal.) from fat; 1.9 g protein; 7.7 g fat (0.9 g sat.); 2.7 g carbo.; 34 mg sodium; 0 mg chol.

Arugula Pesto Quail with Chèvre and Shiitake
Jonathan Hunt and Russell Lowell, Lowell-Thompson Catering

Cooking time: About 50 minutes

Prep time: About 45 minutes

Notes: Purchase basil pesto or make your own.

Makes: 4 main-dish, 8 appetizer servings

8 boned quail (1 1/4 lb. total)

About 1 tablespoon olive oil

8 large unpeeled cloves garlic

1/4 pound fresh shiitake or common mushrooms

1/2 cup chicken broth

5 ounces fresh chèvre (goat cheese)

1/2 cup prepared pesto

1/2 cup lightly packed arugula leaves, rinsed and drained

Additional arugula leaves or basil sprigs

Salt and pepper

1. Rinse quail, pat dry, and rub lightly with olive oil, using about 2 teaspoons total.

2. Place on a grill about 4 inches above hot coals or high heat on a gas barbecue (you can hold your hand at grill level only 2 to 3 seconds). Close lid on gas grill. Cook to brown birds evenly, about 1 1/2 minutes per side. Let cool.

3. In an 8- to 10-inch frying pan, combine 1/2 teaspoon oil and garlic. Cook over medium-low heat, turning cloves occasionally until soft when pressed, 20 to 25 minutes. Remove from pan and let cool.

4. Rinse mushrooms. Trim and discard shiitake stems (use common mushroom stems). Coarsely chop mushrooms and put in frying pan with 1 teaspoon oil. Stir often over medium-high heat until lightly browned, 8 to 10 minutes. Remove from heat and add broth; stir browned bits free. Squeeze garlic from skins into pan. Add cheese and stir until well blended.

5. Stuff cheese mixture equally into each

A FAVORITE *at Lowell-Thompson Catering is grilled eggplant slices dressed with a tomato vinaigrette. The salad holds well at room temperature.*

quail. Set quail in a 10- by 15-inch pan. If making ahead, cover and chill up to 1 day.

6. In a blender, smoothly purée the pesto and ½ cup packed arugula. If making ahead, cover and chill up to 1 day.

7. Spoon pesto equally over quail. Bake in a 450° oven until quail are hot and thigh meat is pink at bone (cut to test), about 20 minutes. Transfer quail to a platter and garnish with arugula leaves. Pour pan juices into a small bowl and serve to spoon over quail, adding salt and pepper to taste.

Per piece: 287 cal., 67% (198 cal.) from fat; 20 g protein; 22 g fat (7 g sat.); 4 g carbo.; 222 mg sodium; 11 mg chol.

Grilled Eggplant with Tomato Caper Vinaigrette

Cooking time: About 30 minutes
Prep time: About 25 minutes
Notes: To make ahead, let cooked eggplant slices stand up to 3 hours, or cover and chill up to 1 day. Two alternatives: grill eggplant instead of baking, or use 2 pounds slender Asian eggplant for smaller pieces.
Makes: 6 salad, 12 appetizer servings

    2   eggplant (about 1 lb. each)
    7   tablespoons olive oil
    1   Roma tomato (about ¼ lb.)
    1   tablespoon red wine vinegar
    1   tablespoon sherry vinegar
    1½ teaspoons minced prepared capers
    1   teaspoon chopped shallots
    1   teaspoon chopped garlic
    1   teaspoon chopped fresh basil leaves
        Fresh basil sprigs
        Salt and pepper

1. Trim and discard eggplant stems. Cut eggplant crosswise in ⅜-inch-thick rounds, and brush slices lightly with oil, using about 3 tablespoons. Arrange slices in a single layer in 2 pans, each 10 by 15 inches.

2. Bake in a 425° oven until slices are browned and soft when pressed, about 25 minutes.

3. Finely chop tomato and mix with remaining ¼ cup oil, wine vinegar, sherry vinegar, capers, shallots, garlic, and chopped basil.

4. Arrange eggplant slices on a platter and moisten evenly with tomato dressing. Garnish with basil sprigs. Add salt and pepper to taste.

Per salad serving: 185 cal., 78% (144 cal.) from fat; 1.9 g protein; 16 g fat (2.2 g sat.); 11 g carbo.; 26 mg sodium; 0 mg chol. ■

By Linda Lau Anusasananan

TWICE-BAKED MUFFIN *chips are very crunchy; munch, or dunk in coffee.*

Only the crisp survives

Getting the edge, and just the edge, on muffins

IF YOUR FAVORITE PART OF A MUFFIN IS the crisp edge around the pan rim, this recipe is for you; it eliminates all that soft stuff.

Instead of baking muffins in cups, spread batter in a wide pan. Once the tender sheet is baked, break it into chunks and dry them in the oven. These crisp hunks store well.

Basic Muffin Chips

Cooking time: About 2 hours
Prep time: About 15 minutes
Makes: 12 pieces

    1½ cups all-purpose flour
    ½   cup sugar
    2   teaspoons baking powder
    ¾   cup milk
        About ¼ cup (⅛ lb.) butter or margarine, melted
    1   large egg
        Flavor ingredients (choices and directions follow)

1. In a bowl, stir flour with sugar and baking powder; set aside. In another bowl, beat to blend milk, ¼ cup butter, and egg. Add to flour mixture along with flavor ingredients; stir just until evenly moistened. Pour batter into a buttered 10- by 15-inch rimmed pan.

2. Bake in a 375° oven until muffin springs back when gently pressed in center, 25 to 30 minutes. Let cool in pan.

3. Tear or cut muffin into 12 pieces of roughly the same size. Place pieces well apart in 2 pans (10- by 15-in. size). Bake in a 250° oven until the muffin chips are dry and crisp to touch, about 1½ hours. Serve warm, or cool on racks. If making ahead, store airtight at room temperature up to 4 days.

Cranberry cornmeal muffin chips. Decrease **flour** to 1 cup and add 1 cup **yellow cornmeal.** To batter, add 1 cup **dried cranberries.** Mix together 2 tablespoons **sugar** and 1 teaspoon grated **orange peel;** sprinkle over batter in pan, then bake.

Per piece: 201 cal., 24% (48 cal.) from fat; 3.1 g protein; 5.3 g fat (3 g sat.); 36 g carbo.; 127 mg sodium; 31 mg chol.

Cherry muffin chips. Mix into batter 1 cup **dried cherries.** Mix together 2 tablespoons **sugar** and 1 teaspoon grated **lemon peel;** sprinkle mixture over batter in pan, then bake.

Per piece: 178 cal., 26 % (47 cal.) from fat; 2.7 g protein; 5.2 g fat (3 g sat.); 31 g carbo.; 127 mg sodium; 31 mg chol.

Pumpkin muffin chips. Increase **sugar** to ¾ cup and add 1 teaspoon **baking soda.** To batter, add 1 cup **canned pumpkin** and ¾ cup chopped **dried apricots.** Sprinkle ⅓ cup **sliced almonds** over batter in pan, then bake. Increase second baking time to about 2½ hours total.

Per piece: 199 cal., 30% (59 cal.) from fat; 3.7 g protein; 6.6 g fat (3.2 g sat.); 32 g carbo.; 197 mg sodium; 31 mg chol. ■

By Christine Weber Hale

A fine seasonal trio: hazelnuts, Satsuma mandarins, and Comice pears.

KEVIN CANDLAND

Just in time for the holidays

How to choose and use three Western treasures—
two kinds of fruit and one nut—in their prime

BY CHRISTINE WEBER HALE

FOR GIFTS, FOR COOKING, OR FOR JUST PLAIN EATING, COMICE PEARS, Satsuma mandarins, and hazelnuts fit the bill. And you'll find them at their best and most plentiful right now.

Comice pears

The buttery smooth texture and intense flavor of freshly harvested Comice pears, grown in several Western states, quickly fade when the fruit is commercially stored.

Like other pears, the Comice is picked firm and must ripen off the tree, but it's ready to enjoy in just a few days. When ripe enough to eat, the pear is fragile and bruises easily, so it's best to buy firm fruit, ignoring minor surface blemishes but avoiding pears with soft spots. Put firm pears (in no more than two layers) in a paper bag, fold top to close loosely, and let stand at room temperature until the fruit gives to gentle pressure on the stem end, two to seven days. Store pears in the refrigerator as long as a week.

Comice flesh darkens rapidly when exposed to air, so rub cut surfaces with lemon juice to slow the browning.

Serving suggestions
• *For salad,* combine peeled Comice slices with leaves of Belgian endive, frisée, and butter lettuce. Moisten salad with a dressing of tart balsamic vinegar and a nut oil (such as walnut, almond, or macadamia oil).
• *For dessert,* top Comice slices with a dollop of regular to nonfat sour cream (let your conscience be your guide) and a sprinkling of dark brown sugar or a splash of maple syrup.
• *For breakfast,* peel Comice pears, cut in half lengthwise, core, and fill hollows with raspberry jam, then top with spoonfuls of crème fraîche or unflavored yogurt.

Satsuma mandarins

Knowing Santas put this handsome, deep burnt gold citrus in Christmas stockings, mound them in bowls for seasonal decor, or tuck them into food gift baskets. Beyond beauty, Satsuma mandarins from Southern California are properly prized for their exceptional sweetness and for having few seeds. And like other mandarins and tangerines, they have a loose, almost zip-off peel.

Satsumas first appear in November and are gone by the beginning of January.

Choose fruit that feels heavy for its size—this promises lots of sweet pulp and juice. Avoid Satsumas with soft spots or split peels. The fruit stays good for several days when held at room temperature; refrigerate Satsumas you want to keep longer.

Serving suggestions
• *For salad,* combine Satsuma mandarin segments, romaine lettuce, thinly sliced red onions, and pitted calamata olives, then dress with lemon juice and extra-virgin olive oil.
• *For juice* to serve at holiday brunches and to combine with other beverages, ream Satsuma mandarins. Garnish glasses with Satsuma segments.
• *For dessert,* combine Satsuma segments with an orange-flavor liqueur or syrup to spoon over raspberry or cranberry sherbet or sorbet.

Hazelnuts

Oregon produces 99 percent of the U.S. hazelnut crop, most of it in the picturesque Willamette Valley. The nut, as well as the shrublike tree on which it grows, was formerly known as a filbert. The trees were first planted in Oregon in 1858 by a retired English sailor. Many existing orchards have been producing for more than half a century.

Hazelnuts in the shell are most available in the fall. They are easy to crack, but the nuts are tightly covered by a paper-thin brown skin that you will want to remove because it has a slightly tannic flavor. Roast the nuts to loosen the skin, get rid of the tannic taste, and enhance the nut flavor. You may find skinned hazelnuts in specialty food stores.

To roast, bake shelled hazelnuts in a single layer in a shallow rimmed pan in a 350° oven until nuts are pale gold under the skin, 15 to 20 minutes. Pour hot nuts onto a towel and rub with cloth to remove as much of the papery skin as you can—some bits will stick. Use nuts warm, or seal airtight until ready to serve; freeze if held longer than a few days.

Serving suggestions
• *For an appetizer,* nibble warm roasted hazelnuts with champagne as the French do. It's a memorable combination.
• *For baking,* use roasted hazelnuts in biscotti or as you would other nuts in cookies, muffins, cakes, granolas, or pies—especially in place of pecans in pecan pie.
• *For salad,* scatter chopped roasted hazelnuts into avocado halves, moisten with hazelnut oil, add a squeeze of fresh lime juice, and sprinkle with kosher salt. ■

GOLDEN ALMONDS AND WALNUTS, *chocolate chips, and orange peel fill a rich crust.*

PAUL HAMMOND

Holiday
nut tarts

Make one large tart for a party or several small tarts as gifts

THE INGREDIENTS ARE BASIC—NUTS, eggs, sugar, butter, and flavorings. But when combined, they result in a tart worthy of the season's grandest festivities.

Use just one type of nut or a collection of your favorites. We tried just about every combination in the *Sunset* test kitchen and all worked well, as did the addition of chocolate chips, dried cranberries or dried apricots, and lemon or orange peel.

We also discovered that flavored fruit syrups, found at coffee bars or specialty shops, offer more intense flavors than some liqueurs.

Flavored Nut Tarts

Cooking time: About 1 hour
Prep time: About 20 minutes

Notes: Add liqueur of a favorite flavor, such as orange, almond, or coffee, or a flavored syrup (almond, apricot, and mandarin flavors work especially well).

Makes: 12 servings (one 11-inch tart, two 7-inch tarts, or six 4-inch tarts)

- 2½ cups nuts, such as whole blanched almonds, whole hazelnuts, walnut halves, or pecan halves
- 1½ cups all-purpose flour
- ¾ cup sugar
- 10 tablespoons butter or margarine, cut into tablespoon-size pieces
- 3 large eggs
- ⅓ cup flavored liqueur or flavored syrup
- 1 teaspoon vanilla
- ½ cup chocolate chips, dried cranberries or cherries, or diced dried apricots (optional)
- 1 teaspoon grated lemon or orange peel (optional)

1. Place nuts in a 10- by 15-inch baking pan; if hazelnuts are among the mixture, place them to one side. Bake nuts in a 350° oven about 15 minutes (or until almonds are just golden); shake pan occasionally. After hazelnuts are toasted, place them in a towel and rub to remove as much skin as possible; discard skins.

2. Meanwhile, in a food processor or a bowl, mix flour and ¼ cup of the sugar. Add 8 tablespoons of the butter; whirl (or rub with your fingers) until mixture forms fine crumbs. Add 1 egg; whirl (or mix with a fork) until dough holds together. Press dough over bottom and sides of one 11-inch, two 7-inch, or six 4-inch tart pans with removable rim.

3. Melt remaining 2 tablespoons butter. In a bowl, combine melted butter with remaining ½ cup sugar, remaining 2 eggs, flavored liqueur or syrup, and vanilla until blended. Stir in toasted nuts and, if desired, chocolate chips or dried fruit, and lemon or orange peel. Pour into tart pan (or pans); if using smaller pans, evenly distribute the nuts and syrup.

4. Bake tart on the bottom rack of a 350° oven until golden brown all over, 45 to 50 minutes. If using several tart pans, place them on a 10- by 15-inch baking pan. Cool tarts on a rack. If making ahead, cool, cover, and store at room temperature up until next day. Remove pan rim; cut tart into wedges to serve.

Per serving: 395 cal., 62% (243 cal.) from fat; 9.4 g protein; 27 g fat (7.8 g sat.); 32 g carbo.; 117 mg sodium; 79 mg chol. ■

By Betsy Reynolds Bateson

PETER CHRISTIANSEN

FINE STRANDS OF CARROT *with cool bean sprouts accompany stir-fried Thai noodles.*

Easy-to-make, easy-to-like Thai noodles

Thin noodles are healthy, hearty, and ready in less than 30 minutes

A PASSION FOR PASTA ISN'T RESTRICTED by nationality. One of Thailand's favorite dishes, *pad Thai*—mildly spiced stir-fried noodles—has achieved considerable popularity in Thai restaurants in the West. This distinctive dish is easy to like, and it's also very easy to prepare. The noodles, made of rice flour—not wheat—are heated with tofu and meats. At the table, diners mix the well-seasoned noodles with crisply contrasting vegetables.

Pad Thai

Cooking time: About 10 minutes
Prep time: About 20 minutes
Notes: Some supermarkets and most

Asian grocery stores carry rice noodles (also called rice sticks or *maifun*) and fish sauce. Soy sauce can be used instead of fish sauce.

Makes: 3 or 4 servings

- ½ pound dried rice noodles, preferably about ¼ inch thick, but thinner noodles will work
- ½ pound firm tofu, rinsed
- 1 cup chicken broth
- 3 tablespoons fish sauce (*nam pla* or *nuoc mam*)
- 3 tablespoons catsup
- 2 tablespoons lime juice
- 2 tablespoons sugar
- ¼ to ½ teaspoon cayenne
- 1 tablespoon salad oil
- 4 cloves garlic, pressed or minced
- 6 ounces lean boneless pork or skinned boned chicken, fat trimmed, thinly sliced
- 1 large egg, beaten to blend
- 6 green onions, ends trimmed, cut into 2-inch lengths
- ¾ pound bean sprouts, rinsed and drained
- 3 to 4 tablespoons minced salted roasted peanuts
- ¼ cup fresh cilantro leaves

- ½ cup finely shredded carrot
- Lime wedges

1. Soak noodles in hot (not boiling) water to cover until pliable, 10 to 20 minutes; drain well.

2. Cut tofu into ½-inch-thick slices; drain well. Set slices on several layers of towels, cover with more towels, and press gently to remove water. Cut tofu into ½-inch cubes.

3. Mix broth, fish sauce, catsup, lime juice, sugar, and cayenne.

4. Place a wok or 12-inch frying pan on high heat. When pan is hot, add 1 tablespoon oil; swirl to coat pan. Add tofu; stir often until browned, about 5 minutes. Lift out tofu with a slotted spoon.

5. Add garlic and pork; stir-fry until meat is lightly browned, about 2 minutes. Push mixture to side of pan and add beaten egg to empty space. Cook until egg begins to firm, then stir to break apart. Add broth mixture, tofu, and drained noodles; stir-fry until noodles are hot, 2 to 3 minutes. Add onions and ½ the bean sprouts. Stir and mix until sprouts barely wilt, about 30 seconds.

6. Spoon noodle mixture equally onto plates; top with peanuts and cilantro. Alongside noodles, mound portions of remaining bean sprouts, carrot, and lime wedges.

Per serving: 552 cal., 28% (153 cal.) from fat; 30 g protein; 17 g fat (3.1 g sat.); 72 g carbo.; 277 mg sodium; 80 mg chol. ■

By Linda Lau Anusasananan

CHEFS OF THE WEST
Adventures with food

Eggnog magic makes pie disappear

Dress up polenta for a holiday brunch and canned clams to sauce a quick pasta

HOLIDAY HOSPITALITY ENTAILS eggnog—but just a little eggnog. Too much kills the appetite, engenders drowsiness, and adds a spare white sidewall around the waist. If you have overestimated your need and have a surplus on hand, try making Barbara Moore's Eggnog Pie. It has the comforting flavor of eggnog, a texture that partakes of both custard and chiffon, and a meringue crust that will absolve you of some of the guilt you incur with the whipped cream topping. (If you are concerned about eating uncooked eggs, note that the egg whites in the pie filling are not heated.)

Eggnog Pie

Cooking time: About 1 hour and 40 minutes

Prep time: 50 minutes to 1 hour, plus about 6 hours for cooling and chilling

Notes: If making the crust a day ahead, let cool, seal airtight and hold at room temperature. Or cover the finished pie and chill it 1 day.

Makes: 8 to 10 servings

4 large egg whites

¼ teaspoon cream of tartar
¼ teaspoon salt
1½ cups granulated sugar
1 envelope unflavored gelatin
¼ cup cold water
3 large eggs, separated
½ cup milk
1 cup eggnog
1 cup whipping cream
2 tablespoons powdered sugar
¼ teaspoon vanilla
Ground nutmeg

1. Make crust: In a deep bowl with a mixer on high speed, whip the 4 egg whites with ¼ teaspoon cream of tartar and ⅛ teaspoon salt until foamy. Continue to beat at high speed while gradually adding 1 cup granulated sugar, 1 tablespoon at a time, then beat until whites hold stiff peaks.

2. Butter a 10-inch pie pan and dust with flour. Spread meringue over bottom and up sides of pan to create a pie shell.

3. Bake in a 275° oven until crust is pale brown and feels dry when touched, about 1½ hours. Let cool.

4. Make filling: In a 1½- to 2-quart pan, mix gelatin and ¼ cup granulated sugar. Stir in water and let mixture stand 5 minutes. Add egg yolks and whisk to mix well, then stir in milk, eggnog, and ⅛ teaspoon salt. Stir over medium-low heat until mixture is thick enough to coat a metal spoon in a thin, even layer, 8 to 10 minutes. Cover and chill until mixture is thick enough to mound slightly when dropped from a spoon.

5. In a deep bowl with a mixer on high speed, whip 3 remaining egg whites until foamy. Continue to beat on high speed and gradually add the last ¼ cup granulated sugar, then beat until whites just hold short, stiff peaks. Gently fold eggnog mixture into whites.

6. Assemble pie: Pour eggnog filling into meringue crust. Cover and chill until filling is set, at least 1½ hours.

7. Whip cream with powdered sugar until it holds soft peaks; stir in vanilla. Swirl cream over pie filling and up against meringue crust. Dust pie lightly with nutmeg and cover without touching it. Chill until filling is firm enough to cut, at least 3 hours.

Per serving: 265 cal., 37% (99 cal.) from fat; 5.7 g protein; 11 g fat (6.5 g sat.); 37 g carbo.; 126 mg sodium; 107 mg chol.

Barbara Moore

Redondo Beach, California

T HE CLASSIC SCRAPPLE (OFTEN called Philadelphia scrapple) is a species of cornmeal mush cooked with pork scraps and spices or pork sausage, then chilled, sliced, fried, and served with syrup.

Lenore Klass here offers a scrapple, sans pork, that resembles the original about as closely as a minuet resembles ice hockey.

Her Cranberry Orange Scrapple was designed as a holiday brunch dish, choosing Native American foodstuffs. But the quality of the dish demands that it be available for other celebrations, whether they are on the calendar or in the family.

Cranberry Orange Scrapple with Sauce

Cooking time: About 35 minutes
Prep time: About 15 minutes; allow at least 1½ hours for polenta to cool and firm (or it can chill until next day).
Notes: For a quick variation, spoon the freshly cooked polenta into bowls, pour the sauce over it, and eat hot. To cook on

the stove, use a 3- or 4-quart pan, bring polenta and water to a boil, then simmer gently, stirring, for about 15 minutes.
Makes: 6 servings.

    1   cup polenta
    3⅔ cups water
    1½ tablespoons grated orange peel
    ¼   teaspoon salt
    1   cup dried cranberries
    ¼   cup firmly packed brown sugar
    1   tablespoon butter or margarine
    ¾   cup orange juice
    2   tablespoons granulated sugar
    ½   teaspoon vanilla
    1   orange (about ½ lb.), peeled and
        sectioned
        Chopped pecans

1. In a 2½- to 3-quart microwave-safe bowl, combine polenta, water, 1 tablespoon orange peel, and salt. Cook, covered, in a microwave oven at full power for 12 to 13 minutes, stirring every 4 minutes.

2. Stir cranberries and brown sugar into polenta, then pour into a lightly buttered 5- by 9-inch loaf pan. Stir after 10 minutes, then spread surface smooth.

3. Cover and chill polenta until firm when pressed, at least 1½ hours or up to 1 day.

4. Invert pan to release polenta. Cut polenta into ¾-inch-thick slices.

5. Melt butter in a 10- to 12-inch frying pan over medium-high heat; add sliced polenta without crowding and brown on both sides, about 20 minutes total; transfer to a platter and keep warm until all slices are browned.

6. Meanwhile, mix remaining ½ tablespoon orange peel, orange juice, granulated sugar, and vanilla in a microwave-safe bowl (at least 1qt.). Heat at full power in the microwave until sauce is steaming.

7. Serve polenta slices topped with orange sauce and sections, and chopped pecans.

Per serving: 247 cal., 12% (29 cal.) from fat; 2.4 g protein; 3.2 g fat (1.6 g sat.); 53 g carbo.; 121 mg sodium; 6.9 mg chol.

Lenore M. Klass

San Bruno, California

T HE VIRTUE OF EXPEDIENCY IS revered most when time presses. And rarely does it press everyday meals more than during the holidays when upcoming celebratory feasts distract the cook. Hence, a bow and a blessing to

Betty Nichols, who has engineered this memorable clam pasta that can be on the table in less than 30 minutes. It uses ever-ready canned clams, but brightens their flavor with bits of fresh ginger and lemon peel. The addition of vegetables, edible-pod peas and green onions makes this a genuine one-dish meal.

Gingered Clam Pasta

Cooking time: About 5 minutes (plus 10 minutes to boil pasta water)
Prep time: 5 to 10 minutes
Notes: Heat from pasta water poured over peas is enough to make them brighter green and tender-crisp.
Makes: 4 servings

    1   tablespoon sesame seed
    2   tablespoons minced fresh ginger
    2   teaspoons sugar
    1   teaspoon grated lemon peel
    ¼   teaspoon hot chili flakes
    ⅓   cup reduced-sodium soy sauce
    1   tablespoon salad oil
    ½   pound edible-pod peas, ends and
        strings removed
    2   cans (each 6½ oz.) chopped
        clams
    8   or 9 ounces fresh cappellini
        pasta
    ¼   cup thinly sliced green onions,
        including tops

1. Stir sesame seed frequently in a 6- to 8-inch frying pan over medium heat until pale gold, 2 to 3 minutes. Pour seed from pan and set aside.

2. In a small bowl, mix ginger, sugar, lemon peel, chili flakes, soy, and oil.

3. Put peas in a colander and set in the sink.

4. Drain clams and save juice.

5. Drop pasta into about 3 quarts boiling water, add clam juice, and cook just until pasta is just tender to bite, 2 to 3 minutes. Pour pasta into colander over peas and drain well. Return pasta and peas to pan and set on low heat. Add clams, ginger mixture, and green onions. Mix well with 2 forks, then pour into warm bowls and sprinkle with sesame seed.

Per serving: 327 cal., 20 % (62 cal.) from fat; 22 g protein; 6.9 g fat (0.9 g sat.); 43 g carbo.; 864 mg sodium; 73 mg chol.

BJ Nichols

Eugene, Oregon
By Joan Griffiths, Richard Dunmire

JALAPEÑO CHILIES *heat up this pepper jelly. For a quick appetizer, serve over cream cheese.*

Bell Pepper Jelly

Marilou Robinson, Portland

1 1/2   pounds red, yellow, or green bell peppers

2   fresh jalapeño chilies (about 1 1/2 oz. total)

1/4   cup balsamic vinegar

1/4   cup white vinegar

3/4   teaspoon cayenne

3/4   cup light corn syrup

1. Stem, seed, and cut bell peppers into 1/4-inch-wide strips. Stem, seed, and chop jalapeño chilies.

2. In a 10- to 12-inch frying pan on medium-high heat, occasionally stir bell peppers and chilies until they are limp, about 7 minutes. Add balsamic and white vinegars and cayenne. Boil, stirring occasionally, until liquid evaporates, about 3 minutes. Add corn syrup and boil, stirring often, until syrup forms a thick, sticky thread when dripped from a spoon, 8 to 10 minutes.

3. Serve jelly warm or cool (it thickens slightly). If making ahead, cover, and chill up to 1 month. Makes 1 1/3 cups.

Per tablespoon: 42 cal., 2.1% (0.9 cal.) from fat; 0.3 g protein; 0.1 g fat (0 g sat.); 11 g carbo.; 15 mg sodium; 0 mg chol.

FRESH-TASTING *canned ingredients and fresh basil make a fast focaccia for supper.*

Fast Focaccia

Sharon Tonnemacher, Red Bluff, California

1   can (14 oz.) diced tomatoes

1   tablespoon olive oil

2   to 3 cloves garlic, minced

3   tablespoons chopped fresh or 1 tablespoon dried basil leaves

1   can (about 4 oz.) sliced ripe olives, drained

2   tablespoons drained prepared capers

1   baked pizza crust (about 1 lb., 12 in. wide)

1/3   cup grated parmesan cheese

1. Drain tomatoes in a colander or fine strainer at least 5 minutes.

2. Mix oil, garlic, basil, olives, and capers.

3. Set pizza crust in a 12-inch pizza pan or on a 12- by 15-inch baking sheet. Combine tomatoes and oil mixture, and spread over crust. Sprinkle evenly with cheese.

4. Bake in a 450° oven until hot and topping is lightly browned, 10 to 12 minutes. Cut into wedges. Makes 12 appetizer or 4 main-dish servings.

Per main-dish serving: 517 cal., 33% (171 cal.) from fat; 6.8 g protein; 19 g fat (4.8 g sat.); 72 g carbo.; 915 mg sodium; 5.2 mg chol.

FOR A LIVELY PILAF, *cook tangy dried tomatoes, sliced mushrooms, and cilantro with rice.*

Dried-Tomato Pilaf

Diane Sandoval, Issaquah, Washington

1   tablespoon olive oil

1/2   pound portabella or common mushrooms, sliced

1   onion (6 oz.), chopped

1   cup long-grain white rice

2 1/2   cups chicken broth

3/4   cup (2 oz.) dried tomatoes, chopped

1/4   cup chopped fresh cilantro

Salt and pepper

1. In a 3- to 4-quart pan, combine oil, mushrooms, and onion. Stir often over medium-high heat until the liquid evaporates and the vegetables are lightly browned, 10 to 12 minutes.

2. Add rice, and stir until opaque, about 1 minute. Add broth and tomatoes. Bring to a boil, then cover and simmer over low heat until rice is tender to bite, 20 to 25 minutes. Stir in cilantro. Add salt and pepper to taste. Makes 5 or 6 servings.

Per serving: 194 cal., 19% (36 cal.) from fat; 6.1 g protein; 4 g fat (0.7 g sat.); 37 g carbo.; 65 mg sodium; 0 mg chol.

Leeks with Cranberries

Dawn Dixon, Tucson

8 leeks (about 1½ in. wide, 3½ to 4 lb. total)

1 can (16 oz.) whole cranberry sauce

¼ cup rice vinegar

Salt

1. Trim root ends and tough dark green tops off leeks. Cut leeks in half lengthwise. Hold under running water and rinse well between layers. Tie each leek half around its center with cotton string.

2. In a 5- to 6-quart pan, bring about 3 quarts water to a boil over high heat. Add leeks, cover, and simmer over low heat until tender when pierced, about 8 minutes. Drain. Remove strings. (If making ahead, cover and chill up to 1 day.)

3. Mix cranberry sauce with rice vinegar. Spoon over warm or cool leeks. Add salt to taste. Serves 8.

Per serving: 140 cal., 1.9% (2.7 cal.) from fat; 1.4 g protein; 0.3 g fat (0 g sat.); 35 g carbo.; 34 mg sodium; 0 mg chol.

POACHED LEEKS *dressed with tart-sweet cranberry sauce make a handsome holiday dish.*

Orange Jicama Salad

Audrey Thibodeau, Mesa, Arizona

6 tablespoons lime juice

¼ cup orange marmalade

⅛ to ¼ teaspoon hot chili flakes

About ½ pound jicama

2 cans (11 oz. each) mandarin oranges

3 quarts bite-size pieces romaine lettuce, rinsed and crisped

1 cup thin slivers red onion, rinsed and drained

Salt and pepper

1. Whisk to blend lime juice, orange marmalade, and chilies.

2. Peel jicama, rinse, and cut into julienne sticks about ¼ inch thick and 3 inches long. Drain mandarin oranges.

3. In a large bowl, mix romaine lettuce, jicama, mandarin oranges, red onion, and marmalade dressing. Add salt and pepper to taste. Serves 8 to 10.

Per serving: 86 cal., 3.1% (2.7 cal.) from fat; 2 g protein; 0.3 g fat (0 g sat.); 21 g carbo.; 18 mg sodium; 0 mg chol.

CRISP JICAMA *and juicy mandarin oranges add texture to romaine salad with lean dressing.*

Lean Chocolate Biscotti

Barbara Tuttle, Beaverton, Oregon

¼ cup (⅛ lb.) butter or margarine, at room temperature

½ cup sugar

4 large egg whites

2 cups all-purpose flour

⅓ cup unsweetened cocoa

2 teaspoons baking powder

⅓ cup powdered sugar

About 2 teaspoons milk

1. With a mixer on high speed, beat butter and granulated sugar until fluffy. Add egg whites and beat until well blended. Stir in flour, cocoa, and baking powder; mix until well blended.

2. On a buttered 12- by 15-inch baking sheet, shape dough down the length of the pan into a flat log 2½ inches wide and ⅝ inch thick.

3. Bake in a 350° oven until crusty and firm to touch, about 20 minutes. Let cool about 5 minutes.

4. On pan, cut log diagonally into ½-inch-thick slices. Lay slices cut side down (they can touch). Return to oven and bake until cookies feel firm and dry, 15 to 20 minutes. Transfer to racks; let cool.

5. Smoothly mix powdered sugar and enough milk to make a pourable icing. Using a spoon, drizzle icing decoratively over biscotti. Let stand until icing is dry, about 15 minutes. Serve, or store airtight up to 1 week. Makes about 20.

Per cookie: 102 cal., 25% (25 cal.) from fat; 2.3 g protein; 2.8 g fat (1.7 g sat.); 17 g carbo.; 86 mg sodium; 6.8 mg chol.

Compiled by Linda Lau Anusasananan

CHOCOLATE BISCOTTI *made with egg whites, but no yolks, have less fat than most.*

By Elaine Johnson

PAUL HAMMOND

Shrimp rolls and other ideas for slim entertaining

HOLIDAY PARTIES ARE UPON US, AND I wouldn't dare suggest you skip the cheese platters, quiches, and cookies, because I'll be enjoying them myself—in moderation, of course. My guests and I will also be noshing on delicious low-fat foods like shrimp rolls.

These Vietnamese-style appetizers get their crunch from fresh vegetables, not frying. Edible rice paper is the wrapper. The transparent rolls go together in assembly-line fashion, look great on a buffet, and will hold if made ahead.

And what party would be complete without a few chips? There's been an explosion of choices in no- and low-fat potato and tortilla chips. Most have 2 grams of fat or less per ounce, compared to up to 10 grams per ounce for traditional chips. At a *Sunset* tasting, we especially liked potato chips by Childers (regular, salt and vinegar, and barbecue) and Snack Appeal (mesquite salsa and black bean), and tortilla chips by Baked Tostitos and Garden of Eatin' California Bakes (regular, and hot and smoky chipotle). Some plain chips can be dry alone but are terrific with no-fat dips such as mashed black beans with salsa and diced red peppers. Look for the chips in upscale grocery and natural-food stores.

One more tip for figure-conscious party goers: remember that alcohol packs in the calories, too. Between the wine (80 cal. per 4 oz.) and eggnog (193 cal. per 4 oz.), I pace myself with mineral water with a splash of cranberry juice or Italian syrup.

Fresh Vegetable and Shrimp Rolls

Cooking time: About 5 minutes
Prep time: About 25 minutes
Notes: Rice paper is sold at Asian markets or specialty foods stores.
Makes: 36 pieces, 6 servings

- ½ cup seasoned rice vinegar
- ¼ cup water
- 1½ teaspoons sugar
- ¾ teaspoon cornstarch
- ¼ teaspoon dried chili flakes
- 12 round sheets (about 8 in. wide, 5 oz. total) edible rice paper
- 36 fresh chives (each about 5 in.)
- 36 peeled, cooked shrimp (¾ lb.)
- ¾ cup finely shredded napa cabbage
- ¾ cup bean sprouts
- ¼ cup shredded fresh mint leaves

1. In a 1- to 2-quart pan over medium-high heat, stir vinegar, water, sugar, cornstarch, and chili flakes until bubbling, 4 to 5 minutes. Pour sauce into a bowl; let cool.

2. Hold rice paper sheets, 1 at a time, under a gentle trickle of water to moisten all over. Lay flat in a single layer and let stand until softened, 2 to 3 minutes. If sheets still feel tough, repeat rinsing and standing.

3. On top of each rice paper, place 3 chives about 1 inch apart with middle chive about 3 inches from 1 edge. Place 3 shrimp in a row, centered over middle chive, forming a line about 5 inches long. Over shrimp on rice papers, arrange equal portions of cabbage, sprouts, and mint.

4. Fold rice paper over both ends of line of shrimp; fold narrower exposed part of paper over shrimp, and roll up tightly.

5. Cut each log diagonally into 3 pieces, with a shrimp in each. Place on a platter (if making ahead, chill, covered with a damp paper towel, up to 2 hours). Dunk in sauce.

Per piece: 28 cal., 3.2% (0.9 cal.) from fat; 2.3 g protein; 0.1 g fat (0 g sat.); 4.2 g carbo.; 88 mg sodium; 18 mg chol.

Articles
Index

Index of
Recipe Titles

Low-fat Recipes

(30% or less of calories from fat)

General
Index

A

Abalone, farm-raised, 179
Acorn squash, chorizo-cornbread dressing in, 250
Agua fresca, watermelon, 188
Ahi margarita, 90
Almond cake, peach-, 155
Almond truffles, date-, 153
Ancho chili sauce, 197
Ancho chili sauce, cranberry–, turkey medallions with, 248
Anise dressing, endive-pear salad with, 234
Appetizers. *See also* Dips and spreads
  asparagus-prosciutto rolls, 145
  date and chorizo rumaki, 282
  fresh vegetable and shrimp rolls, 292
  Mexican potstickers, 20
  orange-cumin chicken pockets, 130
  papaya shrimp tumble, 130
  peppered chèvre crouton wafers, 193
  polenta-pesto bites, 52
  polenta triangles with Chinese sausage, 20
  skewered lamb balls with lime sauce, 129
  spiced flank steak and grapefruit, 282
  spinach balls with mustard sauce, 213
  taco zucchini cups, 144
  water chestnut, 208
Apple(s)
  -cheese cobbler, 21
  cider sherbet, 243
  and currants, sautéed, 23
  pecan scones, 55
  pie for a crowd, 229
  -potato vichyssoise with herbs, 138
  toast, and nuts, salad with, 266
Apricot(s)
  barbecued turkey breast and, 135
  bars, brandied, 278
  -blackberry cobbler, 140
  brie, spirited, 263
  -Dijon glaze, 48
  dried, chutney, 59
  plum tart, 168
Arizona beef and jalapeño chili, 234
Armagnac ice cream, honey-roasted pears with, 247
Aromatic seed mix, 8
Artichoke open face, 192
Arugula pesto quail with chèvre and shiitake, 283
Asian cabbage salad with orange, 21
Asian flavors, barbecued sirloin roast with, 68
Asian noodle salad with grilled chicken, 82
Asian-spiced mango and chicken, grilled, 109
Asparagus
  Milanese, 44
  and mustard vinaigrette, 125
  -prosciutto rolls, 145
Aunt Diane's kielbasa stew, 267

Autumn vegetables in filo, 246
Avocado and chèvre red pepper salad, 62
Avocado salsa, halibut with, 92

B

Bacon, Canadian, frisée salad with, 60
Bacon, melon, and basil salad, 185
Bag-smoked Chilean sea bass, 190
Bag-smoked shrimp with capers, 190
Baguette bagnat, 265
Baked beans, rum, 115
Baked curried lentils, 126
Baked eggplant slices, 114
Baked king salmon with corn and sage stuffing, 246
Baked quesadillas, basic, 210
Baked tomato, sautéed shrimp with fried garlic and, 226
Balsamic basil baste, 181
Banana scones, blueberry, 55
Barbecued chicken legs with spiced lentils, 135
Barbecued salmon fillets, 209
Barbecued sirloin roast with Asian flavors, 68
Barbecued turkey breast and apricots, 135
Barbecue hotline (barbecuing problems), 65
Barbecue sauce, sweet chili, 181
Basic baked quesadillas, 210
Basic muffin chips, 284
Basic roast chicken, *Sunset's*, 48
Basil
  bacon, and melon salad, 185
  baste, balsamic, 181
  –pine nut biscotti, 149
  soup, sweet corn and, 164
Bean(s)
  black, and broccoli frittata, 234
  black, gazpacho, 138
  black, salsa, grilled sturgeon with, 179
  black, steak and, salad, 165
  black, with peppers and tomatoes, 61
  rum baked, 115
Beef
  black bean and steak salad, 165
  Fringale's braised short ribs with parsnips, 31
  fruited pepper steak salad, 117
  ginger ribs, 90
  and jalapeño chili, Arizona, 234
  loin roast, 282
  marinated flank steak, 192
  ribs and corn, Thai, 166
  roasted marrow bones, 270
  spiced flank steak and grapefruit appetizers, 282
  steak and black bean salad, 165
  stuffed chayotes, 56
Beet
  dressing, leeks in, 39
  grapefruit, and romaine salad, 18
  salad, raw fennel and, 44
Bell pepper jelly, 290
Berr(ies). *See also specific berries*
  butter cake, St. Louie ooey-gooey, 158
  cream dessert, Bolognese, 118
  and crème fraîche, hazelnut waffles with berries and, 159
  freezing for use later on, 141

Berr(ies) (*cont'd.*)
  muffins, polenta, 19
  pies (from frozen berries), 141
  rote grütze, 205
  sauce, 89
Beverly's clam chowder, 21
Biscotti
  basil–pine nut, 149
  hazelnut Merlot, 126
  lean chocolate, 291
  rosemary walnut, 149
Biscuits
  buttermilk, 227
  buttermilk herb, 113
  cheese-frosted, 207
  raised sesame seed, 41
Bistro pizza salad, 86
Black and white chicken with sesame slaw, 105
Black bean(s)
  and broccoli frittata, 234
  gazpacho, 138
  with peppers and tomatoes, 61
  salad, steak and, 165
  salsa, grilled sturgeon with, 179
Blackberry
  cobbler, apricot-, 140
  demiglace, roasted pork loin with, 244
  pie, Kitty's mango, 108
  sorbet, 169
Blintzes, cheese, 54
Blintzes, Chinese cheese, 231
BLT omelet, 92
Blue and brie torte, 263
Blueberry
  banana scones, 55
  -coconut crunch muffins, 266
  crisp, cherry-, 140
  torte, white chocolate–, 165
Bok choy, spicy, with fried tofu, 115
Bolognese berry cream dessert, 118
Boysenberry cobbler, 156
Bombe, frozen melon-mint, 184
Braised short ribs with parsnips, Fringale's, 31
Brandied apricot bars, 278
Bran dollar cakes, cinnamon, 116
Brandy sauce, cervena with, 42
Bread and cabbage soup, Gianni's, 214
Bread dressing, Tuscan-style, 49
Breads. *See also* Biscuits; Muffins
  apple pecan scones, 55
  blueberry banana scones, 55
  Janie's herb, 155
  caramel breakfast rolls, 38
  crunchy whole-wheat, 230
  overnight soft herb rolls, 242
Breakfast rolls, caramel, 38
Brie and blue torte, 263
Brie, spirited apricot, 263
Broccoli frittata, black bean and, 234
Broccoli rabe, garlic, and pine nuts, orecchiette with, 227
Broth, winter vegetable, 18
Brownies
  chocolate-raspberry, 235
  Mexican chocolate, with cinnamon, 40
  truffle, 40
Brown rice and sausage dressing, 256
Burgers, curried turkey, 165
Butter cake, St. Louie ooey-gooey berry, 158
Butterflied lamb leg, grilled, with herbs and feta, 67

Cranber(ries) (cont'd.)
  red cabbage with, 270
  sauce, 242
  sauce, orange-, duck breasts with, 244
  spinach salad with pears and, 257
Crayfish, farm-raised, 177
Cream
  dessert, Bolognese berry, 118
  -filled praline pine nut cones or rolls, 277
  Latin-style, types of, 121
  lemon-ginger, strawberry shortcake with, 100
Crème fraîche, hazelnut waffles with berries and, 159
Crisp, cherry-blueberry, 140
Crisp roast goose with giblet gravy, 268
Croutons, cotija, Caesar salad with, 220
Crouton wafers, peppered chèvre, 193
Crumbleberry pie, 247
Crunchy whole-wheat bread, 230
Cucumbers, salted, 147
Cumin chicken pockets, orange-, 130
Currants, sautéed apples and, 23
Curried catfish and chips, 177
Curried couscous salad, 137
Curried lentils, baked, 126
Curried turkey burgers, 165
Curry
  dressing, 137
  paste, yellow, 35
  scallops, and chives, noodles with, 35
Custard
  brûlée, low-fat raspberry, 145
  cooking questions about, 231–232
  flavored soft, 89

D

Dal with cilantro, 111
Date-almond truffles, 153
Date and chorizo rumaki, 282
Desserts. See also Cakes; Cobblers; Cookies; Pies; Tarts
  apple cider sherbet, 253
  blackberry sorbet, 169
  Bolognese berry cream, 118
  caramel dip, 164
  cherry-blueberry crisp, 140
  date-almond truffles, 153
  with frozen berries, 141
  frozen citrus bowls, 169
  frozen melon-mint bombe, 184
  gianduia mousse, 271
  honey-roasted pears with armagnac ice cream, 247
  Jamaican coconut pralines, 191
  lemon curd dip, 164
  low-fat raspberry custard brûlée, 145
  mango granita, 109
  mango sorbet, 169
  pomegranate ice, 243
  pumpkin sundaes, 257
  raspberry sorbet, 169
  rote grütze, 205
  strawberry clouds, 142
  strawberry-rhubarb mousse, 102
  strawberry shortcake with lemon-ginger cream, 100
  strawberry sundae with strawberry-wine syrup, 99
  tropical fruits with two sauces, 89
  tropical pops, 109
  white chocolate–blueberry torte, 165

Dijon glaze, apricot-, 48
Dim sum, dining out on, 10–14
Dips and spreads
  brie and blue torte, 263
  caramel dip, 164
  lemon curd dip, 164
  phkali, 64
  roasted tomato spread, 204
  roasted vegetable spread, 131
  spiced eggplant dip, 130
  spirited apricot brie, 263
  sweet garlic spread, 130
Dollar cakes, cinnamon bran, 116
Dressing. See Stuffings and dressings
Dressings, salad
  anise, endive-pear salad with, 234
  beet, leeks in, 39
  chili balsamic, 63
  curry, 137
  egg-safe spicy tomato, 207
  hoisin, 82
  honey-Dijon, 116
  lime, 93
  Merlot, 125
  no-fat mango, 211
  nonfat vinaigrette, 211
  rice vinegar, 120
  soy, 32
  spicy tomato, 207
  tarragon, 18
Dried apricot chutney, 59
Dried-tomato pilaf, 290
Duck
  breasts with orange-cranberry sauce, 244
  Twin Palms streamlined cassoulet, 30

E

Easy Yucatán enchilada supper, 84
Eaux-de-vie, 238
Eggnog pie, 288
Eggplant
  and carrot cannelloni, 114
  dip, spiced, 130
  grilled, with tomato caper vinaigrette, 284
  pepper and, focaccia sandwiches, 235
  slices, baked, 114
  spiced pork cannelloni with, 114
Egg(s)
  Benedict, herbed, 112
  black bean and broccoli frittata, 234
  BLT omelet, 92
  Chinese noodle cake with, 32
  poached, 113
  salad and mild chili sandwich, hot, 87
Enchiladas, turkey, 267
Enchilada supper, easy Yucatán, 84
Endive-pear salad with anise dressing, 234

F

Fall fruit salad, 236
Fast focaccia, 290
Fennel and beet salad, raw, 44
Fennel-chestnut soup, 243
Feta, grilled butterflied lamb leg with herbs and, 67
Fettuccine alla Norcina, l'Opera's, 94
Fettuccine, mushroom, with Italian sausage, 17

Fila lattice, plum-orange cobbler with, 139
Filo, autumn vegetables in, 246
Finger pizzas, 233
Fireworks tomato salad, 202
Fish. See also specific fish
  bag-smoked Chilean sea bass, 190
  baked king salmon with corn and sage stuffing, 246
  barbecued salmon fillets, 209
  curried catfish and chips, 177
  farm-raised, 170–180
    catfish, 177
    hybrid striped bass, 176
    salmon, 174–175
    sturgeon, 178
    tilapia, 180
    trout, 179
  grilled salmon with papaya-kiwi salsa, 143
  grilled salmon with potato and watercress salad, 132
  grilled sturgeon with black bean salsa, 179
  grilled swordfish with prosciutto and fontina, 194
  halibut with avocado salsa, 92
  oven-fried tilapia with tomato relish, 180
  Patrizio Sacchetto's salt-crust striped bass, 6
  salmon with citrus-mint gremolata, 175
  tuna with mint-mango chutney, 143
  Tuscan-style swordfish with vegetables, 9
Flank steak and grapefruit appetizers, spiced, 282
Flank steak, marinated, 192
Flavored nut tarts, 286
Focaccia
  fast, 290
  grape, 198
  sandwiches, pepper and eggplant, 235
  spiral stuffed, 127
Fontina, grilled swordfish with prosciutto and, 194
Four-in-one roasted tomatoes, 202
Fresh candied peel, 239
Fresh cheese, vermicelli with, 220
Fresh vegetable and shrimp rolls, 292
Fried garlic and baked tomato, sautéed shrimp with, 226
Fried tofu, spicy bok choy with, 115
Fringale's braised short ribs with parsnips, 31
Frisée salad with Canadian bacon, 60
Frittata, black bean and broccoli, 234
Frosty, raspberry, 157
Frozen citrus bowls, 169
Frozen mango-yogurt shake, 109
Frozen melon-mint bombe, 184
Fruit. See also specific fruits
  salad, fall, 236
  salad, tradewinds, 93
  soup, summer, 195
  tropical, with two sauces, 89
Fruited pepper steak salad, 117
Frying pan potato soufflé, Indian, 110

G

Galettes, potato, 25
Game hens, tea-smoked, 161